Deportations in the Nazi Era

Arolsen Research Series

—

Edited by the Arolsen Archives –
International Center on Nazi Persecution

Volume 2

Deportations in the Nazi Era

Sources and Research

Edited by
Henning Borggräfe and Akim Jah

DE GRUYTER
OLDENBOURG

On behalf of the Arolsen Archives

International Center
on Nazi Persecution

The Arolsen Archives are funded by Germany's Minister of State for Culture and the Media (BKM)

ISBN 978-3-11-074230-5
e-ISBN (PDF) 978-3-11-074646-4
e-ISBN (EPUB) 978-3-11-074658-7
ISSN 2699-7312
DOI https://doi.org/10.1515/9783110746464

This work is licensed under the Creative Commons Attribution-Non Commercial-No Derivatives 4.0 Licence. For details go to http://creativecommons.org/licenses/by-nc-nd/4.0/.

Creative Commons license terms for re-use do not apply to any content (such as graphs, figures, photos, excerpts, etc.) not original to the Open Access publication and further permission may be required from the rights holder. The obligation to research and clear permission lies solely with the party re-using the material.

Library of Congress Control Number: 2022941913

Bibliographic information published by the Deutsche Nationalbibliothek
The Deutsche Nationalbibliothek lists this publication in the Deutsche Nationalbibliografie; detailed bibliographic data are available on the internet at http://dnb.dnb.de.

© with the author(s), editing © 2023 Arolsen Archives, Henning Borggräfe and Akim Jah, published by Walter de Gruyter GmbH, Berlin/Boston. This book is published with open access at www.degruyter.com.

Cover image: Photo of the deportation of Jews from Eisenach on 09.05.1942 (Eisenach Municipal Archives) and transport list ‚30. Osttransport', 26.02.1943, from Berlin to Auschwitz (Arolsen Archives). Design Jan-Eric Stephan.
Printing and binding: CPI books GmbH, Leck

www.degruyter.com

Table of Contents

Foreword by Floriane Azoulay —— IX

Foreword by Sigmount A. Königsberg —— XI

Foreword by Petra Rosenberg —— XIII

Akim Jah
Deportations in the Nazi Era – Introduction —— 1

Archival Sources, Online Portals and Approaches

Henning Borggräfe
Sources on Deportations
A General Model and a Methodological Approach for Researching Person-Related Records based on the Berlin Transport Lists —— 29

Kim Dresel and Christian Groh
An Overview of Sources on Deportations of Jews and Sinti and Roma in the Arolsen Archives —— 55

Maximilian Strnad
Potential of Databases for Research and Culture of Remembrance Using the Deportation of Jews under the Nazi Regime as an Example —— 83

Susanne Kill
Deutsche Reichsbahn and Deportation
The Personal Archive of Alfred Gottwaldt —— 103

Aya Zarfati
Interaction, Confusion and Potential
On the Clash between Archives (on Nazi History) and Family Research —— 119

Discussing Visual Sources of Deportations from Germany

Christoph Kreutzmüller
A Deceptive Panorama
    Photos of Deportations of Jews from Germany —— 135

Elisabeth Pönisch
Deportations from the Perspective of the Remaining Jews and the Surrounding Population
    Narratives, Pictures and Films as Reflections of Social Reality —— 155

Racial Registrations, Forced Housing, and Local Deportation Dynamics

Verena Meier
The 'Prevention Department' within the Criminal Police
    An Example of Learning Administrations and the Core of Organizing Transports of Sinti and Roma to Concentration Camps —— 181

Théophile Leroy
'Gypsies' in the Police Eye
    Identification, Census and Deportation of Sinti and Roma from Annexed Alsace, 1940 to 1944 —— 207

Joachim Schröder
Forced Accommodation for Jews in the Context of the Deportations at the Düsseldorf Abattoir (1939–1944) —— 229

Akim Jah
Gerlachstraße Assembly Camp in Berlin, 1942 to 1943
    History, Function, and the Current State of Research —— 249

Michaela Raggam-Blesch
The Fate of 'Protected' Groups during the Last Years of the War
    Deportations from Vienna's Nordbahnhof – a Largely Unknown Site of the Shoah —— 275

Dóra Pataricza
"Put My Mother on the List Too!" – Reconstructing the Deportation Lists of the Szeged Jewish Community —— 297

Trajectories of Deportation and Subsequent Persecution

Kristina Vagt
The Deportation of Sinti and Roma from Hamburg and Northern Germany to the Belzec Forced Labour Camp in the *Generalgouvernement* of 1940 —— 319

Alfred Eckert
Deportation Train 'Da 32' from Nuremberg and its 1,012 Occupants —— 341

Daan de Leeuw
Mapping Jewish Slave Laborers' Trajectories Through Concentration Camps —— 363

Alexandra Patrikiou
Escaping the Death Train
   The Survival Strategies of Errikos Botton —— 385

Johannes Meerwald
The DEGOB Protocols and the Deportations of Jewish Prisoners to the Dachau Camp Complex
   A Critical Source Analysis —— 405

After the Arrival in Ghettos and other Deportation Destinations

Ingo Loose
Deportations of Jews to the Ghetto of Litzmannstadt (Łódź)
   Some Thoughts on the State of Research, on Older Discussions and Open Questions —— 429

Anna Veronica Pobbe
Looking for the Money
   Using a Bank Account of the Litzmannstadt Ghetto as a Source in the History of Deportations —— 449

Tomáš Fedorovič
Preparations for and Organization of the Transports from Terezín to Auschwitz-Birkenau in September 1943 —— 467

Viorel Achim
The Petitions of Roma Deportees as a Source for the Study of the Deportation Sites in Transnistria —— 487

Alexandra Pulvermacher
'Aktion Zamosc' and its Entanglements with the Holocaust —— 509

Contributors —— 529

Foreword by Floriane Azoulay

This publication stems from the international conference of the same name held by the Arolsen Archives from November 2 to 4, 2020. The event was sponsored by Deutsche Bahn AG, and the original plan was to hold the conference at the former Kaiserbahnhof railway station in Potsdam to provide a direct historical link to the former Reichsbahn, the German national railway system, which played a central role in the deportations. However, the pandemic forced us to change our plans, and this conference became the first large event we held online. The advantage of this approach was that it enabled many people to attend who would not have been able to travel to the venue.

One thing that emerged very clearly from the presentations and discussions held by the experts who took part was the very high level of scholarly interest shown in the topic of indexing and cataloging source materials. The Arolsen Archives are the world's most comprehensive archive on the victims of National Socialism, and we hold valuable collections and documents on deportations, which our specialist staff index and make available to the public online. The conference focused on the deportations of Jews and Sinti and Roma, and it brought together various topics that had previously received attention at events in Vienna, Hamburg, and Yad Vashem in Jerusalem. As reflected in the articles in this volume, the event served to gather knowledge about source materials, but it also showed how many questions remain unanswered despite extensive research.

This is particularly noticeable when it comes to visual sources. For the territory of the German Reich, those photographs of German deportations whose existence we were aware of up until now, come from only a small number of localities. The idea for the #LastSeen initiative arose during the conference, born from a desire to bring these pictures together and make everything accessible online. At the request of those involved, the Arolsen Archives undertook to implement the idea quickly, a task that is well suited to us because of our digital expertise. When seen in isolation, the pictures only show the perspective of the perpetrators, so it is important to contextualize the images and put them into relief by providing as much information as possible about the lives of the persecutees in order to give these people's names, their history, and their dignity back to them. Taken between 1938 and 1945, the photos also show very vividly how National Socialist injustice and the exclusion of the victims of persecution took place right before the public's eyes. The pictures throw light on the last moment when the deportees were excluded from German society and show how many people knew about these crimes and even participated. This inevitably leads us to direct our attention to contemporary questions about the various options we have today when we witness injustice. Thus, the goals of the #LastSeen initiative include using a traveling exhibition to bring the pictures to remote rural areas and using the materials to create an interactive low-threshold educational offering that is especially suitable for young people.

As the Nazi period recedes into the ever-more distant past, subsequent generations are less and less able to imagine the atrocities that were committed, and this increases the danger of losing sight of the historical facts. As a recent study commissioned by the Arolsen Archives on 'Generation Z and Nazi History' showed, there is a high level of interest in this period of history and a clear sense of the injustice of everyday racism. At the same time, however, it should be noted that there is little knowledge about the Holocaust, and that antisemitism is mostly neither recognized as a central ideology of National Socialism nor as a separate phenomenon in its own right. But the continuity of antisemitism as a worldview within society remains unbroken, and it persists today without attracting much social protest as a rule. Structural antiziganism and the discrimination associated with it also demonstrate how centuries-old stereotypes still continue to exist today, even in democracies. Many Sinti and Roma and Jews hide their identity because they are afraid of being disadvantaged or resented. The fact that the reasons for the persecution of two of the largest victim groups targeted by the National Socialists are still not a thing of the past although nearly 80 years have passed should give us a pause for thought. By implementing the #LastSeen initiative and projects like the conference on Nazi deportations that draw attention to numerous questions and unearth relevant academic findings, the Arolsen Archives are responding to changes in the culture of remembrance and to the associated political challenges of our time.

Floriane Azoulay
Director, Arolsen Archives – International Center on Nazi Persecution

Foreword by Sigmount A. Königsberg

In recent years, we have come to learn that hate speech and fake news have had a massively adverse impact on society in many countries. We re-encounter conspiracy myths, hatred and prejudice we erroneously thought had faded away. When people taking part in demonstrations today 'adorn' themselves with the 'Yellow Star', when people dare to publicly show the picture of Joseph Mengele, the Auschwitz murderer-doctor, next to a photo of Dr. Christian Drosten, chief virologist of Berlin's Charité hospital, thus comparing the mass murder of European Jewry to public health managers dealing with a pandemic, we recognize that hatred and prejudice are still virulent even 75 years after the liberation from the Nazis. In addition, we recognize that knowledge about antisemitism and the mechanisms of Nazi persecution is limited. For this reason, it is essential that the work done by historians regarding Nazi persecution and – in the case of this publication – especially the history of deportations is accessible to a broad public. We are in a situation where our society is nearing a crossroads. Will we continue to live in an open, liberal and democratic society, or will it drift into an authoritarian and intolerant form we will not be able to endure? It remains to be wished that civil society will respond to the impulses generated by the authors of these contributions in helping to counteract inhuman societal developments.

Sigmount A. Königsberg
Commissioner against Antisemitism, Jewish Community Berlin

Foreword by Petra Rosenberg

The deportations of Sinti and Roma to Nazi concentration camps and their systematic murder were ended more than 75 years ago. Numerous details of these crimes as well as innumerable references to the biographies of those persecuted and murdered have been preserved in the holdings of the Arolsen Archives. These include, for instance, deportation guidelines and transport lists as well as documents from former concentration camps. Next to testimonies of the life-threatening Nazi bureaucracy, one can find letters, which former prisoners of the Dachau concentration camp wrote to their families, as well as documents on the Lackenbach camp, where over 2,000 Sinti and Roma were interned and from where they were deported to be exterminated. Additionally, postwar documents produced by the International Tracing Service (ITS) have been preserved in Bad Arolsen. These so-called correspondence files document, among other things, the search for missing people. They include letters by survivors asking for a written confirmation of their persecution, such as the one my father Otto Rosenberg wrote in 1954 requesting a certificate of his incarceration in Auschwitz and other concentration camps to substantiate his claim in compensation proceedings. Many of these documents offer an insight into the persecution and genocide of Sinti and Roma. These testimonies are shocking and, at the same time, a manifestation of prejudices passed down over centuries. And a look at the postwar documents makes it clear that bias against Sinti and Roma has survived their liberation – among both, people and authorities. This is shown, for example, by discriminatory comments on numerous official documents. Their struggle for a
   public recognition of their persecution finds its expression in the documents as well. Thus, survivors' statements concerning their path of persecution were often called into question, and the German citizenship they had been deprived of in the Nazi era was restored to many on their personal insistence only.
   The systematic stigmatization and disadvantaging of Sinti and Roma continued even decades after the Nazi era had ended. It was only as a result of the civil rights movement initiated by German Sinti and Roma in the Federal Republic in the late 1970s that, in 1982, the Nazi genocide of Sinti and Roma was officially recognized by Chancellor Helmut Schmidt. Nevertheless, members of our minority are massively discriminated against even today. And this happens not only in Germany, but also in many other European countries. What aggravates the still prevailing prejudices is the widely spread lack of knowledge of the genocide of European Sinti and Roma.

For a long time, historical re-appraisal of this genocide had hardly been a topic in historical scholarship and the number of pertinent publications remained limited. I thus appreciate even more that this conference volume includes contributions on the genocide of Sinti and Roma. In addition, I hope that this book will inspire further research projects addressing the numerous pertinent desiderata.

Petra Rosenberg
Chair, Association German Sinti and Roma Berlin-Brandenburg

Akim Jah
Deportations in the Nazi Era – Introduction

We – i.e., my father and I – were picked up from our apartment by a plain-clothed Gestapo officer on September 24, 1942, and taken by tram to the large synagogue in Levetzowstraße. We arrived there towards evening. The seats had been removed from the synagogue and many Jewish families, who had also been arrested, already lay on the floor there. There were young and old, women, girls, children, men. On the morning of September 26, 1942, the Gestapo began to take away the Jews who were kept there, i.e., smaller and smaller troops – around 50 to 100 people – were put together and had to walk to Putlitzstraße [= Moabit freight] train station. […] My father – Bruno Drexler – and I arrived at the train station with the last troop from Levetzowstraße at around noon on September 26, 1942. I seem to remember that Jewish guards – men and women – were appointed, even in the synagogue in Levetzowstraße. […] The train then set off at midday on September 26, 1942 […]. After a train journey of several days and nights, I can't say the exact number now, we could read signs outside saying "Riga". There was crying and praying in the compartments during the journey. […] As I recall, the train stopped in Riga for one night. Then the train suddenly continued its journey. Then a rumor passed through the compartment. Someone had said that the ghetto in Riga was full. People in the compartment said no one knew where to take us and we were sure to be shot now. I personally didn't believe that at the time. […] The train continued and arrived in Raziku [sic] at the crack of dawn, i.e., it suddenly stopped and we could read the sign RAZIKU. I didn't know which country that was in. […] The doors were opened and we had to get out.[1]

Helga Verleger (née Drexler), the author of this description of the transport from Berlin to Raasiku in German-occupied Estonia in September 1942, was 17 years old at the time and among the few survivors of the deportations of Jews to the ghettos and death camps in German-occupied Central and Eastern Europe. Around half of Europe's Jews murdered in the Holocaust were deported there from their last places of residence, regions, or countries by train before being killed. There were also between several ten thousand to several hundred thousand Sinti/Sintize and Roma/Romnja, who were transported, among other places, to the '*Generalgouvernement*' in German-occupied Poland, and to Auschwitz-Birkenau concentration and death camp, where they were murdered.[2] Alongside vic-

---

1 Statement Helga Verleger, 19.02.1968, B Rep. 058, no. 416, Berlin State Archives. Translation by the author. See also Akim Jah: "Strukturelemente – Forschungsfragen – Quellen. Die Deportation der jüdischen Bevölkerung aus Berlin 1941 bis 1945", in Anja Siegemund and Michael Wildt (eds.): *Gedächtnis aus den Quellen. Zur jüdischen Geschichte Berlins. Hermann Simon zu Ehren*, Berlin/Leipzig: Hentrich & Hentrich, 2021, 135–149, here 137.
2 The exact numbers of both deported and murdered Sinti/Sintize and Roma/Romnja are still not secured in research, especially because of the incomplete empirical basis. Most researchers currently refer to around 200,000 murdered persons, however, determining the exact number of

---

∂ OpenAccess. © 2023 the author(s), published by De Gruyter. (CC) BY-NC-ND This work is licensed under the Creative Commons Attribution-NonCommercial-NoDerivatives 4.0 International License.
https://doi.org/10.1515/9783110746464-004

tims from Germany, the deportations above all also involved German-occupied regions and states allied with Germany.

As the transportation took place 'in the shadow' of much more violent experiences at the places of destination, only a small number of descriptions of the transports themselves exist from the few survivors. These testimonies, as well as the perpetrators' administrative documents about the transports and their preparations, have been preserved scattered in various archives in different countries around the world. The statement by Helga Verleger, which was created in the context of court proceedings against former employees of the Gestapo due to their involvement in the deportation of Jews from Berlin, can thus now be found in the Berlin State Archives.[3] However, the transport list containing her name has been preserved in the Arolsen Archives.[4]

The subject of this volume are sources and research on the deportations of Jews as well as Sinti/Sintize and Roma/Romnja during the Nazi era in Europe. Deportations are understood here as those transports beyond borders that ended with the death or murder of the majority of the deportees. The collected contributions are based on presentations at the conference *Deportations in the Nazi Era – Sources and Research* held by the Arolsen Archives in November 2020. In this introduction, the course of research on the two groups of persecutees will be described, followed by a historical outline as well as considerations on perpetrators and research gaps. After the narrowing of the subject, the contributions will be presented.

Research on the Deportation of Jews

The deportation of the Jewish population from the Reich and from German-occupied regions as well as allied countries became an independent field of research of Nazi persecution at a relatively early stage. Immediately after the end of the Second World War, the Jewish Communities, who were in the process of reconstruction, and the American Jewish Joint Distribution Committee (AJDC) began

---

deportees remains a research desideratum. See Karola Fings: "The Number of Victims". Available at: https://www.romarchive.eu/en/voices-of-the-victims/the-number-of-victims/. Last accessed: 03.08.2022.

3 Cf. Akim Jah: "'Unschuldige Mordgehilfen'. Das Bovensiepen-Verfahren gegen ehemalige Mitarbeiter der Stapo-Leitstelle Berlin", in Sabine Moller, Miriam Rürup, and Christel Trouvé (eds.): *Abgeschlossene Kapitel. Zur Geschichte der Konzentrationslager und der NS-Prozesse*, Tübingen: Edition diskord 2002, 187–199.

4 For the transport lists, see the contribution by Henning Borggräfe in this volume.

the research on the destinations of the individual transports and on the fate of those who were deported.[5] Furthermore, governmental commissions were set up in various countries to investigate the crimes committed by the Germans and shed light on what happened to the Jewish population.[6] The sources created at that time are generally available for academic research today.

Within academic research itself, it was Raul Hilberg above all who presented in detail the history of events, key structural elements, and regional specifics of the deportations to German-occupied Europe in a chapter comprising over 400 pages in his groundbreaking overall presentation of the Holocaust, *The Destruction of the European Jews*, which he began as early as 1948 and published in 1961.[7] In 1974, H.G. Adler submitted his study about the deportations from the German Reich, which remains unsurpassed in its comprehensiveness to this day. Adler investigates numerous aspects of the organization and processes of the deportations, including the theft of the deportees' assets. The involvement of the administration in the deportations represents a focal point of his work, whereby he also presented numerous individual fates of victims as examples. Adler, who was himself a survivor of the Theresienstadt ghetto, was above all able to refer to the preserved documents of the Würzburg Gestapo.[8]

Today, a multitude of studies exist that look at the deportation and murder of the Jewish population in individual countries and regions as well as cities and even smaller towns. Alongside academic historical studies,[9] these also include remembrance projects and results from 'lay researchers' relating to the Jewish history of individual locations.[10] Research has also differentiated itself thematically. As a result, there are investigations into the deportation of individual

---

5 See, for instance, for Berlin Larry Lubetsky: *Berlin AJDC Tracing Office 1945–1947*, Berlin: AJDC Tracing Office, 1948. Available at: https://digital-library.arolsen-archives.org/content/titleinfo/7273639?query=Lubetsky&lang=en. Last accessed: 25.02.2022.
6 Cf. as an example for Vojvodina in Yugoslavia Aleksander Bursać: "Material about the Deportation of the Jews of Bača in 1944 in the Archives of Vojvodina, Fonds F. 183. Commission for Investigation of Crimes Committed by the Occupiers and their Collaborators in Vojvodina – Novi Sad (1944–1948), 1941–1950", in idem., Vladimir Todorović, and Peter Đurđev (eds.): *Deportation of the Jews of Bača in 1944*, Novi Sad/Ramat Gan: Archives of Vojvodina/Bar-Ilan University, 257–266.
7 Raul Hilberg: *The Destruction of the European Jews*, 2 volumes, London: W.H. Allen & Co, 1961.
8 H.G. Adler: Der verwaltete Mensch. Studien zur Deportation der Juden aus Deutschland, Tübingen: J.C.B. Mohr, 1974, XVII–XVIII.
9 One example of this is Christian Gerlach and Götz Aly: *Das letzte Kapitel. Der Mord an den ungarischen Juden 1944–1945*, Frankfurt am Main: Fischer Taschenbuch, 2004.
10 See, for example, Arbeitsgruppe Pogromnacht in Warburg at the Warburg Hüffertgymnasium: *Mut zur Erinnerung. Zugang zur jüdischen Geschichte Warburgs*, Warburg: Hüffertgymnasium, 1988.

groups of victims, e. g. Jews living in 'mixed marriages'.[11] Studies into the various agencies involved in the deportations, including those who seized the assets of the deportees,[12] take into consideration the actors, e. g. the regional offices of the Gestapo, Security Police, the SS, and the men who worked there.[13] Attention in research has also increasingly been paid to the forced collaboration of Jewish Communities and their representatives with the responsible Nazi authorities.[14] In addition, memorial books were created that are devoted to the biographies of people deported from a certain geographical entity and to the events in the respective places of arrival, particularly in the ghettos in occupied Central and Eastern Europe.[15] The names and paths of persecution of the deportees, which were often not known at all for a long time, have thus gradually been researched. In this context, the memorial books are increasingly being made available digitally and online.[16] The *Transports to Extinction: Holocaust (Shoah) Deportation Database* project, which is based at Yad Vashem, reconstructs all transports "of Jews from every Jewish community carried out by the Nazi regime during the period of the Shoah".[17] The aim of the project is "to collect reliable and detailed information about each transport route, the bureaucratic system as well as the socio-economic background of the victims, enabling a comprehensive research of the deportation apparatus".[18]

Research literature specifically about the destinations themselves is also still expanding,[19] sometimes also with new research approaches. With her mono-

---

11 Cf., for instance, Maximilian Strnad: *Privileg Mischehe? Handlungsräume "jüdisch versippter" Familien 1939–1949*, Göttingen: Wallstein, 2021.
12 Cf. for instance, Gerald D. Feldman and Wolfgang Seibel (eds.): *Networks of Nazi Persecution. Bureaucracy, Business and the Organization of the Holocaust*, New York/Oxford: Berghahn, 2006.
13 The contributions in the anthology by Gerhard Paul and Klaus-Michael Mallmann are particularly worthy of mention here. See Gerhard Paul and Klaus-Michael Mallmann (eds.): *Die Gestapo im Zweiten Weltkrieg. 'Heimatfront' und besetztes Europa*, Darmstadt: WBG, 2000. See also the recent articles in Thomas Grotum (ed.): *Die Gestapo Trier. Beiträge zur Geschichte einer regionalen Verfolgungsbehörde*, Cologne/Weimar/Vienna: Böhlau, 2018.
14 Cf. Beate Meyer: *A Fatal Balancing Act. The Dilemma of the Reich Association of Jews in Germany, 1939–1945*, New York/Oxford: Berghahn, 2013.
15 Cf., for example, Angela Genger and Hildegard Jakobs (eds.): *Düsseldorf / Ghetto Litzmannstadt 1941*, Essen: Klartext, 2010.
16 See the article by Max Strnad in this volume.
17 Yad Vashem: "The Deportations of Jews Project". Available at: https://www.yadvashem.org/research/research-projects/deportations.html. Last accessed: 25.02.2022.
18 Ibid.
19 The following lexically structured series of books are fundamental here: Wolfgang Benz and Barbara Distel (eds.): *Der Ort des Terrors. Geschichte der nationalsozialistischen Konzentrationslager*, 9 volumes, Munich: C.H. Beck, 2005–2009; United States Holocaust Memorial Museum

graph on the Theresienstadt ghetto in 2020, Anna Hájková thus presented the first comprehensive examination for some time of the transit ghetto, which played an important role in the history of the deportation of Jews from Central and Western Europe. Following the experience-based approach of E.P. Thompson, she also takes into consideration the prison society of the ghetto and the experiences of the Theresienstadt victims.[20] For Hájková, this widening of perspective is part of a "good historical practice, for which it is the key to integrate all participants' perspectives".[21] The integration of microhistorical studies and the presentation of different perspectives, including the perspectives of persecutees, also characterize approaches towards the historiography of the Shoah as demanded and practiced by Saul Friedländer[22] and most recently by David Cesarani.[23] Both Friedländer and Cesarani also focus on deportations from various German-occupied regions. The recently completed multi-volume edition *The Persecution and Murder of European Jews by Nazi Germany, 1933–1945*, published by the Leibniz Institute for Contemporary History, presents comprehensively the persecution of Jews in various countries and territories, including deportations, with a high number of reproductions of relevant sources.[24]

The many works on decision-making processes at the Reich level offer a very precise image of planned, discarded, and implemented considerations regarding the forcible deportation and ultimate murder of the Jewish population from the German Reich, the German-occupied countries of Europe, and the states allied with Germany.[25] The equally very well-researched reciprocal relationship between local party functionaries and the Reich Security Main Office (Reichssicherheitshauptamt, RSHA) in the initiation and preparation of the deportations in the Reich and the activities of local SS functionaries and Nazi representatives

---

(ed.): *Encyclopedia of Camps and Ghettos 1933–1945*, to date 3 volumes, Bloomington: Indiana University Press, 2009–2018.
20 Anna Hájková: *The Last Ghetto. An Everyday History of Theresienstadt*, New York: OUP, 2020.
21 Ibid., 13.
22 Saul Friedländer: *Den Holocaust beschreiben. Auf dem Weg zu einer integrierten Geschichte*, Göttingen: Wallstein, 2007; idem.: *The Years of Extermination: Nazi Germany and the Jews, 1939–1945*, New York: HarperCollins, 2007.
23 David Cesarani: *Final Solution. The Fate of the Jews 1933–49*, London: Macmillan, 2016.
24 Leibniz Institute for Contemporary History (ed.): *The Persecution and Murder of the European Jews by Nazi Germany, 1933–1945*, to date 4 volumes, Berlin: De Gruyter Oldenbourg, 2019–2020. The German original edition comprises 16 volumes: Institut für Zeitgeschichte (ed.): *Die Verfolgung und Ermordung der europäischen Juden durch das nationalsozialistische Deutschland 1933–1945*, Munich/Berlin: De Gruyter Oldenbourg, 2008–2021.
25 See, for example, Christopher Browning: *The Origins of the Final Solution. The Evolution of Nazi Jewish Policy 1939–1942*, London: Arrow, 2005.

in the occupied regions also show the dynamic that existed among the perpetrators in the lead-up to the deportations which further radicalized the antisemitic policy. However, the procedures in the individual countries differed and were sometimes also characterized by asynchronicity due to, among other reasons, the course of war, political developments on site, behavior of the associated governments, and foreign policy-related considerations.

Research on the Deportation of Sinti/Sintize and Roma/Romnja

As with the history of persecution of the minority in the Nazi era as a whole, for a long time little attention has been paid to the deportation of Sinti/Sintize and Roma/Romnja as a subject of research. Even today, the topic is much less differentiated within research than the deportation of Jews. In West Germany, the public discourse on this aspect of history was characterized by racist images and an apologia of the persecution of supposedly 'antisocial' people in the form of 'crime prevention' measures – even decades after the end of the war. In the book *The Destiny of European Gypsies* published in 1972, Donald Kenrick and Grattan Puxon systematically presented for the first time the persecution of Sinti/Sintize and Roma/Romnja in Nazi Germany, in German-occupied Europe and countries allied with Germany during the Second World War. The authors provided a historical event-based overview of the deportations and the camps that were connected to them.[26]

In 1996, Michael Zimmermann presented for the first time a comprehensive study showing the persecution and murder of Sinti/Sintize and Roma/Romnja in German-dominated Europe while taking a detailed look at the deportations by examining the various persecution measures.[27] More recent publications on the persecution of Sinti/Sintize and Roma/Romnja also describe the deportations in more detail by looking into specific aspects such as the treatment of people of mixed descent ('*Mischlinge*') and deferrals.[28] Today, many local studies and biographical accounts concerning the history of the deportation of Sinti/Sin-

---

26 Donald Kenrick and Grattan Puxon: *The Destiny of European Gypsies*, London: Chatto-Heinemann-Sussex University Press, 1972.
27 Michael Zimmermann: *Rassenutopie und Genozid. Die nationalsozialistische 'Lösung der Zigeunerfrage'*, Hamburg: Christians, 1996.
28 See, for example, Guenter Lew: *The Nazi Persecution of the Gypsies*, Oxford/New York: OUP, 2000.

tize and Roma/Romnja uncover the local dynamics in connection with the deportations on site. It is worth mentioning here, for instance, the regional study into the persecution of Sinti/Sintize and Roma/Romnja in Cologne by Karola Fings and Frank Sparing.[29] In addition, names of deportees have been researched and published as part of commemorative initiatives and the creation of memorials over recent years for various places.[30] The publication of the main book (*Hauptbuch*) of the '*Zigeunerlager*' ('gypsy camp') in Auschwitz-Birkenau, which documents the names of the deportees murdered there, is of particular importance.[31] Additionally, the recently begun research project *Encyclopedia to Document National Socialist Genocide of the Sinti/Sintize and Roma/Romnja in Europe*, based at the Antiziganism Research Unit at Heidelberg University, has taken on the task of presenting "the current international status of research in a comprehensive, empirically saturated overview" and bringing together "the widely dispersed, often difficult-to-access historical knowledge of genocide [on Sinti/Sintize and Roma/Romnja] and its causes, structures, and course",[32] which also raises expectations of a detailed description of the various deportations.

Historical Outline of the Deportation of Jews and of Sinti/Sintize and Roma/Romnja

Following years of social, economic, and legal exclusion of the Jewish population in Germany, which above all also aimed at forcing them to emigrate, the Nazi state deported around 17,000 Jews with Polish family background over the German-Polish border at the end of October 1938. This operation was implemented by the local police authorities and named '*Polenaktion*' ('Polish ac-

---

[29] Karola Fings and Frank Sparing: *Rassismus – Lager – Völkermord. Die nationalsozialistische Zigeunerverfolgung in Köln*, Cologne: Emons, 2005.
[30] See, for example, for Hamburg, the article by Kristina Vagt in this volume.
[31] Państwowe Muzeum Auschwitz-Birkenau (ed.): *Memorial Book. The Gypsies at Auschwitz-Birkenau / Księga pamięci Cyganie w obozie koncentracyjnym Auschwitz-Birkenau / Gedenkbuch der Sinti und Roma im Konzentrationslager Auschwitz-Birkenau*, 2 volumes, Munich et al.: K.G. Sauer, 1993. See also the contribution by Théophile Leroy in this volume.
[32] Heidelberg University: "Workshop zur Konzeption Enzyklopädie zum nationalsozialistischen Völkermord an den Sinti und Roma". Available online: https://www.uni-heidelberg.de/de/newsroom/enzyklopaedie-zum-nationalsozialistischen-voelkermord-an-den-sinti-und-roma. Last accessed: 07.03.2022. Translation by the author.

tion').³³ Although it lacked the experienced bureaucracy of the subsequent deportations, it was, as stated by Sybil Milton, the first mass deportation, which required the coordination of the railway, police, diplomacy, and financial authorities.³⁴

Like the Jewish population, Sinti/Sintize and Roma/Romnja – who, even during the Weimar Republic, were not legally equal citizens and had barely any opportunities to leave Germany after 1933³⁵ – were also persecuted and experienced further legal and social exclusion after the Nazis came to power. They also became the victims of raids. In July 1936, in the context of the upcoming Olympic Games, the Berlin police sent around 600 Sinti/Sintize and Roma/Romnja to the newly established *'Zigeunerlager'* in the suburb Marzahn.³⁶ Two years later "over 800 Sinti and Roma were living there in miserable conditions".³⁷ Other major cities also established *'Zigeunerlager'* in the second half of the 1930s, which represented "a special type in the Nazi internment camp system".³⁸ In the context of the Aktion *'Arbeitsscheu Reich'* (operation 'work-shy Reich'), many Sinti/Sintize and Roma/Romnja, like Jews, were taken to Buchenwald, Dachau, and Sachsenhausen concentration camps in the first half of 1938. A good year later, further Roma/Romnja from Burgenland in incorporated Austria were imprisoned in concentration camps in the Reich during another operation. These operations were ordered by Reichsführer-SS and Chief of the German Police Heinrich Himmler and took place as part of what was known as *'polizeiliche Vorbeugehaft'* ('preventive police custody').³⁹

At the time of the German invasion of Poland on September 1, 1939, around two thirds of the more than 500,000 Jews living in Germany in 1933 had emigrated. With the beginning of the war, the already severely restricted legal emigration options were significantly reduced further, as Germany was then at war with many states. At the same time, the number of Jews in the German-controlled territory had increased considerably due to the war, with over two million Jews liv-

---

[33] See most recently Alina Bothe and Gertrud Pickhan: "Ausgewiesen am 28. Oktober 1938 aus Berlin. Die Geschichte der 'Polenaktion'. Eine Einführung", in idem. (eds.): *Ausgewiesen! Berlin, 28.10.1938. Die Geschichte der 'Polenaktion'*, Berlin: Metropol, 2018, 12–29.
[34] Sibyl Milton: "The Expulsion of Polish Jews from Germany, October 1938 to July 1939. A Documentation", in *LBI Year Book* XXIX, 1984, 169–199, here 174.
[35] Cf. Wolfgang Wippermann: *Wie die Zigeuner. Antisemitismus und Antiziganismus im Vergleich*, Berlin: Elefanten Press, 1997, 150.
[36] Patricia Pientka: *Das Zwangslager für Sinti und Roma in Berlin-Marzahn. Alltag, Verfolgung und Deportation*, Berlin: Metropol, 2013.
[37] Wippermann, Zigeuner, 153. Translation by the author.
[38] Ibid. Translation by the author. Cf. Zimmermann, Rassenutopie, 93–100.
[39] Cf. Fings and Sparing, Rassismus, 93–108.

ing in Poland alone. From the viewpoint of the Nazi regime, forced emigration no longer appeared to be a realistic prospect.[40] With this in mind, the RSHA drew up plans to concentrate the Jewish population in a 'reservation' outside the Reich, whereby the deaths of the people affected were considered acceptable. The 'reservation' was initially intended to be in the *'Generalgouvernement'* in occupied Poland, later in Madagascar, which then was part of the French colonial empire, and finally in the occupied Soviet Union. SS-Hauptsturmführer Adolf Eichmann, then head of the Central Agency for Jewish Emigration in Vienna (Zentralstelle für jüdische Auswanderung), actually organized the first transports of Jews from Vienna, Mährisch-Ostrau, and Katowice to Nisko, south-west of Lublin in the *'Generalgouvernement'*, in October 1939. There, the deportees had to build an encampment on site. Even though this operation ultimately failed and the RSHA stopped the deportations there, transports resumed in early 1940.[41] In February 1940, a transport took place from Stettin (Szczecin) to the *'Generalgouvernement'* and, in October 1940, at the same time as the Madagascar plan was discussed, on the initiative of the local *Gauleiters* more than 6,500 Jews were taken from Baden and Palatinate in southwest Germany to Gurs internment camp in the unoccupied part of France at the foot of the Pyrenees.[42] In February/March 1941, around 5,000 Jews from Vienna were transported to the *'Generalgouvernement'*.[43]

The start of the war also meant radicalization of the persecution of Sinti/Sintize and Roma/Romnja. Alongside the aforementioned plans to deport the Jewish population to the *'Generalgouvernement'*, the deportation of Sinti/Sintize and Roma/Romnja to occupied Poland was also considered within the SS in the context of the *'völkische Flurbereinigung'* ('racial consolidation of land') proclaimed by Hitler.[44] An attempt by the chief of the German Criminal Police, Arthur Nebe, to add Sinti/Sintize and Roma/Romnja from Berlin to the Viennese transports of Jews to Nisko failed, however, due to the general cancellation of deportations to

---

40 Cf. Andrea Löw: "Introduction", in idem. (ed.): *The Persecution and Murder of the European Jews by Nazi Germany, 1933–1945. Volume 3: German Reich und Protectorate September 1939–September 1941*, Berlin/Boston: De Gruyter Oldenbourg, 2020, 13–67, here 13.
41 Cf. Jonny Moser: *Nisko. Die ersten Judendeportationen*, Vienna: Edition Steinbauer, 2012.
42 Cf. Memorial and Education Site House of the Wannsee Conference: "Gurs 1940". Available online: https://www.gurs1940.de/en/. Last accessed: 03.03.2022.
43 Dieter J. Hecht and Michaela Raggam-Blesch: "Der Weg in die Vernichtung begann mitten in der Stadt. Sammellager und Deportationen aus Wien 1941/42", in idem. and Heidemarie Uhl (eds.): *Letzte Orte. Die Wiener Sammellager und die Deportationen 1941/42*, Vienna/Berlin: Mandelbaum, 2019, 21–75, here 24–27.
44 Zimmermann, Rassenutopie, 167.

Nisko.⁴⁵ With the '*Festsetzungserlass*' ('detainment decree') on October 17, 1939, however, Himmler ordered a ban on Sinti/Sintize and Roma/Romnja that forbid them to leave their places of residence. Thereafter, camps were set up, which were ultimately used to prepare deportations.⁴⁶ In May 1940, the criminal police finally deported around 2,500 Sinti/Sintize and Roma/Romnja from Northern, Western, and Southwestern Germany to places in the '*Generalgouvernement*'. A shed at the port of Hamburg, the Hohenasperg prison near Stuttgart, and the trade fair center at Cologne-Deutz served as assembly camps; the latter was subsequently also used as an assembly camp for the deportation of Jews.⁴⁷ However, the German administration in the '*Generalgouvernement*' was not prepared for this deportation. The majority of the deportees were ultimately left to their own devices; some managed to return to the Reich for the time being.⁴⁸ Both deportations – of Sinti/Sintize and Roma/Romnja to the '*Generalgouvernement*' and that of Jews between October 1939 and the beginning of 1941 – were locally limited actions. They were all characterized by a certain improvisation on the part of the perpetrators as the whereabouts of the deportees at their destinations were usually not precisely planned. They also cannot be considered 'death transports'. However, without a doubt, they represented a radicalization in the policy against the persecuted groups who were, made possible by the war, forcibly deported across borders. The organizational experiences that the SS, the police, and the Reichsbahn, in particular, made during this time also formed the basis for the systematic transports that began later.

When the Germans invaded the Soviet Union in summer 1941, the Einsatzgruppen began to kill both the local Jewish population and local Sinti/Sintize and Roma/Romnja.⁴⁹ At the same time, in view of the military successes of the

---

45 Fings and Sparing, Rassismus, 195–196.
46 This included the Lackenbach camp in the Austrian Burgenland set up in November 1940, which was subordinate to the criminal police department in Vienna and existed until the end of the war. Up to 4,000 Sinti/Sintize and Roma/Romnja passed through this camp, in which the conditions were catastrophic. Lackenbach was the starting point for transports to both the Litzmannstadt ghetto in 1941 and also to Auschwitz-Birkenau in 1943. Cf. Susanne Urban: "'Dort in der Hölle haben wir fünf Jahre verbracht'. Lackenbach – ein KZ für Roma und Sinti", in Susanne Urban, Sascha Feuchert, and Markus Roth (eds.): *Stimmen der Überlebenden des 'Zigeunerlager' Lackenbach*, Göttingen: Wallstein, 2014, 15–23, here 17.
47 Zimmermann, Rassenutopie, 172–175; Fings and Sparing, Rassismus, 195–236.
48 See the article by Verena Meier in this volume and Zimmermann, Rassenutopie, 176–184.
49 Cf. Bert Hoppe and Hildrun Glass: "Einleitung", in idem. (eds.): *Die Verfolgung und Ermordung der europäischen Juden durch das nationalsozialistische Deutschland 1933–1945. Volume 7: Sowjetunion mit annektierten Gebieten I. Besetzte sowjetische Gebiete unter deutscher Militärverwaltung, Baltikum und Transnistrien*, Munich: De Gruyter Oldenbourg, 2011, 13–89, here 25–45;

German military, Hitler, anticipating victory, issued the order to begin deporting Jews directly instead of, as initially planned, waiting until the end of the war.[50] At the beginning, the focus lay on removing the Jewish population from major cities and thus creating facts. This initially concerned Jews from the '*Großdeutsches Reich*', i.e., from the '*Altreich*', '*Ostmark*' (Austria), and the Protectorate of Bohemia and Moravia as well as Luxemburg. The transports that followed marked the start of the systematic deportations. Systematic here means the comprehensive inclusion of all Jews – and those whom the Nazis considered to be Jewish – that they could find. At the same time, systematic means the establishment of an unparalleled Europe-wide 'deportation machinery', which was organized in a division of labor with the involvement of numerous institutions and individuals. The processes were constantly 'refined, ending in the systematic killing of the deportees in gas chambers.

The first transports left, among other places, Vienna, Prague, Berlin, and Frankfurt am Main heading for the ghetto Litzmannstadt (Łódź) in the second half of October 1941. Five transports with around 5,000 Roma/Romnja were also organized from Austria to Litzmannstadt at the same time. The original plan was that the deportees taken there would later be transported to the occupied Soviet Union. In fact, the deported Jews were housed in the already overcrowded ghetto, where the Nazis had concentrated the local Jews right after the beginning of the war and were later murdered at Kulmhof (Chełmno) and other killing sites.[51] The affected Roma/Romnja were housed in a separate area, the 'small ghetto', within the Litzmannstadt ghetto, where many died of typhoid fever; others were also taken to Kulmhof and killed there.[52]

Minsk and Kovno (Kaunas) followed as destinations for deportations of Jews from the Reich in November 1941, with transports to Riga, places in the '*General-*

Martin Holler: "'Killing Fields'. Der Völkermord an den Roma in Ost- und Südosteuropa am Beispiel der besetzten Sowjetunion und Jugoslawiens", in Karola Fings and Sybille Steinbacher (ed.): *Sinti und Roma. Der nationalsozialistische Völkermord in historischer und gesellschaftspolitischer Perspektive*, Göttingen: Wallstein, 2021, 82–111, here 82–93.
50 Susanne Heim: "Einleitung", in idem. (ed.): *Die Verfolgung und Ermordung der europäischen Juden durch das nationalsozialistische Deutschland 1933–1945. Volume 6: Deutsches Reich und Protektorat Böhmen und Mähren. Oktober 1941–März 1943*, Berlin/Boston: De Gruyter Oldenbourg, 2019, 13–83, here 17.
51 Ingo Loose: "Die Berliner Juden im Getto Litzmannstadt 1941–1944", in Stiftung Topographie des Terrors (ed.): *Die Berliner Juden im Getto Litzmannstadt 1941–1944. Ein Gedenkbuch*, Berlin: Stiftung Topographie des Terrors, 2009, 44–62, here 48, 57–60.
52 Erika Thurner: *National Socialism and Gypsies in Austria*, Tuscaloosa/London: University of Alabama Press, 1998, 102–105.

gouvernement', and Raasiku in occupied Estonia following later on.⁵³ In the first few months, there was no plan to comprehensively murder the deportees at the destinations. Nevertheless, the Nazi regime gladly accepted the vast numbers of deaths resulting from the catastrophic conditions on the trains, in the ghettos, and in the camps at the destinations and the arbitrariness of the local SS-authorities and guards.

In the context of the failed offensive against Moscow and the entry of the USA into the war in December 1941, the decision was ultimately made to systematically murder all Jews living within the German sphere of power.⁵⁴ The deportations thus became a crucial instrument within this plan. At the Wannsee Conference on January 20, 1942, representatives of various state and party agencies discussed the details of the mass murder of European Jews. In the preserved minutes, a total of over 11 million, who were to be deported and murdered, are listed in 31 countries and regions.⁵⁵ The conference also looked at the questions of who was to be included among the people affected and which groups should be temporarily exempt. Among others, this concerned Jews living in 'mixed marriages'.⁵⁶

In February 1942, only a few weeks after the Wannsee Conference and unrelated to it, in a local action an estimated number of 2,000 Sinti/Sintize and Roma/Romnja were brought from Königsberg to Białystok. There they were imprisoned in the city jail. Many of them died due to the catastrophic conditions. Some of the surviving detainees were later released on condition of sterilization. Others were further deported in the fall of 1942, first to a camp in the Reich Commissariat Ukraine and then to the Brest-Litovsk ghetto and finally to Auschwitz-Birkenau.⁵⁷

With regard to the deportation of the Jewish population from the Reich, which continued right after the Wannsee Conference, the deportees were systematically murdered at the destinations from spring 1942 onwards. Many of these transports had been taken to the Lublin District in the '*Generalgouvernement*'.

---

53 Cf. Alfred Gottwaldt and Diana Schulle: *Die "Judendeportationen" aus dem Deutschen Reich 1941–1945*, Wiesbaden: Marix, 2005, 84–259.
54 Cf. Peter Klein: "Die Wannsee-Konferenz als Echo auf die gefallene Entscheidung zur Ermordung der europäischen Juden", in Norbert Kampe and idem. (eds.): *Die Wannsee-Konferenz am 20. Januar 1942. Dokumente, Forschungsstand, Kontroversen*, Cologne/Weimar/Vienna: Böhlau, 2013, 182–201.
55 Protocol of the Wannsee conference, R1000857, page 1, Politisches Archiv des Auswärtigen Amts, printed in Kampe and Klein, Dokumente, 40–54, here 45.
56 Ibid.
57 Zimmermann, Rassenutopie, 228–229.

After a short stay at a transit camp or ghetto there, the Jews were killed at Sobibor and Belcez death camps, which were set up as part of *'Aktion Reinhardt'* ('operation Reinhardt'). From October 1942, all transports 'to the East' headed to Auschwitz-Birkenau concentration and death camp. The deportees were either killed there upon arrival or were selected for slave labor. With the exception of a very small number who survived until liberation, most of the slave laborers perished due to the horrible conditions at work and in the camp.

Aside from a few exceptions, older people over 65 years of age had been exempted from the first transports 'to the East'. In public, these transports were euphemistically justified by the claim that the deported Jews would be conscripted to perform hard labor. Thus, older people could not be included without undermining the argument that older people "did not represent a danger and they were not able to build any roads – many of them actually lived in old people's homes".[58] However, from June 1942, this group of people, as well as highly decorated war veterans and functionaries from the Jewish Communities, were also deported to the Theresienstadt ghetto. According to Nazi propaganda, they were to spend their old age there. In fact, many of them died due to the living conditions they experienced,[59] others were deported to death camps 'in the East', where they were murdered.

At the same time as the mass deportations from the Reich, which lasted until early 1943, the SS and the (occupation) authorities began to deport the respective Jewish populations from occupied countries and satellite states. Auschwitz-Birkenau initially served as the destination for transports primarily from Western Europe, later also as a central death camp for all other transports. Over 100,000 people from the occupied Netherlands were deported there as well as to Sobibor and Theresienstadt, among others, from July 1942, mostly via camp Westerbork.[60] Around 25,000 Jews were deported to Auschwitz from Belgium via the Dossin barracks at Mechelen, and more than 70,000 people reached Auschwitz from the occupied and unoccupied parts of France via the Drancy assembly camp in a suburb of Paris.[61] Among the Jews deported from the West Eu-

---

58 Hilberg, Destruction, volume 2, 450.
59 Anna Hájková: "Mutmaßungen über deutsche Juden: Alte Menschen aus Deutschland im Theresienstädter Ghetto", in Andrea Löw, Doris L. Bergen, and idem. (eds.): *Alltag im Holocaust: Jüdisches Leben im Großdeutschen Reich 1941–1945*, Munich: De Gruyter Oldenbourg, 2013, 179– 198.
60 See also the contribution by Daan de Leeuw in this volume.
61 Cf. Katja Happe, Barbara Lambauer, and Clemens Meier-Wolthausen: "Einleitung", in idem. (eds.): *Die Verfolgung und Ermordung der europäischen Juden durch das nationalsozialistische Deutschland 1933–1945. Volume 12: West- und Nordeuropa Juni 1942–1945*, Berlin/Munich/Bos-

ropean countries were also many who had fled there from Germany in the years before. Jews were also deported to Auschwitz in a relatively small number from Norway.[62]

Some of the Croatian Jews who had not already died in the camps within the German satellite state were also deported to Auschwitz in summer 1942.[63] Transports with a total of almost 58,000 people from Slovakia reached the ghettos in the Lublin District from as early as March 1942, and Auschwitz for the first time in April 1942. The Ostbahn (Eastern Railway) also transported the Jews who were still alive in the '*Generalgouvernement*' ghettos to the '*Aktion Reinhardt*' death camps Belzec, Sobibor, and Treblinka from March 1942, and later also to Auschwitz.[64]

As a consequence of the Auschwitz decree published in December 1943, the criminal police deported 22,600 Sinti/Sintize and Roma/Romnja from Germany and some German-occupied countries to Auschwitz-Birkenau. This also included, for instance, people from the Netherlands, who were deported to Auschwitz via Westerbork, which was primarily used as an assembly camp for the deportation of Jews.[65] The SS imprisoned the deportees in the '*Zigeunerlager*', a separate area in Auschwitz-Birkenau. Those who did not die there as a result of the catastrophic conditions and who were not transported to Natzweiler for medical experiments, either to the Auschwitz I main camp as former members of the Wehrmacht, or to other concentration camps for forced labor were murdered in the gas chambers in the summer of 1944.[66]

Roma/Romnja from Southeastern Europe were also included in deportations. In the 'Independent State of Croatia', several thousand people were thus taken to the Jasenovac concentration camp in early summer 1942, where they were murdered.[67] At the end of 1944, the Arrow Cross regime deported Roma/Romnja from Hungary to sub-camps of Buchenwald and Ravensbrück concentra-

---

ton: De Gruyter Oldenbourg, 2015, 7–83, here 31–83; Katja Happe, Michael Mayer, and Maja Peer: "Introduction", in idem. (ed.): *The Persecution and Murder of the European Jews by Nazi Germany, 1933–1945. Volume 5: Western and Northern Europe 1940–June 1942*, Berlin/Boston: De Gruyter Oldenbourg, 2019.

62 Happe, Lambauer, and Meier-Wolthausen, Einleitung, 13–83.
63 Ivo Goldstein and Slavko Goldstein: *The Holocaust in Croatia*, Pittsburgh: University of Pittsburgh Press, 2016, 362–370.
64 Cf. Stephan Lehnstaedt: *Der Kern des Holocaust. Bełżec, Sobibór, Treblinka und die Aktion Reinhardt*, Munich: C.H. Beck, 2007, 63–76.
65 Zimmermann, Rassenutopie, 314–315.
66 Ibid., 339–344.
67 Holler, Killing Fields, 102–103.

tion camps for forced labor.⁶⁸ In Romania, which was allied with Germany, the fascist military dictatorship under Ion Antonescu deported around 25,000 of the more than 200,000 Roma/Romnja who lived in the country to Transnistria, the area that formerly belonged to the Soviet Union in the east of the country, in summer and early fall 1942. Some of the Roma/Romnja had to use their own horse-drawn carts for transport, supervised by military and police. Many of them died on the journey due to the cold, malnutrition, and exhaustion.⁶⁹ Already in the fall of 1941, Transnistria had become the destination of deportations of Jews. About 150,000 were deported from Bukovina and Bessarabia by the Romanian authorities. In Transnistria the deportees were left to fend for themselves, many perished due to hunger, diseases, and debilitation, others were murdered there by German Einsatzgruppen, Romanian units, members of the 'Volksdeutscher Selbstschutz' and Ukrainian auxiliary policemen.⁷⁰

At the beginning of 1943, several tens of thousands of Greek Jews were deported from the port city of Saloniki, which had a large Jewish population. Other parts of Greece followed shortly afterwards.⁷¹ The last mass deportation concerned Hungary. From the middle of May 1944, over 400,000 people were deported from there, including Jews from the regions occupied by Hungary, particularly Bača, which was previously part of Yugoslavia. The people affected were mostly murdered in Auschwitz-Birkenau; some of them ended up in Germany as forced laborers.⁷²

On Perpetrators and Research Gaps

Despite the parallels between the deportation of the Jewish population on the one hand and of Sinti/Sintize and Roma/Romnja on the other, and also despite specific synchronicities and overlaps, as in the case of the deportations to the Litzmannstadt ghetto in 1941 and the mass murder in Auschwitz-Birkenau,

---

68 Zimmermann, Rassenutopie, 292.
69 Ibid., 286–289. See also the contribution by Viorel Achim in this volume.
70 Mariana Hausleitner, Souzana Hazan, and Barbara Hutzelmann: "Einführung", in idem. (eds.): *Die Verfolgung und Ermordung der europäischen Juden durch das nationalsozialistische Deutschland 1933–1945. Volume 13: Slowakei, Rumänien und Bulgarien*, Berlin/Boston: De Gruyter Oldenbourg, 2018, 13–95, here 59–63.
71 Cf. Iason Chandrinos and Anna Maria Droumpouki: "The German Occupation and the Holocaust in Greece: A Survey", in Giorgos Antoniou and A. Dirk Moses (eds.): *The Holocaust in Greece*, New York: Cambridge University Press, 2018, 15–35.
72 Cf. Gerlach and Aly, Kapitel.

both are to be viewed separately. This not only relates to the chronology of the persecution measures and therefore the deportations, but it is also expressed in the responsibilities on part of the perpetrators. Although all deportations were planned and organized within the system of terror of Reichsführer-SS and Chief of the German Police Heinrich Himmler and within the RSHA established in 1939, the Gestapo was in charge of the deportation of Jews and the Reichskriminalpolizeiamt (RKPA, Reich Criminal Police Office) for Sinti/Sintize and Roma/Romnja. In the – relatively well-researched – RSHA sub-department IV B 4 'Jewish affairs and evacuation matters' (*'Judenangelegenheiten und Räumungsangelegenheiten*'), Adolf Eichmann organized the transports of the Jews, but was also responsible for the mass transports of other groups, including Sinti/Sintize and Roma/Romnja.[73] Within the RKPA, in relation to Sinti/Sintize and Roma/Romnja, the 'Reichszentrale zur Bekämpfung des Zigeunerunwesens' ('Reich Headquarters for the Gypsy Nuisance') was the crucial agency for the issuing of instructions, monitoring, and "communication with foreign agencies".[74] The Reichszentrale operated in close collaboration with the 'Rassenhygienische und bevölkerungsbiologische Forschungsstelle' ('Racial Hygiene and Population Biology Research Unit') at the Reichsgesundheitsamt (Reich Department of Health) under Robert Ritter.

The specific preparation and implementation on site was the responsibility of the respective regional and local agencies. In the '*Altreich*', these were the Stapoleitstellen (state police headquarters) respectively the Stapostellen (state police stations) and the Kriminalpolizeileitstellen (criminal police headquarters) respectively the Kriminalpolizeistellen (criminal police stations); in the occupied countries the offices of the SS Security Police were usually responsible. Further, many actors and agencies in Germany and abroad were also involved in the deportations in one form or another, such as the Reichsbahn or the financial authorities, the Foreign Office, and the governments and local administrations of the states allied with or occupied by Germany. In some cases, Eichmann's employees were directly on site to organize the deportations, whereby they were able to draw from their former experiences in other locations. The best-known example of this is Alois Brunner. Brunner initially organized the systematic deportations from Austria as head of the Central Agency for Jewish Emigration in Vienna between fall 1941 and 1942. He then went to Berlin before going to Saloniki in early 1943 and then to Paris; in 1944 he was in Bratislava. In all the men-

---

[73] Cf. Hans Safrian: *Eichmann und seine Gehilfen*, Frankfurt am Main: Fischer Taschenbuch, 1995; Thurner, National Socialism, 102.
[74] Zimmermann, Rassenutopie, 109. Translation by the author.

tioned places, he was in charge of organizing the deportation of Jews for which he was considered particularly brutal. He took with him his experiences in organizing assembly camps and transports, in the 'selection' and imprisonment of victims, and in the perfidious instrumentalization of the Jewish Communities.[75]

If one looks closer at Brunner's actions, the way the deportations were carried out in the individual locations, despite all their local differences, becomes apparent. We now know relatively precisely not only what the orders of the RSHA and the respective political backgrounds were, but also how the deportations were organized and, in part, what the conditions were like in the assembly camps. Through perpetrator research and local studies, we know a great deal about the biographical backgrounds of the perpetrators, their attitudes, and their behavior. Thus, we can create typologies and identify the functionality of various perpetrator groups in the mass murder and, in particular, also in the implementation of the deportations.[76]

Despite the research situation described, which could only be touched on here, serious research gaps continue to exist. These include, for instance, the events and structures on site, such as individual assembly camps, as well as structural elements, such as a comparative analysis of the various camps and transports. In addition, certain groups of perpetrators have not yet been researched sufficiently, such as bailiffs involved in the seizure of assets. The behavior of the rest of the population, particularly neighbors who were witnesses of raids, also represents a research desideratum. The police system, particularly the interlinking of the various departments and units of the Gestapo, the criminal police, and the protection police, especially in larger cities in the '*Altreich*', is not as well-researched as one might assume. Although the SS in the occupied and allied countries and its collaboration with the Wehrmacht and the local institutions is subject of a series of instructive individual investigations, in which the deportations and ghettos as destinations also play a role, research gaps nevertheless still exist here, too. Overall, it can be said that the research situation for individual countries, regions, and cities and within the stated areas of research differs significantly, and that comparative and comprehensive research approaches continue to represent exceptions. Additionally, a complete identification of, above all, the deported and murdered Sinti/Sintize and Roma/Romnja and Jews is still pending.

---

75 Safrian, Eichmann, 189–319.
76 Gerhard Paul: "Von Psychopathen, Technokraten des Terrors und 'ganz gewöhnlichen' Deutschen", in idem. (ed.): *Die Täter der Shoah. Fanatische Nationalsozialisten oder ganz normale Deutsche?*, Göttingen: Wallstein, 2002, 13–90.

Although numerous first-hand accounts or biographical studies exist, which focus attention on the perspectives of the deportees, a systematical investigation into the situation of the victims is lacking. Within this, in terms of an integrated history of the Shoah and the Porajmos, research should be conducted into the experiences, survival strategies, and also acts of resistance of the deportees before being deported, i.e. in the assembly camps, during transports, and at the destinations.[77] It can be assumed that the conditions sometimes differed significantly and there is no conformity in the experiences of the victims, even for a place like Berlin, because the conditions depended on the time the people were picked up and on the destination of the transports.[78] For instance, some cities in the Reich had permanent assembly camps that existed months or even years, while they were only created on a temporary basis in other places. The conditions in the assembly camps sometimes differed drastically, whereby the situation in the camps where the transports to Theresienstadt were prepared, usually was somewhat better for those affected than in the assembly camps for the 'transports to the East'. The Jewish population was sometimes collected from apartments – quite often 'Jews apartments' ('*Judenwohnungen*') in which several families or individuals had to live together –, homes, or even from labor camps. Furthermore, the conditions in the camps set up by the local administrations for Sinti/Sintize and Roma/Romnja also differed from city to city. Ultimately, as Alfred Gottwaldt and Diana Schulle have written, no transport was the same "as any other with regard to date, departure station, scope, course, destination, and other surrounding circumstances, so that a differentiated consideration and also a detailed description avoiding assumptions are always required in every case".[79] Part of an integrated history would also be to systematically consider the perpetrators on site and make structures and agencies involved the subject of comparison.

About this Publication

This publication addresses the deportations as a specific part of the Shoah and the Porajmos. Deportations – i.e. the transport carried out by means of state

---

[77] Cf. Tanja von Fransecky: *Flucht von Juden aus Deportationszügen in Frankreich, Belgien und den Niederlanden*, Berlin: Metropol, 2014.
[78] Cf. Cesarani, Solution.
[79] Gottwaldt and Schulle, Judendeportationen, 15. Translation by the author.

coercion,[80] which usually took place by train – were a central structural element of the Nazi persecution and of extermination policies as well as a prerequisite for the mass murder of millions. However, as Birte Kundrus and Beate Meyer have written in the special edition of *Beiträge zur Geschichte des Nationalsozialismus* on the deportations of Jews from Germany, the Nazi deportations are "difficult to reduce to a single concept both historically and legally".[81] According to Meyer and Kundrus, it would be a mistake to equate them with 'death transports' because, as explained above, they only gradually developed into these later on.[82] Nevertheless, it is difficult to show a strict separation as the transports were carried out by the same actors and within the same structures; and the conditions for the affected victims at the places of departure were also often the same. In addition, even those deported between fall 1941 and spring 1942 ended up in the Nazi machinery of murder and, in some cases, were killed before the systematic mass murder of the deported Jews from the '*Altreich*' had even begun. Against this backdrop, the articles in this volume relate to aspects of all transports after the beginning of the systematic deportations of the Jewish population in October 1941. They also include the transports of Sinti/Sintize and Roma/Romnja into the '*Generalgouvernement*' in 1940, which were not 'death transports' but often preceded the murder of the deportees far away from their former places of residence. The deportations of Roma/Romnja to Transnistria in 1942 are also addressed in this publication. Here, too, those affected were left to fend for themselves, but a large proportion perished as a direct result of the deportation. However, the contributions do not focus on incarceration in concentration camps, such as in connection with the pogroms of November 1938 or in the first few years after the Nazis came to power as part of '*Schutzhaft*' ('protective custody') or '*Vorbeugehaft*' ('preventive custody') within Aktion '*Arbeitsscheu Reich*'.[83]

The deportations of Jews and of Sinti/Sintize and Roma/Romnja were not the only mass transports of people during the Nazi period. The German authorities

---

80 For the contemporary definition, see Joseph Heimberger: "Deportation", in Alexander Elster and Heinrich Lingemann (eds.): *Handwörterbuch der Kriminologie und der anderen strafrechtlichen Hilfswissenschaften*, volume 1, Berlin/Leipzig 1933, 217–227.
81 Birte Kundrus and Beate Meyer: "Editorial", in idem. (eds.): *Die Deportation der Juden aus Deutschland. Pläne – Praxis – Reaktionen 1938–1945*, Göttingen: Wallstein, 2004, 11–20, here 12. Translation by the author.
82 Ibid.
83 However, Verena Meier also looks at the operation in her article, which concerns the 'prevention department' within the criminal police, in order to present in detail the organizational changes within the criminal police leading to the deportations in 1943.

also used special trains ('*Sonderzüge*') for the '*Umsiedlung*' ('resettlement') of '*Volksdeutsche*' ('ethnic Germans') and for the transport of Wehrmacht soldiers. Millions of forced laborers and prisoners of war were also transported with the Reichsbahn. Although there were direct links such as to the logistics of the Reichsbahn, these transports, with one exception, which is connected to the deportations of the Jewish population,[84] are not the subject of this publication. What was known as the *Krankentransporte* (transport of sick people), which transported people classified as 'disabled' to their deaths, also cannot be looked at here.

The focus of the volume lies on presenting and discussing sources that relate to the deportations, as well as discussing research questions. These generally concern regional or local historical developments that highlight the structure of the deportations and the deportation system: What was the organization of the transports like? Which agencies were involved and what was the division of labor e. g. within the police? How did the deportees react? What route through the camp system was taken by the deportees who were not killed at the place of arrival? How did the Gestapo make use of the infrastructure of the persecutees, such as by using buildings and the labor of employees of the Jewish Communities? These are just a few of the questions investigated in the contributions that follow.

The contributions, which adopt very different methodologies, concern not only very different locations and countries in Nazi-occupied Europe, but also focus on very different periods, and thus show both the temporal and the geographic dimension of the deportations and mass murder.

At the same time, the articles show the abundance of different sources that are accessible and how they can be used for research in a qualitative and quantitative regard. Alongside preserved documents of the perpetrators, the sources also comprise, for example, documents originated from the victims, such as petitions from the Theresienstadt ghetto and from Transnistria,[85] and sources from the post-war period, for instance interviews survivors gave shortly after they returned to their countries of origin.[86] The preservation but also the cataloging of the holdings are very differently developed. While, for example, the documents from the Litzmannstadt ghetto – which is the subject of no less than two contributions – have largely been preserved, and contain, among other things, the

---

[84] See the contribution by Alexandra Pulvermacher in this volume.
[85] See the contributions by Tomáš Fedorovič and Viorel Achim in this volume. On this topic in general, see also Thomas Pegelow Kaplan and Wolf Gruner: *Resisting Persecution. Jews and their Petitions during the Holocaust*, New York/Oxford: Berghahn, 2020.
[86] See the contributions by Johannes Meerwald in this volume.

bank records of the ghetto, the deportation documents for most local Gestapo and criminal police offices on the deportations in the '*Altreich*' do not exist anymore. The transport lists for the deportation of Jews from the Reich are an exception here, as they have not only largely been preserved in the Arolsen Archives but have also been partly extensively indexed and can thus be quantitatively evaluated via metadata.

In view of the complexity of the historical subject, it seems obvious that the articles published here can only cover small geographic and thematic areas, and the selection, which is based on the presentation during the conference, does not express any content-related emphasis and is far from having any claim to comprehensiveness. Nevertheless, they are intended to contribute towards an integrated history of the deportations in the Nazi era.

The first contributions of the volume are devoted to archival sources, online portals, and methodological approaches. Following this introduction, *Henning Borggräfe* outlines a general model of the sources on deportations in a fundamental text. He presents various relevant source categories using eight contexts, from the preparation of a transport to the remembrance of the deportations after the end of the war. Moreover, he shows how spatial concentration processes within Berlin for the Jewish population in the years and months leading up to the deportations can be presented by linking metadata from the transport lists of the deportation of the Jewish population to other sources. The article exemplifies the digital possibilities of how sources can be quantitatively evaluated by cataloging and processing large amounts of data. The transport lists have been preserved in the Arolsen Archives and form part of the relevant holdings stored there regarding the deportations both of Jews and of Sinti/Sintize and Roma/Romnja. These also include documents from the concentration camps as well as post-war compilations and correspondence files from the International Tracing Service, the predecessor institution of the Arolsen Archives.

Many of the contributions printed in this volume refer (in part) to these sources. In their article, *Christian Groh* and *Kim Dresel* offer a systematic overview of these holdings and discuss recent projects in digitizing, indexing, and cataloging material. The majority of the holdings of the Arolsen Archives can now be viewed online and are part of a growing number of resources relating to the deportations on the Internet. In the contribution "Potentials of Databases for Research and Culture of Remembrance Using the Deportation of Jews under the Nazi Regime as an Example", *Max Strnad* investigates various relevant portals and shows how their potential can be better exploited in the future, if information is clearly identifiable and, above all, better interlinked. Alongside the online collection of the Arolsen Archives, Strnad refers to Yad Vashem's *Transports to Extinction: Holocaust (Shoah) Deportation Database*, the *Statistik und Deportation der jüdischen*

Bevölkerung aus dem Deutschen Reich website, and the *Biografisches Gedenkbuch der Münchner Juden 1933–1945*. Besides larger institutions and online resources, documents on the deportations have also been preserved scattered in numerous smaller archives, including private collections. In her article, *Susanne Kill* uses the personal archive of Alfred Gottwaldt to discuss the importance of private archives for research; she also investigates the function of the Reichsbahn and the state of research in this regard. Railway historian Alfred Gottwaldt, who passed away in 2015, was one of the most knowledgeable experts on the history of the deportations of Jews from Germany and of the Reichsbahn in the Nazi era, which organized and carried out the transports throughout Europe. His extensive collection can be viewed in the archive of the Deutsche Bahn Stiftung. Archives and databases are important sources not only for historians but also for family members looking for biographical information about persecuted and murdered relatives, who were often deported before they were killed. From this perspective, *Aya Zarfati*, in her text "Interaction, Confusion and Potential: On the Clash between Archives (on Nazi History) and Family Research", discusses using, above all, relevant databases. She sketches ways in which they and archives in general could better address family members and their needs and make information and insights for biographical research easier available, accessible, and comprehensible.

Two articles are dedicated to preserved visual sources of the deportations of the Jewish population from the German Reich, which represent an independent type of source. *Christoph Kreutzmüller* offers an overview of preserved photographs and contextualizes them in the pictorial tradition in Germany. In her sociological contribution, *Elisabeth Pönisch* analyzes the events before, during, and after the deportation as a social process. The basis is not only photographs, but also film material, narrative passages, and artefacts.

The subsequent articles concern "Racial Registrations, Forced Housing, and Local Deportation Dynamics". *Verena Meier* uses the deportation of Sinti/Sintize and Roma/Romnja from Magdeburg to illustrate the organizational structure within the criminal police while also showing how this changed between Aktion 'Arbeitsscheu Reich' in June 1938 and the deportation to Auschwitz-Birkenau in March 1943 and how the police were able to rely on existing structures. The basis for the study is provided by various sources, including prisoner books from the police prison in Magdeburg. *Théophile Leroy* also looks at the persecution and deportation of Sinti/Sintize and Roma/Romnja over a prolonged period of time (between 1940 and 1944), namely in Alsace, which was annexed by Germany. Local criminal police records, among other documents, are his main sources. Leroy highlights how the escalating persecution and genocidal policies targeting Sinti/Sintize and Roma/Romnja were implemented. He is able to show that the Strasbourg deportation of March 1943 was the result of specific racial identification operations. The local dynamics are also the subject of the article by *Joachim Schröder*. He focuses on the example of Düsseldorf and, on the basis of files from the Gestapo and other local actors, addresses the subject of '*Judenhäuser*' ('Jews houses'), which has so far been largely overlooked within research. The admissions to a '*Judenhaus*', which began in 1939, preceded the deportations and were the expression of the increasing concentration of the Jewish population within cities in the German Reich on the eve of the deportations. In the early 1940s, Jewish old people's homes were also places where many Jewish people lived as a result of persecution. Following the contribution by Henning Borggräfe on the Berlin transport lists, *Akim Jah* shows, using the example of the Jewish Old People's Home in Berlin's Gerlachstraße, how Jewish institutions were misused as assembly camps by the Gestapo. He evaluated transport lists in order to trace the destruction of the old people's home and the deportation of its residents during 1942 and show the use of the buildings first as a temporary and then as a permanent assembly camp for the transports to Theresienstadt. Unlike in Berlin, where this was only the case from the beginning of 1943, in Vienna the mass transports of Jews were largely concluded in October 1942. *Michaela Raggam-Blesch* focuses on the fate of 'protected' groups during the last years of the war in Vienna. Like in Berlin and other places in the Reich, smaller groups remained or were initially protected from being deported following the conclusion of the mass deportations, particularly members of mixed families with a non-Jewish spouse or parent. How they were ultimately deported from Vienna's Nordbahnhof in the years 1943 to 1944 is outlined by Raggam-Blesch using various, above all local sources with different provenances. *Dóra Pataricza* presents and analyzes the fates of the Jewish deportees and returnees in May/June 1944 in the transborder region around Hungarian Szeged, which also includes the Serbian region of Bačka, which was occupied by Hungary. She also outlines an international project, which uses all relevant sources from various archives around the world to identify the names of around 10,500 Jews who were deported from Szeged and to develop a database for them.

Several contributions are dedicated to the persecution routes following deportation in various contexts. *Kristina Vagt* outlines the transports of Sinti/Sintize and Roma/Romnja from Northern Germany to the '*Generalgouvernement*' in 1940. Those affected were taken to Belzec forced labor camp and later left to fend for themselves. Vagt investigates the further persecution of the deportees based, among other sources, on compensation records and documents from the Arolsen Archives. The article was created in the context of research into the names of deportees for the planned documentation center on the site of the former Hannoverscher Bahnhof in Hamburg, from which the deportation transports departed. *Alfred Eckert* looks into the persecution routes of those deported from Nuremberg to Riga in November 1941. He outlines how the deportees were initially imprisoned in various camps in the Riga region and later deported to the Stutthof concentration camp, among other places. In the process, he shows how the deportees gradually died or were killed and discusses the chances of survival by statistically analyzing the social ties of the deportees. The author was able to access unusually good source documents during his investigation, as both the Gestapo files from Würzburg, a field office of the Nuremberg Gestapo, and historic photos from there have been preserved. *Daan de Leeuw* also looks into the trajectories through the concentration camp system as he focuses on a group of Jewish deportees who were initially deported from Westerbork to Sobibor in March 1943. Drawing upon wartime and post-war documents in the Arolsen Archives and survivor testimonies, he reconstructs and visualizes the pathways of the deportees through geographic information system (GIS) and cartographic tools. The subject of the article by *Alexandra Patrikiou* is the history of an individual Jewish deportee, Errikos Botton, who was deported from Athens in August 1944 and managed to escape from the train. Using Botton's typescript memoir and two Oral History interviews, Patrikiou outlines the deportation and escape, and thus addresses the self-assertion of the deportees, a topic to which little attention has been paid within historiography for a long time. The text by *Johannes Meerwald* is also based on post-war sources. In his contribution, Meerwald evaluates interview protocols from the National Committee for Attending Deportees (DEGOB), which held interviews with Hungarian survivors of the Holocaust right after their return. Using the example of the deportations to the Dachau concentration camp complex, he discusses the extent to which the protocols can contribute to a deeper understanding of persecution routes and shows what qualitative information the interviews contain about the deportations.

The last five articles concern the situation in ghettos and other deportation destinations. *Ingo Loose* focuses on the research situation regarding the Litzmannstadt ghetto as a deportation destination for transports from the German Reich in fall 1941 and reflects on the available historical knowledge and existing knowledge gaps. He also discusses the uneven reception and evaluation of the preserved sources, i.e. archival findings as well as survivors' testimonies. *Anna Veronica Pobbe* also concerns herself with the ghetto in Litzmannstadt. She uses the preserved bank records from the ghetto account to present an unusual source on deportations and explains what these can reveal about the functioning of the ghetto. In this way, she shows what money went to companies in the city and the surrounding area that were involved in the deportations. The Theresienstadt ghetto held particular importance among the destinations for the deportation of Jews. It was a transit camp for Czech Jews as well as the destination for *'Alterstransporte'* ('transports of the elderly') from the Reich, among other things. A large proportion of the ghetto inhabitants were actually deported from Theresienstadt to the death camps. How those enlisted for two transports to Auschwitz-Birkenau in September 1943 attempted to be deferred from further transports is shown by *Tomáš Fedorovič* who analyzes preserved petitions. The article by *Viorel Achim* also concerns petitions. When Romanian Roma/Romnja were deported to Transnistria in summer 1942, many of them wrote petitions to the authorities. Hundreds of these petitions have been preserved in various archives. They offer an insight into the situation of those affected by this deportation, during which, as stated above, many people died. Achim discusses the sources with their specificity and potential and he uses them as a basis to investigate the living conditions of the deportees. The combination of the deportation of Jews from Berlin and the transporting of Polish forced laborers from the Zamość region at the turn of the year 1942/1943 is presented in detail by *Alexandra Pulvermacher*. As part of the 'Germanization' of the region in the Lublin District, Poles were transported to Auschwitz and also taken to Berlin as forced laborers, the latter to replace Jewish forced laborers, who were to be deported to Auschwitz at the same time. The contribution, which is based on a Polish-German source edition, highlights not only the planning-related context of both transports, but also of the Holocaust and the 'Germanization', which were both part of the Nazi population policy.

In the articles, it is not always possible to avoid the language of the perpetrators and their designations for groups who have a specific history of persecution. This includes, for instance, the terms 'nomads' and 'sedentary' Roma/Romnja. The same is also true for words that were used euphemistically at the time or were intended to be pejorative, such as *'Osttransport'*, *'Judenhäuser'*, 'Gypsy villages' or 'Gypsy mayor', and – in the reproduction of quotations – the term 'Gypsy'. The terms Jew and Sinti/Sintize and Roma/Romnja are also generally used in the texts for those people who were persecuted as such, regardless of their self-image.

All the quotations in German or other languages have been translated into English; they can be viewed in the stated original when required. For location names, the names commonly used at this time in the respective national language have been used, with the exception of the names of ghettos and camps set up by the Germans in the occupied countries, for which the German term from that time is used.

As mentioned above, the publication is based on a conference of the same name, which the Arolsen Archives organized in November 2020.[87] This event was preceded by two conferences which we could refer to and from which we were able to obtain ideas during our preparations: The conference organized by the Vienna Wiesenthal Institute for Holocaust Studies *Deportations of the Jewish Population in Territories under Nazi Control. Comparative Perspectives on the Organisation of the Path to Annihilation* in Vienna in June 2019 took a systematic look at the deportations of the Jewish population with a transnational perspective that went beyond local research questions.[88] The event *Documenting and Exhibiting Persecution and Deportations in Europe from 1938 to 1945*, which was held under the leadership of Neuengamme Concentration Camp Memorial in Hamburg in February 2020, was devoted to the question of how the deportations of Jews and of Sinti/Sintize and Roma/Romnja can be the subject of exhibitions.[89] We see this publication explicitly as a supplement to these two events and thank the colleagues of the implementing institutions for stimulating discussions. The editors would also like to thank all the authors for their contributions and all of the archives for making the documents available. Sincere thanks also go to the colleagues at the Arolsen Archives, who have contributed to the success of both the conference and the publication with their great commitment in the background: Anette Döhring, Kerstin Hofmann, Christa Seidenstücker, Margit Vogt, and especially Christine Gräser, Christian Höschler, and Christiane Weber.

---

[87] See Jakob Müller and Alina Bothe: "Tagungsbericht: Deportationen im Nationalsozialismus – Quellen und Forschung, 02.11.2020 – 04.11.2020 digital (Potsdam)". Available online: www.hsozkult.de/conferencereport/id/tagungsberichte-8923. Last accessed: 11.03.2022.
[88] See the conference proceeding: Michaela Raggam-Blesch, Peter Black, and Marianne Windsperger (eds.): *Deportations of the Jewish Population in Territories under Nazi Control*, Vienna: NAP, 2022 (forthcoming).
[89] See the conference proceeding: Oliver von Wrochem (ed.): *Deportationen dokumentieren und ausstellen. Neue Konzepte der Visualisierung von Shoah und Porajmos*, Berlin: Metropol, 2022.

Archival Sources, Online Portals and Approaches

Henning Borggräfe
Sources on Deportations

A General Model and a Methodological Approach for Researching Person-Related Records based on the Berlin Transport Lists

Abstract: This paper discusses the existing sources on the history of the deportations of Jews as well as Sinti and Roma and, using the transport lists of the deportations of Jews from Berlin as an example, presents a methodological approach for digital-based research with archival mass data. In the first part, eight contexts will be identified in which different sources on the history of the deportations were produced by various actors. The paper then addresses aspects of provenance and accessibility and distinguishes documentation centers on the between three main categories of sources that have been used to date for different research approaches. In the second part, using archival data from the Berlin transport lists collection held at the Arolsen Archives as well as matchings with archival data from two other holdings, the paper tests how person-related serial records can be analyzed using a Geographic Information System and quantitative data evaluation. Here, the focus is on spatial dimensions of the deportations from Berlin and their dynamics, on concentration processes of the Jewish population in the city prior to deportations, and on the relations between mass data analysis and narrative sources. In the course of the digitization of archives, a growing amount of person-related mass data is being generated. This paper aims to contribute to a broader discussion of the opportunities and limits of their use for historical research using digital tools and methods.

Introduction

In May 1946, a team of the American Jewish Joint Distribution Committee (AJDC), which had set up a tracing office in the former capital of defeated Nazi Germany, found Gestapo transport lists in the basement of a Berlin finance administration building.[1] The lists contained the names, dates of birth, last residential address-

---

[1] Larry Lubetsky: *Berlin AJDC Tracing Office, 1945–1947*, Berlin: AJDC, 1948, 31–36; on the tracing work of the office, see also Akim Jah: "Die Deportation der Juden aus Deutschland 1941–1945. Zur Geschichte und Dokumentenüberlieferung im Archiv des ITS", in Akim Jah and

es and other biographical information of about 49,000 Jews whom the Gestapo had deported from Berlin to ghettos and extermination camps. The financial authorities once had used the lists to liquidate the property that deportees had left behind. The Berlin AJDC office then created a tracing card index based on the lists. The originals initially remained with the financial authorities before being handed over to the International Tracing Service in Arolsen in 1953, which for decades also used the lists for searching and clarifying fates. Today, the Berlin transport lists collection held at the Arolsen Archives has been scanned, indexed in depth, and is available online.[2]

The Berlin transport lists are an example of a certain category of sources on the history of the Holocaust: person-related serial records. Until now, research has hardly analyzed such sources systematically except primarily for individual biographical studies. Holocaust research, in contrast, heavily relies on two other categories of sources: general files of the institutions involved, and ego-documents. For example, volume 6 of the edition 'The Persecution and Murder of the European Jews by Nazi Germany, 1933–1945',[3] covering deportations from Germany and the so-called Protectorate, contains 329 sources of these two categories as well as some newspaper articles, but no source of the aforementioned category. Obviously, standardized lists, forms or index cards are not easy to explore when the research interest is not an individual person. At the same time, it is sources of this category that archives and documentation centers on the Holocaust are digitizing the most – with the result that we have more and larger person-related datasets available. Yet, researchers still need to explore how and to what end we can use this data for writing deportation history.

This paper has two goals. In a first, introductory step, it outlines a general model of the sources on deportations in order to provide a framework. The model is based on the deportation of the Jews from Germany, but for each case, i.e. also for deportations of Sinti and Roma, as well as for deportations from occupied Europe and countries allied with Nazi Germany, the model should make it possible to assess the source situation and to reflect on how it influences

---

Gerd Kühling (eds.): *Die Deportation der Juden aus Deutschland und ihre verdrängte Geschichte nach 1945*, Göttingen: Wallstein, 2016, 11–29, here 21.

2 See the collection *Deportations from the Gestapo area Berlin*, reference code VCC.155.I, available online at https://collections.arolsen-archives.org/en/archive/1-2-1-1_VCC-155-I. Last accessed: 28.02.2022. A CSV export of the archival data for research can be requested from the Arolsen Archives. On this collection, see also the article by Kim Dresel and Christian Groh in this volume.

3 Susanne Heim (ed.): *Die Verfolgung und Ermordung der europäischen Juden durch das nationalsozialistische Deutschland 1933–1945*, volume 6: *Deutsches Reich und Protektorat Böhmen und Mähren, Oktober 1941–März 1943*, Berlin/Boston: De Gruyter/Oldenbourg, 2019.

research possibilities and perspectives. Among other aspects, it will be shown that the ongoing digitization of archival sources and the development of databases for online memorial books and digital memorials not only open up new possibilities for research, but that certain prerequisites must also be met for their productive scholarly use.

In the second, more detailed step, the paper will use the dataset of the Berlin transport lists collection from the Arolsen Archives to present a methodological approach for researching person-related records with digital tools. The paper examines the dynamics of the deportations from Berlin, spatial concentration processes within the city, and experiences of Jewish Berliners through GIS-based and quantitative analyses. For this, the paper will not rely on the data from the transport lists alone but also on a matching with Berlin data from the 1939 census provided by the German Federal Archives – a second set of person-related mass data.[4] Furthermore, I enriched the GIS-model by another matching with metadata from the oral history collection of the United States Holocaust Memorial Museum (USHMM).[5] In addition to presenting the methodological approach and first findings of this explorative case study, the paper thus also aims to raise awareness of the importance of considering testimonies in context in order to better assess their scope for explaining events and processes during the Holocaust.

Eight Contexts of Source Production on Deportations

Considering the overall process of the persecution and murder of the European Jews and the Sinti and Roma, we first have to state that deportations marked an incisive, but only short phase. While this phase is in focus here, sources on other phases of the Holocaust and the Porajmos (and even on the previous and in some cases the later lives of the victims) might be very important for research on deportations as well. Only looking at the history of deportations, with regard to the production of sources, we could distinguish between eight different con-

---

4 See Nicolai M. Zimmermann: "Die Ergänzungskarten für Angaben über Abstammung und Vorbildung der Volkszählung vom 17. Mai 1939", 2013. Available online at: https://www.bundesarchiv.de/DE/Content/Publikationen/Aufsaetze/aufsatz-zimmermann-ergaenzungskarten.html. Last accessed: 04.03.2022. I would like to thank the colleagues at the German Federal Archives for providing the dataset.
5 This concerned all interviews tagged with the keyword *Berlin*. I would like to thank the colleagues at the United States Holocaust Memorial Museum for providing the dataset.

texts, some of which ran in parallel – as shown in fig. 1. Each deportation was marked by a short period, sometimes lasting only a few days or weeks, from the preparation to the liquidation of the remaining property and subsequent registration of the event by various actors. And then there always was a very long period of retrospective source production, which began immediately after liberation, and continues to the present day.[6]

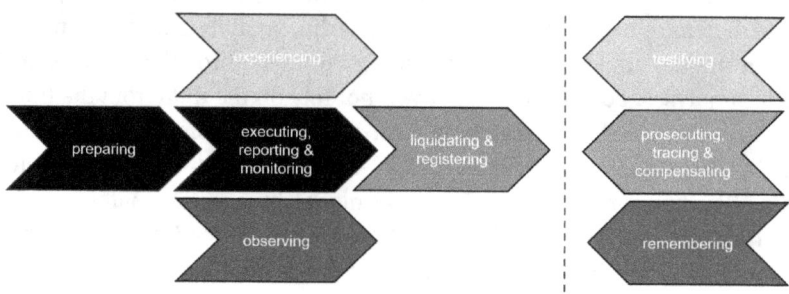

Fig. 1: Eight Contexts of Source Production in the History of Deportations.

Preparing a deportation was the first context: the actors directly involved in this (the Gestapo in case of the Jews, the criminal police in case of the Sinti and Roma) produced files at the state, regional, and local level, containing classic administrative sources, such as correspondence, memorandums, and reports. In addition, sources on deportations also exist in administrative files of other state authorities involved in or informed about the preparations: authorities at the Reich level – see the Wannsee conference for example – and intermediary state authorities, as well as transport operators, and, in case of deferrals (*Rückstellungen*) of Jewish forced laborers, the labor offices and employers. Finally, community organizations – in case of the German Jews the Reich Associ-

---

[6] As mentioned above, the model is based on the deportations of Jews from the German Reich. For published source collections, in addition to Heim, Die Verfolgung und Ermordung der europäischen Juden, also see Akim Jah and Marcus Gryglewski: *"Ihre Grabstätten befinden sich nicht im hiesigen Bezirk." Quellen zur Deportation der Jüdinnen und Juden während des Nationalsozialismus*, Berlin: Hentrich & Hentrich, 2018. While the model will probably not be complete even for the German case, there might be sources only produced in the German setting, whereas there will be other types of sources that originated only in certain countries or occupied territories. See, for example, the article by Viorel Achim in this volume on Roma petitions from Transnistria.

ation of Jews in Germany – were already forcibly involved, as were individual victims who had to fill out property declarations.

A second context, actually three successive steps by those who carried out and accompanied a deportation, can be labelled as *executing, reporting and monitoring*. On the one hand, here we find sources directly triggering the act of deportation – the announcement by the community organization to the individual victims, the actual deportation order by the local Gestapo or criminal police, and the transport list. On the other hand, we find action reports at different levels: from operation reports of the escort command to reports of local to regional as well as regional to top police authorities. Furthermore, the execution of a deportation was monitored by top police and other state authorities and, in the case of deportations from outside the German Reich, also by collaborating regimes, as well as German embassies.

In parallel, marking a third and a fourth context, the victims *experiencing* deportations created other types of sources that are of the highest value for historical research: diary entries, letters, and postcards, sometimes even sent during a transport break or thrown off the train. In addition, deportees wrote petitions to the authorities at some destinations. Relatives and victims who, for example, lived in the neighborhood, in the same house or were waiting in an assembly camp and had not yet been deported created similar sources. The same applies – albeit from a fundamentally different perspective – to those *observing* a deportation, be they neighbors, bystanders at deportation routes to an assembly camp or at train stations, chroniclers of events in the hometown, journalists, or foreign diplomats. However, these observers did not only write diary entries or letters, but in many places photographs, newspaper articles and diplomatic reports have survived, which, among other things, make it possible to assess knowledge about deportations and reactions of the population.

The fifth context consists of various follow-up activities that began shortly after a transport had left. *Liquidating* the assets and property the deportees had to leave behind, meaning state-organized robbery, was an activity in which many sources were created on site, nowadays often serving as a secondary source for missing information on a deportation and its victims. Local and regional financial administrations created lists of previous owners – or, as in the Berlin case, continued to use the Gestapo's lists for their purposes. Financial administration officers kept case files on the liquidation of individual assets. Newspapers announced auctions. Another subsequent activity a number of actors carried out in different places was *registering* a deportation in various card files: card files of the community organization, the municipal resident registration office, the regional police, or the administration of an assembly camp. Moreover, we also find such registrations of a deportation in sources only created many months later. For example, the deportations of hundreds of German Sinti from their hometowns to Auschwitz in early 1943 was recorded on prisoners' registration forms of the Buchenwald concentration camp, the camp they were further transported to in the summer of 1944 to perform slave labor for the German war industry.[7]

Turning to the second, much longer period that began after the end of the Nazi regime and continues to the present day, *prosecuting* the perpetrators as well as *tracing* the victims and *compensating* survivors and relatives all represent a sixth context. Particularly from the mid-1940s to the late 1960s, and again from the late 1980s to the early 2000s, tens of thousands of sources – mostly case files – were created here, which are not only used for research into how the Nazi crimes were dealt with, but also for research into the history of persecution.[8] In many cases, victims of certain transports are only documented in these files, which were created subsequently for and of course shaped by very specific purposes.[9] In many of these files, we find personal accounts as well as originals or copies of primary sources on the deportations, extremely important for writing a history of experience. Case files on prosecutions of perpetrators also include – often apologetic – descriptions of the deportations by, for example, subaltern Gestapo officials, themselves.

In parallel to criminal prosecution, tracing and compensation, where survivors and relatives were involved as witnesses and applicants and therefore had to provide information in given settings, many became active themselves by *testifying* the crimes – a seventh context. Bearing witness took place both out of individual attempts to cope with the horrible experiences and on the initiative of re-emerging Jewish self-organizations, which in a number of places made a concerted effort to collect and record.[10] There were phases of varying intensity, with

---

7 See, for example, Prisoner Registration Form of Willy Blum, 1.1.5.3/5558954/ITS Digital Archive, Arolsen Archives. On the story of Willy Blum, see Anette Leo: *Das Kind auf der Liste. Die Geschichte von Willy Blum und seiner Familie*, Berlin: Aufbau, 2018.

8 In addition to the widely used compensation files in German state archives, the ITS Tracing and Documentation files (T/D-Files), which are kept in the Arolsen Archives, should also be mentioned here.

9 This includes the fact that the documentation of deported Sinti and Roma in compensation case files, due to their long non-recognition as Nazi victims, is much more fragmentary than the one on deported Jews. For the extensive archival material on German compensation in public archives, the German Federal Archive has started to develop a new online portal that will be included in www.archivportal-d.de in the next years.

10 See Laura Jokusch: *Collect and Record! Jewish Holocaust Documentation in Early Postwar Europe*, Oxford: Oxford University Press, 2012; also see the article by Johannes Meerwald in this volume.

peaks in the early postwar period as well as in the 1980s and 1990s, and the techniques changed from questionnaires and newspaper reports to written memoirs and oral history recordings. However, a unifying feature of most sources created here was that survivors presented their entire story of persecution, which is why they often described the deportation only briefly.

Finally, there is an eighth context in which a special kind of secondary source emerged since the 1950s, namely institutionalized *remembering*, which led to the creation of commemorative lists, memorial books, and, increasingly, online databases and digital memorials. This ranges from collections at the municipal level to nationwide works, such as the Memorial Book of the German Federal Archives or the Jewish Monument in the Netherlands, to registries with an international approach, such as the Central Database of Shoah Victims' Names of Yad Vashem or the Holocaust Survivors and Victims Database of the USHMM. All these products and tools of remembrance combine person-related information from various scattered primary sources and have thus become an important type of source in their own right.[11]

Provenance, Accessibility and Categories of Sources

The outlined general model shows the broadest possible spectrum of sources potentially available for researching deportations in the Nazi era. Researchers might use it to compare source situations on deportations of different groups, from different countries, at different periods of time, as well as from individual places. At the same time, the model can serve as an orientation for better assessing the source situation for one's own research project. For this purpose, however, it is also necessary to consider other aspects of the source situation, namely questions of availability and accessibility, but also the different categories of sources.

Regarding availability, provenance is crucial. Quite often, it simply depends on the provenance whether sources still exist today and might be available for research in general. For records of perpetrators (police and other authorities on the state, regional and local level) as well as for other authorities involved (transport operators, financial administrations, labor offices) one key question is what was not destroyed – willingly or by the war. The other is which archive

---

[11] On person-related databases and digital memorials, see also the article by Maximilian Strnad in this volume.

or documentation center preserves surviving documents of these actors today. More than with most other historical topics, the sources on the Holocaust are fragmented. Parts of holdings of a certain perpetrator institution may be located not only at the public archive responsible according to the principle of provenance, but also in public and special archives of the Allied victors, holdings of judicial authorities of various countries, collections of tracing services, as well as documentation centers and memorial sites. In addition, the same collection may be available at two or even more locations in different ways. There might be a collection of original documents non-catalogued and hardly accessible while, at the same time, there might be a fully machine-readable digital copy available elsewhere.[12] This is not only important for researchers, but also for archivists when it comes to making the best use of limited resources. Here, exchanging information, including digital data and images, is key.

Sources created by various institutional actors after liberation (investigation commissions, prosecutors, courts, compensation and restitution authorities, tracing services, but also municipal and state institutions involved in remembrance) are significantly more likely to be preserved. The same is true for sources produced by non-German institutional observers during the war (diplomats, intelligence, foreign press), especially from western countries, as war destruction was less extensive. We will usually find materials of these provenances in public archives, unless they are still with the authorities that created them. The issue of availability for research here is primarily one of accessibility, meaning, on the one hand, the question of whether they are accessible or still classified.[13] On the other hand, if sources are open for research, how are they cataloged and indexed? As will be discussed below, this question takes on much greater significance for researchers using digital methods.

---

[12] This is one of the reasons why the portal of the European Holocaust Research Infrastructure (EHRI) is so important for deportation research. See https://portal.ehri-project.eu/. Last accessed: 03.03.2022. On the emergence of collections archives following World War Two, see: Henning Borggräfe and Isabel Panek: "Collections Archives Dealing with Nazi Victims. The Example of the Arolsen Archives", in Henning Borggräfe, Christian Höschler and Isabel Panek (eds.): *Tracing and Documenting Nazi Victims Past and Present*, Berlin/Boston: De Gruyter/Oldenbourg, 2020, 221–243.

[13] Here, the political work of the International Holocaust Remembrance Alliance (IHRA) regarding the European General Data Protection Regulation (GDPR) was very important. However, it remains to be seen how the GDPR will play out in practice, especially with regard to those sources on the Holocaust that were created in the context of criminal prosecution or compensation only a long time after 1945. On GDPR and Holocaust records, see https://www.holocaustremembrance.com/stories/reference-holocaust-gdpr. Last accessed: 27.02.2022.

For all other sources that are neither from state provenance nor from the provenance of larger organizations, that is, sources of victims and survivors, as well as relatives, but also observers and individual perpetrators, regardless of whether they were created during or after the war, the basic challenge is that we do not know at all who produced such sources on deportations. On top of that, all previously mentioned questions arise, too. It is thanks to decades of work by documentation centers, memorial sites and museums that sources of private provenance have been collected and made available for research. In addition, however, there are still many collections of small community organizations, but also victims associations and individual records of survivors and relatives in possession of private individuals and small organizations. These collections often depend on the commitment of individuals of high age; their future status is therefore fragile. This is why it is all the more important that larger archives and memorials try to secure micro archives and make them accessible.[14] At the same time, many municipal archives and local museums, not only in Europe but all over the world, also hold sources on deportations from private provenances in their collections. In view of this, what is still missing is a portal that virtually brings together such sources, provides background information and makes them digitally accessible. For pictures of Nazi deportations, the Arolsen Archives and partners have just started such an endeavor with the project #LastSeen.[15]

A general model of sources on deportations is not complete without a distinction of the different categories of sources. As shown in fig. 2, we could divide the many types of sources into three main categories, closely connected to certain research approaches.

The first category is general files of all institutions involved (containing correspondence, memos, protocols, reports, etc.). Historians have been evaluating these sources mainly for researching decision-making processes, the actors involved, and responsibilities. There is also a separate archival scholarly discussion on this category of sources, which is probably the most frequently used in Holocaust research.[16] The second category is ego-documents, i.e. sources from the perspective of individual persons, victims as well as bystanders and in-

---

[14] See the corresponding initiative of EHRI: https://www.ehri-project.eu/call-ehri-looking-micro-archives. Last accessed: 03.03.2022. The Arolsen Archives are also open to collaborations for securing small collections.
[15] See https://lastseen.arolsen-archives.org/en/. Last accessed: 04.03.2022.
[16] See for example the EHRI Online Course "Modern Diplomatics of the Holocaust", available at https://training.ehri-project.eu/unit/6-modern-diplomatics-holocaust. Last accessed: 06.03.2022.

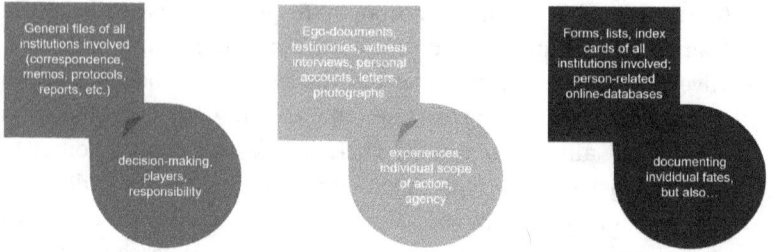

Fig. 2: Three Main Categories of Sources and Methods of Evaluation.

dividual perpetrators. These are diary entries, letters, testimonies, witness interviews, but also photographs.[17] Researchers have been evaluating these sources mainly for a history of experiences of the deportations, for researching individual scope of action, the agency of the victims, but also knowledge about the Holocaust among the non-Jewish population. Here, too, we find a wide range of specialized literature on these sources and their use for research.[18]

The situation, however, is quite different for the third category of sources: person-related documents (case files, forms, lists, or index cards) created for various purposes during and after the war, as well as person-related online-databases built for remembrance. So far, in thousands of cases, researchers have evaluated the enormous number of these sources almost only for the sake of documenting fates of individual deportees. Not only in Holocaust research, but also in the broader field of contemporary history, the methodological-theoretical discussion on researching "person-related records beyond the personal"[19] has just begun.

Yet, as this kind of research necessarily has to be digital, i.e. based on digital tools and methods to cope with the mass of sources and information contained

---

[17] For the history of the deportations, available newspaper reports can also be included here, since they are mostly based on observations. For a topic-independent ideal-typical differentiation of sources, however, published media sources (newspapers, television, radio, Internet) should be treated separately.

[18] On pictures of deportations, see also the contribution by Christoph Kreutzmüller in this volume.

[19] This was the title of an EHRI workshop aimed at discussing this category of sources. See https://arolsen-archives.org/en/news/personal-stories-and-big-data/. Last accessed: 07.03.2022. However, the methodological-theoretical discussion of person-related serial records is still in need of further development. For some basic questions and research approaches using documents on displaced persons, see Henning Borggräfe: "Exploring Pathways of (Forced) Migration, Resettlement Structures, and Displaced Persons' Agency: Document Holdings and Research Potentials of the Arolsen Archives", in *Historical Social Research*, 45–4, 2020, 45–68.

therein, we can at least highlight an important prerequisite. From a researcher's point of view, it is fundamentally important whether archives and other institutions holding digitized collections and hosting digital databases allow for a comprehensive analysis of the data. Will researchers be able to receive datasets of entire collections in a standardized format to enrich, manipulate, and further process them, or will they only be able to carry out pre-defined searches and make use of existing filters in completely digitized holdings via the interface provided, but cannot get the actual data?[20] Provided we will be able to work with whole datasets of archives and digital memorials or online databases, which research questions could we then investigate? Which research methods would be most promising? Which skills would historians need to master? Not least and most important, how would this expand our knowledge of the history of deportations? The second part of the paper approaches some of these questions using the dataset of the Berlin transport lists collection held at the Arolsen Archives.

A GIS-based and Quantitative Analysis of the Berlin Transport Lists

The remaining part of this paper is about testing how we could use the masses of digitized person-related documents, like the Berlin transport lists, for deportation research when the focus is not on individuals. On the following pages, I do not present completed research, but use an experimental project to suggest a methodological approach to this particular type of source. The approach includes processing, visualization and analysis of archival data in a Geographic Information System (GIS), combined with quantitative data evaluations.

Generally, geographical visualization of archival data can pursue three goals: first, we can map archival collections to make them better accessible, so that researchers can find all sources relevant to their place or area of interest regardless of what terms they are indexed or searched with. Second, for remembrance and education, we can make sources on victims visible on a map at the places where they once lived. This simultaneously makes the many places of persecution visible in today's urban space. Third, and this approach is followed here, we can use geographical visualization as an analytical tool to identify pat-

---

[20] The provision of an API or online data repository of the archives would be desirable. At the Arolsen Archives, researchers can currently at least receive a CSV export of data. However, many institutions also have unresolved copyright and data protection issues when it comes to making archive data available.

terns in archival mass data of historical events that would otherwise remain hidden, and from this we can gain new insights into the history we seek to explore. In this sense, data visualization in a GIS is not an end in itself. Rather, it is about understanding and describing historical events more precisely, and thus making experiences visible.[21] The approach presented here has parallels with Tim Cole's and Alberto Giordano's GIS-study of the Budapest ghetto.[22] One main difference is that their project is based on the elaborate composition of many different sources, whereas I am more interested in probing what can be done relatively quickly with existing indexing data provided by archives.

The deportations from Berlin, the subject of this case study, are of particular significance in the history of the persecution and murder of the German Jews. In 68 so-called waves, consisting of 184 individual transports, the Gestapo deported about 50,000 men, women and children from Berlin to the ghettos and extermination camps between October 1941 and March 1945.[23] Berlin formed by far the largest Jewish community in Nazi Germany, and the capital thus accounted for more than a third of all Jews deported from the so-called *Altreich*.[24] Nevertheless, we still know relatively little about the deportations from Berlin. This applies in particular to spatial dynamics and the issue of forced concentration processes of the Jewish population into so-called Jews houses (*Judenhäuser*) prior to deportation.[25]

---

21 See Henning Borggräfe, Lukas Hennies, and Christoph Rass: "Geoinformationssysteme in der zeithistorischen Forschung. Praxisbeispiele aus der Untersuchung von Flucht, Verfolgung und Migration, in den 1930er bis 1950er Jahren", in *Zeithistorische Forschungen/Studies in Contemporary History* (forthcoming, 2022).
22 Tim Cole and Alberto Giordano: "Bringing the Ghetto to the Jew: Spatialities if Ghettoization in Budapest", in Anna Kelly Knowles, Tim Cole, and Alberto Giordano (eds.): *Geographies of the Holocaust*, Bloomington: Indiana University Press, 2014, 121–151.
23 For a chronology and commentary of all transports, see Akim Jah: *Die Deportation der Juden aus Berlin. Die nationalsozialistische Vernichtungspolitik und das Sammellager Große Hamburger Straße*, Berlin: be.bra, 2013, 619–674.
24 Nicolai M. Zimmermann: "Was geschah mit den Juden in Deutschland zwischen 1933 und 1945? Eine Dokumentation des Bundesarchivs", in *Zeitschrift für Geschichtswissenschaft* 64/12, 2016, 1045–1058, here 1055.
25 On the deportations from Berlin and transit camps within the city, see Jah, Die Deportation der Juden aus Berlin; on the connections between housing evictions for the new Reich capital and deportations, see Susanne Willems: *Der entsiedelte Jude. Albert Speers Wohnungsmarktpolitik für den Berliner Hauptstadtbau*, Berlin: Edition Hentrich, 2000; on Jewish forced labor and its connection with the deportations, see Wolf Gruner: *Der Geschlossene Arbeitseinsatz deutscher Juden. Zur Zwangsarbeit als Element der Verfolgung 1938–1943*, Berlin: Metropol, 1997.

As mentioned above and shown in fig. 3, the Berlin transport lists contain information on first and last names, dates of birth, last residential addresses and other biographical information of the deportees. After a deportation train had left Berlin, the Gestapo passed on the respective list to the financial administration for the liquidation of the deportees' property. That the Gestapo had previously used the lists for its own purposes is clear from the fact that the lists also include numerous Jews deported via the German capital from other parts of the Reich and even from occupied countries, for whose property the Berlin financial administration was not responsible.[26]

Before analyzing the Berlin transport list data, it has to be emphasized that the collection kept in the Arolsen Archives is not complete. The lists of the first seven transports in October and November 1941, which presumably affected about 7,000 people, are missing. Information on these deportees is partially available,[27] but not machine-readable. Therefore, this explorative case study refers 'only' to the deportations from January 1942, and to 41,974 people.[28]

Although the person-related information on the lists is machine-readable, it still needs to be prepared for research. Since many people were crossed off lists and reappear on lists of later dates, and since sometimes different lists for the same deportation can be found in the collection, duplicates have to be removed. Furthermore, German *Umlaute* have to be changed, incorrectly transcribed street names have to be corrected, and most importantly, old district numbers and addresses have to be matched with today's addresses. This is quite complicated for Berlin due to postwar reconstructions and the political history of the divided city. However, with the open source software QGIS used for this study, the actual geocoding can afterwards be conducted more or less automatically via a plugin using an OpenStreetMap-API.[29] Once the data is geocoded, we can visualize and examine it in the GIS. Any data can be displayed either as points (i. e. people at addresses), as lines (i. e. movements between two addresses) or as polygons (i. e. boundaries of territories such as city districts). Different datasets are stored

---

26 Spread over the lists, we find 1,789 Jews who were deported via Berlin from towns and communities in Brandenburg and Mecklenburg, from other cities in the Reich, as well as from occupied countries.
27 See https://www.statistik-des-holocaust.de/list_ger_ber_ot1-7.html. Last accessed: 07.03.2022. See also the article by Kim Dresel, and Christian Groh in this volume.
28 For 41,562 Berlin deportees, last residential addresses are available, while this information is missing for 412 other deportees, mainly inmates of the Berlin police prison and people recorded as homeless.
29 The software QGIS is available here: https://www.qgis.org/en/site/. Last accessed: 07.03.2022. The MMQGIS plugin used for geocoding can be installed therein.

Transportliste

Lfd. Nr.	N a m e	Vorname	geb. am	Ort	Beruf	ledig	verh.	Alter	arbeits fähig	Wohnung Ort	Straße	Kennkarten-Nr.	Kennzeichen-Nr.	Bemerkungen
241	Lutz geb.Harris	Therese Sara	15.1.76	Neugutuc USA	ohne	ja	-	66	ja	NO 55,Rykestr.41 II		A152110	12111	
242	Marienthal	Adolf Israel	14.1.74	Packelsheim/Westf.	Arb.	ja	-	68	ja	Halensee,Margraf-Al- brechtstr.14		A427210	12112	
243	Maass	Alfred Isr.	2.3.78	Filehne	ohne	-	ja	64	ja	Wilmdf., Güntzelstr. 17-18		A450297	12114	
244	Maass geb. Angress	Johanna Sara	12.2.76	Berlin	ohne	-	ja	66	ja	dto.		A450298	12115	
245	Levin	Mendel Isr.	14.2.75	Schwerin	ohne	ja	-	67	ja			A709304	12116	
226	Lepcak Leopold	Elli Sara	25.6.75	Krappitz OS.	ohne	ja	-	66	ja	Biesdorf, Scheckla sterstr.90		A052943	12118	
227	Lawitz geb.Cohn	Rosalie Sara	5.3.75	Posen	ohne	ja	-	57	ja	NW 87,Tile Wardenberg str.26a		II.9103/41	12122	
228	Lindemstrauss	Anna Sara	27.9.75	Neuenburg	ohne	ja	-	66	ja	N 58,Hegenauer 14		A 045885	12127	
229	Liebler geb.Meyrowski	Jenni Sara	2.3.76	Guttstadt	Arb.	ja	-	66	ja	NO 55,Winsstr.5		L 93/40	12128	
230	Lewinsohn	Margarete Sara	14.11.75	Berlin	"	ja	-	66	ja	W 15,Konstanzer 3		A564604	12130	
231	Lachmann	Martin Isr.	14.4.75	Nakel	ohne	-	ja	66	ja	Stegl.Eisenstr.24		A5oo277	12131	
232	" geb. Cohn	Hedwig Sara	27.5.80	Berlin	ohne	-	ja	61	ja	Hln. W 30,Traunstei- ner Str.6		A 5oo278	12132	
233	Jontorfsohn geb.Jacobsohn	Regina Sara	10.11.75	Filehne	ohne	ja	-	66	ja	dto.		Aoo438	12145	
234	Keul geb.Mücke	Hedwig Sara	27.9.75	Straussburg	ohne	ja	-	66	ja	Wilm.,Uhlandstr.118		A 039420	12148	
235	Kniebel	Martha Malchen Sara	26.10.75	Schwersenz	ohne	ja	-	66	ja	N 54,Alte Schönhauser Str. 4		A 693 227	12152	
236	Rohr geb.Zanderling	Jachet Sara	27.6.75	Zakopesse	ohne	ja	-	66	ja	Lichtenberg, Tasdorfer Str.71		R.423/38	12158	
237	Sündermann	Irma Sara	10.3.94	Gotheim	ohne	ja	-	48	ja	C 2, Neue Schönhauser Str.16		A 00039	12177	
238	"	Heinz Isr.	6.10.30	Bamberg	ohne	ja	-	11	ja	NO 55,Weißenburger 11		dto.	12178	
239	Beer	Dorothea Sara	1.12.75	Landeck	Arbeiter	ja	-	65	ja	N 54, Schönhauser Allee 186 I		A 187148	12182	
240	Markus	Berthold Isr.	16.2.74	Tangermünde	"		ja	64	ja	Charl.1,Wilmersdorfer Str.32		A 369817	12183	

Fig. 3: Sample List from the Berlin Transport Lists Collection, 1.2.1.1/127187646/ITS Digital Archive, Arolsen Archives.

on different layers, whereby multiple layers can be placed upon each other. The data of each layer can be categorized by color based on values of selected table columns and can also be displayed in aggregated form.

Fig. 4 shows a visualization from the project GIS with the three mentioned forms of representation (points, lines, polygons). However, the multitude of maps created for this study cannot be properly illustrated in this paper – especially since the colors of displayed lines and points are crucial. Therefore, in the following, I refer to a complementary PDF containing a number of visualizations and statistics of the deportations from Berlin, which readers should consult while reading the following chapters of the paper.[30] In addition, it should be emphasized that data visualization and calculation does not always provide immediate answers, but often serves as a kind of question and hypothesis generator. On this basis, further analyses of the data and evaluations of other sources have to be carried out in order to explain patterns.

Centers of Jewish Life in Berlin and Deportation Dynamics

Thanks to previous research, especially by Akim Jah, we know the chronology of the deportations from Berlin, destinations of individual transports, and details about assembly camps within the city. However, we do not yet know where the remaining Jewish population, already reduced by emigration, was living across the city and how deportations were carried out in space and time. From what parts of the city did the Gestapo deport Jews during which periods? Was there a planned spatial approach, in the sense that certain areas were 'cleared of Jews' one after the other? Not least, where was the ongoing disappearance of Jewish neighbors visible, and for how long?

To address these questions, I first created a visualization categorizing the whole dataset by deportation waves.[31] In this map, each dot represents one deportee, here grouped around their last residential addresses. Each color stands for a certain wave. As a result, we initially only see a very colorful picture. One possible way to get a better overview is to use an analysis function in GIS: counting points within certain polygons, meaning deportation addresses

---

30 The PDF is available here: https://www.degruyter.com/document/isbn/9783110746464/html.
31 Ibid., 2.

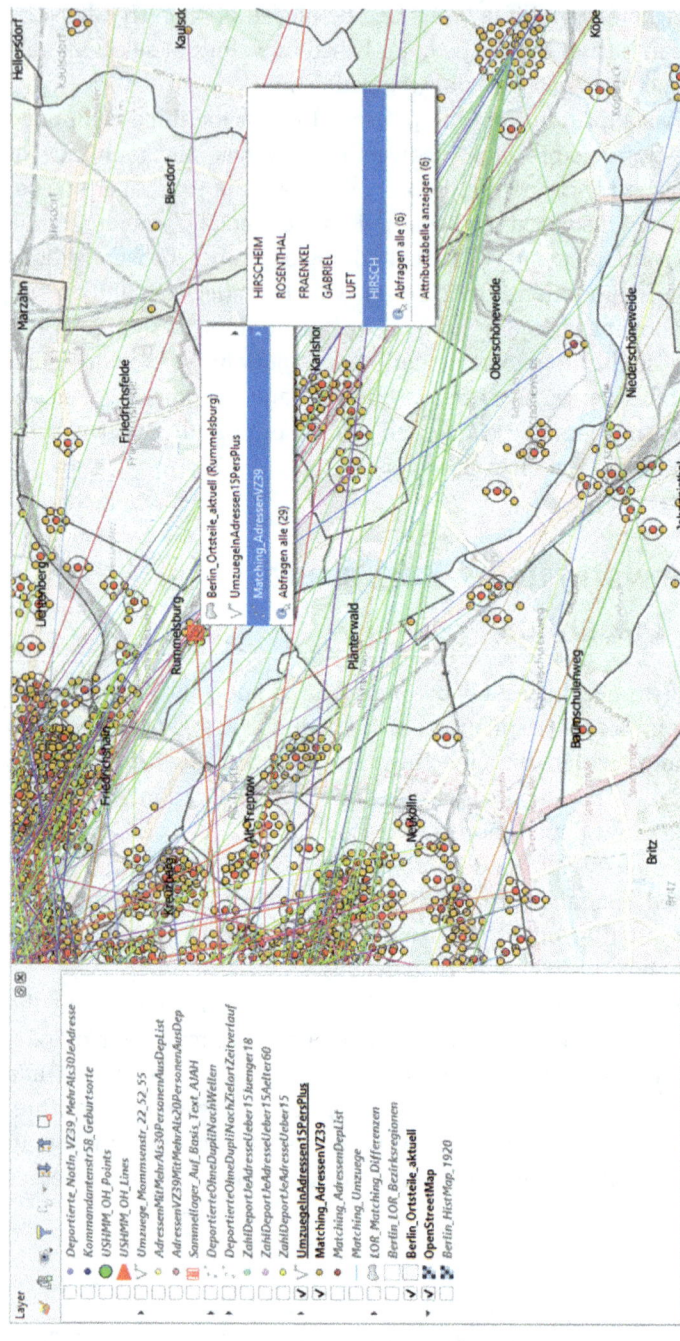

Fig. 4: Points, Lines and Polygons as Basic Display Modes in a GIS.

within city areas.³² Those familiar with Berlin will recognize two main centers of Jewish life: one in the west of the City in southern Charlottenburg, Wilmersdorf and Schöneberg, the other one further east around Alexanderplatz in Mitte and in southern Prenzlauer Berg. A third but smaller center was in Moabit. This map clearly shows the deportation hotspots in Berlin, but it does not tell us anything about deportation dynamics. Therefore, another possible way to further clarify the picture is by switching back to the categorized visualization by waves and then looking at the deportations chronologically and comparatively according to different periods highlighted in previous research.³³ The centers are again clearly recognizable at each period. In addition, we already see special places from where many people were deported repeatedly – north of the city center, for example, the Jewish hospital at Iranische Straße, from where almost 1,000 people were deported in 58 different transports. What we do not see, however, is a clear spatial pattern in the sense of a planned 'de-Jewification' of the city quarter by quarter. On the contrary, we see that the centers of Jewish life, as well as outlying areas, were affected almost permanently, wave after wave.

If we zoom in on a neighborhood, for example the bourgeois so-called Bavarian quarter in Schöneberg,³⁴ we can see from the different colors for different waves that the whole time deportations were taking place from the same neighborhoods, and even from the same houses. Many individual houses were affected in up to 20 and more waves of deportations. The long duration of the deportations from individual quarters becomes even clearer here, too, when comparatively looking at the periods.³⁵ The process of intensive deportation operations lasted for one and a half years until the completion of the so-called *Fabrikaktion* (factory raid) in March 1943.³⁶ Also during the following two years, after the end of the mass deportations, the same neighborhoods were repeatedly affected by deportations. This impressively illustrates the experience of the Jews still living there, namely the permanent uncertainty as to when they themselves would be deported next. On the other hand, for the non-Jewish neighbors in the

---

32 https://www.degruyter.com/document/isbn/9783110746464/html, 3. The representation is not historically correct, because I used a freely available layer of today's neighborhoods, instead of manually drawing a layer of the old *Bezirke*.
33 https://www.degruyter.com/document/isbn/9783110746464/html, 4.
34 Ibid., 5.
35 Ibid., 6.
36 This shows that no clear pattern can be discerned for Gestapo action in terms of urban space – not even after the change in Gestapo personnel in the fall of 1942, which research associates with a more planned and sharper deportation action, see Jah, Die Deportation der Juden aus Berlin, 388–405.

houses as well as the immediate surroundings, the disappearance of the Jews – which was followed by the sealing of the apartments and later the moving in of new neighbors – took place over a long period time and repeatedly and thus could hardly have remained unnoticed. However, in comparison with other cities in Nazi Germany – Cologne, Frankfurt am Main, or Munich – research would have to clarify whether this time-spatial pattern was typical for bigger cities having larger Jewish communities or a Berlin peculiarity, possibly due to the high number of Jewish forced laborers used in industry. It would also be worth clarifying whether this pattern of deportations tended to enable Jewish residents to go into hiding, which seems to have been a more widespread phenomenon in Berlin compared to other cities.[37]

Besides the time-spatial visualization of deportations in a GIS, with quantitative analysis of the transport lists data one could also look more deeply social-biographically at the events, for example by examining social profiles of all deportees at individual phases, from certain neighborhoods or from specific transports, or by researching individual groups, such as minors. A graph of the number of deportees over time, categorized by age groups at the time of deportation, which can be calculated from birth and deportation data, shows not only periods of greater and lesser deportation intensity, but also that the deportations did not strictly follow a specific pattern with regard to age.[38] In addition, it would be important to include gender as a category. However, the deportees' gender was not recorded on the lists, but could only be derived from the given names, which would result in some fuzziness, of course, but would nevertheless be possible with some effort. Certainly, much more could be extracted from the transport lists data for a social history of the deportees than mentioned here. This is especially true for a study of deportation risks of different social groups over time, as well as, derived from this rather than from the destinations of deportation trains, a chronology of the events. In that sense, this paper should be read as an encouragement to further explore research potentials of archival mass data from person-related serial records.

---

37 See Richard N. Lutjens: *Submerged on the Surface. The Not-So Hidden Jews of Nazi Berlin, 1941–1945*, New York: Berghahn, 2019, 16–18; on the number of Jewish forced laborers in Berlin compared to the Reich: Gruner, Der Geschlossene Arbeitseinsatz, 304.
38 https://www.degruyter.com/document/isbn/9783110746464/html, 7.

Forced Concentration Processes Prior to Deportations

A main research topic for Berlin is the spatial concentration of the remaining Jewish population prior to the deportations, especially in connection with the planning and construction work for the new Reich capital. According to Susanne Willem, there was a strong displacement and concentration, but in her book, she did not outline how extensive this phenomenon actually was as well as how and where it actually affected the Jewish population of the city.[39] Closely related is the question of the effects of the Reich law on the tenancy of Jews from April 1939 and the establishing of so-called Jews houses, in other words: forced housing in crowded places, a topic that has been largely unexplored for Berlin both in terms of the numbers of the 'Jews houses' and their locations.[40]

A first approach to the topic of 'Jews houses' is possible if we display the transport lists data not point by point, but aggregated, as shown on the next map.[41] The larger a yellow dot, the more people were deported from a given address. In total, there were 545 addresses across Berlin from where the Gestapo deported more than 15 people, most of them again in the centers of Jewish life. In this way, we can very well identify addresses that would need further investigation with other sources. However, research currently does not know whether a minimum of 15 residents is a good indicator for identifying 'Jews houses'. Furthermore, even if we would have a number, it would remain open whether an address was a 'Jews house', or simply a large building with many Jewish residents, or perhaps an institution of the Jewish self-administration. As demonstrated on another map showing the second center of Jewish life in Berlin, the so-called Spandauer Vorstadt in Mitte, and southern Prenzlauer Berg,[42] a possible way to distinguish 'Jews houses' from institutions of the Jewish self-administration is to calculate the age of the deportees from the transport lists data. In doing so, on additional layers, we can overlay the total number of deportees

---

39 See Willems, Der entsiedelte Jude, 362–363.
40 When 'Jews houses' are mentioned in the following, it must be kept in mind that they were probably often only apartments in larger residential buildings in which the Jews had to live together in cramped conditions. A new research project is currently exploring this topic for Berlin. See Akim Jah, Silvija Kavčič, and Christoph Kreutzmüller: "'Grösse der Wohnung: 1 Leerzimmer'. Eine Projektidee zu den 'Judenwohnungen' und 'Judenhäusern' in Berlin 1939–1945", in Mitgliederrundbrief Aktives Museum, 84, 2021, 3–5.
41 https://www.degruyter.com/document/isbn/9783110746464/html, 8.
42 Ibid., 9.

from certain addresses with the number of residents older than 60 or younger than 18. In this way, it works well to exclude Jewish old people's homes as well as orphanages among the addresses of interest.[43]

If we then add the layer with all deportation addresses to this map again,[44] we come to an important finding regarding the persecution experiences of Jews from Berlin. In parallel with the 'Jews houses', old people's homes and orphanages, meaning dense living in crowded rooms, there were very many houses in which still only a few Jewish residents lived together. The spatial concentration of Berlin's Jews that Susanne Willem emphasizes in her study thus by no means affected the entire Jewish population of the city. A table of the calculated housing density prior to deportations[45] confirms that almost 25,000 deported Berlin Jews, that is, almost 60 percent of the deportees included in this case study, lived at addresses together with fewer than 15 other deportees. Among them, there are more than 6,000 addresses from where only one to five people were deported. For the remaining Jews prior to deportations, there were very different housing situations in the city.

However, if we look only at the data from the transport lists and the housing density, we still do not get an impression of displacement dynamics. Perhaps such differences in housing already existed before – simply as an effect of different social situations. The transport lists alone do not reveal what had actually changed following the 1939 law on the tenancy of Jews and eviction actions by the General Building Inspector (GBI) Albert Speer.[46] In order to find answers to this, I included a second data set into the study, also containing address data of Berlin Jews: the data of the 1939 census kept in the German Federal Archives.[47] Person matching between the two datasets is not quite easy, because of differing name spellings and dates of birth.[48] Nevertheless, I was able to retrieve the 1939 addresses for almost 30,000 of the deportees, which is about 75 percent, and to process and geocode them as well. A map of the addresses of the 1939 census above the deportation addresses of the same people shows many overlaps, but

---

43 Many of these institutions are known and references to them can be found scattered in the research literature on Jews in Berlin. In this way, however, addresses of potential institutions of the Jewish self-organization can be determined automatically even in cases where research is less advanced.
44 https://www.degruyter.com/document/isbn/9783110746464/html, 10.
45 Ibid., 11.
46 On these actions, see Willem, Der entsiedelte Jude, 180–193.
47 On this dataset, see Zimmermann, Die Ergänzungskarten.
48 After experimenting with different identifiers built from the two datasets, I used an identifier consisting of the first three letters of the last name, the first letter of the first name and the date of birth, which had the most hits without producing duplicates due to incorrect matches.

also deviations, meaning moves within the city.⁴⁹ To be more precise, 52 percent of the deportees for whom both addresses are available experienced a change in residence between the 1939 census and deportation about three to four years later. Of all these moves, 55 percent were into houses from which more than 15 people were deported. Consequently, within the group of the 30,000, the proportion of Jewish residents living in houses with more than 15 people increased sharply (from 9.6 percent to 31.4 percent). This again shows the divided housing situation: for many Berlin Jews the housing situation did not change drastically, but many others experienced a forced move into crowded apartments or the influx of strangers into their own houses. One aspect of this was a sharp increase in institutional housing of the elderly.

What did this concentration process mean in terms of urban space? In other words, where did the Jewish population decrease and where did it increase compared to the prewar situation? To approach these questions, we can again use the analysis function of counting points within certain polygons, meaning residential addresses within city areas, for the 1939 addresses as well as the deportation addresses, and then calculating the differences.⁵⁰ It becomes evident that there was a densification in the two main centers of Jewish life, less strongly but still recognizably in the Charlottenburg, Wilmersdorf, and Schöneberg districts, and more strongly in Mitte and Prenzlauer Berg. On the other hand, the Jewish population decreased in many outer neighborhoods, especially in bourgeois residential areas in southwest Berlin.

The data on the 1939 census also helps us to further narrow down potential 'Jews houses' and look at moves into these houses. By generating lines between the residential addresses of the Jewish Berliners available in the two datasets, we can visualize moves within the city. This is, of course, an abstract model, because in many cases there may have been other residential addresses between the two from 1939 and the date of deportation. If we visualize all moves into addresses where more than 15 people were deported from⁵¹, again, we do not see a clear spatial pattern in the sense that, for example, the allocation of housing would have been as close as possible to the previous places of residence, or only into certain areas. On the contrary, the visualization suggests, that the allocation of the remaining living space for Berlin Jews, which the housing advisory office (*Wohnungsberatungsstelle*) of the Berlin branch of the Reich Association of Jews

---

49 https://www.degruyter.com/document/isbn/9783110746464/html, 12.
50 Ibid., 13.
51 Ibid., 14.

did under the control of the Gestapo,[52] rather followed situational logics instead of a plan to concentrate the Jews only in certain areas of the city. If we only look at moves to a few selected 'Jews houses', it becomes clear that although some Berlin Jews moved from the vicinity, for others the move meant not only being brought together with strangers in a crowded space, but also being torn far away from their familiar neighborhood.[53] Since Jews in Nazi Germany were no longer allowed to own bicycles and to use local transport gradually from the fall of 1941 and completely from May/June 1942[54], this meant de facto the severance of previous social relations to remaining non-Jewish as well as Jewish friends. This also seems to be an important experience of many Berlin Jews prior to their deportation.

Testimonies and Mass Data Visualization

As Tim Cole and Alberto Giordano already pointed out in their study on Budapest, "historical GIS provides a context for a better understanding of individual stories."[55] This also applies to the history of the deportations from Berlin, as this final section will briefly illustrate. As a third data set for the explorative case study, I received a metadata export from the oral history collection of the USHMM. The export consists of metadata of 501 interviews tagged with the keyword Berlin, among them 431 containing at least a birth year of the interviewee, which is important for data matching. Matching with the transport lists data[56] leads to only eight hits. This is an interesting finding for the USHMM collection itself, namely that it deals only little with the deportations from Berlin. This makes it even more important to contextualize these few interviews. We find only five of the eight interviewees in the 1939 census data as well. Only three of the five, one of them the well-known survivor Norbert Wollheim, experienced

---

52 See Willem, Der entsiedelte Jude, 376–393.
53 https://www.degruyter.com/document/isbn/9783110746464/html, 15.
54 Wolf Gruner: *Judenverfolgung in Berlin 1933–1945. Eine Chronologie der Behördenmaßnahmen in der Reichshauptstadt*, Berlin: Edition Hentrich, 1996, 79, 83–84.
55 Cole and Giordano, Bringing the Ghetto to the Jew, 151.
56 As the metadata from the interviews is not uniformly comprehensive, I used the first three letters of the last name combined with the year of birth as an identifier and checked the results manually for actual hits.

a change of residence within Berlin between 1939 and the date of their deportation.[57]

These three interviewees who had already lived in Berlin in 1939 and had moved to another address prior to deportation, as well as the three others who cannot be found in the census data, were deported from 'Jews houses' or other addresses were many Jews had to live together. On the contrary, one of the interviewees, Gerald Adler, lived with only five other deportees, among them his parents and his younger brother, at an address in Charlottenburg where he had already lived in 1939, and again from 1941, after returning from a Hachsharah farm. In July 1943, the Gestapo deported him to Theresienstadt.[58] His housing situation in Berlin before deportation does not play any role in the interview. The same is true for interviewee Henry Oertelt, who lived with his mother and another Jewish man at an address in the northern part of Wedding, from where the Gestapo deported him with the same transport to Theresienstadt in July 1943.[59] As we have seen, this kind of housing situation concerned about half of the deportees from Berlin but is represented by only two of the eight interviewees and not even mentioned in the interviews. If we were to work only with these interviews, we would get a very different impression of the extent of the concentration of the Berlin Jews before deportation than we see framed by the analysis of the transport lists data.

As mentioned above, three of the eight interviewees are not included in the 1939 census data, as they did not live in Berlin at that time. From the interviews, we learn that one of them, Gerda Haas, only came to the Jewish hospital at Iranische Straße as a nurse in the winter of 1940/1941, from where the Gestapo deported her to Theresienstadt in May 1943.[60] Artur Posnanski, a native Berliner, had led a Jewish youth group in Brandenburg in 1939 and returned to Berlin as a forced laborer after its dissolution. He was deported to Auschwitz during the '*Fabrikaktion*' in March 1943.[61] And Carol Steinhardt from Frankfurt am

---

[57] For a visualization of the residential addresses of the eight interviewees and the moves of three of them in the context of other addresses and moves, see https://www.degruyter.com/document/isbn/9783110746464/html, 16.
[58] Interview with Gerald Adler. Available at: https://collections.ushmm.org/search/catalog/irn508647. Last accessed: 25.02.2022.
[59] Interview with Henry Oertelt. Available at: https://collections.ushmm.org/search/catalog/irn512459. Last accessed: 25.02.2022.
[60] Interview with Gerda Haas. Available at: https://collections.ushmm.org/search/catalog/irn506701. Last accessed: 25.02.2022.
[61] Interview with Artur Posnanski. Available at: https://collections.ushmm.org/search/catalog/irn502821. Last accessed: 25.02.2022.

Main had to move to Berlin for forced labor only in 1941. Together with a large group of young Jewish women from Hesse and other parts of Germany, she had been placed into a labor camp in Kreuzberg. In March 1943, during the 'Fabrikaktion' she was also deported to Auschwitz.[62] These movements and experiences cannot be gleaned from either the analysis of the transport lists data or the matching with the census data. With these three, therefore, we see how important it is to also frame mass data analysis with qualitative sources.

Even more, these oral history interviews prompt us to take a different look at the mass data and, through further visualization, detect patterns that would otherwise remain hidden. In other words, who were those about 12,000 deportees from Berlin who, like Haas, Posnanski, and Steinhardt, we do not find in the 1939 census data? These were at least three groups: first, Jewish children who were born in Berlin only after the census in May 1939. Their number can be given as 667 from the transport list data. Second, there is an unknown number of people, who had lived in Berlin in 1939, but for whom automated data matching did not work. Finally, as the interviews show us, there was a third relevant group: people who came to Berlin only because of the growing pressure of persecution during the war.

Had those people been mostly forced laborers placed in camps like Steinhardt? To investigate this question, I aggregated only the deportation addresses of these 12,000 persons, again for places where more than 15 of them lived. The visualization points to an interesting finding: If we put the layers of all deportees aggregated by age below,[63] it becomes clear that Steinhard's forced labor camp in Kreuzberg was rather an exception. Instead, there seem to have been strong movements from outside Berlin into Jewish old people's homes – an experience that, simply due to age, cannot be present in any oral history interview recorded since the 1980s. A pattern becomes visible here, which Akim Jah also describes in his contribution on the Jewish old people's home at Gerlachstraße: the persecution-related displacement of especially the elderly Jews into the remaining centers of Jewish life.[64] The starting point for this finding were oral history interviews from a different context – young Jewish forced laborers. This shows once again how important it is not to understand the analyses of quantitative and qualitative sources on deportations as strictly separate approaches, but to relate them to each other in the research process.

---

62 Interview with Carol Steinhardt. Available at: https://collections.ushmm.org/search/catalog/irn47746. Last accessed: 25.02.2022.
63 See https://www.degruyter.com/document/isbn/9783110746464/html, 17.
64 See the contribution by Akim Jah in this volume.

Conclusion

Although often not explicitly reflected in historical studies, there is a close relationship between research questions and epistemological interests on the one hand and the source situation on the other. This paper aimed, first, to sketch a general model of sources for the history of Nazi deportations and to discuss some basic questions of provenance, accessibility and categories of sources. The range of available sources varies greatly, between not only different countries and occupied territories or the deportation of the Jews and the Sinti and Roma, but also between periods, localities and even individual transports. Sometimes, there are almost no or very poorly catalogued sources for some research topics, while for others there are extensive holdings, fully digital and machine-readable. A wider question is how this heterogeneity affects historical research, not only regarding the extent of existing research on certain topics, but also with regard to the topics and approaches that researchers actually choose, and how this shapes our knowledge.

The general model of sources has shown that in various contexts of both contemporary and retrospective source production on the history of deportations, a third category of sources emerged alongside administrative sources and ego-documents: person-related serial records, of which the Berlin transport lists kept in the Arolsen Archives are an example. Large datasets of person-related serial records on the Holocaust are increasingly available digitally, but researchers have hardly explored their potential. Using the deportations from Berlin as an explorative case study, the second part of the paper showed that GIS analyses and quantitative evaluations of this data help to look at historical events more precisely and thereby to contribute to a history of experience of the Holocaust. The chapter on forced concentration processes of Berlin Jews prior to deportation demonstrated that, in addition to evaluations of individual datasets, working with results of person matching between different datasets is particularly promising. Finally, the short chapter on testimonies and mass data visualization made clear that GIS analyses and quantitative data evaluations do not stand alone, but historians ought to conduct them in combination with researching qualitative, narrative sources to write a comprehensive history of Nazi deportations.

Kim Dresel and Christian Groh
An Overview of Sources on Deportations of Jews and Sinti and Roma in the Arolsen Archives

Abstract: The holdings of the Arolsen Archives, the largest collection on all victim groups of Nazi persecution, have a specific history of creation. They contain original material as well as copied documents that were collected and arranged following the needs of the organization's mandate as the former International Tracing Service. This article assists the archives' users in understanding the history of the collection and its consequences for using specific research strategies that differ from the ones in most other archives. While the first part concentrates on the creation and arrangement of the collection in general, the second part presents specific documentation on deportations of Jews, Sinti and Roma. It discusses recent projects in digitizing, indexing and cataloguing of formerly acquired material and related new opportunities for researchers to reconstruct individuals' and groups' paths of persecution as well as an overall picture of the course of deportations from different cities. The subject of the article are documents on individual prisoners, and to a much lesser extent administrative records of various Gestapo authorities. The authors advocate systematic cooperation with other archives to supplement the holdings.

Introduction

With roughly 23 kilometers of documents, the Arolsen Archives hold the largest collection on Nazi persecution, bearing reference to all victim groups. The holdings contain information on those who perished in the Shoah, on other prisoners of concentration and extermination camps, and on forced laborers. Those who survived persecution and found themselves as Displaced Persons (DPs) far away from their countries of origin are also represented in the collection, much of which has already been digitized.

However, despite being the largest collection to cover all victim groups and survivors, the holdings of the Arolsen Archives are by no means exhaustive for

OpenAccess. © 2023 the author(s), published by De Gruyter. This work is licensed under the Creative Commons Attribution-NonCommercial-NoDerivatives 4.0 International License.
https://doi.org/10.1515/9783110746464-006

various reasons: A lot of evidence[1] was destroyed by the Nazis before the end of the war, and the sources that have been preserved to this day are widely spread across various archives, memorial sites etc. Nevertheless, one of the strengths of the Arolsen Archives lies in the fact that all victim groups are represented in their holdings, although in varying detail. As a consequence, it is easy to find series of documents on specific individuals and thus reconstruct their paths of persecution and life stories, even beyond their liberation if they survived. However, the underlying archival history that has led to these strengths also brings difficulties with it at the same time or necessitates unusual research techniques at the very least.

One of the main characteristics of the collections of the Arolsen Archives is that most of the documents contain information about one or more individuals. Since it is therefore a 'person-related' archive, it nevertheless contains sources that provide insights into the administration of the Nazi state. In the first part of this paper, we will outline how the Arolsen Archives' collection has been put together in view of the institutional specifics of the former International Tracing Service (ITS) and give an overview of the different collection groups. The second part presents the sources on deportations of Jews and Sinti and Roma.[2] It reveals how the history of the organization and the special way the collection was processed not only affect the ways it can be used, but also the opportunities for research that it offers.

The Unique Arrangement of the Holdings of the Arolsen Archives

Most archives have a clear territorial jurisdiction: state archives process the documentation of state institutions such as ministries or law courts. These institutions, although they evolve over time, have identifiable and traceable competen-

---

[1] Not all killings and war crimes were documented in the first place; this applies especially to deportations that led to immediate murder.

[2] The traditional term 'gypsy' (*'Zigeuner'*) has pejorative connotations. As a Nazi persecution category, 'gypsy' included various ethnic and linguistic groups. For the sake of simplicity, in this paper we will refer to these persecutees as Sinti and Roma or use the expression 'persons who were persecuted as gypsies', in order to distance ourselves from the negative connotations connected with the term itself. In the archival descriptions, both terms are used. See Sybil Milton: "Hidden Lives: Sinti and Roma Women", in Elizabeth R. Baer, and Myrna Goldenberg (eds.): *Experience and Expression, Women, the Nazis, and the Holocaust*, Detroit: Wayne State University Press, 2003, 53–75, here 54.

ces and responsibilities; they have a commitment to give their documentation to the archives responsible. The Arolsen Archives, formerly known as the ITS, have never been an archive in this sense. Various tracing offices were centralized from 1947, and their work material and documentation were brought to the small town of Arolsen in central Germany.[3] Documents from the International Refugee Organization (IRO), which had been in charge of DPs, also found their way to Arolsen. Furthermore, the US army gave documentation that had been used for war crime trials to the ITS. These are just a few of the sources that gave the ITS documents to enable the institution to fulfill its tasks of providing information, conducting research on missing persons, and issuing certification of imprisonment. Private persons, such as survivors, victims' relatives, former army staff, and lawyers representing former persecutees, also offered documents to the ITS.[4] The depot therefore contains not only originals from liberated concentration camps, ghettos and other places of detention, but also numerous reproductions of documents from various institutions, which the ITS produced itself or acquired to complete its records.

The standard way for an archive to deal with a very large amount of documentation from various sources is to keep any material together that has been provided by one institution, person, or other entity, and then structure its contents. The staff of the ITS, however, created large collections by arranging the documents by topic and including everything that belonged or seemed to belong to a specific topic. No attention was paid to the source of the documents during this process. As a consequence, the provenance, i.e. the context of the transmission of documents to the ITS, has been blurred and often cannot be pieced together any more.[5] Collections numbering hundreds of thousands of papers sometimes contain sub-collections that consist of just a few documents. And as not all

---

[3] For background information on why Arolsen was chosen as the site of the ITS and on the development of tracing bureaus before centralization, see Henning Borggräfe, Christian Höschler and Isabel Panek (eds.): *A Paper Monument. History of the Arolsen Archives*, Bad Arolsen: Arolsen Archives, 2019, 62–71.

[4] Details on the whereabouts and provenances of the respective collections are given in the descriptive texts, both in the database of the Arolsen Archives as well as online. See Arolsen Archives: "Online Archive". Available at: https://collections.arolsen-archives.org/en/search. Last accessed: 01.06.2021.

[5] Henning Borggräfe and Isabel Panek: "Collections Archives Dealing with Nazi Victims: The Example of the Arolsen Archives", in Henning Borggräfe, Christian Höschler and Isabel Panek (eds.): *Tracing and Documenting Nazi Victims Past and Present*, Berlin/Boston: De Gruyter, 2020, 221–244. Available at: https://www.researchgate.net/publication/341688074_Tracing_and_Documenting_Nazi_Victims_Past_and_Present_-_Introduction. Last accessed: 14.07.2022.

the documents given to the ITS were originals, original documents can be found cheek by jowl with copies, microfilms, digital files, and the like.⁶

Provided the arrangement was done well and followed clear criteria, the advantage of this method is that relevant material from various sources can be found in one place. This makes the Arolsen Archives well equipped to serve as an information hub. However, this mix of originals and copies from other institutions in one collection is not only a challenge when it comes to preserving the paper material, it also has legal implications. A lot of documents were given to the ITS on the understanding that they were for the use of fulfilling its mandate to trace fates and give evidence to persecutees and/or their families. This restriction sometimes comes into conflict with the institution's policy of providing free and easy access to all the information stored in the archives.

For decades, cataloguing practices at the ITS were oriented towards the goal of finding person-related information as quickly as possible. Tracing individuals, rather than researching the history of persecution, was the prime motivation for arranging and describing the material. Index cards and later on electronic indexes served the purpose of pointing to documents with information on persecuted individuals. The context and history of the documents was at best noted, but for a long time did not play any important role in cataloguing, and so this information has sometimes been lost for individual documents or even sub-collections.

To attenuate these shortcomings for researchers, the team of cataloguers is currently describing the collections as they now are. The archival descriptions are based on international standards and are in accordance with ISAD(G), but they are not classical finding aids.⁷ The archival staff are not primarily trying to reconstruct the original provenances, but rather focus on reconstructing contexts, describing how and for what purposes the documents were re-arranged, and enabling users to access them. In addition to the millions of indexes for

---

6 As a result, there are – roughly speaking – two types of collections: collections of mixed provenance and collections of the same provenance.
7 ISAD(G) is short for General International Standard Archival Description and was approved by the International Council on Archives. As a structural standard, it represents the basic principles of archival cataloguing as an exemplary type. These include multi-level description, provenance reference, and unambiguity. See Nils Brübach: "Standardisierung im deutschen Archivwesen", in *Scrinium*, 68, 2014, 7–22, here 20.

names, much work has been and is still being done to add topic-related and geographic indexes.[8]

An Overview of the Holdings of the Arolsen Archives

On the following pages we will introduce the different collection groups and their key characteristics. The whole collection is divided into eight main collection groups.[9]

Global finding aids: The first record group contains several finding aids and indexes. Since it is not a collection of historical documents, it is numbered as 'zero'. However, it is worth mentioning here, because it includes the Central Name Index (CNI) with around 50 million cards referring to more than 17.5 million individuals. This group of documents contain among others reference cards with information on all the persons about whom the predecessor organizations of the Arolsen Archives have ever received inquiries. The CNI contains information on deportations and fates of individuals for which no original evidence has been handed down but that have been reported by survivors and witnesses. This information combined with references to holdings of other institutions makes this collection, even if 'only' a finding aid, extremely valuable. The Central Name Index is also an impressive visualization of the dimensions of the archive and of Nazi persecution. Since 2013 it has been part of the UNESCO "Memory of the World" register.

Incarceration and Persecution: The evidence on imprisonment in concentration camps, ghettos, and prisons has been gathered in record group 1. The approximately 12 million documents contain documentation from concentration camps, authorities of the Nazi state, and various other sources, including numerous documents on deportations. The original prisoners' records from the Dachau and Buchenwald camps are among the most valuable sources held by the Arolsen Archives.

---

[8] One of the goals of the cataloguing activities is to make information on persecuted individuals as accessible as possible. In addition, for some years now we have been trying to enable topic-specific research in the database.
[9] See also https://collections.arolsen-archives.org/en/archive/. More detailed information and examples of documents can be found in Suzanne Brown-Fleming: *Nazi Persecution and Postwar Repercussions. The International Tracing Service Archive and Holocaust Research*, Lanham: Rowman&Littlefield, 2016.

Registration of Foreigners and German Persecutees by Public Institutions, Social Security Offices, and Companies (1939–1947): Collection group 2 with its seven million documents (most of them registrations that were made by state, health, and private authorities), comprises proof of the forced stay of individuals of non-German citizenship and of stateless persons in the German Reich. This collection is very useful for research into the fates of so-called civilian forced laborers.

Registrations and Files of Displaced Persons, Children, and Missing Persons: The seven million registration documents in collection 3 refer to survivors, Displaced Persons, and postwar migrants. It reflects the work of the ITS after the liberation, which was to make information available about the fates of individuals who had been persecuted by the Nazi regime. Besides original documentation from the ITS itself, this collection also holds files from other international organizations, such as the United Nations Relief and Rehabilitation Administration (UNRRA) and the IRO, and from Jewish aid organizations. One of the most interesting sub-collections in this record group is that of the IRO's Care and Maintenance (CM/1) files: To receive support, survivors of the Holocaust and other DPs had to fill in questionnaires about their paths of persecution. Therefore, the sub-collection contains numerous references to deportations and other persecution measures that have not been transmitted elsewhere. The activities of the Child Search Branch of the ITS are also documented in a sub-collection of this record group. The latter is thus highly valuable for research into the postwar repercussions of Nazi persecution policies.

Special NSDAP Organizations and Actions: This relatively small collection of more than 50,000 documents contains material from special organizations of the Nazi party. The largest one is the collection on *Lebensborn*, an SS organization that stole children in occupied territories and made efforts to 'Germanize' them.[10] The evidence contained in this collection should be consulted along with documents transmitted to the Federal Archives of Germany (*Bundesarchiv*). Collection 4 also contains some documentation on medical experiments and 'euthanasia'.

Death Marches, Identification of Unknown Dead, and Nazi Trials: In the early years of its existence, the ITS led a large research project on death marches and

---

[10] In the summer of 2021, the Arolsen Archives acquired another *Lebensborn* collection from the author and journalist Dorothee Schmitz-Köster. Included are – among other things – hundreds of interviews Schmitz-Köster conducted with contemporary witnesses, photographs, and personal documents of those affected, as well as recordings made by the author when visiting former *Lebensborn* homes. The collection (reference code 80001001) is currently being processed.

the exhumation of victims of 'evacuation' from concentration camps.[11] The 70,000 documents included in collection group 5 contain, among other things, information from local German authorities on anonymous graves in their area of responsibility, maps of cemeteries, along with names of Jewish, Roma, and Sinti victims of death marches.

Records of the ITS and its Predecessors: Collection group 6, which currently contains more than 14 million documents, is constantly growing and covers the institutional history of the ITS. It comprises the more than two million correspondence files on individual persons the ITS and today's Arolsen Archives have opened since 1947. Each file consists of the entire processing history of the research conducted in connection with (often several) inquiries on the respective person, and the replies that were sent out in response. These so-called T/D files[12] are still highly valuable for tracing purposes and for finding family connections.

Besides reflecting the changing policies for handling inquiries from different victim groups, these files also reflect survivors' individual experiences of persecution and experiences of loss suffered by family members of persecutees, including information for which no further evidence has survived. Thus, the T/D files are useful for research both into individuals' paths of persecution and into the post war politics of compensation and recognition of persecution.

Archival Records of Document Acquisition: In 2019, the archive formed collection group 7 which is sorted by provenance. It gathers various analogue and digital formats from other archives or institutions that the ITS has collected in order to fulfill its mandates and which had not previously been imported into the digital archive. This collection group contains a wide range of materials. They include hundreds of thousands of photocopies, microfilms, floppy disks, and CDs from archives in Germany and Austria, but also copies of materials from archives in states of the former Soviet Union that were made between the 1990s and 2006 thanks to the good relations between the ITS and various national Red Cross societies.[13] Most of this material refers to forced laborers and their

---

11 See Jean-Luc Blondel, Susanne Urban and Sebastian Schönemann (eds.): *Auf den Spuren der Todesmärsche*, Göttingen: Wallstein, 2012.
12 To this day, the Arolsen Archives create a T/D file when they receive an inquiry about a person. T/D stands for tracing/documentation. Every time another inquiry is received about the same person (even decades later) the same file is referred to. T/D files often contain important additional information about a person's life and path of persecution.
13 When selecting documents for filming, the ITS did not follow a uniform line. With a view to acquisition in archives of the former Soviet Union, for example, ITS employees sometimes exclusively created reproductions of papers produced by German authorities, thus tearing them out of

postwar experiences after having returned to their countries of origin. This last collection group also contains recent acquisitions that – breaking with the tradition outlined above – are no longer integrated into the other collections described. Rather, the original context is preserved to create provenance-oriented collections. Searchability is being improved by adding indexes of names, locations, subjects etc.

Records on the Deportation of Jews and Sinti and Roma in the Database

In 2019, the cataloguing team started to process the collections related to the deportations of Jews and Sinti and Roma from Germany, Austria, and the Protectorate of Bohemia and Moravia to ghettos, concentration and extermination camps in the occupied eastern territories, and to Auschwitz-Birkenau.[14] On the following pages, we will discuss typical sources and present some of our recent digitizing, indexing, and cataloguing projects. The latter enable our present-day users to identify the correlations between the various inventories and reconstruct the geography of the transport and deportation routes of individuals or entire groups. Most of the documents about deportations are scattered across collection 1.2 and collection 7, the newly created provenance-based inventory. Other holdings, such as the T/D files in collection 6, and the individual prisoner records in collection 1.1, also provide information on the deportation of individual persecutees. They can be an important source to complement research results, which will be addressed again in the course of this article. The sources on the deportation of Jews and those on the deportation of Sinti and Roma are present-

---

their original inventory context. In other cases, they acquired copies of the entire file including the documents in Russian or Ukrainian from the years after liberation. After completion of the filming work in 2006, the ITS put the large-scale project on hold. The evidence required for compensation thus remained stored – undeveloped – on microfilms and floppy disks in Bad Arolsen for more than a decade. Today, the more than 1.2 million document copies from archives of the former Soviet Union are part of collection 7.2 and are currently being processed.

14 The Yad Vashem Holocaust Deportation Database *Transports to Extinction* and the website *Statistik des Holocaust* provided essential background information that enriched and facilitated the cataloguing of the collections concerned. See Yad Vashem: "Transports to Extinction: Holocaust (Shoah) Deportation Database". Available at: https://deportation.yadvashem.org. Last accessed: 14.12.2021; Thomas Freier: "Statistik und Deportation der jüdischen Bevölkerung aus dem Deutschen Reich". Available at: https://www.statistik-des-holocaust.de. Last accessed: 14.12.2021.

ed below in two separate sections. Another section sheds light on new archival holdings included in collection 7. These materials have been acquired in the context of recent cooperations with small archives and associations and enrich the existing collections on deportations.

The Deportation of Jews Documented in Collection 1.2

The *Deportations and Transports*[15] inventory and the *Gestapo*[16] inventory included in collection 1.2 contain most of the sources the Arolsen Archives hold on the deportations of Jews and a smaller number of documents concerning Sinti and Roma. Since the ITS and its predecessor organizations collected and secured evidence in an extensive manner in order to fulfill their historical function of clarifying individual fates as comprehensively as possible, both inventories contain originals, copies, reproductions, and extracts from different sources.[17]

Deportations and Transports is organized into five sub-collections, four of which are relevant to the topic of this volume: 1.2.1.1 Deportations, 1.2.1.2 AJDC Berlin Index (Deportations), 1.2.1.4 Berlin Index of 'Transports to the East' (Wave 1–7), 1.2.1.5 Registration and Persecution.

The *Deportations*[18] sub-collection (1.2.1.1) contains the majority of the sources the Arolsen Archives hold on the deportations of Jews from the German Reich, Austria, and Bohemia and Moravia. The documentation is arranged by region and covers deportations from twenty-three Gestapo areas (*Gestapobereiche*), including Berlin, Dresden, Düsseldorf, Hanover, and Württemberg-Hohenzollern. Documented for the city of Karlsruhe is the *Aktion 'Arbeitsscheu Reich'*[19]

---

15 https://collections.arolsen-archives.org/en/archive/1-2-1/?p=1. Last accessed: 01.06.2021.
16 https://collections.arolsen-archives.org/en/archive/1-2-3/?p=1. Last accessed: 01.06.2021.
17 Akim Jah's well-researched study on the origins of the included Berlin 'transport lists' is representative of the complex and various archival histories of the inventories. See Akim Jah: "Die Deportation der Juden aus Deutschland 1941–1945. Zur Geschichte und Dokumentenüberlieferung im Archiv des ITS", in Akim Jah and Gerd Kühling (eds.): *Fundstücke. Die Deportation der Juden aus Deutschland und ihre verdrängte Geschichte nach 1945*, Göttingen: Wallstein, 2016, 11–29.
18 Almost the entire *Deportations* sub-collection (1.2.1.1) – nearly 21,000 documents – is available in the online archive. https://collections.arolsen-archives.org/en/archive/1-2-1-1/?p=1. Last accessed: 01.06.2021.
19 See Julia Hörath: *"Asoziale" und "Berufsverbrecher" in den Konzentrationslagern 1933 bis 1938*, Göttingen: Vandenhoeck&Ruprecht, 2017, 306–315.

in June 1938. However, the included list only contains information on the arrested Jewish men and not on those who were persecuted as so-called anti-social elements ('*Asoziale*').[20] The same unit contains detailed documentation of the 'Polenaktion' in the Karlsruhe area in October 1938 and its aftermath.[21]

In rare cases, lists are preserved that were created with a view to planning and carrying out the targeted killing of Jewish patients of so-called sanatoriums and nursing homes.[22]

Most of the lists and correspondence contained in 1.2.1.1 were created by various State Police Offices and State Police Headquarters[23] for the preparation and execution of deportations from autumn 1941 onwards. The sources reflect this process and shed light on the confiscation of assets as an integral part of the deportations. In addition, some extracts from Gestapo files have been preserved as well as entry lists from the Theresienstadt ghetto. The sub-collection also contains directories and correspondence compiled by various Jewish institutions, UNRRA, and by agencies that came into being in the postwar period.

The title of sub-collection 1.2.1.1 was recently changed from *Gestapo Transport Lists* to *Deportations* as this is a more accurate description of the documents it contains. However, a typical source created by the Gestapo is a so-called *Transportliste*. The list shown as fig. 1 documents the deportation of Jews from Berlin to Auschwitz on September 10, 1943.

---

20 https://collections.arolsen-archives.org/en/document/11200764. Last accessed: 24.09.2021.

21 https://collections.arolsen-archives.org/en/archive/1-2-1-1_8229800/?p=1. Last accessed: 01.06.2021. More sources related to the fate of Polish Jews can be found in sub-collection 1.2.1.5, https://collections.arolsen-archives.org/en/archive/1-2-1-5/?p=1. Last accessed: 01.06.2021. For background information on the expulsion/deportations of Polish Jews in 1938 and 1939, see Alina Bothe: "Radikalisierung vor aller Augen. Die 'Polenaktionen' 1938/39", in *informationen. Wissenschaftliche Zeitschrift des Studienkreises Deutscher Widerstand 1933–1945*, 89, 2019, 8–11.

22 One example is a list of 160 Jews who were deported from the 'sanatorium' in Wunstorf on 27.09.1940, see https://collections.arolsen-archives.org/en/archive/1-2-1-1_1471000/?p=1. Last accessed: 01.06.2021. – According to the research on 'euthanasia', the T4 subdivision Gemeinnützige Krankentransport GmbH, Berlin W 9 (GeKraT) and the Deutsche Reichsbahn deported the men and women to the T4 killing center Brandenburg/Havel for murder. See Deutscher Paritätischer Wohlfahrtsverband: "Provinzial Heil- und Pflegeanstalt Wunstorf". Available at: https://www.gedenkort-t4.eu/de/historische-orte/qvp1b-provinzial-heil-und-pflegeanstalt-wunstorf-krh-psychiatrie-wunstorf#karte. Last accessed: 14.05.2021.

23 In this article, *Stapostellen* and *Stapoleitstellen* are translated as State Police Offices and State Police Headquarters.

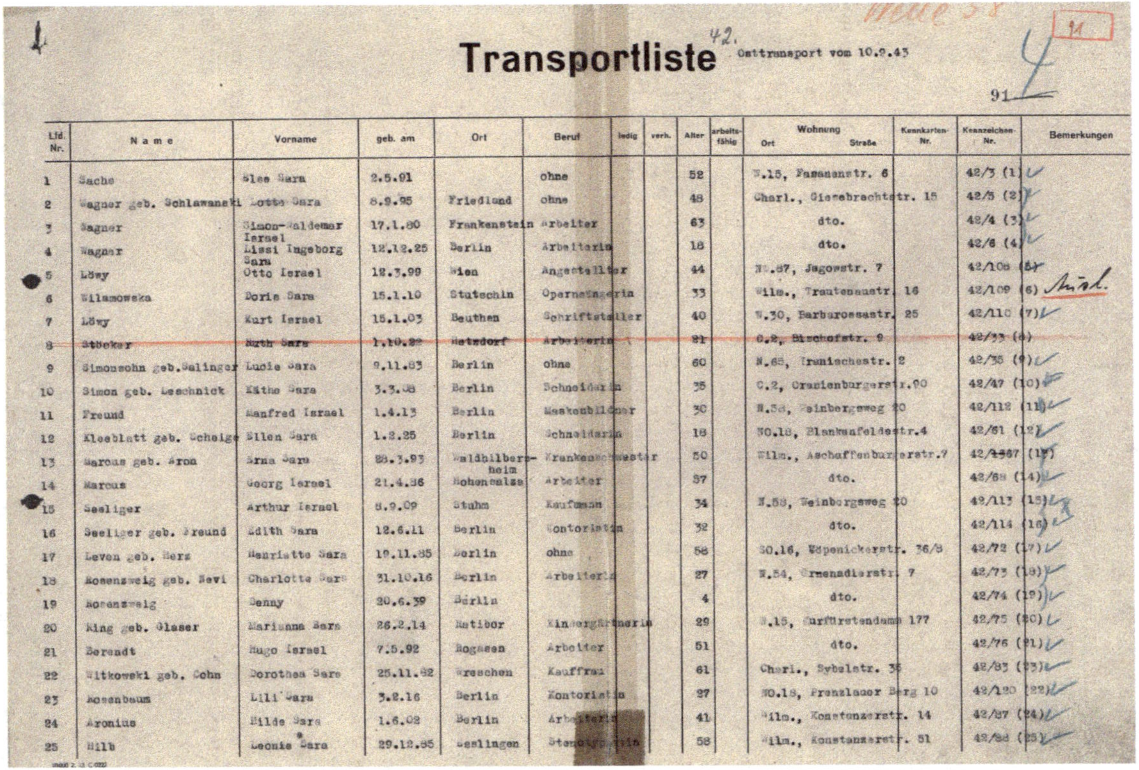

Transportliste Osttransport vom 10.9.43

91

Lfd. Nr.	Name	Vorname	geb. am	Ort	Beruf	ledig	verh.	Alter	arbeitsfähig	Wohnung Ort Straße	Kennkarten-Nr.	Kennzeichen-Nr.	Bemerkungen
1	Sachs	Else Sara	2.5.91		ohne			52		W.15, Fasanenstr. 6		42/3 (1)	
2	Wagner geb. Schlawanski	Lotte Sara	8.9.95	Friedland	ohne			48		Charl., Giesebrechtstr. 15		42/5 (2)	
3	Wagner	Simon-Waldemar Israel	17.1.80	Frankenstein	Arbeiter			63		dto.		42/4 (3)	
4	Wagner	Lissi Ingeborg Sara	12.12.25	Berlin	Arbeiterin			18		dto.		42/6 (4)	
5	Löwy	Otto Israel	12.3.99	Wien	Angestellter			44		NW.87, Jagowstr. 7		42/108 (5)	
6	Wilamowska	Doris Sara	15.1.10	Stutschin	Opernsängerin			33		Wilm., Trautenaustr. 16		42/109 (6)	
7	Löwy	Kurt Israel	15.1.03	Beuthen	Schriftsteller			40		W.30, Barbarossastr. 25		42/110 (7)	
8	~~Stöcker~~	~~Ruth Sara~~	~~1.10.22~~	~~Hetzdorf~~	~~Arbeiterin~~			~~21~~		~~O.2, Bischofstr. 9~~		~~42/33 (8)~~	
9	Simonsohn geb. Salinger	Lucie Sara	9.11.83	Berlin	ohne			60		N.65, Iranischestr. 2		42/35 (9)	
10	Simon geb. Leschnick	Käthe Sara	3.3.08	Berlin	Schneiderin			35		C.2, Oranienburgerstr. 90		42/47 (10)	
11	Freund	Manfred Israel	1.4.13	Berlin	Maskenbildner			30		N.58, Weinbergsweg 20		42/112 (11)	
12	Kleeblatt geb. Scheige	Ellen Sara	1.2.25	Berlin	Schneiderin			18		NO.18, Blankenfeldestr. 4		42/61 (12)	
13	Marcus geb. Aron	Erna Sara	28.3.93	Waldhilbersheim	Krankenschwester			50		Wilm., Aschaffenburgerstr. 7		42/~~1367~~ (13)	
14	Marcus	Georg Israel	21.4.86	Hohensalza	Arbeiter			57		dto.		42/68 (14)	
15	Seeliger	Arthur Israel	8.9.09	Stuhm	Kaufmann			34		N.58, Weinbergsweg 20		42/113 (15)	
16	Seeliger geb. Freund	Edith Sara	12.6.11	Berlin	Kontoristin			32		dto.		42/114 (16)	
17	Leven geb. Herz	Henriette Sara	19.11.85	Berlin	ohne			58		SO.16, Köpenickerstr. 36/8		42/72 (17)	
18	Rosenzweig geb. Levi	Charlotte Sara	31.10.16	Berlin	Arbeiterin			27		N.54, Grenadierstr. 7		42/73 (18)	
19	Rosenzweig	Benny	20.6.39	Berlin				4		dto.		42/74 (19)	
20	King geb. Glaser	Marianne Sara	26.2.14	Ratibor	Kindergärtnerin			29		W.15, Kurfürstendamm 177		42/75 (20)	
21	Berendt	Hugo Israel	7.5.92	Rogasen	Arbeiter			51		dto.		42/76 (21)	
22	Witkowski geb. Cohn	Dorothea Sara	25.11.82	Wreschen	Kauffrau			61		Charl., Sybelstr. 35		42/83 (23)	
23	Rosenbaum	Lili Sara	3.2.16	Berlin	Kontoristin			27		NO.18, Prenzlauer Berg 10		42/120 (22)	
24	Aronius	Hilde Sara	1.6.02	Berlin	Arbeiterin			41		Wilm., Konstanzerstr. 14		42/87 (24)	
25	Hilb	Leonie Sara	29.12.85	Esslingen	Stenotypistin			58		Wilm., Konstanzerstr. 51		42/88 (25)	

Fig. 1: List (extract): Deportation of Jews from Berlin to Auschwitz on September 10, 1943, 1.2.1.1/127213125/ITS Digital Archive, Arolsen Archives.

The collection pertaining to Berlin[24] contains a large number of these original multi-page directories concerning the deportations of Jews to ghettos and camps between October 1941 and March 1945.[25] However, the term 'transport list' is misleading: For each planned deportation, the State Police Headquarters in Berlin drew up a *Transportliste* (in multiple copies) with personal information on the people assigned to that specific transport. These lists were sent to the Chief Treasurer (*Oberfinanzpräsident, OfP*) of Berlin-Brandenburg along with other documents on the confiscation of assets.[26] Therefore, the lists contained in this collection are not the actual transport lists that the Gestapo provided to the deportation trains, as these have not been preserved. According to the historian Joachim Neander, the lists included in this collection could more accurately be described as 'confiscation lists' since the Asset Assessments Office (*Vermögensverwertungsstelle*) used them to organize the confiscation of the property of the deported Jews for the benefit of the Nazi state.[27] However, the archival description uses the term 'transport list' since this is the historical title of the document.

---

[24] Reference code: VCC.155.I, https://collections.arolsen-archives.org/en/archive/1-2-1-1_VCC-155-I/?p=1. Last accessed: 20.09.2021.

[25] The ITS received the originals of the Berlin 'transport lists' with related Gestapo correspondence contained in the Berlin unit at the beginning of the 1950s. Since the originals of the 'transport lists' for the 1st, 3rd and 4th 'transports to the East' (*'Osttransporte'*) to the Litzmannstadt ghetto have not been preserved, the ITS received incomplete copies from the Yad Vashem memorial in the context of the so-called Bovensiepen court process in 1968. Of the 184 deportations from Berlin, a total of 179 lists have been preserved – at least in part. See Jah, Dokumentenüberlieferung, 22–23.

[26] The originals of the so-called declarations of assets (*Vermögenserklärungen*), which the affected persons had to sign at home or in the assembly center (*Sammellager*) shortly before their deportation and which were also sent to the Chief Treasurer, are not included in the holdings of the Arolsen Archives. They are part of around 42,000 personal files contained in collection Rep. 36 A Oberfinanzpräsident Berlin-Brandenburg (II) stored in the Brandenburg State Archive (BLHA) in Potsdam. As part of a large-scale project, the BLHA is currently restoring, digitizing, and evaluating the files. The aim is to make the digitized files available online as comprehensively as possible.

[27] See Joachim Neander: "Die Auschwitz-Rückkehrer vom 21. März 1943", in Antonia Leugers (ed.): *Berlin, Rosenstraße 2–4 – Protest in der Diktatur – Neue Forschungen zum Frauenprotest in der Rosenstraße 1943*, Annweiler: Plöger, 2005, 115–144, here 131. See also Akim Jah: *Die Deportationen der Juden aus Berlin. Die nationalsozialistische Vernichtungspolitik und das Sammellager Große Hamburger Straße*, Berlin: be.bra, 2013, 48.

The Arolsen Archives hold similar directories created by various Gestapo offices with information on deportees from several German cities.[28] However, the inventory regarding deportations from Berlin is somewhat special as it contains mainly originals. It is noteworthy that until recently the digital archive of the Arolsen Archives only contained poorly legible reproductions of the originals, which ITS staff used in the context of tracing activities. The idea of preserving the originals and storing them in a depot rather than using them for answering inquiries makes perfect sense from an archival point of view. However, and this is the problematic aspect, for years it was not the scans of the originals but the scans of those work copies that were integrated into the database. In 2019/2020, the Berlin collection was finally re-digitized and described in detail. It also has been thoroughly indexed, including the following data on the deportees: full name, date and place of birth, marital status, occupation, and the last address.[29] Some additional remarks in the comment section of each 'transport list' have been indexed, too, such as individual activities within the Jewish community, for example, or the Nazi term *'Geltungsjude'*.

The Berlin State Police Headquarters sent the transport lists to the Chief Treasurer of Berlin-Brandenburg together with a letter which referred to the confiscation of the deportees' assets. These letters represent another typical source in the Deportations sub-collection (see fig. 2). Similar correspondence from local Gestapo offices in other cities is included in various units.

One crucial aspect of describing the collections is tagging them with attributes. As mentioned in the letter to the Chief Treasurer, the deportees documented in this type of source were mainly Jews who had been living in 'mixed marriages' until their spouse died or divorced them. Thanks to the subject index, we as cataloguers can ensure that the document can be found in this connection by tagging the related unit with the attribute 'mixed marriage'. In view of the further content of the letters, the unit is also indexed with the subject 'anti-Jewish economic measures'.[30] Researchers can use the subject index to search through the archival descriptions in our database and in the online archive.

---

28 See for example a directory regarding Jews who were deported from Koblenz and the surrounding area to the Izbica ghetto on March 22, 1942, https://collections.arolsen-archives.org/en/document/11196881. Last accessed: 01.06.2021.
29 In this volume, Henning Borggräfe gives one example how this metadata can be evaluated in order to examine deportation dynamics and forced concentration processes within a city.
30 The same attribute is linked to several other collections, e.g. to an index on the deportation of Jews from Hanover to Theresienstadt on 23.07.1942. See https://collections.arolsen-archives.org/en/archive/1-2-1-1_8228902/?p=1. Last accessed: 14.06.2021.

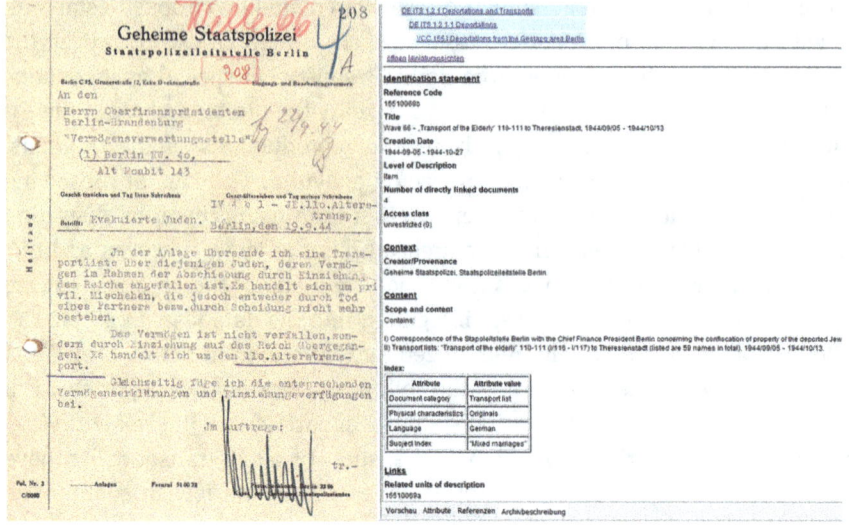

Fig. 2: Letter concerning the deportation of Jews from Berlin to Theresienstadt on September 5, 1944, and their assets, 1.2.1.1/127213269/ITS Digital Archive, Arolsen Archives. The screenshot of the OuS database shows the archival description with the subject index.

By going into hiding, escaping from a transport or committing suicide, thousands of Jews attempted to evade deportation.[31] This circumstance is reflected in the Deportations inventory in the form of lists with correspondence on Jews from various cities. The directory shown as fig. 3 was created by the Düsseldorf State Police Headquarters. It documents those individuals who committed suicide, died, or fled before their planned deportation to Theresienstadt on July 21, 1942.[32]

The directory belongs to the unit concerning deportations from Düsseldorf. The Düsseldorf[33] unit contains original correspondence, statistical lists, and directories from various cities and municipalities in the Düsseldorf Gestapo area concerning the deportation of Jews to the Litzmannstadt ghetto on October 27, 1941. It also includes original directories and transcripts regarding the deportations to Minsk, Riga, Izbica, and Auschwitz between 1941 and 1943, as well as copies of entry lists from Theresienstadt. However, that is not the whole picture. In addition, and this is fairly typical of the way the Arolsen Archives' database is

---

31 See Jah, Dokumentenüberlieferung, 16.
32 The document is tagged with the subjects 'suicides', 'deceased' and 'escape'.
33 Reference code: VCC.155.VII. See https://collections.arolsen-archives.org/en/archive/1-2-1-1_VCC-155-VII/?p=1. Last accessed: 24.09.2021.

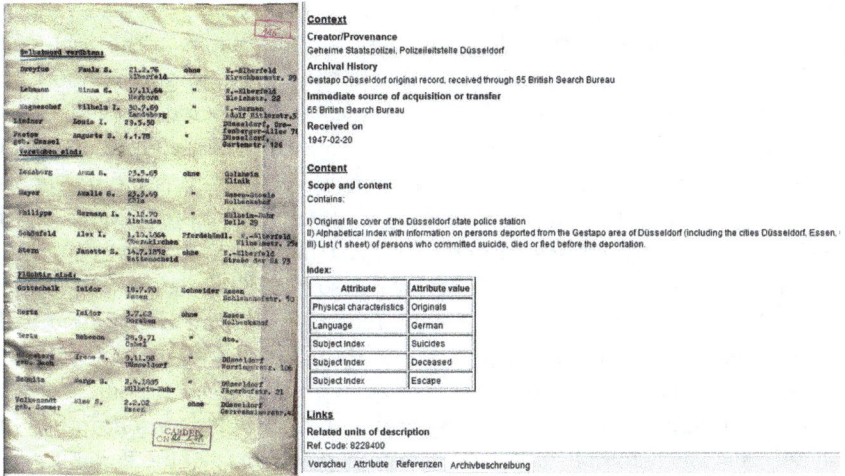

Fig. 3: List: Individuals who committed suicide, died, or fled before their planned deportation to Theresienstadt on July 21, 1942, 1.2.1.1/11198599/ITS Digital Archive, Arolsen Archives. The screenshot of the OuS database shows a part of the archival description with the subject index.

structured, the *Gestapo* sub-collection 1.2.3.0 titled Files and Information on the Gestapo also contains four original files from the State Police Headquarters in Düsseldorf concerning the deportations of Jews from Düsseldorf to Izbica, Sobibor, and Theresienstadt in the years between 1941 and 1943.[34] Among other things, these files include: (1) Orders from the State Police Headquarters in Düsseldorf and statistical evaluations concerning the Jewish population done by various Gestapo field offices and local authorities. (2) Statements on the costs of the deportations, guidelines regarding the confiscation of property, and correspondence on the whereabouts of individual persecutees. (3) Orders and regulations from the Chief Office of National Security (*Reichssicherheitshauptamt*) and various instructions, including some from the Reich Minister of the Interior concerning the alleged identification of certain deportees as being what was called 'hostile towards the people and the state' ('*volks- und staatsfeindlich*').[35]

---

34 Reference codes: 8232301–8232304. See https://collections.arolsen-archives.org/en/archive/1-2-3-0_8232300/?p=1. Last accessed: 24.09.2021.
35 This procedure created a 'legal' basis for confiscating the assets of various groups of deportees, regardless of their nationality or of the deportation's destination.

Not many administrative documents of local Gestapo offices have survived – which makes the Düsseldorf collection particularly valuable.[36] The included sources offer an insight into the extent of bureaucratic planning by various administrative authorities of the Nazi state and indicate the role and cooperation of different (local) Gestapo offices in this process. Some of the originals contained in the *Gestapo* sub-collection (1.2.3.0) are also included in the Düsseldorf Deportations inventory in 1.2.1.1 but – and this is crucial – only as reproductions. Until the revision of the *Deportations* collection in 2020, there was no obvious indication in the database that the Arolsen Archives also hold the originals (see fig. 4 and 5). Today, all the originals matching the reproductions have been identified and the respective archival descriptions link the two units with each other.[37]

Other sub-collections in the Gestapo inventory, namely the various *Gestapo Card Files* of different cities, also include information on the deportation fate of registered Jews. One example is the so-called *Schutzhaftkartei* of the Luxembourg Gestapo in inventory 1.2.3.5.[38]

The *AJDC Berlin Card File (Deportations)* (1.2.1.2)[39] and the *Card File of Berlin Transports to the East (Wave 1–7)* (1.2.1.4)[40] provide a supplementary source of information to the original Gestapo files from Berlin. Unfortunately, both collections contain poorly legible reproductions.[41] The AJDC Berlin Card File is a postwar evaluation of deportation lists and other documents created by the American Jewish Joint Distribution Committee (AJDC). Aside from the personal data of deceased or deported Jews from Berlin, the index cards also include details on their spouses and any next-of-kin as well as deportation data and destinations. The AJDC Card File can be searched by name. The so-called Card File of Berlin Transports to the East (*Osttransporte*) contains personal information on

---

36 Original files from only a few different local Gestapo offices are stored, for example, in the Bavarian State Archives (Gestapo file Würzburg), in the Speyer State Archives (Gestapo file Neustadt/Weinstrasse), and in the State Archives of Lower Saxony (Gestapo file Osnabrück). Cooperations between the Arolsen Archives and these State Archives are therefore crucial.
37 The State Archives of North Rhine-Westphalia (LAV NRW) preserve the largest original collection of personnel files of the State Police Headquarters in Düsseldorf. In the 1960s, the ITS handed over microfilms of the originals preserved in Arolsen to the then Main State Archive Düsseldorf (today's LAV NRW, Rhineland Department). A systematic comparison of the respective holdings (originals and reproductions) of the LAV NRW and the Arolsen Archives is still pending.
38 The collection of the Gestapo Card Files from different cities is not available in the online archive.
39 https://collections.arolsen-archives.org/en/archive/1-2-1-2/?p=1. Last accessed: 24.09.2021.
40 https://collections.arolsen-archives.org/en/archive/1-2-1-4/?p=1. Last accessed: 24.09.2021.
41 The Arolsen Archives hope to obtain high-resolution scans from the Yad Vashem Memorial and the Brandenburg State Archive (BLHA) soon.

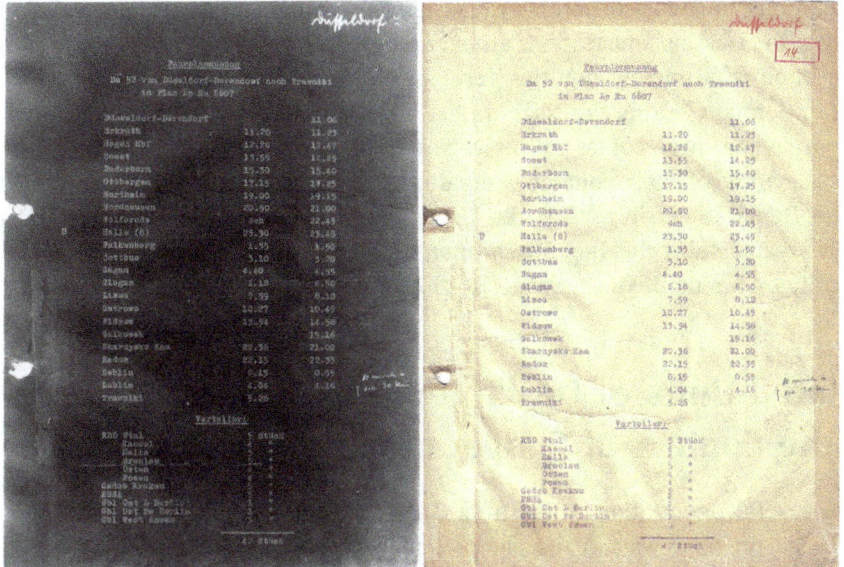

Fig. 4 and **5:** Reproduction (Düsseldorf Deportation collection) and Original Timetable of the train Da 52 from Duesseldorf-Derendorf to Trawniki, undated (*Düsseldorf Gestapo* collection), 1.2.1.1/11199162 and 1.2.3.0/82164555/ITS Digital Archive, Arolsen Archives.

Jews who were deported from Berlin to the ghettos of Litzmannstadt, Minsk, Kaunas, and Riga on the first seven trains in October and November 1941, for which the original archival records are only fragmentary.[42]

Sub-collection *Registration and Persecution* (1.2.1.5)[43] was created in 2020 and includes documents that the predecessor organizations of the Arolsen Archives received up until 2006 in the form of copies from various other archives. Most of them are registration documents and lists of the names of Jews who resided in German cities between the 1930s and the beginning of the 1940s.[44] However, this sub-collection also contains correspondence, applications, certificates,

---

42 See footnote 25 of this article.
43 Most of the 15,227 documents it contains are available in the Arolsen Archives online archive: https://collections.arolsen-archives.org/en/archive/1-2-1-5/?p=1. Last accessed: 01.06.2021.
44 In addition, the sub-collection *Local Lists of Jewish Residents* (1.2.5.1) also contains directories on the fate of Jewish residents of German communities and cities which were created at the request of the ITS. The postwar collection is arranged alphabetically by place name and is being indexed by volunteers of the United States Holocaust Memorial Museum (USHMM). See https://collections.arolsen-archives.org/en/archive/1-2-5-1/?p=1. Last accessed: 24.09.2021.

prohibitions, and lists concerning the residence, naturalization, and expatriation of Jews, their assets, emigration, arrest, and, in rare cases, their deportation. In connection with tracing inquiries and based on the assumption that Jews residing in Germany during the Nazi era had mostly been deported, ITS staff originally assigned these copies to the Deportations inventory (1.2.1.1).[45] Due to the diverse nature of their content compared to the classic collections contained in the Deportations inventory, the documents have been integrated into the newly created sub-collection *Registration and Persecution*. It is arranged alphabetically by the name of the respective town.

Related Units of Descriptions – New Acquisitions in the Context of Cooperations

Since several deportation trains from different cities and Gestapo areas were combined on their way to the camps and ghettos, various sub-collections in the *Deportations and Transports* inventory (1.2.1) are interlinked. Furthermore, they also relate to other collections in our database. A good example is the newly acquired *Collection of the Jewish Community in Leipzig* (7.5.4).[46] It is part of the provenance-based collection 7 and includes digital scans of lists with details of deported Jews that were mentioned in the records of the Saxony-Thuringia District Office of the Reich Association of Jews in Germany.[47] The documentation covers deportations from the geographical area of Saxony, Anhalt, and Thuringia to various ghettos – including Theresienstadt, Warsaw, and Bełżyce – as well as to the concentration and extermination camps Majdanek, Sobibór, and Auschwitz-Birkenau between February 1942 and February 1945.[48]

For the users, the connection between inventories 7.5.4 and 1.2 is not necessarily obvious at first glance. Therefore, we highlight this aspect in the archival description under the heading "Related units of description", which provides information on thematic links to other collections. In addition, the lists included in the Leipzig collection are indexed at document level, which means that they are searchable by name or by the last address of the deportees. This form of index-

---

[45] ITS staff dealt in a similar manner with related documents that had already been integrated into the ITS holdings.
[46] https://collections.arolsen-archives.org/en/archive/7-5-4/?p=1. Last accessed: 24.09.2021.
[47] The *Bezirksstelle Sachsen-Thueringen* of the *Reichsvereinigung* was called *Bezirksstelle Mitteldeutschland* from July 1942 onwards.
[48] https://collections.arolsen-archives.org/en/archive/7-5-4_754002/?p=1. Last accessed: 24.09.2021.

ing, namely the massive linking of metadata with individual documents, is a special method of the Arolsen Archives related to the history of the institution as a tracing service and is still practiced frequently. In this case, the index allows the users to reconstruct different transport and deportation routes.[49]

Another example is the cooperation with the Archive of the Jewish Community in Szeged.[50] In 2020, the Arolsen Archives received digital scans and metadata of a directory regarding Hungarian Jews who were deported from Szeged to Auschwitz and Strasshof in June 1944.[51] The list complements the few sources concerning the deportation of Hungarian Jews in our database.

Both cooperations are part of the Arolsen Archives' new overall strategy. This strategy defines the function of the former International Tracing Service as an 'archival hub', which we hope to strengthen through systematic cooperation with memorial sites, archives, institutions, and associations.[52] As far as the acquisition of documents is concerned, however, the Arolsen Archives still have to establish systematic partnerships with institutions that hold documentation on the persecution of Sinti and Roma.

Records on the Deportation of Sinti and Roma

Similar to the documentation on the deportation of Jews, originals and copies concerning the deportation of Sinti and Roma are scattered across various sub-collections of the 1.2 inventory. Up until recently, most of the collections had only basic and outdated archival descriptions. Therefore, the process of thoroughly cataloguing them is still ongoing. One of the obstacles in identifying the relevant collections is the fact that Sinti and Roma were often sent to concentration camps as so-called anti-social elements (*'Asoziale'*). This prisoner group, however, was rarely mentioned in the original archival descriptions of the ITS, because the German compensation law did not recognize them as eligible and

---

[49] A quick name search in the database for Frieda Horwitz (born 29.04.1878), for example, finds results both in the collection of the Jewish Community in Leipzig (7.5.4) and in the Berlin Deportation inventory (1.2.1.1). Thanks to the two lists, her transport route from Leipzig via Berlin to Auschwitz in February 1943 can be reconstructed, see https://collections.arolsen-archives.org/en/document/128455653 and https://collections.arolsen-archives.org/en/document/127212312. Both last accessed: 24.09.2021.
[50] See Dóra Pataricza's article in this volume.
[51] https://collections.arolsen-archives.org/en/archive/7-9-1_791001/?p=1. Last accessed: 24.09.2021.
[52] Newly acquired collections are usually included in inventory 7.

ITS practices were aligned with its definition of Nazi persecutees. For some years now, we have been working on the designation of documents in the database that concern persecuted groups that received little attention in historical research or in mainstream discourse for decades. Significant results are mainly visible in inventory 1.1 *Camps and Ghettos*. Especially the included collections of individual prisoner records, which the Arolsen Archives preserve from a variety of concentration camps, provide information on the deportation of Sinti and Roma (as well as many Jews) and their individual fates of persecution. Among the documents are prisoner registration cards, prisoner registration forms and personal effects cards, which usually contain the dates of arrest and the arresting authority. In addition, the Camps and Ghettos inventory includes reproductions of the main books of the 'gypsy camp' in the Auschwitz concentration camp with names and dates of birth of the affected individuals,[53] as well as lists regarding deported Sinti and Roma (and Jews).[54] A systematic and comparative approach of the sources, could allow to reconstruct an overall picture of the course of the deportations from different cities (for example with regard to the deportations of Sinti and Roma in March 1943).

The collections mentioned above refer to single individuals or groups. In contrast, some of the following examples illustrate the administration and organization of the deportations. Fig. 6, for example, shows an extract from a 3-page telegram dated October 18, 1939, which contains communication between two SS-Sturmbannführer.[55] They refer to correspondence between Adolf Eichmann and the Chief of the Security Police concerning the bureaucratic planning of the deportations of Sinti and Roma from Ostrava (Mährisch-Ostrau), Kattowice and Vienna. The deportation of 901 Jews from Mährisch-Ostrau to Nisko on October 18, 1939, in the context of the so-called Nisko Aktion is also mentioned.[56] The document is part of sub-collection *Persecution measures against "Gypsies"* (1.2.7.26),[57] which consists of 214 copies concerning the persecution of Sinti

---

[53] https://collections.arolsen-archives.org/en/archive/1-1-2-1_2204001/?p=1 and https://collections.arolsen-archives.org/en/archive/1-1-2-1_2204002/?p=1. Last accessed: 09.09.2021. The originals are stored in the archives of the Auschwitz-Birkenau State Museum.
[54] See for example *List Material of Various Camps* (1.1.47.1): https://collections.arolsen-archives.org/en/archive/1-1-47-1. Last accessed: 09.09.2021.
[55] One of them is presumably SS-Sturmbannführer Rolf Günther, who became Eichmann's deputy in 1941.
[56] For background information on the deportations of Jews in the context of the 'Nisko Aktion' (initiated by Eichmann) as well as the planned deportation of Sinti and Roma to Nisko, which was not carried out, see Jonny Moser: *Nisko – Die ersten Judendeportationen*, Vienna: Edition Steinbauer, 2012.
[57] https://collections.arolsen-archives.org/en/archive/1-2-7-26/?p=1. Last accessed: 01.06.2021.

and Roma. The majority of these sources came to Arolsen in the 1970s and 1980s through the Central Office of the Land Judicial Authorities for Investigation of Nazi Crimes in Ludwigsburg and the Documentation Centre of Austrian Resistance in Vienna (DÖW). The sub-collection is arranged in three units and includes various circulars, orders, and forms issued by the National Criminal Police Office and the Chief Office of National Security between 1938 and 1943, concerning the registration, persecution, and admission of so-called gypsies to concentration camps. There is also correspondence from the police guard battalion and the commander of the Vienna Municipal Police (*Schutzpolizei*) regarding the deportations of Sinti and Roma from Vienna to Auschwitz in March and April 1943. The letters also deal with questions concerning the guards who supervised the deportations. Furthermore, correspondence from police leaders in Latvia and the so-called Reich Commissioner for the East is included, which concerns persecution measures against Sinti and Roma in 1942.[58] Finally, yet importantly, the sub-collection contains postwar correspondence, reports, survivors' testimonies, and court decisions concerning the Lackenbach and Montlhéry camps and compensation for imprisonment.[59]

Sub-collection *List Material Group Prisons & Persecution* (1.2.2.1)[60], which will be revised and processed in the course of 2022/2023, contains nearly 900,000 documents regarding individuals who were imprisoned in various detention facilities such as judicial and Gestapo prisons, so-called labor education camps (*'Arbeitserziehungslager'*) and work houses (*'Arbeitshäuser'*), early concentration camps, as well as forced labor camps. The inventory includes correspondence from the Criminal Investigation Department Hohensalza (Posen) regarding the confiscation of the property of arrested Sinti and Roma and their admission to the 'gypsy camp' in Auschwitz in April 1943[61] as well as camp reports concerning the number of individuals who were incarcerated in the Lackenbach camp as 'gypsies'.[62]

---

58 https://collections.arolsen-archives.org/en/archive/1-2-7-26_9041001/?p=1. Last accessed: 24.09.2021.
59 https://collections.arolsen-archives.org/en/archive/1-2-7-26_9041002/?p=1. Last accessed: 24.09.2021. See Susanne Urban, Sascha Feuchert and Markus Roth (eds.): *Fundstücke. Stimmen der Überlebenden des "Zigeunerlagers" Lackenbach*, Göttingen: Wallstein, 2014.
60 https://collections.arolsen-archives.org/en/archive/1-2-2-1. Last accessed: 01.06.2021.
61 https://collections.arolsen-archives.org/en/archive/1-2-2-1_2392000/?p=1&s=Hohensalza. Last accessed: 01.06.2021.
62 https://collections.arolsen-archives.org/en/archive/1-2-2-1_2704000/?p=1. Last accessed: 01.06.2021.

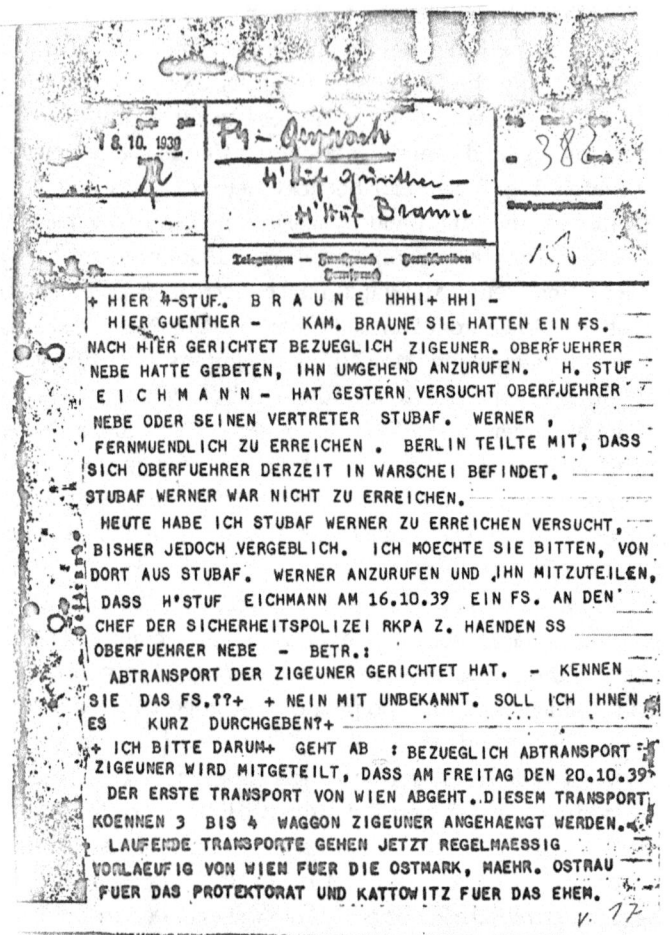

Fig. 6: Telegram (extract) concerning the bureaucratic planning of the deportations of Sinti and Roma from Ostrava, Kattowice and Vienna, October 18, 1939, 1.2.7.26/82342400/ITS Digital Archive, Arolsen Archives.

As mentioned earlier, the *Registration and Persecution* sub-collection (1.2.1.5) also contains relevant sources on Sinti and Roma of which the Arolsen Archives only hold reproductions. Of interest, for example, is a letter from the district administrator of Mosbach, a town close to Stuttgart, which documents the deportation of ten family members to a concentration camp, presumably Auschwitz, on March 23, 1943.[63]

The sources contained in the Deportations inventory 1.2.1.1 on the deportation of Sinti and Roma are mainly copies from other institutions. They include documentation regarding the fate of individual persecutees from Berlin, Hamburg, Frankfurt am Main, Kassel, and Munich. The Hamburg[64] unit contains the majority of sources related to this topic, including copies of directories and correspondence from the Criminal Police regarding Sinti and Roma who were deported from Hamburg to the 'General Government' in May 1940 and to Auschwitz in March 1943.[65] There is also a 60-page copy of the so-called Gypsy File ('*Zigeunerakte*') of the Hamburg Criminal Investigation Department concerning the registration of Roma and Sinti in Hamburg and its surroundings with information on their family members as well as their deportations.[66] The Kassel[67] unit includes a reproduction of an index regarding Roma and Sinti registered in the town in October 1939 with additional comments on 'lifestyle' and employment, and a corresponding letter from the Criminal Police Headquarters in Kassel.[68] The Frankfurt[69] unit includes a note dated December 14, 1940, from the Frankfurt am Main Criminal Police Headquarters concerning four families who were persecuted as 'gypsies' and their allegedly 'voluntary resettlement' to the 'General Government'.[70]

---

[63] https://collections.arolsen-archives.org/en/archive/1-2-1-5_10007241. Last accessed: 15.09.2022. For further sources, see the unit pertaining to Salzwedel: https://collections.arolsen-archives.org/en/archive/1-2-1-5_10009152. Last accessed: 15.09.2022. For a registration card referring to a Sinto residing in Bremen that is not available online, see 1.2.1.5/89204677/ITS Digital Archive, Arolsen Archives.
[64] Reference code VCC.155.VI: https://collections.arolsen-archives.org/en/archive/1-2-1-1_VCC-155-VI/?p=1. Last accessed: 24.09.2021.
[65] https://collections.arolsen-archives.org/en/archive/1-2-1-1_8228010/?p=1 and https://collections.arolsen-archives.org/en/archive/1-2-1-1_3609000/?p=1. Both last accessed: 01.06.2021.
[66] See https://collections.arolsen-archives.org/en/archive/1-2-1-1_1661000/?p=1. Last accessed: 01.06.2021.
[67] Reference code VCC.155.XV: https://collections.arolsen-archives.org/en/archive/1-2-1-1_VCC-155-XV/?p=1. Last accessed: 24.09.2021.
[68] https://collections.arolsen-archives.org/en/archive/1-2-1-1_2098000/?p=1. Last accessed: 01.06.2021. The ITS received both copies (from Frankfurt am Main and Kassel) in the 1960s from the Court of Appeal in Berlin.
[69] Reference code VCC.155.XII: https://collections.arolsen-archives.org/en/archive/1-2-1-1_VCC-155-XII/?p=1. Last accessed: 24.09.2021.
[70] https://collections.arolsen-archives.org/en/archive/1-2-1-1_2097000/?p=1. Last accessed: 01.06.2021.

One of the few original documents concerning the topic in our database is a letter (fig. 7) from the Berlin State Police Headquarters to the Chief Treasurer of Berlin-Brandenburg regarding the deportation of so-called gypsies to Auschwitz on May 5, 1943. The letter also reveals information on how the confiscation of their property was organized. Unfortunately, the accompanying directory with details of the 252 deportees mentioned by the Berlin State Police Headquarters and listed on the cover sheet is not included.

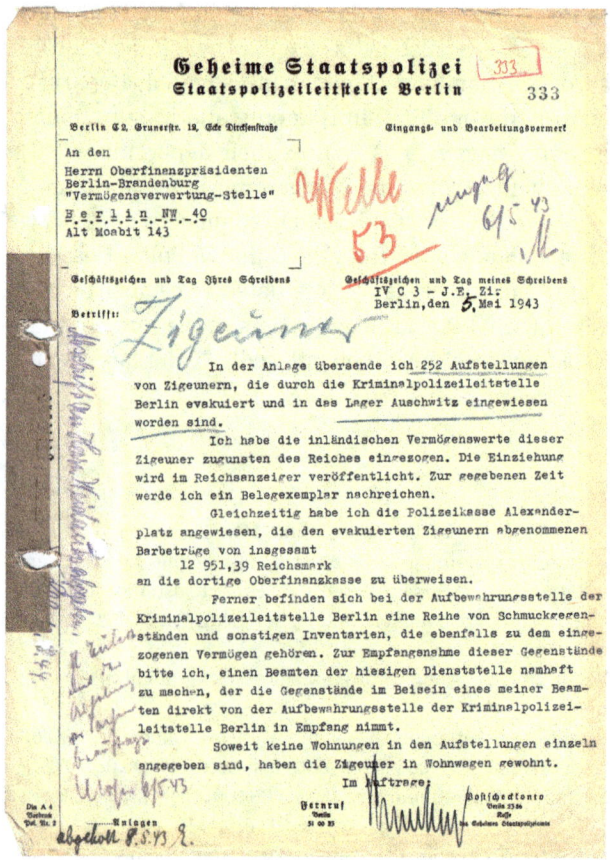

Fig. 7: Letter regarding the deportation of Sinti and Roma from Berlin to Auschwitz, May 5, 1943, 1.2.1.1/127212907/ITS Digital Archive, Arolsen Archives.

The unit regarding deportations from Munich[71] and the surrounding area contains a transcript of an alphabetical list with information about the confiscation of the property and assets of associations and of individuals belonging to various persecution categories. The 98-page, undated postwar directory refers, among other things, to the property of Sinti and Roma. It is based on records of the Asset Assessments Office in Munich and provides, in most cases, details of the name, date of birth, last address, and file number.[72]

After the liberation, German restitution authorities based their decisions on eligibility regarding 'compensation for National Socialist injustice' (*Wiedergutmachung*) on information passed on by the ITS. The legal basis was formed by 'compensation laws' (enacted between the late 1940s and the mid-1950s), which operated with a narrow definition of the term 'persecutee'. ITS staff provided – among other things – certificates of incarceration (*Inhaftierungsbescheinigungen*), in which they quoted categories of imprisonment from concentration camp documents stored in Arolsen without contextualizing them. Since Sinti and Roma were often sent to concentration camps as '*Asoziale*,' they did not receive any restitution from the German Federal Republic. Looking at the topic of *Wiedergutmachung*, the T/D correspondence files included in collection 6.3.3 reveal this problematic aspect of the Tracing Service's activities.[73] However, the documentation also include valuable information concerning the persecution fate of Sinti and Roma and Jews (and other persecutees) that will become more accessible and searchable once the Arolsen Archives realize a planned systematic cataloging of the T/D files.[74]

Finally, yet importantly, the aforementioned *Gestapo sub-collection* 1.2.3 contains cards (see fig. 8) that different Gestapo offices filled out for a large number of various groups of individuals who had 'come to their attention'. Some of them refer to the registration, observation, and deportation of Sinti and Roma. By means of crowdsourcing and optical character recognition (OCR), the Gestapo

---

71 Reference code VCC.155.II: https://collections.arolsen-archives.org/en/archive/1-2-1-1_VCC-155-II/?p=1. Last accessed: 24.09.2021.
72 Part of the directory is a glossary that provides explanations of the abbreviations used for persecution categories, see https://collections.arolsen-archives.org/en/document/11196196. Last accessed: 01.06.2021.
73 See Susanne Urban et al. (eds.): *Fundstücke. Entwurzelt im eigenen Land: Deutsche Sinti und Roma nach 1945*, Göttingen: Wallstein, 2015.
74 In the Arolsen Archives' database, the T/D files (6.3.3.2) are searchable by the name of the person in question. In the online archive, the majority of the files are neither searchable nor available yet. The Arolsen Archives are currently debating on how to make the files more accessible.

Card Files will be linked to a large amount of metadata in the near future. This will make them searchable in connection with the topic of this article.[75]

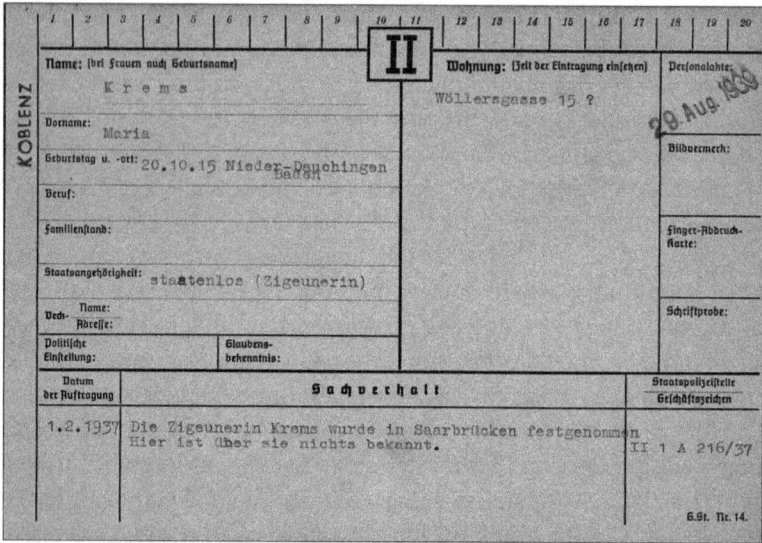

Fig. 8: Gestapo Koblenz Card File for Maria Krems (front page), 1.2.3.3/129178532/ITS Digital Archive, Arolsen Archives. The originals of the Gestapo Koblenz Card File are stored in the State Archives in Koblenz.

Conclusion and Prospects

The intention of this paper was to give an overview of how to navigate through the Arolsen Archives' database in order to find documentation on the deportations of Jews and Sinti and Roma. Considering the immense size of the archive in Bad Arolsen, this paper is an attempt to make the relevant inventories visible but does not claim to be comprehensive. Without a doubt, there is much more to explore and to find. As far as the acquisition of documents as part of the organization's new strategy is concerned, it would certainly be a huge gain for histor-

---

75 The University of Osnabrück is currently evaluating the data fields of the Osnabrück Gestapo Card File in a large-scale project in order to analyze changes in the structural approach of the Gestapo in the course of the Nazi era. The Arolsen Archives hold copies of the collection. See Sebastian Bondzio and Christoph Rass: "Allmächtig, allwissend und allgegenwärtig? Die Osnabrücker Gestapo-Kartei als Massendatenspeicher und Weltmodell", in *Osnabrücker Mitteilungen*, 124, 2019, 223–260.

ical research if especially the collections on the persecution of Sinti and Roma were to grow in the future.

Due to its history as a tracing service, today's Arolsen Archives are primarily a person-related collection. In the past, the organization has made great efforts to make its collections searchable especially by names. These endeavors have taken new forms: As part of the #everynamecounts crowdsourcing project, there are currently 25,662 volunteers around the world indexing data (mostly) from individual prisoner records of the Arolsen Archives' Camps and Ghetto inventory.[76] In addition to a variety of information on single individuals (such as name, date of birth, last place of residence, occupation, nationality, marital status, religion, prisoner number, transfers within the camp system, and family members) the volunteers also transcribe the category of imprisonment to which the persons concerned were assigned in the concentration camp. Once the newly generated metadata will be integrated into the Arolsen Archives' database, the holdings can be searched specifically by certain attributes, which opens up a variety of new research opportunities such as the reconstruction of complex persecution and transfer routes within the concentration camp system of individuals or entire prisoner groups. The metadata will also provide a new basis for research into family biographies of persecution.[77]

---

[76] Arolsen Archives/Zooniverse: "#everynamecounts". Available at: https://www.zooniverse.org/projects/arolsen-archives/every-name-counts/stats. Last accessed: 14.07.2022.

[77] On the potential of the newly generated metadata for future research and the chances and (ethical) challenges of making them available in the online archive of the Arolsen Archives, see Kim Dresel: "What Counts and Who Does It? Crowdsourcing und Arolsen Archives 2.0", in *Medaon – Magazin für jüdisches Leben in Forschung und Bildung*, 15/29, 2021, 1–6. Available at: http://www.medaon.de/pdf/medaon_29_dresel.pdf. Last accessed: 14.12.2021.

Maximilian Strnad
Potential of Databases for Research and Culture of Remembrance Using the Deportation of Jews under the Nazi Regime as an Example

Abstract: Online information sources are influencing our knowledge more and more. However, the insights we can gain from the various online portals on Nazi history are limited by the range of information available, and its quality and format. This is clearly demonstrated in relation to the deportation of Jews under Nazi-rule: Most of the transports, as well as the fate of the majority of the deportees can be reconstructed online. However, the information is stored disparately and is inconsistent. In this article, various examples of databases on the history of National Socialism will be used to show how their potential can be better exploited in the future, if information is clearly identifiable and, above all, better interlinked.

Introduction

The future is digital! This statement has become a truism not only since the coronavirus crisis, but also in the field of Holocaust research and the culture of remembrance. With the temporary closure of reading rooms and the limited admission of users, the need for access to digital sources of information has once again risen sharply.

In addition to archives, educational institutions and private initiatives in particular have set up online portals on the history of National Socialism in recent years, some of them extensive. The information they contain usually offers less access to primary sources than to formatted data – published in the form of memorial books or prisoner databases for example. Powerful databases often lie behind these offerings, which not only reconstruct the history of those people who became victims of Nazi tyranny, but also bring places of remembrance of Nazi history back into public memory[1] or name perpetrators[2]. The provision of de-

---

[1] See for example Federal Agency for Civic Education: "Datenbank Erinnerungsorte". Available at: https://www.bpb.de/geschichte/nationalsozialismus/erinnerungsorte/. Last accessed: 12.01.2022.

ⓐ OpenAccess. © 2023 the author(s), published by De Gruyter. [cc BY-NC-ND] This work is licensed under the Creative Commons Attribution-NonCommercial-NoDerivatives 4.0 International License.
https://doi.org/10.1515/9783110746464-007

tailed information in these knowledge clusters, which are easily accessible to anyone at any time, offers countless research opportunities, the potential of which academics are exploiting more and more to formulate and answer both new and old research questions.

Especially where there are consistent database applications, these can be used in historiography to substantively support analytical results with empirical findings. Most of these are research projects with a regional focus.[3] However, where a higher-level evaluation is aimed at and complex requests to various databases are necessary for this purpose, corresponding inputs often fail in advance due to a number of hurdles. Whilst it is true that earlier problems with the compatibility of different programs can now be largely solved by standardizing export interfaces, the information in the various databases is available in different densities, and is not structured and formatted in a consistent manner. Many databases have grown and expanded over the years, with much of the information stored in them only as full text, and not in the form of uniquely identifiable values, so-called entities.

This can lead to considerable problems with identifying places, institutions and people. However, a subsequent restructuring of the information is time-consuming and out of the question for many projects, if only for cost reasons. The use of artificial intelligence will make it increasingly possible to rise to these challenges in the future, but its use is currently still expensive and not widespread. Apart from technical and content-related problems, data protection and personal privacy requirements in particular often represent obstacles that are difficult to overcome. The fundamental question of whether it is justifiable not only to collect data on those people who were persecuted and murdered by the Nazis, but also to interlink it – i.e. the ethical and moral problems of data collection – is, however, only referred to here; it is not the main focus of this paper.

In addition, many institutions have still not recognized the additional value of sharing information both for themselves and their projects, and have therefore invested few or no resources in exchanging information with other projects, interlinking their data or even providing open access to it. In Germany and Austria

---

[2] See for example Hamburger Behörde für Schule und Berufsbildung: "Datenbank online. Die Dabeigewesenen". Available at: https://www.hamburg.de/ns-dabeigewesene. Last accessed: 12.01.2022.

[3] For Munich, see for example Maximilian Strnad: *Privileg Mischehe? Handlungsräume "jüdisch versippter" Familien 1933–1949*, Göttingen: Wallstein, 2021; Katharina Bergmann: *Jüdische Emigration aus München. Entscheidungsfindung und Auswanderungswege (1933–1941)*, Berlin: De Gruyter Oldenbourg, 2022.

in particular, this also often conflicts with fundamental considerations, for example, concerns that right-wing extremists could misuse the data, or that the data could be used in an inappropriate way due to the loss of control associated with their wide accessibility. The opportunities offered by open-source access, for example, through crowdsourcing for cataloging, reviewing and expansion, or as part of hackathons,[4] as in the case of the Marbles of Remembrance[5] or Visualization of Jewish Life in Berlin projects,[6] are often shelved in light of these concerns.

Databases are created for a unique purpose. In the area of Nazi history, this is usually based on the culture of remembrance and is usually subject to the content-related and geographical focus of the driving institution. However, many users have additional or different interests in terms of knowledge and use and would be keen to use the data for their own research. However, due to the obstacles described above, the potential for higher-level queries to databases that could provide significant new insights for regional comparisons and generalizations, for example, has barely been exploited to date.

In this paper, I will use the deportations of Jews under National Socialism as an example to analyze the potential that using databases offers researchers, and the challenges they face. This analysis is performed from a dual perspective: Firstly, as a member of staff at the Munich Institute for Urban History and Remembrance (IfSE), I am involved in the development of one of the databases examined. Secondly, I always refer back to the relevant databases as knowledge clusters in my own publications.[7] In a second step, the analysis is followed by an attempt to show where there is a need for action, and how new insights

---

[4] For Coding Da V1nc1, the first German hackathon for open cultural data, see German National Library et al.: "Coding Da V1nc1". Available at: https://codingdavinci.de/en. Last accessed: 12.01.2022.

[5] See German National Library et al.: "Marbles of Remembrance". Available at: https://codingdavinci.de/de/projekte/marbles-remembrance-murmeln-der-erinnerung. Last accessed: 12.01.2022. See also the chat bot that resulted from the project: Arolsen Archives: "Get to know Jewish children of the Nazi period with an app". Available at: https://arolsen-archives.org/en/learn-participate/initiatives-projects/marbles-of-remembrance/. Last accessed: 12.01.2022.

[6] See German National Library et al.: "Visualisierung jüdischen Lebens". Available at: https://codingdavinci.de/index.php/de/projekte/visualisierung-juedischen-lebens. Last accessed: 12.01.2022.

[7] For example, in Maximilian Strnad: *Zwischenstation "Judensiedlung": Verfolgung und Deportation der jüdischen Münchner 1941–1945*, Munich: Oldenbourg, 2011; ibid.: "Die Deportationen aus München", in Alan Steinweis (ed.): *Münchner Beiträge zur jüdischen Geschichte und Kultur*, 2, 2014, 76–96. Available at: https://www.jgk.geschichte.uni-muenchen.de/muenchner-beitraege/2014_2/2014_2.pdf. Last accessed: 12.01.2022.

can be generated for research through better formatting and interlinking of information. Using the example of the online memorial to the victims of National Socialism planned in Munich, the paper concludes by illustrating the important momentum that this can provide for research, and in the culture of remembrance.

Comparison of Five Online Portals

This paper was inspired by the outcomes of the round table discussion at the *Deportations in the Nazi Era – Sources and Research* conference in November 2020.[8] At this conference, representatives from five institutions addressed the question of what potential their databases and online portals hold for research on the deportations of German Jews, and what challenges they expect in the coming years.[9] These are the *Memorial Book. Victims of the Persecution of Jews under the National Socialist Tyranny in Germany 1933–1945* in the Federal Archives;[10] the Yad Vashem Holocaust Deportation Database *Transports to Extinction*;[11] the *Statistik und Deportation der jüdischen Bevölkerung aus dem Deutschen Reich* website;[12] the *Biografisches Gedenkbuch der Münchner Juden 1933–1945* web portal[13] and the Arolsen Archives online archive[14].

---

8 I would like to thank Tanja von Fransecky, Sarah Grandke, Thomas Freier, Cornelia Shati-Geißler, and Giora Zwilling for the stimulating discussions, as well as the editors of this omnibus volume, Henning Borggräfe and Akim Jah, for their important input.
9 Like the round table discussion at the conference, this paper is also limited to the geographical area of the 'Altreich' and to the deportation of Jews. Apart from a few regional memorial books in which Sinti and Roma are also mentioned and the memorial book by Jan Parcer there is currently no higher-level database available on Sinti and Roma who were persecuted during the Nazi era. See Jan Parcer: *The Gypsies at Auschwitz-Birkenau.* Munich: Saur, 1993; for the mention of Sinti and Roma in regional memorial books see, for example, Erinnerungswerkstatt Augsburg: "Sinti und Roma". Available at: https://gedenkbuch-augsburg.de/sinti-und-roma. Last accessed: 12.01.2022.
10 Federal Archives: "Memorial Book. Victims of the Persecution of Jews under the National Socialist Tyranny in Germany 1933–1945". Available at: https://www.bundesarchiv.de/gedenkbuch/introduction/en. Last accessed: 12.01.2022.
11 Yad Vashem: "Transports to Extinction: Holocaust (Shoah) Deportation Database". Available at: https://deportation.yadvashem.org/. Last accessed: 12.01.2022.
12 Thomas Freier: "Statistik und Deportation der jüdischen Bevölkerung aus dem Deutschen Reich". Available at: https://www.statistik-des-holocaust.de/. Last accessed: 12.01.2022.
13 Munich Municipal Archives: "Biografisches Gedenkbuch der Münchner Juden 1933–1945". Available at: https://gedenkbuch.muenchen.de/. Last accessed: 12.01.2022.

There are two different types of online databases in particular that are important in terms of the deportations of Jews. These are, firstly memorial books that follow a biographical approach, and secondly, subject-specific portals. The Memorial Book in the Federal Archives belongs to the first category. It is one of the oldest and most widely used tools for personal research on Jewish victims of Nazi persecution in Germany. The data it contains are based on extensive research and include written sources from various provenances. The key biographical data and details of persecution are documented, including information on imprisonment, emigration and deportation. On the subject of deportation, the online database includes details on the "place from which the deportation train departed, including departure date and destination, as well as any other transports, including date and destination"[15]. Using the advanced search function, it is not only possible to search for individual people, but also to generate lists of results on various topics, such as date of departure, place of departure, and destination of the deportations. These lists can also be exported as a CSV file, a facility that is not to be underestimated, especially for the construction and extension of own research databases, but also for data reconciliation. However, the formation of differentiated clusters is only possible to a limited extent as search terms across several categories can only be stated in a general search field and can only be combined with a search in date fields. For example, although it is possible to search for people who were deported from a specific city on a specific day, combination searches of people born in one city and deported from another return unreliable results because the combined search queries both fields for both terms. As no further search or filter functions are available for the search results, it is also not possible to further limit search results and search for people, for example, who were first deported from their hometown to a ghetto, and from there on to an extermination camp at a later date.

Now, by definition, the Federal Archives' online memorial book is designed primarily to locate individual people. However, cluster functions would be particularly helpful for social history research, especially since the memorial book, with its over 175,000 personal records, is the most comprehensive source of information on murdered German Jews. From a technical point of view, it is comparatively easy to provide such search and filter functions, since the corresponding information in the underlying database is structured in individual

---

14 Arolsen Archives: "Online Archive". Available at: https://collections.arolsen-archives.org/en/search/. Last accessed: 12.01.2022.
15 Federal Archives: "Introduction". Available at: https://www.bundesarchiv.de/gedenkbuch/introduction/en. Last accessed: 12.01.2022.

fields, and is available in a standardized format. Another obstacle to further research on the deportations is the fact that the memorial book is a book of commemoration for those who died (also for data protection reasons). Survivors of the deportations cannot be found in this book. Therefore, the results do not reflect the full extent of the deportations.[16]

There is also another problem: Because of its huge volume, the database is not always up to date in spite of consistent and highly research-intensive editing. Let us take the first transport from Munich as an example. According to the current body of information in the Munich Municipal Archives, a total of 997 Jews were deported to Kowno on November 20, 1941 and murdered there on November 25.[17] In the Federal Archives memorial book, however, a corresponding search yields 1,003 hits to be assigned to this transport.[18]

On a subpage of its website, based on the relevant literature, the Federal Archives provides, as an extra source of information, an overview of the chronology of all deportations from the German Reich, including Austria, the Protectorate of Bohemia and Moravia, and the German Sudeten regions, as well as from Belgium, France, the Netherlands, and Luxembourg.[19] For researchers and individuals interested in history, this is an important source of information in terms of the course and extent of the deportations. However, the data correspond to the state of research as it was around 20 years ago. Some users are also missing a function that, proceeding from the chronology, lists all the people included in the memorial book, who were deported on the respective transport. Corresponding lists of results could be stored comparatively easily by linking the various chronology entries with the corresponding database fields 'place of departure', 'date of departure' and 'destination'.

---

[16] The list of residents, which is not accessible online, documents the personal details of all approx. 600,000 people who lived in the '*Altreich*' between 1933 and 1945 and were persecuted for being Jewish. Cf. essentially Nicolai M. Zimmermann: "Was geschah mit den Juden in Deutschland zwischen 1933 und 1945? Eine Dokumentation des Bundesarchivs", in ZfG, 64, 2016, volume 12, 1045–1058.

[17] Cf. Munich Municipal Archives: "Am 22.11.1941 nach Kaunas (Welle I, Transport 379) deportierte Personen". Available at: https://gedenkbuch.muenchen.de/index.php?id=gedenkbuch_transport&ddat=20.11.1941&ziel=Kaunas. Last accessed: 12.01.2022.

[18] Search for place of departure and place of deportation Kowno Munich in conjunction with deportation date 11/20/1941. Eleven people are wrongly assigned to this transport (for example, Manfred Rosenbaum, born on April 26, 1928, in Munich), three are missing (for example, Ilse Sohn, born on March 1, 1921, in Karlsruhe).

[19] Cf. Federal Archives: "Deportation chronology". Available at: https://www.bundesarchiv.de/gedenkbuch/chronology/view.xhtml?lang=en. Last accessed: 12.01.2022.

Some of these functions are offered by the *Biografisches Gedenkbuch der Münchner Juden 1933–1945*, one of the oldest and most comprehensive regional memorial book projects, which also provides further information and short biographies on many people. The memorial book, a first version of which went online in 2012 and was relaunched in November 2020, currently contains 5,026 entries.[20] The editing and deep cataloging of around 5,000 data records is much easier to achieve than with the Federal Archives' memorial book, not least because of its regional focus. It is also possible to search the individual fields separately in the Munich memorial book, and thus create unique clusters. However, in contrast to the Federal Archives' memorial book, searching for imprisonment, emigration and deportation, or according to the place of departure or further deportations, is not possible at present as the corresponding fields in the database have not yet been activated in the online portal. The useful CSV export function is also missing.

In contrast to the memorial book website of the Federal Archives, there is also a separate list for the deportations from Munich, which documents not only the extent of the deportations, but also their composition.[21] The individual transports are each accompanied by a list of the deportees, and the individual entries are in turn linked to the respective data record sheets of the persons concerned. As in the Federal Archives' memorial book, permalinks ensure that the web addresses of the individual data record sheets can be cited, and remain discoverable online. Although this is a book of commemoration for the murdered Jews from Munich, for the sake of completeness these lists also include men, women and children who were deported from other places via Munich, or Jews from Munich who survived. However, because of data protection reasons no personal record sheets are available for them.

While the relational linking of records in the *Biografisches Gedenkbuch der Münchner Juden 1933–1945* has so far been limited to deportations from Munich, and the individual records – as in the case of the Federal Archives' memorial book – are not related to each other, Yad Vashem's *Transports to Extinction* application offers considerably more far-reaching research and contextualization options which, in addition, are not limited to transports from the '*Altreich*'. In contrast to the first two projects mentioned above, this is not a memorial

---

20 Cf. Munich Municipal Archives: "Biografisches Gedenkbuch der Münchner Juden 1933–1945". Available at: https://gedenkbuch.muenchen.de/. Last accessed: 12.01.2022. In the underlying database, 14,292 people are currently recorded.
21 Cf. Munich Municipal Archives: "Die Deportationen aus München". Available at: https://gedenkbuch.muenchen.de/index.php?id=deportationen. Last accessed: 12.01.2022. Gender and last place of residence prior to deportation are indicated.

book, but an online portal that combines various content from the different Yad Vashem database applications by focusing on the deportation of Jews.[22] A basic search allows users to find all places, events, people, and terms relating to the deportations. In contrast to the memorial books where the focus is on the person, here there is a separate data record sheet for each individual transport. The search results are displayed on a map. Places of departure that contain the search result are marked in green and places of arrival in red. The search results can also be displayed in list form for clearer presentation. Search results can be narrowed down further using a timeline and filter functions according to places of departure and arrival. The filter functions offer a convenient quick entry point for a general overview of the regional scope of deportations as well as of deportations from different time periods.

The data record sheets contain different densities of information on the transports, including details of the route, the size of the transport, the deportees, and the perpetrators and institutions involved. They are completed – where available – by bibliographic references and links to various sources from the Yad Vashem digital collections that are connected to the transport in question. These include written sources from the document archive, photographs from the photo archive, and eyewitness interviews from the survivor testimonies archive section. If there are entries in the *Central Database for Shoah Victims' Names* for people deported on this transport, these are also linked.

The variety of information and cross-references are of great value for research and educational work. All the more astonishing then that there are significant gaps in the application, especially with regard to information on deportees: The names of deportees are not listed on the data record sheets, even if this information is known, and a transport list exists and is interlinked to the transports data record sheet.[23] Biographical research on the deportations is therefore

---

[22] For basis and editing status, see Yad Vashem: "About the Holocaust (Shoah) Deportation Database". Available at: https://yadvashem.org/collections/about-deportation-project.html. Last accessed: 12.01.2022.

[23] See, for example, the data record sheet on the first transport from Munich to Kaunas on November 20, 1941. Yad Vashem: "Transport, Train Da 27 from Muenchen, Germany to Kaunas, Lithuania on 20/11/1941". Available at: https://deportation.yadvashem.org/index.html?language=en&itemId=9437950&ind=-1. Last accessed: 12.01.2022. The heading "Victims' Names" only contains links to the Central Database of Shoah Victims' Names, which means that only three entries are listed here for this transport, although some 1,000 people were part of the transport. In the case of the first transport from Vienna, however, on which again over 1,000 people were deported to Nisko, there are 1,697 entries available, since this includes the number of cross-references to the Central Database of Shoah Victims' Names, including in many cases several entries for one and the same person. See Yad Vashem: "Transport from Vienna, Austria to Nisko, Poland

only possible to a very limited extent. Unfortunately, the data record sheets are not stored with permalinks either making it much more difficult for other projects to link to this important source of information.

A search for individual people is not possible on the website *statistik-des-holocaust.de* either. This site actually pursues the aim of making statistical data from primary sources about the Jewish population in the '*Altreich*' available for Holocaust research.[24] The deportations are subdivided according to the various regions, and the individual transports are listed chronologically. Each individual transport has its own data record sheet, which is stored with a permalink and, in addition to statistical data, describes the circumstances and special features of the transports, and addresses open issues. As a rule, the information is based on the surviving deportation lists. If these are not available for a region, the data is reconstructed from various other sources.[25] In addition to the total number, the origin of the deportees is also listed. A search for details of gender and age, which can be found in most deportation lists, and which are of considerable informational value in terms of research, is however futile. Nevertheless, *statistik-des-holocaust.de* contains the largest amount of statistical information on the deportations from the '*Altreich*'. For historians and other interested parties, the website is a central research tool, also especially because of the digital copies of the original deportation lists for each transport gathered from disparate archives.

The Arolsen Archives do not provide a memorial book or a specific research tool on deportations. However, their online archive is also one of the most important portals for deportation research. The collections contain numerous documents that include information on individual transports and deported persons. The Arolsen Archives have digitized most of its collections in the last two decades. Recently, partly with the help of volunteers,[26] the information on individual documents has been indexed. In the run up to the *Deportations in the Nazi Era – Sources and Research* conference, the Arolsen Archives rescanned some of

---

on 20/10/1939". Available at: https://deportation.yadvashem.org/index.html?language=en&itemId=6970463&ind=0. Last accessed: 12.01.2022.

24 Thomas Freier: "Statistik und Deportation der jüdischen Bevölkerung aus dem Deutschen Reich". Available at: https://statistik-des-holocaust.de/index.html. Last accessed: 12.01.2022.

25 As in the case of the people deported from Koblenz and Aachen to Izbica on March 22, 1942, see Thomas Freier: "Koblenz–Aachen nach Izbica". Available at: https://statistik-des-holocaust.de/list_ger_rhl_420322.html. Last accessed: 12.01.2022.

26 See Zooniverse: "#everynamecounts". Available at: https://www.zooniverse.org/projects/arolsen-archives/every-name-counts?language=en. Last accessed: 12.01.2022.

the transport lists preserved in its holdings and subjected them to deeper indexing for the first time.[27]

By drawing on this index data when searching, not only is a list of the primary sources related to the search term displayed. The search function also enables an aggregation of knowledge, as the following example shows. If an indexed transport list is available in the Arolsen Archives online collection, a search by date and destination, for example, will return hits in the two basic search areas 'People'[28] and 'Topics'. While a digital copy of the corresponding primary source is displayed under 'Topics', all the persons mentioned in the source are listed under 'People'. However, there is still a certain lack of clarity as other people may also be included for whom the search terms may occur in a different context. As the index data in the archive database are stored in a general description field, it is not possible to limit the search results. If you search for the first transport from Munich, for example, you will return 1,035 hits instead of the 999 people on the deportation list.[29] This example is good for drawing attention to another problem: Not every transport is easy to find. Cataloging in the Arolsen Archives refers to information as it appears on the respective source. The first transport from Munich to Riga was originally scheduled for November 15, 1941, but was postponed until November 20. The destination was also changed at short notice from Riga to Kaunas. If a user searches for the terms Kaunas and 11/20/1941, they return no hits as the original deportation list still contains the original deportation destination and departure date, and the information on the actual departure date and destination has not been added to the document description.[30] Only a search for Riga and 11/15/1941 returns the desired result. There are similar problems with name searches, as there are often different spellings on the lists.

---

[27] The lists of transports from the German Reich can be found mainly in Collection 1.2.1.1. Cf. also the deportation lists from the archives of the Jewish Religious Community in Leipzig in Collection 7.5.4. See also the contribution of Kim Dresel and Christian Groh in this volume.

[28] Similar to a search in the Yad Vashem Shoah Victims' Names database, all results are displayed here as hits containing the searched name.

[29] Quite a few people are indexed twice, for example, Alfred Alster, born October 7, 1930 in Munich. In fact, only 997 people were deported. See Munich Municipal Archives: "Am 22.11.1941 nach Kaunas (Welle I, Transport 379) deportierte Personen". Available at: https://gedenkbuch.muenchen.de/index.php?id=gedenkbuch_transport&ddat=20.11.1941&ziel=Kaunas. Last accessed: 12.01.2022.

[30] See deportation from State Police district Munich to Riga, 15.11.1941, 1.2.1.1/8227200/ITS Digital Archive, Arolsen Archives.

Cross-Linking Potential

If we take a general look at the research options in the applications presented here, it is striking that all portals limit themselves to the provision of their own results, although it is linking them that offers considerable potential both for research and from a culture of remembrance perspective. This becomes even more obvious when comparing the strengths and weaknesses of the individual applications. While *statistik-des-holocaust.de* and *Transports to Extinction* provide information on the individual transports and related sources but contain little or no information on the deportees themselves, the memorial books and the Arolsen Archives' online collection provide this detailed information but offer little additional information on the individual transports.

The cross-linking of different sources of information is not only user-friendly, it would also allow the closing of gaps that cannot be closed by the respective portal operators by themselves, or only with considerable human resources. Let us take the listing of deportees as an example. Compiling lists of deportees is time-consuming, but even more time-consuming is it to review the names and information they contain. Most of the original deportation lists have already been indexed in the Arolsen Archives, and in the databases behind the different memorial books the information about the people has also been verified. The gaps on deportees in the Arolsen Archives' online database and on *statistik-des-holocaust.de* could therefore be closed comparatively easily in the case of many transports by cross-linking them with the memorial books and/or the cataloged sources from the Arolsen Archives. Reconciling data between the different applications would also make it possible for the different operating institutions and initiatives to double check their own datasets. Let us go back to the different search result for the first deportation from Munich in the memorial books of the Federal Archives and the Munich Municipal Archives. If the different databases were cross-linked, the local memorial books could be of central importance for the Federal Archives in two respects. As a rule, their database is up to date with the latest research and is therefore highly plausible. In addition, the density of information is particularly high there. In any case, it is easy from a technical point of view to identify and link the data records on deported persons using flag fields. These are usually the date of departure, the place of departure and the destination of the deportation.

The need for cross-linking also becomes clear when it comes to making available digitized sources that are scattered across a wide range of archives. This is particularly evident in the case of Yad Vashem's *Transports to Extinction* project, in which, although the provision of documents on the deportations is conceived as a central element, the potential of this important function has so far remained largely unexploited. This is mainly due to the fact that most relevant documents in the Yad Vashem Archives are not yet sufficiently indexed in order to be able to link them to the relevant transports. But even if the corresponding metadata would be available, it is not possible to link the photos, testimonies and documents accessible in Yad Vashem with the relevant transports, especially in the case of person-related sources[31] since, as already explained, most of the deportees' names are not stored in the data sheets.

First and foremost, it is obvious that due to the limitation to individual collections, further sources can only be provided to a limited extent. It is true that like the USHMM and the Arolsen Archives, the Yad Vashem Archives have for decades been acquiring relevant sources from other archives on a large scale, digitizing them and gradually including them in their online services.[32] However, in spite of this large wealth of available sources in the Yad Vashem Archives, many other sources are still only accessible via other archives. Although more and more portals are currently being created, which enable cross-institutional searches, these are generally limited to the reproduction of higher-ranking information on the level of single collections; a search for individual events and people is often not really possible here either at present.[33]

---

31 Yad Vashem too is making more attempts to form clusters in order to structure its data better. Users are encouraged to create a 'personal file' for Holocaust victims by comparing various documents relating to a person. However, only documents contained in the institute's own *Central Database of Shoah Victims' Names* are included, i.e. neither digital copies from the institute's own archives, nor external sources. See Yad Vashem: "We invite you to take part in creating a 'personal file' for Holocaust victims". Available at: https://www.yadvashem.org/newsletters/invitations/clusters-eng.html?utm_source=twitter&utm_medium=organic-english&utm_campaign=research-from-home. Last accessed: 12.01.2022.

32 Not all sources can be put online for legal reasons.

33 For documents relating to the Holocaust, see, for example, EHRI: "EHRI project". Available at: https://www.ehri-project.eu/ and especially "EHRI Portal". Available at: https://portal.ehri-project.eu/. Both last accessed: 12.01.2022. For Jewish history in Europe, see, for example, the Rothschild Foundation Hanadiv Europe: "Yerusha. European Jewish Archives Portal". Available at: https://yerusha.eu/. Last accessed: 12.01.2022. In terms of records, further specific web offerings are planned, for instance the Federal Ministry of Finance has begun setting up a portal that is intended to offer a general standardized digital access to all restitution files, see Federal Ministry of Finance: "Themenportal Wiedergutmachung – Dokumentenerwerb für die Zukunft". Available at: https://www.bundesfinanzministerium.de/Content/DE/Standardartikel/Themen/Oeffentliche_Finanzen/Vermoegensrecht_und_Entschaedigungen/2020-07-07-themenportal-wiedergutmachung-zukunftsaufgaben.html. Last accessed: 12.01.2022.

Challenges in Linking Data

The central problem involved in linking information is its unique identification. It is not only missing or incorrect information that presents obstacles, as described in the case of the first deportation transport from Munich. The unique identification of people in particular is often not possible. Different spellings and discrepancies in dates are just two problems that can now be solved more and more effectively through improved search algorithms. The biggest challenge is to filter out from the often large number of results returned, the search results that actually relate to the person you are looking for. In view of the effort involved in manually linking a large number of people with an even larger amount of information, the linking of sources to people is often omitted, or it remains the user's task to filter out the correct data records from the abundance of hits.

As complex as the unique identification of a person on a document is, it is easy from a technical perspective to establish the relationship between the document and the respective personal data record. To this end, the ID of the relevant personal data record is assigned in the document catalog file for the person named. Cross-database mapping is more complicated because personal data records have different IDs in all applications. To solve this problem, more and more institutions are turning to authority files.[34] If a person is reliably identified, the data record is assigned the corresponding ID from the authority file as an attribute, in addition to the internal database ID.

Authority files now provide a good set of data for better known personalities. On the other hand, there are still no entries for many people – including the majority of those persecuted under the Nazis. It is possible in theory to create relevant data records for individual projects in the various authority files, but, as in the case of places, events etc., the linking of people to an authority file is associated with considerable additional effort in terms of formatting data and cataloging. The corresponding authority data records must firstly be identified or

---

34 In German-speaking countries, the Gemeinsame Normdatei (GND, Integrated Authority File) managed by the German National Library is the best known, cf. German National Library: "Gemeinsame Normdatei". Available at: https://gnd.network/Webs/gnd/EN/Home/home_node.html;jsessionid=1D0EC071C36 A3935B22 A45386799B6E9.internet571. Last accessed: 12.01.2022. Wikidata is gaining increasing acceptance internationally, cf. MediaWiki: "Wikidata". Available at: https://www.wikidata.org/wiki/Wikidata:Main_Page. Last accessed: 12.01.2022. There is also a large number of authority files for various special areas, for example MemArc for the concentration camp complex, see Flossenbürg Concentration Camp Memorial: "Memorial Archives". Available at: https://memorial-archives.international/. Last accessed: 12.01.2022.

created, and in any case needs to be manually linked to the personal data record in the individual database application.

The effort is however worth it. Linking to the authority file ensures that identical IDs are used across projects and applications. Consequently, people are not only uniquely identifiable, they can also be found via relevant interfaces. This makes it possible to link data records, and the information and documents associated with them, automatically across platforms even without manual effort. It is already possible in some German archive portals, to have source references to individual result clusters, which are based on GND authority files, displayed cross-institutionally.[35] The *Memorial Archives* project has shown how identified people– in this case concentration camp prisoners – can be assigned to different groups and deportation transports in this way.[36]

International holocaust research has not yet committed to the use of an integrated authority file.[37] However, the understanding of how to establish functioning communication between the various applications has grown. Not only has the establishment of the *European Holocaust Research Infrastructure* (EHRI) portal contributed to this in a special way, but also the challenges that increasingly arise in the field of digital memory.[38]

---

35 In the Baden-Württemberg State Archives e. g., several online collections of various archives are searchable. See State Archives of Baden-Württemberg: "Online-Findmittelsystem". Available at: https://www2.landesarchiv-bw.de/ofs21/home.php. Last accessed: 12.01.2022.

36 Johannes Ibel: "Vernetztes Forschen in den Memorial Archives", in Jadwiga Pinderska-Lech and Gabriela Nikliborc (eds.): *Transporte polnischer Häftlinge in den KZ-Systemen Auschwitz, Dachau und Flossenbürg / Transporty polskich więźniów w kompleksach obozowych KL Auschwitz, KL Dachau i KL Flossenbürg*, Oświęcim: Państwowe Muzeum Auschwitz-Birkenau, 2020, 58–68, here 62–66 in particular.

37 This is especially true in the case of people. In the case of places, many projects – for example EHRI – now use Wikidata. Cf EHRI: "Using Wikidata to build an authority list of Holocaust-era ghettos". Available at: https://blog.ehri-project.eu/2018/02/12/using-wikidata/. Last accessed: 12.01.2022.

38 Cf. in this respect, for example the *Digital Memory – Digital History – Digital Mapping. Transformationen von Erinnerungskulturen und Holocaust-Education* online conference from September 22 to 24, 2021 at the University of Graz.

Potential Applications Using a Local Example

The digital name memorial for the victims of National Socialism planned in Munich[39] is an example for the opportunities that the cross-linking of various information in different online portals can provide for research and the culture of remembrance. Based on the biographical memorial book for Munich Jews[40], the various databases of victims and memorial books on Jews and other groups for Munich are currently being merged at the Munich Institute for Urban History and Remembrance (IfSE)[41] into the *Victims of National Socialism* (OdN) database, standardized, and supplemented by individual research.[42]

A "contemporary online memorial book" is being developed at the IfSE as the basis for the digital memorial of names,

> which will make all names and personal details of the Munich victims of the Nazi regime accessible to the public. Like the *Biographical Memorial Book for Munich Jews*, this online database is intended not just as place of remembrance, but also as a central research tool for relatives, schools, history workshops, academic institutions and anyone interested in history. The online memorial book is also intended to offer space for participation for those involved in the culture of remembrance.[43]

The aim is to create an application in which the information is closely interlinked. By linking people, places, events, and time periods, complex interrelationships will be presented in a simple way, and formatted for academic evaluation. Different clusters can be formed depending on the relevant interest, which in turn can be correlated with each other. The aim here is not only to clearly

---

39 Originally, a physical memorial was planned but the plan was abandoned in favor of a digital name memorial. The cultural department is currently preparing for a design competition. Cf. conference document no. 14–20/V 03773, plenary session of the Munich City Council July 29, 2015; conference document no. 14–20/V 17642, plenary session of the Munich City Council March 18, 2020, pages 12–14. The documents are accessible online, see City of Munich: "Rats-InformationsSystem". Available at: https://risi.muenchen.de/risi. Last accessed: 12.01.2022.
40 On the basis and genesis of the database, see Munich Municipal Archives: "Das Biografische Gedenkbuch der Münchner Juden 1933–1945". Available at: https://gedenkbuch.muenchen.de/index.php?id=projekt0. Last accessed: 12.01.2022.
41 Work was located at the Munich Municipal Archives until the end of 2021; since the beginning of 2022 it has been focused at the newly founded IfSE. On the founding of IfSE, see conference document no. 20–26/V 03810, plenary session of the Munich City Council July 28, 2021.
42 The extension to other groups of victims was decided in 2009, see city council application no. 02–08/A 04045, plenary session of the Munich City Council March 18, 2009.
43 Conference documents no. 14–20/V 17642, plenary session of the Munich City Council March 18, 2020, page 15. Translation by the author.

show family connections, but also to be able to answer academic questions. In terms of research on deportations, this will mean: In the future, not only will all persons who were deported on a specific transport be issued as a cluster, these clusters will also be able to be further differentiated, for example with regard to their social composition, i.e. their gender, age, marital status or origin, or with regard to their last places of residence. Consequently, it will be possible to investigate hitherto little-known connections between social background, ghettoization and deportation. The georeferenced illustration of the respective clusters is a central element in the project design.[44]

However, the cross-linking of information will not be limited to relationships within the database. In the future, they will be linked to external sources of information as well. There are two main considerations here. The first is pragmatic in nature: In view of the ever-increasing amount of information available on the internet, it no longer seems appropriate that specific information has to be provided in all applications. Take glossaries for example: unknown terms, but also further information on places, events and people can now be looked up in numerous popular knowledge databases,[45] ideally, they are interlinked directly to them.

This is also true particularly for the deportations. Information relating to the individual transports from Munich will be linked directly to the Yad Vashem *Transports to Extinction* portal, and to the deportation lists accessible in the online collections of the Arolsen Archives, Yad Vashem and at *statistik-des-holocaust.de*. In addition, individual personal records will also be dynamically linked to the corresponding personal entries in other online memorial books, such as those managed by the Federal Archives, Yad Vashem or holocaust.cz. Establishing common standards for the continuous exchange of data will be necessary. Successful matching requires the use of authority files and unique terms as well as the reconciliation of data via standardized search queries in specific database fields. The aim is not only to keep the information in the individual

---

[44] Relevant prototypes exist in Vienna for example, see Documentation Centre of Austrian Resistance (DÖW): "Memento Vienna". Available at: https://www.memento.wien/. Last accessed: 12.01.2022. A corresponding application is also currently being developed for Prague, cf. Michal Frankl et al.: "Present and absent: Exploring the Holocaust of Jews in Prague using a mobile application". Available at: https://austriaca.at/0xc1aa5576_0x003c13df.pdf. Last accessed: 12.01.2022.

[45] For example, *Historisches Lexikon Bayerns* or *Deutsche Biographie*. See Bavarian State Library: "Historisches Lexikon Bayerns". Available at: https://www.historisches-lexikon-bayerns.de/Lexikon/Startseite. Last accessed: 12.01.2022; Historische Kommission bei der Bayerischen Akademie der Wissenschaften: "Deutsche Biographie". Available at: https://www.deutsche-biographie.de/. Last accessed: 12.01.2022.

application up to date, but also to interlink them with other portals, to ensure that information on the Munich victims of National Socialism does not become outdated there as well.[46]

Particular importance will be attached to the linking of historical source material. In addition to research, archive records relating to individuals are increasingly being used in education.[47] Pupils usually find it easier to visualize complex relations on the basis of individual fates. Learning outcomes are thus deepened through biographical approaches.[48] The Munich Municipal Archives are therefore currently digitizing those parts of its sources that are important for research into National Socialism, and are integrating them into its online collections.[49] These documents will be linked to the respective personal data records in the memorial book. However, by far the most individual-based documents on the Munich victims of National Socialism are stored in external archives. Source references should be placed here. Where sources are already accessible online, these should be linked directly to the relevant personal data files of the online memorial book. Together with the Arolsen Archives, an initial pilot project will test whether automated matching between the data records from the *OdN* database in Munich and the indexed Arolsen Archives source collections is possible. In addition, the involvement of a volunteer community will be relied upon to supplement and link the information.[50]

---

46 Information from the *Biographical Memorial Book for Munich Jews* in the USHMM Holocaust Survivors and Victims Database is badly out of date, for instance, having been imported on one occasion more than a decade ago. Cf. United States Holocaust Memorial Museum: "Holocaust Survivors and Victims Database". Available at: https://www.ushmm.org/online/hsv/source_view.php?SourceId=20535. Last accessed: 12.01.2022.
47 Cf. Akim Jah: "Biografische Quellen zur nationalsozialistischen Verfolgung: Historisches Lernen mit dem Online-Archiv der Arolsen Archives", in Oliver von Wrochem (ed.): *In aller Öffentlichkeit. Die Verfolgung und Deportation von Juden, Sinti und Roma in Europa 1938–1945. Konzepte der Vermittlung in Ausstellungen und Bildungsarbeit* (working-title, forthcoming).
48 See, for example, the Arolsen Archives' documentED project. Arolsen Archives: "documentED: Material for visits to memorial sites". Available at: https://arolsen-archives.org/en/learn-participate/initiatives-projects/documented/. Last accessed: 12.01.2022.
49 See Munich Municipal Archives: "Online-Archivkatalog des Stadtarchivs München". Available at: https://stadtarchiv.muenchen.de/scopeQuery/suchinfo.aspx. Last accessed: 12.01.2022. Some digitization and cataloging will be carried out in partnership with the Arolsen Archives.
50 Crowdsourcing has been used for a long time in the creation of memorial books, for example, since 1998 in the *Namen statt Nummern. Gedächtnisbuch für die Häftlinge des KZ-Dachau* project. See Dachauer Forum e.V.: "Gedächtnisbuch für die Häftlinge des KZ Dachau". Available at: https://www.gedaechtnisbuch.org/. Last accessed: 12.01.2022. See also the Arolsen Archives #everynamecounts campaign: Arolsen Archives: "everynamecounts". Available at: https://enc.arolsen-archives.org/en/. Last accessed: 12.01.2022.

Summary

The *Transports to Extinction* portal and *statistik-des-holocaust.de* represent two strong tools for researching deportations of Jews in the Nazi era. The Federal Archives memorial book and local online memorial books, like the one in Munich, also offer a great deal of well-formatted information on deportations. As a result of more cataloging, systematic searches for transports and deportees are now also possible in some online archives, such as the one by the Arolsen Archives. The biggest gap is in the recording of the deportees' names. There is no publicly accessible application that allows a complete and, above all, verified allocation of the deportees to the respective transports. Each of the online applications described has strengths and weaknesses. In the meantime, many research questions can be answered through cross-database research, but the individual applications are currently seldom interlinked, which is due not least to the considerable effort required for manual linking between the individual offerings of information. This is not only time-consuming for users. Important information may not be discovered. The scope of the respective applications remains limited. The aim must therefore be not only to provide better interfaces for data exchange, but also to consistently catalog, structure and format individual data records in such a way that links between people, events (such as the deportations), and sources can be established more automatically in the future. To this end, further optimization of search routines will be needed, but also more thought needs to be given to the introduction of authority files for the unambiguous identification of people, places and events.

Information on the deportations that is available on the internet will continue to grow. The map-based web app *Mapping the Lives*, for instance, which illustrates the places where victims of National Socialism lived, already includes a search function on the deportations.[51] In the course of the forthcoming 80th anniversary of the deportations from the German Reich, a digital picture atlas is being created under the title *#LastSeen*,[52] in which existing photos of the deportations will be recorded, deep cataloged, formatted and shown. Another project is the digital memorial platform *deportiert-aus-muenchen.de* comprising individual biographies of Jews, Sinti and Roma deported from Munich, which is being produced by the IfSE together with schools. The Westdeutscher Rundfunk is also

---

[51] Cf. Tracing the Past e.V.: "Mapping the Lives". Available at: https://mappingthelives.org/. Last accessed: 12.01.2022.
[52] See Arolsen Archives: "#LastSeen". Available at: https://lastseen.arolsen-archives.org/en/. Last accessed: 12.01.2021.

planning to add historical material on the deportations to its recently released *Stolpersteine* app.[53] It remains to be seen whether a targeted linking of the various projects can create a network of information that not only offers academics, relatives and people interested in history an access to the available data as simple and broad as possible, but also promotes the formation of new knowledge clusters.

In conclusion: Research and the culture of remembrance on Nazi history have been heading for the digital age for a long time. The present is already digital. In the future, however, it will not be sufficient to limit oneself to reproducing individual research on the internet, nor will it be necessary to find, evaluate and format all available information single-handedly. It will in fact be the task of the respective database and portal operators to interrelate their digital information to the one of others. The future is therefore no longer just about making information available digitally, but about making it easier to find and mapping it correctly. This guiding principle must be anchored more firmly as a central maxim in our work going forward.

---

[53] The material is being collected in partnership with over 150 towns and communities in North Rhine Westphalia. Cf. Westdeutscher Rundfunk: "Stolpersteine NRW – eine WDR-App gegen das Vergessen". Available at: https://presse.wdr.de/plounge/wdr/programm/2021/07/20210728_stolpersteine_nrw.html. Last accessed: 12.01.2021. The web version with database offers numerous filter functions, see Westdeutscher Rundfunk: "Stolpersteine NRW". Available at: https://stolpersteine.wdr.de/web/. Last accessed: 24.01.2021.

Susanne Kill
Deutsche Reichsbahn and Deportation
The Personal Archive of Alfred Gottwaldt

Abstract: Alfred Gottwaldt, senior curator at the German Museum of Technology, was one of the experts on the history of the Deutsche Reichsbahn under the Nazi Regime. His intensive research on the organization of the deportations, his knowledge of operational processes at the Reichsbahn and his great interest in biographical issues made him an in demand internationally advisor for memorials and museums. His private collection was acquired and made accessible with the help of the Deutsche Bahn Stiftung (DB) Foundation. It is now also open for research. His collection is to be seen in context of the progressing research on the deportations with railways in occupied Europe. The active role of the state-owned Reichsbahn in the deportations must also be seen against the background of its economic and bureaucratic procedures in peacetime.

Introduction

October 18, 1941, marks a turning point in the deportation and killing of German Jews. On this Saturday, the Gestapo in Berlin began systematically deporting Jewish women, men and children from Germany. The deportations started at a train station on the outskirts of Grunewald, an exclusive residential suburb of Berlin. There, 1,091 people were loaded into third-class passenger cars and transported to the Litzmannstadt Ghetto. Today, the Track 17 memorial at Grunewald station serves as a monument to those who were deported, with the dates of the transports – 184 in all, starting with October 18, 1941 – inscribed in cast steel plates that line the tracks. Deutsche Bahn AG (DB) dedicated the memorial in 1998. It has since become a place of public and private remembrance. Each steel plate includes the date, the number of deportees and the destination of the transport. In its impressive simplicity, the memorial represents all the deportations that departed from stations in Berlin – from Grunewald, Moabit freight station, and Anhalter Bahnhof.

Grunewald station was firmly entrenched in the memory of the Jewish communities in East and West Berlin as a deportation site. The first memorial here, a plaque "dedicated to the tens of thousands of Jewish citizens of Berlin who were deported from this station to the death camps by henchmen of the ruthless Hitler regime,"[1] was placed at the site by the Association of Persecutees of the Nazi Regime (VVN) in 1953. Over time, the station, which was operated by East German Railways during the Cold War, was all but forgotten as a location for commemoration ceremonies until it began to be used again in the 1980s. In 1993, Alfred Gottwaldt wrote a report for the German railways, which were managed at that time by CEO Heinz Dürr, on the historical topography of the deportation of Berlin Jews at Grunewald station[2] This report was the motivating factor for erecting the memorial on Track 17.

Alfred Gottwaldt's unexpected death in summer 2015, less than a year after he had retired from his job as rail transport curator at the German Museum of Technology in Berlin, was a great loss for the field of historical research on deportations and for Holocaust remembrance, especially in Berlin. Gottwaldt most certainly would have followed the November 2020 conference "Deportations in the Nazi Era" with interest and played a role in it. As the Deutsche Bahn Foundation was fortunate enough to acquire Gottwaldt's collection, this paper discusses his impact, describes his preserved documents – which we have since catalogued almost in full – and shares how it came to be. Drawing on the literature, I will also discuss the role that the Reichsbahn played in the deportations.

Gottwaldt as Researcher and Curator

Alfred Gottwaldt was nearly peerless in his research of the role of the Reichsbahn during the Nazi period. As a jurist and, in his capacity at the Museum of Technology in Berlin, an advocate of examining the history of technology in a sociopolitical context, he had both railway expertise, which he began acquiring in his youth, and a deep understanding of legal and administrative factors. Gottwaldt was a regular at seminars held by Wolfgang Scheffler and Helga Grabitz at the Center for Research on Antisemitism at the Technical University of Berlin, where his insights were a great asset, as they were for museums and memorials whose curators sought pieces for their exhibitions that were as authentic and powerful as possible. A curator himself, Gottwaldt created an exhibit at the Museum of Technology in 1988 that was dedicated to the Holocaust and centered around a historic freight car. At that time, it was still uncommon for museums to address the extermination of European Jews within the context of the history

---

1 Gerd Kühling: *Erinnerung an nationalsozialistische Verbrechen in Berlin. Verfolgte des Dritten Reiches und geschichtspolitisches Engagement im Kalten Krieg 1945–1979*, Berlin: Metropol, 2016, 286.
2 HA-20-Mahnmal-02, Topografie, Historische Sammlung Deutsche Bahn AG (HSDBAG).

of technology. Gottwaldt exhibited the freight car as a memorial site among historical passenger cars and locomotives. He later advised other museums and memorials on the acquisition and restoration of similar pieces.[3]

We will leave the question of whether Alfred Gottwaldt would have considered himself a disciple of Wolfgang Scheffler to others to answer.[4] We do know that he frequently attended Scheffler's colloquia and studied the prosecution of Albert Ganzenmüller, the former State Secretary at the Reich Transport Ministry, in depth. Scheffler served as an expert witness in the criminal proceedings against Ganzenmüller. When looking to determine how deportation trains were organized and who was responsible, Gottwaldt shared Scheffler's assessment in particular of documents and statements from the Düsseldorf public prosecutor's office relating to the charges that Ganzenmüller had aided and abetted the murder of millions of people.[5]

One product of the years-long research projects and in-depth discussions in the context of Scheffler's colloquia was *Die Judendeportationen aus dem Deutschen Reich* ("the deportation of the Jews from the German Reich"), which Gottwaldt published with Diana Schulle in 2005 and which is considered a standard reference work.[6] This annotated chronology provides a systematic overview of the prehistory and background of each of the waves of deportations and then lists and annotates each of the deportation transports from the German Reich to the ghettos and extermination sites in German-occupied Eastern Europe. The book is both a reference work and a memorial, a fact that is sometimes overlooked. On the one hand, its chronology is based on the work of many studies, which were often conducted outside of the university research landscape as part of history workshops and local history projects. Such workshops and projects often focused on the fate of individual Jewish citizens, leading to contact with survivors of the persecution and their descendants. In this way, the local public was made keenly aware that not a single town or city in Germany had protected its Jewish citizens from persecution and deportation, a fact that had long been

---

[3] Alfred Gottwaldt: "Der deutsche 'Viehwaggon' als symbolisches Objekt in KZ-Gedenkstätten", in *Gedenkstättenrundbrief*, 139, 2007. Available at: https://www.gedenkstaettenforum.de/uploads/media/GedRund139_18-31.pdf. Last accessed: 20.10.2020.

[4] I would like to thank Martina Voigt for providing me with information about the Scheffler colloquia.

[5] The complete files on the Ganzenmüller case, which the Düsseldorf prosecutor's office were concerned with, can be found in the Rhineland Department of the State Archives of North Rhine-Westphalia in Duisburg.

[6] Alfred Gottwaldt and Diana Schulle: *Die Judendeportationen aus dem Deutschen Reich von 1941–1945. Eine kommentierte Chronologie*, Wiesbaden: Marix, 2005.

kept in silence. The chronology and its index of places brought this complicity out into the open. On the other hand, the work, with its aim to retrace the timeline of each of the deportations and train movements, is an important addition to the central German Memorial Book, the online version of which is continually updated by the German Federal Archives.[7] The Pan-European Deportation Database,[8] a much more comprehensive research and online project begun by Yad Vashem in 2007, also benefited from Gottwaldt's and Schulle's detailed work, which offered an authoritative summary of research in the field to date.

Many publications by Gottwaldt on railroad history, and especially on locomotive construction, preceded this chronological memorial. In particular, his two books on the impact of Julius Dorpmüller, General Director of the Reichsbahn and Reich Transport Minister, provide context for the deportations. Gottwaldt's interest in the internationally respected railway engineer was driven by the psychologically motivated question of how a national conservative official who considered himself apolitical became entangled with Nazism. Gottwaldt's books *Julius Dorpmüller, die Reichsbahn und die Autobahn* and *Dorpmüllers Reichsbahn*, which are full of illustrations and photographs, introduced an audience familiar with railroad history and technology to the critical history of the Reichsbahn under the Nazis.[9] With equal skill, Gottwaldt's set of popular publications on "trains, locomotives and people"[10] repeatedly called attention to the role that the Reichsbahn and its personnel played in achieving Nazi objectives. In later years, Gottwaldt applied this same skill to researching the fates of Jewish railroad workers – including those who were soon forgotten in postwar Germany. This was the case with railroad engineer Ernst Spiro, who was highly respected in his field and managed to emigrate to England, and with Paul Levy, who, along

---

[7] Federal Archives: "Memorial Book. Victims of the Persecution of Jews under the National Socialist Tyranny in Germany 1933–1945". Available at: https://www.bundesarchiv.de/gedenkbuch/introduction/en. Last accessed: 10.04.2020.

[8] Yad Vashem: "Transport to Extinction: Holocaust (Shoah) Deportation Database". Available at: https://www.yadvashem.org/research/research-projects/deportations.html. Last accessed: 10.04.2021. For both databases, see also the contribution by Maximilian Strnad in this volume.

[9] Alfred Gottwaldt: *Julius Dorpmüller, die Reichsbahn und die Autobahn*, Berlin: Argon, 1995; Alfred Gottwaldt: *Dorpmüllers Reichsbahn – Die Ära des Reichsverkehrsministers Julius Dorpmüller 1920–1945*, Freiburg: EK-Verlag, 2009.

[10] This was the title of an exhibition catalogue. See Alfred Gottwaldt: *Züge, Loks und Leute. Eisenbahngeschichten in 33 Stationen. Ein Katalog*, Berlin: Nicolai, 1990.

with his wife, was deported from the Berlin-Moabit freight depot on February 26, 1943, to Auschwitz, where they were murdered.[11]

In 2009, the German Federal Ministry of Transport commissioned Alfred Gottwaldt for a study of the Reich Transport Ministry's antisemitic policy. Gottwaldt wrote the study with Diana Schulle.[12] In his dissertation, which he began under Wolfgang Scheffler and completed under Wolfgang Benz, he traced the implementation of antisemitic measures at the Reichsbahn in great detail.[13] His analysis of the management structure of the Reich Transport Ministry and Reichsbahn, personnel policy, and implementation of antisemitic measures and laws supports the theory, first developed by Hans Mommsen, of "cumulative radicalization"[14] of institutions and society as it applies to the microcosm of railroad administration and operations. Players in this microcosm made locomotives and railcars available to the SS and police without a second thought as Polish Jews throughout the Reich were being removed to the German-Polish border in October 1938[15] and as Jewish men who had been arrested following the November pogroms were being transferred to German concentration camps. Based on what we know now about the war of extermination, these transports were a precursor to the systematic deportation of Jews by rail in German-occupied Europe. They were the consequence of radicalization, which began with the defamation and exclusion of Jewish employees in 1933 and which quickly made the Reich Transport Ministry and Reichsbahn accessories to the Nazis' criminal goals.

---

11 Alfred Gottwaldt: *Ernst Spiro: ein jüdischer Reichsbahndirektor*, Berlin: Hentrich & Hentrich, 2014; Alfred Gottwaldt: *Paul Levy: Ingenieur der Hedschasbahn und der Reichsbahn*, Berlin: Hentrich & Hentrich, 2014.
12 Alfred Gottwaldt and Diana Schulle: *"Juden ist die Benutzung von Speisewagen untersagt". Die antijüdische Politik des Reichsverkehrsministeriums zwischen 1933 und 1945: Forschungsgutachten*, erarbeitet im Auftrag des Bundesministeriums für Verkehr, Bau und Stadtentwicklung, Teetz: Hentrich & Hentrich, 2007.
13 Alfred Gottwaldt: *Die Reichsbahn und die Juden 1933–1939. Antisemitismus bei der Eisenbahn in der Vorkriegszeit*, Wiesbaden: Marix, 2011.
14 Hans Mommsen: "Der Nationalsozialismus. Kumulative Radikalisierung und Selbstzerstörung des Regimes", in *Meyers Enzyklopädisches Lexikon*, volume 16, Mannheim, 1976, 785–790.
15 In addition to H.G. Adler's *Der verwaltete Mensch. Studien zur Deportation der Juden aus Deutschland*, Tübingen: J.C.B Mohr, 1974, 91–105, it was primarily Sybil Milton's "The Expulsion of the Polish Jews from Germany October 1938 to July 1939. A Documentation", in *Leo Baeck Institute Year Book*, 29, 1984, 169–199, which drew attention to the expulsion of Polish Jews from Germany as a precursor to the deportations.

The Reichsbahn as the Focus of Research

It is important to understand the research context of Gottwaldt's publications in order to place his work, and thus his collections, within a larger context. Like many of his generation, Gottwaldt was greatly influenced by the work of historian Raul Hilberg. Hilberg's seminal work, *The Destruction of the European Jews*,[16] which was published in 1961, and his 1976 study *The Role of the German Railroads in the Destruction of the Jews*, a German translation of which was published by a railway publishing house as *Sonderzüge nach Auschwitz*[17] in 1981, made Hilberg one of the founding fathers of university Holocaust research not only in the English-speaking sphere, but in Germany as well. For the Vienna-born American historian, the technocratic handling of deportation trains, and thus the Reichsbahn more generally, were typical of the bureaucratic actions and highly departmentalized division of labor behind the plundering and extermination of Europe's Jews.[18]

Hilberg's research on how the Reich Security Main Office (*Reichssicherheitshauptamt*, RSHA) and Reich Transport Ministry interacted in the organization of deportation transports has remained unchallenged to this day. When a new, updated edition of his 1961 book *The Destruction of the European Jews* was re-released in Germany in 1990 as part of S. Fischer Verlag's series on the Nazi era, only a few nuances in the accounts of the responsibilities of the Reichsbahn needed to be expanded upon.[19] Additions included a few sources that became public in conjunction with the prosecution of Albert Ganzenmüller, Deputy General Director and State Secretary at the Reich Transport Ministry, and some documents from East German archives, which had long been inaccessible to research-

---

16 Raul Hilberg: *The Destruction of the European Jews*, Chicago: Quadrangle Books, 1961.
17 Idem.: *Sonderzüge nach Auschwitz*, Mainz: Dumjahn, 1981.
18 Christopher R. Browning and Peter Hayes published two of Hilberg's essays on the Reichsbahn and Holocaust, "German Railroads, Jewish Souls" and "The Bureaucracy of Annihilation," for the Holocaust Memorial Museum in Washington, supplementing them with English translations of key primary sources and with two of their own articles providing context. See Christopher R. Browning, Peter Hayes and Raul Hilberg: *German Railroads, Jewish Souls. The Reichsbahn and the Final Solution*, New York and Oxford: Berghahn Books, 2019.
19 Raul Hilberg: *Die Vernichtung der Juden*, Frankfurt am Main: S. Fischer, 1990. In this context, see also the collection Walther Pehle and René Schlott (eds.): *Raul Hilberg, Anatomie des Holocaust. Essays und Erinnerungen*, Frankfurt am Main: S. Fischer, 2016.

ers in the West.[20] They did not significantly change the fundamental image of the Reichsbahn as a "bürokratischer Moloch"[21], however.

Given the highly regulated nature of railroad operations, it should come as little surprise that the Reichsbahn continued to follow regulations and practices that had been developed in peacetime, even as it operated trains outside of the regular civilian or Wehrmacht schedules. In addition to traditional special trains (*Gesellschaftssonderzüge*) for passengers, the Reichsbahn had already operated numerous trains for the Nazi regime in the years leading up to the war. These included special trains for the Nuremberg party rallies, the Reich Harvest Thanksgiving Festival on the Bückeberg near Hamelin, the *Deutsches Turn- und Sportfest* in Breslau (now Wrocław) and other mass Nazi gatherings of millions of enthusiastic participants.[22] Paul Schnell published a detailed description of the policies of the Reichsbahn's special train service in the transport journal *Verkehrstechnische Woche* in 1938.[23] Schnell originally worked in railcar management in Leipzig but transferred to Rail Operations Department 21, *Massenbeförderung* ("mass transport"), at the Reich Transport Ministry in 1936. This was the department that was also responsible for providing deportation trains, which ran on the orders of the SS and police force, beginning in 1941. Direct contact between Adolf Eichmann's department at the RSHA and his transport officer Novak ran through the subordinate department 211 and its head, Amtsrat Otto Stange. The trains, whether they were equipped with passenger cars or freight cars, as was the case later on, were formally planned by the general operating offices (*Generalbetriebsleitungen*) using the same rules that were applied to charter trains.

Managing trains based on civilian rules also had a stabilizing effect on the regime, which was typical of the way bureaucracy was used in the Nazi period. Reichsbahn functionaries may have forced people onto trains with complete disregard for their victims' humanity, but they did so under the guise of officially sanctioned 'resettlement' and 'evacuation,' and they translated their actions into a procedure that was familiar to them and therefore seemed legal. There

---

20 The compiled files of the Reich Transport Ministry are part of the R5 database of the German Federal Archives in Berlin.
21 Raul Hilberg, Vernichtung, 1990, 428.
22 Klaus Hildebrandt: "Die Deutsche Reichsbahn in der nationalsozialistischen Diktatur 1933–1945", in Lothar Gall and Manfred Pohl (eds.): *Die Eisenbahn in Deutschland*, Munich: Beck, 1999, 165–250, here 217.
23 Paul Schnell: "Der Reisesonderzugdienst der Deutschen Reichsbahn und die zu seiner Bewältigung getroffenen Maßnahmen, insbesondere auf dem Gebiet der Personenwagenbewirtschaftung", in *Verkehrstechnische Woche*, 32, 1938, 125–134.

was a set group of offices authorized to order trains. This meant that there were also official billing addresses. Special reduced fares were arranged for orderers based on the number of people transported and the number of kilometers traveled. The expulsion of Polish Jews from Germany in 1938, the deportation of Jews from Baden and the Palatinate to Gurs in 1940 and of Sinti and Roma from Cologne that same year, the deportation of Vienna's Jews in early 1941, and not least the resettlements, expulsions, and deportations in Poland once World War Two began were all organized in this way.

Soon after the invasion of the Soviet Union in 1941 began, the Reich Transport Ministry issued a decree specifying in more detail how special passenger trains were to be billed.[24] The rules were updated in part to restrict who could order special trains and to prevent local Gestapo and SS offices from interfering in processes relating to train operations. Twelve institutions of the Nazi state were authorized to order trains, including the Reichsführer SS, the Chief of the Security Police and the SD, the Gemeinnützige Krankentransport GmbH Berlin (a euphemistically named 'charitable ambulance' service), the Reich Labor Minister, and state employment offices. The new rules also specified the minimum number of people that could be transported and the price that would be billed to orders of special trains.[25] The decree was based on procedures for and experience with resettlement, expulsion, and prisoner transports carried out before October 1941. Gottwaldt summarized these various precursors to systematic deportation from the German Reich.[26] No further formal orders were needed. Reichsbahn trains would run – and everyone, including the initiators and participants of the Wannsee Conference on January 20, 1942, could count on that. Peter Longerich has described the Wannsee Conference as aiming to make a number of important Reich offices accessories to and jointly responsible for the RSHA's plan to deport all Jews in the areas under German control to the East, where they would be exposed to extremely difficult living conditions and ultimately worked to death or murdered.[27] But if this was the primary purpose of the conference, it was not necessary in the case of the Reich Transport Ministry. The RSHA had its assurance in the Reichsbahn's catchy 1935 slogan 'Dem Reiche

---

[24] The following is summarized from the exhibition catalogue Andreas Engwert and Susanne Kill: *Sonderzüge in den Tod. Die Deportationen mit der Deutschen Reichsbahn*, Cologne: Böhlau, 2009.
[25] Decree dated July 26, 1941, on the pricing of special trains, reprinted in Engwert/Kill, Sonderzüge in den Tod, 47.
[26] Gottwaldt and Schulle, "Judendeportationen", 26–51.
[27] Peter Longerich: *Politik der Vernichtung. Eine Gesamtdarstellung der nationalsozialistischen Judenverfolgung*, Munich: Piper, 1998, 466.

wir dienen auf Strasse und Schienen' (roughly: serving the Reich by road and by rail). The law of February 10, 1937, formally establishing government control of the Reichsbank and Reichsbahn,[28] made official what had long been common practice. The head office of the Reichsbahn was now a department of the Reich Transport Ministry instead of an independent company of the Reich.

Thomas Kuczynski has examined whether the Reichsbahn profited from the deportation trains and from transports of roughly 12 million forced laborers.[29] This question might seem strange at first since the Reichsbahn was not expected to generate a profit as it had been during the Weimar years. The Deutsche Reichsbahn-Gesellschaft, which was founded in 1924 and which operated independently and paid reparations under the Dawes Plan, was in practice quickly relegated to history in 1933. Following the laws passed in 1937, a new Reichsbahn Act dated July 4, 1939, explicitly stressed the importance of the Reichsbahn as part of the Reich's administration: It was supposed to work "for the benefit of the German people and the German economy."[30] Even in peacetime, the sheer number of tasks required of the Reichsbahn by the government threatened to result in underfunding of the responsibilities that a civilian transport operator would be expected to carry out.[31] To be sure, this does not change the fact that income was generated with each train. However, the question of how exactly and to what extent orderers paid the arranged fares for the deportation trains to the Reichsbahn accounts, remains unanswered. The invoices and letters that have survived are too few in number for us to draw any serious conclusions about the amount of income generated. The Reichsbahn's 1942 statistical report lists a share of 0.04 percent, or nearly 3.8 million Reichsmarks, under "Special trains for individual orderers, etc."[32] It is difficult to identify the transfer amounts that were to be paid when deportation trains from Belgium, France and the Netherlands

---

28 "Gesetz zur Neuregelung der Verhältnisse der Reichsbank und der Deutschen Reichsbahn vom 10.2.1937", in *RGBl.*, 1937 II, No. 8, 47 et seq.
29 Thomas Kuczynski: "Dem Regime dienen – nicht Geld verdienen. Zur Beteiligung der Deutschen Reichsbahn an Deportationen und Zwangsarbeit während der NS-Diktatur", in *Zeitschrift für Geschichtswissenschaft*, 57, 2009, 510–528.
30 "Gesetz über die Deutsche Reichsbahn (Reichsbahngesetz) vom 4.7.1939", in *RGBl.*, 1939 I, No. 123, 1205–1210, here 1206. Translation by the author.
31 Alfred Mierzejewski: *The Most Valuable Asset of the Reich. A History of the German National Railway*, volume 2, 1933–1945, Chapel Hill/London: The University of North Carolina Press, 2000, 57–76 and 166.
32 Deutsche Reichsbahn: *Statistische Angaben über die Deutsche Reichsbahn im Geschäftsjahr 1942*, Berlin, 1943, 53. Translation by the author.

were billed via the official travel agency Mitteleuropäisches Reisebüro (MER).³³ The Reichsbahn bureaucracy and Reich Transport Ministry used a peacetime instrument here, too. The travel agency was responsible for billing European transports and transferring the money for the individual transport services to the participating railways based on their share of the services performed. The majority shareholder in the MER was the Reichsbahn, or, in other words, the German state. The amounts that were transferred and the railways that received payments via the MER have so far not been determined.³⁴

The payment practices of individual government orderers of special trains left much to be desired from the perspective of the Reichsbahn accounting office. Its first postwar financial report for the US and British sectors shows accounts receivable of nearly 570 million Reichsmarks.³⁵ The balance sheets included a section entitled "Receivables from the Reich, Wehrmacht, NSDAP, etc. and doubtful accounts."³⁶ Hilberg summarized the issue of revenues thusly: "And trains could be dispatched before payment was received; in other words, the SS was entitled to credit."³⁷ His wording is less monocausal and more careful than Christopher Browning's assertion that the Reichsbahn's business with the SS was very profitable.³⁸

The bureaucratic billing of fares stands in contrast to the utter disregard for the misery on board trains to the ghettos and extermination sites. It could have given railroad officials the impression that they were following the rules, which could have left them feeling exonerated. However, billing needs to be considered in the larger context of the plundering of Jews by the Reich. Each deportation began with theft.³⁹ The Reich Finance Ministry and RSHA spared no effort when it came to appropriating every last possession of Jewish citizens and mak-

---

33 Telegram from the Referat für Personentarife dated July 14, 1942, reprinted in Engwert/Kill, Sonderzüge in den Tod, 49.
34 The few surviving business records of MER and Deutsches Reisebüro are located at the Hessisches Wirtschaftsarchiv in Darmstadt.
35 "Geschäftsberichte der Deutschen Reichsbahn im vereinigten Wirtschaftsgebiet über die Geschäftsjahre 1945–1948 (Mai 1945 bis 20. Juni 1948), Offenbach am Main, 1949", 58, MB-05-IRa/b70/1945/48, DB Museum Nuremberg.
36 Ibid. Translation by the author.
37 Raul Hilberg: "German Railroads, Jewish Souls", in Browning, Hayes, and Hilberg, German Railroads, 19–49, here 29.
38 Christopher Browning: "Raul Hilberg and Other Historians of the German Railways during the Nazi Era", in Browning, Hayes, and Hilberg, German Railroads, 104–120, here 110.
39 Martina Voigt: "Die Deportation der Berliner Juden 1941–1945", in Zentrum für audio-visuelle Medien (ed.): *Die Grunewald-Rampe – Die Deportation der Berliner Juden*², Landesbildstelle Berlin, Berlin: Edition Colloquium, 1993, 23–46, here 31.

ing money through a wide variety of channels. Especially perfidious was the RSHA's method of forcing the Reich Association of Jews in Germany to open a special account 'W'. This account would collect donations from "participants in evacuation transports," allegedly to finance the care of the "emigrants."[40] In fact, the revenues were used to finance the cost of transport and to enrich the Reich. Beginning in December 1938, Jewish emigrants were also forced to pay an 'emigration fee' to the local Jewish community, in addition to the Reich Flight Tax (*'Reichsfluchtsteuer'*).[41] The RSHA had access to the accounts where the funds from these fees were kept. Jews were also charged 50 Reichsmarks to have "Evakuiert" (evacuated) stamped on their identification cards before deportation. This fee was to be paid in cash, if they even had any cash.[42] The money was then collected before the transport by members of the Gestapo or by the transport head of the escort unit. This method encouraged individuals to keep the cash for themselves. As Beate Meyer has demonstrated, it was very much in the RSHA's interest for the Reich Association of Jews in Germany and their district offices to pay for their so-called transport costs through account 'W'.[43] Otherwise there was a risk of cash disappearing into the pockets of escort unit men, which were normally staffed by members of the SS and the Gestapo as well as policemen (*Ordnungspolizei*).

Alfred Mierzejewski notes that operating deportation transports posed no challenges for the Reichsbahn in comparison with the total number of trains operated during the war.[44] However, we must not forget the active role that the Reichsbahn played. The operating offices insisted that trains be deployed effectively, regardless of which trains were being used. This was the only way to make trains 'pay off' from a logistical standpoint, justifying the use of rolling stock, locomotives and personnel. No one appears to have cared about the morality of it, even when 5,000 people were being squeezed onto a train with no more

---

40 Adler, Der verwaltete Mensch, 526, 563 et seq.; Beate Meyer: *Tödliche Gratwanderung. Die Reichsvereinigung der Juden in Deutschland zwischen Hoffnung, Zwang, Selbstbehauptung und Verstrickung (1939–1945)*, Göttingen: Wallstein, 2011, 126–210.
41 Fees could be quite high, as in the case of Reichsbahn Director Ludwig Homberger and his wife. The files of the offices responsible for restitution (*Wiedergutmachungsämter*) relating to Homberger are located at the Berlin State Archive (B_Rep_025–01_Nr_1655_50) and the state office for unresolved property issues (*Landesamt für Vermögensfragen*).
42 This was the procedure recorded by the *'Judenreferent'* of the Gestapo in Frankfurt am Main while in custody; 'transport funds' were later paid by check, as was done by the Jewish community in Cologne. See Jewish Museum Frankfurt: *"Und keiner hat für uns Kaddisch gesagt." Deportationen aus Frankfurt am Main 1941 bis 1945*, Frankfurt am Main: Stroemfeld, 2004, 124.
43 Meyer, Tödliche Gratwanderung, 126–210, 278.
44 Mierzejewski, The Most Valuable Asset, 128.

than 60 cars. At any rate, the surviving sources from the Reich Transport Ministry and minutes of meetings of the General Operating Office do not even hint at any objections that anyone might have voiced on the matter.[45]

Cataloguing and Using the Gottwaldt Collection

The bureaucratic structure of the Reichsbahn, so aptly described by Raul Hilberg in its technocratic attitude toward railway service and its view that the Reichsbahn's role was to serve the Nazi regime, was something that also interested Alfred Gottwaldt. However, he quickly homed in on the people who kept the bureaucracy and operations going. Shortly before his death, Gottwaldt prepared a brief synopsis of a publication he was planning and submitted it to the Deutsche Bahn Foundation. It was to be a continuation of his dissertation. He intended to continue his examination into 1945, focusing primarily on analyzing the role of the Reichsbahn and its leadership in carrying out the deportations from the German Reich and occupied countries. His aim was to present a strictly source-based view of the role of the railroad in the extermination of Europe's Jews in World War Two. He wanted to study not only the role of the Reichsbahn, but also the involvement of other national railways in occupied and allied countries. He planned to structure his work chronologically, dividing it into 12 six-month periods from September 1939 to May 1945. He had also planned to publish an accompanying collection of documents. The Deutsche Bahn Foundation promised to provide initial assistance for the necessary groundwork. It was an ambitious undertaking that would have closed a gap in research, or at a minimum compiled knowledge that had been gathered in different contexts – particularly if Gottwaldt had succeeded in drawing on sources and literature on other state railways, as had already been attempted for the French national railway.[46] It is important to note that there has been very little study of the perspective from within

---

45 The minutes of the meetings of the operating offices are also in the R5 database of the Federal Archives in Berlin. Questioning in the indictment of Albert Ganzenmüller and Franz Novak is also revealing.
46 For a discussion of the French national railway see Marie-Noëlle Polino: "Der Zusammenhang von Transport und Vernichtung – ein ungelöstes Problem für Historiker", in Ralf Roth and Karl Schlögl (eds.): *Neue Wege in ein neues Europa. Geschichte und Verkehr im 20. Jahrhundert*, Frankfurt am Main, Campus, 2009, 281–300. The files of SNCF are available at: https://www.sncf.com/en/group/history/sncf-archives. Last accessed: 03.12.2021.

the railways in occupied countries.⁴⁷ The Dutch national railway only recently commissioned the NIOD Institute for War, Holocaust and Genocide Studies in Amsterdam to conduct a pilot study in light of calls to pay compensation to Holocaust victims and their families.⁴⁸ The study will doubtless need to determine what leeway, if any, was given to the Dutch railway to make its own decisions under German occupation. Still, it is extremely discouraging to see that the system developed in peacetime for moving cars back and forth and billing cross-border services through the MER worked just as well for deporting European Jews, in a practice that was as effective as it was cruel. Gottwaldt was unable to conduct his own studies on Europe's railways or their role in the Holocaust.

When it became clear that Gottwaldt's collection might otherwise be lost, the Deutsche Bahn Stiftung was persuaded to acquire it and most notably to provide the funds needed to catalogue its contents. This decision was not without risk since there was no way to assess the size or quality of the private collection, which was being stored in a shipping container. After thorough discussion and an initial examination, all parties agreed that Gottwaldt's collections on railroad history and his preliminary work for future publications on the history of the Reichsbahn in Nazi Germany should be kept and made public.⁴⁹ It proved to be an advantage that the DB Museum in Nuremberg, which is part of the Foundation, had long collaborated with Gottwaldt in his capacity as a Museum of Technology curator and private collector. The Foundation was able to fund two sub-projects. Jan-Henrik Peters, also an expert in the technical and political history of the Reichsbahn and its sources, took on the task of cataloguing the extensive collection of photographs. The photographs have now been tagged with metadata and are accessible at the DB Museum in Nuremberg and DB's historical collection in Berlin. There are just over 5,400 photographs, with most of the twentieth-century photographs from the collectionss of railroad employees. There are also over 100 prewar postcards showing train stations, which are of particular historical value because many of the stations no longer exist. Design drawings, maps and brochures relating to Prussian locomotive and railcar-building history are gradually being catalogued at the DB Museum.

---

47 This became obvious in Ralf Roth and Henry Jocolin (eds.): *Eastern European Railways in Transition. Nineteenth to Twenty-First Centuries*, Farnham: Ashgate Publishing, 2013.
48 Nederlands Spoorwegen: "Preliminary research by NIOD". Available at: https://www.ns.nl/en/about-ns/dossier/ns-during-the-second-world-war/preliminary-investigation-niod.html. Last accessed: 03.12.2021.
49 I would like to express my gratitude to Diana Schulle, Jörg Schmalfuss, Ulrich Tempel, and the staff of the DB Museum.

Diana Schulle, who is likely more familiar with Gottwaldt's methods than anyone else, was willing to undertake the second sub-project. She sorted, evaluated and indexed Gottwaldt's typescripts and research documents on the history of the Reichsbahn in Nazi Germany. Ultimately, Schulle came to the sobering conclusion that the collection did not include a cohesive manuscript on the European scale of the deportations or the role of the railways and their leadership. To be sure, there was a collection of copies of documents and typescripts that Gottwaldt had created for the second part of his history of the railroad during the Nazi era. In all there are more than 1,500 typed pages on the history of the Reichsbahn between 1939 and 1945. It is an extensive collection, but there is great variety to the contents, and large portions have already been published. The information that has already been published primarily concerns the history of the deportations to Auschwitz and Theresienstadt in 1942 and 1943 and the deportation of the Jews from East Prussia.[50] Gottwaldt's preliminary work did not address other questions, such as the evacuation of the camps, the transport of internees by rail to other locations near the end of the war, or cooperation among the RSHA, Wehrmacht and Reichsbahn as the war drew to a close. Diana Schulle and I ultimately came to the unfortunate conclusion that it would not be possible to publish a posthumous work. Any such work would not have come close to the standards that Gottwaldt set for his own work.

Gottwaldt's collection of biographical information about functionaries involved with Reichsbahn and deportation matters could be helpful for prosopographic studies. Gottwaldt created biographical notes and short biographies and compiled career histories over many years. He focused primarily on functionaries who worked at Reichsbahn divisions in the occupied East during the Nazi period, particularly the Reichsbahn divisions in Minsk, Opole, Poznań, Riga and Warsaw and the General Directorate of the Eastern Railway ('*Generaldirektion der Ostbahn*', Gedob) headed by Adolf Gerteis in Krakow. And finally, Gottwaldt searched for Reichsbahn functionaries who were involved, or might have been involved, in deportations at individual Reichsbahn divisions, including those in Berlin, Essen, Kassel, Königsberg, Munich, Saarbrücken, Stuttgart, Szczecin, Wrocław, and Wuppertal. The result is an arresting, though not seamless, picture of the career paths of the Reichsbahn functionaries involved in the deportations, which extends even into the years after World War Two.

---

50 Most recently Alfred Gottwaldt: "Die Deportation der Juden Ostpreußens 1942/1943", in Uwe Neumärker and Andreas Krossert (eds.): *"Das war mal unsere Heimat ..." Jüdische Geschichte im preußischen Osten*, Berlin: Stiftung Denkmal für die ermordeten Juden Europas, 2013, 125–137.

Anyone who knows how hard it is to research biographical information on employees of large government agencies and companies will appreciate this preliminary work. It is available for use in research projects, such as a project currently being conducted by the Leibniz Institute for Contemporary History for the German Federal Ministry of Transport on "continuities and transformations during the National Socialist dictatorship, the East German regime, and new democratic beginnings"[51] and projects undertaken by the Gesellschaft für Unternehmensgeschichte.[52] Precisely because the employees of the Nazi-era Reichsbahn cannot collectively be considered 'uncompromising' in Michael Wildt's use of the term,[53] questions about the careers of Reichsbahn functionaries and their courses of action could create divergent views of the railroad employee profession under the Nazi regime.

However, we cannot expect the history of the deportations to be reevaluated based on the collection. The work of Raul Hilberg and H.G. Adler was truly pioneering thanks to the authors's vast knowledge of sources and profound understanding of the role of bureaucracy in the Nazi state. Alfred Gottwaldt made sure to explain in many talks that every deportation train had its own story: the story of the people who were forced to board the trains, and the story of the people who made sure that the trains ran.

Alfred Gottwaldt's collections has largely been catalogued and is available for use. The written documents, which have been pared down to 350 files, are now part of Deutsche Bahn's historical collection in Berlin, as are over 5,000 photographs. Because the material was private and not actively given to us, we have chosen not to digitize it or publish the metadata of the research work. However, Deutsche Bahn Stiftung would be delighted for the collections to be used and for it to serve as motivation for further research.

---

[51] IfZ München: "Kontinuitäten und Transformationen zwischen NS-Diktatur, SED-Herrschaft und demokratischem Neubeginn". Available at: https://www.ifz-muenchen.de/aktuelles/themen/das-deutsche-verkehrswesen/. Last accessed: 20.11.2020. Translation of the title by the author.

[52] Gesellschaft für Unternehmensgeschichte: "Unternehmensgeschichten – laufende Projekte". Available at: https://unternehmensgeschichte.de/mbH-Unternehmensgeschichten-laufend. Last accessed: 24.05.2021.

[53] Michael Wildt: *Generation der Unbedingten. Das Führungskorps des Reichssicherheitshauptamtes*, Hamburg: HIS, 2002.

Aya Zarfati
Interaction, Confusion and Potential

On the Clash between Archives (on Nazi History) and Family Research

Abstract: Deportation lists and databases based on them are a central source for descendants trying to research the history and fates of their relatives who were persecuted under the National Socialist Regime. And yet finding available sources and more so, understanding the sources and the context in which they were produced, is not an easy task. Not only are most family members neither historians nor experts on the Nazi-era and the Shoah, they are often trapped in their own family stories and tend to overlook information that contradicts the family narrative. Combining the perspectives of an academic, an educator, and a descendant of victims to Nazi persecution, Zarfati uses her own experiences in researching the persecution and deportation of her relatives in Austria and Croatia in order to describe the challenges and obstacles which descendants find themselves facing during such research. Aiming for future collaboration between descendants and archives, she also sketches ways in which archives and databases could better address family members and their needs and make information and insights for biographical research more available, accessible and comprehensible.

Introduction

On January 26, 1942, my great-grandfather wrote a letter from Vienna, addressed to a non-Jewish acquaintance in his Austrian hometown Leoben, whose identity remains unknown:

> Dear gracious Madam!
>
> [...] I cannot put down in writing, what I am going through here. The room is a frozen pit, not a bit of wood and coal. [Indecipherable sentence] One is not allowed into any store or restaurant. No smoking material. No newspapers are allowed to be bought. I receive 15 RM a week from the Jewish Welfare Office [*Jüdische Fürsorge*] and then lunch once a day. The food in the so-called soup kitchen is absolutely inedible and the milieu that comes along – I would have liked you, dear lady, to see it once – a human being endures a lot. You can imagine, when [sic] I decided to write you, Madam. I'll be glad when it's over, one day, and I have eaten as much bread as I wanted to. But since I still have the 3 little children, unprovided for, I must live. But life is not worth living. To be reunited with the family is a

utopia at the moment, and my wife writes me in her penultimate letter, that even if I can come, I shouldn't, the Jews there are subjected to the same persecutions as here. The winter is especially difficult for us. Every day we have the fear of being taken and sent to Poland. That is the worst. Within 3 hours and only taking along what is most needed, everything else is left behind.[1]

This is the last surviving letter of the 56-year-old Max Werdisheim, written – as I learned through the Arolsen Archives – 11 days before his deportation with the 16th transport from Vienna to Riga on February 6, 1942.

Max (Maximilian) Werdisheim was born in 1886 in Moravia, at the time part of the Habsburg Empire. In March 1938, as German troops marched into Styria, he was living with his wife Berta and two daughters (22 and four and a half years old) in the small town of Leoben, where he had a successful business. His wife was pregnant with twins, to be born in June that same year. The oldest daughter was able to flee illegally to Palestine shortly before the November Pogroms (the so-called *Kristallnacht*) and became the addressee of most of Max and Berta's letters. Most letters were sent from Yugoslavia, where the family with all in all 13 immediate and extended family members escaped to. Apart from the oldest daughter, who was in Palestine, only one of them survived – my grandmother.

Prompted by a project on flight and escape at the Memorial and Educational Site House of the Wannsee Conference, where I work as a research associate, my research on the biography of Max Werdisheim began a few years back. It combined three different perspectives: that of an academic, an educator, and a descendant. These perspectives influenced the way I conducted the research; the time, energy and funds invested in various aspects of the story I deemed important to highlight; as well as the questions I posed the sources. In the course of the research process, I have had very different experiences with databases, online portals, and archives' staff. Those differences were highly dependent on the archive's size, funding, staff, number of requests, and technical capabilities. These experiences have raised many questions that are relevant for a possible future cooperation between descendants of the deported Jews and archives – and are the topic of this paper.

Deportation lists and databases based upon information found in those lists are pivotal for descendants who try to research the history and fate of their relatives who were persecuted by the Nazi regime. As mentioned, most members of the Werdisheim family fled to Yugoslavia: Max and his wife Berta, their mothers, their children, and six of Max Werdisheim's siblings. The last surviving letter

---

[1] Max Werdisheim to an unknown woman, Vienna, 26.01.1942, Private Collection of the Zarfati Family, Tel Aviv. Translation by the author.

of Berta Werdisheim from March 1941 places her in Ruma, today Serbia, back then soon to be part of Ustaša controlled Croatia. Initially, I had planned to reconstruct further biographies of family members who fled to Yugoslavia. However, it was hardly possible to reconstruct the specific stations of their persecution, as they are not recorded on any deportation list or other record I could find. In this case, gaps in information could not have been bridged by archive material. Max Werdisheim, however, was captured in Zagreb either in December 1939 or in January 1940 and sent back to the German Reich for a trial. "Due to defamation, I was brought to Graz, my brother as well, and we were kept in custody for 17 months. The fallacious nature of this slander came to light, and both of us were acquitted"[2], he wrote to the same unknown lady in Leoben on January 12, 1942. He spent about four weeks in Vienna before being deported – the deportation to Riga being just one stage in a long odyssey of persecution. But with the help of archives and digital databases I could put together and comprehend many of the stages of his life (and not just death).

The first question that should be addressed when discussing the intersection between archives (on Nazi history) and family research is the meaning of the research for the descendants. Albeit appearing banal at first, it is the key to understanding the research process of descendants and their ability to process the information found in archives. Such research is often a confrontation with discrepancy – the discrepancy between the family narrative and the actual facts and concrete path of persecution.

At the end of August 2020, the young Israeli Oded Pshetetzki, who lives in Berlin, wrote in a Facebook post that through the Arolsen Archives, his family learned that Mendel Pshetetzki, his grandfather's youngest brother, who was thought to have perished in the Holocaust, actually survived Nazi persecution and was living in Austria under the name Marian Pshetetzki. Despite Corona travelling restrictions, Oded was able to meet this 94-year-old man in a nursing home in Innsbruck in August 2020. Interesting in the account shared on Facebook is that at the beginning of the correspondence with Arolsen, the family's response to the new information shared by the archive's staff was that they (the staff) must have made a mistake, "Marian is not a Jewish name anyway"[3]. This exemplifies a larger phenomenon of descendants, being 'trapped' or captured in their family narratives. This narrative is usually accepted as is and

---

2 Max Werdisheim to an unknown woman, Vienna, 12.01.1942, Private Collection of the Zarfati Family, Tel Aviv. Translation by the author.
3 Oded Pshetatzki, Facebook, 30.08.2020. Available at: https://www.facebook.com/oded.pshetatzki/posts/10158992092944767. Last accessed: 02.05.2021. Translation by the author. The post became viral with over 3,000 likes and 344 shares.

viewed uncritically and even a-historically. This means that family members need more support and guidance when searching archives and should be considered and addressed as a separate target group.

In 1957, Max Werdisheim's daughter Alice – who in Israel married and became Aliza Zarfati – submitted a testimony page to Yad Vashem, stating that her father perished in Auschwitz. That is also what she told me, her granddaughter, and therefore, the 'knowledge' I grew up with regarding the fate of Max Werdisheim. For a long time, I did not question this story and had no reason to do so. What prompted the Pshetetzkis to turn to the Arolsen Archives was an article in the Israeli newspaper *Haaretz*, informing its readers of the possibility to find documents which have not yet been published. In my case, it was an entry in the 2013 published book *Archiv der Namen. Ein papierenes Denkmal der NS-Opfer aus dem Bezirk Leoben* by Austrian historian Heimo Halbrainer, in which short biographies of the Jews from the Leoben district are listed. According to the biographies of Berta and Max Werdisheim, Max was arrested during the November Pogroms, sent to the concentration camp of Dachau and released in March 1939.[4] An arrest of her father in Dachau was never mentioned by my grandmother and seemed like a detail too significant for her to ignore or to forget to mention – yet even if it was true, it did not stand in contradiction to other information she shared with her family. Although assuming the information in the book was false, I submitted an inquiry to the Dachau Memorial archive.

The entry on Max Werdisheim in Halbrainer's book also reads that "on February 6, 1942, he [Max] was deported to Riga and murdered"[5]. Reading it, I was confronted for the first time with information that contradicted the family narrative. The fact that Riga, and not Auschwitz, was mentioned as the place of deportation was a piece of information I first failed to grasp and only became conscious of after receiving a copy of the deportation list and correspondence file from the International Tracing Service (ITS), today Arolsen Archives. It was the staff of the archive of the Dachau Memorial who referred me to the ITS after not being able to find a prisoner under that name. Coming across Halbrainer's book provoked a need to know more.

---

4 Heimo Halbrainer: *Archiv der Namen: Ein papierenes Denkmal der NS-Opfer aus dem Bezirk Leoben*, Graz: Clio Graz, 2012, 80.
5 Ibid. Translation by the author.

Research Process and Signposts: Where Does One Start (and How Does One Proceed)?

The first archive that I 'visited' was my own family archive. In 1997, shortly after my grandmother's sister, the one who had fled to Palestine, passed away, her son found a cache of old letters and documents in the attic of her apartment in Tel Aviv and passed them on to my grandmother. The letters were written in old German current handwriting that my grandmother, who was born in Austria in 1933, could not read, as she never attended a German school. But the dates, the places from which the letters were sent and the signatures at the bottom proved that they were written by her parents during the time in which they were persecuted by the Nazi regime. My mother immediately made sure that the letters were translated into Hebrew. At the time, I read them once and never looked at them again.

The fact that the letters were kept during all these years is not to be taken for granted. While they serve as historical documents for us, for the people they were addressed to, they were a reminder of a tragedy and were possibly connected with survivor's guilt and even with a sense of failure for not being able to save those who were left behind.[6] In a discussion with Berlin educators in June 2018, Peter Fischer, the former commissarial executive director of the Central Council of Jews in Germany, shared that "[i]n 1945, my father had burned all the documents, all the exchange of letters my mother had with her family, of which no one survived, because he could not live with the memory"[7]. My grandmother's sister not only systematically kept the letters of her deceased parents, but also postwar correspondence about her persecuted parents, the search for her sister and the *Rückstellungsakten*, as the files on restitution are referred to in Austria. The combination of family letters and additional related documents, which include direct references to dates, places, people and sometimes institutions, functioned as an initial guideline for my research in the archives. They were central for the methodology of the research, as they helped reconstruct the chronology of the family's attempts to escape both Austria and Europe and to sketch the geographical scope in which those attempts took place – as well as the concrete

---

6 Survivor's guilt was first described by psychoanalyst William G. Niederland in 1961. For further reading see, for example, William G. Niederland: *Folgen der Verfolgung: Das Überlebenden-Syndrom, Seelenmord*, Frankfurt am Main: Suhrkamp, 1980.
7 Peter Fischer in a meeting with Berlin educators as a preparation for a seminar in the Memorial Yad Vashem, 15.06.2018, at the Regional Agency for Civic Education (Landeszentrale für politische Bildung). Translation by the author.

path of persecution of Max Werdisheim. My starting point was, therefore, undoubtedly advantageous to that of others. But what about interested descendants who do not hold such documents?

There are already archives and online portals offering important information and insights for biographical research but unfortunately, there is no portal or website serving as an extensive guideline encompassing and linking all available sources and search options. My research was often characterized by lack of structure and by coincidence. It was, for example, an unfortunate coincidence, that I entered the German version of the website of the Austrian State Archives as only on the English version one finds the category "Family Research"[8]. Some discoveries of truly brilliant tools happened completely by chance and at a very late stage of the research. They would have saved me valuable time had I known of their existence at the beginning of it. An entry portal for biographical research, especially for the target group of descendants, is currently being planned at the Arolsen Archives. Such a portal would eventually serve not only descendants, but also young researchers, students, educators and memorial associations.

A future online portal for family research should address the potential for further discovery of sources to be found in archives, as well as a commentary to the historical value of documents which descendants might possess at their own households – and are sometimes unaware of the value these hold to others beyond themselves. Another aspect of the research, which I have not yet resolved and which such a portal could address, is the correct preservation of documents in family archives. Our documents are sadly still held in clear film in an ordinary folder.

One of the main obstacles which characterizes family research is part of a broader problem of Holocaust research in general, namely, the wide dispersal of the archival source material. As victims of Nazi persecution were sometimes forced to go on a long journey through different places, it is very unlikely that sources concerning a certain person would be kept in just one place. In fact, dominant principles of the international archive community demand exactly the opposite. "[T]here is no such thing as a 'general card index' of all persons, objects and places stated in the archival records stored. […] Contrary to what […] people might hope, they [=archives] do not provide collections of material

---

[8] Austrian State Archives: "Family Research". Available at: https://www.statearchives.gv.at/family-research.html. Last accessed: 04.05.2021. The category "Family Research" does appear in the German version of the website under "Benutzung > Forschungshinweise > Familienforschung". In contrast, on the English version, it is immediately visible on the upper bar.

on certain persons or topics at the push of a button"[9], as can be read on the Website of the Austrian State Archives.

Whereas this is true for conventional archives, as collections archives, the large documentation centers on the Holocaust, Yad Vashem, the United States Holocaust Memorial Museum and the Arolsen Archives, break with this principle and have always placed great emphasis on name-related indexing. For this reason, they also integrate large holdings of copies from other archives (organized according to the principle of provenance) into their collections.[10]

An online portal designed to face the fragmentation of Holocaust historiography is the EHRI-project, the European Holocaust Research Infrastructure. Its aim is to improve access to Holocaust sources, first and foremost by making them visible. As EHRI's main target group is researchers its primary impact is scientific.[11] Therefore, its user interface poses more of a challenge for family research than a source simplifying the research process.

Are Family Members of Persecuted People a Target Group of Archives at All?

All three mentioned large documentation centers on the Holocaust address family members explicitly as a target group. On its website, under the sub-category 'Inquiries', the Arolsen Archives offer specific information for relatives of victims of Nazi persecution. Next to an inquiry form that can be sent directly, information is offered on how the archives respond to inquiries, stating that although the many requests submitted each year prolong the waiting times for information, priority is given to survivors and their close relatives.[12] It is also possible to

---

[9] Austrian State Archives: "User Information – Archive Basics". Available at: https://www.statearchives.gv.at/user-information/archive-basics.html. Last accessed: 13.05.2021.
[10] Henning Borggräfe and Isabel Panek: "Collections Archives Dealing with Nazi Victims: The Example of the Arolsen Archives", in Henning Borggräfe, Christian Höschler and Isabel Panek (eds.): *Tracing and Documenting Nazi Victims Past and Present*, Berlin/Boston: De Gruyter Oldenbourg, 2020, 221–244. Available online at: https://www.degruyter.com/document/doi/10.1515/9783110665376-013/html. Last accessed: 28.08.2021.
[11] EHRI (European Holocaust Research Infrastructure): "EHRI's Mission. What is the European Holocaust Research Infrastructure?". Available at: https://www.ehri-project.eu/about-ehri. Last accessed: 13.05.2021.
[12] Arolsen Archives: "Information for Relatives of Victims of Nazi Persecution". Available at: https://arolsen-archives.org/en/search-explore/inquiries/information-for-relatives. Last accessed: 28.08.2021.

search independently in the online archive, although this search might be difficult without further help. Priority "to survivors, their families, and families of victims"[13] is also given by the United States Holocaust Memorial Museum, which offers free research services in finding information about the fates of individuals.

Yad Vashem's Central Database of Shoah Victims' Names also addresses family members of victims and survivors directly and provides an extremely helpful tool – a simple list of frequently asked questions regarding this database. Neither new nor innovative, this simple online tool completely transforms the user-experience. Not only is one directly addressed and acknowledged, but one also finds answers to core questions which might (and often do) arise when using the database. The questions are divided into three sub-categories: historical questions, questions about the database, and questions on how to use it. The answers point out possible errors, duplications, or gaps in information, and provide general information about the Holocaust. Under the third category one finds the question "Is Yad Vashem interested in corrections of the information?"[14] – with the inviting answer that it is.

Austrian victims of Nazi persecution are recorded in the victims' Database of the Documentation Center of Austrian Resistance (DÖW). Easily accessed online, it offers a search of victims' names. It gives information – as far as these are known – in the following categories: first name, surname, birth date, place of birth, place of residence, deportation, date of death, place of death and the remark 'did not survive'. No interaction with descendants or other users of the database is being held on the DÖW website and it is impossible to add information to existing names or to add new names of people who are not listed as Austrian victims, but were, in fact, such.

Max Werdisheim's youngest children, the twins Harry Peter and Walter Hans, who were born on June 5, 1938, less than three months after the incorporation of Austria into the German Reich, do not appear in the DÖW's victims' database, presumably because their names were not listed on a deportation list. In the Yad Vashem's database they appear with a testimony page given by my grandmother, containing very few details. The name Werdisheim produces eleven entries in the DÖW database – six of them of women. I was looking for one with the same birth date as Max Werdisheim, as his daughter remembered him having a

---

13 United States Holocaust Memorial Museum: "Research Services". Available at: https://www.ushmm.org/remember/resources-holocaust-survivors-victims/individual-research/services. Last accessed: 28.08.2021.
14 Yad Vashem: "FAQs – Names' Database". Available at: https://www.yadvashem.org/archive/hall-of-names/database/faq.html. Last accessed: 28.08.2021.

twin sister. Her guess as to which of the sisters was the twin turned out false. I could form a list of all of Max's siblings, and learn that Helene Porges, who does not appear in any victim's database with her maiden name Werdisheim, was Max's twin sister through the archive of the Jewish Community of Vienna (*Israelitische Kultusgemeinde Wien*, IKG), which proved to be a valuable source. It holds the *Matrikel* – birth, marriage and death register – of all the Jewish communities in Austria, as well as other personal sources, such as the *Auswanderungsfragebögen*, the emigration questionnaires Austrian Jews addressed to their representative body. Establishing that Helene Porges was Max Werdisheim's sister, I now knew that he spent the last weeks before his deportation sharing a so-called ghetto-apartment with his sister and also, that the siblings were deported together with the 16th transport. Yet the DÖW database offered no invitation to share these details.

It is important to note that the involvement of users, regardless of whether they are personally connected to the victims or not, raises new challenges, such as who should verify the information integrated in the database. An extreme example of the misuse of the privilege to participate is the case of the German historian and blogger Marie Sophie Hingst, who in 2013 submitted 22 false Pages of Testimony to Yad Vashem – a falsification which was revealed in 2019 by the German weekly magazine *Der Spiegel*.

But what about information that is already available? Can descendants, who are not historians or experts on the Holocaust and Nazi persecution understand information presented to them? As already mentioned, one of the personal information on victims to be found on the DÖW database is an address given under 'place of residence'. Nevertheless, this is the last known address, meaning the address which appears on the Gestapo deportation lists. This address does not correspond with the actual place where those Austrian Jews mentioned on the deportation lists resided before being forced to leave their homes and move to Vienna, or to a different apartment inside the capital in 1938. However, this is not clear to all descendants. This information is by no means hidden and can be found on the DÖW website – but not directly when using the search tool. Thus, this important fact escapes many. This can lead to descendants trying to lay *Stolpersteine* (stumbling stones) at this forced address – although their relatives were not really residing here. It can also lead to false images.

According to my grandmother, her grandparents had lived in Vienna, in an apartment to which she – along with her mother and siblings – had moved after the November Pogroms of 1938. Family members still living in Vienna today also mentioned this address on the famous *Mazze-Insel* (Mazze-Island), the name Viennese Jews gave the second district, Leopoldstadt, as the address of Max Werdisheim's parents. Placing the parents in Vienna's second district, known for inhabiting strict orthodox Eastern European Jews, provoked the false impression that they were strictly Orthodox, unmodern '*Ostjuden*' who lived in the cultural ghetto of the Leopoldstadt. In fact, Max's parents, Jakob Samuel and Charlotte Werdisheim, lived in Graz, and were themselves forced by the Nazi Regime to leave Styria and resettle in Vienna. I was able to find two photos of them: one was found in the cache of letters, the second one was sent to me by distant relatives. Both undated, they were probably taken in the early 1920s and in the second half of the 1930s respectively. Both of them show modern assimilated Jews.

As already mentioned, it was through the Arolsen Archives (back then ITS), that I learned about Max's deportation to Riga. It took over a year to receive an answer to my submitted inquiry form. Inquiry Team 7 sent me the correspondence file regarding Max Werdisheim, along with two further PDF-files. The first was a personalized letter with an apology for the long processing time and the important reference to the e-Guide on the ITS website. The second PDF was a FAQ with essential questions regarding the archive and the documents it holds (i.e., why are there different spellings and information about the same person on the documents?). The e-Guide exemplary explains the different sections, abbreviations and symbols of personal documents found in the archive, such as identification documents of concentration camp inmates, forced laborers or Displaced Persons (DPs). It was less helpful for the sources found regarding Max Werdisheim, but it is an impressive and helpful tool for anyone reading and analyzing such documents.[15] The correspondence file of the ITS contains a request for information submitted by the ITS to the Office of Victim Welfare of the Vienna Provincial Government in 1959. The ITS received the response that Max Werdisheim "is believed to have died in Kaiserwald in 1943."[16]

The response of the Office of Victim Welfare was based on a witness testimony – this testimony being the only document providing information on the last station of Max Werdisheim's life apart from the deportation list: a death declaration by the Vienna Regional Court for Civil Matters (*Landesgericht für Zivilrechtssachen Wien*), issued on September 20, 1949.[17] In the cache of family documents, I found a translated copy of this decision on Max Werdisheim's death certificate. It did not include the material upon which the decision was made,

---

15 Arolsen Archives: "e-Guide". Available at: https://eguide.arolsen-archives.org/en/. Last accessed: 28.08.2021.
16 Request for Information from the Office of Victims Welfare of the Vienna Provincial Government to the ITS, 28.09.1959, 6.3.3.2/106165614/ITS Digital Archive, Arolsen Archives. Translation by the author.
17 Death declaration, resolution of 20.09.1949, Max Werdisheim, 48 T 1123/47, Wiener Stadt- und Landesarchiv, Landesgericht für ZRS, Wien.

but the translation into Hebrew mentioned that the proceedings took place in the Palace of Justice, in a certain department 48. A staff member of the archive of the Jewish Community in Vienna referred me to the Vienna Regional Court for Civil Matters.

The court's decision relied on one testimony given by Lea Singer, an Austrian Jew, who, according to her own statement, was deported with Max and his sister to Riga on February 6, 1942. It was Dagobert Werdisheim, the only Werdisheim sibling to survive the Holocaust, escaping to France instead of Yugoslavia, who filed the request for a death declaration for both Max and Helene just a year earlier, on February 28, 1947. He suggested Singer "who was in the concentration camp in Riga, together with my two mentioned siblings" as a "person of reference [*Auskunftsperson*]".[18] He must have met Singer in Vienna after the war, when searching for information on his siblings and their destinies. According to the minutes of her testimony in October 1947 at the Regional Court (*Landesgericht*), she was 49 years old at the time. Lea Singer describes her time with Max Werdisheim and his sister Helene in the following words:

> After their expulsion [*Aussiedlung*] from Graz, Max Werdisheim and Helene Porges lived with me on II. Lilienbrunngasse 9. Together we were taken by the Gestapo in February 1942 and deported with a transport to Riga.
>
> Helene Porges was transported away from the station in Riga by a car. These cars were equipped with a device for gassing the occupants, so I can state with complete certainty that Helene Porges had already died on the date of her arrival in Riga on February 10, 1942. I can remember the date because the trip took exactly 4 days.
>
> By chance, I was [spared] this kind of death and arrived via foot march to a concentration camp in Riga with my husband and the remaining transport participants. There I repeatedly met Max Werdisheim.
>
> We eventually came to the concentration camp of Kaiserwald, where Max Werdisheim died of hardship and hunger in the summer of 1943.
>
> Taking my further deportation into account, I can conclude that Max Werdisheim certainly did not survive September 31, 1943.
>
> I did not see Max Werdisheim's corpse myself, but only very few escaped this time of horror, altogether 16 persons out of 1,200 from that transport, in the concentration camp Riga.[19]

A woman with the name of Lea Singer does not appear on the transport list of February 6, 1942, but her name does appear on a list of survivors from that trans-

---

18 Death declaration of Max Werdisheim, Memorandum of 28.02.1947, 48 T 1123/47, Wiener Stadt- und Landesarchiv, Landesgericht für ZRS, Vienna. Translation by the author.
19 Ibid. Translation by the author.

port, published by Gertrude Schneider née Hirschhorn.[20] The Hirschhorn family was also forced to live on Lilienbrunngasse 9 and was deported to Riga on the same transport as Max Werdisheim and Helene Porges. Schneider, who was 14 in 1942, later became a historian. In her research, she mentions that "the two Brunners [=the SS-men in charge of organizing the transports] had a habit of adding Jews at the last minute, Jews who went unrecorded in the general chaos, and while the figures of transports always hovered around the magic number of 1,000, it is extremely difficult to give an exact number."[21] She also speaks of "a group of about twenty Jews, men and women, kept separate from us, who had been deported once before and were now being deported again. Not one of them appeared on our actual transport list."[22]

Since 2015, the Arolsen Archives, as the largest archives on victims of Nazi persecution, publish more and more of their holdings online. A search for Lea Singer yielded a scanned copy of a prisoner registration form of a prisoner with that name, born in Vienna on February 23, 1903, who was transferred from the Riga ghetto (Berlinerstraße 7) to the Stutthof concentration camp on July 19, 1944, where she received the prisoner number 49473.[23] According to the form, she was arrested on August 15, 1941. Even though the year of birth given in the registration form does not match the one for Lea Singer who testified to Max's death in Kaiserwald, the signature in the file is clearly from the same woman.

Max Werdisheim had a business and properties and therefore left behind a huge corpus of documentation regarding the expropriation of his property. At the beginning of the research, I was expecting to find records produced by the perpetrators, representing their perspective. Contrary to my expectations, I also found documents that Max Werdisheim had written personally. One such document is an application for a passport that he submitted to the Gestapo in April 1938, and which is mentioned in the book *Archiv der Namen* by Halbrainer.[24] Following the principles guiding archival work, the application was archived ac-

---

20 Gertrude Schneider: Exile and Destruction: The Fate of Austrian Jews, 1938–1945, Westport CT: Praeger, 1995, 175.
21 Ibid., 58.
22 Ibid., 59.
23 Prisoner registration form Lea Singer from Stutthof, 1.1.41.2/4640580/ITS Digital Archive, Arolsen Archives. In the summer of 1944, SS personnel of the Kaiserwald concentration camp were forced to leave Riga due to the advancing Red Army. With the inmates who could still be transferred and with some of the inmates' files they headed to the concentration camp of Stutthof near Danzig. However, many of the files were lost in the chaos.
24 Halbrainer, Archiv der Namen, 80.

cording to the appropriate authority – and not under the name of the individual who submitted it. It took a thorough search by the archive's staff in order to find it.²⁵ I would have never come across it, let alone found it, had I not been aware of its existence.

Reuniting Families Postmortem

There is much that I did not find. Not all original documents to copies kept in the family archive could be (re)located in the corresponding archives. It was extremely disappointing to come to dead ends in such cases, despite having solid proof of the existence of documents, knowing exactly which authority issued them or even having their archival number. Some of the sources found in the family archive are not only of significance for me as a descendant of Max Werdisheim but carry their own weight. One of them is a copy of an interrogation of Julius Werdisheim, Max's brother, by the Prosecutor's Office at the Regional Court of Graz. It is part of a court file regarding "Anton Pacholegg-Guttenberg and others".²⁶ The others were Pacholegg's brother-in-law Karl Stepanel and "the two Jews, the brothers Max Israel Werdisheim and Julius Israel Werdisheim", who "had to stand trial for the crime of foreign exchange [*Devisenverbrechen*]".²⁷ I was particularly interested in this criminal case because in April 1942, the same Anton Pacholegg who according to Julius Werdisheim's interrogation deceived the brothers, was sent to the concentration camp of Dachau, where he worked for (and with) the infamous SS doctor Sigmund Rascher in 'Station No. 5'. Rascher was responsible for various experiments, among them high-altitude experiments, made with Dachau prisoners from February 1942 to March 1944 – many of them ending lethally.²⁸ The same Pacholegg gave a testimony about these experiences on May 13, 1945 – a testimony which entered the Nuremberg Trials and which the historian Joachim Neander convincingly proves as

---

25 I would like to express my sincere gratitude to Franz Mittermüller of the Landesarchiv Steiermark and the rest of the archive's staff for their intensive search of this record.
26 Criminal case against Pacholegg-Guttenberg and others, interrogation of the accused, 15.05. 1941, reference number 4 St 4318/39, Private Collection of the Zarfati Family, Tel Aviv. Translation by the author.
27 "Devisenverbrecher verurteilt", in *Kleine Volks-Zeitung*, 01.11.1941, 8. Translation by the author.
28 Albert Knoll: "Humanexperimente der Luftwaffe im KZ Dachau: Die medizinischen Versuche Dr. Sigmund Raschers", in Neuengamme Memorial (ed.): *Wehrmacht und Konzentrationslager*, Bremen: Edition Temmen, 2012, 139–148, here 139.

worthless.²⁹ The Werdisheim's account on Pacholegg sheds light on aspects of Pacholegg's biography that were previously unknown. All of my efforts to locate the full file of this investigation and judicial process proved futile.

Not every family has a similar set of documents, and yet my family is certainly not the only one. If descendants were asked to make their own family collections available, such sources would be accessible to all. The Holocaust tore families apart. It was interesting to observe that their stories and fates are still torn apart – being dispersed among various archives in different countries. It is the new era of online accessibility to digital sources which can bring them back together.

---

29 Joachim Neander: "A Strange Witness to Dachau Human Skin Atrocities: Anton Pacholegg a.k.a. Anton Baron von Guttenberg a.k.a. Antoine Charles de Guttenberg", in *Theologie.Geschichte: Zeitschrift für Theologie und Kulturgeschichte*, 4, 2009. Available at: https://theologiegeschichte.de/ojs2/index.php/tg/article/view/472/511. Last accessed: 19.08.2022.

Discussing Visual Sources of Deportations from Germany

Christoph Kreutzmüller
A Deceptive Panorama

Photos of Deportations of Jews from Germany

Abstract: The paper analyses the visual traces of the deportation of Jews from 37 communities in Germany and argues that the pictures of deportations follow a pictorial tradition. Marching people as well as Jews being taken to an unknown destination were a set motif – or even a *sujet* – in Nazi Germany. As millions of Germans and thousands of police precincts had cameras, it rather seems surprising that so few photographs of deportations have been found, yet. The corpus of photos we know today offers a rather deceptive panorama of the deportations. The visual sources stage the perpetrators, humiliate the victims and offer a glimpse of the onlooking neighbors. The perspective of the deported Jews is not represented. They were being looked at but were not in a position to take pictures themselves. The paper shows that the photographs are disproportionately scattered: The cities with a large Jewish population are completely underrepresented. The larger the Jewish community was, it seems, the less likely it is that photographs of the deportation exist. Apart from a geographical there is a chronological bias, too, as we do not have any photographs of deportations of Jews from 1943 to 1945.

Introduction

On October 13, 1941, shortly after her escape from camp Gurs in southern France and, incidentally, just a few days before the systematic deportations of Jews from Germany began, Carola Loeb recalled her experiences. In a long letter to her children, she reviewed how her neighbors in Mutterstadt had treated her and what had happened to her during the deportation to southern France one year before:

> We went by bus to the courtyard of the Maxschule in Ludwigshafen, money was exchanged there, there was not enough for us. There was food; soup, bread and sausage. We couldn't eat anything. [...] I sat on the floor in the middle of our luggage like a gypsy mother. People took photos and gawked. We were indifferent to it.[1]

---

[1] Letter from Carola Loeb to her children, 13.10.1941, printed in Christoph Kreutzmüller (ed.): *Gurs 1940. Die Deportation und Ermordung von südwestdeutschen Jüdinnen und Juden/Expulsion*

Racist clichés about Sinti and Roma aside, in the eyes of Loeb, being deported went hand in hand with being photographed. Even so, at first sight it seems astonishing just how many pictures of deportations were made, survived the war and were (and are) kept in local archives and private collections.[2] One of the reasons why there are so many pictures, I will argue, is that the motif was customisable. Pictures of deportations followed a pictorial tradition and can be viewed as part of a certain *sujet*. This will be discussed in the first part of my paper. Taking the corpus of photos of deportations known today, I will then develop a panorama, discuss what was photographed by whom and what is missing. The focus will be on pictures of deportations of Jews from Germany, excluding Austria as well as the deportation of Sinti and Roma that deserve a deeper analysis.[3] My *tour d'horizon* is not only limited in its scope, it is somehow preliminary, too. The project "#LastSeen. Pictures of Nazi Deportations" that was established after my presentation in the conference "Deportations in the Nazi Era – Sources and Research" in November 2020 is likely to trace more pictures and will be able to offer much more information; on the photos of the deportation of Sinti and Roma, too. The project and valuable hints after my talk have already contributed to the following.

Looking at the photos, the structural violence that the pictures show and their making expresses immediately leaps to the eye. Plain to see, nearly all photographers were close to the perpetrators and/or part of the crime. Their cameras had become weapons that further degraded the depicted. Even though Loeb maintained she was "indifferent" to it, she noticed being photographed – and was not asked for consent.[4] Whether or not to show these photos taken "against their will"[5] and "regard [...] the pain of others"[6] is a difficult ethical question,

---

et Assasinat de la population Juive du Sud-Quest de L'Allemagne, Berlin: House of the Wannsee-Conference, 2021, 27. Translation by the author.

2 Klaus Hesse and Philipp Springer: *Vor aller Augen. Fotodokumente des nationalsozialistischen Terrors in der Provinz*, Essen: Klartext 2002; Klaus Hesse: "Bilder lokaler Judendeportationen. Fotografien als Zugänge zur Alltagsgeschichte des NS-Terrors", in Gerhard Paul (ed.): *Visual History. Ein Studienbuch*, Göttingen: Vandenhoeck & Ruprecht, 2006, 149–168.

3 Frank Reuter: *Der Bann des Fremden. Die fotografische Konstruktion des "Zigeuners"*, Munich: Oldenbourg, 2014.

4 Letter from Carola Loeb to her children, 13.10.1941, in Kreutzmüller, Gurs, 27.

5 Cornelia Brink: "Vor aller Augen: Fotografien wider Willen in der Geschichtsschreibung", in *Werkstatt Geschichte*, 47, 2008, 61–74.

6 Susan Sontag: *Regarding the Pain of Others*, London: Penguin, 2003.

today.⁷ However, at times, the discussion obscures the fact that using them in an illustrative sense can do violence to the images (and the people depicted), too. Neglect, after all, is a form of violence. So is disdain. After all, photos are an extremely important source. Well read, they can reveal information that cannot be obtained by studying written or oral sources. In the end, the Shoah was an extremely violent process, and we have to face the violence but treat the photos and the human beings on them with respect.

Shooting Pictures: The Camera

Photography became a mass phenomenon in the 1920s.⁸ In the preface to the second edition of his bestselling handbook *Der Photo-Amateur*, Hans Windisch rightly stated in 1936 that the "photo amateur of today works differently [...] than ten years ago".⁹ Technical developments – above all the introduction of small frame cameras – made photography easier and cheaper. The number of camera owners rapidly increased in Germany. In 1927, their number is estimated at almost two million, i.e. around three percent of the population. By 1939, it is said to have been ten percent.¹⁰ Of course, not everybody could afford a Leica. Many just used simple box cameras.¹¹ Colour films were expensive and the standard black and white films had a light sensitivity of just 64 Asa, which in turn meant the photographers had to rely on a fair amount of light to take a picture.

The extent to which technical factors limited even professionals in the early 1930s, becomes clear from a photo that Georg Pahl, owner of the ABC Press Agency, took on January 30, 1933.¹² Carefully composed along the diagonal, it shows SA men marching from the top left to the bottom right. As we read photos like Latin print the men were marching forward – into the picture and into the

---

7 Jennifer Evans: "Photography as an Ethics of Seeing", in idem., Paul Betts, and Stefan-Ludwig Hoffmann (eds.): *Photography and Twentieth-Century German History*, New York/Oxford: Berghahn, 2019, 1–22.
8 Harriet Scharnberg: *Die "Judenfrage" im Bild. Der Antisemitismus in nationalsozialistischen Fotoreportagen*, Hamburg: Hamburger Editionen, 2019, 27–33; Janina Struk: *Photographing the Holocaust. Interpretations of the Evidence*, London/New York: I.B. Tauris, 2004, 16–19.
9 Hans Windisch: *Der Photo-Amateur. Ein Lehr- und Nachschlagebuch*, Munich: Photo-Schaja, 1936², 5. Translation by the author.
10 Timm Starl: *Die Bildgeschichte der privaten Fotografie in Deutschland und Österreich 1880 bis 1980*, Munich: Koehler & Amelang, 1985, 98.
11 Hans-Dieter Götz: *Box Cameras Made in Germany. Wie die Deutschen fotografieren lernten*, Gilching: VfV, 2002.
12 Photo by Georg Pahl, 30.01.1933, 102–02985 A, German Federal Archives, Berlin.

city. Yet, the light sensitivity of film and lens were not sufficient for an atmospheric night photo and the flash was not strong enough. The smoke from the torches obscured the view. Since the SA men were also not 'properly' aligned and the attitude of the bystanders was by no means clear, the SA march was re-enacted at least twice. This produced images that seemed more appropriate to the occasion – and are still being reproduced today.[13]

What could be photographed by whom was usually determined by racist criteria, always relied on proximity to the Nazi Party, local standing and, of course, the motif. Officially, only fortifications and aerial views were subject to a ban on images in 1930's Germany.[14] In March 1942 pictures of motorways, railway tracks and trains were also banned.[15] Still, shooting violent acts needed the consent of the offenders and/or the cover of the police. As early as 1933, the author of a handbook for press photographers, Carl Dietze, addressed obstructions to photographers and explicitly mentioned that police officers did not have the right to 'snatch' cameras if they thought someone ought not to have taken a picture.[16] Seemingly that had already become common practice. During the pogrom-like riots in Berlin in the summer of 1935, a Danish journalist was attacked by the crowd. Investigating the case, the police chief claimed that he had been attacked "because of his Jewish appearance" and because "he tried to photograph the crowd while standing in his car. By this behaviour he was bound to incur the displeasure of the crowd, which was itself agitated".[17] Needless to say, the film was destroyed. To this day only two fairly nondescript pictures of the riots have been found.[18]

Being assaulted, it was often impossible but always dangerous for Jews to take pictures and thus depict their view. Some still did. En route from Berlin to Amsterdam in August 1935, Fritz Fürstenberg took more than two dozen photographs of town entrance signs on which Jews were forbidden to enter. Natural-

---

13 "Der Siegeszug durchs Brandenburger Tor wie am 30. Januar 1933", in *Völkischer Beobachter*, 31.01.1936. Available at: https://www.dhm.de/lemo/bestand/objekt/fackelzug-durch-das-brandenburger-tor-1936.html. Last accessed: 21.10.2021.
14 Windisch, Photo-Amateur, 193. Cf. Bernd Boll: "Das Adlerauge des Soldaten. Zur Fotopraxis deutscher Amateure im Zweiten Weltkrieg", in *Fotogeschichte*, 22, 2002, 75–87, here: 80.
15 "Photographierverbot", in *Kleinfilm-Foto. Hefte für Kleinfilmphotographie und –Projektion*, 5, 1942, 74–75.
16 Carl Dietze: *Presse-Illustrations-Photographie. Fachweiser für die Verwertung der Gebrauchsphotographie im Dienste aller Gebiete, Wissenszweige und Berufe*, Leipzig: Carl Dietze, 1933[8], 38.
17 Letter from Helldorf to the Ministry of the Interior, 28.08.1935, R. 100269, Political Archive of the Foreign Ministry, Berlin. Translation by the author.
18 Christoph Kreutzmüller, Hermann Simon, and Elisabeth Weber: *Ein Pogrom im Juni. Fotos antisemitischer Schmierereien in Berlin 1938*, Berlin: Hentrich, 2013, 26–27.

ly, the Jewish entrepreneur had to act secretly. For fear of the Gestapo's long arm, the face of his fiancée was whitened when the pictures were presented in a "lantern slide show on the German refugee problem" in Amsterdam.[19] During the pogroms of November 1938 basically the only motif left for Jews was the inside of their – ravaged – homes.[20] In November 1941, just when systematic deportations had started, Jews were banned from owning cameras even though not all of them followed the Reich Security Main Office's orders.[21] It is a telling fact that leaflets explicitly stated that cameras were not allowed to be taken onto the deportation trains.[22]

Staging Deportation: The Development of the Motif

Pictures of deportation follow a certain pictorial tradition: In the nineteenth century the expulsion of Jews had become a widespread motif on antisemitic postcards. Viciously, these cards presented individuals or groups being kicked out of cities or being sent across a border to an unknown destination – sometimes literally into the desert.[23] Most of the postcards presented drawings. This was partly because the exodus of Jews was just a racist phantasy and partly because it only became possible to photograph masses of moving people in the late nineteenth century.

Having made a big technical leap photography was recognized as an important weapon of propaganda in the First World War. Accordingly, hundreds of pictures of men joining the army and soldiers boarding trains were taken.[24] Taking up the military tradition, the Nazi 'party soldiers' marched continuously until, in

---

19 Christoph Kreutzmüller and Theresia Ziehe: "Crossing Borders in 1935. Fritz Fürstenberg's Photographs of Persecution in Nazi Germany", in *Leo Baeck Yearbook*, 64, 2019, 73–89.
20 Christoph Kreutzmüller: "Bilder der Bedrohung. Von Juden aufgenommene Fotos der Verfolgung", in *Medaon*, 12, 2018, 1–6.
21 "Order by the Central Security Office, 13.11.1941", in Joseph Walk (ed.): *Das Sonderrecht für die Juden im NS-Staat. Eine Sammlung der gesetzlichen Maßnahmen und Richtlinien. Inhalt und Bedeutung*, Heidelberg: UTB, 2013², 355.
22 Leaflet by the Jewish Association, Inv. No. 2003/81/3, Jewish Museum, Berlin.
23 Johannes Heil: "'Deutschland den Deutschen'. Judenvertreibungen und Vertreibungsphantasien im Postkartenformat", in Helmut Gold and Georg Heuberger (eds.): *Abgestempelt. Judenfeindliche Postkarten auf der Grundlage der Sammlung Wolfgang Haney*, Heidelberg: Umschau/Braus, 1999, 241–250.
24 Hermann Rex: *Der Weltkrieg in seiner rauen Wirklichkeit*, Oberammergau: Hermann Rutz, 1927, 9–24.

the end, death marches became the murderous swan song of the NS-Regime. The afore-mentioned pictures of the re-enactment of the march of SA men through the Brandenburg gate were used as a symbol of what the Nazis referred to as the 'national awakening'. In the propaganda film *Triumph of the Will* Leni Riefenstahl staged near endless parades of various formations in 1935. Soon the rapidly growing Wehrmacht joined in. Apart from parades, the viewfinders of the cameras caught religious and carnival processions.[25] How to organize an 'Aufmarsch', a proper march, was even discussed in dance magazines.[26]

While becoming an ever stronger symbol of inclusion, marching was used as a form of exclusion, too. In 1933 political opponents and/or Jews were being marched through the streets – and quite frequently photographed especially in small towns.[27] Yet, in April 1933 police manhunt in the poor Jewish quarter "Scheunenviertel" east of Alexanderplatz in Berlin was not only covered by press photographers but also by the radio because sound could transmit something light could not. Aired were the voices of men that were not native German speakers in order to 'prove' the propaganda claim that Jews were not Germans.[28] In 1935, marches shaming Jewish/non-Jewish couples were – as in the case of Norden (near Emden) – not only photographed, but the photographs were sold and send as postcards.[29] Due to constant mobbing and recurring violence, more and more Jewish families decided to leave their homes, often moving to larger towns in Germany.[30]

Early 1936, the ghastly antisemitic weekly *Der Stürmer* received a series of seven prints of the departure of the "last three Jews" of Roth, near Nuremberg, to nearby Regensburg.[31] One print is stamped "Photo Müller". Whether this was

---

25 Linda Conze, Ulrich Prehn, and Michael Wildt: "Sitzen, baden, durch die Straßen laufen. Überlegungen zu fotografischen Repräsentationen von 'Alltäglichem' und 'Unalltäglichem' im Nationalsozialismus", in Annelie Ramsbrock, Annette Vowinckel, and Malte Zierenberg (eds.): *Fotografien im 20. Jahrhundert. Verbreitung und Vermittlung*, Göttingen: Wallstein, 2013, 270–298; Linda Conze and Sandra Starke: "Die visuelle Chronik einer Kleinstadt. Fotografien zwischen Öffentlichkeit und Privatheit", in Thomas Medicus (ed.): *Verhängnisvoller Wandel. Ansichten aus der Provinz 1933–1949. Die Fotosammlung Biella*, Hamburg: Hamburger Editionen, 2016, 65–98.
26 Erich Jantetz: "Der Aufmarsch", in *Gymnastik und Volkstanz*, 12, 1937, 15–16.
27 Hesse and Springer, Vor aller Augen, 42–66.
28 A partial transcription of the radio report can be found in Eike Geisel: *Im Scheunenviertel. Bilder, Texte, Dokumente*, Berlin: Severin und Siedler, 1981, 138–139.
29 Christoph Kreutzmüller and Julia Werner: *Fixiert. Fotografische Quellen zur Verfolgung und Ermordung der Juden in Europa. Eine pädagogische Handreichung*, Berlin: Hentrich, 2016, 23.
30 Jewish Museum Berlin: "Topography of Violence". Available at: https://www.jmberlin.de/topographie-gewalt/#/en/info. Last accessed: 21.10.2021.
31 Inscription on the back of the photo, 31.12.1935, E 39, 56/1.

the photographer or the shop that made the print is unknown. It is also unknown who send the pictures to the *Stürmer*. But he or she certainly knew a lot about the family.[32]

Fig. 1: Unknown Photographer, Roth, December 31, 1935, E 39, 56/7, Stadtarchiv Nürnberg.

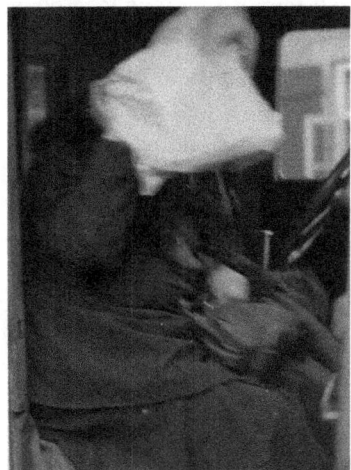

Fig. 2: Unknown Photographer, Roth, December 31, 1935, E 39, 56/4, Stadtarchiv Nürnberg.

---

32 Unknown photographer, Roth, 31.12.1935, E 39, 56/1–7, Stadtarchiv Nürnberg (StAN). Just like many other photos send to the *Stürmer* the series was not published.

The series shows the family leaving their house in a narrow alleyway among neighbors standing and staring. After the moving truck had been loaded it left the town "mit Vollgas" (at full throttle), as the writing on the back had it. On the back of another print of the series the sender remarked with a self-righteous meanness so typical: "She does not let herself be photographed". Six years later, the resilient woman, Emilie Freising, was deported via Nuremberg to Theresienstadt where she perished on August 23, 1943.[33]

When in October 1938 some 25,000 Jews were expulsed to the Polish border, this was photographed, too, albeit – as far as we know – only in Dortmund, Nuremberg and Rendsburg.[34] The expulsion was a sign of the ever more radical approach the Nazi regime took and eventually produced the pretext for the November pogroms. Again, marches accompanied plunder, destruction and murder. On November 10, 1938, Jewish men were being photographed while they were being walked through the streets in many places from Baden-Baden to Bautzen.[35] The onlookers doubled as cordon and audience – needed to complete humiliation. As the photos from Baden-Baden show, some onlookers had taken their cameras along.[36]

At the same day in 1938 in Edenkoben (near Speyer), an unknown photographer took a series of six pictures that shows Jewish men from the village being forced by SA to board a bus. "To Palestine" a sign decorated by a little swastika flag reads.[37] Though many men in the bus certainly wished to have had a chance to emigrate, the bus only took them to nearby Karlsruhe and left them stranded there. Some were deported to Dachau others returned home and were deported to Gurs two years later.

Clear to see, the expulsion of the unwanted had become a set motif by 1938. So had the boarding of trains: Pictures and postcards of soldiers getting onto trains (eventually similar carriages that were used for mass-deportations from 1942 on) were widely spread in and after the First World War. From 1933 on special trains (*Sonderzüge*) became a frequent sight again; be it on Nazi organized

---

33 German Federal Archives: "Entry Emilia Freising, born 18.09.1864", in *Memorial Book. Victims of the Persecution of Jews under the National Socialist Tyranny in Germany 1933–1945*. Available at: https://www.bundesarchiv.de/gedenkbuch/en868980. Last accessed: 21.10.2021.
34 Andrea Löw and Kim Wünschmann: "Film and the Recording of City Space in Nazi Germany: The Demolition of the Munich Main Synagogue", in Natalia Aleksiun and Hana Kubátová (eds.): *Places, Spaces, and Voids in the Holocaust*, Göttingen: Wallstein, 2021, 25–54.
35 Hesse and Springer, Vor aller Augen, 110–116.
36 Christoph Kreutzmüller: "Photographing Bystanders", in Christina Morina and Krijn Thijs (eds.): *Probing the Limits of Categorization. The Bystander in Holocaust History*, New York/Oxford: Berghahn, 2018, 131–147.
37 Unknown photographer, Edenkoben, 10.11.1938, X3, 2925–2931, Landesarchiv Speyer.

summer holidays, at the party rallies in Nuremberg or – from 1939 – during the so-called resettlement of Germans from Rumania or the USSR. How to capture a departure by train was known amongst photographers.[38]

Alongside humiliating pictures capturing Jews as mere objects there are quite a few pictures taken by Jews, too: On September 1, 1936, Herbert Sonnenfeld took a series of 42 photographs of Jewish teenagers on their journey from Berlin's central station, the Anhalter Bahnhof, to Palestine. Working for the Zionist weekly *Jüdische Rundschau* Sonnenfeld joined the youth on their way to Marseille and took a few pictures out of the train, thus preserving a rare view back onto the platform and the people who stayed behind.[39]

Fig. 3: Photo by Herbert Sonnenfeld, September 1, 1936, FOT 88/500/106/015, Jewish Museum Berlin.

Picturing Deportation: The Corpus of Photos

Deporting 'unwelcome aliens' back to Poland or 'Russia' or maybe to put those who could not be deported in some kind of a 'concentration camp' was being dis-

---

38 Elizabeth Harvey: "Documenting Heimkehr. Photography, Displacement and 'Homecoming' in the Nazi Resettlement of Ethnic Germans", in Evans, Betts, and Hoffmann, Ethics of Seeing, 79–107.
39 Maren Krüger: *Herbert Sonnenfeld. Ein jüdischer Fotograf in Berlin*, Berlin: Nicolai, 1990, 139–142. Thanks to Theresia Ziehe, Berlin, for additional information.

cussed in Germany as early as 1920.⁴⁰ Against this backdrop it is not surprising that the first mass-deportation of the Nazi regime was the expulsion of 25,000 Polish Jews in October 1938.⁴¹ As mentioned above, in Dortmund, Nuremberg and Rendsburg this was photographed. While there are no photographs of the deportations from Stettin and Schneidemühl to occupied Poland in February 1940, there are visual sources from eight places of the deportations from Southwest-Germany to Gurs eight month later.⁴² In 1941 and 1942, the deportations "to the East" were photographed in at least 24 places. Then the traces disappear. The last visual record of a deportation is a film by a member of the lab staff of the famous camera producer Zeiss-Ikon who filmed the forced transfer of Jews from Dresden to a nearby labour camp in November 1942 – which strictly speaking was only indirectly linked to the deportation.⁴³ There are neither photos of the murderous climax of deportation of Jews from Germany in early 1943, nor from the scattered smaller deportations until March 1945.

The time the pictures were taken determines which deportation destinations were depicted. The deportations to Gurs stand out with particularly dense visual traces. Strongly featured are also the deportations to Riga, whereas the deportations to Theresienstadt and the ghettos in occupied Poland (both the General Government and the Warthegau) are underrepresented. There is no visual source of the deportations to Kowno and Minsk in 1941/1942 and no single photo is known of the deportations to Auschwitz-Birkenau. The transports of Jews from Germany to the 'metropolis of death' (Otto Dov Kulka) only had started in autumn 1942 – just when the visual traces disappear.

Taking into account that in Dortmund and Nuremberg photos were taken both in 1938 and in 1942, photographs of the deportation of Jews exist from at least 33 German communities: Bielefeld, Birkenfeld, Brandenburg (Havel), Breslau (now Wrocław), Bretten, Bruchsal, Coesfeld, Dortmund, Eisenach, Emden, Fulda, Gailingen, Hanau, Hattingen, Hohenlimburg, Kerpen, Kippenheim, Kitzingen, Laupheim, Lörrach, Ludwigshafen, Moers, Munich, Neustadt/Saale, Nu-

---

40 "Konzentrationslager für Ausländer", in *Vossische Zeitung*, 04.01.1920; "Ausländerkonzentrationslager Ohrdruf", in *Vossische Zeitung*, 07.03.1921.
41 Alina Bothe and Gertrud Pickhan (eds.): *Ausgewiesen. Die Polenaktion. Berlin, 28.10.1938*, Berlin: Metropol, 2018.
42 Kreutzmüller, Gurs 1940, 24–25.
43 Norbert Haase, Stefi Jersch-Wenzel, and Hermann Simon: "Einleitung", in idem. (eds.): *Die Erinnerung hat ein Gesicht*, Leipzig: Kiepenheuer, 1998, 9–18, hier: 12; "Erich Höhne mußte Film über 'Judenlager' drehen", in *Dresdner Neueste Nachrichten*, 07.08.1997. See also the contribution by Elisabeth Pönisch in this volume.

remberg, Regensburg, Rendsburg, Siegburg, Tauberbischofsheim, Weingarten, Wetzlar, Wiesbaden, and Würzburg.[44]

In addition, five film-sequences can be traced: Four of departures (Bruchsal, Dresden, Hildesheim, and Stuttgart) and one clip of the arrival of exhausted occupants of a train from Magdeburg in the ghetto of Warsaw.[45] As both a film and a photo from Bruchsal exist, there is a total of 37 communities with visual sources of deportations known today. Only twelve of these places – i.e. less than one third – had more than 100.000 inhabitants and counted as cities.[46] As Klaus Hesse put it, photographing deportation was a "small town sensation".[47] Considering that the majority of Jews lived in cities (a fact that was further amplified by rural exodus due to persecution in the 1930s), this is a surprising find. To take the argument even one step further: Of the five cities with the largest Jewish communities only one (Breslau) is represented – with just two photographs. So far we do not know of neither pictures from Frankfurt am Main, Hamburg, Cologne, nor from Berlin.

The astonishing misrepresentation indicates that the corpus of photographs is scattered and the panorama dented. This might be partly due to the fact that photos were regarded as second-class sources or mere illustrations and were therefore not collected systematically for a long time. By chance, the photo-albums from Würzburg were discovered and preserved by Isaac Wahler as early as 1947.[48] But most of the other pictures were handed over to the archives in

---

[44] Klaus Hesse lists 27 communities where photos were taken between 1940 and 1942. Cf. Klaus Hesse: "Die Bilder lesen. Interpretationen fotografischer Quellen zur Deportation der deutschen Juden", in idem. and Philipp Springer, Vor aller Augen, 185–212, here 187. Not listed are Breslau, Bretten, Tauberbischofsheim, Nuremberg, and Weingarten. Cf. Katharina Friedla: *Juden in Breslau/Wrocław 1933–1949. Überlebensstrategien, Selbstbehauptung und Verfolgungserfahrungen*, Cologne et al: Böhlau, 2015, 432.
[45] Hesse included Bruchsal, Dresden, and Stuttgart but not Hildesheim and Magdeburg in his list. For Hildesheim see "Deportation of the Jews of Hildesheim". Available at: https://collections.ushmm.org/search/catalog/irn1003952. Last accessed: 21.10.2021. For Magdeburg see "Jewish Deportees from Magdeburg in the Warsaw Ghetto". Available at: https://encyclopedia.ushmm.org/content/en/film/jewish-deportees-from-magdeburg-in-the-warsaw-ghetto. Last accessed: 21.10.2021.
[46] As cities counted Bielefeld, Breslau, Dortmund, Dresden, Ludwigshafen, Magdeburg, Munich, Nuremberg, Regensburg, Stuttgart, Wiesbaden, and Würzburg.
[47] Klaus Hesse, Die Bilder lesen, 187. Translation by the author.
[48] Sworn Statement Isaac Wahler, 05.09.1947, Die Evakuierung der Juden aus Würzburg, Rep. B-2, Nachlass Wahler, 1, Archive of the House of the Wannsee-Conference, Berlin; Herbert Schultheis and Isaac Wahler: *Bilder und Akten der Gestapo Würzburg über die Judendeportation 1941–1943*, Bad Neustadt a.d. Saale: Rötter, 1988. See also the contribution of Alfred Eckert in this volume.

the 1970s/1980s, sometimes coupled with the statement that the photos had been taken secretly even if simple appearances refute this.[49]

More research still needs to be done how the photographs were presented or meant to be presented. We know that sometimes pictures were put into albums and therefore assembled to form a narrative. Arranging the album in Würzburg, police secretary Elfriede Röllich quoted a popular folk song (that Elvis Presley would cover 18 years later) as a caption – and knowingly or not – perpetuated a tradition of antisemitic postcards.[50] The director of the city museum in Bielefeld added some snide remarks onto the pages of his "war chronic".[51]

While in 1940 photos were still also taken by onlookers, the majority of pictures after 1941 seems to have been made by policemen or professional photographers for internal documentation and as a proof of performance. Just like in Würzburg, it was often a member of the identification service who worked at the camera.[52] In Bielefeld the assistant police officer Georg Hübner actually worked for the director of the city museum.[53] In Eisenach, too, the pictures were made for the municipality. It is very likely that Theodor Harder, a local photographer, who had worked for the town before, took the photos in May 1942.[54]

In Kitzingen, where the first deportation had already been photographed by the Würzburg police in March 1942, the Nazi Kreisleiter asked his son to "take a few photos of the removal of the 'last Kitzingen Jews'"[55] in September 1942. When the train departed, the 16-year old had taken two photos and reached the end of his film. Only the first half of the last frame was exposed.

Moving freely and taking pictures at will, the unknown photographer who took a series of thirteen pictures of the deportation from Hattingen (near Dortmund) in April 1942 obviously worked for an official agency. Yet the quality of the equipment (or his/her training) was rather poor. Nearly half of the photos

---

49 See, for example, the description of the photographs from Wiesbaden. Available at: https://photos.yadvashem.org/photo-details.html?language=en&item_id=97784&ind=11. Last accessed: 21.10.2021.
50 Protocol, 29.03.1949, 407I (volume 5), StA Würzburg; Heil, Deutschland den Deutschen, 243.
51 Helmut Gatzen: *Befehl zum Abtransport, Juden und "Mischlinge 1. Grades" 1933–1945 in und um Gütersloh*, Gütersloh: Flöttmann, 2001, 72–75.
52 Protocol, 29.03.1949, 407I (volume 5), StA Würzburg; Heil, Deutschland den Deutschen, 243.
53 Stadtarchiv Bielefeld: "Die Bielefelder Polizei 1933–1950. Deportation von Juden 1941–1945". Available at: https://www.stadtarchiv-bielefeld.de/Portals/0/PDFs/Online-Ausstellungen/Ordnung%20und%20Vernichtung/04_Deportation.pdf. Last accessed: 21.10.2021; Gatzen, Befehl zum Abtransport, 72–75.
54 Order of the mayor of Eisenach, 18.08.1937, Hauptamt 11–002–13, Stadtarchiv Eisenach.
55 Letter Lothar Heer to Staatsarchiv Würzburg, 22.06.1995, Lichtbildersammlung, 289, StA Würzburg. Translation by the author.

A Deceptive Panorama — 147

Fig. 4: Photographs by Lothar Heer, Kitzingen, September 21, 1942, Lichtbildersammlung, 289, StA Würzburg.

are blurred.⁵⁶ However, by chance he or she caught a glimpse of the entrance door of the forced residence being sealed or locked by an official in uniform, marked with a star.

Fig. 5: Unknown photographer, Hattingen, April 28, 1942, 0126, Stadtarchiv Hattingen.

It was probably an even bigger coincidence that the transport to Zamosc to which the Jews were added was photographed in Dortmund, too. It is unclear who took the two photographs of the Jews on a football green on April 28 and, two days later, marching through the city. But as he or she kept distance, these photos might have been actually taken clandestinely⁵⁷ – just like another picture taken in Regensburg.⁵⁸

The photos differ considerably in their quality and scope. Again, Würzburg stands out because of the sheer number (139). In many places the photographer seemingly filled a film roll of twenty plus frames, but sometimes only one or two pictures were taken (or survived). What the pictures share is their panoramic view. Only a dozen or so were taken in portrait mode. In Wiesbaden, an unknown policeman portrayed an old, but well-dressed man with a walking stick and dark glasses who might have been blind but certainly was confused and walked in the 'wrong direction'. Just like his colleagues in Auschwitz did in

---

56 Thomas Weiss: "'Sie hat mich auch gesehen und mir zugewunken'. Das Ende der Synagogengemeinde in Hattingen", in Ralf Piorr (ed.): *Ohne Rückkehr. Die Deportation der Juden aus dem Regierungsbezirk Arnsberg nach Zamość im April 1942*, Essen: Klartext, 2012, 109–130, here 117.
57 Rolf Fischer: *Verfolgung und Vernichtung. Die Dortmunder Opfer der Shoah. Ein Gedenkbuch*, Essen: Klartext, 2015, 174–175 and 215.
58 Unknown photographer, Regensburg 1942, 104 AO7, Yad Vashem, Jerusalem.

Fig. 6: Unknown photographer, Dortmund, April 28, 1942, 502–01/032–21–01, Stadtarchiv Dortmund.

the album that has become known as the Lili Jacob Album, he portrayed the handicapped, the odd one out.[59] Maybe he was even making mean fun, playing with the fact that the Jew did not know, could not see, what he knew and foresaw.

As they were made as an internal proof of achievement, the photos present an orderly, smooth running process without any disturbances, without any resistance on the side of the heavily loaded, elderly deportees. Yet, while in 1940 the photos focus on the Jews being led away from their homes and being taken to (and then from) the assembly points like schools, most series from 1941 onwards focus on the trains. All series feature the guards (ordinary police as well as Gestapo) but hide the physical violence that was part of the deportation. Also mis-

---

59 Tal Bruttmann, Stefan Hördler, and Christoph Kreutzmüller: *Die Fotografische Inszenierung des Verbrechens. Ein Album aus Auschwitz*, Darmstadt: Wissenschaftliche Buchgesellschaft, 2019, 145–146.

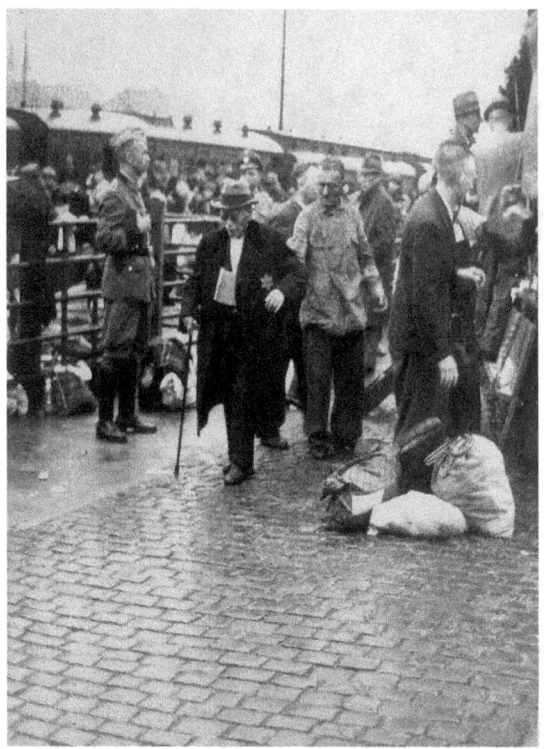

Fig. 7: Willi Rudolph (?), Wiesbaden, August 29, 1942, 1046/6, Yad Vashem, Jerusalem.

sing are the bureaucratic routines that led to the deportation – from timetable conferences to mission briefings. Even though some policemen took shots of the registration, the luggage and body searches the deportees had to undergo, most photographers focussed on 'the action', the walk to the station and embarkation. Doing paperwork, after all, is not an exciting motif. Often taking place indoors, it was more difficult to capture. Due to the technical limitations – or the timetables –, most photographers took their pictures at daytime and outside. Only in Coesfeld, Munich and Würzburg the photographers worked with artificial lighting or with a flash.

The trains we see are (old) third class coaches. So far, no photos have been found showing the deportees getting onto freight trains. Some of the series taken in 1941 and 1942 show deserted stations or side tracks, others were taken in regular stations. As they got on the regular train to Weimar, the deportees even mixed with the non-Jewish passers-by on the forecourt and in the railway station of Eisenach. As mentioned, the picture was taken by a local photographer. In-

Fig. 8: Theodor Harder (?), Eisenach, May 9, 1942, 41.3-J-491, Stadtarchiv Eisenach.

conceivable that a policeman would have taken such a picture, showing an – albeit short – loss of control

So far, neither pictures of the shunting nor rolling trains have emerged or have been recognized. Missing too are views into the carriages. The only exception known so far is not from the Reich. It is a short sequence of a film Rudolf Breslauer took for the commandant of the transit camp Westerbork in the Netherlands in 1944, which of course might have included Jews from Germany that had fled to the Netherlands before 1940 and were then deported, too.[60]

Apart from three pictures showing the arrival of unidentified transports walking from the nearby train station to Theresienstadt and a sequence staging the arrival of Jews from Magdeburg in the Warsaw ghetto there is only scattered visual material of the arrival of deportees in ghettos,[61] shooting sites and camps. On some photos taken in the Litzmannstadt ghetto, German Jews can be spotted

---

60 Film "Uitgaand Transport", 1944. Available at: https://www.youtube.com/watch?v=cnA_NdgWII4. Last accessed: 21.10.2021.

61 Václav Krejza: "Photographies of the transport of Jewish men and women to Terezin". Available at: https://collections.jewishmuseum.cz/index.php/Detail/Object/Show/object_id/31629, https://collections.jewishmuseum.cz/index.php/Detail/Object/Show/object_id/31635, and https://collections.jewishmuseum.cz/index.php/Detail/Object/Show/object_id/31637. Last Accessed: 22.11.2021. Thanks to Aletta Beck for this information.

with the yellow star on their left breast.⁶² In a series SS-Hauptscharführer (sergeant) Bernhard Walter took for an album with the title *Die Umsiedlung der Juden aus Ungarn* (The resettlement of the Jews from Hungary) on May 15 or 16, 1944, in Auschwitz' spoil-collection point Kanada I, luggage of a transport from Theresienstadt can be seen. One inscription on a suitcase reads "III/1", the number of the first transport from Cologne to Theresienstadt in June 1942. On another the name Ricke Flatauer can be reconstructed. The 73-year-old woman had been deported from Berlin to Theresienstadt on August 25, 1942, and perished there less than five months later. Her suitcase was then apparently passed on and taken by someone else on what most probably was his or her last journey.⁶³

We know that SS photographer Walter also got his camera in the Kanada-complex in Auschwitz. It probably had been taken there by a deported Jew and was then stolen. We also know that the films in cameras taken to Auschwitz as well as the prints were immediately destroyed.⁶⁴ No one will ever know how many visual sources were burned in the pits of Auschwitz. However, one thing is certain, being deported among many other monstrosities meant the loss of all photographs for the Jews. This, of course, is yet another reason why the visual sources made by Jews are lacking. There are only very few exceptions: Just before she decided to go into hiding Annemarie Kuttner took a picture of her mother and herself in their apartment at Uhlandstraße in Berlin. Although she knew it might be the last picture she decided to focus on a certain normality and photographed herself and her mother sitting around a table that is decorated by a cloth. A portray of the deceased father/husband on the desk completes the picture. Only the fact that the foot end of the bed cranes into the picture betrays how cluttered the room was and that the picture was taken in a '*Judenwohnung*', a forced residence.⁶⁵

---

62 Ingo Loose: *The Face of the Ghetto. Pictures taken by Jewish Photographers in the Litzmannstadt Ghetto, 1940–1944*, Berlin: Topography of the Terror Foundation, 2010, 57, 65–66.
63 Bruttmann, Hördler, and Kreutzmüller, Die Fotografische Inszenierung, 241–247.
64 National Committee for Attending Deportees (DEGOB): "Report by a woman from Budapest, born 1915". Available at: http://www.degob.org/index.php?showjk=701. Last accessed: 21.10.2021.
65 Kreutzmüller, Bilder der Bedrohung, 5.

Conclusion: A Deceptive Panorama

Photographs are considered 'windows to past realities' but they never simply depict what happened.[66] Just as photos often stage what they pretend to only record, taking pictures was (and is) often voyeurism in the disguise of documentation. Nevertheless, photographs are also instructive sources, but – like any other source – they have to be read critically. Since photographs can in principle be reproduced at will and because for a long time they were considered a secondary source – if not even mere illustrations – the history of transmission and the historical context of the pictures have all too often been lost and can nowadays only be reconstructed with great effort. This complicates the analysis. One of the tasks of future research – as for example with the project "#LastSeen. Photos of Nazi Deportations" – will be to reconstruct context and establish precise object biographies for all the photos.

Marching people were a set motif – or even a *sujet* – in Nazi Germany. Picturing Jews being taken to an unknown destination followed a tradition, too. And millions of Germans had cameras. The number of photos known today are just the tip of the iceberg. We can expect to discover more photographs of deportations. The panorama presented in the photographs we have so far is not only deceptive in reproducing the view the perpetrators wanted to keep, i.e. blanking out violence as well as any other disturbance. It is also biased. Firstly, while photographing deportation seems a 'small town sensation' it is almost certain also a small-town collection. In smaller municipalities archives seem to have been more successful collecting photos. As most photographs were acquired in the 1970s and 1980s when local initiatives in West Germany were busily researching 'their past', West German municipalities are overrepresented. There are fewer photographs in local archives of the former GDR and nearly no visual sources of the deportation of the towns and cities in what is now Poland or Russia.

The second bias is connected to the first but poses a paradox in its own right. The larger the Jewish community was, it seems, the less likely it is that photographs of the deportation exist. The biggest void is Berlin where more than one third of the Jews in Germany lived and from where approximately 50,000 Jews were deported.[67] We know that out of fear that unwelcome pictures might be published by the international press, the Nazi regime kept a tight con-

---

66 Jens Jäger: *Fotografie und Geschichte*, Frankfurt am Main: Campus, 2009, 83.
67 Akim Jah: *Die Deportation der Juden aus Berlin. Die nationalsozialistische Vernichtungspolitik und das Sammellager Große Hamburger Straße*, Berlin: Be-Bra, 2013.

trol on photography in the German capital. We also know that the files of the Berlin Gestapo were destroyed at the end of the war. Still, it seems unlikely that no one took a photo of one of the far more than 100 transports. In May 2019, the House of the Wannsee Conference published a call for photos which drew quite a lot of media attention but was not met with success. Still, recent examples of Vienna and camp Vught in the Netherlands show that new photos can be found.[68]

The third bias is perhaps the most confusing and important one. Why do we not have any photographs of deportations of Jews from 1943 to 1945? Was it that the would-be photographers had gotten used to deportations and therefore did not regard the motif as worthy of photographing anymore? Or did the growing intensity of air raids and the destruction of cameras, films and the growing fear of losing the war play a role? Or was it that camera-owners (like everybody else in Germany) knew all too well in 1942/1943 that the deported would be murdered on arrival? Or was it a mix of all aspects?

The corpus of photos we know today offers a rather deceptive panorama of the deportations. The visual sources stage the perpetrators, humiliate the victims and offer a glimpse of the onlooking neighbors. The presence of spectators certainly influenced Klaus Hesse's choice of the title of his important study. *Vor aller Augen* (in plain sight) is apt and catchy, but it reflects only the perspective of the non-Jewish part of the society, perpetrators and onlookers alike. The perspective of the deported Jews is not represented. They were being looked at – but could not photograph back!

---

68 Dieter Hecht, Michaela Raggam-Blesch, and Heidemarie Uhl (eds.): *Letzte Orte. Die Wiener Sammellager und die Deportationen 1941/42*, Vienna: Mandelbaum, 2019; "Voor het eerst kijk je recht in het gezicht van de gedeporteerde Joden uit kamp Vught. Hoe doken deze unieke beelden ineens op?", in *De Volkskrant*, 25.05.2021.

Elisabeth Pönisch
Deportations from the Perspective of the Remaining Jews and the Surrounding Population

Narratives, Pictures and Films as Reflections of Social Reality

Abstract: This article focuses on the behavior and perception of the remaining Jews and the surrounding population during the deportation of the Jewish population within the German Reich between 1941 and 1945. This research interest emphasizes that the disenfranchisement and exclusion of the Jewish population and the resulting isolation, deportation and murder, were not only a political, but rather a social process. Therefore, deportations should also be considered as such. For this purpose, I analyze the processes before, during and after the deportation. Contemporary diaries and oral history interviews as well as deportation notices and other deportation artifacts of the impending deportations are the main sources to be examined in this article. The consideration of the gaze of the others further illustrates the objectified exclusion of the deported Jews. Spatial visibilities of the deportation that took place were also the sealing of apartments or rooms, accumulations of suitcases or signs on the doors like 'Here resided the Jew/the Jewess ...'. Through the analysis of film material, the visual visibility of the deportation will also be taken into account.

Introduction

How did the remaining Jews experience the deportations of their former Jewish cohabitants, neighbors, their family and friends? In the collective memory of the remaining Jews and the non-Jewish population surrounding them, specific images have influenced and consolidated the perception of the deportations. Victor Klemperer described in his diary on July 13, 1942, the following deportation situation in the Henriettenstift at Güntzstraße 24 in Dresden that functioned as a 'Judenhaus' ('Jews house').[1]

---

[1] The results of this article are part of a dissertation project that deals with life in the so-called Judenhäuser in Nazi Germany between 1939 and 1945.

OpenAccess. © 2023 the author(s), published by De Gruyter. This work is licensed under the Creative Commons Attribution-NonCommercial-NoDerivatives 4.0 International License.
https://doi.org/10.1515/9783110746464-011

> Beautiful Dresden – handsome squares, gardens, the Henriettenstift, an imposing building, also has a large garden. In a fairly gloomy entrance hall: a mêlée, no space to move, chaos. Tied-up mattresses, trunks, evacuation luggage [...] piled up everywhere, in between them the toing and froing of star-wearing helpers, half the Community seemed to be helping the old ladies.[2]

Visually comprehensible is the same 'toing and froing' illustrated in a film, which shows another roundup at the Güntzstraße 24 in Dresden. The film of about 30 minutes documents how the Jewish inhabitants of the building were brought to the *'Judenlager'* (*'Jewish Camp'*) *Hellerberg* on November 23 and 24, 1942. In the first few minutes, the inhabitants with *'Yellow Stars'* on their coats carry suitcases, with their names written on them, together with pieces of furniture to a truck (see fig. 1[3]). Hellerberg, which was built in cooperation with Zeiss-Ikon AG and served as a labor and residential camp between November 1942 and March 1943, was located approximately seven kilometers outside of Dresden. The construction of the camp was initiated by the company and the local Gestapo.[4] Thus, it was not a site of the deportations in the classical sense. Rather, Dresden-Hellerberg was "the first evidence of a labor and residential camp that was supported jointly by the Gestapo and private industry and at the same time regarded as a collection camp for deportation".[5]

Fig. 2[6] shows a situation on the streets of Würzburg: Jewish men and women walking as a group, fully packed with bags and suitcases, through the streets to the train station. On the left side of the picture, two uniformed policemen are visible guarding the march; on the right side, passers-by can be recognized. Both, the still of the film and the photo, show different narratives of the expulsion of the Jewish population from Germany, each claiming interpretive sovereignty. The first picture is part of a film that illustrates the chaos but also the external control of the situation whereas the second photo exemplifies the

---

2 Victor Klemperer: *I Will Bear Witness: A Diary of the Nazi Years 1942–1945*, New York: Modern Library, 1999, 99.
3 "Deportation of Dresden Jews to Hellerberg", 2016.518, RG-60.0199, USHMM Film Archive, Washington. Available at: https://collections.ushmm.org/search/catalog/irn599830. Last accessed: 21.01.2022.
4 Cf. Wolf Gruner: *Jewish Forced Labor Under the Nazis: Economic Needs and Racial Aims, 1938–1944*, Cambridge: Cambridge University Press, 2006, 78–79.
5 Ibid., 79.
6 "Wuerzburg, Germany, German policemen leading deportees to the train station", 25.04.1942, 7900/53, Yad Vashem Photo archive, Jerusalem. Available at: https://photos.yadvashem.org/index.html?language=en&displayType=image&strSearch=7900/53. Last accessed: 21.01.2022.

Fig. 1: Still image from the film Deportation of Dresden Jews to Hellerberg (timescale: 10:02:28:17), Stiftung Sächsische Gedenkstätten (StSG). **Fig. 2:** Jews being marched through the streets of Würzburg to the train station, Staatsarchiv Würzburg.

deportation as a structured process that underlies a planned force and imposed external logic.

As different as the various deportations were, so different were the resulting images surrounding the deportations of the Jewish population from German cities from 1941 onward. Based on this, my research interest is driven by the question of how the deportees perceived the different situations. Precisely, this refers to their interactions in the various places of deportation: the houses from which people were deported, the streets on which they were brought to the train stations, the assembly points where they had to wait for the trains 'to the East', the train stations from where they were sent off and the assembly camps that served as the last stop, as well as the social relations in these various places. The questions guiding the research are hereby: How did the Jews who stayed behind and the non-Jewish population perceive the deportations? Which social relations become visible in the different (micro-)situations of the deportations? More abstractly, this is followed by the sociological question of which normatively valid order is reflected during the deportations? These questions aim at the inherent social order of the deportation. These questions emphasize that the disenfranchisement and exclusion of the Jewish population and the resulting isolation, deportation and murder, were not only a political, but rather also a social process.[7] Consequently, in this article, the main focus will be on the social inter-

---

[7] Frank Bajohr bases his research on Alf Lüdtke's analysis of Nazi rule as 'social practice'. By this, Lüdtke means that the sharp separation of rulers and ruled is not considered, but rather the diverse forms of action and behavior in society need to be analyzed. Cf. Frank Bajohr: "Vom antijüdischen Konsens zum schlechten Gewissen: Die deutsche Gesellschaft und die Judenverfol-

actions during the deportation. For this purpose, the relationship constellations between all people involved in the deportation must also be considered.

In order to answer my research questions, first, I will examine written testimonies of those who participated in the deportations as observers. Secondly, I will analyze narrative perceptions, visual material and specific artifacts to show how the phenomena of exclusion and deportations were objectified in the apartments and 'Judenhäuser', where the deportees had to live before they were deported. For that matter, the central assumption of this contribution is that the analysis of narratives and visual material on the deportation is suitable for reconstructing the specific situation of the deportation and for presenting the behavior of the people involved in a differentiated way. In the following, I will illustrate this primarily with examples from the deportations from Dresden and Leipzig[8] but also with reference to other cities, for example Hamburg or Würzburg. To strengthen my argumentation, I use a sociological approach. As a methodological basis for the analysis of the narratives,[9] images, films, and artifacts I apply the documentary method of Ralf Bohnsack.[10]

In the first part of this article, I briefly discuss the contextual and methodological basis of my reflections to unfold thematic considerations to deportations as the research object. Afterwards, I present the course of the deportations and thus the events surrounding them as a social situation. On this basis, I analyze the moving and still images as well as perceived impressions. Finally, in a summary, the view will be directed to the individuals in the deportation event and the chances, potentials, and difficulties of visual material on the deportations will be concretized.

---

gung 1933–1945", in idem. and Dieter Pohl (eds.): *Der Holocaust als offenes Geheimnis: Die Deutschen, die NS-Führung und die Alliierten*, Munich: Beck, 2006, 20–79, here 16.

8 In this article, I will not describe the specific deportation events of the different cities. This has already been done by other studies. I will only go into the specifics of the urban deportations to the extent that it supports my argument.

9 All interviews of the Werkstatt der Erinnerung at the Forschungsstelle für Zeitgeschichte in Hamburg were anonymized by the Forschungsstelle.

10 The method examines not only what is represented but above all how the documents, images and films are created and produced and how they are used in everyday life. The focus is on the reconstruction and interpretation of immanent (imaginable) meaning of narrative, interaction and discourse processes, but also of visual experience. The aim of this method is to reconstruct the action-guiding experiential knowledge in the everyday lives of individuals and groups in order to identify the interplay of social structures and individual or collective actions. See Ralf Bohnsack, *Rekonstruktive Sozialforschung: Einführung in qualitative Methoden*. Opladen: Budrich, 2010; Ralf Bohnsack, *Qualitative Bild- und Videointerpretation: Die dokumentarische Methode*. Opladen: Budrich, 2011.

Deportations: Contextualization and Methodological Considerations

For the sociological question of the concrete spatial experiences of the deportations, the respective destination of the deportations is subordinated. Therefore, it seems appropriate to examine not only the deportations from the German Reich to the ghettos and killing sites in German occupied Central and Eastern Europe[11] between 1941 and 1945 (and locally limited deportations in 1940), but also to analyze the enforced expulsions from Jews from their homes and the incarceration in camps within Germany, which preceded the actual deportation, such as the expulsion to Hellerberg. Of course, the fundamental differences between deportations to 'the East' and expulsions within Germany should not be concealed here. For example, people were allowed to take furniture with them during the latter, as the film material on the forced relocation to the Dresden Hellerberg camp shows. Contrary, in case of the deportations to 'the East' in general only a suitcase with a strictly limited kg quantity was allowed. There were also differences in the extent to which people were informed about the destinations; so the Dresden Jews in the film knew exactly where they would be taken. As different as the various contexts are, I will concentrate in this article on the concrete spatial experiences and thus I will focus on the publicly visible eviction from the deportees out of their last inhabited apartment and the reactions of those witnessing it.

Furthermore, this article focuses on the deportations from the so-called *Judenhäuser* ('Jews houses'). The 'Law on Tenancies with Jews' of April 30, 1939, created the basis for dissolving tenancies with Jewish tenants without notice. As a result, certain buildings in most large cities were declared '*Judenhäuser*'. In these tenant buildings families and individuals, who were often strangers to each other, had to share an apartment. An exact number of the Jewish population that had to live in such houses is difficult to reconstruct and thus remains uncertain. Nevertheless, the numbers for certain cities can be reconstructed. For example, Beate Meyer estimates that in mid-1942 about half of the Jews still living in Hamburg had to live in '*Judenhäuser*'.[12] This concentration fundamentally

---

11 See Wolf Gruner, "Von der Kollektivausweisung zur Deportation der Juden aus Deutschland (1938–1945): Neue Perspektiven und Dokumente", in *Die Deportation der Juden aus Deutschland: Pläne – Praxis – Reaktionen 1938–1945*, edited by Birthe Kundrus, and Beate Meyer, 21–62. Göttingen: Wallstein, 2004.
12 See Beate Meyer, "Judenhäuser", in *Das jüdische Hamburg: Ein historisches Nachschlagewerk*, edited by Kirsten Heinsohn, 130–132. Göttingen: Wallstein, 2006, 132.

changed the urban configuration because, in many cities, these houses were centered in certain residential quarters. Thus, places of "Jewish presence"[13] were created.

This approach allows two extensions of the research focus. Deportations are not defined by their destination, but rather by characteristic events in those places where they began. In addition, the focus on the '*Judenhäuser*' brings deportation situations into view, in which a larger number of people were fetched at the same time and at the same place. These deportations were necessarily more visible in the cityscape and attracted more attention, since a large number of people, accompanied by local police and Gestapo, had to vacate their apartments and houses.

The development of a sociological perspective on the roundups in Nazi Germany up to 1941 evokes a specific methodological approach that combines the various sources, that means both visual and narrative descriptions of what was perceived. Thereby, I argue for a close connection of visual material with these descriptions.

In this contribution, three types of sources and their particular approaches are considered: (1) moving and still images as social practice, (2) narrative passages by the deportees and the remaining Jews as descriptions of the sensually perceived and (3) artefacts as materialized human expression. I will analyze visual material of the deportations, such as film documents and photographs. For this purpose, I will primarily examine the film material which shows how the Jews from the '*Judenhäuser*' in the Güntzstraße 24 and Sporergasse 2 in Dresden were brought into the camp at Hellerberg between November 23 and 24, 1942, but also photographs from the Yad Vashem archive, for example, showing the deportation of the Würzburg Jews.[14] Based on written testimonies, diaries or interviews I reconstruct statements about the perception of the visual impressions of the deportation, specifically the collection from domicile. The artifacts that were produced specifically around the situation of the deportations constitute a third group of material to be analyzed. These documents, lists, labeled suitcases and sealed doors are analyzed in their impact on the participants. Here, both

---

[13] "Holocaust ghettoization involved both the removal of 'Jews' from large swathes of the city (and thus the creation of spaces of 'Jewish absence') and their relocation to one particular place – the ghetto (and thus the creation of spaces of 'Jewish presence')." Tim Cole, "Ghettoization", in *The Historiography of the Holocaust*, edited by Dan Stone, 65–87. Basingstoke: Palgrave Macmillan, 2004, 80.
[14] For the deportations from Würzburg and other Franconian cities see the contribution by Alfred Eckert in this volume.

the described artifacts in the diaries, memories or interviews and the depicted objects in pictures and in the film come into focus.

Previous research on Holocaust images and films in general and the deportations in particular has unfolded two analytical problems. First of all, photographs of the Holocaust have often been treated rather superficially in scholarly literature as they were primarily used as illustrations, thus they have hardly been the focus of historical analysis in the past.[15] Only recently this has changed. A second aspect that anyone researching visual material must deal with is that, as with all sources, the specific history of creation must be reflected. Photographs and films do not show much about the life of the victims but more about the view of the perpetrators. While the diaries and interviews focus on the perspective of the Jewish bystanders during the deportations, the film and visual material clearly show the perpetrator's perspective. Nevertheless, I argue in this article that also objectified statements about the content of pictures presumably taken by perpetrators are possible, which neither refer purely to the intention of the author nor to the – impossible to ascertain – perceptions of the portrayed.

The Perceived Impressions and Specific Visual Images Around Deportations

Raul Hilberg stated in *The Destruction of the European Jews:* "Each city has its own deportation history, and each history reveals a great deal about the mechanics of the deportations and the psychological environment in which they took place".[16] It is not the aim of this article to unify the different deportation histories. Rather, I intend to highlight similarities, without disguising the differences.[17]

---

15 Cf. Norbert Haase, Stefi Jersch-Wenzel and Hermann Simon: "Die Erinnerung hat ein Gesicht: Anmerkungen zu einem Filmdokument", in idem. (eds.): *Die Erinnerung hat ein Gesicht: Fotografien und Dokumente zur nationalsozialistischen Judenverfolgung in Dresden 1933–1945*, Leipzig: Kiepenheuer, 1998, 9–18, here 11. See also the contribution by Christoph Kreutzmüller in this volume.
16 Raul Hilberg: *The Destruction of the European Jews*, volume 2, Chicago: Quadrangle Books, 1961, 320.
17 For a general view see Dieter Pohl: "Die Deportation von Juden aus dem Deutschen Reich 1941–1943", in Albrecht Liess (ed.): *Wege in die Vernichtung: Die Deportation der Juden aus Mainfranken 1941–1943*, Munich: Generaldirektion der Staatlichen Archive Bayerns, 2003, 57–72; Birthe Kundrus and Beate Meyer (eds.): *Die Deportation der Juden aus Deutschland: Pläne – Praxis – Reaktionen 1938–1945*, Göttingen: Wallstein, 2004, 20; Andrea Löw: "Die frühen Deportati-

The deportations differed, for example, in their organization – i.e., with the actors and institutions involved –, their concrete processes, and the destinations.

The actual deportations were preceded by rumors of forced relocation. The deportation included these rumors, the roundups and raids itself, the transfer to assembly camps and the deportation to the various ghettos, concentration and extermination camps. In addition, the events after the deportation were also part of the actual process. The deportation from a situationist perspective – i.e. the specific processes within the social situation of the deportation with the present and absent participants, the spatial setting and the atmosphere –, appeared as followed.

The first rumors about possible deportations represent an initial moment of the deportation situation. The news that other Jewish residents in other cities or neighborhoods would be deported spread,[18] but they knew neither where they would be deported to nor what was waiting for them at the destination.[19] These rumors become particularly clear in the diary of Victor Klemperer.[20] In general, the transports were not organized city by city or district by district, but rather simultaneously throughout the Reich and over a longer period of

---

onen aus dem Reichsgebiet von Herbst 1939 bis Frühjahr 1941", in *"Wer bleibt, opfert seine Jahre, vielleicht sein Leben". Deutsche Juden 1938–1941*, Göttingen: Wallstein, 2010, 59–76; Roland Maier: "Die Verfolgung und Deportation der jüdischen Bevölkerung", in Ingrid Bauz, Sigrid Brüggemann and Roland Maier (eds.): *Die Geheime Staatspolizei in Württemberg und Hohenzollern*, Stuttgart: Schmetterling-Verlag, 2013, 259–304. For a rather regional view on Hamburg, see Frank Bajohr (ed.): *Die Deportation der Hamburger Juden: 1941–1945*, Hamburg: Forschungsstelle für Zeitgeschichte/Institut für die Geschichte der Deutschen Juden, 2002²; idem.: "Die Deportation der Juden: Initiativen und Reaktionen aus Hamburg", in Beate Meyer (ed.): *Die Verfolgung und Ermordung der Hamburger Juden 1933–1945: Geschichte, Zeugnis, Erinnerung*, Hamburg: Landeszentrale für politische Bildung, 2006, 33–41; Beate Meyer: "Die Deportation der Hamburger Juden 1941–1945", in idem., Verfolgung und Ermordung der Hamburger Juden, 42–78; idem.: "'Ihre Evakuierung wird hiermit befohlen'. Die Deportation der Juden aus Hamburg und Schleswig-Holstein 1941–1945", in Rainer Hering (ed.): *Die "Reichskristallnacht" in Schleswig-Holstein: Der Novemberpogrom im historischen Kontext*, Hamburg: Hamburg University Press, 2016, 257–276. For a regional view on Leipzig and Dresden, see Ellen Betram: "Die Deportation aus Leipzig und Dresden am 21. Januar 1942", in Wolfgang Scheffler and Diana Schulle (eds.): *Buch der Erinnerung. Die ins Baltikum deportierten deutschen, österreichischen und tschechoslowakischen Juden*, Munich: Saur, 2003, 799–831.

18 Cf. interview by Mery Sagal, interview #45075, Visual History Archive, USC Shoah Foundation.

19 Cf. Else R. Behrend-Rosenfeld and Siegfried Rosenfeld: *Leben in zwei Welten: Tagebücher eines jüdischen Paares in Deutschland und im Exil*, Munich: Volk, 2011, 108.

20 Cf. Victor Klemperer: *I Will Bear Witness: A Diary of the Nazi Years 1933–1941*, New York: Modern Library, 1999, 615. In his diary entry from December 5, 1941, he wrote: "But the 'evacuations' continue, it can hit us any day."

time. In Leipzig and Dresden all residents of certain Jewish houses received deportation orders one after the other. Thus, after each of the nine deportations from Leipzig between 1942 and 1945, the number of '*Judenhäuser*' was reduced.[21] Reports about the deportations found their way to the other Jewish city residents. In general, no news was received from those who had already been deported, and if there were some, it usually was a short letter or postcard saying that everything was fine and that those who had stayed at home should send food and clothing.[22] From what is known about letters from other camps it can be assumed that they were written mostly by order and were also censored. When Else Behrend received the first news about the deportation of the Jews from Stettin and Pommern to Lublin in early 1940, she was shocked how 'primitive' the former neighbors had to live there and that they suffered from frostbites.[23]

And then suddenly the terrible news turned from a rumor affecting others to a fact in one's own life. The own deportation was initiated by the deportation order. In many cases, people had only a few days or even hours to leave their apartments or rooms in the '*Judenhäuser*', as Eva Wollenberg remembered.[24] Controlled by the Gestapo, the former residents left the building, carrying their suitcases in front of passers-by to the trucks or in the direction of the train stations from which they were driven to an unknown place.[25] In some cases people walked to the assembly camps, in other cases they were taken to the points by omnibuses, streetcars or trucks.[26] Henry Musat who was also forced to live in a '*Judenhaus*' and observed a deportation described a scene he wit-

---

[21] For Leipzig, a total of nine deportations can be documented between 1942 and 1945. Cf. Manfred Unger: "Juden in Leipzig: Verfolgung und Selbstbehauptung in archivalischen Quellen 1933–1945", in *Archiv Mitteilungen*, 38/5, 1988, 149–156, here 151; deportation lists, RG-14.035, reel 11 and 14, USHMM Archive, Washington.
[22] Cf. Behrend-Rosenfeld and Rosenfeld, Leben in zwei Welten, 110.
[23] Cf. ibid., 108. The transport went first to Lublin from where the deportees were taken to various smaller towns, mainly to Piaski.
[24] Cf. interview by Eva Wollenberger, interview #19675, Visual History Archive, USC Shoah Foundation.
[25] Cf. "Deportation of Dresden Jews to Hellerberg", 2016.518, RG-60.0199, USHMM Film Archive, Washington. Available at: https://collections.ushmm.org/search/catalog/irn599830. Last accessed: 21.01.2022.
[26] Cf. interview by Richard Marx, interview #15534, Visual History Archive, USC Shoah Foundation; Akim Jah: *Die Deportation der Juden aus Berlin. Die nationalsozialistische Vernichtungspolitik und das Sammellager in der Großen Hamburger Straße*, Berlin: be.bra Wissenschaft, 2013, passim.

nessed in Leipzig in January 1942, in which the deportees walked through the streets to the assembly camp with everything they could carry.[27]

Bystanders watched or insulted those departing. Inge Weinke remembered how bystanders applauded as the bedridden residents of the Warburg-Stift nursing home in Hamburg were escorted to trucks.[28] Regina Rubinstein reported how some children clapped and shouted: 'The Jews go to Palestine!'[29] Most of the bystanders, however, ignored the situation; very few expressed pity or indignation.

The local Gestapo was responsible for making sure that the departure went as planned and inconspicuous as possible. Their last movement in the once familiar city led the deportees to one of the deportation assembly camps.[30] For example, on February 16, 1943, Leipzig Jews were taken to the 32nd elementary school at Yorckstraße 2/4, which had also served as an assembly place during the previous deportations. Here they met former neighbors and friends, who wanted to help them one last time with food or blankets.[31] Regina Rubinstein remembered, for example, how her aunt Marta Höriger helped her family. This aunt brought sandwiches to the assembly camp in Leipzig on the day of the deportation but was immediately sent away by the Gestapo or the police on guard duty under threats.[32]

From the assembly camps, people were brought to the train stations by buses, trucks or on foot and were then deported to the ghettos and camps in passenger or freight trains.[33] Some of the deportations were accompanied by physical and psychological violence, or they rather differed in the degree of brutalization: "The removal of the old people's home to Theresienstadt brutal [sic].

---

[27] Cf. interview by Henry Musat, interview #1889, Visual History Archive, USC Shoah Foundation.

[28] Cf. interview by Inge Weinke, interview #34, Werkstatt der Erinnerung at the Forschungsstelle für Zeitgeschichte in Hamburg (FZH).

[29] Cf. interview by Regina Rubinstein, interview #44414, Visual History Archive, USC Shoah Foundation.

[30] Letter from Ernährungsamt, 17.01.1942, collection: Ernährungsamt, No. 6, p. 121, City Archive Leipzig.

[31] Cf. interview by Rolf Kralovitz, interview #29877, Visual History Archive, USC Shoah Foundation.

[32] Cf. interview by Regina Rubinstein, interview #44414, Visual History Archive, USC Shoah Foundation.

[33] Cf. Gruner, Kollektivausweisung, 21; interview by Renata Adler, interview #12684, Visual History Archive, USC Shoah Foundation; interview by Regina Rubinstein, interview #44414, Visual History Archive, USC Shoah Foundation.

Truck with benches, crowded together, only the tiniest bundle could be taken, cuffs and blows".[34]

As can be seen impressively from Victor Klemperer's diary, those Jews who stayed behind had no illusions about their own fate. He knew that they had been spared only this time. He walked past the sealed rooms of their former roommates and remembered how just days before they had sat together with them in the evenings and talked.[35] The sealings[36] and the signs 'Here resided the Jew/Jewess ...'[37] made him aware of the situation again and again.[38] From now on he waited in the '*Judenhaus*' without illusions that they too would face the same fate as the former roommates and neighbors who had just departed. For some Jews, this was precisely the moment when they went underground.[39]

Basically, the atmosphere surrounding the deportations was characterized by uncertainty, differing degrees of physical and psychological violence, and perceptible exclusion, which was also reflected and spatially objectified in the deportation itself.

Deportation Situation as Depicted in the Film "Deportation of Dresden Jews to Hellerberg"

Even though the pickup of the Dresden Jews was not a deportation to the concentration or extermination camps, the case of the incarceration at Hellerberg camp shows exemplary moments of the exclusion of Jews from a situational perspective. By examining specific sequences of the film, the immanent meaning of narrative, interaction, and discourse processes can be reconstructed and interpreted. The specific deportation situation will be traced in its components through the transition from 'what' to 'how'. In a first step the aim is to work

---

34 Klemperer, I will bear witness 1942–1945, 90 (diary entry from 02.07.1942).
35 Cf. ibid., 132 (diary entry from 25.08.1942).
36 Cf. interview by Eva Wollenberger, interview #19675, Visual History Archive, USC Shoah Foundation.
37 Cf. Klemperer, I will bear witness 1942–1945, 29 (diary entry from 16.03.1942).
38 Cf. interview by Erwin Michalies, interview #568, Werkstatt der Erinnerung at the FZH.
39 Cf. Wolfgang Benz: "Überleben im Untergrund 1943–1945", in idem. (ed.): *Die Juden in Deutschland 1933–1945. Leben unter nationalsozialistischer Herrschaft*, Munich: C.H. Beck, 1993³, 660–701; idem. (ed.): *Überleben im Dritten Reich: Juden im Untergrund und ihre Helfer*, Munich: Beck, 2003.

out which themes and subthemes are presented in the film.⁴⁰ Subsequently, the contents of the film are interpreted.

The film of about 30 minutes shows the deportation of the Dresden Jews from two 'Judenhäuser' to the Hellerberg camp on November 23 and 24, 1942. Each section of the film has a title reflecting the respective deportation situation: *Abholen des Gepäcks* (picking up the luggage), *Entlausung* (delousing), *Ankunft am Hellerberg* (arrival at Hellerberg), *Einige Beispiele jüdischer Ordnung* (some examples of Jewish order). Cameraman was Erich Höhne, born in Dresden in 1912, who worked at Zeiss Ikon in Dresden from 1942 onwards under the direction of Walter Riedel, the head of the film laboratory.⁴¹ The function and the reception of the film is not conclusively clarified; so there is no information about who ordered the production of the film.⁴² The transport from the '*Judenhäuser*' Sporergasse 2 and Güntzstraße 24 comprises a total of 31 scenes and lasts three and a half minutes, so the proportion of these scenes takes up only a tenth of the entire film. All scenes were recorded without sound. In addition, some filmic settings, such as the camera position, were repeated. The film does not allow any assumptions to be made about the chronological sequence of events.

In the first six scenes, there are no people to see. After the title of the first section of the film, 'Picking up the luggage', has been faded in, two images are shown: the street name "Sporer-Gasse" and the house number 2. Then, in the fourth scene, three overflowing garbage cans are shown, with things to be disposed of lying next to them.⁴³ In the seventh to seventeenth scenes, Jewish inhabitants with the 'Yellow Star' on their coats carry suitcases with names, pieces of furniture and household articles to a truck.⁴⁴ Repeatedly, men with the star on their jackets carry belongings out of the house in the Sporergasse and go back into the house. Two men wearing hats and trench coats face each other at the house entrance and watch (or rather guard) this process.

A long shot is usually chosen as the image section, whereat the camera filming inclines from above. Thus, the camera is not at eye level with the people being filmed. In some scenes, the camera follows the movements of the persons,

---

40 Cf. Bohnsack, Qualitative Bild- und Videointerpretation, 56–58.
41 Cf. Haase, Jersch-Wenzel, and Simon, Die Erinnerung hat ein Gesicht, 11–12.
42 Cf. ibid., 12.
43 Cf. "Deportation of Dresden Jews to Hellerberg", 2016.518, United States Holocaust Memorial Museum (USHMM) Photo archive, Washington. Available at: https://collections.ushmm.org/search/catalog/irn599830. Last accessed: 21.01.2022. Timescale: 10.00.15 till 10.00.47.
44 Cf. ibid. Timescale: 10.00.47 till 10.01.54.

which indicates that it is not a consistently fixed still camera.[45] In the following scene, the camera changes the position to a more ground level location.[46] This scene shows only the footpath and the body of a man, but not his face. A 'Yellow Star' is attached to his clothing. He carries suitcases with white-painted names to the truck. In addition, an unknown pedestrian is walking by in the background. In the following scene, the position of the camera is a bit higher up, but at first one can only see the lower half of the people. During this scene, the camera moves upwards so that the upper half of the people is becoming visible.[47] For the first time, a person looks directly into the camera. The next two scenes show close ups of suitcases with names and addresses being taken away from a person that cannot be identified and a piece of fabric on a board with the inscription "Kinderbett für's Lager"[48] (crib for the camp) as well as a rack with wheels.[49] The camera setting is fixed in these scenes. The cameraman then films from inside the house entrance to the outside while men carry belongings into a truck. Conspicuous is a man who stands at the entrance and seems to be observing the procedure. A man with an umbrella passes the house entrance and seems to take no notice of the proceedings (see fig. 4).[50]

The following scenes show the deportation of the residents of the 'Judenhaus' Güntzstraße 24. There are a total of four different camera positions. In the first position, the camera is at ground level diagonally behind the truck at the other side of the street.[51] In these scenes, people carry laced bags or suitcases to a truck. In addition, two other categories of people can be seen here: those who seem to be rather in control of the process and those passing by such as a woman with a small child in her arms.[52]

Similar to the first shot, the camera in the following scene is positioned diagonally behind the truck across the street. However, the scene is shot from a more distant location so that the entrance of the forecourt to Güntzstraße 24 is now visible. During the scene, in which several people carry the belonging to a truck, the camera moves in the direction of the truck. It seems to be very windy so that a man's hat flies off and he and another man run after it.[53]

---

45 Cf. ibid. Timescale: 10.00.47 till 10.01.41.
46 Cf. ibid. Timescale: 10.01.41 till 10.01.54.
47 Cf. ibid. Timescale: 10.01.47 till 10.01.54.
48 Cf. ibid. Timescale: 10.02.05.
49 Cf. ibid. Timescale: 10.01.54 till 10.02.08.
50 Cf. ibid. Timescale: 10.02.08 till 10.02.14.
51 Cf. ibid. Timescale: 10.02.15 till 10.02.22, 10.02.37 till 10.02.56, 10.03.34 till 10.03.39.
52 Cf. ibid. Timescale: 10.02.49 till 10.02.56.
53 Cf. ibid. Timescale: 10.03.19 till 10.03.34.

In a third position, the camera is placed at ground level outside the house and directed towards the entrance of the building. In this shot, the camera films how people with 'Yellow Stars' on their clothes carry packages out of the house and how others enter the house again empty-handed. The peculiarity here is that due to the position of the camera, the people coming out look directly into it.[54]

In the fourth shot, the camera is positioned diagonally behind the truck but films from the sidewalk. Here several people can be seen stowing the belongings carried out of the house in the truck; one person is in the truck.[55]

The mentioned scenes are designed to seemingly capture an 'ordinary' situation. The images are not initially specified by written additions; only later in the film there is a section that is introduced with the cynical sentence 'Some examples of Jewish order'. Nevertheless, the antisemitic character is clear, especially in view of the fact that overflowing garbage cans are shown at the beginning of the film.

The focus of these sequences lies on three groups of actors: First of all those persons who are marked with a 'Yellow Star' on their clothing and who, for the most part, take on the task of carrying the belongings out of the houses. A second group form those who do not wear a 'Yellow Star' but nevertheless stay longer at the depicted places. These persons – most likely members of the Gestapo or block guards – observe the situation. The third group are the passers-by, none of them stopping. With a few exceptions where the filmed persons look into the camera, the cameraman and the persons do not interact directly with each other.

(In)Visibilities of the Deportation Situation

In the following, I direct my analytical focus to three moments in the chronology of time to show how written memoirs, artifacts and non-verbal expressions materialized uncertainties and exclusion in the situation of the deportation. Although these processes are always intentional and directed – after all, they are conditioned by the Nazi policy of persecution and deportation – they also have unintended and contingent consequences. First, I consider the uncertainty inherent before the actual deportation, which also manifested itself visually. Subsequently, I will look at the specific situation of the deportation itself. The social relations between the present actors and the exclusion of the Jews were

---

54 Cf. ibid. Timescale: 10.02.22 till 10.02.37, 10.02.56 till 10.03.10.
55 Cf. ibid. Timescale: 10.03.10 till 10.03.19, 10.03.39 till 10.03.44.

objectified through the averting and pitying gaze of the non-Jewish bystanders. Finally, the spatial consequences of the deportation will be examined.

Before the Deportation: Materialized Change Between Certainties and Uncertainties

The deportations were characterized by constant uncertainty. This was caused by the fact that temporary certainty was often quickly expired by opposing orders. In their memoirs, survivors very often write about the problematic handling of these permanently changing conditions associated with the deportations:

> Lissy Meyerhof unexpectedly included among those to be evacuated. Furniture confiscated for auction. Transport (to Poland or Russia) scheduled for November 27, postponed at the last moment, it is said until January. No one knows any detail, not who will be affected, nor when, nor where to. Every day news from many cities, departure of large transports, postponement, then departures again, sixty-year-olds, without sixty-year-olds – everything seems arbitrary. Munich, Berlin, Hanover, Rhineland [...]. The army needs the trains, the army has released trains [...]. Everyone wavers, waits from day to day. Today an urgent communication from the National Association: Who has war decorations? Will that be of any use against deportations?[56]

Through *bulletins* at the building of the Jewish Community or *personal deportation orders*, the remaining Jews in German cities were informed that they were being 'evacuated' or would have to 'emigrate' ('*abwandern*'). Esra Jurmann, who lived as a child in a '*Judenhaus*' in Dresden, recalls the official wording:

> You are scheduled for evacuation transport on [...] January 20, 1942. You are allowed one piece of luggage per person. You must deposit 150 Reichsmarks for the trip. We again emphatically point out the regulation that strictly forbids the transfer of Jewish property.[57]

Victor Klemperer, who had to live with his wife in a house for Jews and non-Jews in 'mixed marriages', drew attention to a similar aspect in his diary:

> Kätchen gave me the documents to read that are handed out to those listed for transportation. Their property is confiscated, they have to make an inventory on printed forms. These forms go into the most wretched detail: "Ties ... shirts ... pajamas ... blouses ..."[58]

---

56 Klemperer, I Will Bear Witness 1933–1941, 612 (diary entry from 28.11.1941).
57 Interview by Esra Jurmann, interview #36824, Visual History Archive, USC Shoah Foundation. Translation by the author.
58 Klemperer, I Will Bear Witness 1942–1945, 12 (diary entry from 09.02.1942).

However, certainty existed only with regard to the deportation itself taking place – the destination and detailed purpose of the deportation usually remained unclear to the Jews. The accompanying uncertainty was therefore not resolved by the lists and individual deportation orders. Lucille Eichengreen from Hamburg, for example, remembered that the deportation order meant for them that they might be sent to Poland, but could continue their lives there with some degree of normality.[59]

This uncertainty manifested itself visually. Victor Klemperer's description of the "tied-up mattresses, trunks, evacuation luggage" and the "toing and froing of star-wearing helpers"[60] was already cited above. In addition, on November 30, 1941, he wrote in his diary:

> Chaotic conditions in the deportation business; transports leave, are cancelled, leave after all. Those designated drag their suitcases to the station, drag them back, wait – in Hanover the women from an old people's home are sitting on their suitcases.[61]

Of course, Klemperer's description cannot be generalized to all deportations in the German Reich – after all, he describes a specific situation in November 1941. However, it illustrates an important point that can be abstracted. Here, too, uncertainty about chaotic conditions materializes as the people are moving through the streets with their suitcases, heading for ever-changing destinations.

Another visible sign of this was the objectification of chaos because of the uncertainties of the place to which they were being taken. Regarding the luggage and what to take with them, there was a high level of uncertainty among the deportees. Elena Bork remembered that her mother packed canned food,[62] Regina Rubinstein that her mother forbade packing mattresses.[63] Inge Weinke memorized how she helped the elderly in the Warburg-Stift to pack and label their suitcases in the course of their deportation. She sewed a lady's fur coat into a muff so that she could take it with her.[64] Thea Meixner was surprised, for example, that a woman, while packing her suitcase, absolutely wanted to take perfume with her but forgot to do so:

---

59 Cf. interview by Lucille Eichengreen, interview #52330, Visual History Archive, USC Shoah Foundation.
60 Both quotes Klemperer, I Will Bear Witness 1942–1945, 99.
61 Ibid., 614 (diary entry 30.11.1941).
62 Cf. interview by Elena Bork, interview #112, Werkstatt der Erinnerung at the FZH.
63 Cf. interview by Regina Rubinstein, interview #44414, Visual History Archive, USC Shoah Foundation.
64 Cf. interview by Inge Weinke, interview #34, Werkstatt der Erinnerung at the FZH.

Mrs. Möllerich was insanely excited because she no longer knew which clothes to take with her. I can still hear her crying out: "For God's sake, I didn't pack my perfume". In 1943 we received pre-printed cards from the people of Litzmannstadt asking us to send them money. My father did that, but then we heard nothing more.[65]

Another example illustrates the uncertainty associated with the deportation even more concrete. Victor Klemperer wrote in his diary on July 16, 1942:

Seliksohn here yesterday afternoon. He now appears to live in large part from his work as a hairdresser and he goes about it with great eagerness. He did the hair of the whole Henriettenstift before they were transported, this coming Monday afternoon he will deal with all the inhabitants of our house.[66]

Thus, the uncertainty about the destination and purpose of the impending deportation could be seen on the faces of the inhabitants of the 'Judenhäuser'. Besides the haircut, the choice of clothing for the deportation is also illustrative: "And all pull on, one on top of the other, as many clothes, pieces of underwear and socks as they possibly can".[67]

Thea Meixner remembered the deportations from the Israelite Hospital in Schäferkampsallee in Hamburg, which at that time functioned as a 'Judenhaus', that she witnessed as a 26-year-old. She described a pictorial situation that most probably happened on February 23, 1945, when 194 people in so-called mixed marriages were deported: "When a transport was announced, the first thing that was done was to move the beds into the corridor because of the expected suicide cases".[68] She did not describe personal circumstances or the suffering of particular people, rather she recalled the image of the beds being pushed into the corridors as a visible sign for the general desperation of people in the face of the impending deportations. Meixner does not recall the exact function of these beds. Constitutive for the situation before and even during the deportation was thus the permanence of uncertainty.

---

[65] Interview by Thea Meixner, interview #11, Werkstatt der Erinnerung at the FZH. Translation by the author.
[66] Klemperer, I Will Bear Witness 1942–1945, 102 (diary entry from 16.07.1942).
[67] Ibid., 131 (diary entry 23.08.1942).
[68] Interview by Thea Meixner, interview #11, Werkstatt der Erinnerung at the FZH. Translation by the author.

During the Deportation: Exclusionary Gaze – Between Contempt, Aversion and Pity

The non-Jewish population knew about the deportations but mostly tried to *dispute* and *deny* what was happening. This was illustrated in the film material of the deportations from Dresden. The pictures do not allow any guess about why those passing by did not pay attention to the deportation, i.e. showed neither approval nor disapproval.[69] They rather leave room for speculations about how this indifference affected the situation itself and those who were to be deported. Any communication requires a common definition of the situation by every participant. If a certain situation does not cause outrage or revolt, this does not necessarily imply consent, but it does send a certain signal to those involved. "If men define situations as real, they are real in their consequences"[70] according to the Thomas theorem. For the evaluation of the situation, it did not matter whether the bystanders agreed with or were actually disgusted by or opposing the deportation. Thus, the situation was determined by the fact that there was no significant resistance from the non-Jewish population. As long as there were no visible or perceivable protests against the deportations, they could be conducted without major problems. The possibilities for protest or even resistance of the deportees themselves were limited to going underground or fleeing to avoid deportation.

The Jewish Community felt separated from the rest of the population during the Nazi period – and they were indeed spatially and socially disconnected. This perceived status as strangers was reinforced by two different processes that related to the gaze of others during the deportations: On the one hand the refused or ignored gaze and on the other hand the compassionate gaze of others. Two stills, taken from the film material of the deportation from Dresden, show how passersby hurriedly walk by and do not give the scene a glance (see fig. 3[71] and fig. 4[72]). In fig. 4, it is apparent that a man nevertheless attends the scene as an observer. However, this person can be seen several times, which indicates that he is not a

---

[69] Frank Bajohr examined whether the deportations were perceived as casual everyday incidents or as extraordinary events. As a result, he described the aura of the sensational and extraordinary that surrounded the deportations and attracted especially young people. Cf. Bajohr, Vom antijüdischen Konsens zum schlechten Gewissen, 48–49.
[70] William Issac Thomas and Dorothy Swaine Thomas: *The Child in America: Behavior Problems and Programs*, New York: Knopf, 1928, 572.
[71] Cf. Norbert Haase, Stefi Jersch-Wenzel and Hermann Simon: "Momentaufnahmen aus einem Film", in Haase, Jersch-Wenzel, and Simon, Die Erinnerung hat ein Gesicht, 19–86, here 26.
[72] Cf. ibid., 31.

passer-by, but rather a police officer in civilian clothes. During all scenes, this person monitors the events without interacting with the people who carry the belongings to the trucks or even helping them. Passers-by however completely ignored the situation of deportation. The 'we didn't know about it!'[73] rather meant 'we knew, but we didn't want to know about it!'

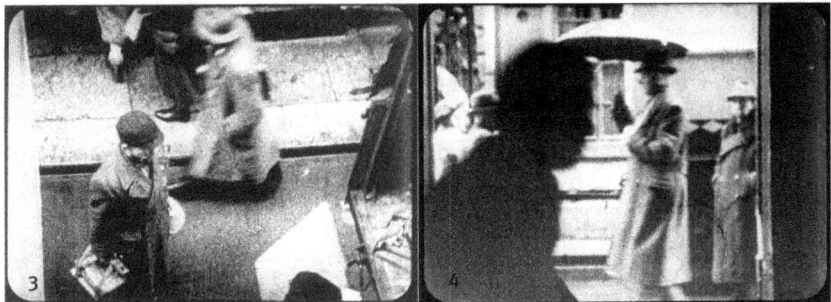

Fig. 3 and **Fig. 4:** Still images from the film *Deportation of Dresden Jews to Hellerberg* (timescale: 10:01:05:24 and 10:02:14:08), StSG.

Another picture, already referred to by historian Konrad Kwiet, shows the image of a young girl who witnessed the deportation of the Jews from Kerpen.[74] There was a second form of reactions by the non-Jewish population that the excluded perceived: contact through the other's expression of solidarity or condolences. However, these forms of interaction also only cemented the status of the excluded in their perception that they were no encounters of equal value. The averted gaze increased the distance and separation of the participants from each other and at the same time objectified this social relationship status.

As a result, the exclusionary look was the visible sign for those involved (i.e. both for the guarding authority and for those deported) that there would be no obstacles for the process of deportation on part of the population. The question of whether the deportations were a public or a non-public process is not the central one, even though in this case it can clearly be described as a public process. The deportations were visible to all; it was not under the cover of night or in secret that the perpetrators had to act. The film and the descriptions show that it

---

[73] Cf. Peter Longerich: *"Davon haben wir nichts gewusst!" Die Deutschen und die Judenverfolgung 1933–1945*, Munich: Siedler, 2006.
[74] Cf. Konrad Kwiet: "Without Neighbors: Daily Living in Judenhäuser", in Francis R. Nicosia (ed): *Jewish Life in Nazi Germany: Dilemmas and Responses*, New York: Berghahn Books, 2010, 117–148, here 130.

was not necessary to deport the Jewish population in secret. It rather shows that even a societal crime, which the deportations undoubtedly were, can be turned into a public event through denial and ignorance. Acceptance and even support, mostly illustrated by the active observation passers-by, were further possible reactions of the non-Jewish population.

In most situations, the deportees apparently avoided eye contact with the passers-by. However, it is also noticeable that the deportees looked directly into the camera at several points in the film.[75] It is clear from both the written narratives and the film footage that the people did not interact with the passers-by. The few gazes of those who carry the belongings from the former houses reveal that they were aware of the recording. These brief interactions between the filmed and the camera – it remains open to what extent the cameraman was seen by the filmed – illustrates a distanced relationship.

After the Deportation: Sealing As a (Failed) Attempt to Make Jews Invisible

The next step after picking-up the Jews was the deprivation of the assets of the deportees. With the deportation of the Jewish population, the social process of deportation was not yet completed. What remained were their belongings like furniture and objects of value in uninhabited rooms, which lingered as traces of their former owners. These remaining belongings made it impossible to immediately eliminate the memory of the Jewish deportees; they were still present through these belongings.

The ongoing deportation was also accompanied by another sign: the names on the suitcases. In a longer shot, they can also be seen in the film (see fig. 5[76] and fig. 6[77]). Klemperer noticed them in his hallway as well:

> Her trunk, with "Jenny Sara Jacoby" in big letters, is already in the hall. That is all that is left to her of the grand villa. Beside it is another suitcase: "Rosa Sara Eger." She is the old mother of [Robert] Eger, who is married to an Aryan; they own the big clothing store.[78]

---

75 Cf. "Deportation of Dresden Jews to Hellerberg", 2016.518, United States Holocaust Memorial Museum (USHMM) Photo archive, Washington. Available at: https://collections.ushmm.org/search/catalog/irn599830. Last accessed: 21.01.2022. Timescale: 10:01:53 and 10:03:08.
76 Cf. Haase, Jersch-Wenzel, and Simon, Momentaufnahmen aus einem Film, 28.
77 Cf. ibid., 29.
78 Klemperer, I Will Bear Witness 1942–1945, 137 (diary entry from 04.09.1942).

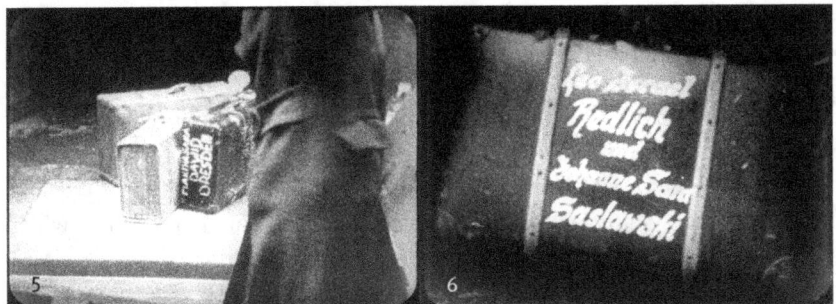

Fig. 5 and **Fig. 6:** Still images from the film *Deportation of Dresden Jews to Hellerberg* (timescale: 10:01:42:13 and 10:01:55:07), StSG.

If a resident or an entire family had to move out of their room because of the deportation order, the Gestapo usually sealed the rooms, in Dresden even with a 'No Entry!'sign.[79] Victor Klemperer described his visit to the *'Judenhaus'* Strehlener Straße in his diary on March 16, 1942:

> So, yesterday afternoon in the Judenhaus in Strehlener Strasse. A notice on every door: "Here resided the Jew Weiler ..." – "Here resided the Jewess ...". These are the people who have been evacuated, whose household goods have been sealed up and are gradually being removed.[80]

Seven months later, he reported in his diary the now *familiar* sight of these signs:

> Today in beautiful, mild autumn weather went to see Neumark a second time because of the hat left me by Neumann, this time successfully: I met Neumark at one o'clock, and we chatted for a whole hour. The beautiful heirloom was hanging in the hall, on the room to the side the familiar seal, more precisely two red fiscal stamps holding a strip of brown paper stretched across door and doorframe and the familiar "here lived the Jew ... and the Jewess ...".[81]

Objectivations of the deportation that had taken place were the sealing of and the signs on the doors. The seals[82] and the signs made the remaining Jews

---

79 Cf. interview by Erwin Michalies, interview #568, Werkstatt der Erinnerung at the FZH.
80 Klemperer, I Will Bear Witness 1942–1945, 29 (diary entry 16.03.1942).
81 Ibid., 151 (diary entry 07.10.1942).
82 Cf. interview by Eva Wollenberger, interview #19675, Visual History Archive, USC Shoah Foundation; interview by Hans-Joachim Recker, interview #15, Werkstatt der Erinnerung at the FZH.

aware of the situation repeatedly.[83] Thus, from now on, they waited without illusions that they too would meet the same fate as the former roommates who had just departed. They walked past the sealed rooms of their former roommates and remembered how they had sat and talked with them every evening just days before.[84] "Before a deportee goes, the Gestapo seals up everything he leaves behind. Everything is forfeit."[85]

However, the sealing also had another important latent meaning, which must be examined in connection with the remaining belongings of the deportees. Paradoxically, the sealing involved two opposing processes: On the one hand the sealing amounted to making the Jews and the former Jewish presence invisible. Therefore, it aimed at preventing all remembrance. Artifacts have inherent, often symbolic meaning. The seal is an artifact of the Gestapo; only they were entitled to enter a room after sealing it and then to seal it again. Sealing limited who could enter the rooms of the former residents. To seal something is the act of closing something in such a way that others can no longer gain entry unnoticed.

On the other hand, the process of sealing itself and the subsequent asset liquidation process were designed to redistribute Jewish property and thus to recall the former Jewish presence. The phrase 'We didn't know about it' is thus once again exposed as false. The exploitation of the property of the deportees as the institutionalized process of asset taking (*Vermögensverwertung*) was an integral part of the deportations. Frank Bajohr negotiates this social practice under the term 'interest activation through persecution of Jews'.[86] Around this social process of exploitation arose special visual impressions. Thereby this was not only an economic process of the robbery but involved also a temporal social reorganization. In Leipzig, for example, there were approximately 14 days between deportation and realization of assets, with the exception of the deportation on January 13, 1944, when 43 days passed between deportation and auction.[87] During these days, the rooms, apartments, and houses of the deportees were usually sealed. Sealing has so far been negotiated in scholarly discourse more as a proc-

---

83 Cf. interview by Erwin Michalies, interview #568, Werkstatt der Erinnerung at the FZH.
84 In his diary, Victor Klemperer wrote on 25 August 1942: "The sealed ground floor, the solitude in the house – we were never especially intimate with Elsa Kreidl – the ending of our evening visits downstairs: la maison juive morte." (Klemperer, I Will Bear Witness 1942–1945, 132).
85 Ibid., 9 (diary entry from 21.01.1942).
86 Cf. Bajohr, Vom antijüdischen Konsens zum schlechten Gewissen, 30–34.
87 Cf. Thomas Ahbe: "Das Versteigerungshaus Hans Klemm und die Ausplünderung der Leipziger Juden im 'Dritten Reich'. Opfer – Täter – Nutznießer", in Susanne Schötz (ed.): *Leipzigs Wirtschaft in Vergangenheit und Gegenwart: Akteure, Handlungsspielräume, Wirkungen 1400–2011*, Leipzig: Leipziger Universitätsverlag, 2012, 305–325, here 311.

ess of 'Aryanization' and economic plunder of the Jews than of a process that reveals a social order of exclusion.[88]

Concluding Remarks

This analysis of the visually perceived during the deportations can contribute to answering the question how the Jews who stayed behind and the non-Jewish population experienced the deportations. The analysis of the deportations has shown that processes of exclusion, antisemitism and insecurity materialized in it.

The deportations were recognizable as deportations in many ways. It was not an 'ordinary' procession, rather the deportees were aware that they were going to an unknown place where their situation would probably worsen. The deportations were accompanied by uncertainty and insecurity for the Jews who stayed behind as well. Both contemporary diaries and oral history interviews as well as deportation notices and other deportation artifacts were examined in this article. Spatial visibilities of the deportation that had taken place were also the sealing of apartments or rooms, accumulations of suitcases, or signs on doors ('Here lived the Jew ...'). They all illustrate the inherent uncertainty of the deportation situation, but also the exclusion and the attempt by the Nazis to banish the deported Jews from memory. These moments can be reconstructed by analyzing the visual material or the situational perceptions of the participants reflected in diaries or oral history interviews. Subsequently, insights into spatial reassignments and regionalization can be made.

But even for the surrounding non-Jewish population the deportations were recognizable as deportations. Accordingly, the attempts to normalize this situation or to integrate this deportation into everyday life required active efforts by those involved. The situation of the deportation in itself contains a fundamental antisemitic attitude, which becomes apparent through the various ways in which the individual actors distance themselves from the situation, for example through the various forms of gaze. The people who were to be deported were not strangers like forced laborers. They were former friends, colleagues, and neighbors. Distancing oneself from people who were once known to one because of their 'Jewish' status required an active distancing.

---

88 In Leipzig, the auctions and sealings were mainly organized by the Chief Financial Office Leipzig (Oberfinanzpräsidium Leipzig). Ahbe, Versteigerungshaus Hans Klemm, 311; Christiane Kuller: *Finanzverwaltung und Judenverfolgung: Die Entziehung jüdischen Vermögens in Bayern während der NS-Zeit*, Munich: C.H. Beck, 2008.

In this article, I focused more specifically on the space and the visual aspects of the deportations by examining narrative descriptions, visual material, and artifacts. Images, photographs, and films involve also specific risks, because they pursue an inherent political purpose, can manipulate and burn themselves deeply into the social (national) memory. Therefore, more intensive research is needed on the role and intent of film and visual material surrounding the various types and aspects of deportations.

**Racial Registrations, Forced Housing, and Local
Deportation Dynamics**

Verena Meier
The 'Prevention Department' within the Criminal Police

An Example of Learning Administrations and the Core of Organizing Transports of Sinti and Roma to Concentration Camps

Abstract: The criminal police transported Sinti and Roma to concentration camps based on a division of labor and relying on older and well-established infrastructures for prisoner transports, in which concentration camps and special trains (*Sonderzüge*) were integrated. Comparing the transports organized by the criminal police Magdeburg in the course of the 'work-shy Reich' action (*Aktion 'Arbeitsscheu Reich'*) in June 1938 and the deportation to Auschwitz-Birkenau in March 1943, this micro-historical analysis highlights the structures within the apparatus of the criminal police. It is further argued that with the criminal police's option to incarcerate people in concentration camps on the basis of 'police preventive detention', special 'prevention departments' (*'Vorbeugungsreferate'*) for this task were created on all levels of the police to which departments as well as case officers for 'gypsy questions' (*Dienststellen für 'Zigeunerfragen'* and *Sachbearbeiter für 'Zigeunerfragen'*) were attached.

Introduction

The genocide of Sinti and Roma was a state-organized crime by the Nazis that was implemented in a division of labor.[1] The core of the network of perpetrator collectives[2] was the scientific-police complex[3] consisting of the criminal police and the *Rassenhygienische und bevölkerungsbiologische Forschungsstelle* (Racial

---

[1] Herbert Jäger: "Arbeitsteilige Täterschaft. Kriminologische Perspektiven auf den Holocaust", in Hanno Loewy (ed.): *Holocaust: Die Grenzen des Verstehens. Eine Debatte über die Besetzung der Geschichte*, Hamburg: Rowohlt, 1992, 160–165; idem.: *Verbrechen unter totalitärer Herrschaft. Studien zur nationalsozialistischen Gewaltkriminalität*, Hamburg: Suhrkamp, 1966.
[2] Frank Bajohr: "Neuere Täterforschung", in *Docupedia-Zeitgeschichte. Begriffe, Methoden und Debatten der zeithistorischen Forschung*. Available at: http://docupedia.de/zg/bajohr_neuere_taeterforschung_v1_de_2013. Last accessed: 31.01.2022.
[3] Michael Zimmermann: *Rassenutopie und Genozid. Die nationalsozialistische "Lösung der Zigeunerfrage"*, Hamburg: Christians, 1996.

Hygiene and Population Biology Research Center, RHF). This chapter sheds light on the actions of the perpetrators within the criminal police, who were responsible for transfers of Sinti and Roma to concentration camps. A special focus is put on the Kriminalpolizeistelle Magdeburg[4] and the transports of Sinti and Roma from the Magdeburg area to concentration and extermination camps in 1938 and 1943.[5] The organization of the transports from Magdeburg in the course of the 'work-shy Reich' action (*Aktion 'Arbeitsscheu Reich'*) to the concentration camps of Buchenwald and Sachsenhausen in June 1938 as well as the deportation to the 'gypsy family camp' in the Auschwitz-Birkenau extermination camp in March 1943 are diachronically analyzed in this chapter both from the perspective of institutional and regional history.

Analyzing two temporally and structurally different transfers of Sinti and Roma to concentration camps makes the main responsibilities within the 'prevention department' (*'Vorbeugungsreferat'*) of the criminal police evident. Furthermore, this essay argues that this specific department in fact emerged after 1938 due to the increasing number of transfers the criminal police organized to concentration camps. Its evolution as a specialized task force thus was highly dependent on experience gained throughout the years. Its role in the context of the deportations will not only be analyzed on the vertical level from the highest criminal police department within the Reichskriminalpolizeiamt (RKPA, see fig. 1[6]) in the Reichssicherheitshauptamt (Reich Main Security Office, RSHA), via the intermediate Kriminalpolizeileitstellen to the subordinate Kriminalpoli-

---

[4] The superordinate criminal police office in this region was the Kriminalpolizeileitstelle Halle, which was in charge of the Kriminalpolizeistellen Halle, Magdeburg, Erfurt, Dessau, and Weimar. See region map of the *Reichskriminalpolizei* with the regions of the *Kriminalpolizeileitstellen* and the subordinate *Kriminalpolizeistellen*, R 58/9711, n.p., Bundesarchiv (BArch). According to IV (4) of the circular decree for the structural reorganization of the criminal police in the Reich from 20 September 1936 a Kriminalpolizeileitstelle was at the same time the Kriminalpolizeistelle for that respective city. See reorganization of the state's criminal police, circular decree of the Reich Minister of the Interior, Pol. S. – V 1–272/36-, 20.09.1936, R 58/241, sheets 71–76, here 74, BArch. In this essay, the English term 'criminal police' is used when generally referring to this institution. The German term Kriminalpolizeistelle Magdeburg is mainly used when the rank of the Kriminalpolizeistelle in Magdeburg is relevant to the implementation of measures as well as in distinction to the responsibilities of the superordinate Kriminalpolizeileitstelle.

[5] This focus is due to the author's dissertation project *Kriminalpolizei und Völkermord. Die nationalsozialistische Verfolgung von Sinti und Roma in Magdeburg und die Aufarbeitung dessen unter den Alliierten sowie in der DDR*.

[6] Chart created by the author based on an organizational chart of the Kriminalpolizeistelle Magdeburg, as of January 1, 1945, K 14, no. 299, n.p., Landesarchiv Sachsen-Anhalt (LASA); Arthur Nebe: "Organisation und Meldedienst der Reichskriminalpolizei", in *Schriftenreihe des Reichskriminalpolizeiamtes Berlin*, 1, 1939, 21–22.

zeistellen. It will also be examined on the horizontal level within the Kriminalpolizeistelle Magdeburg and within relation to other departments such as the identification department (*Erkennungsdienst*) and the reporting department (*Meldedienst*), as well as the female criminal police (*Weibliche Kriminalpolizei*) and the case officers for 'gypsy questions' (*Sachbearbeiter für 'Zigeunerfragen'*) (see fig. 2).

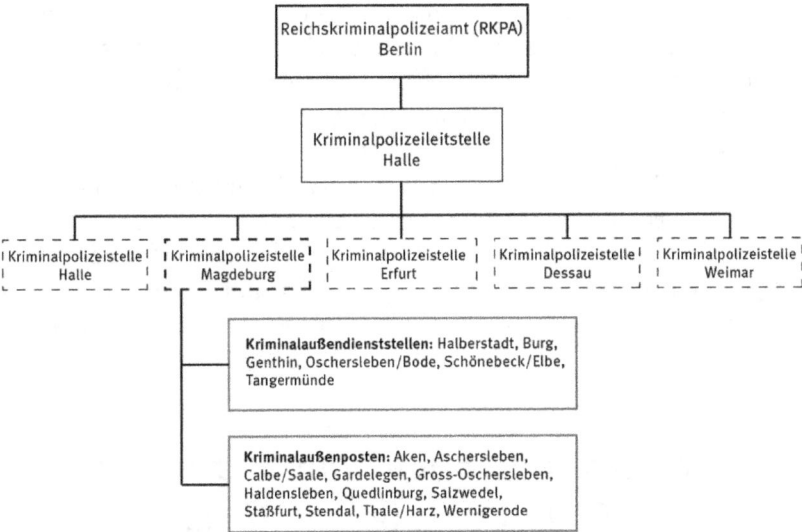

Fig. 1: Organization of the criminal police on the vertical level from the RKPA to the Kriminalpolizeistelle Magdeburg.

In existing studies on the persecution of Sinti and Roma, generally, no differentiation is made between the various departments of the criminal police. Where differentiations are discussed within the police apparatus, they primarily concern demarcations of the Kripo from the Gestapo and the uniformed Schutzpolizei. Analyses of the internal structures of the criminal police therefore represent a desideratum in the still young research on the Nazi persecution of Sinti and Roma, Yenish, or others who fell under the stigmatizing term 'gypsy' (*'Zigeuner'*). By including the female criminal police, the current chapter also makes an important contribution to hitherto scarcely existent gender-historically differentiated research on the persecution of Sinti and Roma. The responsibility of female perpetrators in the genocide has so far been addressed primarily in relation to female employees of the RHF and the Youth and Welfare Offices.[7]

In the following, the mass arrests and transports will be historically classified and the question will be asked to what extent earlier experiences from the prisoner transport system of the police and judiciary as well as the police and court prisons played a role in the implementation of these transports. By comparing both transfers with regard to a) regulations and implementations in Magdeburg, b) the role of the police prison and provisional assembly spaces, as well as transports with the Reichsbahn, and c) selection criteria, this essay argues that there was a crucial difference between collective transports and deportations into concentration and extermination camps in the course of mass arrests such as 1938 and 1943.

In this chapter, the term 'transport' is used to describe the transfers of people by the criminal police to SS-run concentration and extermination camps in general. The term 'deportation' on the other hand refers to the systematic and forced mass transportation to and incarceration of persecuted Sinti and Roma in camps and ghettos in occupied Central and Eastern Europe with the ultimate death of the deportees.

'Police Preventive Detention' and 'Prevention Departments' within the Criminal Police

The legal basis for the criminal police's admissions to concentration camps was the 'police preventive detention' (*'polizeiliche Vorbeugungshaft'*). Similar to the Gestapo's 'protective custody' (*'Schutzhaft'*), it was a detention for an indefinite period of time without prior judicial proceedings, without judgment and without legal protection of the person to be detained.[8] This form of incarceration was first used in Prussia on the basis of a secret decree issued by the Prussian Ministry of the Interior on November 13, 1933, for the 'application of police preventive deten-

---

[7] Karola Fings and Frank Sparing: "Vertuscht, verleugnet, versteckt. Akten zur NS-Verfolgung von Sinti und Roma", in Christoph Dieckmann: *Besatzung und Bündnis. Deutsche Herrschaftsstrategien in Ost- und Südosteuropa*, Berlin: Verlag der Buchläden, 1995, 181–201, here 187; Josef Henke: "Quellenschicksale und Bewertungsfragen. Archivische Probleme bei der Überlieferungsbildung zur Verfolgung der Sinti und Roma im Dritten Reich", in *Vierteljahrshefte für Zeitgeschichte*, 1, 1993, 61–77.

[8] Karl-Leo Terhorst: "*Polizeiliche Überwachung und polizeiliche Vorbeugungshaft im Dritten Reich. Ein Beitrag zur Rechtsgeschichte vorbeugender Verbrechensbekämpfung*", Heidelberg: C. F. Müller Juristischer Verlag, 1985, 4–7.

tion against professional criminals'. Between 1933 and 1937, a development phase followed with different mechanisms for implementing police preventive detention in the different Länder of the Reich. The 'Basic Decree on Preventive Crime Control by the Police' issued by the Reich Ministry of the Interior on December 14, 1937, established a uniform Reich-wide regulation for 'police preventive detention' as well as 'police planned surveillance' and extended it to other groups of persons such as those designated as 'asocials'.[9] With this decree, the criminal police was given the legal basis for more 'freedom of action' and thus increasingly took over the functions of the judiciary.[10]

The police's 'prevention mandate' was significantly expanded under the Nazi regime. This was also reflected in the new self-image of the police apparatus. The deputy chairman for police law in the Academy for German Law, Reinhard Höhn, wrote in 1937 on the old and new conception of police law:

> Thus, the criminal police had changed from a police force that, according to liberal principles, was oriented towards defense against individual cases to a police force that proceeded from the protection of the Volksgemeinschaft and that could organize this protection of the community in a planned manner.[11]

In the first volume of the series of publications of the *RKPA* in 1939, Arthur Nebe, head of the criminal police, also clarified the new field of activity of the criminal police, emphasizing the importance of 'police preventive detention':

> Crime investigation and crime prevention are the fields of work in which the criminal police will be active in the new Reich. […] [In addition to solving crimes], it is also to act preventively and in a forefending way according to dutiful discretion in the sense of the idea of averting harm to the general public.[12]

To this end, the "police preventive detention" and the "planned surveillance of habitual and sex offenders, and of all antisocial elements in general"[13] served this purpose. The investigation of the causes of crime as well as the genesis of criminality was to be the starting point of the 'preventive work'. By this, Nebe understood above all hereditary biology and demanded that the criminal police

---

9 Wolfgang Ayaß: *"Asoziale" im Nationalsozialismus*, Stuttgart: Klett-Cotta, 1995.
10 Terhorst, Polizeiliche Überwachung, 4–7, 56–59.
11 Reinhard Höhn: "Altes und neues Polizeirecht", in Hans Frank (ed.): *Grundfragen der deutschen Polizei*, Hamburg: Hanseatische Verlagsanstalt, 1937, 21–34, here 31. Translation by the author.
12 Nebe, Organisation, 21–22. Translation by the author.
13 Both quotes ibid., 22. Translation by the author.

should be placed "more and more in the service of race and hereditary research".[14]

For the implementation of this new mission, special task forces were created within the criminal police departments between 1938 and 1940. Thus 'prevention' was not just a concept but structurally embedded in the criminal police apparatus. Their fields of focus were the two main measures of 'prevention': the 'police preventive detention' and 'police planned surveillance'. These measures were directed against all people who were classified as 'professional criminals' ('*Berufsverbrecher*') or 'habitual criminals' ('*Gewohnheitsverbrecher*') as well as Sinti and Roma and so-called asocials. A 'prevention department' had existed on the level of the RKPA since 1938, then called S-KR.3. Since 1939/1940 a specialized 'prevention' group abbreviated as 'VB' dealt with this task. This group was reorganized in March 1941 and now operated as V A 2 under the section 'criminal politics and prevention'.[15] This reorganization of the structures of the criminal police apparatus also becomes evident in testimonies of former criminal police officers. They demonstrate that this department was created at the RKPA in the course of the mass arrests and transports during the 'work-shy Reich' action.[16]

Until 1940, on the regional and local level, most Kriminalpolizei(leit)stellen did not have a distinctive 'prevention commissariat', instead the criminal police inspectorates were in charge of ordering 'police preventive detention' and 'police planned surveillance'. In the daily work routine, criminal police officials of the commissariats for the investigation and persecution of specific crimes started an individual case by collecting relevant documents and creating a 'criminal resume'. They then reported the case to the director of the police inspectorate for a decision, e.g., whether someone should be taken into custody. The request for a detention arrangement was throughout all its years of operation signed by the head of the respective Kriminalpolizei(leit)stelle. The final decision of the individual case, however, would be taken in the RKPA as they needed to confirm the order. The implementation of the decision was then conducted by the reporting commissariats and their case officials in the Kriminalpolizeistellen.[17] Thus, with their request for a detention arrangement to the RKPA, the local criminal

---

14 Ibid., 21. Translation by the author.
15 Zimmermann, Rassenutopie, 114.
16 Interrogation of Ferdinand Hardegen, former criminal police officer of the RKPA, 28.03.1966, B 057–01, no. 449, sheet 156, Landesarchiv Berlin (LAB).
17 Interrogations of Hermann Keil, 26.01.1966, Karl Lorenz, 27.01.1966, and Johannes Pfaar, 01.02.1966, B 057–01, no. 449, sheets 63, 65–66, and 83, LAB.

police authorities played a decisive role in the selection of people to be transferred to a concentration camp on the basis of 'police preventive detention'.

This subject matter was in later years appointed to specific 'prevention commissariats' on the level of the Kriminalpolizei(leit)stellen as well as a special 'prevention working group' on the level of the RKPA. Whereas the working group of the RKPA was established parallel to the mass transports to concentration camps in June 1938, the subordinate Kriminalpolizei(leit)stellen subsequently created similar organizational structures. Furthermore, the years between 1938 and 1940 show an important shift in the structural organization of the case officers at the Kriminalpolizeistellen and the departments for 'gypsy questions' at the Kriminalpolizeileitstellen altogether.

This structural reorganization also started on the level of the RKPA. The 'Zigeunerpolizeistelle' Munich (formerly 'Zigeunernachrichtenstelle'), which had collected identification material of Sinti and Roma since 1899 for all regions of Germany and was attached to the identification department at the criminal police in Munich, was moved to the RKPA in November 1938. There it formed a new department called 'Reichszentrale zur Bekämpfung des Zigeunerunwesens'.[18] It was integrated in the aforementioned 'prevention working group' within the RKPA. Thus, the close connection between the 'prevention department' and the 'Reichszentrale zur Bekämpfung des Zigeunerunwesens' was clearly expressed on a structural institutional level.[19]

A mirroring structural reorganization is apparent on the subordinate levels of the Kriminalpolizei(leit)stellen from 1940 (see fig. 2).[20] At the Kriminalpolizeileitstelle Hamburg for instance the commissariat BK 2 focused on 'police preventive detention' and 'police planned surveillance' of whom they considered as 'gypsies', 'asocials' and prostitutes since 1940. Attached were 'criminal genealogical researches' (*Kriminalgenealogische Forschung*') as well as the – since renamed and now called – 'Zigeunerdienststelle'. Before this structural reorganization and the attachment to the new 'prevention commissariat', the then named 'Zigeunernachrichtendienststelle' had been part of the identification department.[21]

---

18 Zimmermann, Rassenutopie, 108–109; Karola Fings and Frank Sparing: *Rassismus – Lager – Völkermord. Die nationalsozialistische Zigeunerverfolgung in Köln*, Cologne: Emons, 2005, 241.
19 Organizational chart of Office V (RKPA) of the RSHA from 1941, R 58/1055, sheet 1, BArch.
20 Organizational chart, C 29 Annex I, segment 3 no. 154, volume 12, n.p., LASA. See also organizational chart of the Kriminalpolizeistelle Magdeburg, as of January 1, 1945, K 14, no. 299, n.p., LASA.
21 Interrogation of Kurt Wedeking, 13.01.1966, B 057–01, no. 449, sheets 119a–119k, LAB.

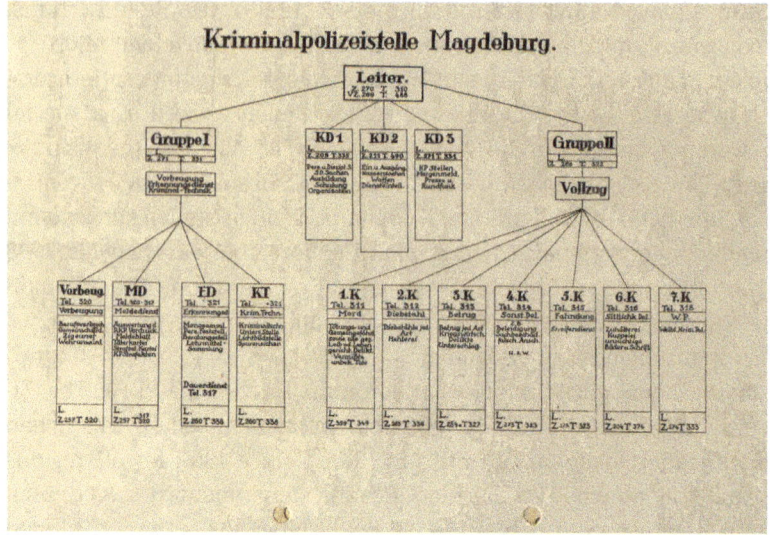

Fig. 2: Organizational chart of the Kriminalpolizeistelle Magdeburg, as of April 1, 1942, C 29 Annex I, segment 3 no. 154, volume 12, n.p., Landesarchiv Sachsen-Anhalt.

The Kriminalpolizeileitstellen, other than the Kriminalpolizeistellen, created at least two 'prevention commissariats', which focused on different groups of persecutees.[22] Six to seven officers worked in the 'prevention commissariats' here, whereas at the level of the Kriminalpolizeistellen three positions can be made out and only one 'prevention commissariat' existed.[23] Thus, a clear organizational shift is apparent on all levels of the criminal police: With the reorganization, the case officers for 'gypsy questions' were linked to the 'prevention commissariats' or 'prevention working group' and the attachment to the identification department or to the reporting department was dissolved. Many of these criminal police officers working as case officers had thus been experts in the field of identification and in sharing personal information of wanted people across borders.[24] Kriminalinspektor Josef Eichberger[25] and Kriminalkommis-

---

22 Interrogation of Kurt Wedeking, 13.01.1966, B 057–01, no. 449, sheets 119a–119k, LAB; interrogation of Hans Espenschied, 22.02.1966, B 057–01, no. 449, sheet 231, LAB. At the Kriminalpolizeileitstelle Hamburg two 'prevention commissariats' existed, whereas the Kriminalpolizeileitstelle Berlin had four.
23 See interrogation of Hans Gassner and his estimation of staff for the Kriminalpolizeileitstelle Stuttgart, 06.04.1966, B 057–01, no. 449, sheet 179, LAB.
24 Interrogation of Karl Lorenz, 27.01.1966, and interrogation of Peter Kenten, 04.03.1966, B 057–01, no. 449, sheets 65–67 and 108, LAB.

sar Wilhelm Supp[26] were criminal police officers of the 'Reichszentrale zur Bekämpfung des Zigeunerunwesens' at the RKPA in Berlin and both had been working for the identification department and for the reporting department before. After the war these perpetrators characterized their work in the 'Reichszentrale' as continuous tasks from the fields of the identification department and the reporting department and thereby downgraded their responsibilities in racial persecution.[27]

However, this structural reorganization also highlights the enforcement of racial-biological paradigms in police work since 1938. Two decrees from 1938 and 1939 were crucial for making racial-biological paradigms the foundations of practical police work and the persecution of Sinti and Roma by the criminal police. With his decree of December 8, 1938, Heinrich Himmler announced that the "gypsy question must be tackled from the essence of the race"[28] and therefore decreed institutional cooperation with the Reich Health Office. With the socalled *Festsetzungserlass* the RSHA ordered on October 17, 1939, the registration of all Sinti and Roma between October 25 and 27, 1939.[29] This registration required the information the identification departments had gathered since the 1920s. In Magdeburg, the case officer for 'gypsy questions' was also mainly responsible for organizing the registration in 1939. He arranged the collected data according to areas and finally forwarded it to the 'Reichszentrale zur Bekämpfung des Zigeunerunwesens' via the 'Dienststellen für Zigeunerfragen' at the Kriminalpolizeileitstelle Halle. At this highest level of authority, the material was then evaluated and 'racial reports' ('*Rassegutachten*') were passed on from the RHF. Thus, alongside the registration, a racial categorization was carried out

---

25 "Schreiben Josef Eichbergers an die Spruchkammer IV München", 22.07.1948, SpK box 344, Staatsarchiv Munich. Eichberger had worked since 1930 for the criminal police in Munich and initially for the identification department. In 1937, he was transferred to the 'Zigeunerpolizeistelle München'.
26 Supp had been case officer of the reporting department (*Kriminalnachrichtendienst*) and in the tracing division (*Fahndungsabteilung*) at the Kriminalpolizeileitstelle Nuremberg-Fürth from 1935 to 1941. The 'Zigeunerdienststelle' was a subordinate institution. He transferred to the RKPA in February 1941 and became its manager. See "Personalakte Supp LKA Bayern", LKA, no. 219, Bayerisches Hauptstaatsarchiv.
27 Interrogation of Wilhelm Supp, October 1963, B Rep. 057–01, 2692, 2713–2714, LAB.
28 Circular Decree, 08.12.1938, in *Ministerialblatt des Reichs- und Preußischen Ministeriums des Innern*, 51, 1938, columns 2105–2106. Translation by the author.
29 Urgent instruction by the RSHA – diary no. RKPA. 149/1939 g, 17.10.1939, concerning 'gypsy registration', C 30 Osterburg A, no. 161, sheets 29–30, LASA.

by the medical staff in this institution of the Reich Health Office.[30] Members of the RHF came to Magdeburg between February 2 and 5, 1939, for an inspection and racial examination of 35 Sinti and eight Roma on the spot.[31]

The learning administration of the criminal police had a crucial impact on the organization of the transfers of Sinti and Roma to concentration and extermination camps in 1938 and 1943, which will be analyzed subsequently with a focus on the Kriminalpolizeistelle Magdeburg.

Instructions for and Implementation of the Incarceration in Magdeburg in 1938

The basic decree issued by Reich Minister of the Interior Wilhelm Frick on 'Preventive Crime Control by the Police' on December 14, 1937, as well as the urgent instruction from Reinhard Heydrich in the Reich Criminal Police Office to the State Criminal Police Offices of June 1, 1938, formed the legal basis for the mass arrests and transports to concentration camps in the course of the 'workshy Reich' action.[32] At least 200 men, who were able to work but were classified as 'asocials' in the view of Nazi ideology, were to be placed in 'police preventive detention' in the region of each Kriminalpolizeileitstelle.[33] Among them mostly people who the responsible police officers classified as 'vagrants', 'beggars', 'gypsies' or 'pimps' were to be arrested. Exempted were those who were in permanent employment. Additionally, all male Jews who fined imprisonment of at least a month were to be incarcerated in this action between June 13 and 18, 1938.

The Kriminalpolizeistelle Magdeburg forwarded this basic decree together with additional orders by the Kriminalpolizeileitstelle Halle to their subordinate

---

30 Karola Fings: "Gutachten zum Schnellbrief des Reichssicherheitshauptamtes – Tgb. Nr. RKPA. 149/1939 -g- – of 17.10.1939 betr. 'Zigeunererfassung' ('Festsetzungserlass')", 2–3. Available at: https://sintiroma.org/images/sinti-roma/zr_2020_karola_fings_gutachten_festsetzungserlass.pdf. Last accessed: 03.06.2021.
31 "Sinte-Zigeuner Liste", no. 1 to 35, and "Türken-Liste III", no. 501 to 508, n.p., R 165/108, BArch.
32 Basic decree on 'Preventive Crime Control by the Police', Pol. S-Kr.3, no. 1682/37–2098, 14.12.1937, n.p., R 187/399, BArch; urgent instruction by the RKPA on 'Preventive Crime Control by the Police', Tgb. Nr. RKPA 60^{01}/295.38, 01.06.1938, n.p., R 187/399, BArch.
33 Urgent instruction by the RKPA on 'Preventive Crime Control by the Police', Tgb. Nr. RKPA 60^{01}/295.38, 01.06.1938, n.p., R 187/399, BArch; implementation order by the *Kriminalpolizeileitstelle* Halle, K 1. K, 02.06.1938, n.p., C 30 Osterburg A, no. 163, LASA.

criminal police departments on June 4.³⁴ These additional orders by the Kriminalpolizei(leit)stellen Magdeburg and Halle further reveal local dynamics. The intermediate department in Halle ordered that the number of registered people in their area was to be increased to 250 in total as exemptions were predictable. For the Kriminalpolizeistelle Magdeburg the superordinate department in Halle calculated, based on the population, 60 'asocials' and Jews to be considered. This number could have been "arbitrarily exceeded but not undershot".³⁵ The number of imprisoned people was to be reported to Halle by June 19, distinguishing between Jews and 'asocials'. The Kriminalpolizeistelle Magdeburg further specified the people affected for their district: predominantly 'gypsies' as stated in the RSHA order as well as all male Jews that had been fined with imprisonment for at least one month in the past. Generally, only people able to work were to be registered and eventually transported.

The transport of a total of 96 persons designated as 'work-shy' from Magdeburg to the concentration camps took place in three waves on June 14, 17 and 20, 1938.³⁶ Contrary to the guidelines of April 1938, the transports were not only heading towards the Buchenwald concentration camp but also to the Sachsenhausen concentration camp.³⁷ The reasons for the change from the order have not yet been identified. The prison record book shows that the Kriminalpolizeistelle Magdeburg began to carry out this action already two days before the date set by Heydrich. On June 11 and 12, 1938, 13 people from Magdeburg, 11 of whom were Jewish, were arrested and taken to the police prison. From there the majority was transported to a concentration camp; two were released again.³⁸ In the early morning hours of June 13, 1938, between 6:30 a.m. and 7:00 a.m., officers of the Kriminalpolizei and Schutzpolizei Magdeburg arrested a total of 29 male Sinti and Roma and two persons designated as 'vagrants' (*'Landstreicher'*) at

---

34 Implementation order by the Kriminalpolizeistelle Magdeburg, L 2538/38, 04.06.1938 and implementation order by the Kriminalpolizeileitstelle Halle, K 1. K, 02.06.1938, both n.p., C 30 Osterburg A, no. 163, LASA.
35 Order *Kriminalpolizeistelle* Magdeburg, L 2538/38, 04.06.1938, C 30 Osterburg A, no. 161, LASA. Translation by the author.
36 The quantitative evaluation here is based primarily on the entries in the prison record book of the Magdeburg police prison. See C 29 Annex III, no. 9, LASA.
37 Guidelines to the basic decree on 'Preventive Crime Control by the Police' by the RKPA, Tgb, Nr. RKPA 60⁰¹25/83, 04.04.1938, in Kameradschaft Verlagsgesellschaft mbH,(ed.): *Kriminalpolizei. Sammlung der für die kriminalpolizeiliche Organisation und Tätigkeit geltenden Bestimmungen und Anordnungen*, Berlin: Kameradschaft Verlagsgesellschaft Gersbach & Co., 1937, section VII.7 to VII.39, here VII. 23.
38 Prison record book, C 29 Annex III, no. 9, list no. 546–552, 556–558, 565–567, LASA.

the municipal detention camp for Sinti and Roma on Holzweg in Magdeburg.[39] Twenty-two of them were transported to a concentration camp, the seven others were released again.[40] The first transport from Magdeburg in the course of the action then took place at 1:30 p.m. on June 14, 1938, to Buchenwald concentration camp with a total of 33 people of the aforementioned arrests.

A second transport left Magdeburg to the concentration camp in Sachsenhausen on June 17, 1938, with a total of 30 persons designated as 'work-shy'. Among them were eight Sinti and Roma who had been arrested in the municipal detention camp in a raid in the late afternoon of June 13.[41] Other arrested people who were designated as 'work-shy' followed till June 16 to the police prison. The second transport to the Sachsenhausen concentration camp left Magdeburg on June 17. The third transport left Magdeburg three days later, on June 20, for the Sachsenhausen concentration camp with 33 people. The majority of those brought to Sachsenhausen with the second and third transports did not live in Magdeburg but came from the areas of the criminal field offices (Kriminalaußendienststellen) in Genthin, Halberstadt, Oschersleben, Schönebeck, and Tangermünde or the field offices (Kriminalaußenposten) in Quedlinburg, Thale, and Wernigerode. Among them were three Sinti aged 38 to 50 from Quedlinburg.[42]

The orders for 'preventive detention', together with the alleged individual reasons for the arrests noted on them, were always signed by the head of the Kriminalpolizeistelle, Kriminaldirektor Friedrich Wilhelm Oberbeck.[43] The medical officer of the Kriminalpolizeistelle Magdeburg, Dr. Haubner, confirmed that those arrested in the Magdeburg area were "fit for camp detention and work".[44] For the criminal field offices and posts, the local medical officers signed

---

39 Prison record book, C 29 Annex III, no. 9, list no. 570–599, LASA.
40 Michael Zimmermann recorded for the Kriminalpolizeistelle Magdeburg that at least 44 male Sinti and Roma and 12 other male Magdeburg residents were among the deportees. See Zimmermann, Rassenutopie, 115.
41 Prison record book, C 29 Annex III, no. 9, list no. 606–610, LASA.
42 Prison record book, C 29 Annex III, no. 9, list no. 661–663, LASA.
43 "Anordnung der polizeilichen Vorbeugungshaft", L 2676/38, 13.06.1938, personal file, C 29 Annex II, no. 135/1, sheet 3, LASA. According to the NSDAP Gau card index (*Gau Kartei*), Oberbeck moved to Magdeburg in 1938 and joined the NSDAP local group there on 22 November 1938. In 1942, he moved to Bochum to head the local Kriminalpolizeistelle. Cf. Gau card index of Friedrich Wilhelm Oberbeck, R 9361– IX Kartei/30951364, BArch; RSHA address list of 01.10.1941, R 58/9804, sheet 14, BArch; "Verzeichnis Dienststellen von 1943–1944", R 58/9706, sheets VI/4 (Bochum) and VI/43 (Magdeburg), BArch.
44 Certification by a medical professional to be 'fit for camp detention and work', L 2677/38, 13.06.1938, personal file, C 29 Annex II, no. 127/1, sheet 8, LASA. Translation by the author.

a corresponding certificate.⁴⁵ On all relevant forms for requesting the incarceration on the basis of 'police preventive detention' the initials of Kriminalkommissar Kläbe can be found; on some forms Kriminalkommissar Klaus confirmed the accuracy of the information with his initials. Both were members of the identification department. Klaus had also been responsible for obtaining the information in advance from the criminal register at the public prosecutor's office in charge. While mainly the lower ranks of the civil service took part in the arrests, higher officials filled out documents for the imposition of 'police preventive detention'.

Instructions for and Implementation of the Deportation from Magdeburg to Auschwitz-Birkenau in 1943

The instructions for the deportations to Auschwitz-Birkenau in 1943 were different and only affected Sinti and Roma. On December 16, 1942, *Reichsführer-SS* and Chief of the German Police Heinrich Himmler ordered that Sinti and Roma were to be sent to the concentration and extermination camp at Auschwitz-Birkenau. The implementing regulations, which can be taken from the RSHA circular of January 29, 1943, ordered that the "preparatory measures (i.e., selection of individual persons, dispatch and filling out of forms, etc.) [...] are to begin immediately so that the action can take place on March 1, 1943".⁴⁶ The main action was to be completed by the end of March 1943.⁴⁷ The main book (*Hauptbuch*) of the so-called gypsy family camp in Auschwitz-Birkenau lists 470 arrivals from Magdeburg, 219 men and boys and 251 women and girls.⁴⁸

Prisoner records attest to the fact that the Kriminalpolizeistelle Magdeburg began implementing the deportation order on February 23.⁴⁹ Kriminalkommissar

---

45 Certificate by the director of the health office in Quedlinburg, 13.06.1938, personal file, C 29 Annex II, no. 98/1, sheet 6, LASA.
46 Transcript of urgent instruction of the RSHA, V A 2 no. 59/43 g, 29.01.1943, sheets 385–391, Ms 410, Institut für Zeitgeschichte (IfZ). Translation by the author.
47 Ibid.
48 Reimar Gilsenbach: *From Tschudemann to Seemann. Two Trials from the History of German Sinti*, Berlin: Edition Parabolis Gogoli, 2000, 161.
49 Files on the implementation of prison arrest and the transfer of Anna Rose from the court prison to the police prison in preparation for the deportation, personal file, C 29 Annex II, no. 224, sheets 31–39, LASA.

Schmidtke of the reporting department and the 'prevention commissariat' started the transfer of two Sinti women from the court prison to the police prison in Magdeburg "for the purpose of imposing preventive measures".[50]

Only a few individuals were affected by these preparatory arrests, whereas the vast majority of the Sinti and Roma deported from Magdeburg were arrested during the so-called Main Action ('*Hauptaktion*') on March 1, 1943, in the municipal detention camp in Magdeburg. Interviews with eyewitnesses reveal that in the early morning hours of that day, around 4 or 5 a.m., the police came to the camp with about 10 to 15 trucks and surrounded it with dogs. From there the victims were taken to the Magdeburg police headquarters where they remained in a large room. Sinti and Roma from subordinate departments of the Magdeburg Kriminalpolizeistelle were also brought there. Afterwards, they were all deported by train from Magdeburg freight station to Auschwitz-Birkenau.[51] Between the arrest on March 1 and the transport to Auschwitz-Birkenau on March 2 only one day passed. The train with the deportees eventually arrived in Auschwitz-Birkenau on March 6.[52]

The reporting department and the 'prevention commissariat' were thus mainly responsible for the organizational implementation of the deportations in Magdeburg. The reporting department maintained a basic collection and evaluation activity and, together with the identification department's collections and the personal files, formed "the center of the police information system".[53] Preparatory measures and later transports were organized by Kriminalkommissar Schmidtke of the reporting department and the 'prevention commissariat' in Magdeburg. Schmidtke's signature is found on most documents relating to the implementation of the deportation measures in 1943, which hints at main responsibilities at the level of higher-ranking police officers. In the prison record books, Schmidtke and another subordinate member of the reporting department, Kriminalinspektor Karl Frenzel, noted under 'departure' that the prisoners, who had been arrested before, were transferred to the Auschwitz-Birkenau concentration camp on March 1, 1943.[54]

---

50 Ibid. Translation by the author.
51 Interview with Günther St., 30.08.1991, no.18, sheet 14, Stiftung niedersächsische Gedenkstätten.
52 Gilsenbach, Tschudemann, 161.
53 Stephan Heinrich: *Innere Sicherheit und neue Informations- und Kommunikationstechnologien. Veränderungen des Politikfeldes zwischen institutionellen Faktoren, Akteursorientierungen und technologischen Entwicklungen*, Berlin: LIT-Verlag, 2007, 145. Translation by the author.
54 Notice on the arrest in the police prison, personal file, C 29 Annex II, no. 568, sheet 1(r), LASA. This information corresponds to the entries in the prison record book: Kriminalsekretär

Furthermore, officers of the identification department were responsible for a registration if this had not been done in the course of the '*Festsetzungserlass*' or if deportees were registered at another criminal police office.[55] Some of the registrations were carried out by the identification department in the course of the mass arrests on March 1 and 2, 1943, when the would be deportees were first brought to the Magdeburg police prison.[56] There they were held for the time of consultation with the Kriminalpolizei(leit)stellen of the previous place of residency until the responsible authority arranged for further action.

The case of two sisters from Halle shall be emphasized at this point as it highlights the work between different criminal police commissariats and within the institution in Magdeburg. The two sisters Maria and Katharina M. were picked up by the station police (*Bahnhofspolizei*) in Magdeburg on February 27, 1943.[57] According to the so-called *Festsetzungserlass* from 1939, they were not allowed to leave their place of residence in Halle. Interrogation records reveal that their mother had sent them to Magdeburg to fetch food and that they had received a letter from their father in a Magdeburg prison. Since the children were minors, the case was taken up by the female criminal police, to be precise by Kriminalkommissarin Paris, head of the female criminal police, and Kriminalsekretärin Ladage. The sisters were picked up in Magdeburg by an officer of the female criminal police from the Kriminalpolizeileitstelle Halle, only to be brought back there via a collective transport.[58] Later, they were deported from Halle to Auschwitz-Birkenau.[59]

In contrast to the transports in the course of the 'work-shy Reich' action, the detention records from 1943 and the accompanying internal correspondence

---

Hanke was noted here as the admitting officer, Kriminalkommissar Schmidtke as the transporting officer, and the identification department was named under 'remarks'. See prison record book, C 29 Annex III, no. 18, list no. 4692–4799, LASA.

[55] Notice on the arrest in the police prison, personal file, C 29 Annex II, no. 568, sheet 1, LASA.

[56] Prison record book, C 29 Annex III, no. 18, list no. 4692–4799, LASA.

[57] In this esay, the names of those natural persons are stated anonymously if the date of death was less than 30 years ago or the date of birth was less than 110 years ago. With these data protection provisions, the author follows the currently valid provisions of the Landesarchiv Sachsen-Anhalt of June 28, 1995. See Land Sachsen-Anhalt: "Archivgesetz Sachsen-Anhalt". Available at: https://www.landesrecht.sachsen-anhalt.de/bsst/document/jlr-ArchGST1995rahmen. Last accessed: 11.01.2022.

[58] Notice on the arrest in the police prison, personal file C 29 Annex II, no. 570, LASA; prison record book, C 29 Annex III, no. 18, list no. 4761–4762, LASA.

[59] "Seite aus dem Hauptbuch des sog. Zigeunerlagers des KL Auschwitz-Birkenau (1943–1944): Weibliche Häftlinge (Nummernserie 1–10849)", registration numbers 1494 and 1497, 1.1.2.1/530982/ITS Digital Archive, Arolsen Archives.

show that responsibilities for imposing detention were distributed differently on the vertical axis and within the authorities' hierarchical order from the Kriminalpolizeistelle to the Reichskriminalpolizeiamt. According to the urgent instruction from January 29, 1943, and different from 1938, a confirmation of detention did not have to be requested from the RKPA.[60] A speedy implementation could be ensured by relaxing the requirements for the imposition of 'police preventive detention' of December 14, 1937. The Kriminalpolizeistellen did not have to submit an application with attachments to the RKPA for the imposition of 'police preventive detention', which no longer had to be approved by the supreme criminal police authority before the person was transported to a concentration camp. The heads of the intermediate Kriminalpolizeileitstellen were primarily responsible for the implementation of this measure and the compliance with the conditions for the deportations in 1943. The RKPA had sent the 'racial report' by the RHF before, which were crucial for the selection at the level of the intermediate Kriminalpolizeileitstellen. In contrast to the authorities in the Rhineland, no written evidence of regional conferences at which selection criteria were discussed and deportation lists were subsequently drawn up could be found for the Magdeburg or Halle criminal police offices.[61] Officers of the Kriminalpolizeileitstelle in Berlin reported after the war that the head Leo Karsten created lists of deportees based on their index cards and files. This list was then sent for approval to the RKPA.[62]

Furthermore, subsequent transports after the deportations in March 1943 reveal the larger network of perpetrators involved in the persecution. The transport of a 13-year-old Roma boy from Magdeburg to the 'Polish youth detention camp' in Litzmannstadt was implemented in June and July 1943 by the female criminal police in cooperation with the 'Reichszentrale zur Bekämpfung der Jugendkriminalität' and the 'Reichszentrale zur Bekämpfung des Zigeunerunwesens' as well as the welfare and youth office in Magdeburg.[63] Another case is Paul Gerste, as

---

[60] Transcript of urgent instruction of the RSHA, V A 2 no. 59/43 g, 29.01.1943, sheets 385–391, Ms 410, IfZ. Translation by the author.
[61] Fings and Sparing, Rassismus, 298.
[62] Interrogation of Oskar Bülow, 19.11.1965, B 057-01, no. 448, sheet 117, LAB; Patricia Pientka: *Das Zwangslager für Sinti und Roma in Berlin-Marzahn. Alltag, Verfolgung und Deportation*, Berlin: Metropol, 2013, 162.
[63] Personal file, C 29 Annex II, no. 524, LASA. The 13-year-old Rom of Croatian citizenship and his family were excluded from the deportations to Auschwitz-Birkenau on March 2, 1943, on the basis of the foreign citizenship certificate. On June 16, 1943, the Kriminalpolizeistelle Magdeburg filed an application for admission to this camp, which was confirmed by the Reichskriminalpolizeiamt and the 'Reichszentrale zur Bekämpfung der Jugendkriminalität' ('Reich Central Office for Combating Juvenile Delinquency') on July 9, 1943. On July 16, 1943, the transport from Mag-

his transport from Magdeburg to Auschwitz on October 12, 1943 highlights the cooperation of the criminal police with other branches of the police. Gerste had been wanted by the Staatspolizeileitstelle Magdeburg (Gestapo) for breach of his employment contract.[64] Since further admissions to the camp in Auschwitz were not possible, placement in a 'labor education camp' ('*Arbeitserziehungslager*') was agreed upon by telephone with Kriminalrat Richmann of the Gestapo. There he was to be "beneficially employed"[65] in the meantime.[66]

Infrastructures of Detaining and Transporting: Prisons, Provisional Assembly Spaces, and Transports by the *Reichsbahn*

In 1943, as in the 'work-shy Reich' action, the police prison became an important space for the exercise of police power and repression and was of central importance for the preparation and organization of the deportations. After the arrests in June 1938, the persons designated as 'work-shy' were first taken to the police prison. During their time in custody there, the criminal police officers filled out all the necessary paperwork for the disposition of the 'police preventive detention'. The prison record books of the police prison show that those to be transported were generally placed in larger group cells.[67]

However, during the deportation of the Sinti and Roma from the municipal detention camp in Magdeburg in 1943, the officers of the Magdeburg criminal police did not resort to the police prison. Point IV.2 on the imposition of preventive detention in the urgent instruction by the RKPA from January 29, 1943, explicitly referred to the need to avoid prolonged detention prior to deportation: "In order to avoid prolonged police detention, the arrest of gypsy persons is not to take place until their immediate removal to the concentration camp is assured"[68].

---

deburg took place. At that time, there was an admission stop in the 'gypsy family camp' in Auschwitz-Birkenau.
64 Telegram from the Kriminalpolizeileitstelle Hannover to the Kriminalpolizeistelle Magdeburg, pp hvr nr. 123 1075 1245, 10.06.1943, personal file, C 29 Annex II, no. 413, sheet 20, LASA.
65 File note and transcript of a letter from the Kriminalpolizeistelle Magdeburg to the Staatspolizeileitstelle Magdeburg, K. MD. 2246/43, 23.06.1943, personal file, C 29 Annex II, no. 413, sheet 26, LASA. Translation by the author.
66 See footnote 92 on page 201.
67 Prison record book, C 29 Annex III, no. 9, file nos. 613, 614, 618, LASA.
68 Transcript of urgent instruction of the RSHA, V A 2 no. 59/43 g, 29.01.1943, sheets 385–391, Ms 410, IfZ. Translation by the author.

Points VI.2 and VI.3 again refer to the timetable and emphasize that the preparatory measures such as the selection of individuals, clarification of transportation and guarding issues, as well as sending and filling out the forms should be started immediately. Eyewitnesses also remembered that they were shortly kept in a larger assembly room in the criminal police station, to which also Sinti and Roma from other regions around Magdeburg had been taken.[69] Similarly as during the deportations of Jews and their brief transit ('*Durchschleusung*', 'channeling') through the assembly camps,[70] belongings and valuables were taken from Sinti and Roma before the transport.[71] This is remarked upon in the files of three persons who had been registered in Berlin – according to the '*Festsetzungserlass*' from October 1939 – and who subsequent to the raid in the Magdeburg municipal detention camp were transferred from the police prison in Magdeburg to Auschwitz-Birkenau with a collective transport on March 9, 1943.[72] The Gestapo handed over larger personal belongings and objects of the deportees to the Oberfinanzdirektion for further utilization.[73] The identification cards were taken from the deportees and their money and valuables were confiscated.[74] For the Kriminalpolizeileitstelle Breslau a former female employee of the criminal police remembered after the war that she was delegated from the 'prevention department' to the case officer for 'gypsy questions' in the course of the deportations for three days for this task only. Her duty was to register in lists all the belongings that had been confiscated from the deportees.[75]

The criminal police and SS could rely on well-established transport mechanisms within the criminal justice system for integrating new transports to con-

---

69 Interview with Günther St., 30.08.1991, no.18, sheet 14, Stiftung niedersächsische Gedenkstätten.
70 Philipp Dinkelaker: *Das Sammellager in der Berliner Synagoge Levetzowstraße 1941/1942*, Berlin: Metropol, 2017, 73–83; Martin Friedenberger: *Fiskalische Ausplünderung. Die Berliner Steuer- und Finanzverwaltung und die jüdische Bevölkerung 1933–1945*, Berlin: Metropol, 2008.
71 Zimmermann, Rassenutopie, 319; Hans-Dieter Schmid: "'… wie Judensachen zu behandeln': die Behandlung der Sinti und Roma durch die Finanzverwaltung", in *Zeitenblicke*, 3, 2004. Available at: https://www.zeitenblicke.de/2004/02/schmid/schmid.pdf. Last accessed: 16.01.2022.
72 Prison record book, C 29 Annex III, no. 18, file nos. 4773, 4778, 4779, LASA.
73 Lutz Miehe: "Die Verfolgung von Sinti und Roma", in Ministerium des Inneren des Landes Sachsen-Anhalt (ed.): *Vom Königlichen Polizeipräsidium zur Bezirksbehörde der Deutschen Volkspolizei. Die Magdeburger Polizei im Gebäude Halberstädter Straße 2 zwischen 1913 und 1989*, Halle: Mitteldeutscher Verlag, 2010, 62–77, here 75.
74 File note and transcript of a letter from the Kriminalpolizeistelle Magdeburg to the Kriminalpolizeileitstelle/'Zigeunerdienststelle' Berlin, K.MD. 633/43, 04.03.1943, personal file, C 29 Annex II, no. 564, sheet 1, LASA.
75 Interrogation of Else Pohl (former criminal police employee at the Kriminalpolizeileitstelle Breslau), 04.04.1966, B 057–01, no. 449, sheets 170–171, LAB.

centration camps. The transfer of prisoners from police prisons to correctional facilities, known in the jargon of the judiciary and the prison system as *Schub* (pushing), had been regulated since the late nineteenth century by a wide variety of regulations concerning routes, connecting trains, guarding, wagon queuing, and cost accounting.[76] On April 24, 1939, a circular of the Reichsführer-SS and Chief of the German Police, issued together with the Reich Minister of Justice, newly regulated prisoner transports throughout the Reich.[77] According to these 1939 regulations, case-by-case decisions were to apply to the execution of special transports.[78] This referred to deportations, for which the Reichsbahn provided special trains (*Sonderzüge*) that ran independently of timetables and were prepared in terms of planning at the central level of the RSHA and the Reichsbahndirektionen.[79]

In the mid-1930s, the Deutsche Reichsbahn owned 64 prisoner cars with room for 28 to 30 people in each wagon.[80] The newer wagons with four axles could transport 56 inmates. These were built in 1936, and in 1938 the Reichsbahn only operated two of them: one for ring I in Berlin and another one for ring VIII in Cologne.[81] Until 1937, the Länder were responsible for the financial expenses of these transports but with the centralization of the police apparatus the administration under Heinrich Himmler took over.[82]

Transports were organized from the transport office of the Ordnungspolizei and officers of this police branch acted as transport escorts. The police and judiciary – and also the SS – had to follow the regulations of the Reichsbahn for such collective transports. The Reichsbahn published its own course books for prisoner wagons, according to which the collective transports of the police and judiciary were based.[83] These collective transports played a crucial role in preparatory measures for the transports and deportations in 1938 and 1943, as

---

76 Dietmar Schulze: "'Sonderzug nach Lichtenburg' – Häftlingstransporte ins Konzentrationslager", in *Hallische Beiträge zur Zeitgeschichte*, 41, 2007, 39–54.
77 Der Reichsführer SS und Chef der Deutschen Polizei: *Dienstvorschrift für den Gefangenentransport. Gültig vom 1. Juni 1939 an*, Berlin: Berlin Buchdruckerei des Gefängnisses Plötzensee, 1939, 5.
78 Ibid.
79 Alfred C. Mierzejewski: The Most Valuable Asset of the Reich. A History of the German National Railway 1933–1945, volume 2, Chapel Hill: University of North Carolina Press, 2000, 116–119; Zimmermann, Rasseutopie, 167–173.
80 Reichbahndirektion Berlin: *Kursbuch für die Gefangenenwagen. Gültig vom 16. Mai 1938*, Berlin: Reichsbahndirektion Berlin, 1938; Schulze, Sonderzug, 42.
81 Schulze, Sonderzug, 42.
82 Ibid.
83 Ibid.

Sinti and Roma who were not in Magdeburg were brought to the police prison there via these collective transports.[84] Furthermore, the Kriminalpolizeistelle relied on collective transports and this well-established system when transferring people to concentration camps in 'police preventive detention' after the mass arrests and transports.[85]

The Reichsbahndirektion had to provide special trains for the mass transports and deportations. This was in accordance with the urgent instructions from January 20, 1943, (VI.5) for the deportations to Auschwitz-Birkenau and it was the same practice as during the deportations of the Jewish population. If it was not possible to provide such special trains, not less than 50 persons were to be deported in one transport. This was the minimum number of a group fare (*Sammelfahrschein*) for half of the price of a third class ticket for regular passenger cars (*Personenwagen*).[86] The deportees were transported in passenger cars and in Magdeburg trains coming from Hannover and Braunschweig were coupled.[87]

For the transports from Magdeburg to the Buchenwald and Sachsenhausen concentration camps in June 1938, the number of people who were transferred was between 30 and 33, which resembles the highest number of people that could fit into a wagon for the collective transports of prison inmates. It is unclear, however, whether the criminal police relied on these trains for collective transports or on special trains, as the release time of the police prison in Magdeburg does not match the schedule of such trains mentioned in the course book from 1938.[88] Since the establishment of the early concentration camps, the police apparatus (in particular the SA and Gestapo) relied on special trains for the mass transport of people who were placed in 'protective custody' ('*Schutzhaft*') into concentration camps. In his analysis of the transports to the concentration camp Lichtenburg (Prettin), Dietmar Schulze concluded that special trains were always used for mass transports of several hundred people. Already for

---

[84] Prison record book, C 29 Annex III, no. 9, file nos. 613, 614, 618, LASA.
[85] Prison record book, C 29 Annex III, no. 18, file nos. 4773–4779, LASA.
[86] This was the case in the deportation of Sinti and Roma from Mosbach, Herbolzheim, Karlsruhe, and other cities in the southwest between March 23 and 27, 1943. See Zimmermann, Rassenutopie, 318; train connection Herbolzheim–Auschwitz, B 698/5 no. 5195, Landesarchiv Baden-Württemberg/Staatsarchiv Freiburg. Schmid was also able to reconstruct this for Hannover and Braunschweig, cf. Schmid, Judensachen, 2. The deportation route from Hannover via Magdeburg to Auschwitz-Birkenau was the same, though the timetable has not yet been found.
[87] Testimony of Adolf P. in the investigation procedure against Willi Rudolf Sawatzki, 17.11.1966, N 2403/1645, sheets 65–69, here 65–66, BArch.
[88] Reichsbahndirektion Berlin, Kursbuch, 22–23, 50–51.

the first transport of 450 persons on 20 June 1933, the number of transportees was so large that a quarter of all trains for collective transports in the entire German Reich would have been needed to conduct the transportation to this camp.[89] For the mass arrests in June 1938 in Berlin, eyewitnesses remember that special trains were used there as well.[90]

Thus, the means of transportation is not a criterion that distinctively differentiates the transfers into concentration and extermination camps in 1938 and 1943. For both transfers it seems like the criminal police and SS relied on special trains, which were provided by the local Reichsbahndirektion. Special trains were also used for the deportation of Sinti and Roma to the Generalgouvernement in May 1940.[91] The persecution history and the subsequent transport of individual Sinti and Roma from Magdeburg to the camp complex in Auschwitz finally highlights that the criminal police again relied on the system of collective transports for transfers to concentration and extermination camps.[92] Thus, similarly to the Gestapo, which organized the transportations and deportations of Jews, the criminal police could rely on a well-established infrastructure for prisoner transports in which concentration camps and special trains were integrated.

Registration, (Re-)Categorization, and Selection: Responsibilities and Authorities between the Center and the Peripheries

Registering, defining, and selecting played a central role in the preparatory measures of the transportations, both in the 'work-shy Reich' action in 1938 and in the deportation to Auschwitz-Birkenau in 1943. Whereas in the case of the trans-

---

89 Schulze, Sonderzug, 43.
90 Report by Mr. Z. from Berlin, protocol from a beneficial organization sent to the Foreign Office in London, 28.10.1938, in Christian Faludi: *Die 'Juni Aktion' 1938. Eine Dokumentation zur Radikalisierung der Judenverfolgung*, Frankfurt am Main: Campus, 2013, 250.
91 Fings and Sparing, Völkermord, 175.
92 One example is Paul Gerste, who was ordered to be transported to Auschwitz on October 12, 1943, but who arrived in mid October in the 'gypsy family camp' of Auschwitz-Birkenau after the sanitary closure had been lifted. See file note by Kriminalsekretär Bernhard Michaelis, K. Vorb. 2246/43 Mi, 25.10.1943, and file note and transcript of a letter from the Kriminalpolizeistelle Magdeburg to Kriminalpolizeileitstelle Halle, K. Vorb. 2246/43 Mi, 20.10.1943, personal file, C 29 Annex II, no. 413, sheets 18, 35, LASA; "Seite aus dem Hauptbuch des sog. Zigeunerlagers des KL Auschwitz-Birkenau (1943–1944): Männliche Häftlinge (Nummernserie 1–10094)", 1.1.2.1/ 530982/ITS Digital Archive, Arolsen Archives.

ports in June 1938 there was still a stronger influence of the Kriminalpolizeistelle Magdeburg on the selection of those to be transported, this was eliminated in 1943 in favor of the intermediate Kriminalpolizeileitstelle; additionally, the information the *RHF* and RKPA provided on the racial status of the deportees became more important. While in 1938 the selection of persons was made locally at police headquarters, by the time of the raid on March 1, 1943, it was already clear who would be deported. This meant that the deportation to Auschwitz-Birkenau could take place within a short period of time, whereas the three transports in 1938 to the Buchenwald and Sachsenhausen concentration camps lasted more than a week.

In the deportations of 1943, the use of 'racial research' and 'hereditary biology' by the criminal police also prevailed, as evidenced by the selection criteria and institutional cooperation with the RHF. For the selection of those to be deported, 'racial-biological' criteria played a decisive role in 1943. A list of criteria for the exclusion makes clear that aspects such as social conformity and employment situation had to be taken into consideration prior to selections for deportations;[93] decorated war veterans were exempted, too. The main criteria that prevented a deportation were if one could prove that he or she was what the Nazis called a '*reinrassige*' Sinti and Lalleri or if they were married to a partner of 'German blood'. The cooperation with the RHF was therefore crucial to the selection process. If a racial report by the RHF was not present, the Kriminalpolizei(leit)-stellen gave an evaluation themselves and judged according to heredity, lifestyle, and appearance. As the RKPA did not ask for a specific number of deportees, the scopes of action for implementation were wider.[94] A systematic analysis of the selection process for the deportations from Magdeburg is still pending.

As in Cologne, Sinti or Roma with foreign citizenships or those married to partners of 'German blood' were not deported. However, the latter needed to agree to be sterilized.[95] According to the racial report by the RHF, a Roma family should have been deported but the family managed to get a confirmation letter by the Croatian ambassador in Berlin a few days before that, confirming the Cro-

---

93 Transcript of urgent instruction of the RSHA, V A 2 no. 59/43 g, 29.01.1943, sheets 385–391, Ms 410, IfZ. Translation by the author.
94 Fings and Sparing, Lager, 298.
95 Files notes and transcripts of letter exchanges between the Kriminalpolizeistelle Magdeburg and the Ortspolizeibehörde Quedlinburg regarding the forced sterilization, June–August 1943, personal file, C 29 Annex II, no. 96/1, sheets 85–89, LASA.

atian citizenship of the family. This non-German citizenship exempted them from being deported.[96]

The three leading officers of the 'Reichszentrale zur Bekämpfung des Zigeunerunwesens' – Heinrich Böhlhoff, Johannes Otto, and Wilhelm Supp – visited the 'gypsy family camp' in Auschwitz-Birkenau in 1943 at least twice. In 1960 and 1963, Supp remembered during interrogations that one of their tasks was to check whether the inmates were 'rightfully' deported by the Kriminalpolizei(leit)stellen or whether they fell under the exemptions.[97] This underlines again that the Kriminalpolizeileitstellen implemented the deportations mainly independently. The Kriminalpolizei(leit)stellen, however, always sought the advice and order for forced-sterilization in the cases of non-deported Sinti and Roma from the superordinate 'Reichszentrale'.

In contrast to these 'racial-biological' criteria, social and economic criteria were predominant in 1938. The practical implementations of 'police preventive detention' of 'work-shy' in Magdeburg in June 1938 confirm the thesis that this action aimed at providing labor resources for the concentration camps and that the context of the *Vierjahresplan* (four-year plan) was elementary for this action.[98] Mainly younger people were transported and most of them were not providing wage labor but were self-employed. This kind of occupation was not regarded as proper work by the police officers and was grounded in a specific anti-gypsy sentiment.[99] This action was characterized by many local specificities as the selection of the people to be transferred and the number of arrested and transported varied immensely on the local level. All in all, way more than the ordered number of at least 200 people per Kriminalpolizeileitstelle was reached in many areas, so that a lot more than 10,000 people were transported to the concentration camps.[100] These local specificities are in general characteristic of the mass transports in 1938.

Subsequent transports to concentration camps after the deportations in March 1943 – for instance when further admissions to the 'gypsy family camp' in Auschwitz-Birkenau were not possible due to the medical and sanitary conditions between spring and fall 1943 – were implemented in accordance with the measures for the 'police preventive detention' and the RKPA needed to confirm

---

96 File notes and transcripts of letter exchanges between the Kriminalpolizeistelle Magdeburg and the Kriminalpolizei-Außenposten Teplitz-Schönau, April 1944, personal file, C 29 Annex II, no. 522, sheets 40–45, 50, LASA.
97 Personal file of Wilhelm Supp, B Rep. 057–01, no. 2692, sheets 1638–1639, 2734–2735, LAB.
98 Ayaß, Asoziale, 161–165.
99 The same observations were made for Cologne; see Fings and Sparing, Lager, 95–105.
100 Ibid.

the request for incarceration. In order to be transferred to a concentration camp on the basis of 'police preventive detention', a recategorization of the person had to be undertaken and the label 'asocial' was added. Personal files from Magdeburg reveal that the Kriminalpolizeistelle asked the 'Reichszentrale zur Bekämpfung des Zigeunerunwesens' how to deal with these cases.[101] Subsequently, they asked for a request of transfer to a concentration camp for someone labeled as 'asocial' on the basis of 'police preventive detention'. On the level of the RKPA, special case officers for 'police preventive detention' collected the relevant material from the Kriminalpolizeistellen for their own data collection and made a proposal for a case decision. The 'prevention department' and working group directors Kriminalrat Heinrich Böhlhoff and his deputies Kriminalrat Johannes Otto or Kriminalrat Hans Maly (the latter between January and September 1943 only) were then in charge of confirming the transport to a camp on the basis of 'police preventive detention'.[102]

Conclusion

The investigation of the arrest and deportations of Sinti and Roma in 1938 and 1943 with a focus on the division of labor among the perpetrators in the Kriminalpolizeistelle Magdeburg shows the diversity of the officers involved. The fine-grained analysis also demonstrated that the extent of involved officers in the persecution of Sinti and Roma was much larger than the few specializing in what the Nazis called 'gypsy questions'. It has become clear, however, that the 'prevention commissariats' and 'prevention departments' on all levels of the criminal police played a central role in the transfers to concentration camps. This structural component, however, only emerged with the mass transports to concentration camps in 1938 within the criminal police apparatus. The comparison of the transfers thus highlighted the fluidity of practical police work and how a learning administration created structures that matched ideological foundations and later 'racial biological' paradigms.

The comparison reveals the special features of the deportation to the 'gypsy family camp' in Auschwitz-Birkenau. The analysis also shows the advantages of taking institutional structures – besides (collective) biographies – into consider-

---

101 Letter from the Kriminalpolizeistelle Magdeburg to the 'Reichszentrale zur Bekämpfung des Zigeunerunwesens' concerning 'immigrant gypsy', K. ED./43, 03.09.1943, personal file, C 29 Annex II, no. 582, LASA.
102 Regulation concerning the organization and staff of the department V A 2 in the RKPA for the RSHA trial investigation (1 Js 13/65), B 057–01, no. 461, sheet 103, LAB.

ation when researching Nazi crimes from a perpetrator's perspective. Overall, this essay has shown how approaches of new perpetrator research and a precise evaluation of the responsibilities of local criminal police officers can contribute fresh insights not only into the deportations but also into the practice of persecution in general. For future research, such a view can be fruitful in order to avoid the disappearance of perpetrators behind passive constructions or the reference back to the institution of 'criminal police' in general.

Théophile Leroy
'Gypsies' in the Police Eye
Identification, Census and Deportation of Sinti and Roma from Annexed Alsace, 1940 to 1944

Abstract: In annexed Alsace, the destruction and dislocation of Sinti and Roma families, labelled as 'gypsies', were part of the broader genocidal dynamic triggered by the German authorities during the winter of 1942/1943. Using Strasbourg criminal police records, Arolsen Archives materials and the documentation of the Rassenhygienische Forschungsstelle (Racial Hygiene Research Center, RHF) in Berlin, the main aim of this contribution is to shed light on how escalating persecution and genocidal policies targeting Sinti and Roma were implemented in a western borderland space. Racial registrations and uses of the 'gypsy' category are analysed to document police methods and identification practices in a former French territory. By underlining the circulation and exchange of collected data on 'gypsy' individuals between central institutions and regional police stations, this article intends to show that the Strasbourg deportation of March 1943 was the result of specific racial identifications operations aiming to eliminate German Sinti and Roma families living in annexed Alsace.

Introduction

On March 22, 1943, 61 individuals reached Auschwitz-Birkenau. From pages 353 to 356 of the women's registration book of the *'Zigeunerlager'* ('gypsy camp'), 35 newly arrived individuals were recorded.[1] On that same day, the men's register reported 26 new entries.[2] Among the 61, 33 were under the age of 15. Within this group, seven different family names were mentioned: Rosenbach, Franz, Wesel, Blum, Gerste, Braun, and Freiwald (see fig. 1). These names reappear on fourteen death certificates issued by the registry office of the Auschwitz camp administration.[3] These documents indicate that all of them were domiciliated in Alsatian

---
[1] Pages 353 to 356 of the women's *Hauptbücher des 'Zigeunerlagers'* of Auschwitz-Birkenau, 22.03.1943, 1.1.2.1/531497–531498/ITS Digital Archive, Archives Nationales.
[2] Pages 146 and 147 of the men's *Hauptbücher des 'Zigeunerlagers'* of Auschwitz-Birkenau, 22.03.1943, 1.1.2.1/530981–530982/ITS Digital Archive, Archives Nationales.
[3] For one example, see death certificate for Robert Blum, 29.10.1943, Auschwitz-Birkenau, 1.1.2.1/568532/ITS Digital Archive, Archives Nationales.

OpenAccess. © 2023 the author(s), published by De Gruyter. This work is licensed under the Creative Commons Attribution-NonCommercial-NoDerivatives 4.0 International License.
https://doi.org/10.1515/9783110746464-013

cities before their deportation: eight lived in Strasbourg, four in Cronenbourg and two in Colmar. Moreover, prisoner registration cards of four other members of this deportation convoy, created later when they were transferred to Buchenwald, mentioned that they had been arrested as 'work-shy gypsies' (*'Arbeitsscheue Zigeuner'*) by the Strasbourg criminal police (Kriminalpolizei, Kripo) in March 1943.[4] Although these documents are linked to specific individuals – either dead or transferred –, such spatial and administrative indications hint at the geographic provenance of the entire group. They constitute a first lead to explore local applications of deportation policies targeting 'gypsies' implemented in Western Germany's territorial margins.

By the end of 1940 and following the defeat of France, the former Bas-Rhin and Haut-Rhin departments were annexed to the German territory and Strasbourg progressively became the new administrative and political centre of the Gau Oberrhein, which united Baden and annexed Alsace. This borderland territory of the Rhine area was perceived as a fundamental space in the Nazi policy, which intended to reshape racial European frontiers. Alsace was meant to become a Western march built for the defence of Germanness.[5] Thus, the Alsatian lands were subjected to Germanization policies that affected individuals considered as 'gypsies' within this territory.[6] People labelled as 'gypsies' were mainly musicians, basket-makers, fairground artists and trailer dwellers linked to the travelling worlds of this transfrontier area between France, Germany, and Switzerland: Sinti, Manouches, Roma and Yenish experienced familial dislocations and endured persecution policies throughout the war.

The main aim of this article is to shed light on how racial and genocidal policies targeting Roma and Sinti were implemented in annexed Alsace where different legal conceptions of categories framing and criminalising itinerant professions had overlapped since the second part of the nineteenth century, inherited both from German and French police practices. The term 'gypsy' used in this paper refers to the term *'Zigeuner'* used by the German authorities during the Second World War to label people that were stigmatized as racially inferior aliens meant to disappear from the German area. It was as 'gypsies' that many families were persecuted, and it is as such that they appear in the sources used for this study. The choice not to capitalize this term intends to emphasize that this

---

[4] For one example, see prisoner registration card for Hugo Wesel, Buchenwald, 1.1.5.3/7407285/ ITS Digital Archive, Archives Nationales.
[5] Isabel Heinemann: *Rasse, Siedlung, deutsches Blut. Das Rasse- und Siedlungshauptamt der SS und die rassenpolitische Neuordnung Europas*, Göttingen: Wallstein, 2003, 305–356.
[6] Lothar Kettenacker: *Nationalsozialistische Volkstumspolitik im Elsass*, Stuttgart: Deutsche Verlags-Anstalt, 1973, 249–267.

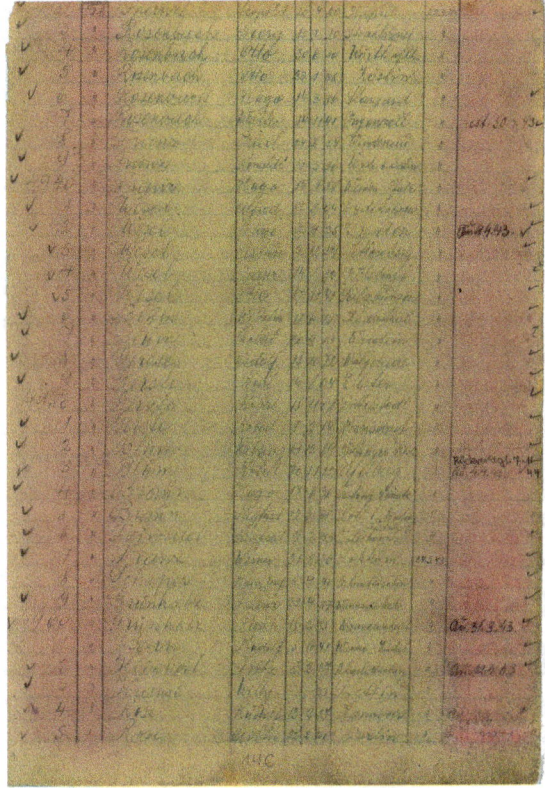

Fig. 1: Page 146 of the men's *Hauptbücher des Zigeunerlagers* of Auschwitz-Birkenau, March 22, 1943, Archive of the State Museum Auschwitz-Birkenau in Oświęcim.

exonym is first and foremost the result of a social categorization elaborated by state laws and shaped by administrative, bureaucratic and police practices starting as early as the nineteenth century which does not refer to any stable collective identity claimed by the individuals concerned.[7]

---

[7] On the racialisation of the 'gypsy' category since the nineteenth century, see Leo Lucassen: "'Harmful Tramps'. Police Professionalization and Gypsies in Germany, 1700–1945", in *Crime, History & Societies*, 1, 1997, 29–50; Ulrich F. Opfermann: "Preußen – Kaiserreich – Weimar, Umbrüche und Kontinuitäten", in *Zigeunerverfolgung im Rheinland und in Westfalen 1933–1945. Geschichte, Aufarbeitung und Erinnerung*, Paderborn: Ferdinand Schöningh, 2012, 37–52; Juliane Tatarinov: *Kriminalisierung des ambulanten Gewerbes: Zigeuner- und Wandergewerbepolitik im späten Kaiserreich und in der Weimarer Republik*, Frankfurt am Main: Peter Lang, 2015.

In the historiography of the persecution of Roma and Sinti, Alsace has rarely been the focus of scholarly attention. Although Marie-Christine Hubert's pioneering thesis addresses the Alsatian case, French academic publications mainly analyse the internment policy for 'nomads' in the occupied and non-occupied zones, relegating this borderland area as a shadow zone.[8] Michael Zimmermann's groundbreaking study of the Roma and Sinti genocide in Europe raises the Alsatian question and provides us with its major repressive framework but without mentioning any deportation to Auschwitz-Birkenau from this annexed territory.[9] Using a microhistorical perspective, recent studies have emphasized the need to consider annexed or German-ruled borderland areas as autonomous case studies going beyond traditional national borders to reveal the local dynamics of persecution practices.[10] Similarly, the biographical study of Heiko Haumann on the trajectory of Zilli Reichmann, arrested in 1942 in Alsace as a 'gypsy', deported to Lety and later to Auschwitz, reveals the integration of this annexed territory within the Nazi camp system.[11] Thus, the methodological approach in this paper is to study the margins to understand the core of repressive policies towards Sinti and Roma in Europe. It was indeed within border areas that the question of identification became more acute: who, in the eyes of the German authorities, had to be categorized as 'gypsy' in annexed Alsace? What criteria did the Germans use to identify the 61 individuals labelled as 'workshy gypsies' and to deport them to Auschwitz-Birkenau in March 1943? How did the police services concretely implement the policies to repress them?

---

8 Marie-Christine Hubert: *Les Tsiganes en France 1939–1946. Assignation à résidence, internement, déportation*, Paris: Paris 10 University, 1997, 87–90.
9 Michael Zimmermann: *Rassenutopie und Genozid: Die nationalsozialistische "Lösung der Zigeunerfrage"*, Hamburg: Christians, 1996, 214–218. He wrote that "transports from Alsace, as well as from Lorraine and Luxembourg, have not been documented so far" (ibid., 309). Both translations by the author.
10 Claire Zalc and Nicolas Mariot's study on the persecution of the Jewish families living in Lens, a northern French city located in the *zone interdite* (forbidden zone), shows the specificities of the anti-Jewish measures and persecution practices in this territory ruled by German authorities which united Belgium and two northern French departments (Nord and Pas-de-Calais). See Nicolas Mariot and Claire Zalc: *Face à la persécution: 991 Juifs dans la guerre*, Paris: Odile Jacob, 2010. The work of Monique Heddebaut on 'gypsy' families deported by a convoy from Malines to Auschwitz-Birkenau in January 1944 underlines the dynamics of deportation policies targeting Sinti and Roma set up in the same military zone. See Monique Heddebaut: *Des Tsiganes vers Auschwitz: le convoi Z du 15 janvier 1944*, Paris: Tirésias-Michel Reynaud, 2018. For a study on the German police in annexed Moselle, see Cédric Neveu: *La Gestapo en Moselle: une police au coeur de la répression nazie*, Metz: Serpenoise, 2012.
11 Heiko Haumann: *Die Akte Zilli Reichmann: Zur Geschichte der Sinti im 20. Jahrhundert*, Frankfurt am Main: S. Fischer, 2016.

The dynamics between central decisions and regional applications regarding the escalating Sinti and Roma persecution policies will be analysed through the Alsatian lens. By delving into the archive records of the Strasbourg Kripo from 1940 to 1944 and racial investigations led by the Rassenhygienische und bevölkerungsbiologische Forschungsstelle (Racial Hygiene and Population Biology Research Center, RHF) in specific Rhine cities between 1937 and 1942, I intend to show that police identification practices and deportation policies towards so-called gypsies followed specific criteria depending on the temporality of the war and did not affect all itinerant families living in Alsace with the same intensity. While one might have thought that the German police had a clear vision of whom to arrest, given the racial policies they had put in place against Sinti and Roma in Germany prior to 1940, it appears that the identification of 'gypsies' living in Alsace was a more complex process involving several authorities.

The repressive frameworks will first be introduced to contextualize the regional situation at the very beginning of the annexation and to document the use of the 'gypsy' category in the implementation of expulsion policies to unoccupied France. This part will be based on correspondences and monthly reports of the German police deployed in Alsace that are held in the French departmental archives in Strasbourg and Colmar but also in the National Archives in Washington. Then, the temporality of the repression towards the 'gypsy presence' shall be studied by referring to the arrest cards and mugshots made by the Strasbourg Kripo in 1942. Finally, following the deportation order of 'gypsies' to Auschwitz issued by Heinrich Himmler on December 16, 1942, the spatial and chronological applications of this decision will be analysed by taking as a case study the constitution of the Strasbourg convoy of March 1943 and by referring to Arolsen Archives documents. The aim is to understand which families were targeted by such policies by comparing the deportees' names of this convoy with the RHF documentation kept in the German Federal Archives in Berlin.

Expulsion Practices and the Use of the 'Gypsy' Category by the Germans in Conquered Alsace, 1940 to 1941

Shortly after German troops entered Strasbourg on June 19, 1940, the Reich Security Main Office (*Reichssicherheitshauptamt*, RSHA) set up the *Einsatzgruppe* III (mobile police intervention group) to secure Alsace before its annexation to the *Reich*. Under the authority of a Commander of the Security Police (*Befehlshaber der Sicherheitspolizei und des SD*, BdS), the *Einsatzgruppe* III was divided into two territorial units operating in the Bas-Rhin and Haut-Rhin: the *Einsatzkommando* III/1 with its headquarters in Strasbourg and the *Einsatzkommando* III/2 with its offices in Mulhouse. These police forces, composed of Gestapo and Kripo agents, supervised the actions of the territorial gendarmeries and were responsible for the implementation of expulsion policies against populations deemed undesirable in Alsace.

During the first weeks of the military occupation of Alsace, expulsion practices targeted Sinti and Roma among other groups perceived by the Germans as 'undesirable elements'. On July 1, 1940, BdS Gustav-Adolf Scheel ordered his police officers to draw up lists of "professional criminals and asocial individuals present in Alsace for their future evacuation".[12] Two weeks later, he specified the modalities of application and quoted the profile of the individuals that were to be identified and expelled: "professional criminals, beggars, vagrants, asocial pimps and gypsies".[13] At this time, the use of the 'gypsy' category by the German police deployed in Alsace was incorporated into common criminal behaviour patterns and did not support any autonomous specific policy, targeting so-called gypsy families as such.

During the next month, the identification of so-called gypsies started to be associated with itinerant economic activities perceived as a threat to regional security and stability. On 14 August 1940, Alexander Landgraf, criminal commissioner and head of the Strasbourg police, informed his agents of the details regarding the forthcoming operation aiming to "cleanse Alsace of asocial, criminal and gypsy elements": men identified as "gypsies" or "having the gypsy type" were to be taken, along with their wives and children, to the *Sicherungslager* (security camp) of Schirmeck-Vorbruck.[14] In August 1940, 41 'asocial elements' living in Obernai, a municipality located in the southwest of the Strasbourg area, were transferred to this camp. This group consisted of four families with the sur-

---

12 BdS-Elsaß to the Einsatzkommando III/1 and 2, 01.07.1940, 9379992, T-175/513, National Archives and Records Administration, Washington (henceforth NARA). Translation by the author. The order is also quoted in Zimmermann, *Rassenutopie und Genozid*, 214. Translation by the author.
13 BdS-Elsaß to the Einsatzkommando III/1 and 2, 20.07.1940, 9380004, T-175/513, NARA. Translation by the author.
14 Einsatzkommando III/1 leader to the Strasbourg criminal police, 14.08.1940, 938005, T-175/513, NARA, Washington. Translation by the author. For a study on the Schirmeck-Vorbruck camp, see Jean-Laurent Vonau: *Le "Sicherungslager Vorbruck-Schirmeck" un camp oublié en Alsace*, Strasbourg: Éditions du Signe, 2017.

name Gargowitsch.[15] According to the French census, these families were registered as residents in this city in 1936.[16] In the police report, all of them were presented as basket-makers (*Korbmacher*), an itinerant profession based on mobility – itinerant trade, sale on markets – that constituted a reason for 'asociality' and a pretext for further expulsion. Although the word '*Zigeuner*' does not appear on this document, the Gargowitsch were treated as 'gypsies' and taken to the Schirmeck security camp. This specific case illustrates the overlapping use of police categories that targeted the 'gypsy' presence in annexed Alsace.

To set up the expulsion lists, the officers of the Einsatzgruppe III relied on former French police archives. In August 1940, Landgraf justified his delay in drawing up the expulsion lists by referring to "the ramified classification of French police files".[17] It can be assumed that they targeted so-called gypsy families by using the 'nomad' records issued by the French prefectures.[18] In the absence of French police records, the German authorities resorted to field investigations: on July 11, 1940, the Landkommissar (civil territorial leader) of Altkirch, a city in the south of Mulhouse, required the municipal authorities under his jurisdiction to identify "asocial individuals [...] and above all the gypsies" because "the criminal records had been removed since the outbreak of the war".[19] In response, the mayor of Durmenach provided a 'gypsy list' ('*Zigeunerliste*') composed of 36 individuals.[20] But the existence of such lists specifically targeting Sinti and Roma remains very rare during this period and seems to have resulted from local initiatives. Thus, many identification lists used the 'gypsy' category among others to quell the presence of people who could not belong to the '*Volksgemeinschaft*' as conceived by the Nazi ideology. In the summer of 1940, the German security offices were mainly devoted to expelling any individual related to social or economic marginality schemes.

---

15 List of the 'asocial elements' living in Obernai, 16.08.1940, 1.1.40.1/4397075/ITS Digital Archives, Archives Nationales.
16 Obernai population census, 1936, 364D 4, Archives départementales du Bas-Rhin, Strasbourg (henceforth ADBR).
17 Strasbourg criminal commissioner to the BdS-Elsaß, 18.08.1940, 9379996, T-175/513, NARA. Translation by the author.
18 In 1912, the 'nomad' category was created by the French authorities to collectively target, register and monitor families with an itinerant activity and a mobile lifestyle. This legislation was applied in Alsace and Moselle after the First World War. On the 1912 law, see Emmanuel Filhol: *Le contrôle des Tsiganes en France (1912–1969)*, Paris: Karthala, 2013, 59–106.
19 Altkirch Landkommissar to the Mulhouse criminal police, 11.07.1940, 1AL3 213, Archives départementales du Haut-Rhin, Colmar (henceforth ADHR). Translation by the author.
20 Durmenach mayor to the Altkirch Landkommissar, 18.07.1940, 1AL3 213, ADHR.

On the Durmenach list were the names of Joseph Lafertin, his wife Marie, and their four children. Joseph Lafertin was born in 1892 in Aspach-le-Haut, near Thann, in southern Alsace. In May 1921, he was registered as a *musicien ambulant* (itinerant musician) and categorized as a 'nomad' by the Haut-Rhin prefecture.[21] He was then forced to carry a specific anthropometric identity booklet and have it stamped in every locality he travelled to. Labelled as *'Zigeuner'* by the German local authorities during the summer 1940, Joseph and his family were expelled to the unoccupied French zone. On June 20, 1941, considered by the French authorities as 'nomads' coming from Alsace, the Lafertin family, with nearly 330 other Alsatian itinerants, were conducted to Rivesaltes, an internment camp located in the Pyrénées-Orientales and administered by the Vichy regime.[22] The trajectory of the Lafertins illustrates the interweaving of repressive measures against Alsatian itinerants by French and German authorities from the very beginning of the war.[23]

In the following months, through their research in former French police archives and field investigations, the German security forces began to gather information on the presence of 'gypsies' in Alsace and started to establish reports on the racial condition of the travelling families living in the region. On September 27, 1940, the Altkirch gendarmerie sent a note to the Mulhouse Kripo on a basketmaker family living in Henflingen and stated that they must not be considered as "racial gypsies" because the head of the family had "a good reputation"[24]. This statement underlines the scope of action that local police forces had to racially qualify individuals who carried out an itinerant activity according to behaviour and lifestyle criteria.

Incrementally, the German policy targeting 'gypsy' families became more and more precise as police authorities gathered knowledge on the Alsatian po-

---

21 Individual anthropometric notice, Antoine Lafertin, 26.05.1921, 1AL2 1148, ADHR. Between 1920 and 1921, following the end of the First World War, the three prefectures of Moselle, Bas-Rhin and Haut-Rhin implemented the French 1912 law on the regulation of itinerant professions. The sixteenth mobile brigade dedicated to these identification procedures labelled 1,161 individuals as 'nomads' and matriculated 109 trailers in all three departments. See Report of the sixteenth mobile brigade to the ministry of Interior, 28.12.1921, 157AL 131, ADHR.
22 Pages 342 to 377 of the entry register of the Rivesaltes camp, 20.06.1941, 1260W 78, Archives départementales des Pyrénées-Orientales.
23 For further information on the internment of expelled itinerant families from Alsace in southern France, see Emmanuel Filhol and Marie-Christine Hubert: *Les Tsiganes en France. Un sort à part, 1939–1946*, Paris: Perrin, 2009; Alexandre Doulut: *Les Tsiganes au camp de Rivesaltes (1941–1942)*, Paris: Lienart, 2014.
24 Altkirch gendarmerie to the Mulhouse criminal police, 27.09.1940, 1AL3 213, ADHR. Translation by the author.

pulation. On November 18, 1940, arguing a criminality rise in Alsace, the Einsatzgruppe III organized a new wave of expulsions targeting "undesirable elements"[25] living in the Strasbourg area. On November 21, the Strasbourg Landkommissar mobilized its territorial gendarmerie networks and ordered to report the presence of "asocials, work-shy people, gypsies or gypsy-like people, vagrants, homosexuals and beggars".[26] In response, several gendarmerie services such as Mommenheim, Brumath or Wolfisheim sent back their lists using distinct categories to class the names. Relying on these lists, the police spotted and expelled 664 individuals from the Strasbourg area to the unoccupied France in December 1940.[27] When the Strasbourg police sent the final results of these expulsion operations to the Einsatzgruppe III services in January 1941, it attached three separate lists relating to "homosexuals", "asocials" and "gypsies".[28] Although these lists remain undiscovered to this day, the fact that, for the first time, police regional authorities set up a distinct list dedicated to expelled 'gypsy' individuals shows how progressively the use of the 'gypsy' category became more specific in the eyes of the German police.

These forced and massive evacuations targeting Sinti and Roma among other categories of 'undesirable elements' continued with various intensity until January 1941. This policy shift coincided with an administrative change. Indeed, the police services and attributions were reorganized to correspond to the bureaucratic architecture of the German apparatus police: criminal police stations were settled in Alsace as permanent offices and took over the security missions originally applied by the Einsatzgruppe III. The first *Meldeblatt* (police internal report) of the Strasbourg Kripo was issued on February 24, 1941.[29] After the coordinated expulsion operations, Kripo agents took over the repression towards 'gypsy' individuals and carried out preventive arrests and targeted expulsions.

---

25 BdS-Elsass to the Strasbourg, Erstein, Haguenau, Sélestat, Saverne and Wissembourg Landkommissar, 18.11.1940, 9380011, T-175/513, NARA. Translation by the author.
26 Strasbourg Landkommissar to the Wolfisheim gendarmerie, 21.11.1940, 400D 77/27, ADBR. Translation by the author.
27 Strasbourg Kriminalkommissar to the BdS-Elsaß, 14.12.1940, 9380016, T-175/513, NARA.
28 Strasbourg Kriminalkommissar to the BdS-Elsaß, 09.01.1941, 9380022, T-175/513, NARA. Translation by the author.
29 *Meldeblatt* of the Strasboug criminal police, 1, 24.02.1941, 400D 77/11, ADBR.

The Strasbourg Criminal Police and the Census of the 'Gypsy' Presence in Annexed Alsace, 1941 to 1943

As Alsace was incorporated into the *Reich* in the months following its annexation, German authorities progressively applied their criminal legislation and police laws. Scholars have underlined the involvement of the Kripo services in the implementation of racial policies in Germany against individuals perceived as 'gypsies'.[30] In Alsace, the 8th office of the Strasbourg criminal police was charged with the "preventive fight against crime" and had to repress the "gypsy presence".[31] Therefore, Kripo agents adopted former police practices used in Germany to precisely target travelling families and to identify 'gypsies' using racial standards.

On July 9, 1941, the December 1937 decree on crime prevention was issued in Alsace.[32] Two days later, the Strasbourg police internal report relayed the methods to be adopted to settle this policy: 'gypsies' and 'mixed-race gypsies' (*'Zigeunermischlinge'*) were to be registered by the Kripo services before the end of the month.[33] Thus, from the summer of 1941 onwards, in police discourses and practices, 'gypsies' were no longer mingled with 'asocials' and 'homosexuals' as repressive categories but were now subjected to a separate, targeted, and specific persecution. Although the result lists of this first racial census in the summer of 1941 remain unknown, the arrest cards of the Strasbourg Kripo, kept in the Bas-Rhin departmental archives centre, reveal the intensity and the temporalities

---

[30] For the involvement of the German criminal police in racial policy implementation, see Patrick Wagner: *Volksgemeinschaft ohne Verbrecher: Konzeptionen und Praxis der Kriminalpolizei in der Zeit der Weimarer Republik und des Nationalsozialismus*, Hamburg: Christians, 1996. For the specific persecution towards 'gypsies', see idem.: "Kriminalprävention qua Massenmord. Die gesellschaftsbiologische Konzeption der NS-Kriminalpolizei und ihre Bedeutung für die Zigeunerverfolgung", in Michael Zimmermann (ed.): *Zwischen Erziehung und Vernichtung. Zigeunerforschung und Zigeunerpolitik im Europa des 20. Jahrhunderts*, Stuttgart: Franz Steiner, 2007, 379–392; Marc von Lüpke-Schwarz: *"Zigeunerfrei!" Die Duisburger Kriminalpolizei und die Verfolgung der Sinti und Roma 1939–1944*, Saarbrücken: Dr. Müller, 2008; Johannes Kaiser: *Verfolgung von Sinti und Roma in Karlsruhe im Nationalsozialismus. Die städtische und kriminalpolizeiliche Praxis*, Karlsruhe: Info, 2020.
[31] "Organisationsplan der Kriminalpolizei Strassburg", 05.07.1941, R70-Elsass 19, Federal Archives, Berlin-Lichterfelde (henceforth: BArch). Translation by the author.
[32] Guenter Lewy: *The Nazi persecution of the Gypsies*, Oxford: Oxford University Press, 2000, 81.
[33] *Meldeblatt* of the Strasbourg criminal police, 11, 11.07.1941, 400D 77/11, ADBR.

of the 'gypsy' policy on an urban scale and document police identification practices in annexed Alsace.

Composed of nearly 5300 individual cards, the Strasbourg Kripo arrest file unveils the repressive devices against criminality and provides information on the civil status (surname, first name, date, place of birth) and the circumstances of the arrest (year, place and motive) of individuals arrested between 1940 and 1944 in Alsace, mainly around the Strasbourg area.[34] The arrest motive constitutes a methodological key to enlighten the modalities of repression: it makes it possible to identify who, in the eyes of the Kripo, was perceived as a 'gypsy'. By collecting the cards which contain the term '*Zigeuner*' or '*Ausweisung*' (expulsion) as an arrest motive, the corpus of people arrested following these two categories comprises 232 individuals. Among them, 165 were arrested in the Strasbourg district in 1942.

Studying these 165 arrest forms outlines the evolution of the categories used by Kripo agents to treat the 'gypsy' presence during this specific year: 90 were categorized as 'gypsies' and 75 were expelled. Although only the year of the arrest is documented, each card contains two anthropometric mugshots (face and profile) with a unique identification number. This number refers to the chronological order of the mugshots taken by the Strasbourg Kripo photographic unit. By focusing on this data, it is then possible to discern a more precise temporality of the persecution policies towards 'gypsies'. For instance, Maria Reinhardt, born in 1912 in Bildstock (Sarre), was arrested in Strasbourg in 1942 as '*Zigeunerin*'. The number 66/42 appears on her mugshot which means that she was the 66th person to be photographed in 1942.[35]

The Kripo mugshots of 1942 help to understand the temporality of the repression and the shift in the methods employed. By comparing an arrest card with the entry register of the Strasbourg prison, the moment of arrest can be determined. As an example, Rosa Siegler, born in 1905 in Strasbourg, was identified as '*Zigeunerin*' by the Kripo services in 1942 with the number 748/42.[36] She was incarcerated in the Strasbourg prison on August 8, 1942.[37] Thus, it can be assumed that other mugshots with a relatively close number were also taken in early August 1942. But connecting an identification number with a precise date remains uneasy since arrested individuals labelled as 'gypsies' were not necessarily incarcerated in the Strasbourg prison. Nonetheless, the chronological evolution of the arrest motives used by the Kripo can be approximated with this

---

34 Arrest cards of the Strasbourg criminal police, 1940–1944, 757D 68–107, ADBR.
35 Arrest card Maria Reinhardt, 1942, 757D 76, ADBR.
36 Arrest card Rosa Siegler, 1942, 757D 77, ABDR.
37 Custody register of the Strasbourg prison, 08.08.1942, 1184W 62, ADBR.

method and hints at a crucial policy shift regarding the police treatment of the Sinti and Roma population in annexed Alsace.

Table 1: Distribution of Arrest Motives Used by the Strasbourg criminal police in 1942 According to the Mugshot Number

Category Mugshot Number	*'Ausweisung'* (expulsion)	*'Zigeuner'* ('gypsy')	Total
0–747 (before 8 August 1942)	75	9	84
748–1272 (after 8 August 1942)	0	81	81

Before the 748th mugshot of Rosa Siegler taken on August 8, 1942, the Strasbourg Kripo unit had used the category expulsion 75 times whereas the 'gypsy' category was only used 9 times. Indeed, during the first part of 1942, expulsion practices remained the main means used by the German authorities to eliminate Alsace from its 'asocial and criminal elements' The itinerary of the Geiger family exemplifies the first phase of 1942. Louis Geiger, a basket-maker born in 1881 in Alsace, was identified as a 'nomad' in 1928 by the French Haut-Rhin prefecture in Colmar.[38] In 1942, he was arrested in Strasbourg by the Kripo and photographed with the 429/42 mugshot number.[39] With his wife Caroline Secula and his two sons, he was later expelled to unoccupied France and reached Lyon on June 19, 1942 with a convoy of 132 individuals, composed mainly of Alsatian families who exercised an itinerant activity.[40] On June 20, 1942, in a report sent to the RSHA, the Strasbourg police stated that "125 gypsies"[41] were evacuated to France during the previous week, and it is quite probable that this report referred to this specific expulsion convoy.

From the summer of 1942, the use of the 'gypsy' category by Kripo agents became exclusive. The German authorities in annexed Alsace decided to stop the expulsions and started to spot and immobilize Sinti and Roma families while awaiting a future decision. This shift corresponds to an order of the Stras-

---

38 Individual anthropometric notice for Louis Geiger, 18.08.1928, 3AL2 118, ADHR.
39 Arrest card Ludwig Geiger, 1942, 757D 87, ADBR.
40 List of the 132 individuals expelled from Alsace, 19.06.1942, 3W 71, Archives départementales de la Moselle, Metz.
41 Strasbourg criminal police to the RSHA, 20.06.1941, 2963003, T-175/413, NARA. Translation by the author.

bourg Kripo issued on June 28, 1942 requiring a complete census of 'gypsies', 'mixed-race gypsies' and 'gypsy-like persons' to "definitively solve the gypsy question in Alsace".[42] The local police stations received concrete instructions: they were asked to register all 'gypsy' persons over the age of six and to duly notify the nationality of the recorded individuals who were forbidden to leave their place of residence until further notice. To carry out this registration procedure, Kripo agents had to use the RKP 172 form, a specific document created in 1939 to implement the repressive measures established by Heinrich Himmler's decree for 'fighting the gypsy plague' (*'Bekämpfung der Zigeunerplage'*) issued on December 8, 1938, in Germany. These nominative reports contained individual data such as civil status, family ties and nationality. However, the information collected on this form was adapted to the presumed 'gypsy' lifestyle: the 'gypsy nickname' (*'Zigeunername'*) is noted as well as the type of housing and the regional travel areas of the censused person. No such reports have been identified yet for Alsace but the required use of this specific form by Kripo agents enlightens the transfer of the same German police methods regarding the 'gypsy' policy in an annexed territory. It can be presumed that this racial registration in Alsace was the expression of a broader and coordinated census operation of the Sinti and Roma present in the recently conquered territories as a similar event occurred in Prague in July 1942 when German criminal police forces decided to achieve a racial registration specifically dedicated to identifying 'gypsy' people living in this urban area using the same identification methods.[43]

After the December 16, 1942, order of Heinrich Himmler – known as the 'Auschwitz Decree' – and following the January 15, 1943, meeting regarding the execution of the collective deportation of Sinti and Roma from the Reich,[44] the RSHA issued a report to all Kripo departments (except Vienna) on January 29, 1943, to specify the conditions of the identification of individuals concerned by this measure.[45] In this document, Alsace was specifically mentioned as a ter-

---

42 Strasbourg criminal police to the Mulhouse criminal police, 28.06.1942, 3AL3 24077, ADHR. Translation by the author.
43 Aletta Beck and Michal Schuster: "Die Verfolgung von Roma und Sinti im Protektorat Böhmen und Mähren". Available at: https://www.holocaust.cz/de/geschichte/rom/die-verfolgung-der-roma-nach-der-errichtung-des-protektorats-boehmen-und-maehren/. Last accessed: 09.05.2021.
44 On this meeting, see Karola Fings: "A 'Wannsee Conference' on the Extermination of the Gypsies? New Research Findings Regarding 15 January 1943 and the Auschwitz Decree", in *Dapim. Studies on the Holocaust*, 27, 2013, 174–194.
45 Report of the RSHA on the "Einweisung von Zigeunermischlingen, Rom-Zigeunern und balkanischen Zigeunern in ein Konzentrationslager", 29.01.1943, 1.2.7.26/82342449–82342453/ITS Digital Archive, Archives Nationales.

ritory where the deportation order should be implemented. To apply this central decision, the Strasbourg Kripo made several targeted arrests of Sinti and Roma families and deported 61 individuals, labelled as 'gypsies', to the *'Zigeunerlager'* of Auschwitz-Birkenau on March 22, 1943. However, not all the people recorded by the police 'gypsy census' of the summer 1942 were deported from annexed Alsace as the mention *'Zigeunererfassung'* ('gypsy census') appears 105 times on the Kripo arrest cards. The central hypothesis – as will be explained in the following section – is that the deportation only affected censused 'gypsies' with at least one relative who had been previously racially registered and identified as a 'mixed-race gypsy' in Germany during the pre-war years.

Racial Identifications and the Deportation of 'Gypsies' from Annexed Alsace, 1943 to 1944

Rosenbach, Franz, Wesel, Blum, Gerste, Braun and Freiwald: as mentioned above, these are the seven family names of the 61 deportees arrested by the Strasbourg Kripo and sent to Auschwitz in March 1943. Genealogical and patronymic investigations made by Kripo officers played a key role in the racial identification and selection of 'gypsies' to be deported from annexed Alsace. These police inquiries relied on the racial surveys conducted by a central institution created in 1936 and dedicated to the registration of Sinti and Roma living in Germany: the RHF.[46]

On 5 February 1941, Robert Ritter, head of the RHF, published an article whose title translates to "The inventory of gypsies and mixed-race gypsies in Germany".[47] There he unveiled his project for the identification and subsequent registration of Sinti and Roma living in Germany. The idea of collecting data regarding the racial characteristics of an entire group is connected to a broader dynamic of total census and classification of the German population promoted

---

[46] On the RHF see Zimmermann, Rassenutopie und Genozid, 125–146; Martin Luchterhandt: *Der Weg nach Birkenau. Entstehung und Verlauf der nationalsozialistischen Verfolgung der "Zigeuner"*, Lübeck: Schmidt-Römhild, 2000, 123–137; Eve Rosenhaft: "Wissenschaft als Herrschaftsakt. Die Forschungspraxis der Ritter'schen Forschungsstelle und das Wissen über Zigeuner", in Zimmermann (ed.): Zwischen Erziehung und Vernichtung, 329–353; Karola Fings and Frank Sparing: *Rassismus – Lager – Völkermord: Die nationalsozialistische Zigeunerverfolgung in Köln*, Cologne: Emons, 2005, 109–194.

[47] Robert Ritter: "Die Bestandsaufnahme der Zigeuner und Zigeunermischlinge in Deutschland", in *Der Öffentliche Gesundheitsdienst*, 21, 477–489, 611/3/10, Wiener Library, London. Translation by the author.

by the Nazi authorities.⁴⁸ In his article, Ritter argued for the necessity of labelling 'gypsy' people to implement racial policies and presented his methodology to distinguish 'pure gypsies' from 'mixed-race gypsies'. According to him, the census of the entire 'gypsy' population could be completed in a year since, so far, 10,000 racial individual reports had been sent by the RHF to the Reichskriminalpolizeiamt (Headquarters of the Criminal Police, RKPA), the main office responsible for the 'fight against the gypsy plague' ('*Bekämpfung des Zigeunerunwesens*'). The results of racial surveys conducted by members of the RHF in previous years were used as reference records by the criminal police stations. Ritter's statements underline the key role of the RHF in the identification and racial determination process of the targeted 'gypsies' and the decisive involvement of this research center in the Sinti and Roma genocide.⁴⁹ For instance, in 1937 and 1938, RHF agents conducted several racial censuses and investigations in multiple Rhine cities such as Karlsruhe, Mannheim, Freiburg or Herbolzheim. Using genealogy and anthropometry, RHF racial anthropologists and Kripo police officers worked together to identify, register, and categorize more than 1,000 Sinti living in the Rhine area using a complex racial classification with numerous variations between a 'pure gypsy', a 'mixed-raced gypsy' and a 'non-gypsy'.⁵⁰

The racial inquiries realized by the RHF for Alsace were most likely based on the results of the Strasbourg police 'gypsy census' which recorded 105 individuals between the summer of 1942 and spring 1943. To achieve this racial census, Kripo agents completed the RKP 172 questionnaires and sent the documentation to RHF services in Berlin for further racial investigations. As the RHF collected and gathered anthropometrical and genealogical data on the 'gypsy' families living in Alsace, members of this institution carried out inquiries within their centralized records and archives. The case of the Gerste family exemplifies the circulation of collected data between central institutions and local police stations regarding 'gypsy' individuals. At the beginning of 1943, six members of the Gerste family were arrested in the Strasbourg area and labelled as 'gypsies' by

---

48 Götz Aly and Karl Heinz Roth: *Die restlose Erfassung. Volkszählen, Identifizieren, Aussondern im Nationalsozialismus*, Frankfurt am Main: S. Fischer, 2000.
49 On Robert Ritter, see Joachim S. Hohmann: *Robert Ritter und die Erben der Kriminalbiologie. "Zigeunerforschung" im Nationalsozialismus und in Westdeutschland im Zeichen des Rassismus*, Frankfurt am Main: Peter Lang, 1991, 133–216; Tobias Schmidt-Degenhard: *Vermessen und Vernichten. Der NS-"Zigeunerforscher" Robert Ritter*, Stuttgart: Franz Steiner, 2012.
50 "Hilfskarteien: Sinti aus Süddeutschland, Rheinland, Mitteldeutschland", 1937–1940, R165 6, BArch.

the Strasbourg Kripo (see fig. 2).[51] According to their birthplaces, the Gerste family was originally from Thuringia. The presence of three of them in Mainz was documented in February 1938 as their names were mentioned on a blood exam list compiled by Gerhart Stein, one of the main racial investigators of the RHF.[52] Consequently, RHF researchers built up the genealogical tree of the Gerste family in 1942 and proved that they should be considered as 'mixed-race gypsies'.[53] Therefore, according to the instructions sent by the RSHA on January 29, 1943, the Gerste family was concerned by the deportation order as they could be identified as German 'mixed-race gypsies'. Arrested by the Strasbourg Kripo, the Gerste family was deported to Auschwitz on March 22, 1943, where none of them survived.

Similarly, previous racial registrations conducted by the RHF led to the identification of the Wesels who were also considered as 'mixed-race gypsies' by the genealogical investigations of the RHF.[54] According to the death certificate issued by the Auschwitz registry office, Alfred Wesel (born 1904 in Eydtkuhnen) and Maria Winter (born 1902 in Leipzig) had their fifth child in November 1941 in a Moselle town named Château-Salins, which proves that this family was present in the annexed area during the war.[55] A few months earlier, on February 13, 1941, Rudolf Wesel, Alfred's father, was summoned to the Berlin Kripo station to be questioned about his family ties.[56] Presented as a 'mixed-race gypsy', Rudolf Wesel was forced to give all the information he knew about his relatives (names, surnames, nicknames, places and dates of birth) and to specify the relationships between them. He recognized that the Wesel patronym was an alias and that his parents were in fact named Höhdel. Upon identifying his six children, he stated that he did not know where his son Alfred lived. The police report of Rudolf Wesel's interrogation highlights what Michael Zimmerman defined as a "scientific-police complex"[57] by underlining the close connections between the Kripo's genealogical inquiries and racial research aimed at identifying 'gypsy' families conducted by the RHF across Germany. Therefore, the arrest and identification of the Wesels in Alsace demonstrate the ability of the Kripo services to

---

51 For one example, see: Arrest card Adolf Gerste, 1943, 757D 87, ADBR.
52 Nominative list of the blood exams conducted in Mainz by Gerhart Stein, February 1938, R165 38, BArch.
53 Genealogical materials Gerste, 1942, R165 145, BArch.
54 Genealogical materials Wesel, 1942, R165 148, BArch.
55 Death certificate for Otto Wesel, 1.1.2.1/514697/ITS Digital Archive, Archives Nationales.
56 Police interrogation report of Rudolf Wesel, 13.02.1941, in File of the Berlin criminal police on the Wesel family, 1.2.2.1/12102896/ITS Digital Archive, Archives Nationales.
57 Zimmermann, Rassenutopie und Genozid, 147–155, here 147. Translation by the author.

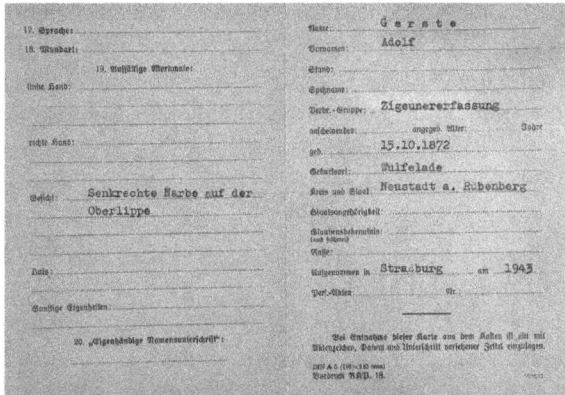
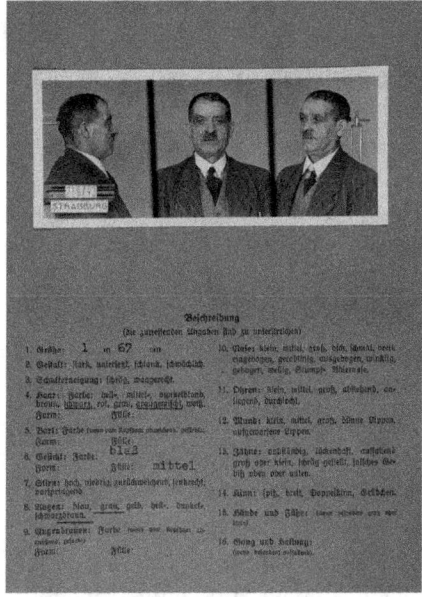

Fig. 2: Arrest card of Adolf Gerste, 1943, 757D 87, Archives départementales du Bas-Rhin, Strasbourg.

weave a network of data exchanges concerning 'gypsy' families all across Germany, including recently annexed territories.

In annexed Alsace, the deportation of March 1943 concerned exclusively 61 individuals who had already been spotted by the Kripo offices and the RHF in previous years. It was because these families were formerly registered in German police records and racial archives as 'mixed-race gypsies' that the Strasbourg Kripo deported them to Auschwitz-Birkenau in 1943. On the contrary, some families who were identified during the 'gypsy census' of 1942 were not deported because the German authorities did not have records on them and were not able to issue genealogical findings linked to the racial 'gypsy' classification. According to their birthplaces during the interwar period, the non-deported individuals censused had mainly pre-war French anchorages whereas the 61 deportees essentially came from Germany. Therefore, in March 1943, the principal target of the Strasbourg Kripo – when it came to carry out the roundups and organize the deportation – was firstly directed towards individuals previously identified as 'mixed-race gypsies' and of German origin.

Of the seven members of the Wesel family deported to Auschwitz on March 22, 1943, only one survived the concentration camp system. In 1955, Hugo Wesel, born in 1925 in Dresden, filled out inquiry forms to the International Tracing Service (ITS) for his relatives and stated that he and his family had been arrested in Strasbourg on March 11, 1943.[58] This postwar information on the temporality of the urban arrestations given by a survivor is a fundamental clue to document precisely the chronology of the deportation policy in Alsace as the regional archives do not unveil any chronological information on the Strasbourg Kripo arrest practices at this very moment. In the same perspective, the Buchenwald prisoner registration form of Georg Rosenbach identifies March 14, 1943, as his arrest date in Colmar.[59] Moreover, the inquiry form regarding the fate of Conrad Franz sent by the Munich state compensation office to the ITS in 1956 stated that he was arrested in 1943 in Strasbourg during a '*Zigeuneraktion*' (police action against 'gypsies').[60] Although these are fragmentary or postwar materials, they roughly shape the chronological framework of the roundups and suggest that the Kripo agents may have executed the targeted arrests in less than a week.

The spatiality of these urban persecutions can be traced with the death certificates issued by the Auschwitz registry office. Although there are a few variations, four deceased deportees indicate "Kronenburg, Oberhausbergerstrasse Nr. 74"[61] as their last residence. This location is confirmed by the Buchenwald prisoner registration card of Toni Franz which mentions "Strassburg-Kronenburg

---

[58] Tracing inquiry from Hugo Wesel, 26.04.1955, in T/D file Alfred Wesel, 6.3.3.2/99448520/ITS Digital Archive, Archives Nationales.
[59] Prisoner registration form of Georg Rosenbach, Buchenwald, 1.1.5.3/6946697/ITS Digital Archive, Archives Nationales.
[60] Tracing inquiry for Conrad Franz, 22.05.1956, in T/D file Conrad Franz, 6.3.3.2/101646933/ITS Digital Archive, Archives Nationales.
[61] For an example, see death certificate for Amanda Franz, Auschwitz-Birkenau, 1.1.2.1/578185/ITS Digital Archive, Archives Nationales.

Hausbergerstr. 74"[62] (see fig. 3). Furthermore, this address is noted for individuals tied to different families, meaning that they were present together at the same place before being deported from Strasbourg.

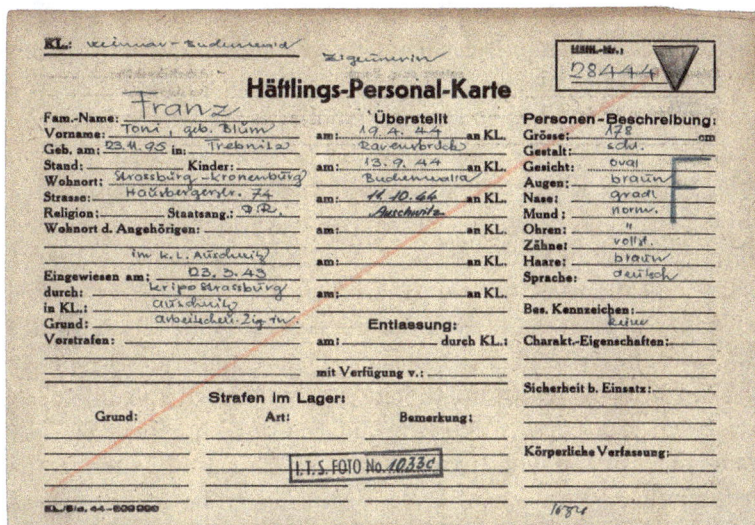

Fig. 3: Prisoner Registration Card of Toni Franz, Buchenwald, 1.1.5.4/7562572/ITS Digital Archive, Archives Nationales, Paris.

Comparing these geographical data with the resident registration file of the Strasbourg municipality allows us to map more precisely the presence of the deported families inside the urban area. These resident registration cards attest that out of all 61 deportees, 39 of them were housed in Cronenbourg and 11 in Strasbourg.[63] They were registered at these two specific locations between November 17, 1942, and March 5, 1943. And on March 19, 1943, each card indicates the same phrase: "has been deported to a labor camp for an unknown period with his family"[64].

The Cronenbourg place is in the northwestern suburbs of Strasbourg, beyond the central railway station. According to the city's 1939 street directory,

---

62 Prisoner registration card of Toni Franz, Buchenwald, 1.1.5.4/7562572/ITS Digital Archive, Archives Nationales.
63 Resident registration file of the Strasbourg municipality, 1940–1944, 624MW 1–67, Archives de Strasbourg.
64 For an example, see resident registration form for Leopold Franz, 1943, 624MW 16, Archives de Strasbourg. Translation by the author.

this address refers to a former military hospital built in 1891 and composed of five barracks and one administrative building.[65] In 1929, the Strasbourg municipality acquired this site, surrounded by its original wall, to convert it into social housing.[66] It can be assumed that in 1943, the Strasbourg Kripo authorities used this facility, which could be easily secured and guarded, to gather 'gypsy' families arrested in the area. The assumption that Cronenbourg's former military hospital was a place of assignment can be sustained by the information given by a Gerste relative after the war. When submitting inquiries to the ITS for the deported Gerste family in 1958, August Gerste indicated that they resided near Saarlouis, in Saarland, before being arrested in 1943.[67] The arrest of the Blum family is a further argument for thinking that the Cronenbourg address may not have been the real residence of the deported 'gypsy' families. Their mugshots provide time and spatial indications as they were taken outdoor.[68] Moreover, the Kripo photographer added a blackboard behind the individual with the exact date and place. The women of the Blum family were photographed on October 22, 1942, in Haguenau, a town located in northern Alsace. Furthermore, one of the deportees gave birth to a child in the city's hospital in February 1942.[69] The birth certificate issued by the Haguenau municipality indicates that the mother was domiciled in Ittlingen, in Baden, whereas her death certificate in Auschwitz points out the Cronenbourg address.[70] The gathering of spatial data with Arolsen materials and local sources regarding the deportees from the Strasbourg area in March 1943 confirms that the targeted families lived in different places in Alsace and Sarre. Their arrests were probably due to their economic mobility at a time when the Strasbourg Kripo was keeping a watchful eye on the 'gypsy question'. As such, the arrested families may have been 'preventively' gathered at Cronenbourg for further racial examinations in late 1942 and early 1943 before being selected and deported.

---

65 Street directory of Strasbourg, 1939, 1BA 1939, Archives de Strasbourg.
66 Former Cronenbourg military hospital: housing development project, 1929–1930, 843W 616, Archives de Strasbourg.
67 Tracing inquiry from August Gerste, 28.08.1958, in T/D file Alwine Gerste, 6.3.3.2/104406185/ ITS Digital Archive, Archives Nationales. On the death certificate issued by the Sonderstandesamt (special registry office) in Arolsen in 1971, the place of residence of Alwine Gerste is Saarlouis.
68 For an example, see Arrest card of Pauline Blum, 20.10.1942, 757D 69, ADBR.
69 Birth certificate for Waltraud Freiwald, 19.02.1942, Mairie de la ville de Haguenau.
70 Death certificate for Emma Freiwald, 16.11.1943, Auschwitz-Birkenau, 1.1.2.1/578308/ITS Digital Archive, Archives Nationales.

Conclusion

The Strasbourg criminal police's racial identifications played a key role in the deportation of Sinti and Roma from Alsace as police services progressively collected knowledge on the 'travelling worlds' of this borderland area. Using census methods and referring to the records of the *Rassenhygienische Forschungsstelle* in Berlin, Kripo services first led the repression towards the identified and selected German 'gypsy' individuals who had been previously registered. The Strasbourg deportation of March 1943 was embedded in the broader context of the Sinti and Roma genocide as coordinated deportation convoys were organized in Western Germany. For instance, on March 10, 1943, the Karlsruhe criminal police planned the deportation of a convoy from Herbolzheim scheduled for March 24, 1943.[71] Similarly, on March 15, 1943, a convoy left the Stuttgart railway station for Auschwitz-Birkenau.[72] The destruction and dislocation of these families were part of the genocidal dynamic triggered by the German authorities in spring 1943. With the involvement of Kripo officers, this policy was at the same time applied in annexed Alsace.

The 61 deportees from Strasbourg arrived at Auschwitz-Birkenau on March 22, 1943, where the death of 33 of them was documented between April 4, 1943, and May 21, 1944, within the registry book of the 'gypsy camp'. The fate of 14 individuals remains unknown whereas 14 others were later transferred to Buchenwald or Ravensbrück. The examination of ITS inquiries shows that at least nine of them survived through the war. While there are no administrative records, correspondences or police orders related to the deportation of this group in the French departmental archives, documents from the Arolsen Archives shed light on the spatial and chronological trajectories of this specific group. The study of the implementation of the genocidal policies in annexed Alsace underlines the methods used by the German repressive forces to project onto this borderland space their own conception of 'gypsies', product of their racial imaginary and former police methods. Registration of presumed 'gypsies', gathering of individual and familial data, transmission of records from Stras-

---

71 The Documentation and Cultural Centre of German Sinti and Roma: "'Rassendiagnose: Zigeuner'. Der Völkermord an den Sinti und Roma und der lange Kampf um Anerkennung". Available at: https://www.sintiundroma.org/de/set/022211a/?id=2591&z=13. Last accessed: 08.05. 2021.
72 Magdalena Guttenberger and Manuel Werner: *"Die Kinder von Auschwitz singen so laut!" Das erschütterte Leben der Sintiza Martha Guttenberger aus Ummenwinkel*, Norderstedt: Books on Demand, 2020, 204.

bourg to Berlin, inquiries into genealogical materials, and selections for deportation: these police and bureaucratic operations show how brutally the German racial ideology found its own spatial expression in a recently annexed Western European borderland territory.

Joachim Schröder
Forced Accommodation for Jews in the Context of the Deportations at the Düsseldorf Abattoir (1939–1944)

Abstract: During the period 1941 to 1944, the former Düsseldorf abattoir served as an assembly camp for almost 6,000 Jewish men, women and children from the administrative district of Düsseldorf prior to their deportation. Their deportation was the end of a long process of disenfranchisement and social isolation, the penultimate stage of which was eviction from their own or rented housing and confinement in forced accommodation: a *'Judenhaus'* ('Jews house', a tenement building where Jews were housed), communal accommodation or a camp. This paper investigates for the first time the background to and the process of 'residential segregation' in this region. It names the various actors of local municipal authorities and the NSDAP involved and uses examples to describe the situation faced by those who were persecuted.

Introduction

Around 8,000 people persecuted for being Jewish were deported from the Düsseldorf administrative district to the ghettos, concentration and extermination camps in German-occupied East Central Europe between 1941 and 1944. This corresponded to around a third of the Jewish population in the region, based on the year 1933.[1] For almost 6,000 of these people, the Düsseldorf abattoir served as the central assembly camp for the whole of the administrative district. Like many other such assembly camps in the German Reich, the Düsseldorf abattoir was set up as a transit camp only on a temporary basis. Regular slaughtering operations were not interrupted during the process. The Gestapo worked closely with the abattoir's management to organize the *'Schleusung'* ('channeling') of the Jews who were brought here, which means they were registered and deprived

---

[1] In 1933, with around four million inhabitants, the Düsseldorf administrative district was one of the most densely populated administrative districts in the German Reich, with the major cities of Duisburg, Essen, Gladbach-Rheydt (now: Mönchengladbach), Krefeld, Mülheim an der Ruhr, Oberhausen and Wuppertal. The proportion of (registered) Jews in the total population of the administrative district was 0.6 percent.

∂ OpenAccess. © 2023 the author(s), published by De Gruyter. This work is licensed under the Creative Commons Attribution-NonCommercial-NoDerivatives 4.0 International License.
https://doi.org/10.1515/9783110746464-014

of their remaining possessions and signed a waiver relinquishing their assets.[2] The would-be deportees spent no more than 24 hours at the site. After the rigmarole, they had to stay a night in the cattle market hall, which was dirty and had no heating. Seven deportations in total led to the ghettos in Łódź, Minsk, Riga, Izbica, and Theresienstadt, or to work camps run by the Todt Organization in Lenne and Zeitz. Only around 400 people survived their deportation.[3]

The site of the former abattoir is now home to the campus of the Düsseldorf University of Applied Sciences. At the site of the former assembly camp, in the cattle market hall, the Alter Schlachthof Memorial Centre now researches these crimes and commemorates those who were deported and murdered. The events that took place on the site are documented in a permanent exhibition. How the deportations took place, and which players from which authorities and agencies had a significant involvement in them, are the central questions asked.

Not only is the fate that awaited the deportees in the ghettos researched and documented, but also what these people experienced prior to their deportation. Deportation was merely the culmination of a series of discriminatory measures and interventions to which the Jewish population had been subjected since 1933. Following bans on exercising certain professions, 'Aryanization', and exclusion from social and cultural life, Jews were driven out of their own (or rented) homes and placed in forced accommodation. There were different types of forced accommodation in which Jews were housed prior to their deportation, which are differentiated as follows:

'*Judenhäuser*' ('Jews houses')[4]: These houses were established in residential buildings (formerly) belonging to Jewish owners.

---

[2] For a definition of the term '*Schleusung*' see Akim Jah: *Die Deportation der Juden aus Berlin. Die nationalsozialistische Vernichtungspolitik und das Sammellager Große Hamburger Straße*, Berlin: be.bra, 2013, 136–137.

[3] See, in detail, Joachim Schröder: *Alter Schlachthof Memorial Centre. Exhibition Catalogue*, Düsseldorf: Droste, 2019; Bastian Fleermann and Hildegard Jakobs: *Düsseldorfer Deportationen*, Düsseldorf: Droste, 2015; Holger Berschel: *Bürokratie und Terror. Das Judenreferat der Gestapo Düsseldorf 1935–1945*, Essen: Klartext, 2001.

[4] Use of the Nazi term '*Judenhaus*' is inconsistent within existing research. More recent works avoid this term altogether and refer to 'ghetto houses' – a term which, however, insinuates proximity to the living conditions in the ghettos in German-occupied East Central Europe. The term '*Judenhaus*' will be retained in the following for now. A comprehensive account of the subject is not yet available, but there are numerous regional works, based on the work of Gerhard Botz: *Wohnungspolitik und Judendeportation in Wien 1938–1945. Zur Funktion des Antisemitismus als Ersatz nationalsozialistischer Sozialpolitik*, Vienna/Salzburg: Geyer-Edition, 1975, and Marlis

Sammelunterkünfte (communal accommodations) and residential camps: The term Sammelunterkunft is used here to describe buildings that were not previously residential buildings, such as administrative buildings of the Jewish Communities or former department stores. Residential camps were barracks used and set up especially for Jews, such as the Holbeckshof camp in Essen or the Much camp in Siegerland.[5]

Assembly camps: These camps, often set up in buildings of the Jewish Communities or in (public) halls or other big 'suitable' buildings were established for the immediate preparation of the deportations (for example, the Große Hamburger Straße camp in Berlin and the assembly camp at the Düsseldorf abattoir).

The first two types served to segregate Jews from the rest of society and keep them together under surveillance in certain locations. As a rule, they existed for at least several months and were permanently occupied, sometimes with a high turnover. However, in the assembly camps set up for immediate preparation for deportation, people did not usually stay for longer than one or a few days.[6] This paper looks at the first two types, *'Judenhäuser'* and communal accommodation/ residential camps in the administrative district of Düsseldorf.

As it turned out, confinement in forced accommodation was usually the last step prior to deportation. How much such forced accommodation there was in the city or in the administrative district of Düsseldorf is not yet known; the subject is still largely unexplored at a regional level.[7] Nor is it known in detail how

---

Buchholz: *Die hannoverschen Judenhäuser. Zur Situation der Juden in der Zeit der Ghettoisierung und Verfolgung 1941 bis 1945*, Hildesheim: A. Lax, 1987.

5 There had already been a comprehensive camp system in the German Reich since 1938, set up by various agencies, into which Jews were conscripted for forced labor, or retrained. See Wolfgang Gruner: *Der Geschlossene Arbeitseinsatz deutscher Juden. Zur Zwangsarbeit als Element der Verfolgung 1938–1943*, Berlin: Metropol, 1997, 217–272. The (work) camps referred to here were set up from 1941/1942 onwards, in the run-up to the pending deportations, cf. ibid., 249–272.

6 In individual cases, there are also overlaps between type 2) and type 3) (for example, in Munich, Milbertshofen camp, Cologne, Fort V in Müngersdorf).

7 However, some information can be found in local studies, for example Stefan Rohrbacher: *Juden in Neuss*, Neuss: Galerie Küppers, 1986, 210; Günther Erckens: *Juden in Mönchengladbach. Jüdisches Leben in den früheren Gemeinden M. Gladbach, Rheydt, Odenkirchen, Giesenkirchen-Schelsen, Rheindahlen, Wickerath und Wanlo*, volume 1, Mönchengladbach: Stadtarchiv, 1988, 736–746; Claudia Flümann: *"... doch nicht bei uns in Krefeld!" Arisierung, Enteignung, Wiedergutmachung in der Samt- und Seidenstadt, 1933 bis 1963*, Essen: Klartext, 2015, 243–254. For Düsseldorf, only brief passages from Bastian Fleermann: "Vom Pogrom zum Abtransport. Die Situation der Juden im Reg. Bez. Düsseldorf zwischen November 1938 bis April 1941", in Angela Genger and Hildegard Jakobs (eds.): *Düsseldorf. Getto Litzmannstadt. 1941*, Essen: Klartext, 2010; important preparatory work was done in Düsseldorf by Dr. Barbara Suchy, who, with the help of surviving house books, drew up a list of apartments in which Jewish residents of Düsseldorf had

the multi-layered process of 'evicting' the Jewish population and keeping them together in forced accommodation took place in the region, and which players from which agencies and authorities were involved.

Identifying and documenting forced accommodation has a significant value in terms of remembrance culture as these places offer starting points for historical and political educational and remembrance work. In three research seminars to date, students at the Department of Social/Cultural Sciences did research on the history of *'Judenhäuser'* in the region. The prospective social workers and social education workers, who will be active in a wide variety of social settings in their future professions, were now confronted with a very special, historical social setting, and attempted to find answers to the following questions: Where was such forced accommodation in the region? What did 'being sent to a *'Judenhaus'* mean for the people concerned? What were the living conditions like? How long did the people live here? The findings of the research seminars have been incorporated into this paper. This paper is intended to provide initial answers to the questions raised but should still be considered a work in progress.[8]

'Aryanization' of Jewish Housing: Legal Basis and Developments

There were two aspects to the Nazi expropriation and eviction policy in the area of housing. Firstly, the Nazi rulers were involved in expropriating or 'Aryanizing' Jewish-owned property, where the intention was to transfer the resulting profits to government coffers. Secondly, the Nazis sought to separate Jews from the rest of society: Jewish and non-Jewish tenants were not to live under the same roof, and non-Jewish tenants were not to live in apartments owned by Jewish land-

---

lived. Dr. Suchy also kindly provided the author with an (unpublished) paper on a *'Judenhaus'* in Düsseldorf.

[8] The initial clues as to the location of much of the forced accommodation were the surviving deportation lists available online in the Arolsen Archives, which often include the last addresses of the deportees (Collection 1.2.1.1). This information is supplemented by other sources, such as the house books already mentioned, and other sources. Reports on the seminars (with my colleague Alexander Flohé, Düsseldorf University of Applied Sciences) can be found at https://www.erinnerungsort-duesseldorf.de. The ongoing research project at the Alter Schlachthof Memorial Centre on forced accommodation in the region was also supported by research carried out by historian Dr. Mareen Heying, to whom sincere thanks is expressed at this point.

lords. Hovering over these measures, as before, was the declared overall aim of inducing even more Jews to emigrate.[9]

The systematic expropriation of 'Jewish housing' began virtually at the same time as the "elimination of the Jews from German economic life"[10] – as per the wording of the decree issued on November 12, 1938, immediately after the November pogroms. It prohibited Jews from exercising any managerial or business activity from January 1, 1939 onwards. It was followed on December 3, 1938 by the Verordnung über den Einsatz jüdischen Vermögens[11] (Decree on the Utilization of Jewish Property). This decree forced Jewish owners to sell their businesses, property, jewelry, etc.

In his subsequent decree of December 28, 1938,[12] the Reich's Minister of Economics, Hermann Göring, referring to an "order from the Führer", emphasized that the "Aryanization" of Jewish housing, i.e. the dispossession of Jewish house and apartment owners, but also, in a broader sense, the expulsion of Jewish tenants from buildings belonging to non-Jewish owners, was to take place last. This was to avoid chaotic circumstances caused by too many Jews becoming homeless. At the same time, "Jewish-owned" property could serve as collateral for financing the emigration of destitute Jews, for example. Jewish tenants in buildings owned by non-Jews were to be evicted and moved into houses owned by Jews. Jews who were married to non-Jews were exempt from these regulations in two cases: if the husband was 'Aryan', or if the husband was Jewish and there were children. Overall the intention was to avoid a concentration of large numbers of such forced accommodation or a "ghettoization" in certain parts of the city – Hitler was obviously concerned about German and international opinion here.[13]

---

9 Saul Friedländer: *Das Dritte Reich und die Juden. Die Jahre der Verfolgung 1933–1939*, volume 1, Munich: Beck, 1998, 310. Re. 'Wohnraumarisierung' (residential segregation), cf., in addition to the works of Buchholz and Botz (footnote 5), Wolf Gruner: "Die Grundstücke der 'Reichsfeinde'. Zur 'Arisierung' von Immobilien durch Städte und Gemeinden 1938–1945", in *Jahrbuch zur Geschichte und Wirkung des Holocaust*, 2000, 125–156; Michaela Raggam-Blesch: "'Sammelwohnungen' für Jüdinnen und Juden als Zwischenstation vor der Deportation, Wien 1938–1942", in *Dokumentationsarchiv des österreichischen Widerstands (DÖW), Annual Report*, Vienna, 2018, 81–100.
10 Reichsgesetzblatt I, 1938, 1580.
11 Reichsgesetzblatt I, 1938, 1709.
12 Published in Susanne Heim (ed.): *Die Verfolgung und Ermordung der europäischen Juden durch das nationalsozialistische Deutschland*, volume 2, Munich: Oldenbourg, 2009, Doc. 215, 583–584.
13 Friedländer, Das Dritte Reich und die Juden, volume 1, 310–313.

Even before December 1938, the steadily worsening antisemitic climate and the increasing economic difficulties associated with this had led to Jewish tenants having to leave larger apartments in order to find new, often smaller living accommodation in buildings owned by Jewish landlords. This is evidenced by the house books that have survived in the Düsseldorf Municipal Archives, with the help of which the movements of Jewish tenants into and out of individual houses can be easily traced.[14]

The 'residential segregation' and confinement of Jews in forced accommodation only really gathered pace with the *Gesetz über die Mietverhältnisse mit Juden* (Law on Leases Contracted with Jews) adopted on April 30, 1939,[15] and its implementing decree issued by the Reich Ministry of Labor [sic!] and the Reich Ministry of the Interior on May 4, 1939.[16] The law abolished protection for Jewish tenants. However, an 'Aryan' landlord could only terminate a Jewish tenant's lease if he had obtained a certificate from the relevant municipal authority stating that alternative accommodation was available.[17] Jewish landlords were also forced to declare empty or unused rooms. Jews who had been made homeless could then be moved into these rooms even against the landlord's will or the will of the tenants themselves. The Düsseldorf-based Nazi newspaper Rheinische Landeszeitung explained:

> Since a household cannot comprise both German compatriots and Jews, the option has been created to remove Jews from German residences even against their will. Then again, Jews occupying an excessive amount of living space in proportion to their population, while many German compatriots and their families are still without accommodation, or have to make do with unsatisfactory accommodation, cannot be justified. Hence the need to accommodate those Jews, who have to be removed from German apartments, and who do not wish to, or are unable to avail themselves of the opportunity to emigrate, in Jewish houses, in order to take advantage of the space available to Jews in these houses – which in some cases is particularly abundant – by taking in other Jewish families.[18]

---

14 Cf. for example, the house books of the '*Judenhäuser*' at Adersstraße 8, Rochusstraße 57 or Teutonenstraße 9 in the Düsseldorf Municipal Archives (Collection: 'house books'). For Vienna, this process is described by Raggam-Blesch, Sammelwohnungen, 87.
15 Reichsgesetzblatt I, 1939, 864–865. Also in 0–1–4–12314, sheets 5–9, Düsseldorf Municipal Archives (referred to in the following as StAD).
16 Ministerialblatt des Reiches und Preußischen Ministeriums des Innern No. 19 of April 10, 1939, 996–997 (also: 0–1–12314, sheet 49–50, StAD).
17 Friedländer, Das Dritte Reich, volume 1, 313.
18 Rheinische Landeszeitung, May 4, 1939: "Keine Juden in deutschen Wohnungen". Translation by the author.

The antisemitic motivation of both the Nazi rulers and the editor, who considered it inadmissible that Jewish men and women were provided with housing that was unspecified in size, but allegedly "abundant", is clearly apparent here. In order to promote the bringing together of Jews in buildings belonging to Jewish owners, subletting to Jews was facilitated to a large extent. Jews were subsequently allowed to conclude subletting agreements even without the permission of the (Jewish) landlord – at the same time, they could only rent to Jewish subletters. The *Rheinische Landeszeitung* goes on to say:

> Having said that, the municipal authority has been given broad powers enabling it to house Jews subject to eviction as planned. In addition to the power to impose the conclusion of tenancy and subletting agreements between Jews, the municipal authority also has the right to demand the registration of any rooms that are let to Jews, or which may be eligible for accommodating Jews.[19]

Municipal leaders, i.e. mayors, were charged with implementing the *Gesetz über die Mietverhältnisse mit Juden* and also with the utilization of the apartments that became available. In carrying out this task, they were to "liaise appropriately with the competent party authority in order to ensure that the measures proceed in an orderly manner".[20] The fundamental idea of the statutory regulations was to group Jews together in certain houses. In the process, houses that were already predominantly inhabited by Jews were to be preferentially designated as 'Judenhäuser': "However, the designation of these houses was not to lead to an undesirable formation of ghettos."[21]

Identification of 'Jewish Housing'

The municipal leaders were charged with implementing the law, but the agencies who then put these laws into practice were quite different in the cities and local authorities. As the surviving records show, there was an exchange of information between individual towns and cities as to which authorities had been charged with implementing the law.[22] In Mönchengladbach, for example, the mayor assigned this task to the municipal police department.[23] In the regional capital,

---

19 Ibid. Translation by the author.
20 Rheinische Landeszeitung, May 10, 1939: "Judenhäuser – aber keine Ghettobildung". Translation by the author.
21 Ibid.
22 Cf. 0–1–4–12314, sheet 31 (Essen), sheet 56 (Bielefeld), StAD.
23 Erckens, Juden in Mönchengladbach, volume 1, 737.

Düsseldorf, the mayor, Dr. Helmut Otto, entrusted the Office for Economic Affairs with the task of implementing the *Gesetz über die Mietverhältnisse mit Juden* on May 23, 1939. Within the municipal Office for Economic Affairs (office 65), this task was assigned to the 'Pricing Authority for Rents and Leases for Residential and Commercial Premises'. The pricing authority was hived off and raised to the rank of a separate office (office 64) after the beginning of the Second World War.[24] The former head of the Office for Economic Affairs, Dr. Hermann Binstadt, a staunch Nazi and '*Alter Kämpfer*' (early member) of the NSDAP, was put in charge.[25] As a few of the surviving records from Office 64 show, a reliable party comrade, former front-line soldier, Dr. Walter Uhrhahn, who was seriously injured during the war, was also responsible for '*Mietverhältnisse mit Juden*' ('leases contracted with Jews').[26]

The first task was to identify houses owned and rented by Jews. As ordered in the implementing decree of May 4, 1939, the 'Pricing Authority for Rents and Leases' published an announcement in the regional press on June 2, 1939, in which all non-Jewish landlords were asked to register living space rented to Jews by June 15, 1939. All Jewish landlords were required to report: living space rented to 'non-Jews', living space rented to Jews, their own living space, empty living space, and space that became available after May 4, 1939: "Any person who deliberately or negligently fails to register in a timely manner shall be punished with a fine or imprisonment".[27]

At the same time, the pricing authority also tried to involve the Gestapo, the financial administration, the police and the district leadership of the NSDAP in the laborious work of creating this list. The Gestapo was not involved, however, at least not at this early stage. Inspired by corresponding orders from Berlin and suggestions by the pricing authority, NSDAP district leader, Karl Walter, in a joint meeting with councilor Brückmann and Dr. Hermann Binstadt,[28] was particularly interested in the question of closing off individual streets and residential areas to Jews. The pricing authority itself had suggested closing off Königsallee, Scha-

---

24 0–1–4–12314, sheet 10, StAD. The individual areas of responsibility of the new office can be found in the city of Düsseldorf 1940 directory: "Pricing and monitoring of rents and leases for residential and commercial premises. Conversion of apartments into premises of a different kind. Procurement of housing for large families, lease agreements with Jews. Consulate matters."
25 Binstadt joined the NSDAP on December 1, 1931. He was decorated on several occasions during the war. Cf. his personnel file: 0–1–5–31096, sheet 432, 452, 470, StAD.
26 Uhrhahn had a doctorate in law, held various offices in the city of Düsseldorf between 1924 and 1955; was denazified in Group V after the war; his leading role in the confinement of Jews in forced accommodation is not evident from his personnel file. Cf. 0–1–5–33793, StAD.
27 0–1–4–12314, sheet 11, StAD. Translation by the author.
28 It is possible that Dr. Walter Uhrhahn also attended the meeting in his place.

dowstrasse, Jägerhofstrasse, Ernst-vom-Rath-Strasse and the entire Hofgarten district, all located in the city center, to Jews. The NSDAP district leader also wanted to include Schlageterstadt, a housing development in the north of Düsseldorf where mainly NSDAP members lived.[29] At the same time, he promised to involve local NSDAP groups in the listing of "Jewish apartments".[30] As it turned out, however, the NSDAP leadership lacked the necessary capacities for such identification work, but it did ask for the completed list to be handed over.[31]

The Düsseldorf Financial Administration, which was also asked for assistance, merely sent the pricing authority a list of the "administrators of foreign real estate residing in Düsseldorf" on June 21, 1939.[32] The pricing authority carried out the task of actual identification over the next few weeks, mainly on its own, with help from the landlords' responses to the request for information, and possibly also with support from the police (residents' registration office).[33] Some of the 138 Jewish house owners listed in a surviving, undated complete list compiled by the authority were already living abroad or had emigrated. The residents of their houses were both Jewish and non-Jewish. In addition to the two Jewish Community properties at Bilker Straße 25 and Grafenberger Allee 78, there were only twelve properties housing exclusively Jewish tenants, and five others housing almost exclusively Jewish tenants.[34] At the same time, thanks to the requests for information, the authority identified a total of 550 apartments with Jewish tenants in "non-Jewish properties".[35]

---

29 File note dated May 30, 1939, 0-1-4-12314, sheet 12, StAD. The Schlageterstadt housing development in the district of Golzheim was built during the 'Productive People' exhibition in 1937 (known today as Golzheimer Siedlung).
30 Cf. note by administrative staff member Dr. Uhrhahn on a conversation in the NSDAP district administration on May 30, 1939, 0-1-4-12314, sheet 14, StAD.
31 Cf. internal note, concerning "rented property with Jews", after a meeting between Dr. Binstadt and Dr. Uhrhahn at the NSDAP district administration, June 23, 1939, 0-1-4-12314, sheet 25, StAD.
32 Cf. Head of Düsseldorf Financial Administration to the city of Düsseldorf, office 64, June 21, 1939, 0-1-4-12314, sheet 26, StAD. Why the Financial Administration provided such a list is unclear, a list of Jewish owners was explicitly requested on June 10, 1939 (ibid., sheet 18).
33 This is indicated by a note handwritten by a pricing authority employee (ibid., sheet 20).
34 Cf. "Register of Jewish home owners" (no date), 0-1-4-12316, StAD. Jewish tenants only: Gartenstraße 112, Germaniastraße 28, Goethestraße 12 and 18, Grunerstraße 19, Grupellostraße 8 and 29, Horst-Wessel-Straße 60, Kreutzstraße 58, Reichsstraße 69, Steinstraße 60, Wagnerstraße 7; predominantly Jewish tenants: Karlstraße 95, Geibelstraße 39, Martin-Luther-Platz 19, Steinstraße 82, Teutonenstraße 9 (strangely, Kurfürstenstraße 59, later the largest 'Judenhaus' in the city, is not in the register).
35 Letter from Dr. Binstadt to Mayor Dr. Haidn, July 17, 1939, 0-1-4-12314, sheet 36, StAD.

Consequently, there were numerous properties with 'mixed' residents, and this 'problem' was not easy for the rulers to solve, since the protection for non-Jewish tenants continued to exist even in properties with Jewish owners, so they could not simply be given notice, and neither could Jewish tenants married to non-Jews. Point 7 of the implementing regulation applied here: "The free right of landlords to let remains [...] unaffected". The law and the implementing regulation had given the city administration the necessary means to forcibly evict Jewish tenants if necessary and to accommodate them in other properties. Which property was now declared a '*Judenhaus*' was selected in the coming months by the pricing authority from the list that had been compiled. In addition, pricing authority employees, in agreement with the Gestapo, inspected all Jewish apartments, especially in buildings owned by Jews, in order to determine how much living space could be used to accommodate Jewish families from 'Aryan' houses.[36]

Like the city administration, the Nazi rulers counted on the fact that the process of evicting Jewish tenants from houses belonging to non-Jewish owners would proceed largely without their intervention, and that they would only occasionally have to resort to coercive measures. This was also recommended in the implementing regulation (point 5), and there is evidence that it worked, at least initially. In the summer of 1939, for instance, the pricing authority refrained from compiling registers of apartments and rooms in "non-Jewish houses", "as the circumstances are constantly changing due to the departure and relocation of Jewish tenants".[37]

By December 1940, the eviction process had progressed further, due to the relocation of Jewish tenants within the city and emigration, which although limited by the start of the war, was still ongoing. There were still around 1,400 Community members in 741 'households', where every furnished room was counted as a household.[38] And the eviction process continued to accelerate, as the pricing authority informed the NSDAP district legal department on April 22, 1941. The district legal department wanted "to find a solution to the Jewish housing issue" and to requisition the remaining '*Judenhäuser*' in order to give them to the families of "front line soldiers and workers":

---

[36] Letter from the pricing authority to the NSDAP district legal department, April 22, 1941, 0–1–4–12314, sheet 60, StAD.
[37] Letter from Dr. Binstadt to Mayor Dr. Haidn, July 17, 1939, 0–1–4–12314, sheet 36, StAD.
[38] Handwritten note by a pricing authority employee, 0–1–4–12317, sheet 44, StAD.

It is contrary to good common sense that often non-working [sic!] Jews live in palatial apartments, while hard-working compatriots and large families often to have make do with apartments that are damaging to their health.[39]

The pricing authority then notified that "just recently there has been an increase in changes of apartment by Jewish apartment owners, in that Jews from Aryan houses are moving into Jewish houses, and Jewish apartment owners are taking in Jews as subtenants more than was previously the case".[40] The fundamental idea of grouping Jews together in certain houses, by force if necessary, was being put into practice more and more. Notices of termination enforced by order began to play an increasingly important role. As far as can be seen, the executing body was now the Gestapo, which had not been involved previously, and which registered all Jewish tenants in 'Aryan' houses.[41] If the Gestapo gave notice of termination, the apartment that had become vacant was immediately reported to the municipal welfare office which was supposed to pass this on to 'compatriots' in need.[42]

Incidentally, as the case of Dr. Ernst Blankenstein, who was in a 'privileged mixed marriage' shows, the Gestapo also disregarded the applicable legal provisions here as and when it saw fit. It was a thorn in the side of the Gestapo that Dr. Blankenstein lived with his non-Jewish wife in an apartment "in one of the best residential areas".[43] So although "there was no legal basis for the compulsory implementation of this measure", as Gestapo official Pütz himself noted, it arranged for the landlord to give Dr. Blankenstein notice to vacate the apartment. And it ordered the couple to move into a very run-down apartment at Grimmstrasse 36, a 'Judenhaus'.

The total number of 'Judenhäuser' in the city of Düsseldorf, or even in the administrative district of Düsseldorf, has not yet been determined. A conserva-

---

39 Head of the NSDAP district legal department to the Mayor of Düsseldorf, April 7, 1941, 0–1–4–12314, sheet 59, StAD. Translation by the author. Corresponding letters were apparently also received in other cities in the administrative district, cf. for Mönchengladbach (there in August 1941): Erckens, Juden in Mönchengladbach, volume 1, 741.
40 Letter from the pricing authority to the NSDAP district legal department, April 22, 1941, 0–1–4–12314, sheet 60, StAD.
41 Presumably, it arranged for this registration work to be carried out by the Jewish community in Düsseldorf, which 'cooperated' out of necessity. The community itself issued an instruction to all members that changes of residence were to be reported to it immediately. Cf. circular from the Board of the Jewish Religious Community, May 9, 1940, 0–1–23–1370, StAD.
42 0–1–4–12317, sheet 48–49, StAD. Police chief constable Kinzel and police commissioner Hürdelbrink were responsible.
43 Note Gestapo Düsseldorf, April 21, 1943, RW 58/3429, sheet 13, NRW regional archives. Translation by the author. Thanks to Frank Sparing (Düsseldorf) for pointing out this file.

tive estimate of around 25 to 30 '*Judenhäuser*' can be assumed for the city area, although not all of them existed for the same length of time. Only those houses that were completely or predominantly occupied by Jewish residents are considered '*Judenhäuser*' here.[44]

Housing Shortage and Deportations

It would be a very comprehensive task to trace in detail the movements of displacement and concentration that began in all cities and communities in the administrative district in the years following the introduction of the *Gesetz über die Mietverhältnisse mit Juden*. They ended the same way in all cases. Smaller towns and communities announced that they were 'Jew-free' after the last Jewish residents had been deported or had fled to the nearest large city where Jews were still living, or where there were still larger Jewish communities.[45] In the larger cities, the number of '*Judenhäuser*' and the number of residents forced to occupy them initially grew. The deportations that began in October 1941 led to a clear stimulation of the whole process.

To what extent, and if at all, the housing shortage that prevailed in the large cities of the Rhein-Ruhr region accelerated the process of forced eviction of the Jewish population cannot yet be assessed. However, it should be assumed that the parties responsible for providing the population with housing in the municipal administrations – Housing Department and Welfare Department – kept an eye on the apartments occupied by Jews, and were very well informed about developments. This is documented in Düsseldorf by a meeting of department heads of the city administration on matters relating to air-raid protection on October 27, 1941 – the day of the first mass deportation from the Düsseldorf administrative district. In connection with aid for victims of bomb damages, Welfare Department Director Otto Buchholz announced "that he would like to negotiate with the Head of the Financial Administration about the purchase of furniture from

---

44 The estimate is based on the few surviving pricing authority file fragments (StAD, 0–1–4–12317) as well as on the transcription of the house books made by Suchy (see footnote 8).
45 Like the Mayor of Hilden on January 8, 1942, for example, after the last Hilden Jews had been deported to Riga and others had moved to Düsseldorf. Arbeitskreis Stolpersteine Hilden (ed.): "*Steine gegen das Vergessen. Stolpersteine in Hilden*", Hilden, 2013, 18–19. Available at: https://docplayer.org/54287642-Steine-gegen-das-vergessen.html. Last accessed: 14.11.2021.

the Jewish apartments that are now becoming vacant".⁴⁶ His report, a few days later, said:

> I would like to take this opportunity to talk about the evacuation of around 1,000 Jews from Düsseldorf, a matter which is probably already generally known. The extent to which housing will be freed up as a result of this cannot yet be determined. What is certain is that the generally cherished hopes are far from being fulfilled. We can expect between 100 and 120 apartments to become vacant. They will initially be offered by the Geheime Staatspolizei [i.e. the political police] to the city administration to house families that have been the victims of air raids.⁴⁷

The Düsseldorf pricing authority kept a file with lists of the Jews "leaving" [sic!] on October 27 to "Litzmannstadt" and November 11, 1941, to Minsk, divided according to districts or city areas and addresses.⁴⁸ Many of the addresses were '*Judenhäuser*', but numerous Jews were still living in 'mixed' houses at this time, although often in cramped conditions. The apartments that became vacant were then, as mentioned above, requisitioned by the Gestapo and made available to the Welfare Department for passing on to those in need. On the one hand, this concerned apartments owned by non-Jewish landlords, but on the other hand a whole series of former '*Judenhäuser*' in Düsseldorf were closed or 'Aryanized' following the deportation of November 10, 1941, such as the houses at Adersstraße 8, Rochusstraße 57, Reichsstraße 69 and Fürstenwall 198.⁴⁹

The extent to which residents of 'mixed' houses were 'preferentially' selected when the deportation lists were compiled cannot yet be determined. One thing is for sure: The process of concentrating Jews in fewer and fewer '*Judenhäuser*' and communal accommodation was greatly accelerated by the deportations. This can be illustrated well using the example of a somewhat smaller town like neighboring Neuss. Until the first deportation to the Łódź ghetto on October 27, 1941, the Jews who were still in Neuss had lived in a total of eight '*Judenhäuser*'. Three of these houses were closed, i.e. 'Aryanized' shortly after the deportation: Büttger Straße 18 (October 27, 1941), Büchel 31 and Drususallee 81 (both on October 30, 1941). The residents who had not yet been deported were distributed among the remaining '*Judenhäuser*' in which the Gestapo had 'freed up' living space with

---

46 Minutes of the meeting on matters relating to air-raid protection, October 27, 1941, 0–1–4–474, sheet 13, StAD. Translation by the author.
47 Report of November 1, 1941, on the state of care for the homeless, ibid., sheet 50. Translation by the author.
48 "Nachweisungen der 'ausreisenden' Juden und deren Wohnungen, 1941", 0–1–4–12317, StAD.
49 See the relevant Gestapo forms at the end of the file, ibid.

this first deportation, which 18 Jews from Neuss had been forced to join. The next closures took place after the deportation to Riga on December 11, 1941, which affected 24 Jews from Neuss. The *'Judenhäuser'* at Niederwallstraße 15 (December 10, 1941), Kapitelstraße 1 (December 13, 1941) and Kanalstraße 65 (December 17, 1941) were then closed, i.e. 'Aryanized'. The remaining eleven people lived in the *'Judenhäuser'* at Büchel 5 and Küpperstrasse 2. The property belonging to Emil Lehmann at Büchel 5 was expropriated by the authorities in May 1942, two of the residents were sent to the nursing home in Düsseldorf, two others were sent to Küpperstraße 2, where all the remaining seven Neuss Jews now lived – until they were deported to the Theresienstadt ghetto on July 21, 1942.[50]

As a rule, moving into a *'Judenhaus'* was extremely depressing for those affected, as they usually had to part with most of their possessions and drastically downsize. It was the multiple changes in particular that wore people down, as Richard Kaufmann, the last leader of the Jewish Community in Mönchengladbach, explained in a letter to a friend in March 1942. He had just moved into the *'Judenhaus'* at Hindenburgstraße 360: "I will say nothing about our apartments. Although it is true to say that it is not quite as bad here now as it was when we first moved in. In fact, we would even be satisfied if we didn't have to change again".[51] Kaufmann was deported to the Izbica ghetto in the *'Generalgouvernement'*, German-occupied Poland, on April 22, 1942. What Kaufmann says in his letter about life in the *'Judenhaus'* is not all negative. He talks particularly about the community and the closeness to fellow community members, which he, like many others for sure, found comforting. However, sources can also be quoted that talk about the cramped conditions, the lack of intimacy, the often tetchy atmosphere in the *'Judenhäuser'* where people waited anxiously to see whether or not they would have to join the next deportation.[52]

At the end of the eviction process, fewer and fewer Jews in mixed marriages were ultimately concentrated in only a few *'Judenhäuser'* in the large cities, although there were exceptions here too that proved the rule. It was, as Victor Klemperer described in his "LTI" study published after the war:

> The number of Jews is getting smaller and smaller. Both individually and in groups, the younger ones are disappearing to Poland and Lithuania, and the older ones to Theresienstadt. Very few houses are sufficient to accommodate those that are left in Dresden. This is also expressed in the language used by the Jews; it is no longer necessary to give the full

---

50 Cf. Rohrbacher, Juden in Neuss, 210–212.
51 Erckens, Juden in Mönchengladbach, volume 1, 591. Translation by the author.
52 Cf. for example, for Düsseldorf, Mark Roseman: *"Du bist nicht ganz verlassen." Eine Geschichte von Rettung und Widerstand im Nationalsozialismus*, Munich: DVA, 2020, 140.

address of each Jew, only the street number is given of the few houses located in different parts of the city: he lives at number 92, at number 56.[53]

Living in Communal Accommodation: Department Stores, Community Centers, Barracks

Not only apartment buildings, most of which were privately owned, were used as forced accommodation, but also administrative buildings, former Jewish schools or former department stores. In Düsseldorf, for example, the Reich Association of Jews in Germany building in Bilker Straße served as communal accommodation until the end of March 1942. The residents who had not yet been deported by then were moved to the Jewish nursing home at Grafenberger Allee 78. Turnover among the residents was high here too; places that had become 'vacant' after deportations were quickly filled by new arrivals from the surrounding area or from the city. After the deportation to Theresienstadt on July 21, 1942, the Düsseldorf Jewish nursing home was closed. Nursing homes also served as communal accommodation in Wuppertal (Straße der SA 73) and Mönchengladbach-Rheydt (Horst-Wessel-Straße 80).[54] In the case of Mönchengladbach, it was a former school of domestic science for Jewish women. The school had already been closed in 1937 and even before the introduction of the law on leases contracted with Jews served as communal accommodation for mostly elderly Jews from Rheydt and the surrounding area.[55] All residents were deported, and the two homes were closed following the deportations to Theresienstadt on July 21 and 25, 1942.

Jewish community centers were also used as communal accommodation in other cities in the administrative district, such as in Mülheim an der Ruhr, for example. The building at Löhstraße 53 was used for various community purposes. After the synagogue had been destroyed, the community held religious services here. Jewish tenants also lived here before the law was introduced, and from 1939 onwards, the building was used as forced accommodation, housing

---

53 Victor Klemperer: *LTI. Notizbuch eines Philologen*, Leipzig: Reclam, 2005[21] (first ed. 1946), 237. Translation by the author.
54 Today respectively: Friedrich-Ebert-Straße.
55 House Book Friedrich-Wilhelm-Straße (today Friedrich-Ebert-Straße). Including a letter from senior civil servant Schilling to the Rheydt District Court, March 3, 1966, StA Mönchengladbach.

at least 14 Jews prior to their deportation.⁵⁶ In Essen, a large building at Hindenburgstraße 22 was owned by the Jewish Community. Some of the space was used for Community administration, and for various Jewish groups and associations. From August 1942, however, it was also used as communal accommodation after the Holbeckshof barracks (see below) were closed down.⁵⁷

In Duisburg, the former Winter department store at Baustrasse 34 served as communal accommodation for at least 85 people from the beginning of 1939 until 1942. They lived there under extremely cramped conditions, as Holocaust survivor Herbert Salomon recalled: "In this empty building, they had divided bunks with wooden boards, each of which housed a family in an area measuring 10–12 square meters. Beds, couch, stove and some linen were allowed. The inmates [sic] were watched constantly by the Gestapo".⁵⁸ They had to be in the building at curfew and were only allowed to shop in a single store nearby between 4 and 5 pm. They were not allowed to receive visitors, but members of the *Bund* resistance group managed to get into the building to give some of the residents food and clothes.⁵⁹

Regular barracks were set up for Jews in two cities in the administrative district, Essen and Mönchengladbach,⁶⁰ where those affected sometimes had to live for just a few days, and sometimes for several weeks or months. In Mönchengladbach, the camp was located at Kabelstraße 93. It was the city's homeless shelter. At least two of the barracks there functioned as forced accommodation for Jews – the earliest admission date was February 24, 1942, and others arrived at the beginning of March 1942. 14 people were deported to the Izbica ghetto in the Lublin district of the *'Generalgouvernement'* via the Düsseldorf abattoir on April 21, 1942, and three others to Theresienstadt on July 25, 1942. None of them survived.⁶¹

---

56 The building was completely destroyed during a bombing raid on June 23, 1943. Today, there is a primary school on the site. Cf. Joachim Schröder: *Spurensuche III – Nachbarschaft, Vertreibung, Erinnerung. 'Judenhäuser' im Regierungsbezirk Düsseldorf (1939–1945)*. Available at: www.erinnerungsort-duesseldorf.de. Last accessed: 14.11.2021.
57 See the list of people living at the Holsbeckshof barracks, in Hermann Schröter: *Geschichte und Schicksal der Essener Juden. Gedenkbuch für die jüdischen Mitbürger der Stadt Essen*, Essen 1980, 432–458.
58 Quoted in Evangelischer Kirchenkreis Duisburg/Evangelisches Familienbildungswerk (ed.): *Stolpersteine in Duisburg*, volume 1, Duisburg 2005, 36. Translation by the author.
59 Ibid., 37; Roseman, Du bist nicht ganz verlassen, 140.
60 Gruner lists 38 such camps throughout the Reich, including the Holbeckshof camp (and the Much camp mentioned above), but not the camp in Mönchengladbach. Cf. Gruner, Der Geschlossene Arbeitseinsatz, 250.
61 Book of Remembrance (Izbica, Theresienstadt), StA Mönchengladbach.

The camp in Essen was set up in April 1942 in the district of Steele and was the starting and assembly point for the deportation of Jews from Essen, before they were brought to the Düsseldorf abattoir. After several houses in the city had been damaged by Allied bombing raids in April 1942, and numerous people had lost their homes, the pressure on 'Judenhäuser' in the city increased considerably.[62] Eventually, the city of Essen decided to evacuate numerous 'Judenhäuser' and to house their residents in empty barracks on the grounds of the former Deimelsberg colliery, which had previously been used for French prisoners of war. The camp consisted of nine wooden barracks, was surrounded with barbed wire, and guarded by members of the SA. The inmates were allowed to leave the camp during the day, but in the evenings and at night they were subject to a curfew like all other Jews. The barracks were divided into several rooms. Where five prisoners of war had previously lived, up to 15 Jews were now crammed into one space.[63]

The camp's residents' cards that have been preserved contain around 350 names. These residents were deported in three waves: the first were deported to Izbica on April 21/22, 1942 – they were first taken to the main train station in Essen,[64] from there to the Düsseldorf abattoir, and then transported from the freight station the following morning. No one survived this deportation. On June 15, 1942, a further 65 Jews from Essen were deported to Sobibór and murdered as soon as they arrived there. On July 20, 1942, the Gestapo deported a further 191 people; they also had to go firstly to the Düsseldorf abattoir, from where they boarded trains the following morning, this time for Theresienstadt. Among them was 72-year old Leopold Sternberg, who wrote a farewell letter to his children from the Holbeckshof barracks:

> Yes, dear children, you meant well for us, you had the best of intentions to enhance our twilight years, but it has all turned out differently. Mother drew the better lot, she has been resting in the ground for two and half years now, and is spared all of the misery.

---

62 Cf. Letter from Gestapo Essen to Gestapo Düsseldorf, April 14, 1942, regarding bomb damage in Essen due to air raids (April 12/13, 1942), 1.2.3.0/82164583/ITS Digital Archive, Arolsen Archives.
63 Cf. Schröter, Geschichte und Schicksal der Essener Juden, 54 (with incorrect date, intended date: May 1, 1942).
64 Imo Moszkowicz, an Auschwitz survivor who later became known as a director, describes the harrowing scene of parting with his mother and three siblings at Essen central station. He was also housed in Holbeckshof. Imo Moszkowicz: *Der grauende Morgen*, Regensburg: Boer, 1996, 42–43.

[...] Last night the list was read out, Aunt Fanny and I are on it. [...] I send heartfelt kisses to you all and hereby bid you farewell, Your Father and Grandfather.[65]

The Holbeckshof camp was closed on August 5, 1942. The few remaining Jews in Essen, who were still serving the war effort and therefore spared deportation, were distributed among only a few *'Judenhäuser'*, including primarily the buildings at Gänsemarkt 18, Maschinenstraße 19, Hindenburgstraße 22 and Weberstraße 8.

Traces: Former *'Judenhäuser'* and Communal Accommodation in Remembrance Culture

The former *'Judenhäuser'* and communal accommodation have left only few traces. This may come as a surprise, since they existed in all cities and even in smaller towns. The concentration in specific areas of increasingly disenfranchised Jewish neighbors happened right 'next door', in public, in front of everyone's eyes. One reason for forgetting may be that the monstrosity of what followed the confinement of Jews in forced accommodation, namely their deportation to the ghettos and death camps, overshadowed everything that had gone before. Certainly after the war many people did not want to be reminded that persecution had taken place right on their own doorstep. Not to mention those who themselves had profited from the displacement and robbery of the Jews, and lived in apartments and buildings that had previously belonged to or were occupied by Jews, perhaps even with furniture and household effects acquired at auction.[66]

Many of the former *'Judenhäuser'* and spaces of communal accommodation no longer exist because they did not survive the bombings in the Second World War or the demolition frenzy in the 1950s and 1960s. They were replaced by new buildings, office blocks, nurseries and even parking lots. Others still stand, without major changes, and yet nothing is usually known about their history. In our research seminars, students interviewed passers-by, local residents and neighbors. It was a rare exception when they met someone who knew something about the existence of the *'Judenhäuser'* at that time. Inquiries among current

---
[65] Letter from Leopold Sternberg from the Holbeckshof barracks, July 12/13, 1942, AR 0918, old synagogue Essen. Translation by the author.
[66] Cf., for example, regionally: Wolfgang Dreßen (ed.): *Betrifft: "Aktion 3": Deutsche verwerten jüdische Nachbarn. Dokumente zur Arisierung*, Berlin: Aufbau, 1998.

owners rarely led to positive responses, either because they were afraid of public discussion or even restitution claims, or because they had no interest in the subject.

Only a few buildings formerly used as forced accommodation have commemorative plaques.[67] *Stolpersteine* (stumbling stones), which have become popular in German remembrance culture, are in most cities laid in front of the last voluntary places where victims of Nazi persecution resided, i.e. not in front of former '*Judenhäuser*' (only if the person in question had lived there prior to 1939). How, and whether, such forced accommodation will be remembered at all in the future is open to debate and was also discussed in the university seminar. A group of students wanted to fill the gap they felt by creating an interactive website on which at least the previously known '*Judenhäuser*' in Düsseldorf could be marked on a city map.[68] The process of concentrating the Jews, at the end of which was their assembly at the Düsseldorf abattoir and their deportation to the ghettos and death camps, is illustrated here in a particularly vivid way. The forced accommodation is thereby snatched from the jaws of oblivion, and at the same time it should inspire further research: on the local circumstances in the administrative district, on the players and profiteers involved in the 'residential segregation' process, and on the living conditions in the individual spaces of communal accommodation about which we still know far too little.

---

67 Cf., for example, Küppersstraße 2 in Neuss, or Klosterstraße 1 in Kleve ('Former Finance Office'), the latter of which has already been the subject of antisemitic graffiti on several occasions.
68 So far, only the prototype is available online: http://steffiveenstra.de/judenhaeuser.html. Last accessed: 14.11.2021. A website is planned that will record all the '*Judenhäuser*' and communal accommodation in the Düsseldorf administrative district.

Akim Jah
Gerlachstraße Assembly Camp in Berlin, 1942 to 1943

History, Function, and the Current State of Research

Abstract: Between August 1942 and the beginning of 1943, the former Jewish old people's home in Gerlachstraße near Berlin's Alexanderplatz acted as an initially temporary, later permanent assembly camp (*Sammellager*) for arranging transports of Jews to Theresienstadt. With up to 2,500 people being 'channeled' there, Gerlachstraße was a rather small assembly camp, of which Berlin had 15. However, as a temporary central site for preparing 'transports of the elderly', it had a crucial importance among the Berlin assembly camps. At the same time, Gerlachstraße is paradigmatic of the conversion of Jewish homes into assembly camps by the Gestapo. The article briefly outlines the history of the old people's home, which has been almost completely unresearched up to now, discusses the deportation of the residents at the beginning of 1942 and in the summer of 1942, and ultimately investigates the conversion of the building into an assembly camp. The key research findings are then highlighted with regard to their importance for deportation research. Furthermore, research desiderata and approaches for further research into the camp history are shown.

Introduction

Paula Jonas, 74 years of age, wrote to the Berlin tracing office of the *American Jewish Joint Distribution Committee* (AJDC) on November 12, 1946:

> In response to your original document dated 9.11.46, I would like to inform you that I was with Ms. Friedericke [sic] Jachmann at the home in Gerlachstr., Ms. Jachmann was unfortunately collected one year earlier than me, in 1941, allegedly to be taken to Silesia, although, to our dismay, we were told that this transport never arrived at its destination and all those aboard [had been] killed on the way instead. We, my husband and I, came to T[h]eresienstadt with all of the occupants only in '42. Yours sincerely, Ms. P. Jonas.[1]

---

[1] Postcard from Paula Jonas to the tracing office of the American Joint Distribution Committee, 12.11.1946, 6.3.3.2/85500657/ITS Digital Archive, Arolsen Archives. Translation by the author.

The AJDC tracing office was set up in in the second half of 1945 to clarify, in close contact with the reestablished Jewish Community, what had happened to the Jews deported from Berlin during the years of National Socialism. To this end, the office evaluated the preserved transport lists held by the financial authorities, responded to inquiries from family members, and corresponded with other institutions and survivors, who it hoped could provide further information.[2] The office thus also approached Paula Jonas. The starting point for the search was an inquiry from the relatives of Friederike Jachmann from Tel Aviv, which had been transferred via the Search Department of Irgun Olej Merkaz Europa (Organization of Immigrants from Central Europe).

The correspondence shows how little knowledge there was about the whereabouts of the around 50,000 Jewish deportees one and a half years after the end of the Second World War. At the same time, the other documents in the so-called correspondence file, which today is preserved in the Arolsen Archives, show that the tracing office was already able to trace the destinations and circumstances of individual transports at that time. It was thus able to pass information on from Paula Jonas to Tel Aviv while also refining the details. According to this, Friederike Jachmann was deported on January 25, 1942, to Riga – not to Silesia, although Paula Jonas could not have known that.

Paula Jonas, the author of the postcard (see fig. 1), was deported to Theresienstadt seven months later, on August 17, 1942, with what was known as the '*1. Große Alterstransport*' ('1st large transport of the elderly').[3] The same transport included not only her husband, Sali Jonas, but also the majority of all remaining residents of the Gerlachstraße old people's home, which thus ceased to exist as a welfare facility and henceforth served as an assembly camp to prepare transports to Theresienstadt. Paula Jonas survived, returned to Berlin following liberation, and lived at Iranische Straße 3 opposite the Jewish Hospital in the borough of Wedding. The building, in which there was also a Jewish old people's home until the second half of 1942, was used by the reestablished Jewish Community, among other things, to house Jewish Displaced Persons, who had fled from Poland after the end of the war.[4] In her application for assistance by the Interna-

---

[2] Akim Jah: "Die Deportation der Juden aus Deutschland 1941–1945. Zur Geschichte und Dokumentenüberlieferung im Archiv des ITS", in Akim Jah and Gerd Kühling (eds.): *Die Deportation der Juden aus Deutschland und ihre verdrängte Geschichte nach 1945*, Göttingen: Wallstein, 2016, 11–29, here 21.

[3] Transport list '*1. Großer Alterstransport*', 17.08.1942, 1.2.1.1/127204926/ITS Digital Archive, Arolsen Archives.

[4] Angelika Königseder: *Flucht nach Berlin. Jüdische Displaced Persons 1945–1948*, Berlin: Metropol, 1998, 43.

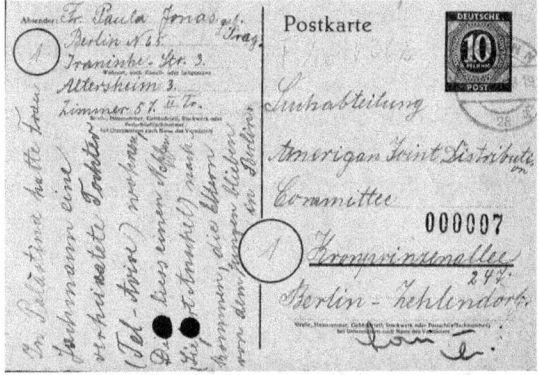

Fig. 1: Postcard from P. Jonas to tracing office of the American Joint Distribution Committee dated December 11, 1946, T/D file for Friederike Jachmann, 6.3.3.2/85500657, ITS Digital Archive, Arolsen Archives.

tional Refugee Organization, Paula Jonas later stated that she wanted to emigrate to Palestine.[5] Sali Jonas died in Theresienstadt in 1944.[6]

---

5 CM/1 file of Paula Jonas, 3.2.1.1/79235502/ITS Digital Archive, Arolsen Archives.
6 Index card of Sali Jonas, 2.3.1.2/130607722/ITS Digital Archive, Arolsen Archives; German Federal Archives: "Entry Sali Jonas, born 04.05.1867", in *Memorial Book. Victims of the Persecution*

Although the various transports from Berlin have now been researched more or less comprehensively, the history of the Gerlachstraße home and the fate of its residents have virtually been forgotten. This is all the more remarkable as the location temporarily acted as *the* central Berlin assembly camp for the transports to Theresienstadt and was right in the middle of the city, just a short distance from Alexanderplatz.

This article is intended to outline, for the first time, the main aspects of the extermination history of the home and subsequent assembly camp, and to investigate the whereabouts of the deportees from the building.[7] I will look into the founding of the home in 1931 and its function from 1933 to 1941, outline the deportation of the home residents in the first eight months of 1942, present the use of the home as a temporary assembly camp during what were known as the '*Große Alterstransporte*' ('large transports of the elderly') in the summer/fall of 1942, and finally take into account the function of the building as a permanent central assembly camp at the end of 1942/beginning of 1943. At the end of the article, I will discuss resolved, unanswered, and new research questions while referring to relevant sources.

The aim of the article is to close research gaps in local and regional history while also stimulating further in-depth research into Gerlachstraße. At the same time, the article hopes to present in detail the research questions that also relate to the organization of the transports from the German Reich and their preparations as a whole. I would also like to refer in this article to the potential that the various holdings at the Arolsen Archives offer for conducting local and regional research into the history of deportations.

The Jewish Old People's Home at Lietzmannnstraße/Gerlachstraße 18–21

The Jewish old people's home in Gerlachstraße was built in different construction phases in different neighboring houses at what was then Lietzmannstraße 19–21 and inaugurated on November 1, 1931. The neighboring plot no. 18 was

---

of Jews under the National Socialist Tyranny in Germany 1933–1945. Available at: https://www.bundesarchiv.de/gedenkbuch/en1084633. Last accessed: 15.03.2022.

7 A short version of this text was published in German in 2021: Akim Jah: "Das vergessene Sammellager am Alex", in Bezirksamt Mitte von Berlin, Stadtentwicklungsamt, Fachbereich Stadtplanung (ed.): *KM-Magazin für das Fördergebiet Karl-Marx-Allee, II. Bauabschnitt*, March 2021, 8–9.

added in 1932. At that time, the institution comprised over 120 beds, with five employees working there. Alongside single rooms, there were also communal rooms and a richly decorated synagogue.[8] The sponsor of the institution was the association Jüdische Altersheime für die Provinzen Brandenburg und Grenzmark – Berlin (formerly Landsberg a./W.) e.V., which had been founded in 1929. The home was one of several Jewish welfare facilities, which were run by an association, distributed across Berlin supplementing the large network of welfare institutions of the Jewish Community. The association's board members included Community rabbi Martin Salomonski and the subsequent chair of the Jewish Community, Heinrich Stahl.[9]

Just a few months after the institution was founded, it, like the other Jewish old people's homes in the city, was faced with a growing number of people in need. When the Nazis came to power in 1933, the antisemitic political atmosphere intensified significantly. As part of the persecution measures against the Jewish population, many Jewish residents lost not only their work and income, but often also their apartments; many became impoverished. This was combined with an aging population within the Jewish community due to the emigration of mainly younger people and an influx from rural regions to Berlin.[10] All of this led to a larger number of mainly older Jews, who were in need of somewhere to live and were accommodated, among other places, in the Jewish homes.[11] Long before deportations began, the homes had "lost the former character of retirement homes"[12] and had become accommodation for people in need, whose new residents in fact were not exclusively older people. At the same time, the economic situation in the homes and thus also the conditions for the residents had deteriorated since the Nazis had taken power.[13] The situation was exacerbated by officially ordered home clearances and mergers. In the middle of April 1942, the

---

8 Cf. Birgit Gregor: "Ein verschwundener Ort – das Altersheim in der Litzmannstraße[sic]/ Gerlachstraße", in Horst Helas (ed.): *Juden in Mitte. Biografien – Orte – Begegnungen*, Berlin: Trafo, 2000, 158–165. The further presentation of the history of the home until 1941 is also based on research by Gregor.
9 *Jüdisches Adressbuch für Gross-Berlin*, reprint of the 1931 edition, Berlin: Arani, 1994, 20; Beate Meyer: "Gratwanderung zwischen Verantwortung und Verstrickung – Die Reichsvereinigung der Juden in Deutschland und die Jüdische Gemeinde zu Berlin 1938–1945", in idem. and Hermann Simon: *Juden in Berlin 1938–1945*, Berlin: Philo, 2000, 291–337, here 302.
10 See also the contribution by Henning Borggräfe in this volume.
11 Akim Jah: *Die Deportation der Juden aus Berlin. Die nationalsozialistische Vernichtungspolitik und das Sammellager Große Hamburger Straße*, Berlin: be.bra Wissenschaft, 2013, 165–173.
12 Susanne Willems: *Der entsiedelte Jude. Albert Speers Wohnungsmarktpolitik für den Berliner Hauptstadtbau*, Berlin: Metropol, 2000, 400–401. Translation by the author.
13 Ibid.

number of residents in the Gerlachstraße home reached 206 persons and was thus much higher than when the institution was founded.[14]

The home residents who had moved from outside Berlin included married couple Leopold and Thekla Borower, born in 1872 and 1882 respectively. They had come to the capital in July 1939 from Schwiebus (now: Świebodzin) in Lower Silesia and lived at the home in Lietzmannstraße. Just under a year before, Leopold Borower had been arrested as part of the *Juniaktion* ('June operation') and imprisoned at Sachsenhausen concentration camp for two months.[15] The move to Berlin may have also particularly taken place in order to seek a certain amount of protection from antisemitic hostility in the capital city, where there was also a large Jewish community with an existing welfare network.

At the beginning of 1939, almost all of the independent Jewish associations and institutions that still existed at the time were formally dissolved by the authorities and integrated into the newly founded Reichsvereinigung der Juden in Deutschland (Reich Association of Jews in Germany), a compulsory association to which all persons considered Jews according to the Nuremberg Laws had to belong.[16] The home Gerlachstraße thus actually fell under the administration of the Jewish Community of Berlin,[17] which became part of the Reichsvereinigung and, like this, was under the control of the Gestapo. In the same year, Lietzmannstraße was renamed Gerlachstraße.

Deportation of the Old People's Home Residents to Riga

In October 1941, the Gestapo began the systematic deportation of the Jewish population from the German Reich, initially to the ghettos in German-occupied Central and Eastern Europe. On January 25, 1942, the Berlin Gestapo[18] deported

---

14 "List Alters- und Siechenheime der Jüdischen Kultusvereinigung zu Berlin", 15.04.1942, R-8150, No. 480, Federal Archives Berlin (BArch).
15 "Liste der am Donnerstag, den 23.6.1938 eingelieferten Arbeitsscheuen", 1.1.38.1/4093727– 4093729/ITS Digital Archive, Arolsen Archives; "Veränderungsmeldung", 25.08.1938, 1.1.38.1/ 4093824/ITS Digital Archive, Arolsen Archives.
16 Beate Meyer: *A Fatal Balancing Act. The Dilemma of the Reich Association of Jews in Germany, 1939–1945*, New York/Oxford: Berghahn, 2013.
17 Jewish Community Berlin, *Haupt-Etat 1941*, 1, 75 A Be 2, No. 52/1, # 278, Centrum Judaicum Archiv (CJA).
18 As the regional Gestapo office for Berlin, it was also known as *Stapoleitstelle Berlin* or *Staatspolizeileitstelle Berlin* (State Police Headquarters Berlin).

23 residents of the home in Gerlachstraße to Riga with the '*10. Osttransport*' ('10th deportation transport to the East'), including Friederike Jachmann, who was mentioned in the introduction. The majority of the deportees were older people over 65 years of age, who due to their age did not belong to one of the groups of people scheduled initially for deportation by the Reich Security Main Office (RSHA), which organized the deportations throughout the Reich. The Gestapo nevertheless placed them, as well as the residents of other old people's homes, on the transport list in violation of the guidelines[19] – a procedure that was characteristic of this phase of the deportations and is also known from other cities.[20]

The people concerned were picked up in Gerlachstraße by policemen a few days before the transport departed and taken to the synagogue in Levetzowstraße in the Moabit neighborhood, which had been converted into an assembly camp. There, they were searched by members of the '*Judenreferat*', the 'department for Jewish affairs' of the Gestapo Berlin, which was responsible for organizing the transports within the Berlin Gestapo.[21] Any valuables found were confiscated. Those scheduled for deportation also had to submit a declaration of assets, on the basis of which their property was later confiscated in a "pseudo-legal act".[22] This examination, which, according to information from survivors, took place on long tables in Levetzowstraße, was referred to by the Gestapo as 'channeling' ('*Durchschleusung*').[23] This procedure formed a structural feature of the deportations and took place in a similar manner at each assembly camp in Berlin and the German Reich. At Levetzowstraße, the people concerned, together with around 1,000 other people who were also taken there, had to sleep on the floor. Food was to be organized by the Jewish Community. On January 25, 1942, the inmates were transferred by the Gestapo to Grunewald train station, where they had to climb aboard a freight train. This reached Riga-Skirotava

---

19 Transport list, '*10. Osttransport*', 25.01.1942, 1.2.1.1/127187493, 127187510–127187513, 127187536/ITS Digital Archive, Arolsen Archives. See Jah, Deportation, 271–272 and 625–626.
20 Cf. Wolf Gruner: "Von der Kollektivausweisung zur Deportation der Juden aus Deutschland (1938–1945). Neue Perspektiven und Dokumente", in Birte Kundrus and Beate Meyer (eds.): *Die Deportation der Juden aus Deutschland. Pläne, Praxis, Reaktionen 1938–1945*, Göttingen: Wallstein, 2004, 21–62, here 53; Rita Meyhöfer: "Berliner Juden und Theresienstadt", in Miroslav Kárny, Raimund Kemper, and Margita Kárná (eds.): *Theresienstädter Studien und Dokumente*, Prague: Sefer, 1996, 31–51, here 37.
21 Jah, Deportation, 87–110.
22 Martin Friedenberger: *Fiskalische Ausplünderung. Die Berliner Steuer- und Finanzverwaltung und die jüdische Bevölkerung 1933–1945*, Berlin: Metropol, 2008, 273. Translation by the author.
23 Jah, Deportation, 136–137.

train station on January 30, 1942.²⁴ Not all of the deportees, as Paula Jonas assumed, were killed on the way, but many died on the journey "from cold, hunger, and exhaustion".²⁵ Others, "mentally confused"²⁶ by the cold, were shot following arrival at the train station. Those who were still alive were initially taken to the Riga ghetto. Absolute torture awaited those who had survived the conditions in the ghetto at the camps in Salaspils, Kaiserwald, Auschwitz, and Stutthof.²⁷ The exact circumstances of Friederike Jachmann's death are not known; due to her age, it is to be assumed that she was either among those killed at the train station or she died at the Riga ghetto. The whereabouts of the other home residents, including the aforementioned married couple Leopold and Thekla Borower, who arrived at the old people's home in 1939 from Schwiebus and were also deported on this transport, are also unclear.²⁸ According to Alfred Gottwaldt and Diana Schulle, a total of only 13 people from this transport survived.²⁹

Another deportation from the old people's home in Gerlachstraße took place in June 1942: 53-year-old Herta Scharlinski was deported, among other people from Berlin and surrounding area to the Lublin District on June 13, 1942. This '*15. Osttransport*' ('15th deportation transport to the East') was also arranged at Levetzowstraße and probably dispatched from Moabit freight station.³⁰ Herta Scharlinski was the only person from Gerlachstraße on this transport; however, the deporting of residents from other Jewish welfare institutions on this transport indicates that the Gestapo were increasingly turning their attention to the Jewish

---

24 Alfred Gottwaldt and Diana Schulle: *Die "Judendeportationen" aus dem Deutschen Reich 1941–1945*, Wiesbaden: Marix, 2005, 134.
25 Letter from the American Joint Distribution Committee to Irgun Oley Merkas Europa, 23.01. 1947, 6.3.3.2/85500655/ITS Digital Archive, Arolsen Archives. Translation by the author.
26 Gottwaldt and Schulle, Judendeportationen, 134. Translation by the author.
27 Wolfgang Scheffler: "Das Schicksal der in die baltischen Staaten deportierten deutschen, österreichischen und tschechoslowakischen Juden 1941–1945. Ein historischer Überblick", in Wolfgang Scheffler and Diana Schulle (eds.): *Buch der Erinnerung. Die ins Baltikum deportierten deutschen, österreichischen und tschechoslowakischen Juden*, volume 1, Munich: Saur, 1–43. See also the contribution by Alfred Eckert in this volume, on those deported from Nuremberg to Riga just a few weeks earlier.
28 Cf. German Federal Archives: "Entry Thekla Borower, born 30.04.1882", in *Memorial Book. Victims of the Persecution of Jews under the National Socialist Tyranny in Germany 1933–1945*. Available at: https://www.bundesarchiv.de/gedenkbuch/en1041697. Last accessed: 15.03.2022; ibid: "Entry Leopold Borower, born 19.06.1872", in *Memorial Book. Victims of the Persecution of Jews under the National Socialist Tyranny in Germany 1933–1945*. Available at: https://www.bundesarchiv.de/gedenkbuch/en1041484. Last accessed: 15.03.2022.
29 Gottwaldt and Schulle, Judendeportationen, 134.
30 Alfred Gottwaldt: *Mahnort Güterbahnhof Moabit. Die Deportation von Juden aus Berlin*, Berlin: Hentrich&Hentrich, 2015, 32.

homes and their residents at this time, when the transports carrying predominantly older people began heading to Theresienstadt.[31] The profession of Herta Scharlinski is stated on the transport list as "Hausangestellte"[32] (domestic worker), which could mean that she not only lived in the home but also worked there, and was thus among the 14 employees who were working at the home in spring 1942.[33] In Lublin, some of the men were taken to the Majdanek concentration camp, while others, presumably all those who remained, were transferred to the Sobibor death camp,[34] where Herta Scharlinski was also murdered.[35]

Beginning of the 'Transports of the Elderly' to Theresienstadt

The Gestapo arranged the first transport to Theresienstadt on June 2, 1942. Until then, older men and women over 65 years of age had been largely excluded from the deportation transports 'to the East', which had been justified with a labor assignment there,[36] although, as we have seen above, there were exceptions. The older people, as well as holders of the *Verwundetenabzeichen* ('Wounded Badge') and bearers of higher military awards and decorations, were now taken to the Theresienstadt ghetto.[37] As they were no longer able to work, they were supposed to spend their retirement years there, according to Nazi propaganda. Also, senior officials from the Jewish Community and the Reichsvereinigung were deported to Theresienstadt and not 'to the East'.

---

31 Jah, Deportation, 629.
32 Transport list, *'15. Osttransport'*, 13.06.1942, 1.2.1.1/127187839/ITS Digital Archive, Arolsen Archives.
33 Cf. *Alters- und Siechenheime der Jüdischen Kultusvereinigung zu Berlin*, 15.04.1942, R-8150, BArch.
34 Gottwaldt and Schulle, Judendeportationen, 215–216.
35 Cf. German Federal Archives: "Entry Herta Scharlinski, born 26.04.1889", in *Memorial Book. Victims of the Persecution of Jews under the National Socialist Tyranny in Germany 1933–1945*. Available at: https://www.bundesarchiv.de/gedenkbuch/en1150372. Last accessed: 13.01.2022.
36 Cf. "Reichssicherheitshauptamt, Schnellbrief an alle Staatspolizei(leit)stellen im Altreich", 31.01.1942, 1.2.3.0/82164542–82164544/ITS Digital Archive, Arolsen Archives.
37 "Reichssicherheitshauptamt, Richtlinien zur technischen Durchführung der Evakuierung von Juden in das Altersghetto Theresienstadt", 15.05.1942, 1.2.3.0/82164705–82164712/ITS Digital Archive, Arolsen Archives.

Many of those taken to Theresienstadt actually died just a short time after arriving, due to the miserable conditions there.[38] Others were deported by the SS from there to the death camps, where they were murdered.[39] The beginning of the transports to Theresienstadt meant that the older Jewish people living in Berlin were no longer protected from deportation; in particular, the people living in the Jewish homes had now attracted the attention of the Gestapo. At approximately 2,300 men and women, they represented around a sixth of all of the Jewish population over 65 living in Berlin at that time.[40]

The first transport from Berlin to Theresienstadt on June 2, 1942, consisted, like the second on June 4, 1942, of residents from the old people's home in Große Hamburger Straße. This home was the oldest nursing home of the Community, with a central location close to Hackescher Markt. Following the deportation of the majority of the residents, it was converted into the central assembly camp for the transports to Theresienstadt by order of the Gestapo,[41] while the former synagogue in Levetzowstraße continued to be used to prepare the transports 'to the East'. The Community's employees who worked at the Große Hamburger Straße old people's home remained in the building and now had to help prepare the transports. They were subordinate to the 'Jewish camp management' ('Jüdische Lagerleitung') appointed by the Gestapo, which also initially had to supervise 15 Jewish *Ordner* ('wardens'), which were also employees of the Community. These had to accompany the Gestapo men when rounding people up, carry the luggage of the people concerned, and help the infirm to walk. The Gestapo maintained a constant presence in the building to supervise the assembly camp and organize the transports.[42] The building itself was not initially converted for its new role, the furniture was retained, the beds were now used to accommodate those whose deportation was imminent and only had to stay in the building briefly, i.e. at least one day, for 'channeling'.

If a transport was scheduled, the people concerned were taken from Große Hamburger Straße to Anhalter train station on a special streetcar. This station,

---

38 Anna Hájková: "Mutmaßungen über deutsche Juden: Alte Menschen aus Deutschland im Theresienstädter Ghetto", in Andrea Löw, Doris L. Bergen, and Anna Hájková (eds.): *Alltag im Holocaust: Jüdisches Leben im Großdeutschen Reich 1941–1945*, Munich: De Gruyter, 2013, 179–198.
39 Anna Hájková: *The Last Ghetto. An Everyday History of Theresienstadt*, New York: OUP, 2020, 201–238.
40 Cf. Gerd Lüdersdorf: *Es war ihr Zuhause. Juden in Köpenick*, Berlin: Edition Roots, 1998, 23.
41 Akim Jah: "Vom Altenheim zum Sammellager. Die Große Hamburger Straße 26, die Deportation der Berliner Juden und das Personal der Stapoleitstelle", in *Theresienstädter Studien und Dokumente*, 2007, 176–219.
42 Jah, Deportation, 299–305.

which was Berlin's largest at the time, served as a departure station for the transports to Theresienstadt, with separate cars being attached to regular trains to Karlsbad (Karlovy Vary).

The '4. *Alterstransport*' ('4th transport of the elderly') on June 9, 1942, marked the start of the 'regular' transports to Theresienstadt.[43] These transports, which initially comprised 50, then 100 people from the beginning of July and departed five times a week, were used by the Gestapo to deport both men and women who lived in apartments, including the flats in 'Jews houses' ('*Judenhäuser*'),[44] and also residents of the various Jewish homes in the city. However, the individual homes were not cleared all at once, but instead these people were gradually added to the transport lists on an individual basis, whereby the criteria for selection remain unknown. As a result, three residents from the home in Gerlachstraße were already on the stated '4. *Alterstransport*'.[45] Only little is known about the biographies of the three, Bruno Landsberger and the Glogauer married couple. Bruno Landsberger died in Theresienstadt about half a year after the deportation.[46] In 1964, his granddaughter attempted – in vain – to ascertain the exact date of death from the International Tracing Service (ITS), which she required to assert claims for compensation.[47] Heimann Glogauer also died in Theresienstadt; in his case, his date of death, December 10, 1942, i.e. around a year after he arrived there, was registered.[48] However, nothing at all is known about the whereabouts of his wife Cäcilie.

Three days after this transport, on June 12, Heinrich Stahl, one of the main sponsors of the old people's home, was also deported to Theresienstadt with the '5. *Alterstransport*' ('5th transport of the elderly'). He died there on November 4, 1942.[49] A further nine residents of the Gerlachstraße old people's home were deported between June 26 and July 21 1942 on five of the Theresienstadt transports.

---

[43] The '3rd Theresienstadt transport' was a 'penal transport' in response to the arson attack carried out by Jewish resistance groups in the Lustgarten. Cf. Jah, Deportation, 636.
[44] For 'Jews houses', see also the article by Joachim Schröder in this volume.
[45] Transport list, '4. *Alterstransport*', 09.06.1942, 1.2.1.1/127187877/ITS Digital Archive, Arolsen Archives.
[46] Cf. *German Federal Archives:* "Entry Bruno Landsberger, born 03.10.1860", in *Memorial Book. Victims of the Persecution of Jews under the National Socialist Tyranny in Germany 1933–1945*. Available at: https://www.bundesarchiv.de/gedenkbuch/de1098325. Last accessed: 13.01.2022.
[47] T/D file for Bruno Landsberger, 6.3.3.2/108369882/ITS Digital Archive, Arolsen Archives.
[48] Card from the Terezin card file for Heimann Glogauer, 1.1.42.2/5030424/ITS Digital Archive, Arolsen Archives.
[49] Meyer, Balancing Act, 211.

The 'Large Transports of the Elderly' and the Clearing of the Gerlachstraße Old People's Home

At the end of July 1942, the Gestapo stopped collecting people from the homes and began preparing for three special transports to Theresienstadt, each comprising around 1,000 people, which were to be dispatched within three months. In contrast to the previous transports comprising a smaller number of deportees, the Gestapo referred to these three as *'Große Alterstransporte'* ('large transports of the elderly'). These transports were accompanied by the complete clearance of the remaining old people's homes in the city.[50]

As the capacity for 'channeling' in the Große Hamburger Straße assembly camp was inadequate for such a large number of people, the Gestapo used eight Jewish homes as temporary assembly camps. This concerned the home for the deaf and dumb at Parkstraße 22 in Weißensee, the former community center and old people's home for the Orthodox Adass Jisroel Community at Artilleriestraße 31 (now Tucholskystraße), the old people's homes at Mahlsdorfer Straße 94 in Köpenick, Schönhauser Allee 22 in Prenzlauer Berg, and Friedenstraße 3 at Volkspark Friedrichshain, the homes at Brunnenstraße 41 and Gormannstraße 3, each in the borough of Mitte, and finally Gerlachstraße 18–21.[51] Just like a few weeks before at Große Hamburger Straße, the respective residents in the individual institutions were first deported and then – sometimes also in parallel – the building was used to 'channel' other people who were brought there. This means that the latter spent the night in the beds of the former home residents, who had only just been deported themselves.

In contrast to the procedures at the permanent Levetzowstraße and Große Hamburger Straße assembly camps, which are well documented, little is known about the details of the 'channeling' procedure in the temporary camps. The reason for this is the lack of sources regarding the conditions for inmates, the procedure, the specific locations of 'channeling,' and surveillance. There are no indications of a permanent Gestapo presence in the buildings, nor of the buildings being converted or having grating fitted at this time. It is also unclear who actually collected the people concerned at home and brought them to the homes and how they got from there to the train station. It is only known that the Gestapo planned to transport the deportees to the station

---

50 Note from Philipp Kozower about a consultation with the *Geheime Staatspolizei, Staatspolizeileitstelle Berlin*, 29.07.1942, R-8150, Film 52407/No. 23, BArch.
51 Akim Jah: "Die Berliner Sammellager im Kontext der 'Judendeportationen' 1941–1945", in *Zeitschrift für Geschichtswissenschaft*, 3, 2013, 211–231; Jah, Deportation, 315.

"with motor vehicles from the motor pool"[52] of the police and that the transports were arranged at Moabit freight station. The employees of the Jewish Community, as was previously also the case at the permanent assembly camp, had to help with the preparations and look after the people.[53]

The '*1. Große Alterstransport*', a special train with passenger cars, left Berlin on August 17, 1942, with a total of 997 people.[54] 201 of these had been 'channeled' at Gerlachstraße; 176 of them were residents of the home.[55] The remaining 25 people were brought from their apartments to the old people's home for 'channeling'.

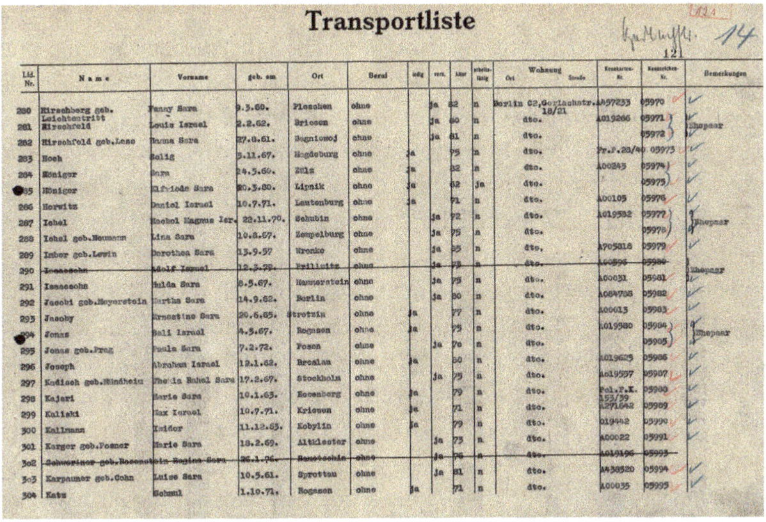

Transportliste

121

Lfd. Nr.	Name	Vorname	geb. am	Ort	Beruf	ledig	verh.	Alter	arbeitsfähig	Wohnung Ort Straße	Kennkarten-Nr.	Kennzeichen-Nr.	Bemerkungen
280	Hirschberg geb. Leichtentritt	Fanny Sara	9.3.60.	Pleschen	ohne		ja	82	n	Berlin C2, Gerlachstr. 18/21	A597233	05970	
281	Hirschfeld	Louis Israel	2.2.62.	Briesen	ohne		ja	80	n	dto.	A019266	05971	Ehepaar
282	Hirschfeld geb. Lese	Emma Sara	27.8.61.	Bagniewoj	ohne		ja	81	n	dto.		05972	
283	Hoch	Selig	3.11.67.	Magdeburg	ohne	ja		75	n	dto.	Fr.F.28/40	05973	
284	Höniger	Sara	24.5.60.	Zülz	ohne	ja		82	n	dto.	A00245	05974	
285	Höniger	Elfriede Sara	20.3.80.	Lipnik	ohne	ja		62	ja	dto.		05975	
286	Horwitz	Daniel Israel	10.7.71.	Lautenburg	ohne	ja		71	n	dto.	A00105	05976	
287	Ichel	Hochel Magnus Isr.	22.11.70.	Schubin	ohne		ja	72	n	dto.	A019532	05977	Ehepaar
288	Ichel geb. Neumann	Lina Sara	10.8.67.	Zempelburg	ohne		ja	75	n	dto.		05978	
289	Imber geb. Lewin	Dorothea Sara	13.9.57	Wronke	ohne		ja	85	n	dto.	A705818	05979	
290	~~Isaacsohn~~	~~Adolf Israel~~	~~12.3.79.~~	~~Prillwitz~~	~~ohne~~		~~ja~~	~~73~~	~~n~~	~~dto.~~	~~A00596~~	~~05980~~	Ehepaar
291	Isaacsohn	Hulda Sara	8.5.67.	Hammerstein	ohne		ja	75	n	dto.	A00031	05981	
292	Jacobi geb. Meyerstein	Martha Sara	14.9.62.	Berlin	ohne		ja	80	n	dto.	A084738	05982	
293	Jacoby	Ernestine Sara	20.6.65.	Strotzin	ohne	ja		77	n	dto.	A00013	05983	
294	Jonas	Bali Israel	4.5.67.	Rogasen	ohne	ja		75	n	dto.	A019980	05984	Ehepaar
295	Jonas geb. Praz	Paula Sara	7.2.72.	Posen	ohne		ja	70	n	dto.		05985	
296	Joseph	Abraham Israel	12.1.62.	Breslau	ohne	ja		80	n	dto.	A019625	05986	
297	Kadisch geb. Windheim	Thekla Rahel Sara	17.2.67.	Stockholm	ohne		ja	75	n	dto.	A019557	05987	
298	Kajari	Marie Sara	10.1.63.	Rosenberg	ohne	ja		79	n	dto.	Pol.P.K. 153/39	05988	
299	Kaliski	Max Israel	10.7.71.	Kriewen	ohne	ja		71	n	dto.	A271642	05989	
300	Kallmann	Isidor	11.12.63.	Kobylin	ohne	ja		79	n	dto.	019442	05990	
301	Karger geb. Posner	Marie Sara	18.2.69.	Altkloster	ohne		ja	73	n	dto.	A00022	05991	
302	~~Schweriner geb. Rosenstein~~	~~Regina Sara~~	~~26.1.76.~~	~~Samotschin~~	~~ohne~~		~~ja~~	~~76~~	~~n~~	~~dto.~~	~~A019196~~	~~05993~~	
303	Karpauner geb. Cohn	Luise Sara	10.5.61.	Sprottau	ohne		ja	81	n	dto.	A438520	05994	
304	Katz	Schmul	1.10.71.	Rogasen	ohne	ja		71	n	dto.	A00035	05995	

Fig. 2: Extract from the transport list, *'1. Großer Alterstransport'*, August 17, 1942, 1.2.1.1/127204926/ITS Digital Archive, Arolsen Archives.

Jenni Frankenstein was also among the deported home residents. At the beginning of 1942, she had lived in the former Jewish school at Große Hamburger Straße 27, which at the time served as a home to accommodate those in need of somewhere to live. Her name already featured on the transport list for the de-

52 Note from Philipp Kozower about a consultation with the *Geheime Staatspolizei, Staatspolizeileitstelle Berlin*, 29.07.1942, R-8150, Film 52407/No. 23, BArch. Translation by the author.

53 Jah, Sammellager im Kontext, 216.

54 Transport list, *'1. Großer Alterstransport'*, 17.08.1942, 1.2.1.1/127204914 – 127204958/ITS Digital Archive, Arolsen Archives.

55 Jah, Deportation, 317.

portation transport on January 25, 1942, on which the first residents of the old people's home in Gerlachstraße were deported to Riga. For unknown reasons, however, she was not deported at that time and was instead taken from Große Hamburger Straße to the home in Gerlachstraße, where places had become available due to this very transport. In 1948, her daughter, who was living in the United Kingdom at that time, contacted what was then the ITS in Arolsen concerning the whereabouts of her mother. The response, written in English, shows how little was known about this transport and the history of the Gerlachstraße home at that time. The daughter, who had her mother's last address in Berlin in Gerlachstraße, received the following response: "At the said address [Gerlachstraße 20] formerly was a Jewish asylum of old-aged persons, who are said to have been taken to Theresienstadt in 1943 [sic]. Further investigation and a check with the Jewish Community absolutely failed".[56] Also Paula Jonas, who was mentioned in the introduction, was one of the deported home residents; she was one of only 16 people who survived this transport.[57] The other deportees died either in Theresienstadt or were murdered in the death camps. For instance, Amalja Anschel, born in 1860, was dead just eleven days after arriving in Theresienstadt.[58] As Alfred Gottwaldt and Diana Schulle have shown, 377 people from the transport were already deported on to the Treblinka death camp in September and October 1942. And more were sent to Auschwitz in 1943 and 1944.[59] The former also included then-74-year-old Gertrud Arner, who left Theresienstadt on September 19, 1942, with a transport to Treblinka.[60]

Immediately before the '*1. Große Alterstransport*', on August 15, 1942, the Gestapo had deported nine residents of Gerlachstraße to Riga with the '*18. Osttransport*' ('18th transport to the East'). These were a domestic worker, a cook with her 13-year-old daughter, and five older home residents, three of whom were over 65 years of age.[61] What reasons prompted the Gestapo to assign the three older people to this transport rather than deporting them to Theresienstadt is unknown.

Following the '*1. Große Alterstransport*', the buildings in Gerlachstraße were largely cleared. One month later, the former old people's home was used, like the

---

[56] T/D file for Jenni Frankenstein, 6.3.3.2/105283006/ITS Digital Archive, Arolsen Archives.
[57] Gottwaldt and Schulle, Judendeportationen, 310.
[58] Card from the Ghetto Theresienstadt Card File, Amalja Anschel, 1.1.42.2/4964087/ITS Digital Archive, Arolsen Archives.
[59] Cf. Gottwaldt and Schulle, Judendeportationen, 309–310.
[60] Card from the Ghetto Theresienstadt Card File, Gertrud Arner, 1.1.42.2/4964482/ITS Digital Archive, Arolsen Archives.
[61] Transport list, '*18. Osttransport*', 15.08.1942, 1.2.1.1/127204851–127204903/ITS Digital Archive, Arolsen Archives.

other homes stated above, as an assembly camp for the '*2. Große Alterstransport*' ('2nd large transport of the elderly'). It left Berlin on September 14, 1942, and comprised exactly 1,000 people, predominately Jews, who did not live in a home.[62]

On October 3, 1942, the Gestapo arranged the '*3. Große Alterstransport*' ('3rd large transport of the elderly') in the same way. It comprised 1,021 people.[63] Gerlachstraße was also used as an assembly camp for this transport. It cannot be said for certain, either for the '*2*'. or for the '*3. Große Alterstransport*', how many people were 'channeled' there in each case. If we take the size of the transports and the number of camps available as a reference, it can be assumed that it was around 200 each. The asset files of the Asset Utilization Office of the Chief Finance Authority of Berlin-Brandenburg (*Vermögensverwertungsstelle des Oberfinanzpräsidenten Berlin-Brandenburg*) that have been preserved in the Brandenburgisches Landeshauptarchiv (Brandenburg Main State Archive, BLHA) in Potsdam, which often contain the name of the assembly camp, serve as evidence that the building actually functioned as an assembly camp.

People were also detained at Gerlachstraße between the three transports. An unknown number of inmates, who were not immediately attached to the next transport after being rounded up, had to spent several weeks there. At least one suicide is known from this 'interim period.' Berthold Pulvermann took his own life in Gerlachstraße on September 5, 1942.[64]

During the period of the three '*Große Alterstransporte*', the smaller transports to Theresienstadt, which were still being arranged in Große Hamburger Straße, continued. Those deported also included two residents from Gerlachstraße. They were deported with the '*50. Alterstransport*' ('50th transport of the elderly') on August 25, 1942.[65] During this period, two residents from Gerlachstraße, who were under 65 years of age, were also deported to Riga on September 5 and to Raasiku on September 26.[66]

---

62 Transport list, '*2. Großer Alterstransport*', 14.09.1942, 1.2.1.1/127205123–127205166/ITS Digital Archive, Arolsen Archives.

63 Transport list, '*3. Großer Alterstransport*', 14.09.1942, 1.2.1.1/127207315–127207355/ITS Digital Archive, Arolsen Archives.

64 Cf. Stolperstein-Initiative Eichenkamp: "Berthold Pulvermann". Available at: https://www.stolpersteine-berlin.de/de/biografie/3708. Last accessed: 10.02.2022.

65 Transport list, '*50. Alterstransport*', 25.08.1942, 1.2.1.1/127204997/ITS Digital Archive, Arolsen Archives.

66 Transport list, '*19. Osttransport*', 05.09.1942, 1.2.1.1/127205075, 127205242/ITS Digital Archive, Arolsen Archives; transport list, '*20. Osttransport*', 26.09.1942, 1.2.1.1/127205242/ITS Digital Archive, Arolsen Archives.

Following the 'large' transports to Theresienstadt, the Gestapo had the majority of the homes cleared in order to enable them to be used for Nazi organizations. However, Gerlachstraße was initially excluded from this. People who were still at the other homes were now brought to the home in Gerlachstraße, which now acted as an 'interim assembly camp'. From there, along with some remaining previous residents of the old people's home in Gerlachstraße, they were deported via Große Hamburger Straße in the following weeks.[67]

At the end of October 1942, the Gestapo deported a larger number of Community employees, who were previously mainly employed at the various welfare institutions, as part of what was known as the *Gemeindeaktion* ('community raid'). Given that the Jewish population had been decimated by deportation and homes had been closed, the Gestapo now considered these employees to be 'superfluous'. Fifteen-year-old Margot Noafeldt was also among the deportees. She presumably worked as a nurse at the Levetzowstraße assembly camp between December 1941 and October 1942 and came to the Gerlachstraße assembly camp in the same role in October 1942. On October 28, she was deported to Theresienstadt with her parents.

The end of the *Gemeindeaktion* marked the start of a new phase for the former home in Gerlachstraße as an assembly camp, which was closely linked to the planned deportation of the Jews still performing forced labor in the armaments factories and the visit by Eichmann's confidant Alois Brunner from Vienna.

Brunner in Berlin: Gerlachstraße as a Permanent Assembly Camp

By the end of October 1942, around a year after the deportations from Berlin had begun, over 15,000 Jews had been deported 'to the East' and around 10,000 to Theresienstadt. However, approximately an equal number of people, whose deportation was scheduled by the Gestapo, were still in Berlin at that time. These included thousands who had to perform forced labor in the armaments factories. As their work was critical to the war, this group was initially largely excluded from deportation. However, in September 1942, based on an initiative by Hitler,

---

[67] Cf., for example, transport list, '75. *Alterstransport*', 20.11.1942, 1.2.1.1/127207564/ITS Digital Archive, Arolsen Archives; transport list, '76. *Alterstransport*', 15.12.1942, 1.2.1.1/127207668– 127207671/ITS Digital Archive, Arolsen Archives; transport list, '77. *Alterstransport*', 16.12.1942, 1.2.1.1/127207673–127207674/ITS Digital Archive, Arolsen Archives.

plans began to include these '*Rüstungsjuden*' ('armaments Jews') in the deportations and replace them with foreign forced laborers.[68] RSHA and the General Plenipotentiary for Deployment of Labor (*Generalbevollmächtigter für den Arbeitseinsatz*) Fritz Sauckel planned to organize two transports a week, each with 1,000 people, from Berlin to Auschwitz from the beginning or middle of November 1942 over a prolonged period of time in exchange for the same number of Polish forced laborers, who were to be transported to Berlin from the Zamosc region.[69] This increased workload for the Gestapo coincided with an embezzlement affair within the Berlin Gestapo, as a result of which the '*Judenreferat*', which was responsible for the deportations, was thinned out in terms of personnel. As a replacement, Eichmann's confidant Alois Brunner and other SS men came from Vienna to Berlin to push forward the deportation of the '*Rüstungsjuden*.' Although the 'strike' against the '*Rüstungsjuden*' ultimately only took place at the end of February/beginning of March 1943 – one reason was that far fewer Polish forced laborers could be rounded up – Brunner began restructuring the assembly camps in the middle of November 1942. The former old people's home in Große Hamburger Straße, which had previously been used for the transports to Theresienstadt, was used to prepare the trains to Auschwitz in the future. Gerlachstraße was assigned the role of a central assembly camp for the Theresienstadt transports.[70] Employees of the Jewish Community had to make the necessary structural changes there.

Like in the other assembly camps, a Jewish *Ordner* service also existed in Gerlachstraße. When the deportations had begun in 1941, the officials from the Community had decided to set aside employees for this role in the – ultimately futile – hope of being able to influence what happened with the deportations and ease the conditions for the people concerned.[71] Three *Ordner* who had previously worked at the Große Hamburger Straße assembly camp had to train the other *Ordner*.[72] The *Ordner* service in Gerlachstraße comprised 15 people. In ad-

---

68 Wolf Gruner: *Der geschlossene Arbeitseinsatz deutscher Juden. Zur Zwangsarbeit als Element der Verfolgung 1938–1943*, Berlin: Metropol, 1997, 307.
69 Akim Jah: "Alois Brunner in Berlin – On the Deportations of Jews from Berlin, October 1942 to February 1943", in Michaela Raggam-Blesch, Peter Black, and Marianne Windsperger (eds.): *Deportations of the Jewish Population in Territories under Nazi Control, Beiträge des VWI zur Holocaustforschung*, Vienna 2022 (forthcoming). See also the contribution by Alexandra Pulvermacher in this volume.
70 The home at Gormannstraße 3 was initially intended to take on this role, although this plan was changed at the last minute and Gerlachstraße was instead designated as an assembly camp. Cf. Jah, Deportation, 420.
71 Meyer, Balancing Act, 110–115.
72 Note by Richard Rockmann, 25.11.1942, 2B1, No. 5, CJA.

dition to them, the Community also had to appoint a typist and a doctor.[73] The *Ordner* service also included Max Kiewe, who, as the janitor, had lived in one of the buildings since the time of the old people's home with his wife and his son. All three now had to help look after the inmates. In contrast to them, the other *Ordner*, where known, did not have to live in Gerlachstraße, but remained in their apartments. Under the threat of the most severe penalties, the *Ordner* were forbidden to "pass on verbal or written messages, packages, and the like to or from"[74] the assembly camp. The first 'channeling' took place in Gerlachstraße on November 18, 1942, which had now been converted into a permanent assembly camp, and the first transport left the former old people's home for Theresienstadt on November 1, 1942.

Little is known about the details of the structural changes, the division within the building, i.e. which parts were actually used for the assembly camp, and – here too – about the conditions for the prisoners there. There is also inadequate documentation regarding the process of transferring people to Anhalter station, from which the transports continued to leave for Theresienstadt. What we know from the preserved Community's files, however, is that two to three rooms, each for twelve people, were originally to be prepared as an assembly camp.[75] However, if we assume that the transports each comprised 100 people, a much larger part of the buildings must have actually been used as an assembly camp, most likely the sections of the building at Gerlachstraße 20 and 21.[76] It is also known from the Community files that the kitchen was closed and the prisoners were supplied with provisions via the home at Gormannstraße 3, which also provided food to Große Hamburger Straße camp. Like in Große Hamburger Straße, at Gerlachstraße Brunner had the furniture removed from the building. A sickbay was also set up. The room, which had previously been used for 'channeling' the '*Große Alterstransporte*', was reactivated for this. The Community's repair workshop now had to affix grating to the windows. During the frequent bomb alerts that took place at this time, the inmates had to remain in the rooms, which exposed them to an increased risk.[77]

---

73 List, *Wohnungsstelle und Abwanderung*, undated/beginning of the year 1943, 1, 75 A Be 2, No. 14/1, CJA.
74 *Aktennotiz* by Moritz Henschel, 11.12.1942, 2B1, No. 5, CJA. Translation by the author.
75 Note from Philipp Kozower about a consultation with Mr. Dobberke at the old people's home Große Hamburgerstraße 26, 16.11.1942, R-8150, Film 52407/No. 23, BArch.
76 This is based on an evaluation of the affidavits of service in the individual files of the Asset Utilization Office of the Chief Finance Authority of Berlin-Brandenburg (Vermögensverwertungsstelle des Oberfinanzpräsidenten Berlin-Brandenburg) in the BLHA. Cf. Jah, Deportation, 420.
77 Note by Richard Rockmann, 25.11.1942, 2B1, No. 5, CJA; Jah, Sammellager im Kontext, 218.

Until the beginning of 1943, Gerlachstraße acted as an assembly camp for arranging the Theresienstadt transports. Probably a total of 1,141 people were deported via Gerlachstraße between November 1942 and February 1943. The names of the deportees can be found on the transport lists in the Arolsen Archives.[78] These also show that, alongside older people over 65 years of age and veterans with higher military awards and decorations, the transports also included many Community employees, a consequence of the further reduction in Community employees following the *Gemeindeaktion*. Also the board members of the Community and the Reichsvereinigung Paul Eppstein, Philipp Kozower, and Leo Baeck, who were deported at the end of January 1943 in conjunction with the formal dissolution of the Community were among those deportees. Eppstein became the 'Elder of the Jews' ('*Judenältester*') and thus the head of what was known as the Jewish 'self-administration' in Theresienstadt.[79] On Brunner's instructions, the deportees also included residents of the Jewish homes for the infirm.[80] The people concerned usually only spent a few days in Gerlachstraße. As there were sometimes longer intervals between individual transports, some of them nevertheless had to spend several weeks there.

After the *Fabrikaktion*

On February 27, 1943 – the Viennese SS men had left Berlin around a month before, and the Gestapo's '*Judenreferat*' had been reestablished with new personnel – the Jews performing forced labor in the armaments factories were finally picked up 'in one fell swoop', mainly from their workplaces in the factories, and deported to Auschwitz with their family members within a few days. Alongside Große Hamburger Straße, temporarily created assembly camps were used to arrange the transports.[81] The raid has become known as the *Fabrikaktion* ('factory raid').

People who fulfilled the RSHA criteria for deportation to Theresienstadt and had been arrested during the *Fabrikaktion* and in the following days were not, however, initially deported, but instead taken to Gerlachstraße and Große Hamburger Straße, where they were 'channeled.' On March 17, 1943, they were finally

---

78 Cf. Arolsen Archives: "Subcollection 'Deportations from the Gestapo area Berlin' (1.2.1.1)". Available at: https://collections.arolsen-archives.org/en/archive/1-2-1-1_VCC-155-I. Last accessed: 03.03.2022.
79 Hájková, Ghetto, 28.
80 Note by Joel Sänger, 27.01.1943, 2B1, No. 5, CJA.
81 Jah, Sammellager im Kontext, 220–227.

deported to Theresienstadt with the '*4. Großer Alterstransport*' ('4th large transport of the elderly'), comprising a total of 1,164 people.[82] This transport was probably the last time that Gerlachstraße served as an assembly camp.[83] Große Hamburger Straße was then the sole assembly camp for the transports both to Auschwitz and Theresienstadt. At the beginning of 1944, the camp moved to the site of the Jewish Hospital in Wedding.[84]

Inmates who had not initially been deported were still present in Gerlachstraße after March 17, 1943. In April 1943, they were transferred to the building at Auguststraße 17, where Jews who had already been deferred were located.[85] The *Ordner* who worked in Gerlachstraße also moved from there to Auguststraße, some of them also to Große Hamburger Straße.[86] When Auguststraße was closed in May 1943, the Gestapo also deported the remaining *Ordner*, who had previously worked in Gerlachstraße.[87] These included Herbert Levy, who held a senior position within the *Ordner* service at the Gerlachstraße assembly camp, and former janitor Kiewe, his wife, their 16-year-old son, and their adult daughter. The latter ultimately had to work at the Auguststraße camp as an *Ordner*.

At the end of April 1943, the buildings in Gerlachstraße were eventually cleared by order of the Gestapo. As of May 1, 1943, they were transferred into the ownership of the Nationalsozialistische Volkswohlfahrt (National Socialist People's Welfare, NSV).[88] However, the buildings no longer contained any furnishings from its time as an old people's home. As the Reichsvereinigung wrote to the fire insurance company, they had "already been almost universally used elsewhere or sold off when the old people's home was converted into an assembly camp." The "property of the home residents" also no longer came "into consideration" as insured objects at this time, along with the "synagogue

---

82 Gottwaldt and Schulle, Judendeportationen, 352; Jah, Deportation, 462–463 and 651–652.
83 While the described use of Gerlachstraße is substantiated in connection with the *Fabrikaktion*, only the 'channeling' of some of the people concerned at Große Hamburger Straße can be verified in the sources. The role of Gerlachstraße with regard to the '4. Große Alterstransport' thus represents a research desideratum.
84 Jah, Deportation, 551–564.
85 Jah, Deportation, 501–503.
86 Cf. list of accommodation office and emigration [undated, beginning of 1943], 1, 75 A Be 2, No. 14/1, CJA.
87 A large proportion of them came to Theresienstadt with the '88th transport of the elderly' on May 18, 1943, a transport that also included other Community employees. See transport list, '88. Alterstransport', 18.05.1943, 127212938–127212940/ITS Digital Archive, Arolsen Archives; Jah, Deportation, 502–503.
88 Letter from Adolf Cohn to Mr. Guttmann, 27.04.1943, 1, 75 A Be 2, No. 112, # 341, CJA.

furnishings".[89] When the building was transferred to the NSV, there was an unknown number of, presumably non-Jewish, tenants in the building at Gerlachstraße 18, although nothing is known about their backgrounds and further whereabouts.[90]

From Birgit Gregor we know that the old people's home buildings were completely destroyed in the war, presumably in May 1944, although the neighboring building of the home's synagogue still existed in the early 1960s. However, the synagogue was torn down as part of the construction work at Alexanderplatz between 1965 and 1969, and the street Gerlachstraße disappeared with it.[91] The historic site is located approximately where Berolinastraße is today, in the area to the rear of the Haus der Statistik. A short distance from there, at Mollstraße 11, is a memorial stone for the victims of the pogrom in 1510. The panel displayed on it was affixed to the external wall of the home in 1934 by the aforementioned Martin Salomonski and now forms, albeit indirectly, the only permanent visible reference to the former welfare institution in the urban area.[92]

Final Remarks: Resolved, Unanswered, and New Research Questions

The former Jewish old people's home and subsequent assembly camp in Gerlachstraße represents a central historic site of the deportation and murder of the Jewish population from Berlin. Up to 2,500 people were 'channeled' there[93] in two different phases: Firstly, during the '*Große Alterstransporte*' in summer/fall 1942, when the buildings, like other homes in the city at that time, were used as a temporary assembly camp. Secondly, between November

---

89 Letter from the Reichsvereinigung der Juden in Deutschland, Bezirksstelle Berlin, to Richard Winter Insurance, 03.05.1943, 1, 75 A Be 2, No. 112, # 341, CJA. Translation by the author.
90 Letter from the Reichsvereinigung der Juden in Deutschland, Bezirksstelle Berlin, to the tenants in the Gerlachstraße 18 building, 27.04.1943, 1, 75 A Be 2, No. 112/1, # 14218, CJA.
91 Gregor, Ort, 161.
92 Ibid.
93 As a systematic evaluation has not yet been conducted, this number is based on approximate estimates: 384 residents whose last place of residence was stated on the transport lists as Gerlachstraße 18–21 (or one of the house numbers), including those deported 'to the East'; 25 'channelings' of non-home residents for the '1st large transport of the elderly' and 200 each for the '2nd' and '3rd' transport of the elderly' and 580 for the '4th' transport of the elderly' as well as 1,141 'channelings' during the permanent assembly camp phase until February 1943. The number given elsewhere (Jah, Sammellager im Kontext, 231; Sammellager am Alex), a total of at least 1,141, is much too low an estimate.

1942 and March 1943, when Gerlachstraße was the central, sole assembly camp for preparing the Theresienstadt transports. There is a close connection between the assembly camp function and the fate of the former home residents, the majority of whom were deported directly from the home with the '*1. Große Alterstransport*' in August 1942. However, the Gestapo deported a larger group of residents to Riga before this, in January 1942. In addition, individual residents or employees of the home were frequently added to a transport list 'to the East' over the course of 1942 – what is not presented in full in this text. Many of those deported to Theresienstadt were transported from there to death camps, where they were murdered. The historic site of Gerlachstraße is thus not only inextricably linked to Theresienstadt, but also to Riga, Sobibor, Treblinka, and Auschwitz.

The example of the home and assembly camp at Gerlachstraße and the paths of persecution of the old people's home residents allow many structural elements of the deportations to be highlighted, which are evident not only in Berlin but also in other places within the Reich. The persecution-related concentration of the Jewish population in major cities and the increase in the population of Jewish welfare institutions as a result of persecution are two developments that preceded the deportations and ultimately played into the hands of the Gestapo's logistics when preparing the transports. Other Jewish welfare institutions in Berlin, both those belonging to the Community and those funded independently, acted as (temporary) accommodation for Jews who had become homeless, including locations such as the Jewish school at Große Hamburger Straße 27 and the *Kleiderkammer* (clothing storage room) at Choriner Straße 26 in the borough Prenzlauer Berg. The details of the institutions' history have often not yet been researched. The Berlin practice of admitting people to homes and the organization of a place to live by the Jewish Community also represents a research desideratum, analogous to the occupancy of the '*Judenwohnungen*' ('Jews apartments'),[94] which has also not yet been researched in depth.

The example of Gerlachstraße clearly demonstrates that the Gestapo actually did not deport all Jews over 65 to Theresienstadt, but also 'to the East' and that only detailed research into the individual fates can clarify their actual whereabouts. The example of Gerlachstraße also shows that the Gestapo set up both permanent and temporary assembly camps as required. Although the change in function at Gerlachstraße from a temporary assembly camp, which was

---

94 Akim Jah, Silvija Kavcic, and Christoph Kreutzmüller: "'Größe der Wohnung: 1 Leerzimmer'. Eine Projektidee zu den 'Judenwohnungen' und 'Judenhäusern' in Berlin 1939–1945", in Aktives Museum Faschismus und Widerstand in Berlin e.V. (ed.): *Mitgliederrundbrief*, 8/4, January 2021, 3–5.

used at the same time as comparable buildings, to the central Berlin assembly camp for the Theresienstadt transports is specific to this site, it also indicates the Gestapo's common practice of using the buildings of Jewish institutions as assembly camps. Many Jewish homes in Berlin were thus used for this purpose – and the history of these camps is also largely unresearched. The Gestapo's (additional) use of the infrastructure in Gerlachstraße, i.e. the buildings, the institution, and the personnel down to the janitor, took place in a similar way in Große Hamburger Straße just a few months before and is typical of the Gestapo's approach to the deportations, as is also shown by looking at other assembly camps within the Reich.[95] In the case of Gerlachstraße, it is particularly clear to see how the deportations were interlinked with the simultaneous destruction of the respective institutions. And, as looking at the preparations for the '*1. Große Alterstransport*' on August 17, 1942, shows, the functions of old people's home and transport preparation sometimes merged. The 'channeling' carried out at all assembly camps as an intrinsic and, in the perpetrators' view, 'necessary' step in organizing the deportations, i.e. the primary function of the assembly camps, becomes apparent when looking at Gerlachstraße.

Many questions nevertheless remain unanswered.[96] This is particularly true of the conditions for the people deported from or via Gerlachstraße. During the 'channeling' for the '*Große Alterstransporte*' in the summer/fall of 1942, the old people's home infrastructure was still intact, as it was before in the Große Hamburger Straße camp. This means that the conditions in the buildings then used as (temporary) assembly camps for the Theresienstadt transports cannot be compared with the extremely precarious conditions in the temporary assembly camps, such as during the *Fabrikaktion* in February/March 1943, in terms of sanitary facilities, sleeping facilities, climatic conditions, and presumably also food. However, we do not know anything about the forms of surveillance, presence, and behavior of the Gestapo employees in Gerlachstraße.

The unanswered questions also apply to the phase in which the site was a permanent assembly camp from November 1942 onwards. Although, as shown, there is evidence of structural changes such as grating on the windows and the situation certainly deteriorated for the prisoners, we know little about the prisoners' conditions. In view of the brutal approach by the SS under Alois Brunner during the same period when rounding people up and his violent behavior at the Große Hamburger Straße assembly camp, where the transports to Auschwitz

---

95 Cf. Jah, Deportation, 147–156.
96 A further research desideratum are the *Heimeinkaufsverträge* (home purchasing contracts), which the residents of the old people's home had to conclude for Theresienstadt by order of the authorities.

were arranged, research into the conditions at the Gerlachstraße assembly camp is also relevant as it can provide information about the extent to which the appearance of a 'transfer of residence' to Theresienstadt (at that time) continued to be maintained. With this in mind, a differentiated examination of the various assembly camps and their respective function – and the collections and transfers to the train station – also appears to be indispensable. This brings me to the role of the Gestapo in Gerlachstraße.

The absence of the Gestapo is conspicuous in the preserved sources concerning the Gerlachstraße assembly camp – records, letters, and notes from the Jewish Community[97] and the Reichsvereinigung[98] as well as statements by witnesses and defendants in a postwar trial against former Gestapo employees due to involvement in the deportations from Berlin.[99] This is in stark contrast with the (other) permanent assembly camps, for which there are, for instance, extensive descriptions of the policemen who worked there.[100] This could indicate that the Gestapo did not have a permanent presence in Gerlachstraße, nor did the police in charge of the deportations stay there regularly. Instead, employees of the Jewish Community may have had to organize the 'running' of the camp as well as – at least in some cases – transferring people to the train. The latter is indicated in a memorandum from the Community, which shows that the Gestapo instructed Community members to transfer inmates from one assembly camp to another by themselves.[101]

The unanswered questions relating to the Gerlachstraße assembly camp ultimately also include research into the perspectives of the people concerned, i.e. the experiences of the residents of the old people's home, inmates, and Community employees, who had to spend a prolonged period of time at the assembly camp. The postcard from Paula Jonas cited in the introduction gives us a vague idea of what the residents of the home experienced: The residents, for some Gerlachstraße already served as 'emergency accommodation,' had to cope with the increasing overcrowding of the home and the worsening economic

---

97 These are preserved in the archive of the Centrum Judaicum in collection 1.75 A Be 2.
98 These are preserved in the Federal Archives in collection R-8150 and in the archive of the Centrum Judaicum in collection 2 B 1.
99 These are preserved in collection B Rep 58 in the Berlin State Archives. See also Akim Jah: "Die Mitarbeiter der Stapoleitstelle Berlin und das Bovensiepen-Verfahren", in Andreas Nachama (ed.): *Reichssicherheitshauptamt und Nachkriegsjustiz. Das Bovensiepen-Verfahren und die Deportation der Juden aus Berlin*, Berlin: Hentrich&Hentrich, 2015, 55–79.
100 Cf. Akim Jah: "Gesicht der Berliner Deportationen: Walter Dobberke", in *Lernen aus der Geschichte*, 2, 2022. Available at: http://lernen-aus-der-geschichte.de/Lernen-und-Lehren/content/15244. Last accessed: 23.02.2022.
101 "Aktennotiz Moritz Henschel", 25.11.1942, 2B1, No. 5, CJA.

situation of the institution – in addition to the general consequences of the antisemitic persecution policy. At the beginning of 1942, they then learned how some of them – with an unknown destination – were deported and had to live with the constant fear of being next. How did the start of the transports to Theresienstadt change this perception and how was the ghetto talked about at the home? And finally: to what extent was it possible for the former residents to support each other during the transport and relate to each other even after arriving at the destination? It can be considered certain that the experiences differ significantly from each other depending on the time of the transport and the destination, and that there is no 'conformity of experiences',[102] even in this relatively small group of home residents.

However, the conditions for further research into the Gerlachstraße home and assembly camp and comparable locations are better than ever. As the transport lists that are preserved in the Arolsen Archives are now indexed down to the level of street names, the names of the former residents of the home can be found very easily. There is no need to search through the lists manually anymore. The asset files in the Asset Utilization Office of the Chief Finance Authority of Berlin-Brandenburg stored in the BLHA are also currently being digitalized and indexed, which will also make identifying and evaluating relevant files much easier in the future.[103] An evaluation of the documents for the four 'Große Alterstransporte' could thus unearth further information about their arrangement and preparation and clarify the function of Gerlachstraße in connection with the '4. Große Alterstransport' in March 1943.

Also, for the 'channelings' from November 1942, an evaluation of the files could yield information about the – respective and average – period of time spent in the assembly camp and thus provide an indication of the conditions during the time of the permanent camp. References to further suicides may also be found this way. Finally, as Henning Borggräfe has shown, a GIS-based evaluation of the sources, i.e. linking the metadata of the transport lists with other sources[104], could also determine quantitatively when exactly the number of home residents increased and where they had previously lived, i.e., whether Gerlachstraße was their freely chosen place of residence. It would also be possible to clarify to what extent the deportation of home residents to Riga in January 1942 helped the Gestapo make space in the old people's home to 'relieve' or close any other existing Community accommodation or welfare homes. The biogra-

---

102 David Cesarani: *Final Solution. The Fate of the Jews 1933–49*, London: Macmillan, 2016.
103 Cf. Brandenburg Main State Archive: "Das OFP-Projekt". Available at: https://blha.brandenburg.de/index.php/projekte/ofp-projekt/. Last accessed: 05.08.2022.
104 See the contribution by Henning Borggräfe in this volume.

phies, including the lives of the few survivors, can also be researched by drawing on the correspondence files archived in Bad Arolsen, such as the postcard from Paula Jonas or other personal sources. Although we know much more about the former home and assembly camp and the deportation of its residents today than the AJDC in 1946, there continue to be research gaps – and a lack of historical awareness among the population about the so far largely forgotten sites of the deportation of the Jewish population from Berlin.[105]

---

[105] However, the awareness of the historical site is increasing. The artist R. Stein Wexler has recently launched a project on the Gerlachstraße assembly camp dedicated to the memory of the deported residents of the old people's home, which also includes a temporary installation at the historical site. Cf. R. Stein Wexler: "Fügung des Schicksals/Twist of Fate". Available at: https://www.rsteinwexler.com/projects/fuegungdesschicksals. Last accessed: 05.08.2022.

Michaela Raggam-Blesch
The Fate of 'Protected' Groups during the Last Years of the War

Deportations from Vienna's Nordbahnhof – a Largely Unknown Site of the Shoah

Abstract: After the end of mass deportations in Austria in October of 1942, the Jewish Community in Vienna was officially dissolved by Nazi authorities and reorganized as the so-called Council of Elders, who was put in charge of all remaining people defined as Jewish by Nazi racial laws, independent of their denomination. The majority of the people left behind were protected from deportation because they were members of an intermarried family with a non-Jewish spouse or parent. A small fragment of the Jewish population was able to remain in Vienna as employees of the Council, working as doctors, nurses, cooks, caregivers, cleaning staff, or clerical workers in the remaining institutions of the former Jewish Community. In addition, a tiny fraction of the remaining Jewish population was protected by foreign citizenship. The protection of this heterogeneous group was often temporary, since diplomatic considerations regarding foreign citizenship were subject to changes and the number of Council employees was continuously reduced by orders of the authorities. This article focuses on the deportations of previously protected groups from Vienna's Nordbahnhof – until recently a largely unknown site of deportations.

Introduction

On January 5, 1943, a small transport of about 100 people left Vienna's Nordbahnhof for Theresienstadt.[1] It was the first one of a total of 33 deportation transports from this railway station until the end of the war. In the years before, during the time period of 1941/1942, the majority of the Austrian Jewish[2]

---

[1] Jonny Moser: "Österreich", in Wolfgang Benz (ed.): *Dimension des Völkermords: Die Zahl der jüdischen Opfer des Nationalsozialismus*, Munich: Oldenbourg, 1991, 67–93, here 81; Alfred Gottwaldt and Diana Schulle: *Die "Judendeportationen" aus dem Deutschen Reich 1941–1945: Eine kommentierte Chronologie*, Wiesbaden: Marix, 2005, 347.
[2] In this paper, the term 'Jewish population' will be applied to all people defined as Jewish by Nazi racial laws, who faced persecution by the National Socialist regime, independent of their denomination.

population – approximately 45,527 people[3] – had been deported in mass deportation transports from Vienna's Aspangbahnhof. Among the 100 people on the transport early January 1943 was 14-year-old Gerty Taussig, who had been left behind in Vienna after falling sick shortly before the deportation of her family:

> I myself stayed very long [in Vienna], because just before they sent my parents away, which was in September of 1942 / October 1942, I got sick [...] I think it was Diphtheria [...]. And they sent me to a hospital, so I shouldn't infect the rest of the people. And while I was in the hospital, they shipped my parents to the concentration camp. And they forgot me. They forgot that I existed. [...] And I was there until January of 1943. [...] I was sent to Terezín. And... it was a very small transport. It was the left-over Jews, and I was one of them, you know. Just like a hundred of us. There were very few transports after the time that I went. Because we were just the last few Jews that were still around.[4]

At the end of October 1942, the Jewish Community in Vienna was officially dissolved by Nazi authorities and reorganized as the so-called Council of Elders, who was put in charge of all remaining people defined as Jewish by Nazi racial laws, independent of their denomination.[5] The majority of the people left behind were protected from deportation because they were members of an intermarried family with a non-Jewish spouse or parent. Thus, the composition of the former Jewish Community changed significantly, since more than half of the Council's members were, in fact, not Jewish by religious denomination.[6]

A very small fragment of the Jewish population was able to remain in Vienna without the protection of non-Jewish family members. They worked as doctors, nurses, cooks, caregivers, cleaning staff, or clerical workers in the remaining institutions of the former Jewish Community, because those protected from deportation – as anyone defined Jewish – were barred from general hospitals and nursing facilities. Therefore, the Jewish Community and its successor organiza-

---

3 Moser, Österreich, 67–94; Dieter J. Hecht and Michaela Raggam-Blesch: "Der Weg in die Vernichtung begann mitten in der Stadt: Sammellager und Deportationen aus Wien 1941/42", in Dieter J. Hecht, Michaela Raggam-Blesch and Heidemarie Uhl (eds.): *Letzte Orte: Die Wiener Sammellager und die Deportationen 1941/42*, Vienna: Mandelbaum, 2019, 20–75, here 74–75.
4 Gerty Meltzer (née Taussig), Interview 1686, Visual History Archive (VHA), USC Shoah Foundation, 24.03.1995. Gerty Taussig was reunited with her family in Theresienstadt. They were deported to Auschwitz together in the fall of 1944. She is the sole survivor of her family.
5 Aktennotizen, 10.10. and 01.11.1942, Joseph Loewenherz Collection, IKG Wien Memos 1941–1945, AR 25055, Leo Baeck Institute (LBI), New York.
6 Dieter J. Hecht, Michaela Raggam-Blesch and Eleonore Lappin-Eppel: *Topographie der Shoah: Gedächtnisorte des zerstörten jüdischen Wien*, Vienna: Mandelbaum, 2018², 484–490; Bericht über die Tätigkeit des Ältestenrates der Juden in Wien, January 1944, A/W 117, Central Archives for the History of the Jewish People (CAHJP), Jerusalem, 31–34.

tion, the Council of Elders, was made responsible for their care.[7] A tiny fraction of the remaining Jewish population was protected by foreign citizenship.[8] The protection of this heterogeneous group, however, was often only temporary and employees of the Council were continuously reduced on orders of the authorities. In addition to these groups, a sizeable number of Jews in Vienna tried to survive in hiding. When they were caught, they were deported immediately. Against this backdrop, smaller deportation transports continued until the end of the war.

This article focuses on the late stage of deportation transports from Vienna's Nordbahnhof – until recently a largely unknown site of deportations.[9] These transports have often been neglected in Holocaust research in Austria, since they were much smaller in scope and size: Between January 1943 and March 1945 a total of 1,760 Austrian Jews[10] were deported in 33 transports from Nordbahnhof.[11] Among them were former employees of the Council, individuals with foreign citizenship, people who had tried to escape deportations by going into hiding as well as members of 'mixed families' who lost their protection. In addition, about 151 Jewish and 55 non-Jewish Gestapo prisoners as well as presumably about 2,000 Roma and Sinti[12] were deported from Nordbahnhof station to Auschwitz.[13]

---

[7] Bericht über die Tätigkeit des Ältestenrates der Juden in Wien, January 1943, A/W 116, CAHJP, Jerusalem, 18, I –III; Michaela Raggam-Blesch: "Survival of a Peculiar Remnant: The Jewish Population of Vienna During the Last Years of the War", in *Dapim. Studies on the Holocaust*, 29/3, 2015, 197–221.
[8] Statistics from 15.04.1943 listed 235 members of the Council with foreign citizenship. Aufstellung betreffend Zugehörigkeit der in Wien lebenden Juden zu folgenden Gruppen: privilegierte Mischehe, nicht privilegierte Mischehe, Geltungsjuden, Ausländer, 15.04.1943, A/W 414, CAHJP, Jerusalem.
[9] While the Nordbahnhof has been known as a site of deportation in research since the studies of Jonny Moser, there is no commemoration or memorial to date.
[10] This definition not only includes people of different denominations persecuted as Jews but also Jews of different citizenship with residence in Austria.
[11] Gottwaldt and Schulle, Judendeportationen, 456–467.
[12] Regarding the deportation of Roma and Sinti, there is little documentation available. The majority of the 2,760 Austrian Roma and Sinti registered in Auschwitz in 1943 were presumably deported from Vienna's Nordbahnhof. Staatliches Museum Auschwitz-Birkenau in Zusammenarbeit mit dem Dokumentations- und Kulturzentrum Deutscher Sinti und Roma, Heidelberg (eds.): *Gedenkbuch. Die Sinti und Roma im Konzentrationslager Auschwitz-Birkenau*, Munich: Saur, 1993; Volkshochschule der burgenländischen Roma: "Nationalsozialismus". Available at: https://www.burgenland-roma.at/index.php/geschichte/nationalsozialismus. Last accessed: 18.09.2021.

This article is situated in microhistorical studies, which have made a significant contribution to Holocaust research in recent years.[14] Microhistory encourages us to take a closer look at particularities and unusual cases in order to gain a deeper understanding not only of regional differences, but also of the multilayered realities of the Holocaust.[15] The Nordbahnhof as a site of deportations is connected to spatial studies, which have gained increasing importance in Holocaust research by demonstrating how the destruction of Jewish life also had a profound geographic dimension.[16] During deportation transports, Jewish victims were violently relocated from their homes to unknown destinations. The overwhelming majority of the deportees did not survive.[17]

Deportations from Nordbahnhof

The mass deportation transports in the years 1941 to 1942, which left from Vienna's Aspangbahnhof, had been organized by the *Zentralstelle für jüdische Auswanderung* (Central Office for Jewish Emigration). Originally founded by Adolf Eichmann in August of 1938 to speed up the process of appropriation and expulsion, the *Zentralstelle* had been the central authority for the implementation and coordination of the anti-Jewish policies in Austria and had also been in charge of deportations.[18]

---

13 According to Jonny Moser, all transports from Vienna to Auschwitz left from Nordbahnhof station. Moser, Österreich, 86–87. I would like to thank Wolfgang Gasser and Wolfgang Schellenbacher (Dokumentationsarchiv des österreichischen Widerstandes, DÖW) for their estimate on the number of non-Jewish prisoners deported to Auschwitz.
14 See e. g.: Omer Bartov: *Anatomy of a Genocide. The Life and Death of a Town Called Buczacz*, New York: Simon & Schuster, 2018; Tim Cole: *Holocaust City. The Making of a Jewish Ghetto*, New York/London: Routledge, 2003; Jan Tomasz Gross: *Neighbors. The Destruction of the Jewish Community in Jedwabne, Poland*, Princeton: Oxford University Press, 2001.
15 Claire Zalc and Tal Bruttmann (eds.): *Microhistories of the Holocaust*, New York/Oxford: Berghahn, 2017, 1–13.
16 Anne Kelly Knowles, Tim Cole and Alberto Giordano (eds.): *Geographies of the Holocaust*, Bloomington: Indiana University Press, 2014; Natalia Aleksiun and Hana Kubátová (eds.): *Places, Spaces, and Voids in the Holocaust*, Göttingen: Wallstein, 2021, 9–20.
17 Simone Gigliotti: *The Train Journey. Transit, Captivity, and Witnessing in the Holocaust*, New York/Oxford: Berghahn, 2009, 1–5; Hecht and Raggam-Blesch, Weg in die Vernichtung, 74–75.
18 Doron Rabinovici: *Instanzen der Ohnmacht: Wien 1938–1945. Der Weg zum Judenrat*, Frankfurt am Main: Jüdischer Verlag, 2000, 60–92; Gabriele Anderl and Dirk Rupnow: *Die Zentralstelle für jüdische Auswanderung als Beraubungsinstitution*, Vienna/Munich: Oldenbourg, 2004, 112–119; Hecht, Lappin-Eppel, and Raggam-Blesch, Topographie der Shoah, 177–180.

After the last mass transport with more than 1300 persons had left Vienna's Aspangbahnhof on October 9, 1942, for Theresienstadt,[19] smaller transports were organized from Nordbahnhof until the end of the war. This railway station had previously been used by the Gestapo for the deportation of *'Schutzhaft'* ('protective custody') prisoners to Auschwitz.[20] The euphemistic term 'protective custody' applied to opponents of the Nazi regime and other 'undesired persons', who were imprisoned solely on the basis of police orders. While many of these prisoners were not Jewish, the majority of 'protective custody' prisoners deported to Auschwitz were Jews, who often had been arrested for imputed crimes. Among them were also persons who had tried to evade deportations by going into hiding.

In March of 1943, the *Zentralstelle* was being dissolved and its staff send off to other operation sites in Europe, where their expertise was used for the deportation of other local Jewish communities.[21] In Vienna, the Gestapo headquarters (*Gestapoleitstelle*) took over the agendas of the *Zentralstelle*. By early April 1943, the last assembly camp located in a former Jewish girl's school in Vienna's Second district (Malzgasse 7) was closed down. From this time onwards, Jewish victims were usually picked up directly from their homes before their deportation and transferred to the Nordbahnhof station by open trucks.[22]

Larger transports from Nordbahnhof mostly went to Theresienstadt, smaller transports and 'protective custody' transports were sent to Auschwitz. All trains belonged to the former Austrian Federal Railways, which had become part of the German Reichsbahn. The deportees usually left Vienna in passenger coaches, guarded by the Vienna police forces *('Schutzpolizei')*. Transports of 'protective custody' prisoners to Auschwitz were conducted in prison cars. The number of deportees of these prison transports was usually in single-digits.[23]

Between January 1943 and March 1945, about 1,303 Austrians who were defined as Jewish were deported in 22 transports to Theresienstadt.[24] In contrast to

---

19 Moser, Österreich, 80; Gottwaldt and Schulle, Judendeportationen, 454.
20 Moser, Österreich, 87.
21 Hans Safrian: *Die Eichmann Männer*, Vienna: Europa Verlag, 1993, 225–319.
22 Aktennotizen, 29.03.1943, LBI; Hecht and Raggam-Blesch, Weg in die Vernichtung, 73.
23 Gottwaldt and Schulle, Judendeportationen, 390–391, here 347. Raul Hilberg: "The Bureaucracy of Annihilitaion", in Christopher R. Browning, Peter Hayes and Raul Hilberg (eds.): *German Railroads, Jewish Souls: The Reichsbahn, Bureaucracy, and the Final Solution*, New York: Berghahn, 2020, 1–18; Winfried Gronwald (ed.): *Kursbuch für die Gefangenenwagen (Gültig vom 06.10.1941 an). Dokumente zur Eisenbahngeschichte*, Mainz: Dumjahn, 1979.
24 Gottwaldt and Schulle, Judendeportationen, 456–467; Jonny Moser indicated the total number of deportees to Theresienstadt during the years 1943–1945 with 1,299. Moser, Österreich, 81–82.

the 13 mass transports to Theresienstadt during the previous year, these transports were smaller in size, as customary in other cities of the German Reich.[25] Until then, all deportation transports from the *Ostmark* had departed exclusively from Vienna, where the majority of the Austrian Jewish population had been concentrated. From June 1943 onwards, a number of small transports from Austrian provinces to Theresienstadt were enforced. A total of 47 people were deported from cities and towns such as Graz, Linz, Kremsmünster and Waidhofen, often consisting of less than five people, most of whom were spouses of dissolved 'mixed marriages'.[26]

Theresienstadt was considered a 'privileged destination' for the elderly, former employees of the Jewish Community and the Council of Elders, war veterans and members of dissolved 'mixed marriage families'. The alleged 'privilege' was short-lived, since a large number of the people deported to Theresienstadt were later transferred to Auschwitz and other killing sites. Others, especially elder persons and former residents of the old people's homes, perished soon after arriving in Theresienstadt due to the catastrophic living and poor hygienic conditions.[27]

Auschwitz was the main destination for Jewish and non-Jewish Gestapo prisoners. During the years 1943 to 1944, about 151 individuals defined Jewish were deported to Auschwitz in '*Schutzhaft*' transports from Vienna's Nordbahnhof.[28] In addition, about 457 Jewish Austrians were deported in a total of 11 'regular' Auschwitz transports during the years 1943 to 1944.[29]

---

25 Smaller transports were in conformity with the deportation guidelines for Theresienstadt issued in May 1942. Gottwaldt and Schulle, Judendeportationen, 271, 347.
26 Gottwald and Schulle, Judendeportationen, 458–467; Jonny Moser indicated the number of deportees of this transport with 46. Moser, Österreich, 81–82; Hecht and Raggam-Blesch, Weg in die Vernichtung, 74.
27 Hecht, Lappin-Eppel, and Raggam-Blesch, Topographie der Shoah, 473–483; Anna Hájková: "Mutmaßungen über deutsche Juden: Alte Menschen aus Deutschland im Theresienstädter Ghetto", in Andrea Löw, Doris L. Bergen, and Anna Hájková (eds.): *Alltag im Holocaust: Jüdisches Leben im Großdeutschen Reich 1941–1945*, Munich: De Gruyter, 2013, 179–198; Wolfgang Benz: *Theresienstadt: Eine Geschichte von Täuschung und Vernichtung*, Munich: C.H.Beck, 2013.
28 For these transports hardly any further documentation (such as dates and numbers of deportees for each transport) is available. Moser, Österreich, 86.
29 These transports were documented with deportation lists. Gottwaldt and Schulle, Judendeportationen, 456–465; Moser, Österreich, 86; Transports 47 a–h: 8 deportations to Auschwitz, 03.03.1943–01.09.1944, 1.2.1.1/11204193–11204204/ITS Digital Archive, Arolsen Archives.

'Mixed Families' and their Precarious Respite from Deportations

After the dissolution of the Jewish Community in the fall of 1942, about 8,000 people defined as Jewish still remained in Vienna. The vast majority of them were intermarried spouses with a non-Jewish partner.[30]

Intermarriages between Jews and non-Jews, as well the presence of their 'half-Jewish' children, were perceived as a threat to the professed racial homogeneity of the Nazi regime. In conjunction with the so-called Final Solution, this 'unsolved problem' played an important role in the discussions during the infamous Wannsee Conference in January 1942 and its follow-up meetings in March and October of the same year. Internal disagreements within the Nazi party and concerns that 'Aryan' family members would cause public unrest ultimately spared this group from the full force of the radical measures applied to the rest of the Jewish population, even if plans for the ultimate inclusion of 'half-Jews' and Jewish partners of 'mixed marriages' in the Final Solution were never abandoned.[31]

After the November Pogroms and the surge of anti-Jewish legislation, Nazi authorities decided to provide privileged treatment to certain 'mixed marriages' in order not to evoke objections from broad non-Jewish circles. Privilege depended on gender and the religious denomination of their offspring. Families, where the non-Jewish spouse was male (head of the household) were declared 'privileged'. 'Mixed marriages' with children, who were categorized as *'Mischlinge'*[32]

---

30 A report from 01.01.1943 lists 7,989 people defined as Jewish. Among them, 5,564 individuals were married to a non-Jewish partner and 334 persons were protected through their employment at the Council of Elders. Bericht, A/W 116, CAHJP, 18. The demographics from April 1943 also list 1,151 *'Geltungsjuden'* and 235 persons who were protected by a foreign citizenship. Aufstellung betreffend Zugehörigkeit der in Wien lebenden Juden, 15.04.1943, A/W 414, CAHJP.
31 Cornelia Essner: *Die "Nürnberger Gesetze" oder: Die Verwaltung des Rassenwahns 1933–1945*, Paderborn: Schöningh, 2002^{10}, 384–442; Raul Hilberg: *Die Vernichtung der europäischen Juden*, volume 2, Frankfurt am Main: Fischer TB, 2007, 436–445; Jeremy Noakes: "The Development of Nazi Policy Towards the German-Jewish 'Mischlinge' 1933–1945", in *Leo Baeck Institute Yearbook*, 34, 1989, 291–354.
32 The *First Supplementary Decree of the Nuremberg Laws*, issued on 14.11.1935, defined individuals with a Jewish and an 'Aryan' parent either as so-called *Mischlinge* of the first degree or as *'Geltungsjuden'* – depending on their religious denomination. Children of 'mixed marriages' who were either baptized or non-denominational were classified as *'Mischlinge'* by the Nazi regime. They were neither considered 'Aryan' nor Jewish and literally personified the status of being 'in between'. Joseph Walk (ed.): *Das Sonderrecht für die Juden im NS-Staat: Eine Samm-*

by the Nazi regime were also 'privileged' – regardless whether the father or the mother was 'Aryan'. They received the same food ration cards as the general non-Jewish population and were usually able to remain in their apartments.[33]

Intermarried families who, together with their children, were members of the Jewish Community, were declared 'non-privileged mixed marriages' and therefore subjected to a similar treatment as the general Jewish population. Their children, even though technically also 'half-Jews' according to Nazi ideology, were classified '*Geltungsjuden*' ('de facto Jews') due to their religious denomination.[34] Together with the Jewish population, 'non-privileged' families were gradually excluded from staple foods and evicted from their homes.[35] From September 1941 onwards, Jewish spouses of 'non-privileged mixed marriages' and their children had to wear the yellow star on their outer garment, thereby publicly identifying them as Jews and making them vulnerable to assaults in public.[36]

In the course of the mass deportations between February 1941 and October 1942, the majority of the Austrian Jewish population had been deported from Vienna. Jewish spouses of 'mixed marriages' as well as their children were deferred from these transports, as long as the marriage remained intact. If the marital bond was dissolved due to divorce or death of the non-Jewish spouse, this protection ended. While Jewish spouses of dissolved 'privileged mixed marriages' – according to deportation guidelines – were deferred from deportations 'to the East', they were designated for deportation transports to Theresienstadt starting in June of 1942.[37] The same applied to adult '*Geltungsjuden*', who lost their protection if they were not living in the same household as their 'Aryan' parent.[38] Jewish spouses of dissolved 'non-privileged mixed marriages' as well as dis-

---

lung der gesetzlichen Maßnahmen und Richtlinien – Inhalt und Bedeutung, Heidelberg: Müller, 1981, 127, 139–140.
33 'Privileged mixed marriages' were also exempt from some of the anti-Jewish laws and taxes. Noakes, Development of Nazi Policy, 337.
34 'Half-Jews', who were registered with the Jewish Community at the time of the introduction of the Nuremberg Laws were considered '*Geltungsjuden*'. Walk, Sonderrecht, 139–140, 347.
35 Ibid., 312, 318–319, 346, 378, 380.
36 Noakes, Development of Nazi Policy, 337; Walk, Sonderrecht, 347–348.
37 Childless 'privileged mixed marriages' were also included in deportations 'to the East', since deportation guidelines only exempt Jewish spouses of dissolved 'mixed marriages' who did not have to wear the yellow star. This privilege ended when the 'mixed marriage' had been childless. "Polizeiverordnung über die Kennzeichnung der Juden, 01.09.1941", in RGBl. I, 547; Deportation guidelines of 11.10.1941, 31.01.1942 and 15.05.1942, in Gottwaldt and Schulle, Judendeportationen, 56–58, 140–144, 268–275.
38 "Deportation guidelines, 15.05.1942", in ibid., 270; "Deportation guidelines for Theresienstadt, 20.02.1943", in Wolf Gruner: *Widerstand in der Rosenstraße: Die Fabrik-Aktion und die Verfolgung der "Mischehen" 1943*, Frankfurt am Main: Fischer TB, 2005, 50–52.

solved childless 'privileged mixed marriages' were included in the deportations to ghettos, camps and murder sites in the 'East', as Max Strnad has shown with his recent publication on 'mixed marriages' in Germany.[39] Jewish spouses of dissolved 'mixed marriages' were only exempt from deportations altogether, if they had under-aged children classified as *'Mischlinge'*.[40]

Deportation Transports of Previously Protected or Eluded Groups during 1943

Given the significantly smaller scale of the deportations from Nordbahnhof with previously protected groups, these transports provide the opportunity to add personal stories to transport numbers and dates. In the following chapters, the precarious conditions of protection and the occasional arbitrariness of Nazi authorities will be analyzed on the basis of exemplary cases, which will be shown chronologically during the last years of the war. They also give an overview of the different groups that enjoyed protection for varying periods of time – among them foreign citizens, residents of old people's homes, people of mixed descent and Council employees.

On January 8, 1943, the second deportation transport from Vienna was leaving Nordbahnhof station for Theresienstadt.[41] Among the people in that transport was Hildegard Gutfreund with her son Kurt, who had turned five just two days before their deportation. The two of them had been living in hiding for several months, before they were arrested by the Gestapo in December 1942.[42] Life underground was difficult, as the non-Jewish population rarely was ready to take the risk of hiding Jews. Food was rationed and hard to obtain, and there always was the danger of being betrayed by informers.[43] The Gestapo reports in the

---

[39] Max Strnad: *Privileg Mischehe? Handlungsräume "jüdisch versippter" Familien 1933–1945*, Göttingen: Wallstein, 2021, 262–276.
[40] The guidelines specify *'Mischlinge* of the first degree' under the age of 14 in the same household. Deportation guidelines, 15.05.1942, in Gottwaldt and Schulle, Judendeportationen, 268–275.
[41] Up to that time, only 'protective custody' transports had left from Nordbahnhof.
[42] Both of them survived in Theresienstadt. Kurt Gutfreund, Interview 12716, VHA, USC Shoah Foundation, 08.03.1996.
[43] Hecht, Lappin-Eppel, and Raggam-Blesch, Topographie der Shoah, 417–418, 531–543.

years 1943 to 1944 are full of arrests and many were deported from Nordbahnhof. Only a few managed to remain under cover until the end of the war.[44]

Among the people in hiding were also some persons, who had been deported in the course of the early transports from Vienna in the spring of 1941 to open ghettos in the Generalgouvernement and who had managed to return to Vienna, in order to escape the catastrophic living conditions they had encountered there.[45] The sisters Deborah and Brandel Feuer had been deported to Kielce on 19 February 1941. After their 'illegal' return back to Vienna they were hidden by Clara Daler, a 70-year-old widowed Jewish woman, who presumably had been protected by a prior intermarriage.[46] All three of them were arrested by the Gestapo on October 12, 1942. At that time, mass deportations from Vienna had just been concluded. Clara Daler was transferred in a 'protective custody' transport to Auschwitz, where she was murdered on January 12, 1943.[47] Deborah and Brandel Feuer remained in custody until their deportation on March 3, 1943 – the first 'regular' Auschwitz transport leaving from Nordbahnhof. They did not survive.[48]

A few weeks later, Hertha Pollak was deported together with her daughters Helga and Elisabeth. Hertha had been able to evade deportation the year before due to her non-Jewish father Clemens von Pronay, who had connections to higher Nazi circles. While having been baptized after birth, she was defined as '*Geltungsjüdin*' on account of her marriage to the Jewish physician Paul Pollak.[49] After the escape of her husband to Italy, Hertha was left behind with her two

---

[44] Of about 1,600 people who are known to have tried to survive 'underground', about a third was arrested and deported. The historian Brigitte Ungar-Klein estimates the total number of failed attempts, however, to be considerably higher. Brigitte Ungar-Klein: *Schattenexistenz: Jüdische U-Boote in Wien 1938–1945*, Vienna: Picus, 2019.

[45] Hecht and Raggam-Blesch, Weg in die Vernichtung, 24–26; Walter Manoschek: "Februar/ März 1941: Die frühen Deportationen aus Wien in das Generalgouvernement", in Hecht, Raggam-Blesch, and Uhl, Letzte Orte, 95–109.

[46] Gestapo, Tagesbericht (TB) daily report 5, 13.–15.10.1942, 8479, DÖW, 7; Gottwaldt and Schulle, Judendeportationen, 269–270, 364.

[47] While the exact date of her deportation is not known, her death was recorded in Auschwitz. Documentation Centre of Austrian Resistance (DÖW): Database of Austrian Shoah and Gestapo Victims (DBSHOAH). Available at: http://www.doew.at/personensuche. Last accessed: 18.06.2021.

[48] List of the deportation transport 47a to Auschwitz on March 3, 1943, A/VIE/IKG/II/DEP/Deportationslisten/3/13, VWI; Gestapo, TB 5, 13.–15.10.1942, 8479, DÖW, 7; DBSHOAH: http://www.doew.at/personensuche. Last accessed: 18.06.2021.

[49] According to the 'First Supplementary Decree of the Nuremberg Laws', '*Mischlinge*' who were married to people defined Jewish were also considered '*Geltungsjuden*'. After the onset of deportations, they lost the protection from their non-Jewish parent. See RGBl. I, 125, 14.11.1935, 1334.

Fig. 1: Herta Pollak (left) with her daughter Helga (born 1929) and her mother-in-law Ernestine Pollak (1869–1942 Treblinka), Vienna 1934, private collection.

daughters, who were raised in the Jewish faith. They were deported to Theresienstadt on March 30, 1943, where all three of them survived. In an interview, her daughter Helga Feldner-Busztin (née Pollak) described their transfer to the assembly camp in Malzgasse 7 only weeks after her 14th birthday. There she met a group of Slovakian Jews, who had been caught hiding on coal cars, trying to cross the Austrian border to Switzerland. In the assembly camp she first found out what was happening in Auschwitz, since the Slovakian captives were already well informed about the ongoing mass murder. Helga recalled that neither she nor any of the adults could believe this and dismissed it as scare stories.[50] Her account is confirmed in a Gestapo report, which mentioned 30 Jews from Bratislava, who had been caught on January 12 and 15, 1943, at the Swiss border and transferred to Vienna Gestapo headquarters.[51] They were recorded on the deportation list and deported together with other Austrian Jews on March 3, 1943 to Auschwitz.[52]

---

50 Helga Feldner-Busztin, Interview 48947, VHA, USC Shoah Foundation, 20.12.1998; Anna Goldenberg: *Versteckte Jahre: Der Mann, der meinen Großvater rettete*, Vienna: Zsolnay, 2018.
51 Gestapo, TB 1, 29.01.– 01.02.1943, 8479, DÖW, 4–6.
52 List of the deportation transport 47a to Auschwitz on March 3, 1943, A/VIE/IKG/II/DEP/Deportationslisten/3/13, Archive of the Vienna Wiesenthal Institute for Holocaust Studies (VWI), Loan from the Archive of the Jewish Community Vienna (IKG-Archiv Wien).

Foreign citizenship only provided temporary protection from deportation and was subject to changes in diplomatic considerations throughout the war years.[53] The majority of the people on the second 'regular' Auschwitz transport from Nordbahnhof on March 31, 1943, were individuals who had been protected by their Romanian citizenship up to the change of deportation guidelines for foreign Jews in February 1943.[54] They were arrested in a round-up on March 25, 1943, which was followed by a sweep of Croatian, Slovakian and Romanian Jewish citizens in Berlin less than two weeks later on April 6, 1943.[55] This led to protests of the Romanian legation in Berlin and Vienna, demanding German authorities to provide Romanian Jews the same treatment given to Hungarian Jews. Political considerations moved the Ministry of Foreign Affairs to comply – under the condition that Romanian Jews returning from occupied territories would subsequently be transferred to Transnistria. On April 30, 1943, arrests of Romanian citizens were largely halted.[56] For the approximately 60 Romanian Jews in Vienna, who had been arrested in the round-up, those diplomatic changes came too late. Among the people deported was 50-year-old Dora Katz, whose son Martin managed to evade the transport by hiding.[57] Most of the people in this transport, among them Dora Katz, were killed upon arrival.[58]

One of the larger transports in 1943 left Vienna's Nordbahnhof station on May 25, 1943, with a total of 205 individuals for Theresienstadt.[59] Most of the people deported were inhabitants of the last two Jewish old people's homes in Seegasse 9 and 16, which were closed down soon afterwards.[60] This was the only

---

53 Beate Meyer: "Protected or Persecuted? Preliminary Findings on Foreign Jews in Nazi Germany", in Aleksiun and Kubátová: Places, Spaces, and Voids, 87–114.

54 Up to this time, only stateless persons and citizens of Poland and Luxembourg had been included in the deportations from the German Reich. Meyer, Protected or Persecuted?, 110–111; Gottwaldt and Schulle, Judendeportationen, 56–58, 140–144, 148–155, 170–177, 268–275, 318, 376.

55 Akim Jah mentions a deportation transport from Berlin with a total of 30 Romanian citizens on 19.04.1943. Akim Jah: *Die Deportation der Juden aus Berlin. Die nationalsozialistische Vernichtungspolitik und das Sammellager Große Hamburger Straße*, Berlin: be.bra, 2013, 470.

56 Radu Ioanid: *The Holocaust in Romania. The Destruction of Jews and Gypsies under the Antonescu Regime, 1940–1944*, Chicago: Ivan R. Dee, 2000, 259–270. I would like to thank Julie Dawson for referring me to this publication.

57 Martin Katz was arrested in April 1943 and was saved by the Romanian consul general Konstantin Mareş, who organized a last-minute conscription for military labor employment in Romania. Hecht, Lappin-Eppel, and Raggam-Blesch, Topographie der Shoah, 300–302.

58 DBSHOAH: http://www.doew.at/personensuche. Last accessed: 18.06.2021.

59 Gottwaldt and Schulle, Judendeportationen, 357. Jonny Moser indicated the number of deportees of this transport with 203. Moser, Österreich, 81.

60 Hecht, Lappin-Eppel, and Raggam-Blesch, Topographie der Shoah, 240–260.

transport, where one of the homes – the former building of the Swedish Mission at Seegasse 16 – seemed to have functioned as an assembly camp.⁶¹ The fact that this particular deportation transport was one of only two documented transports leaving Vienna in boxcars instead of passenger coaches appears all the more unsettling, considering the composition of the transport with frail and elderly persons.⁶² Among the other people in the transport was Alfred Kocian (born 1927) with his mother Paula, who had been divorced from his 'Aryan' father since the early 1930s. Due to the fact that Alfred had been registered with the Jewish Community at birth, he was defined as *'Geltungsjude'* and therefore could not provide protection from deportation.⁶³

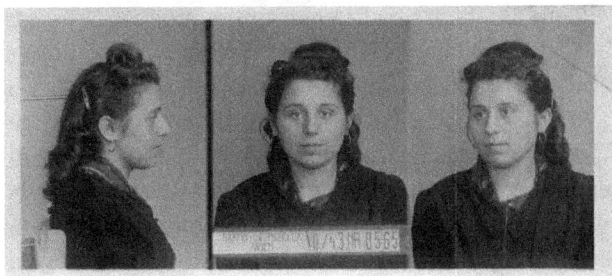

Fig. 2: Selma Gmerek (born 1920), mug shot index of the Vienna Gestapo, 23 July 1943, Wiener Stadt- und Landesarchiv, WStLA.

The Nordbahnhof also served as a deportation site for Roma and Sinti, who were deported from there to Auschwitz starting in 1943.⁶⁴ While documentation and lists of these transports have not yet surfaced, one specific case was recorded in the Gestapo daily reports following an arrest. On July 9, 1943, 15 people were detained after attempting to cross the border to Hungary illegally. Among them, 14 were categorized *'Zigeunermischlinge'* (people of Roma or Sinti decent),

---

61 This is indicated in survivor testimonies: Alfred Kocian, Interview 26579, VHA, USC Shoah Foundation, 29.01.1997; Susanne Vybiral, Interview 26960, VHA, USC Shoah Foundation, 11.12.1996.
62 The second documented transport leaving Vienna in boxcars was on 24.06.1943 for Theresienstadt. Moser, Österreich, 81, 83; Gestapo, TB 8, 22.–26.05.1943, 8479, DÖW, 10; Gestapo, TB 8, 24.–28.06.1943, 8479, DÖW, 3.
63 Alfred and Paula Kocian survived in Theresienstadt. Alfred Kocian, 26579, VHA.
64 This can be traced back to the 'Auschwitz edict' on 16.12.1942 by Heinrich Himmler, who decreed the deportation of the remaining Roma and Sinti within the German Reich to Auschwitz. Udo Engbring-Romang: *Die Verfolgung der Sinti und Roma in Hessen zwischen 1870 und 1950*, Frankfurt am Main: Brandes und Apsel, 2001, 342–347.

who had fled from Berlin in order to escape their impending forced sterilization procedure and/or their imminent deportation, as it was stated in the Gestapo report.[65] According to the report, they were three generations of two families, who were musicians by profession – among them 74-year-old Alexander Gmerek and 12-year-old Elisabeth Gmerek. The fifteenth person was Charlotte Alandt, fiancée of Jakob Gmerek, who was missing in the report. They were deported to Auschwitz with a 'protective custody' transport in September of 1943. The members of the Höpfner and Gmerek family were transferred to the 'Zigeunerlager Auschwitz' in Birkenau, where conditions were particularly abominable.[66] Only Auguste (born 1902), Andreas (born 1897) and 20-year-old Robert Höpfner survived.[67]

Since the Council of Elders constantly had to reduce the number of its employees on orders of the authorities, many staff members kept a packed suitcase in their rooms in order to be ready for deportation at any time.[68] In November of 1943, two transports left to Theresienstadt. Many of the deportees had been employees of the Council. Among them was the cemetery gate keeper Josef Bäck together with his wife Hermine and their 23-year-old daughter Gertrude Bäck, who were deported with the transport on November 11, 1943.[69] The family had lived on the Jewish cemetery to take care of the grave sites and the cultivation of vegetables for the Council of Elders.

In fact, the cemetery had become an important recreation area for the remaining Jewish population, which was excluded from parks and woods. The Council used the space at the cemetery to grow much-needed vegetables for its institutions to supplement the meager food supplies the Jewish population received at that time. Children from the Jewish children's home and other youth helped with the cultivation and harvest and used the time outside to

---

65 Gestapo, TB 8, 27.–29.07.1943, 8479, DÖW, 5–7.
66 Staatliches Museum Auschwitz-Birkenau und Dokumentations- und Kulturzentrum Deutscher Sinti und Roma: Gedenkbuch; Romani Rose (ed.): "*Den Rauch hatten wir täglich vor Augen*". *Der Nationalsozialistische Völkermord an den Sinti und Roma*, Heidelberg: Wunderhorn, 1999.
67 Alexander (born 1869), Elisabeth (born 1931), Franz (born 1897), Maria (born 1894), Selma (born 1920) and Walter Gmerek (born 1922) as well as Lola (born 1927) and Robert Höpfner (1892) became victims of the Porajmos. The fate of four people remained unknown. DBSHOAH: http://www.doew.at/personensuche. Last accessed: 18.06.2021.
68 Hecht and Raggam-Blesch, Weg in die Vernichtung, 71–74; Maria König (pseudonym), in DÖW (ed.): *Jüdische Schicksale: Berichte von Verfolgten*, Erzählte Geschichte, volume 3, Vienna: DÖW, 1993², 245; Rosa Müller (pseudonym), in ibid., 251; Franzi Löw, in ibid., 197.
69 The family was murdered in Auschwitz in the fall of 1944. DBSHOAH: http://www.doew.at/personensuche. Last accessed: 18.06.2021.

play.⁷⁰ Jewish youngsters used the cemetery as a place to get together and flirt with each other, while forgetting their precarious situation for a short while. Among them were Elizabeth Welt, who was protected by her Romanian citizenship⁷¹, and Herbert Neuhaus, whose father, Heinrich Neuhaus, was in charge of the laboratory at the Jewish hospital.

In her diary, Elizabeth confessed her growing infatuation with Herbert, who was something like a heartthrob for many of her friends.⁷² On November 11, 1943, the Neuhaus family was deported to Theresienstadt, after his father Heinrich had been denounced for harboring Jews who had escaped from Poland and were trying to cross the border into Hungary illegally.⁷³ In his unpublished memoirs, Herbert Neuhaus recalls his deportation from Vienna:

> One month after our imprisonment, on Thursday, 11 November 1943 at 8 am, we were taken from our cell [...] and led to a fairly big assembly room where at last we saw my mother again. [...] After a tearful reunion we were driven in a police car to the detention center [at] Malzgasse 7,⁷⁴ across the street from the hospital, where we were told that we had been assigned to a transport to the K.Z. Theresienstadt, which was to leave in the afternoon. [...] As Vienna by that time was practically *'Judenrein'* (free of Jews) there were no longer any mass transports, as in the past [...] but only small groups were deported, whenever a worthwhile number of victims had 'accumulated'. Thus, our group consisted of 91 persons and we were placed in regular 3rd class railroad cars and given lunchboxes by the *Ältestenrat* [Council].⁷⁵

Leopold Moses, chief archivist of the Jewish Community and the Council of Elders, was also involved in hiding the group of Polish Jews together with Heinrich Neuhaus.⁷⁶ As the Neuhaus family was deported to Theresienstadt, Moses was

---

70 Hecht, Lappin-Eppel, and Raggam-Blesch, Topographie der Shoah, 309, 506, 514.
71 During the March 1943 round-up (in her autobiography she dates it with June 1943), Elizabeth and her father had been hiding in the Romanian consulate. They both enjoyed the protection of the consul general Mareş, who provided them with false papers. Elizabeth W. Trahan: *Geisterbeschwörung. Eine jüdische Jugend im Wien der Kriegsjahre*, Vienna: Picus Verlag, 1996, 151–156.
72 Diary of Elizabeth Welt, 14.09.1943, AR 25038, Folder 5, LBI; Hecht, Lappin-Eppel, and Raggam-Blesch, Topographie der Shoah, 310–311.
73 Gestapo, TB 5, 15.–18.10.1943, 8479, DÖW, 2–4.
74 During this time, the assembly camp had already been closed and the building was used as an old people's home for the Council of Elders. According to several testimonies, a section of the building still seemed to have served as a Gestapo prison. See also: Hecht, Lappin-Eppel, and Raggam-Blesch, Topographie der Shoah, 246, 260, 412, 501.
75 Herbert Neuhaus, unpublished memoirs, transmitted via email to Dieter J. Hecht in February 2010. Heinrich, his wife Wanda and Herbert Neuhaus survived in Theresienstadt.
76 Gestapo, TB 5, 14.–16.03.1943, 8479, DÖW, 2–4.

Fig. 3: Elizabeth Welt (1924–2009) and her friend Lotte Freiberger (born 1923) at the Jewish cemetery, Vienna, presumably 1941, private collection.

kept in Vienna for a few weeks longer. On 1 December 1943 he was deported to Auschwitz, where he subsequently was murdered.[77] While the exact details of his or Neuhaus's involvement in the 'crime' were not mentioned in the Gestapo report, other sources reveal that Leopold Moses had a more leading role in the assistance of the Jews trying to cross the border to Hungary.[78] There was, nevertheless, often an aspect of the arbitrariness in the assignment of individuals to

---

[77] DBSHOAH: http://www.doew.at/personensuche. Last accessed: 18.06.2021.
[78] An article by Jonny Moser reveals that the historian Leopold Moses also had ties with the Aid and Rescue Committee (Vaada) in Budapest. Jonny Moser: "Flucht über Wien 1942/43", in *DÖW Jahrbuch 2011. Schwerpunkt: Politische Verfolgung im Lichte von Biographien*, Vienna, 2011, 264–271.

transports destined for Auschwitz or Theresienstadt on part of the Nazi authorities.

Dissolved 'Mixed Marriages' and Denunciations – Deportation Transports During 1944/1945

At the beginning of 1944, the RSHA deported Jewish spouses of dissolved 'mixed marriages' in a concerted operation throughout the German Reich.[79] Most deportees of the first Theresienstadt transport from Vienna in 1944, which left Nordbahnhof on March 10, 1944, therefore came from intermarriages, where the 'Aryan' spouse had previously died or divorced their Jewish partner.[80]

The next transport to Theresienstadt followed on April 28, 1944, with a total of 80 people.[81] The deportation list suggests that many of the people in this transport might have had protection through a foreign citizenship until that time.[82] Among the other deportees of this transport were the seven Schwarz siblings, whose 'Aryan' mother had been eager to get rid of them. Four of the siblings, Margarethe, Maria, Anna and Kurt Schwarz, had been housed in the Jewish children's home because their mother Rosa Schwarz had started a relationship with a fanatical National Socialist, who would not tolerate them. She also denounced her older children Erwin and Hilda for not wearing the mandatory yellow star. As a result of these accusations, all seven siblings, including 16-year-old Berta, were deported to Theresienstadt in April 1944.[83] Their father, Michael Schwarz, had already been arrested in the previous year after having been denounced by his wife Rosa as an alleged communist. He was deported

---

[79] This followed an RSHA edict from 18.12.1943, where these deportations of dissolved 'mixed marriages' were mandated. Walk, Sonderrecht, 401. In Berlin, the first one of these transports left already on 10.01.1944 with 329 persons, who were arrested after a coordinated round-up. Strnad, Privileg Mischehe, 269–270; Jah, Deportation der Juden aus Berlin, 530–532.
[80] This was also mentioned in the Gestapo daily report: Gestapo, TB 5, 14.–16.03.1944, 8479, DÖW, 5.
[81] Gottwaldt and Schulle, Judendeportationen, 463. Jonny Moser indicated the number of deportees of this transport with 79. Moser, Österreich, 82.
[82] Almost half of the deportees (37 of a total of 80 people) had a birthplace outside of Austria, among them many with possibly Hungarian and Slovakian citizenship. This coincides with the German occupation of Hungary and the imminent deportations of Hungarian Jews.
[83] Hecht, Lappin-Eppel, and Raggam-Blesch, Topographie der Shoah, 510; Herbert Dohmen and Nina Scholz: *Denunziert: Jeder tut mit: Jeder denkt nach: Jeder meldet*, Vienna: Czernin, 2003, 9–20.

to Auschwitz, where he perished in November 1943.⁸⁴ Maria Gabrielsen (née Schwarz), one of the younger siblings, described the roundup at the orphanage and their deportation from Vienna in her autobiography:

> Now the others came from the children's home – both the children and the adults – and said goodbye to each of us. It was a very difficult moment for all of us. We were given some food parcels and later someone slipped us some sweets to take with us on the trip. Everyone was crying quietly. […] At an appointed time, a truck drove up. A few men in uniform directed us to board the platform. Then we were driven to a railway station. There everything was busy. Constantly new trucks with people arrived. In the end, everything was full with Jewish people. The yellow stars were glaring at us. A few were standing there and discussing something. Others appeared quite despondent and had seated themselves on their suitcases. […] Men in uniforms were shouting and calling out commands in all directions, while their dogs with their sharp barking joined in. The entire scene made us scared.⁸⁵

The seven Schwarz siblings survived in Theresienstadt. After their return to Vienna, they reported their mother Rosa Schwarz, who was sentenced to six years imprisonment in one of the first people's court trials after the war.⁸⁶

The last transport from Vienna's Nordbahnhof to Theresienstadt left the railway station on March 19, 1945. Among the 11 women on the transport was Cornelia Salzer, who had been living in hiding together with her husband Karl for three years. They were arrested by the Gestapo on November 25, 1944. All 11 deportees, who arrived in Theresienstadt less than two months before liberation, survived. Cornelia Salzer's husband Karl, however, was transferred to Mauthausen concentration camp and murdered in Ebensee in April 1945, just a few weeks before the end of the war.⁸⁷

---

84 DBSHOAH: http://www.doew.at/personensuche. Last accessed: 18.06.2021.
85 Maria Gabrielsen and Oddvar Schjolberg: *Angezeigt von Mama: Die Geschichte einer Denunziation*, Berlin: Metropol, 2018, 56–58. Translation by the author.
86 Hecht, Lappin-Eppel, and Raggam-Blesch, Topographie der Shoah, 510; Dohmen and Scholz, Denunziert, 9–20.
87 Dokumentationsarchiv des österreichischen Widerstandes (DÖW) and Institut Theresienstädter Initiative (eds.): *Theresienstädter Gedenkbuch. Österreichische Jüdinnen und Juden in Theresienstadt 1942–1945*, Prague, 2005, 597; Gestapo, TB 4, 24.–30.11.1944, 8479, DÖW, 14; DBSHOAH: http://www.doew.at/personensuche. Last accessed: 18.06.2021.

Precarious Protection during the Last Years of the War

During the last years of the war, the remaining Jewish population found themselves under increased scrutiny. For preliminary protected groups, even trivial infractions against Nazi laws could lead to imprisonment and deportation. Julius Kalmus, who was protected by an intermarriage with a non-Jewish spouse, was arrested in March 1943 for an alleged 'refusal to work' in his forced labor assignment as a coal carrier. While the details of his fate are not clear, he eventually perished under unknown circumstances.[88] His daughter, 21-year-old Stefanie Kalmus, was arrested in October of the same year. According to the Gestapo record, she was accused of having an 'illegitimate relationship' with a 'German-blooded' man.[89] 'Half-Jewish' descendants of intermarriages were particularly targeted with a number of marriage stipulations regarding their most personal decisions, which became objectives of state control.[90] Stefanie Kalmus was deported to Auschwitz with a 'protective custody' transport and murdered in October of 1944.[91] Even activities like going to the movies could be dangerous, since it was forbidden to Jews and one could only enter if one removed the yellow star, which was itself a major offense. Marie Glaser, who was married to a non-Jewish man, was arrested by the Gestapo on March 5, 1943, on the basis of a 'forbidden cinema visit'. Her fate remains unknown.[92]

The wide-ranging anti-Jewish stipulations led to a criminalization of normal, daily activities, since survival strategies, such as getting extra food from the black market to supplement the meagre food rations, were dangerous. This can be seen in the increased number of arrests quoted in the Gestapo daily reports during the final years of the war.[93] Lilli Gampl, who was protected by an intermarriage, was arrested in November of 1942, after being caught purchasing

---

[88] DBSHOAH: http://www.doew.at/personensuche. Last accessed: 18.06.2021.
[89] Gestapo, TB 8, 26.–28.10.1943, 8479, DÖW, 3.
[90] *'Geltungsjuden'* such as Stefanie Kalmus were subjected to the same anti-Jewish legislation as the general Jewish population, prohibiting them from having sexual relationships with 'Aryans'. Walk, Sonderrecht, 127, 139–140. For *'Mischlinge'*, the decree forbidding these relations followed in the summer of 1942. Ibid., 382.
[91] DBSHOAH: http://www.doew.at/personensuche. Last accessed: 18.06.2021.
[92] DBSHOAH: http://www.doew.at/personensuche. Last accessed: 18.06.2021.
[93] Statistik der Staatspolizeileitstelle Wien für den Monat Januar 1944, Gestapo, TB 1, 01.–06.01.1944, 8479, DÖW; Raggam-Blesch, Survival of a Peculiar Remnant, 212–213.

provisions that were forbidden to her from farmers in the countryside. She was deported to Auschwitz, where she was killed in April 1943.[94]

At times, the surge of anti-Jewish legislation also led to absurd accusations: In December of 1943, Otto Lauterbach, who was protected through his marriage to a woman of Catholic decent, was denounced for illegally wearing of a traditional Austrian folk suit *(Trachtenanzug)* – which was forbidden to Jews – and for listening to foreign radio stations. He was deported to Auschwitz and survived.[95]

For preliminary protected groups, survival, in fact, was not guaranteed until the very last hours of the Nazi regime. Margarete Mezei, an employee of the Vienna Jewish Community, had stayed behind in Vienna with her two children after the escape of her husband, the writer Moritz Mezei (1886–1944).[96] With the beginning of deportations and forced labor assignments in 1941, she managed to secure jobs for her children at the Jewish Community: Ilse got a position at the telephone switchboard, while Kurt volunteered at the technical department.

On March 12, 1945, the bomb shelter in the basement of the Jewish Community was hit during an air raid. Ilse Mezei, who had taken refuge there together with her mother, was instantly killed, while Margarethe Mezei survived severely injured. Kurt Mezei, her twin brother, had to attend the funeral alone, since their mother was still in the hospital. When the fighting in Vienna became particularly violent during the last days before liberation, he took refuge in a cellar near his apartment together with eight other Jewish neighbors. On April 12, 1945 – only hours before liberation by the Red Army – they were discovered by raging SS troops and murdered.[97]

Conclusion

The deportations from Nordbahnhof were significantly smaller in scale than the mass transports during the years 1941 to 1942. Considering the fact that most of

---

[94] As with many 'protective custody' transports, the exact date of her deportation is not known. Her death was recorded in Auschwitz. DBSHOAH: http://www.doew.at/personensuche. Last accessed: 18.06.2021; Gestapo, TB 7, 20.–22.11.1942, 8479, DÖW, 9.
[95] Gestapo, TB 3, 07.–09.12.1943, 8479, DÖW, 5. Hecht, Lappin-Eppel, and Raggam-Blesch, Topographie der Shoah, 406–407.
[96] The writer and journalist Moritz Mezei fled to Italy in 1939. From there he was deported to Auschwitz and killed in 1944. Hecht, Lappin-Eppel, and Raggam-Blesch, Topographie der Shoah, 299–300.
[97] Hecht, Lappin-Eppel, and Raggam-Blesch, Topographie der Shoah, 545–548.

Fig. 4: The twins Ilse and Kurt Mezei (born 1924), Vienna, presumably 1941, Dokumentationsarchiv des österreichischen Widerstandes, DÖW 09443/7.

those deported had been previously protected by family relations to non-Jews, employment with the Jewish community organization or Council of Elders, citizenship or by the ability to evade deportations in hiding, these transports give the opportunity to analyze the precarious conditions of protection and add personal stories to transport numbers and dates. They also illustrate the Nazi authorities' arbitrariness when assigning individuals to specific transports: While Hildegard Gutfreund and her son Kurt were deported to Theresienstadt, other persons who had been caught while living in hiding – such as the sisters Deborah and Brandel Feuer – were deported to Auschwitz. Even if details of the Holocaust were not yet known or considered as scare stories – as Helga Feldner-Busztin remembered – people still had an understanding that a deportation to Auschwitz implied some sort of 'punishment' while Theresienstadt was perceived a 'privileged destination'. In the beginning of 1943, foreign citizenship came in the center of attention and protection for Jewish citizens of many countries waned. During the last years of the war, members of 'mixed families' found themselves under increased scrutiny and even trivial infractions against Nazi laws could lead to imprisonment and deportation. Finally, denunciation also had an impact. The case of the 'half-Jewish' Schwarz siblings, who were reported by their 'Aryan' mother, was, however, more of an exception, which also drew attention in the immediate postwar years.[98]

With the liberation by the Red Army on April 13, 1945, about 6,512 Austrians classified as Jewish had survived Nazi persecution in Vienna.[99] Among them were about 195 people who had been protected through employment with the Council of Elders. More than 40 percent of the 334 employees registered in January 1943 had been deported in the meantime.[100] Foreign citizenship proved to be the most fragile protection: From 235 individuals protected by foreign citizenship in April 1943, only 13 individuals had been able to remain in Vienna.[101] The majority – about 5,300 Austrians of Jewish descent – survived as members of intermarried families.[102] From 6,715 Jewish spouses of 'mixed marriages' and '*Geltungsjuden*' in the beginning of 1943, more than 1,400 individuals had either died or been deported between 1943 and 1945.[103] Another approximately 1,000 people had managed to survive in hiding. According to the historian Brigitte Ungar Klein, more than 500 persons can be determined, who had attempted life in hiding and became victims of the Shoah. She estimates the actual number of individuals who were deported after being discovered much higher.[104]

Considering that the Viennese Jewish Community had been one of the largest in Central Europe – 167,249 members before the Nazi takeover in 1938 – only a very small number was able to survive in Vienna.[105]

---

98 Willy Krell, "Kinder klagen an", in *Der Neue Weg*, 3/4, 01.02.1946, 7.
99 According to Jonny Moser, the number of Austrians was 5,512. An additional 1,000 persons survived in hiding. Jonny Moser, *Demographie der jüdischen Bevölkerung Österreichs 1938–1945*, Vienna: DÖW 1999, 56; Brigitte Ungar-Klein: "Jüdische U-Boote und ihre Helferinnen und Helfer in Wien", in Hecht, Raggam-Blesch, and Uhl, Letzte Orte, 171–185, here 171–173.
100 At least 139 former employees of the Council of Elders were deported between 1943 and 1945. Aufgliederung der in Wien und Niederdonau lebenden Juden, 01.01.1945, A/W 415, CAHJP; Bericht, A/W 116, CAHJP, 18.
101 Among them 2 Bolivian, 1 British, 2 Palestinian, 2 Romanian, 2 Slovakian, 2 Turkish, 1 Hungarian and 1 US citizen of Jewish decent. Ibid; Aufstellung betreffend Zugehörigkeit der in Wien lebenden Juden, 15.04.1943, A/W 414, CAHJP. See footnote 8.
102 An additional approximately 118 individuals who were members of intermarried families survived in the region of Lower Austria. Aufgliederung, A/W 415, CAHJP.
103 In January 1943, a total of 5,564 individuals were registered as spouses with a non-Jewish partner. Another 1,151 were descendants of 'mixed marriages' (*'Geltungsjuden'*). Bericht, A/W 116, CAHJP, 18.
104 Ungar-Klein, Jüdische U-Boote, 171–173.
105 Moser, Demographie, 16.

Dóra Pataricza
"Put My Mother on the List Too!" – Reconstructing the Deportation Lists of the Szeged Jewish Community

Abstract: The Jewish Community of Szeged, Hungary has a rich cultural and historical heritage hearkening back two centuries. Like most Jewish cities in Europe, much of the Szeged Jewish population was destroyed in the Holocaust. Szeged was the main deportation centre for Csongrád County (southern Hungarian villages) and parts of current Northern Serbia (Bačka region). Most of the Szeged Jewish Communities' archive stayed intact. Recently the documents of this archive were catalogued, indexed, and partly digitized in a two-year project, including deportation lists and lists of survivors. Currently, in an international project funded by the Jewish Claims Conference, all available records are compiled to build a database and to identify all the ca. 10,500 Jews who were deported from Szeged. The project aims to integrate genealogical and historical data culled from Yad Vashem as well as oral (the USC Shoah Foundation) and written testimonies (e.g., degob.org by the National Committee for Attending Deportees) to reconstruct the deportation events of May and June 1944. The paper aims at presenting and analyzing the fates of the Jewish deportees and returnees of the Holocaust in the transborder region around Szeged.

Introduction

In June 1944, five Jewish leaders were sitting in a shed in the brick factory of Szeged and, by German command, made various lists of their fellow Jews. Without knowing the purpose of the lists, they decided who ought to get a chance of survival.[1] After the war, the lists created by them got lost. In a research project in 2020/2021, an international research team led by the author of the current article tried to reconstruct the final list created by the Jewish leaders and the other transportation lists of Jews deported from Szeged in the last days of June 1944. The research was conducted based on archival material and testimonies, complemented by state-of-the-art data science. The current paper describes the

---

[1] Lipót Löw, one of the compilers of the list: "Testimony". Available at: http://www.degob.hu/index.php?showjk=3618. Last accessed: 06.09.2021.

OpenAccess. © 2023 the author(s), published by De Gruyter. This work is licensed under the Creative Commons Attribution-NonCommercial-NoDerivatives 4.0 International License.
https://doi.org/10.1515/9783110746464-017

events around the deportation and the process of the reconstruction of the deportation list(s).

Szeged's Jewish Community in Hungary was established more than two centuries ago and has a rich cultural and historical heritage. Similar to other Jewish populations in Europe, several Jewish citizens from Szeged were killed during the Holocaust. The Hungarian authorities deported 437,000 Hungarian Jews in less than two months,[2] and in many cases, no records have survived on the deportation, neither on the Hungarian side, nor at the destination, which in most cases was Auschwitz. The majority of the deported were killed within 24 hours upon arrival, with no records.[3] As a major regional centre in Southern Hungary, the city of Szeged was the main deportation centre for the surrounding villages (Csongrád County) and parts of current Northern Serbia, the Bačka region, at that time under Hungarian occupation. Approximately 2,000 Jews living near Novi Sad in Bačka were ultimately transported to Auschwitz or Strasshof in April and May 1944 via Szeged. In June 1944, 8,617 people, including all the Jews of the surrounding cities and villages, were deported from Szeged in only three days.

The first train went to Auschwitz, with most victims being murdered. The second train was uncoupled, with half going to Auschwitz and half to Strasshof, a labor camp north of Vienna, while the third train was sent to Strasshof too, with most of the Jews surviving. A third destination was Budapest, for a small group consisting of 66 people, they too were transported with the third train. The setup of the three transports resulted in the fact that the Jewry of Szeged was after the war one the most intact Jewish communities in the Hungarian countryside with an exceptionally high, an estimated 50 to 60 percent rate of survival, including babies, children, and elderly. In the case of Szeged, this also means that a relatively large number of testimonies and memoirs from people of all ages and backgrounds is available.

Several questions can be raised regarding both the process of the deportations and the reconstruction of the events: How were decisions made on who was to be transported with which train? How precise are the testimonies? Are the estimations of the number of deportees accurate? Were cases of birth and death kept track of in the assembly camps? What raised the chance of survival in the case of Szeged's Jewry? Is there a correlation between certain aspects,

---

[2] Randolph L. Braham and Zoltán Tibori Szabó (eds.): *A magyarországi holokauszt földrajzi enciklopédiája*, volume 1, Budapest: Park, 2007, 7–92.
[3] Laurence Rees: *The Holocaust. A New History*, London: Viking, 2017, 392.

such as occupation and the rates of survival? Can the network of Szeged's Jewry be reconstructed based on the documents related to the Holocaust?

The current article describes the methodology of an ongoing research project[4] conducted in the Szeged Jewish Community (SzJC), describing how missing vital sources on the Holocaust such as the non-existing lists of deportation can be reconstructed based on different sources. These sources are the newly catalogued, indexed and partly digitized archives of the Szeged and Novi Sad Jewish Communities,[5] the regional and national archives, the already existing background literature, oral and written testimonies from several sources, various Holocaust-related online databases as well as genealogical sites. The project aims to identify and recreate the names of those 10,600 Holocaust victims deported from or via Szeged[6] and reconstruct who was deported with which train by using, merging, and reconciling every available source. The project also aims to find patterns and combine personal stories and big data to reconstruct the happenings of May and June 1944.

This article presents the methodology and the findings of this research focusing on the approximately 4,000 deportees belonging to the Szeged Jewish Community. The article aims to present innovative solutions for central methodological issues, provide a valuable framework for novel directions in Holocaust research,[7] and describe how to use and, if needed, replace missing primary documents when reconstructing the history of the Holocaust.

---

4 The author wishes to thank the Conference on Jewish Material Claims against Germany (the Claims Conference) for making the research project possible.
5 The digitization project was made possible with the support of the Rothschild Foundation Hanadiv Europe.
6 The extensive list of Jews deported from the Bačka region was recently published, see Alexander Bursać, Vladimir Todorović and Petar Đurđev (eds.): *Deportation of the Jews of Bačka in 1944*, Novi Sad/Ramat Gan: Archiv Vojvodine – Bar-Ilan University, the Sal Van Gelder Center for Holocaust Research & Instruction, 2021. Although some of the sources include male forced laborers, the scope of our research does not include collecting their names.
7 The author would like to express her gratitude to Mrs. János Horváth, née Terézia Löw, Mrs. George Gara, née Vera Pick, István Salamon and Katalin Varga, who recounted their memories of the deportation process in Szeged in June 1944.

Previous Research

The history of the deportations from Szeged has been researched mainly by Judit Molnár, partly from the view of the perpetrator.[8] Júlia Dunainé Bognár together with Ferenc Kanyó has published the names of the victims of Szeged, which was supplemented by a second volume of names by Ferenc Kanyó in 2000.[9] However, both books list victims of the Holocaust together with military and civilian casualties. The lists are not complete, nor do they contain the list of survivors. The books were composed based on the list of martyrs on the memorial hall of the Szeged New Synagogue, the death registers, and articles published in the *Délmagyar* newspaper from 1945 to 1948, where missing people were listed.[10] Meanwhile, new documents have emerged, and it turned out that there are several mistakes in these registers (e. g., people with the same names were not identified, survivors were listed as being murdered, some victims' names are missing); thus, it is high time to revise these lists.

In 2004, the Hungarian Research group of Yad Vashem Archives, led by László Karsai and Judit Molnár, together with Kinga Frojimovics, the director of the Hungarian Section in Yad Vashem Archives at that time, had made a basic categorization and had also put onto microfilm the documents of the Szeged Jewish Community related to the Holocaust. A copy of these microfilms is in the Szeged Jewish Community, and another copy, together with a digitized copy of it, is available on site at Yad Vashem. However, none of these is publicly accessible through Yad Vashem's website.

---

8 Judit Molnár: *Zsidósors 1944-ben: az V. (szegedi) csendőrkerületben*, Budapest: Cserépfalvi, 1995; idem.: *Csendőrök, hivatalnokok, zsidók: válogatott tanulmányok a magyar holokauszt töténetéből*, Szeged: Szegedi Zsidó Hitközség, 2000; Kinga Frojimovics and Judit Molnár: *Szeged – Strasshof – Szeged: Tények és emlékek a Bécsben és környékén "jégre tett" Szegedről deportáltakról. 1944–1947*, Szeged: Szegedi Tudományegyetem Állam- és Jogtudományi Kar Politológia Tanszék; Szegedi Magyar–Izraeli Baráti Társaság, 2021.
9 Volume 1: Júlia Dunainé Bognár and Ferenc Kanyó: *A második világháború Szegedi hősei és áldozatai. Tanulmányok Csongrád Megye XXIII.*, Szeged: Szeged Csongrád Megyei Levéltár, 1996; volume 2: Ferenc Kanyó: *Szeged és környéke második világháborús hősei és áldozatai. Tanulmányok Csongrád Megye Történetéből. XXIII/A*, Szeged: Szeged Csongrád Megyei Levéltár, 2000.
10 Dunainé Bognár and Kanyó, *Hősei és áldozatai*, 145–147.

The Events in Szeged in May and June 1944

One of the core focuses of our ongoing project is the reconstruction of the events and the circumstances under which the ghettoization list and the list of transports were created, even though or exactly because the latter has not survived. Who, how, and when compiled the list, and what aspects and factors were considered when deciding whom to include?

The German army occupied Hungary on March 19, 1944, and the fate of the Jews of Hungary has been finalized. In Szeged, on April 29, 1944, chief count Sándor Tukats instructed deputy mayor Béla Tóth to establish the city ghetto. The mayoral decree on the ghettoization of Jews was issued on May 17, and the ghettoization of the local Jews was planned to be started on May 22.[11] The ghetto consisted of designated buildings around the Old and the New Synagogue with the synagogues and the community building in its center.[12] At the request of the local Christian leaders, Jews who had converted to Christianity were accommodated in three buildings outside the ghetto.[13]

The public administration had no chance (and will) in Szeged to neglect the orders against the Jewish population since there was a German consulate in the city. In the nearby city of Hódmezővásárhely, deputy mayor Pál Beretzk interpreted the orders differently and decided not to send the local Jewry to the ghetto.[14] This decision, of course, did not save them from deportation, but they were allowed to stay in their homes until then.

The evacuation of the ghetto started on June 16, 1944, when the Jews were taken to the territory of the Szeged brick factory, a transit ghetto. The Jewry of nearby settlements had been already taken there, thus there were altogether 8,617 people in the brick factory. Eventually, out of the 3,827 people sent to the ghetto, 3,095 Jews went to the brick factory. There were 737 people exempted from deportation for various reasons: 127 people had been interned in the meantime, 57 had died, 22 became exempted from the regulation, and four had been granted Swedish citizenship. In addition to them, there were also 505 converted Jews and 22 so-called prominent people who got an exemption from the interior

---

11 Randolph L. Braham: *A magyar holocaust*, volume 2, Budapest: Gondolat Kiadó, 1988, 55.
12 Hungarian Jewish Museum and Archive: "Report cards of the Jewish communities in the Hungarian countryside". Available at: https://library.hungaricana.hu/hu/view/ZsidoSzervezete kIratai_1944_D_5_1/?pg=728&layout=s. Last accessed: 05.05.2021.
13 Molnár, Csendőrök, 79.
14 Imre Makó and János Szigeti: *"Vihar és vész közepette". A holokauszt hódmezővásárhelyi áldozatai*, Hódmezővásárhely: Magyar Nemzeti Levéltár, 2014, 22.

minister.[15] Among the 22 Jews exempted from deportation were university professors, high ranked military officers, and those regarded as counterrevolutionaries in the Aster Revolution of 1919.[16] An exemption could only be granted to those who applied for it in writing, so conversion and intermarriage did not mean exemption automatically from ghettoization and deportation. In many cases, even filing a request to be considered as an exempt did not help either, because the decision on the requests depended on the Hungarian officials. In some cases, people under exemption were deported. In other cases, the approved decision on exemption was sent out after the deportation.[17]

The most important source for our research is the ghettoization list written in May 1944, consisting of 94 typewritten pages. It is with the help of this list that we can reconstruct the fate of the Szeged Jewry. Since the actual deportation list did not survive, the only way to reconstruct it is to compare testimonies and the ghettoization list. Thus, what happened to whom in those four to five weeks between the ghettoization and the deportation can be pieced together, and the process and aspects considered when people were chosen for the three transports become evident. Pap was the president of the Jewish Community in Szeged until the German occupation, after that one of the members of the Jewish council. His account describes how he was forced to compile the list:

> Two weeks before moving in, a statement had to be made who is to move into the ghetto. I was in a terrible situation because a couple of medical doctors, university professors, and military exempts did not have to move to the ghetto, and I did not put them on the list. However, they [the Hungarian authorities] told me that according to another regulation, no one could be omitted [from being added to the list], so patients who had a surgical operation two days earlier and women who just gave birth were also brought into the ghetto.[18]
> I fought a great fight not to take at least these patients [to the ghetto], they promised to leave them [in the hospital], but it seems the higher forum did not allow them to do so, and on the last day, they were also taken out to the brick factory.[19]

The ghettoization list mentioned and compiled by Pap contains all Jewish residents of Szeged who officially had an address in Szeged at that time. It does

---

15 Molnár, Zsidósors, 172.
16 Ferenc Kanyó: "A szegedi zsidóság holocaustja", in *Szeged*, June 1994, 46.
17 Molnár, Csendőrök, 129–130.
18 This claim is supported by Ilona Müller, a survivor from Szeged, quoted in an article in Délmagyar.hu. See Arany T. János, Dombai Tünde and Szabó C. Szilárd: "Ott álltunk anyaszült meztelenül". Available at: https://www.delmagyar.hu/szeged-es-kornyeke/ott-alltunk-anyaszult-meztelenul-2528608. Last accessed: 01.04.2021.
19 Róbert Pap: "Testimony". Available at: http://www.degob.hu/index.php?showjk=3560. Last accessed: 28.04.2021. Translation by the author.

not list the Jews living in the surrounding towns. In 2018, eight researchers, including the author of this article, copied the list into an excel spreadsheet in a few months so that it can be used for research purposes. The original document can be found at the office of the Jewish Community of Szeged, and the digitized and transcribed material was handed over to be made available on jewishgen.org, ushmm.org and the online archive of the Arolsen Archives.[20]

The list includes the names of men and, in most cases, the married names of women, including previous names, place and date of birth, occupation, address before the ghettoization, and remarks, for example, concerning forced labor, exemption or 'mental problems'. Kathy Glatter from Gratz College did extensive research in 2019 to restore the identities of the married women on the list. With the help of the digitized marriage records available on the website macse.hu, a database of Hungarian vital records, she researched the maiden names of approximately 700 women.

The ghettoization list has 3,881 names altogether, including names that were added later in handwriting. 1,178 people were born in Szeged; 57 percent female and 43 percent male. Besides these data, there are pencil-marked notes on the papers. However, the meaning of these pencil marks (check marks, round shapes, and hyphens) has not been deciphered yet, nor do we know who made the notes when; thus, further analysis is necessary. The marks might have been added at the time of the move to the ghetto when compiling the transportation lists or upon the return of survivors to Szeged. Some names are not marked, some are marked twice, and others are marked with two different marks. Based on the use of the marks, it can be excluded that they indicate who survived and who died.

Although according to the filing jacket the list is referred to as a deportation list, it was written before the deportation at the time of ghettoization.[21] The exact determination of the date of creation is possible through deceases of which the dates are known. The death certificates of Szeged are openly accessible on familysearch.org, a webpage displaying vital and other registers. Thus, Ilona Szabó, who had been added to the list, had already died on May 3, 1944. Her death was reported only on May 5, indicating that her name was added to the list before May 5 or that the Community was informed later about her death. Several other cases of death in May 1944 give us a hint on the dates. While Mrs Miksa Wertheimer's name appears on the list, her husband, Miksa Wertheimer, who

---

20 USHMM: https://www.ushmm.org/online/hsv/source_view.php?SourceId=49350. Last accessed: 12.09.2022.
21 On the misleading term deportation list (*Deportationsliste*), see the article by Christian Groh and Kim Dresel in this volume.

died on May 10, 1944, is omitted, indicating that the list was compiled after May 10 and thus only the name of the newly widowed Mrs Wertheimer was added. Szidónia Wilhelm's name is also included on the list, although she died on May 30, 1944. Thus, it can be concluded that the ghettoization list was written in about 20 days, between May 6 and May 30, and that circulation of the information was difficult at that time.

The Szeged Jews, at least those who were also obliged to wear a Jewish Star on their clothes, 3,827 people in total, had to move into the ghetto of the city within eight days starting from May 22, 1944, according to the order of vice mayor Béla Tóth, thus by then, the ghettoization list ought to have been ready. The Jews were allowed to bring 50 kilos of luggage and food for 14 days into the ghetto.[22]

A recurring motif in the testimonies is that of the suicides committed on the night before the move to the brick factory and that on the same night many people converted to Roman Catholicism. Despite the rabbi's efforts of convincing his fellow Jews not to leave their religion last minute, in the end, he even had to assist them converting:

> Around four AM, a pilgrimage started towards my apartment. Dozens of people came and asked for falsified certificates that they had converted in the past. In vain did I explain that it could not help them either. All I could do was hand out a stack of ministerial paper (250 pcs.), my fountain pen, and the seal of the rabbinate. I told them to write whatever they want to, and I will sign everything. Lest they believe that me refusing to give them a certificate will aggravate their fate. That morning I was taken out to the sports complex, from there to the brick factory. Later I heard that after that, the Christian priests indeed entered the [brick factory] and baptised indiscriminately.[23]

---

22 Molnár, Zsidósors, 79–82.
23 Rabbi Frenkel remembered the events and described them to his predecessor. See rabbi József Schindler in a letter quoted by Zsolt Markovics, rabbi of Szeged. Available at: https://www.orzse.hu/resp/mtud2005-markovics-frenkeljeno.htm. Last accessed: 22.03.2021. Translation by the author. See also József Schindler: "Megjegyzés a 'Zsidómisszió vagy zsidóüldözés' című cikkhez", in *Theologiai Szemle*, 7/8, 1960, 243–244. The oral testimony of Vera Gara (née Pick) confirms the series of events. See Vera Gara: "Ottawa Holocaust Survivors Testimonial 2016". Available at: https://www.youtube.com/watch?v=Y62rEDkR-bw&t=575s. Last accessed: 19.05.2021. See also Vera Gara: *Least Expected Heroes of the Holocaust*, Ottawa: Vera Gara (self-published), 2011, 8–9.

The Compilation of a List for the Third Transport

The first transport left Szeged on June 25, 1944, with 3,199 people. Based on the testimonies it seems, that certain groups were automatically included in that group, such as converts and ill (especially mentally ill people). Mrs. Ferenc Szendrei, née Zsuzsanna Német (born 1920 in Hódmezővásárhely) had to work as a nurse in the brick factory. Later she was transported to Auschwitz with the first transport. She gave an extensive account of both the days in the brick factory and how people for the first transport were selected. According to her, the patients treated in the temporary hospital-like institution in the brick factory, the poor and the mentally ill people were sent off with the first transport. She also claimed that Jews who had converted to Christianity too had been transported on June 25:

> My two relatives and I were among those meant to be first transported from the brick factory. [...] As far as I could judge there, the first transport taken included those who converted to Christianity, the poor and those who did not have good relations with the members of the Jewish council. For this reason, my grandmother's siblings and family members did not get into the first transport because there was a doctor and a lawyer among them, and they were wealthy compared to us. [...] All of the patients treated in the "hospital" and all the mentally ill Jews in the brick factory were sorted into the first transport.[24]

In the meantime, the selection of people to be transported to Strasshof also took place: On June 20, Argermayer[25], an SS-Hauptsturmführer appeared at the gate of the ghetto, called the five representatives of the communities, and handed them a letter written by Ernő Szilágyi, a leading member of the Zionist Rescue Committee (Va'ada). In the German-language letter, Szilágyi asked them to select 3,000 Jews from the people in the ghetto, prioritising the following: families with many children, families of laborers, relatives of prominent Jews.

Testimonies often describe even minor events and enable the reconstruction of the series of events. However, these first-hand accounts are often not precise, and in some cases, they originate from survivors who were children at the time of the Holocaust, yet their testimonies too are essential to find out about the details. The accounts of the personal experiences describe different aspects of the selection criteria and highlight the series of events uniquely. The testimonies reflect

---

24 Makó and Szigeti, Vihar és vész, 127–130. Translation by the author.
25 An alternative spelling is Angermayer. The Hauptsturmführer could not be identified and there are no official documents proving the existence of a German officer with this name who served in Szeged at that time. Molnár, Zsidósors, 147.

strategies of predominancy and how, when and based on what motivation pre-existing networks were used to ensure that a family's members would be added to the list of the third transport.

One of the essential sources in this genre is the written testimony of Lipót Löw (born 1889 in Szeged, died 1966 in Jerusalem), the son of chief rabbi Immánuel Löw, who was one of the five-membered commission preparing a list of notable people who were intended to be sent to Strasshof instead of Auschwitz. He gave an extensive account of how the original order of compiling a list of 3,000 names, supposed to be sent to Strasshof yet unbeknownst to the members of the commission, was changed. Once the list of 3,000 was ready but not yet made public, the German Hauptsturmführer limited the number to 2,400 without giving a reason:

> Naturally, as committee members, we had no idea that the selection was a decision between life and death. We did not know either about the death camp in Auschwitz, that our brethren in Szeged would be transported there, or that the people on the list would be sent to Austria to chiefly benevolent people. [...] Apart from the Jews of Szeged primarily the Jews scattered around in the neighbouring towns and villages were gathered in the brick factory: from Makó, Hódmezővásárhely, Mindszent, Kistelek, Dunapataj, Kiszombor, Csanádpalota, Pitvaros, Magyarcsanád, Földeák, and Újkécske.[26]

Attached to Szilágyi's letter was a list with the names of 160 prominent Jews in the Szeged ghetto, compiled in Budapest by the Zionist Rescue Committee. Instead of 160 prominent personalities, only 66 were placed in Kasztner's special group, and this was because the compilers of the list were not allowed to see the original instruction. Lipót Löw found out about this only later: "We noticed that when the captain had given us the order to prepare the list for the entrainment, he let us see the original instruction; also, the fact that he failed to give us the official dispatch and did not let us consult it either. We were sure that the dispatch listed even more names."[27]

Teréz Löw, the granddaughter of chief rabbi Immánuel Löw, was one of the 66 prominent to be saved by Kasztner due to the merits of her grandfather. She has vivid memories of the transportation:

---

[26] Lipót Löw: "Testimony". Available at: http://degob.org/index.php?showjk=3618. Last accessed: 09.05.2021.

[27] Randolph L. Braham: *A népirtás politikája. A holocaust Magyarországon*², volume 2, Budapest: Belvárosi, 1997, 697–698. Lipót Löw lists only the heads of the family and the number of family members to be included, however, due to this fragmentary information it is difficult to reconstruct the 66 names. See Lipót Löw: "Testimony". Available at: http://degob.org/index.php?showjk=3618. Last accessed: 09.05.2021.

> In the end, it was only one wagon of people, and then, all of us [were deported]. We arrived at the outskirts of Budapest, and then our wagon was opened; it was not sealed. And the train went on, we stayed there, and they put us in, I do not know anymore, probably in a bus, and so we got on the Aréna Road, to the synagogue where there were already people from Kolozsvár, and it turned out that those who were concentrated there were, in principle [...] meant to be sent to Palestine sometime.[28]

Due to Immánuel Löw's critical condition – he contracted bilateral pneumonia in the brick factory while lying for days on the floor[29] – the Löw family did not reach the Mandatory Palestine but stayed in Budapest where Immánuel Löw died a couple of weeks later.

József Radó, president of the Hódmezővásárhely Jewish Community, also gave an extensive account of how the list of the third transport was created. In August 1945, he described the same dilemmas that he as the leader of the Hódmezővásárhely Community had to face and why the five-member committee decided not to include converted people into the third transport. His testimony is also a vital source that reveals that after the arrival in Strasshof no difference was made between people who were chosen to be taken to Strasshof (third transport) and those who ended up in Strasshof by accident (second transport):

> To compile the final third list, the captain decided that we could now stick to the original Szilágyi intentions, and the families would not have to be torn apart. We continued to work, dead exhausted. [...] The secrecy was over, people rushed, and everyone demanded from me that I add them to the list. There were 880 members of the Hódmezővásárhely community, and I could not admit more than 300 with any soul. I tried to keep to Szilágyi's instructions. [...] It does not, therefore, include those who have left the community of faith and thereby have denied our community of destiny. [...] Anyway, we still had the hope that they would take me to Palestine, and those who flee their own Jewry would not be there.[30]

Irma Bognár was deported with her baby girl and her mother to Strasshof. She described the experience that initially only her ten-months-old baby was supposed to be included on the list of exempted and the confusion that the announcement caused:

---

28 Mrs. János Horváth, née Terézia Löw, and Tamás Ungvári: "Interview", in Máté Hidvégi and Tamás Ungvári: *Löw Immánuel Válogatott Művei*, Budapest: Scolar Kiadó, 2019, 280–291, here 281. Translation by the author.
29 Hidvégi Máté: "Löw Immánuel utolsó hónapjai". Available at: https://remeny.org/remeny/2015–4-szam/hidvegi-mate-low-immanuel-utolso-honapjai/. Last accessed: 21.02.2021; László Marjanucz: "Löw Immánuel tragikus sorsa a háború végén. Adalékok a zsidó törvények szegedi végrehajtásához", in *Acta Universitatis Szegediensis*, 114, 2002, 115–124, here 122.
30 Makó and Szigeti, Vihar és vész, 131–134. Translation by the author.

> Then another announcement: whose parents are on the list can sign up; the same goes for the parents of the children listed. One must check in at the office at three in the afternoon. As soon as the news was heard, the well-informed rumoured that there were only a thousand and four hundred spots on the list. Those who were above the quota would stay behind. At the set hour, people were pushing, treading, beating each other in the hallway in front of the office door. [...] By the way, no one knew exactly what this list was, whether it was good to get on it, or maybe we would just seal our death sentence with it. I saw a good friend of ours in the office, engineer Szívós, who typed the names. I did not have enough time to stop at the window, and the crowd moved on. I shouted: Elemér! Put my mother on the list too![31]

The final list with 2,400 names was read aloud on June 26, 1944, and whoever was not mentioned was included in the second transport, which left the next day.[32]

Circulating information and keeping track of people must have had its challenges. The number of the population in the contemporary documents is based on daily roll calls, the so-called *Appelle*. People were counted every day. We do not have information on how the gendarmerie kept a trace of babies born in the ghetto, those who were sick and were unable to stand in the yard during the roll calls, and those who died.

Jenő Ligeti recalled that many babies were born in the brick factory: "a musty little tool chamber was set up to conduct the births. I do not have an accurate report, but the number of new Hungarian citizens born in the brick factory's dust is about 60".[33] The birth registers of 1944 cannot be researched according to the Hungarian archival law due to their strictly personal content and the fact that the vital registers include the sensitive data of living individuals. However, the number of newborn babies mentioned in the testimony seems to be an overstatement considering that the average number of live births in 1944 must have been around 19/1000. This rate would mean seven to eight births in two weeks and 9,000 people.[34]

---

[31] Irma Bognár: "*Adjanak hálát a sorsnak ...*" *Deportálásunk története*, Budapest: Sík Kiadó, 2004, 16–20. Translation by the author.
[32] Lipót Löw: "Testimony". Available at: http://www.degob.hu/index.php?showjk=3618. Last accessed: 15.12.2021.
[33] Jenő Ligeti: "Testimony". Available at: http://www.degob.hu/index.php?showjk=3555. Last accessed: 17.05.2021. Translation by the author.
[34] Hungarian Central Statistical Office: "Népesség, népmozgalom (1900–)". Available at: https://www.ksh.hu/docs/hun/xstadat/xstadat_hosszu/h_wdsd001a.html. Last accessed: 15.12.2021.

The Calculation of Survivors and Victims

The primary aim of our research project is to trace back the individual fates of people who were deported from Szeged. This is only possible if the ghettoization list written in 1944 is compared with all possible sources to determine who survived the war and who vanished in the Holocaust. The data and the numbers in different both primary and secondary sources are contradicting.

The Szeged Jewish Community had 2,852 members in April 1944, according to a survey that the communities had to fill in.[35] Based on documents from 1944, Braham stated that 8,617 Jews had been concentrated in the Szeged ghetto, slightly less than half of whom originally lived in the city.[36] Between April and June 1944, more than 1,000 Jews must have moved to Szeged. The remaining approximately 4,000 Jews came from nearby settlements. They were transported in three days to three different locations: Auschwitz, Budapest and Strasshof.

The list of trains going through Kassa (today: Košice) is available online.[37] István Vrancsik, the commander of the Kassa train station, compiled this data. He made notes on the trains passing through Kassa and the number of deportees.[38] Vrancsik recorded every day at the station how many trains passed through the railway station, from which area of Hungary they came, and how many Jews the trains carried. According to him, the wagons were opened at the station, and people were counted and handed over to the German and Slovakian railway staff. The rail car doors were then resealed. Vrancsik's acquaintance, lawyer Gaskó, helped in preserving these records.[39] As such, this is one of the most important sources on the number of victims of the Hungarian Holocaust.

According to these lists, the first train that left Szeged on June 25 arrived in Kassa on the 26. It had 3,199 passengers, out of whom 2,747 were killed. The subsequent transport left on June 27 to Auschwitz, to which wagons from the Bác-

---

35 Kinga Frojimovics and József Schweitzer, *Magyarországi Zsidó Hitközségek – 1944. április. A Magyar Zsidók Központi Tanácsának összeírása a német hatóságok rendelkezése nyomán. Adattár*, vol. 1. Budapest: MTA Judaisztikai Kutatócsoport, 1994, 636.
36 Randolph L. Braham, *A népirtás politikája. A holocaust Magyarországon*^{2}, vol. 2. Budapest: Belvárosi, 1997, 694.
37 Quoted without reference to the archival number of the Yad Vashem Archive by Michael Honey, "Research Note on The Hungarian Holocaust". Available at: http://www.zchor.org/hungaria. Last accessed: 15.12.2021.
38 Molnár, Csendőrök, 193–194, footnote 37.
39 Gellért Ádám: "Csatári László és az 1944 – es kassai deportálások", in *Betekintő*, 3, 2014, 209–246, here 209.

salmás ghetto were also attached. Thus, a total of over 6,000[40] people were sent to Auschwitz. Part of this train was disconnected at Felsőzsolca under circumstances still unclear, and 2,737 of its passengers were directed to Strasshof. The other part of the train passed through Kassa with 3,737 passengers, out of whom an estimated 3,332 did not survive.[41] The numbers indicated have been calculated according to the Vrancsik list and Michael Honey's estimations.[42] The third train, with 1,684 people which left Szeged on June 28, never reached Auschwitz since it was directed straight to Strasshof. In Budapest, a group of 66 people travelling in the last 'selected' car was disconnected. They were transported to the ghetto set up in the Aréna Road Synagogue. According to Braham, based on Lévai, 5,739 people in the second and third transports were sent to the Strasshof camp in Austria, and the majority survived the ordeal.[43]

Since the data in various lists and databases are different and even contradicting, further research and analysis are necessary to combine the available data and the information gained from the testimonies to determine the exact number of deportees and survivors. Some of the below numbers refer to the number of Szeged Jewry only, while the higher numbers include Jews from other villages. The numbers below demonstrate the complexity and the problems involved when trying to reconstruct the exact data, both in regard of the total number of deportees and the other number referring only to Szeged.

Jewish population of Szeged in 1941[44]	4161
Survey, number of members of the SzJC, April 1944[45]	2852
Ghettoization list of Szeged, SzJC, May 1944	3881
Jews in the Szeged ghetto, May and June 1944[46]	3827
Jews from Szeged in the brick factory[47]	3095

---

40 Molnár, Csendőrök, 194.
41 According to these data, the number of people in the second transport is 2,737 + 3,737 = 6,474 people.
42 Michael Honey: "Research Notes on The Hungarian Holocaust". Available at: http://www.zchor.org/hungaria. Last accessed: 08.05.2021.
43 Braham, Magyar Holocaust, volume 2, 57.
44 "National census of 1941". Available at: https://library.hungaricana.hu/hu/view/NEDA_1941_demogr_adatok_kozsegek/?pg=27&layout=s. Last accessed: 06.09.2021.
45 Kinga Frojimovics and József Schweitzer: *Magyarországi Zsidó Hitközségek – 1944. április. A Magyar Zsidók Központi Tanácsának összeírása a német hatóságok rendelkezése nyomán. Adattár*, volume 1, Budapest: MTA Judaisztikai Kutatócsoport, 1994, 636.
46 Document nr. 847/1944, Csongrád County Archive, quoted by Molnár, Zsidósors, 93.
47 Molnár, Zsidósors, 172.

Ferenczy report, June 29, 1944, total number of Jews in the brick factory[48]	8617
First train with Jews from Szeged and surrounding, June 25, 1944[49]	3199
Second train leaving Szeged, calculated as per account of Lipót Löw[50]	3018
Second train with Jews from Szeged and Bácsalmás, June 27, 1944[51]	ca. 6000 or 6474
Third train with Jews from Szeged and surrounding, June 28, 1944[52]	2400
Lévai, Jews deported from Szeged to Strasshof[53]	5739
List of survivors in Szeged, SzJC, number of index cards	1760
List of survivors, SzJC, number of survivors mentioned on the index cards	1894
List of survivors from Szeged, Arolsen Archives	1105
Names of the victims in the memorial hall of the Szeged New Synagogue[54]	1910
Szeged Jewish population in 1946[55]	2332
Szeged Jewish population in 1949[56]	2124

---

48 Quoted in Braham, Népirtás, volume 2, 686.
49 List by István Vrancsik quoted in Michael Honey: "Research Notes on the Hungarian Holocaust". Available at: http://www.zchor.org/hungaria. Last accessed: 15.12.2021.
50 Lipót Löw: "Testimony". Available online: http://www.degob.hu/index.php?showjk=3618. Last accessed: 10.01.2022. The sum can be calculated as followed: 8,617 (number of Jews in the brick factory according to the Ferenczy report) minus 3199 (the number of people in the first transport) minus 2,400 (the number of people in the third transport) which equals 3,018.
51 See footnote 41 of the current article for the calculation.
52 Including Jews from the list of the third transport. Out of 2,400, 66 Jews were taken to Budapest.
53 Jenő Lévai: *Zsidósors Magyarországon*. Budapest: Magyar Téka, 1948, 264, quoted in Braham, Népirtás, volume 2, 699.
54 The names in the memorial hall include forced laborers, Jews born in Szeged but not deported from Szeged, relatives of Jews who restarted life in Szeged and wanted to commemorate the victims of their families even if they were deported from another village. There are also names on the memorial wall that were added by mistake, such as survivors.
55 Braham, Népirtás, volume 2, 712, footnote 69.
56 Theodore Lavi (ed.): *Pinkas Hakehillot Hungariya, Encyclopedia of Jewish Communities. Hungary*, Jerusalem: Yad Vashem, 1976, 393.

Zombori, list of Jews from Szeged, killed between 1941 and 1945[57]	2214
Dunainé Bognár/Kanyó[58]	2214+400 to 500
Kanyó[59]	2519

Lists of Survivors and the Creation of a Database

Several sources can be regarded as suitable for the reconstruction of the list of survivors from Szeged. Besides various correspondence and requests, there exist two extensive sets of data. One are the returning survivors' report cards kept at the Szeged Jewish Community (SzJC), consisting of 1,760 cards, transcribed into an excel table in 2019. The information on returning survivors was recorded at the railway station in the summer of 1945 upon arrival. Teréz Löw, aged 14 in 1945, remembers filling in the cards: "I was also among those who received people returning from deportation at the Szeged station, we asked them where they had been, with whom, whose fate they were aware of. I didn't know I was an employee of Degob [the abbreviation of Deportáltakat Gondozó Országos Bizottság, eng.: National Committee for Attending Deportees]".[60]

The transformation of the individual report cards of the Archive of the Szeged Jewish Community into a unified excel sheet included several challenges: the details of the relatives of the returning individuals were listed on the same cards. Thus, this information also had to be added to the database. Children did not have their own report cards, but their data was often listed on several documents – for example, on the report cards of both returning parents –, thus 1,760 cards hold information of altogether 1,894 people (i.e., 134 underaged children). Thus, several names occurred multiple times in the database, and these had to be merged. Individuals were assigned a unique ID code consisting

---

57 István Zombori: *A szegedi zsidó polgárság emlékezete*, Szeged: Móra Ferenc Múzeum, 1990, 163–200. The list includes the names of men in forced labor and Zombori did not try to reconciliate clashing data (e.g., people with the same names).
58 Dunainé Bognár and Kanyó, Hősei és áldozatai, 146. Dunainé Bognár and Kanyó republished Zombori's list of 2,214 plus an additional "400–500 names" (ibid., 146) of Jews who were born in Szeged but were not necessarily deported from Szeged. The list includes forced laborers, and names of Jews who committed suicide before the deportation.
59 Kanyó, Szeged és környéke, 11. The list includes forced laborers, and names of Jews who committed suicide before the deportation.
60 Email correspondence between the author and Mrs. János Horváth, née Teréz Löw, 19.05. 2021. Translation by the author. On the Deportáltakat Gondozó Országos Bizottság (Degob), see the contribution by Johannes Meerwald in this volume.

of their names and year of birth. With the help of a data cleaning desktop app, data consistency was improved by faceting, clustering (e.g., measuring Levenshtein distances detecting minor differences between two unique ID codes), and sorting the information.

We tried to extract as much data as possible from these listings: the birthdate of listed relatives was not indicated, only their age (in years or, in the case of babies, in months). Nor was their fate written down straightforwardly, thus it had to be assumed that they shared the fate of their returning relatives, i.e., they had been deported on the same train to the exact location and returning from the same concentration camp. Assumed information is indicated as such in the database. The record cards also include information on those who have disappeared or died since the survivors listed all their relatives. In several cases, the same person was listed on many report cards, and duplicates had to be eliminated. The gender of individuals had to be added manually.

There is no date on the report cards when they were created. Based on the cases of surviving babies,[61] for example, those born in the months before the deportation or even on the train at the time of the deportation, the age indicated at the time of the return, the date (year and month) of the creation of the cards can be deducted. Thus, the report cards were written after May 1945, most probably in June/July 1945. The cards function as a catalogue of people returning to Szeged, but the text does not state that they were also deported from Szeged.

The other list of survivors is kept at the Arolsen Archives, indicating the family name and the maiden name of the survivors, their year and place of birth, and their parents' names, as well as the address and occupation after the return.[62] This list records only survivors, 1,105 people. The list is not dated, but the Central Tracing Bureau, the predecessor institution of the Arolsen Archives, received it in April 1946 from the World Jewish Congress and the Jewish Agency for Palestine in Budapest. No information is included on the circumstances of its compilation.

For the database, the ghettoization list and the two lists of returnees had to be merged. All data were put into separate columns, and typos were cleaned. The whole database was translated into English, including information on family relations and occupations. To enable merging for people registered on various lists, an individual ID has been created consisting of the first name and last name and the year of birth of individuals. Once the IDs were created, they were clustered

---

61 Due to the protection of privacy, we do not include the names of these individuals.
62 List of Jewish survivors in Szeged (Hungary), 15.04.1946, 3.1.1.3/78774448 – 78774504/ITS Digital Archive, Arolsen Archives. Available at: https://collections.arolsen-archives.org/en/archive/3-1-1-3_676000/. Last accessed: 17.05.2021.

based on various algorithms, and duplicates were filtered with the help of a facet. The overlap between the ghettoization list and the list of survivors of the Arolsen Archives is 495 out of 3,881 names, and in the case of the report cards, the number is compared to the ghettoization list 1,011 out of 3,881. These ratios might be explained by the fact that not all survivors returned to Szeged and that there were survivors who were not included on the ghettoization list because they had lived in a small village close to Szeged but returned to Szeged and not to their respective hometown. The two lists of survivors were recorded at different times, and survivors might have migrated in this period. Further investigation and analysis are needed to find out about the reasons behind these numbers.

There are several additional data hidden in the lists of survivors. A rough ontology of primary social status can be compiled that reflects the social position with at least acceptable uncertainty and that enables following the changes by comparing the occupations to those indicated in the ghettoization list. The address of the individuals at the time of the ghettoization can refer to the financial situation, as there were neighbourhoods that were better off than others in Szeged. The current research can be the basis for developing a social network model, which can function as a sample network for the computerized exploration and analysis of the genealogy and network of Szeged's Jewry. Comparing social networks with the fate of individuals during the Holocaust, considering age, relationships, health and other factors, the research will be able to answer whether higher socio-economic status represented advantage or disadvantage in the changing historical situation, such as, for example, did a medical doctor or a lawyer have a higher or lower chance of survival than a seamstress or a merchant.

The research project combines historical-philological methodologies with methods from the digital humanities and data science. Naturally, when attempting not only to gather but to combine different data and information, as shown above, several challenges are to be overcome: the multitude of sources, the changes in the data, and the quality of the data are to be taken into consideration, before preparing for the in-depth analysis of the material. From the point of view of computer science, the multitude of sources must be overcome by the fusion of many sources containing fragmented and frequently uncertain data. The evolving field of graph databases helps deal with such unstructured large amounts of data by describing individual data elements and their relations from the historical records. Whenever a relation between two data can be detected, a whole network of relations can be revealed, which interconnects the knowledge fragments for example, the relations of neighbors (relation based on location), a particular profession, age groups, and the branches of families.

Modern analysis methods used in knowledge discovery for revealing the regularities in such networks are widely used in business analytics or social network-based pattern recovery. In the case of the Holocaust, these methods are promising as well. However, the entire historical context needs an active contribution of historians. An example of this is handling different family names. During the lifetime of the generations of Jews living at the time of the Holocaust, there was a wave of name changes, the originally Germanized surnames were changed to Hungarian-sounding ones, and this trend peaked at the end of the 1930s under the government of Gyula Gömbös. Members of the same family would even use different Hungarian surnames.

Similarly, Jewish people had two different names, one for civilian use and one as their Hebrew names. Depending on the level of observance, they preferred to use one of these. In the case of the primarily Orthodox Jewish community of Makó, the Jews preferred using their Jewish names instead of the civil ones. The task of a historian obviously includes dealing with all these issues, such as tracing and recording alternative name forms and name modifications and other changes that can occur during a lifetime, and the tools of information technology can aid traceability.

Conclusion

The core aim of the current research is to create the most extensive list of individuals who were deported through Szeged with their numeric and demographic information and allow a possibility to analyze the material in-depth and allow for further analyses. One potential outcome is a social network model that can direct genealogy-based social research as a sample network. Comparing this with the fate of individuals during the Holocaust, considering the age and health-related factors, we might be able to answer whether the higher socio-economic status represented any advantage in the changing historical situation and how it affected the chance of survival.

Several decisions were made even last minute before the deportation. Birth and death cases occurred in the ghetto and the transit camp and on the train, which were not tracked in all cases. Connections, previously existing networks, social status, and employment by the Jewish communities significantly raised the chances of survival. Despite the chaos, individuals who found a way to be included on the third transportation list in the Szeged transit ghetto turned out to have a 75 percent chance of survival. Most people on the third transport must have known each other either through family connections or through other networks. Many aspects related to the reconstructed transportation lists need further investigation and analysis.

A fine granular analysis can target how individuals' social and economic status influenced their fate during the Holocaust. This needs the fusion of the information hidden in different data repositories and searching for typical patterns along the timeline and the level of social-economic embedding. Digital historical fine granular database investigation is a continuous process of information fusion, ordering, clustering, and finding contradictions or nontrivial phenomena necessitating further information, thus triggering further research, data collection and conclusions based on the new sources and once again triggering new research.

Trajectories of Deportation and Subsequent Persecution

Kristina Vagt
The Deportation of Sinti and Roma from Hamburg and Northern Germany to the Belzec Forced Labour Camp in the *'Generalgouvernement'* of 1940

Abstract: On May 16, 1940, criminal police offices in three different regions of the Reich arrested up to 2,500 Sinti and Roma and, over the days that followed, deported them to the *'Generalgouvernement'*. Up to 1,000 people in northern Germany – Hamburg, Schleswig-Holstein, Bremerhaven, and the Weser-Ems region – were affected. They were deported to the Belzec forced labor camp, then to another camp after a few weeks, and then left to fend for themselves. For most of them, a story of persecution ensued through various ghettos and concentration camps. Many of those concerned were murdered. This deportation of Sinti and Roma persecuted on racial grounds is still relatively unknown. This article provides an account of the discrimination and registration of the Sinti and Roma by the Criminal Police and the Rassenhygienische Forschungsstelle illustrated using the example of northern Germany. It highlights new approaches to the research. Accessing personal documents such as compensation records and the inventories of the Arolsen Archives has made it possible to research individual persecution destinies. It is a process that was implemented for the *denk.mal Hannoverscher Bahnhof* documentation centre project in Hamburg. A memorial site was inaugurated there in 2017, listing the names of the Jews and the Sinti and Roma deported from Hamburg and northern Germany between 1940 and 1945.

Introduction

In a landmark compensation case brought in January 1956, the Federal Court of Justice (Bundesgerichtshof, BGH) ruled that "the resettlement of gypsies from the border zone and neighbouring areas to the *'Generalgouvernement'* ('General Government of Poland') carried out in April 1940 does not constitute a Nazi act of violence on racial grounds pursuant to § 1 of the *Bundesentschädigungsgetz* (Federal Compensation Act)".[1]

---

[1] Judgements of 07.01.1956, reprinted in Bundesgerichtshof and Zentralrat Deutscher Sinti und Roma (Eds.): *Doppeltes Unrecht – eine späte Entschuldigung. Gemeinsames Symposium des Bun-*

The measure carried out in May 1940, euphemistically referred to as a 'resettlement' by the Nazis (a term re-employed in the 1956 ruling), was the first such family deportation of Sinti and Roma, and it affected a total of some 2,500 women, men, adolescents, and children. Included in the number were as many as 1,000 affected persons from northern Germany, approximately 930 from western Germany, and approximately 490 from south-western Germany. They were arrested without prior notification, not as early as April 1940 as cited in the quotation, but on 16 May 1940, and then taken to three central assembly centres in Hamburg, Cologne and Hohenasperg (north of Stuttgart). From there they were subsequently deported to three different destinations in '*Generalgouvernement*' between May 20 and 22.

A striking aspect of the grounds given for the 1956 ruling issued by West Germany's supreme court – apart from the fact that it is riddled with antiziganist stereotypes – is that it denied the Sinti and Roma any recognition as a victim group and judged the persecution and deportation to be legitimate in that it was a strategy aimed at 'crime prevention'. Indeed, "experience has shown" that the persons concerned "had exhibited a tendency to criminality, particularly theft and fraud; they frequently lacked the moral urges of respect for the property of others since, like primitive beings, they had inherent within them an uninhibited instinct for occupation".[2] The judgement meant that a female plaintiff and a male plaintiff were denied compensation payments for their deportation from the Rhineland in May 1940.

The judgement was revised in 1963, but it was not until 2015 – i.e. 59 years after the 1956 landmark ruling of the BGH – that BGH President Bettina Limperg issued an official apology to the Central Council of German Sinti and Roma, finding strong words at a symposium jointly organized by the BGH and the Central Council in 2016: "It is a ruling to be ashamed of, and an indefensible dispensation of justice".[3]

---

desgerichtshofs und des Zentralrats Deutscher Sinti und Roma zu den Urteilen vom 7. Januar 1956, Karlsruhe, 2016, 46–67, here 46. Translation by the author.
2 Ibid., 62. Translation by the author.
3 Detlev Fischer: "Die Urteile des Bundesgerichtshofs vom 7. Januar 1956 – Entscheidung, Vorgeschichte und Entwicklung", in Bundesgerichtshof and Zentralrat Deutscher Sinti und Roma (eds.): *Doppeltes Unrecht – eine späte Entschuldigung. Gemeinsames Symposium des Bundesgerichtshofs und des Zentralrats Deutscher Sinti und Roma zu den Urteilen vom 7. Januar 1956*, Karlsruhe 2016, 25–40. Translation by the author. Cf. the condensed assessment of the discriminatory practices against the Sinti and Roma group and the insufficient compensation payments, in Karola Fings: *Sinti und Roma. Geschichte einer Minderheit*, Frankfurt am Main: C.H. Beck, 2016, 96–98.

The deportation and the ensuing period of persecution during which many deportees were sent to ghettos as well as concentration and extermination camps where they were later murdered, the treatment of this persecuted group by society after 1945 and the restitution and compensation practice all had far-reaching consequences for the survivors and their families as well as the victims' relatives. Using the example of the May 1940 deportation from northern Germany, this contribution aims to outline the research as it currently stands and present the results from the project *denk.mal Hannoverscher Bahnhof documentation centre* in Hamburg.[4] After a brief overview of the existing research and the desiderata, I will look at the process of name reconstruction, describe the campaign of arrests in Hamburg and northern Germany, and the deportees' enforced stay at the Belzec[5] labor camp. I will then focus on the survival strategies adopted by the deportees following their release and their subsequent fate during the Nazi era before finally addressing the public remembrance of the May 1940 deportation.[6]

Existing Research and Desiderata

The historian Michael Zimmermann had previously looked at the May 1940 deportation for his groundbreaking study entitled *Rassenutopie und Genozid* (Racial Utopia and Genocide), based on a wide variety of source material.[7] Karola Fings and Frank Sparing have comprehensively presented the process of exclusion and, among others, the deportation from Cologne and the Rhineland.[8] Ulrich Prehn has taken a closer look at, in particular, the co-operation between the Hamburg criminal police, the welfare authorities, and other offices and au-

---

4 The documentation centre will be part of the Foundation of Hamburg Memorials and Learning Centres Commemorating the Victims of Nazi Crimes.
5 The German spelling of the forced labor camp is being used rather than the Polish spelling of the town of Bełżec in order to highlight the fact that we are dealing here with a German camp.
6 Translation of this article by Stephen Grynwasser, Vienna.
7 Michael Zimmermann: "Rassenutopie und Genozid. Die nationalsozialistische 'Lösung der Zigeunerfrage'", in *Hamburger Beiträge zur Sozial- und Zeitgeschichte*, 33, 1996. See also the account of the May 1940 deportation in Karola Fings: Die Bedeutung der "Mai-Deportation" für den Verfolgungsprozess und ihre Deutung nach 1945. Lecture given at the seminar "Die Verfolgung der Sinti und Roma im öffentlichen Gedächtnis" in Mannheim on 22.05.2010 (unpublished manuscript), 13–17. I am grateful to her for her kind permission to use the manuscript.
8 Karola Fings and Frank Sparing: "Rassismus, Lager, Völkermord. Die nationalsozialistische Zigeunerverfolgung in Köln", in *Schriften des Dokumentationszentrums Köln*, 13, 2006.

thorities in Hamburg.⁹ With regard to northern Germany, previous research into the May deportation focused mainly on Hamburg as the departure point.

For the May 1940 deportation from northern Germany as a whole, especially from Schleswig-Holstein, Bremerhaven, and the Weser-Ems region, on the other hand, numerous research questions remain open, even though greater attention has been paid in recent years to the group of persecuted victims in these regions. Various individuals and initiatives have conducted research on site into those affected by persecution and deportation, and the mechanisms of persecution. In some cases, this was done also in contact with relatives and in consultation with Sinti and Roma associations.¹⁰

With regard to the institutions involved in the organization, numerous research desiderata remain relating not just to the region of northern Germany, but also to the persecution of the Sinti and Roma as a whole. At the level of the Reich, this is true of the Reichszentrale zur Bekämpfung des Zigeunerunwesens (Reich Central Office for Combating the Gypsy Nuisance) at the Reichskriminalpolizeiamt (RKPA, Reich Criminal Police Office) as well as the Rassenhygienische Forschungsstelle in Berlin. At the local level, it concerns the Dienststellen für Zigeunerfragen (Departments for Gypsy Issues) at the Kriminalpolizeistellen (Criminal Police Investigation Departments) and Kriminalpolizeileitstellen (Criminal Police Headquarters) as well as various local offices and authorities. Another set of questions concerns the subsequent fates of the deportees as of autumn 1940; indeed, after the transfer from the Belzec forced labor camp and after an enforced stay of several weeks at the Krychow prison, the deportees were left to

---

9 Cf. Ulrich Prehn: "'… dass Hamburg mit als erste Stadt an den Abtransport herangeht.' Die nationalsozialistische Verfolgung der Sinti und Roma in Hamburg", in *Die Verfolgung der Sinti und Roma im Nationalsozialismus – Beiträge zur Geschichte der nationalsozialistischen Verfolgung in Norddeutschland*, 14, 2012, 35–54. My warmest thanks to Ulrich Prehn for reading this contribution and for his advice. See also Roger Repplinger: "'Hat sich besondere Kenntnisse in der Bearbeitung des Zigeunerunwesens erworben.' Der Kriminalinspekteur Krause im Nationalsozialismus und in der Bundesrepublik", in *Zeitschrift für Geschichtswissenschaft*, 12, 2017, 1049–1070.
10 For example, the initiatives and private individuals in Neumünster, Lübeck, and Hans Hesse in Bremerhaven and Oldenburg sought to get in touch with survivors and descendants of the deported. Investigative research into individual deportees is currently under way in Lübeck and is to be incorporated into a publication. Email from Elisabeth Esser to the author, 09.06.2021, cf. also the brochure by Manfred Bannow-Lindtke: *Bruder Sinti, Schwester Roma. Ein Jahrhundert zwischen Diskriminierung und Verfolgung. Zur Geschichte der Sinti und Roma im 20. Jahrhundert in Lübeck*, Lübeck: Interkulturelle Begegnungsstätte Lübeck, 2000.

their own devices.¹¹ What happened to the deportees? Where did they stay? How many died, and how many survived?

Reconstructing the Names

Any systematic study of the persecution destinies of those affected by the deportation is predicated on knowing their names. A large number of those deported in May 1940 from northern Germany to the Belzec forced labor camp via Hamburg were successfully researched for the memorial site *denk.mal Hannoverscher Bahnhof* and within the context of the preparations for its eponymous documentation centre. The memorial established in 2017 at the site of the former Hamburg railway station known as the *Hannoverscher Bahnhof* commemorates more than 8,000 Jews, Sinti and Roma who were deported to ghettos, concentration camps and extermination camps in Central and Eastern Europe. The plaques at the memorial also list all those who lived beyond the Hamburg greater metropolitan area and were deported via Hamburg.¹²

However, it has proved impossible to find all the names of those deported to Belzec as there is no known overall transport list. But a list of names with Hamburg residents has been preserved, apparently reconstructed by the RKPA after the original list had been destroyed as a result of the effects of war.¹³ The archives of the Amt für Wiedergutmachung (Office for Restitution and Compensation) of the Committee of Former Political Prisoners were also consulted as a complementary source.¹⁴ In addition, first-person documents and interviews

---

11 No systematic research has yet been carried out in the Polish archives.
12 Oliver von Wrochem: "Gedenkort und Dokumentationszentrum denk.mal Hannoverscher Bahnhof in Hamburg: Entstehungsgeschichte und Vermittlungskonzept", in Alexander Kraus, Aleksandar Nedelkovski and Anita Placenti-Grau (eds.): *Ein Erinnerungs- und Lernort entsteht. Die Gedenkstätte KZ-Außenlager Laagberg in Wolfsburg.* Frankfurt am Main/New York: Campus, 2018, 195–213.
  The memorial plaques also mention the names of the Jews deported from Hamburg and those of the more than 300 Sinti and Roma who had been deported to camp section BIIe at the Auschwitz-Birkenau extermination camp in March 1943. The names of some 30 people – mostly children – who were deported to the same destination in April 1944 are also listed.
13 Gypsies previously resident in Hamburg and resettled to the '*Generalgouvernement*' on 20.05. 1940, 331–1 II Police Authorities II 456, Staatsarchiv Hamburg (StAHH). The deportation lists are said to have been destroyed in summer 1943. Cf. e.g. Kriminalamt an das Amtsgericht in Hamburg-Altona, Betr. Maria Winter, alias Emma Rosenbach, 16.02.1957, 331–1, 1782, StAHH.
14 The original files are in the archive of the Union of Persecutees of the Nazi Regime/Federation of Antifascists Land Association of Hamburg and were digitized by the Neuengamme Concentration Camp Memorial.

Fig. 1: *denk.mal Hannoverscher Bahnhof* memorial site with *Fuge* (gap, fugue) and plaques. Photograph: Kati Jurischka.

with survivors were included for the purposes of matching up and identifying the names of Hamburg residents.[15]

Of those deported from Schleswig-Holstein, 207 names complete with biographical details are known from a list compiled after 1945, based on 'racial reports' of the Rassenhygienische Forschungsstelle.[16] After the memorial was completed, it also proved possible to research the names of the Sinti and Roma living in Flensburg, Bremerhaven, and the Weser-Ems region who had been deported via Hamburg in May 1940.[17] The names of the approximately 41 deportees from Flensburg were reconstructed using street registers from the Flensburg municipal archives in which the deportees had been identified using the handwrit-

---

15 In the project *Transgenerational Transmission of History. Building Blocks for the Future of the Recollection of National Socialism in the Migration Society* of the Neuengamme Concentration Camp Memorial, Karin Heddinga conducted interviews with descendants, also on the subject of the persecution of the Sinti and Roma.
16 Expert opinions of the Race Hygiene Research Centre of the Reich Health Office in Berlin-Dahlem (transcript, undated), 331–1_II_928, StAHH. The list also includes those who had remained at their place of residence as well as individuals who had been deported to the Auschwitz extermination camp via Hamburg on March 11, 1943.
17 These names are to be added to the plaques at the *denk.mal Hannoverscher Bahnhof* memorial site at a later date.

ten note "Deported on 16.5.40"[18]. A total of 257 persons are known to have been deported from Schleswig-Holstein.[19] For the partial transports from Bremerhaven and the Weser-Ems region, the historian Hans Hesse has so far managed to research 138 names on behalf of the Neuengamme Concentration Camp Memorial, mainly by analysing compensation records in the Oldenburg and Bremen state archives.[20] On the strength of this research, Hesse presented a memorial book in 2021 with the names of the women, men and children deported from Bremerhaven and the Weser-Ems region.

These new findings show that the number previously assumed by the research, i.e. 910 persons, was too low and that up to 1,000 people in total were affected.[21]

Campaign of Arrests in Hamburg and Northern Germany

The May 1940 deportation was preceded by a gradual process of definition of the term *'Zigeuner'* ('gypsy') over many years, of recording people who were then

---

18 My thanks to the Flensburg municipal archives for identifying and providing the street registers in January 2018: I D 156 Streets, Vol. 194 (Valentinerallee), Flensburg Municipal Archives. In addition, two more families comprising a total of nine persons from the Flensburg and Schleswig area are known from various sources. Cf. Stephan Linck: *Der Ordnung verpflichtet. Deutsche Polizei 1933–1949. Der Fall Flensburg*, Paderborn: Ferdinand Schöningh, 2000, 94–96; Umzugs-Abmeldebestätigung der Stadt Schleswig, 02.12.1941, Archiwum Akt Nowych Waszawa AAN, 433.
19 For Schleswig-Holstein, the assumption has so far revolved around 200 persons, cf. Zimmermann, Rassenutopie, 73.
20 Hans Hesse: "... *Wir sehen uns in Bremerhaven wieder ...*" *Die Deportation der Sinti und Roma am 16./20. Mai 1940 aus Nordwestdeutschland, Gedenkbuch zur nationalsozialistischen Verfolgung der Sinti und Roma aus Nordwestdeutschland, Teil 1*, 27, Bremerhaven Municipal Archives: Bremerhaven, 2021.
21 Zimmermann indicates 200 persons for Schleswig-Holstein, cf. Zimmermann, Rassenutopie, 173. In doing so, he also refers to the 'Übersicht über die in Deutschland lebenden Zigeuner und Zigeunermischlinge', reprinted in Hermann Arnold: *Die NS-Zigeunerverfolgung. Ihre Ausdeutung und Ausbeutung. Fakten – Mythos – Agitation – Kommerz*, Aschaffenburg, undated, 32. The original is to be found in Zsg 142/22–1, BA. I am indebted to Karola Fings for the reference to the printed source. A total of 257 people from Schleswig-Holstein were researched as part of the denk.mal Hannoverscher Bahnhof project. It cannot be ruled out that other individuals or families were deported. The urgent instruction is reprinted in Linde Apel (ed.): *In den Tod geschickt. Die Deportationen von Juden, Roma und Sinti aus Hamburg 1940 bis 1945*, Berlin: Metropol, 2009, 74.

persecuted as such, of disciplining them through compulsory labor, of ousting them from the urban environment, and of criminalizing this particular group of people as a whole.[22] The process itself did not simply begin the moment the Nazis came to power; indeed, it had gradually been gathering pace and given a legal underpinning from 1933 onwards. In June 1938, some 100 male Sinti and Roma were arrested in Hamburg among other cities as part of a Reich-wide campaign entitled '*Arbeitsscheu Reich*' ('Reich work-shy'). Plans for a camp in the Hamburg metropolitan area were drawn up as of the summer of 1939. By this point, forced labor camps had already been established in other cities.[23] But in autumn 1939, the Hamburg plans were shelved when, during an internal meeting, the police commissioner Walter Bierkamp gave notice of the contents of an urgent instruction dated October 17, 1939.[24] Indeed, it set out an arrest decree with which the Reich Main Security Office ordered the registration of all 'gypsies' and 'gypsies of mixed blood' on fixed days from October 25 to 27, 1939 and also their 'final removal' at a time as yet undefined.[25] The local police authorities and gendarmeries were to instruct Sinti and Roma not to leave their place of residence. They collected their personal data and compiled the database for subsequent deportations. The database itself was further expanded in co-operation with the Rassenhygienische Forschungsstelle established at the Reich Health Office in Berlin in 1936, to which we will return later.

It was in this situation that the Hamburg Gauleiter, Karl Kaufmann, took the initiative for the deportation of all Hamburg Sinti and Roma. His plans were to have 1,000 Sinti and Roma deported 'to Poland' from the Hamburg metropolitan

---

[22] Extensive research on the measures adopted to exclude and persecute the Sinti and Roma group in Hamburg was carried out in the inventories of the Hamburg State Archives as part of the exhibition 'In den Tod geschickt. Die Deportationen von Juden, Roma und Sinti aus Hamburg 1940 bis 1945'. See the exhibition catalogue: Apel, In den Tod geschickt.
[23] A camp in Cologne-Bickendorf, completed in 1935, became a template for other cities, see Karola Fings and Frank Sparing: "Rassismus, Lager, Völkermord. Die nationalsozialistische Zigeunerverfolgung in Köln", in *Schriften des Dokumentationszentrums Köln*, 13, 2006, 68–80. In northern Germany, too, Sinti and Roma were required to move, sometimes forcibly, as for example in Flensburg in 1935, cf. Sebastian Lotto-Kusche: "'… daß für sie die gewöhnlichen Rechtsbegriffe nicht gelten'. Das NS-Zwangslager für 'Zigeuner' in Flensburg und dessen Wahrnehmung in der Stadtbevölkerung", in *Demokratische Geschichte. Jahrbuch für Schleswig-Holstein*, 28, 2017, 225–238.
[24] Minutes of the meeting on 20.10.1939 with the Reich Governor, 351–10 I, AF 83.73, StAHH, quoted in Prehn, Abtransport, 51, footnote 43.
[25] Urgent instruction issued by the Reich Main Security Office, Berlin, to the State Criminal Police – Criminal Police Headquarters and Departments, 17.10.1939, 153–154, 331–1 II, 455, StAHH.

area.[26] To this end, Bierkamp contacted Bruno Streckenbach, the former head of the Hamburg Gestapo who was, at that point, the commander of the Sicherheitspolizei (Security Police) and SD in Krakow, to explore ways of expelling said Sinti and Roma from Hamburg.[27]

Initiatives in favor of, and negotiations on, the expulsion and deportation of Sinti and Roma are also known from other cities. In January 1940 for instance, Richard Zaucke, an employee of the Reichszentrale zur Bekämpfung des Zigeunerunwesens (Reich Central Office for Combating the Gypsy Nuisance), was in Graz for the planned deportation of Sinti and Roma from the Burgenland to the '*Generalgouvernement*', scheduled for February 1940.[28] Zaucke was meant to be on site in Hamburg in May 1940 on behalf of the Reich Criminal Police Office for the deportation of the Sinti and Roma from Hamburg and northern Germany.[29]

However, the plans to deport Sinti and Roma as well as Jews from the Reich territory to the '*Generalgouvernement*' initially failed due to the resistance of '*Generalgouverneur*' Hans Frank, who was keen to prevent the newly created administration of the '*Generalgouvernement*' now under his administration from becoming 'overstretched'.[30] By early 1940, there were differing interests within the various Nazi institutions with regard to the Sinti and Roma. The Wehrmacht wanted to expel the Sinti and Roma from the regions near the border, fearing that this particular group might engage in espionage. The espionage attributed to the Sinti and Roma was a trope that went back a long way in history.[31] By con-

---

[26] Minutes of the meeting between police commissioner (senior government advisor Bierkamp, superintendent Lyss, police inspector Schmidt) and the social services administration (senior senate councillor Bornemann) on 12.12.1939, 351–10 I, AF 83.74, StAHH.
[27] Meeting between police commissioner and social services administration, 12.12.1939, 351–10 I, AF 83.74, StAHH, cf. Prehn, Abtransport, here 42–43.
[28] Gerhard Baumgartner: "Projektentwurf: Dezentrale nationalsozialistische 'Zigeunerlager' 1939–1945 auf dem Gebiet des heutigen Österreich", 6–7. Available at: https://www.doew.at/cms/download/8v3s6/gb_projektentwurf.pdf. Last accessed: 24.07.2022.
[29] Zaucke was presumably transferred from the RKPA to Vienna in 1941. That year, he was the criminal director of the Vienna Criminal Police Headquarters and, in that capacity, involved with the 'Lackenbach Gypsy Camp'. He was there on site when, on November 4, 1941, the first transport convoy of Sinti and Roma to the Litzmannstadt (Lodz) ghetto was dispatched, cf. Florian Freund, Bertrand Perz and Karl Stuhlpfarrer: "Das Ghetto in Lodz", 63–64, 66. Available at: https://zeitgeschichte.univie.ac.at/fileadmin/user_upload/i_zeitgeschichte/Publikationen/Endbericht-Lodz_ro.pdf. Last accessed: 24.07.2022.
[30] Zimmermann, Rassenutopie, 176.
[31] See the sub-chapter "Die Wehrmacht und das Klischee vom spionierenden Zigeuner" in Zimmermann, Rassenutopie, 193–199; also, Karola Fings: "Die Bedeutung der 'Mai-Deportation' für den Verfolgungsprozess und ihre Deutung nach 1945". Lecture given at the seminar "Die Verfol-

trast, by January 1940, the head of the Rassenhygienische Forschungsstelle, Robert Ritter, was urging forced sterilization. This measure was also favoured by Reich Medical Leader Leonardo Conti as a Nazi policy instrument towards the Sinti and Roma aimed at excluding them from the '*Volksgemeinschaft*', or national community.[32]

In view of the Reich-wide plans for deportation, Ritter pushed ahead with the registration and examination of 2,000 Sinti and Roma from early 1940 onwards. The results were to be included in a 'gypsy clan archive'. From March to early May 1940, task forces called on the homes of Sinti and Roma residents in western and northern Germany to sound out their personal data and family kinships and take anthropological measurements.[33] To this end, staff members determined the hair and eye colour, measured body parts, recorded the data on special index cards, took fingerprints, and photographed each individual. For those examined in this way, these procedures were a humiliation and an indignity. Records show that one such task force was in Hamburg over the period April 25 to May 4, 1940. Shortly thereafter – on May 6 and 7, 1940 – Robert Ritter, Karl Moravek and at least one assistant – presumably Eva Justin – interviewed at least 21 residents of a Sinti and Roma wagon yard in Neumünster.[34]

Heinrich Himmler's Rapid letter dated April 27, 1940 referencing the previous such instruction dated October 17, 1939 finally gave orders for the deportation of 2,500 individuals across the Reich. The relevant 'Guidelines for the Resettlement of Gypsies' contained criteria for the selection of those to be deported and the implementation method.[35] The administration of the '*Generalgouvernement*'

---

gung der Sinti und Roma im öffentlichen Gedächtnis" in Mannheim on 22.05.2010 (unpublished manuscript).

32 Zimmermann, Rassenutopie, 159, 171; Fings and Sparing, Rassismus, 196–198.

33 Fings and Sparing, Rassismus, 201; cf. on the research practice also Barbara Danckwort: "Wissenschaft oder Pseudowissenschaft? Die 'Rassenhygienische Forschungsstelle' am Reichsgesundheitsamt", in Judith Hahn, Silvija Kavčič and Christoph Kopke: *Medizin im Nationalsozialismus und das System der Konzentrationslager*, Frankfurt am Main: Mabuse, 2005, 140–164.

34 Lists of Sinti and Roma registered by the *Rassenhygienische Forschungsstelle* in Hamburg and Neumünster, R 165–45, BArch. In Hamburg the registration dates were April 25, 26, 27, 29, 30 and May 1, 2, 3; in Neumünster: 06. and 07.05.1940. Some of the daily lists bear the stamp "Collection of H. Arnold" Surviving index cards of medical examinations in Hamburg and Neumünster bear the abbreviation "Dr. Mo" for Dr Karl Moravek, R 165–211, BArch. Photographs of the interventions at the wagon yard in Neumünster have also survived: Film Archives of the Federal Archives, R 165, 72 IV (old signature), BArch. On the photographs Robert Ritter and presumably Eva Justin are seen.

35 Urgent instruction issued by the RFSSuChdDtPol in RMdI, Berlin, to the Criminal Police Headquarters and Departments in Hamburg, Bremen, Hanover, Düsseldorf, Cologne, Frankfurt

was not included in the planning and was to be notified only shortly before the actual deportation.³⁶

At 4 am on May 16, 1940, criminal police officers assisted by ordinary policemen began arresting women, men, adolescents and children in their homes across northern Germany and took them to the local police stations and, from there, to Fruit Warehouse C in the Free Port of Hamburg. In her testimony before the Hamburg Committee of Former Political Prisoners in 1946 Therese Rosenberg gave an insight into what it was like to experience the ordeal of this utterly surprising and violent raid:

> The police officers burst into the flat brandishing pistols and demanded that we immediately accompany them to the *Stadthaus*. My husband explained that if anyone had to go to the station, it was him, and that his wife and children should stay at home. My husband was then threatened with truncheons. So I now had to get myself and the children ready and we were then put into a car and driven to the *Stadthaus*. There we were interrogated and then taken to Fruit Warehouse C. Even though we had a doctor's report stating that one of the children was seriously ill with double pneumonia and that three were bedridden with measles and were not fit to be transported, Krause declared that the children had to come along.³⁷

Those to be deported were selected by officers of the criminal police headquarters and the criminal police stations. Many families with children were affected, but also individuals. Also among the deportees were some 25 women without husbands, with a total of around 100 children of different ages. Some of the husbands had already been arrested as part of the '*Arbeitsscheu Reich*' campaign in 1938 and had not returned from concentration camp detention.³⁸ A number of individual persons joined the transport voluntarily, such as a married couple

---

am Main and Stuttgart on 27.04.1940, 331–1 II, 455, re: resettlement of gypsies, folio 165–168, StAHH.
36 Zimmermann, Rassenutopie, 176–177.
37 Statement given by Therese Rosenberg, 06.07.1946, folio 7, StAnw LG – Strafsachen, 19075/64, 213–11, StAHH. Translation by the author. This statement and others incriminated *Kriminalobersekretär* Kurt Krause, former head of the *Zigeunerdienststelle* (Department for Gypsy Affairs) at *Kommissariat* BK 2 of Criminal Investigation Division I A of the Hamburg Criminal Investigation Department, who at the time was still in the police service.
38 Author's own count and from random sampling. Example of Bertha Bamberger, whose husband Julius Bamberger died in 1940. Also Dunga Otto, whose husband Stefan Otto had been arrested during the '*Arbeitsscheu Reich*' campaign and died at Mauthausen concentration camp on 12.05.1940. See Freies Radio Neumünster: "Zeitreise: Wir erinnern heute an Elisabeth Otto genannt 'Lilli'". Available at: https://freiesradio-nms.de/2020/zeitreise-wir-erinnern-heute-an-elisabeth-otto-genannt-lilli/. Last accessed: 24.07.2022.

from Flensburg who, because of their old age, could have stayed but chose to accompany their adult children and their families.³⁹

As an employee of the Reichskriminalpolizeiamt in Berlin, the aforementioned Richard Zaucke was seconded to the Hamburg Fruit Warehouse; at the Reichszentrale zur Bekämpfung des Zigeunerwesens he was responsible for the deportation of 'anti-social elements', prostitutes, Roma and Sinti to concentration camps.⁴⁰ It is unknown whether an employee of the Rassenhygienische Forschungsstelle was on site as planned.⁴¹

At the Hamburg Fruit Warehouse, all those detained there were registered in a 'master list' complete with serial number. Identification papers such as ID cards, work books and military passes were confiscated "to prevent escape attempts wherever possible".⁴² Instead, certificates were issued for all persons aged 14 and over, specifying their first name, surname and name at birth, date and place of birth, the classification '*Zigeunermischling*' or '*Zigeuner*', a fingerprint of the right index finger, and a serial number assigned to each person. They also bore the signature "Dr Zaucke"⁴³ and an RKPA rubber stamp. Affixed to the back of the certificate was the person's photograph, stamped by the Hamburg Criminal Investigation Department. Thereafter, the holders were required to carry the certificates with them wherever they went so they could identify themselves at all times.

Those detained at the Fruit Warehouse were promised houses, land and cattle in Poland.⁴⁴ This information, designed to assuage, was also provided in Cologne to those interned there on the trade fair premises.⁴⁵ By the same token,

---

39 Transcript of the interview with Helene K. née Weiss, No. 47/2, 2, Sinti and Roma in Lower Saxony collection of interviews, Lower Saxony Memorials Foundation.
40 Patrick Wagner: "Volksgemeinschaft ohne Verbrecher. Konzeptionen und Praxis der Kriminalpolizei in der Zeit der Weimarer Republik und des Nationalsozialismus", in *Hamburger Beiträge zur Sozial- und Zeitgeschichte*, 34, 1996, 340. In Cologne, Josef Ochs of the RKPA was in charge of the overall supervision, cf. Fings and Sparing, Rassismus, 202, 211.
41 In Cologne, a total of 120 people, including criminal police officers and ordinary policemen, soldiers, SS men, and other auxiliary staff such as nurses were deployed for the arrest and medical examination, Fings and Sparing, Rassismus, 203.
42 Urgent instruction issued by the RFSSuChdDtPol in RMdI, Berlin, to the Criminal Police Headquarters and Departments in Hamburg, Bremen, Hanover, Düsseldorf, Cologne, Frankfurt am Main and Stuttgart on 27.04.1940, re: resettlement of gypsies, folio 167, 331–1 II, 455, StAHH. Translation by the author.
43 Archiwum Państwowe w Lublinie, Generalgouvernement, Lublin District, 203.
44 Prehn, Abtransport, 45.
45 Fings and Sparing, Rassismus, 206.

Fig. 2: Certificate for Sophie Berta Rose, née Laubinger, State Archive Bremen, 4,54-E-7295.

they were forbidden from returning and threatened "to be taken into preventive police custody if they were to return without permission".[46]

The mass arrest of some 550 people in Hamburg and their transport in buses through the Hamburg metropolitan area did not go unnoticed by the population. Luise Solmitz, a resident of Hamburg whose husband was persecuted as a Jew, recorded the following in her diary on May 16, 1940: "At the Handlungshilfenverein[47] large omnibuses drove past us, – at last some excursionists. With the police

---

46 State Criminal Police to the District Administrator of Verden District, Re: Resettlement of Gypsies, 13.11.1940, 3/18d, Verden District Archives. Translation by the author.
47 The reference is actually to the *Handlungsgehilfenverein* (association of sales assistants).

at the front and then the gypsies, and last of all their belongings. Evidently, they are being put in some camp somewhere."⁴⁸ On May 20, 1940, she also mentioned the Sinti and Roma in connection with the air raids on Hamburg:

> With every description I get, I am more and more convinced that Hamburg has been taken by surprise, or has allowed itself to be taken by surprise, that since the tremendous battle in the West, the defences have been weaker, that the flak and searchlights have lessened. [...] People blame talkative gypsies; some have observed their deportation.⁴⁹

This statement could be an indication that, as with the population of Cologne, the Sinti and Roma were blamed for the air raids. In Cologne, they had allegedly used bed sheets to signal the location of a chemical factory to the British planes.⁵⁰ This invoked once again the 'cliché of the spying gypsy', which the Wehrmacht had invoked already during the first half of 1940 to promote the deportation of the Sinti and Roma from the western territories.⁵¹

Belzec Forced Labor Camp in the *'Generalgouvernement'* of 1940

The commander of the Ordnungspolizei in Krakow had informed the internal administration of Lublin District of the transport's imminent arrival, but only two days before it was scheduled to depart Hamburg. A telegram stated: "1,000 gypsies to arrive between 22nd and 24th. Destination station Belzec Tomaszow District"⁵². They were to be housed at the newly established forced labor camp at Belzec in the border area with Soviet-occupied western Galicia. A few days later, the first Jews arrived from nearby.

Once the train had arrived from Hamburg, the men among the deportees were forced to dig an antitank ditch on the orders of the SS border guards' construction command. According to survivors, 70 to 80 deportees died of weakness over the first few weeks, including many children.⁵³

---

48 Diary of Luise Solmitz (transcripts), entry dated 16.05.1940, 551, Archive of the Research Centre for Contemporary History in Hamburg (FZH). Translation by the author.
49 Ibid., entry dated 20.05.1940, 553. Translation by the author.
50 Fings and Sparing, Rassismus, 227.
51 Zimmermann, Rassenutopie, 171–172.
52 Handling of gypsies 1939–1940, police teletype, Lublin Regiment, 18.05.1940, 203, Archiwum Pantswowe w Lubline. Translation by the author.
53 According to the survivor Luise Schalle in her statement of 1946, cf. Prehn, Abtransport, 44.

SS men – including *Volksdeutsche* (ethnic Germans) – guarded the camp and inflicted all manner of violence on the prisoners. The SS locked the deportees inside a large shed, along with Polish Roma and Jews who presumably arrived a little later from Lublin and Piaski. Due to the catastrophic living conditions, the upper echelons of the administration hierarchy decided in mid-July 1940 to transfer the German Sinti and Roma to the former Polish prison at Krychow, north-east of Lublin. In the justification for the decision, particular mention was made of the fact that, among those who had arrived from the Reich, were "war veterans and also party comrades", some of whom were even married to "German women".[54] The Polish Roma, for their part, had to remain at the Belzec forced labor camp, which was dissolved in October 1940. It was near this site that the SS established the Belzec extermination camp in late 1941, in which initially Jews from eastern Poland, but then also Roma, were murdered.[55]

In Krychow, the deportees were assigned to moor drainage and canalisation work. Most of them were released in autumn 1940. It is still unclear whether this was done solely on the instructions of the SS or whether it was a joint decision with the civil administration.[56] From this point on, the deportees from Hamburg went their separate ways and developed different strategies in order to survive.

Survival Strategies and Murder

In his study *Rassenutopie und Genozid* (Racial utopia and genocide), Michael Zimmermann had described patterns of survival strategies and the persecution destinies of the deportees from northern Germany in May 1940.[57] For decades, however, systematic access to personal sources that could have provided information about these persecution stories was blocked. These dossiers have become more easily accessible in recent years. They include files from the inventories of the Amt für Wiedergutmachung (Office for Restitution and Compensation),

---

54 Niederschrift der Dienstversammlung der Kreis- und Stadthauptleute des Distrikts Lublin, 18.07.1940, ZS, AR 540/83, 95–96, cited in Zimmermann, Rassenutopie, 180 (translation by the author); Agnieszka Caban and Ewa Koper: *Die Geschichte der Rom*nja und Sint*izze in den Arbeits- und Vernichtungslagern in Bełżec*, Bełżec: Ministry of Administration and Digitalization in Poland, 2020.
55 Robert Kuwałek: *Das Vernichtungslager Bełżec*, Berlin: Metropol, 2014, 59–78.
56 Zimmermann, Rassenutopie, 180–181.
57 Zimmermann has analyzed extensive files on the fate of the Hamburg and northern German deportees from the Lublin and Warsaw municipal archives, which my colleague Sarah Grandke also examined on site for the purposes of our project: Archiwum Akt Nowych Waszawa, AAN, 433.

which are now kept by the Hamburg State Archives and are largely accessible in an online database.[58] The inventories of the Arolsen Archives are also relevant to the question of which stops came after the first two camps and which individuals became caught up in the concentration camp system.[59] As part of the *denk.mal Hannoverscher Bahnhof* project, the more than 900 names known to date have been compared with the inventories held by the Arolsen Archives to verify the personal data and obtain quantitative and qualitative data on the subsequent stops after the forced detention at the Belzec forced labor camp. The aim was to provide a systematic overview of how many of the 1,000 or so people became caught up in the camp system and lost their lives, and how many survived. By evaluating the individual case files in the inventories held by the Arolsen Archives – a process which is, however, still ongoing – as well as the compensation files, it has been possible to obtain a more precise idea of the persecution destinies after the first two stops, namely the Belzec forced labor camp and the Krychow labor camp.

In principle, those deported from the Reich were supposed to find accommodation with farmers in the immediate vicinity following their detention in the autumn of 1940 and then try and make a living for themselves. The individuals in question tried to hold their own under the most difficult circumstances and to ensure their survival as well as that of their families. While there are no known instructions for the systematic persecution and murder of the Sinti and Roma deported from Germany to Poland in 1940[60], many people did get caught up in the concentration camp system and a large number of them were murdered.

Some of the deportees attempted to obtain official recognition as Reich Germans within the '*Generalgouvernement*' in order to be able to apply for clothing or food ration cards. Time and again, the men sought to emphasize their status as world war servicemen. Rudolf and Robert Weiss from Hamburg for instance, who worked at a sawmill in Starachowice, applied for food ration cards from the Main Food and Agriculture Department of the government of the '*Generalgouvernement*' in Krakow on December 13, 1942. The men stated their occupation as skilled workers, referred to themselves as 'Reich Germans' and produced their ID papers. They further substantiated their status by mentioning their serv-

---

58 State Archives Hamburg: "Online Recherche". Available at: https://recherche.staatsarchiv.hamburg.de. Last accessed: 02.02.2022.
59 Remote access has made it possible to conduct research into all the names of the deportees known to date. This resulted in 640 hits in the database, many of which comprised reference cards.
60 Zimmermann, Rassenutopie, 183.

ice record as soldiers in the First World War. However, the arguments they put forward fell on deaf ears with the authorities and, eventually, the Schutzpolizei withdrew their ration cards and their identity papers.[61]

Others tried to return to their place of residence within the Reich. Several such cases from Hamburg, Schleswig-Holstein, Bremerhaven and the Weser-Ems region are known.[62] Mention should be made, by way of example, of Katharina Rose, who prior to her deportation had lived with her partner and three children in a village near Flensburg. In autumn 1940 her partner, who as a non-Sinto had not been deported, applied to the local authorities for her return. When this was not granted, he sent her the tickets, whereupon she managed to return to her partner with two daughters while her son was deemed as missing in Poland. Back in the Reich, however, she was arrested once again after just a few weeks. Richard Zaucke of the Reich Criminal Police Office was again responsible, as he had ordered her 'preventive police detention' in a letter dated January 24, 1941.[63] Katharina Rose was arrested in 1941 and sent to Ravensbrück concentration camp, where she lost her life in June 1944.[64]

Other individuals and families who returned to the Reich territory were arrested already in the border region. The aforementioned Therese Rosenberg and her family were caught on the other side of the border and sent to prison. From there her husband was dispatched to Sachsenhausen concentration camp, where he died in 1942. Therese Rosenberg was sent to Ravensbrück concentration camp. Her children were later sent to camp section BIIe at the Auschwitz-Birkenau death camp[65], the so-called gypsy camp, which had been set up separately for the Sinti and Roma in spring 1943.[66] Rigo Rosenberg's prisoner index card from Buchenwald concentration camp indicates that he was commit-

---

[61] Application submitted by Rudolf and Robert Weiss, Starachowice, for the issue of German food ration cards, 08.04.1943, AAN 433, Archiwum Akt Nowych Waszawa.
[62] Cf. also on Fridolin and Auguste Laubinger with their children and a brother of Auguste Laubinger: Hesse, Bremerhaven, 110–113.
[63] Investigation proceedings 2 a Js 175/49 by the Flensburg public prosecutor's office, RKPA letter, 24.01.1941, 354/784, Landesarchiv Schleswig-Holstein (LASH).
[64] Linck, Ordnung, 94–96; Björn Marnau and Stephan Linck: "'Im Januar 1944 in Kielce/Polen verstorben'. Die Flensburger 'Zigeuner' in den Jahren 1922 bis 1945", in *Ausgebürgert. Ausgegrenzt. Ausgesondert. Opfer politischer und rassischer Verfolgung in Flensburg 1933–1945*, Flensburg: Stadt Flensburg, 1998, 190–222.
[65] Office for Restitution and Compensation, file on Rigo Rosenberg, 351–11_46472, StAHH.
[66] TD file on Marie Rosenberg, 6.3.3.2/86845652/ITS Digital Archive, Arolsen Archives. The youngest daughter was born in Grünberg in Silesia in February 1941.

ted to Auschwitz concentration camp by the Breslau Kriminalpolizei, presumably on 5 May 1942.[67] Seven children were murdered in Auschwitz.

As the family of Richard Weiss from Hamburg shows, many families were literally torn apart. The family had initially remained longer in Krychow than other families as Cilentia Weiss was giving birth at the time of their release. They moved to Chelm, 40 km away, where Richard Weiss found employment as a forestry worker. He was subsequently arrested during a raid by the SD and taken back to Krychow; his family was sent to the Siedlce Ghetto. Richard Weiss fled from Krychow and, according to his own statement, hid with partisans. In the end, he managed to return to his family in Siedlce. His wife was later murdered at Treblinka extermination camp. When the Siedlce ghetto was established, Weiss went to Radomek with his three surviving children. During an SD raid, Ernst and Erich Weiss were arrested. Richard Weiss was forcibly recruited into the SS special unit Dirlewanger.[68] He fled from there, searched for his two surviving sons and returned with them to Hamburg in June 1944.[69]

In summer 1944, a number of those who had been deported from Hamburg to the '*Generalgouvernement*' returned to the Hanseatic City. On September 11, 1944, for example, the Department IV Economics and Food of the Inner City Office in Hamburg reported 16 such 'returning emigrants' from Lublin. They had come to the Department's notice when they applied for food ration cards.[70] In the letter it is assumed that they represent an 'undesirable influx (gypsies)'. The returning male Sinti and Roma were assigned to work as part of Organization Todt; the women were put to work in the waste materials industry.[71]

By contrast, other individuals or families remained in Poland and, in some cases, returned only years later to the Federal Republic of Germany or the German Democratic Republic.[72] Others still remained in Poland altogether, such

---

67 Rigo Rosenberg's prisoner index card from Buchenwald concentration camp, 1.1.5.3/6949008/ITS Digital Archive, Arolsen Archives.
68 The Dirlewanger *Sondereinheit* (special unit), named after Oskar Dirlewanger, was a notorious unit into which Sinti and Roma were drafted, especially towards the end of the war. It was deployed in the fight against the Soviet army, see Zimmermann, Rassenutopie, 296 and 347.
69 Office for Restitution and Compensation, file on Richard Weiss, 351–11_55870, StAHH.
70 Notification regarding the influx of returning emigrants, 11.09.1944, 377–10_I_A_b_IV_7_n, StAHH.
71 Re: influx of gypsies from Lublin who at the time were resettled in the East at the instigation of the Reich Criminal Police Office Berlin, 01.09.1944, folio 1, 377–10_I_A_b_IV_7_n, StAHH. Translation by the author.
72 This is true, for example, of Katharina Rose's son, who was eight years old at the time of the deportation. Through the tracing service of the German Red Cross, contact was made in the 1960s with a sister in the Federal Republic of Germany and another in the German Democratic

as Adolf Brühl, who was deported from Lübeck as a child together with his mother and siblings.⁷³

The preliminary analysis of compensation files and inventories in the Arolsen Archives suggests that more people survived the Belzec forced labor camp, the subsequent enforced stay at Krychow and other stays than had previously been assumed. Earlier estimates that 80 per cent of those deported from Hamburg to Belzec did not survive seem to have been overestimated.⁷⁴

Remembrance Culture

Commemorative reminders in the public space that reference the lives and persecution of the Sinti and Roma and their deportation in May 1940 are still few and far between. This is particularly true of Hamburg and the region of northern Germany as a whole. In Hamburg, for example, very few memorial plaques mark the sites of persecution. The first plaque in Hamburg's urban environment to refer to the May 1940 deportation is located at the site of the former Nöldekestrasse police station in the Harburg borough. It was inaugurated in 1986 by the Rom und Cinti Union Hamburg and commemorates those deported from Hamburg-Harburg. A second plaque was created in 2001 as part of the programme of *Sites of Persecution and Resistance 1933–1945* of the Hamburg Department for the Protection of Historical Monuments. It marks the location of the Fruit Warehouse as an assembly centre for those deported in May 1940 and also refers to the two further deportations of Sinti and Roma in 1943 and 1944 to the Auschwitz-Birkenau extermination camp.⁷⁵ The aforementioned main memorial *denk.mal Hannoverscher Bahnhof* to the memory of the two per-

---

Republic. He moved to the GDR in the mid-1960s, cf. interview with Beate K., 05.12.2017, M2019–0015, Archive of the Neuengamme Concentration Camp Memorial.
73 Cf. the account given by the grandson of Karl Brühl, Andrzej Luczak, in Agnieszka Caban and Ewa Koper, Geschichte der Rom*nja und Sint*izze, 63–64.
74 Michael Zimmermann, Rassenutopie, 183–184, footnote 150; Zimmermann relies on an estimate by the Committee of Former Political Prisoners.
75 The plaque is the initiative of Viviane Wünsche, a schoolgirl who, as part of a history competition, had previously studied the story of the survivor Gottfried Weiss's persecution, cf. Viviane Wünsche: "'Als die Musik verstummte ... und das Leben zerbrach'. Das Schicksal der Harburger Sinti-Familie Karl Weiss im Dritten Reich, dargestellt nach Gesprächen mit Gottfried Weiß (2001)", in Viviane Wünsche, Uwe Lohalm and Michael Zimmermann: *Die nationalsozialistische Verfolgung Hamburger Roma und Sinti. Vier Beiträge*, Hamburg: Landeszentrale für politische Bildung, 2002, 81–102.

secuted groups who were deported, i.e. Jews and Sinti and Roma, has only existed since 2017.

Several plaques situated beyond the Hamburg city limits commemorate the May deportation: Bremerhaven since 1994[76], Kiel since 1997[77], Flensburg since 2008[78] and Neumünster since 2021.[79] In Bełżec, too, a commemorative plaque to the memory of the murdered Sinti and Roma at the former forced labor camp was inaugurated in 2012, thanks in particular to the initiative of local protagonists. Employees of the museum and memorial in Bełżec, which primarily but not exclusively feels that it has the responsibility for the site of the former extermination camp in Belzec, are also involved locally in commemorating and remembering the Sinti and Roma deported to the forced labor camp in 1940.[80]

Outlook

As we have shown, much of the history of the deportation from Hamburg to Belzec in May 1940 has been researched. But there are still research desiderata. In particular, the subsequent fate of these deportees has thus far only been re-

---

[76] Dokumentations- und Kulturzentrum Deutscher Sinti und Roma: "Gedenktafel für die deportierten und ermordeten Bremerhavener Sinti und Roma". Available at: https://verortungen.de/gedenkorte/bremerhaven-karlsburg/. Last accessed: 24.07.2022.
[77] Heiko Weis: "Gedenkstein für die deportierten und ermordeten Sinti und Roma". Available at: https://sh-kunst.de/gedenkstein-fuer-die-deportierten-und-ermordeten-sinti-und-roma/. Last accessed: 24.07.2022.
[78] Dokumentations- und Kulturzentrum deutscher Sinti und Roma: "Gedenktafel für die aus Flensburg deportierte Sinti-Familie Weiß". Available at: https://verortungen.de/gedenkorte/flensburg-norderstrasse-sinti/. Last accessed: 24.07.2022.
[79] The relevant initiative came from Ingo Schumann, to whom I am also indebted for many references to the fates and destinies of Sinti and Roma deported from Neumünster. See also the features on Elisabeth Otto, Maria Busch, née Weiß, and Wilhelm Thormann: Freies Radio Neumünster: "Zeitreise: Wir erinnern heute an Elisabeth Otto genannt 'Lilli'". Available at: https://freiesradio-nms.de/2020/zeitreise-wir-erinnern-heute-an-elisabeth-otto-genannt-lilli/. Last accessed: 24.07.2022; ibid: "Zeitreise: Wir erinnern heute an Maria Busch, geborene Weiß". Available at: https://freiesradio-nms.de/2020/zeitreise-wir-erinnern-heute-an-maria-busch-geborene-weiss/. Last accessed: 24.07.2022; ibid.: "Zeitreise. Wir erinnern heute an Wilhelm Thormann genannt 'Sperling' aus Neumünster". Available at: https://freiesradio-nms.de/2020/zeitreise-wir-erinnern-heute-an-wilhelm-thormann-genannt-sperling-aus-neumuenster. Last accessed: 24.07.2022.
[80] The brochure in four languages also describes the construction and official inauguration of the memorial, see Caban/Koper, Bełżec, 80–88.

searched for some of those affected, and there is a lack of reliable information on how many of the deportees were later murdered. It would also be expedient to focus more on the experiences of the deported Sinti and Roma and their retrospective interpretations of the events that occurred in the *'Generalgouvernement'*. This would entail consulting and analysing first-person documents, existing interviews and published recollections.[81] A systematic assessment of compensation files might be helpful in this regard as often they contain early written reports on the persecution destinies. This would also allow an analysis of how the 1956 BGH ruling was reflected in the practice of the reparations offices.[82]

It would also be promising to examine the May deportation from a comparative perspective: the deportations from the three different regions of origin in northern Germany, in western Germany and in south-western Germany to the three different regions within the *'Generalgouvernement'*. For example, what sort of leeway did the local criminal police offices have in selecting those to be deported, and how did individual persecutees initially manage to escape deportation? Under what conditions did they continue to live in their places of residence, and what forms of persecution did they experience in the years that followed? As mentioned earlier, while many new insights into the deportees' regions of origin have been gained in recent years, they need to be studied further, particularly with regard to the way in which the deportations were organized by the institutions and officials involved. More research into the deportees' persecution destinies within the *'Generalgouvernement'*, to be conducted among Polish regional archives, would be apposite.

Finally, contextualising the May deportation with the first deportations of Jews from Vienna, Moravian Ostrava, and Katowice to Nisko in autumn 1939 and from Szczecin in February 1940 could provide new insights into the start of the deportations, their planning and implementation, and the subsequent persecution destinies of the deported victims in the *'Generalgouvernement'* and be-

---

81 Several interviews are to be found in the collections of the Workshop of Memory at the Research Institute for Contemporary History in Hamburg and the Lower Saxony Memorials Foundation in Celle. In recent years, descendants of those deported have published the stories of their families' persecution as well as the ways in which the families have addressed these issues: Tornado Rosenberg: *Vom Glück im Leben. Die Geschichte von Lani Rosenberg und Mama Blume*, Berlin: epubli, 2019; Ricardo-Lenzi Laubinger: *Und eisig weht der kalte Wind. Das Schicksal einer deutschen Sinti-Familie*, Berlin: KLAK, 2019.
82 The historian Sebastian Lotto-Kusche is currently investigating this issue using the example of applications for compensation for Sinti and Roma deported from Flensburg: See: Sebastian Lotte-Kusche: Zur Deportation der Sinti und Roma am 16. Mai 1940 aus Flensburg. Opferschicksale, Kämpfe der Überlebenden um Entschädigung und Strafverfolgung, in: *Grenzfriedenshefte*, 69, 2022, 3–38, 24.07.2022.

yond. Last but not least, the May 1940 deportation should also be viewed in conjunction with the deportations of Sinti and Roma in the wake of the Auschwitz Decree in December 1942.

One remit pertaining to commemoration policy might be to anchor the event more strongly among the general public through commemorative reminders in public spaces or through reporting, for example on the occasion of memorial days.

Alfred Eckert
Deportation Train 'Da 32' from Nuremberg and its 1,012 Occupants

Abstract: The article concerns deportation train 'Da 32' and the fate of its 1,012 Jewish occupants. The first mass transport from Franconia (Northern Bavaria) left Nuremberg for the Riga-Jungfernhof concentration camp (Latvia) with the Deutsche Reichsbahn on November 29, 1941. Only 52 people survived. The gradual destruction of the Nuremberg group is placed in the context of the Nazi 'Final Solution'. After presenting the available sources, the article focuses on researching the biographical personal details of the victims and reconstructing the further paths of persecution following deportation. Within this, the events at the place of departure, Nuremberg, and at the destination, Riga-Jungfernhof, are examined along with the time spent by them in the Riga ghetto and their further deportation to the concentration camps. The chances of survival for those who were deported are additionally discussed and statistically analyzed by assessing social ties.

Introduction

November 2021 marked the 80th anniversary of the first deportation of the Jewish population from Franconia. 1,012 men, women, and children were deported with '*Judentransport*' ('Jew transport') number 'Da 32'[1] from Nuremberg to Riga in German-occupied Latvia with the Deutsche Reichsbahn on November 29, 1941.[2] On

---

[1] On the meaning of the code 'Da' cf. Alfred Gottwaldt and Diana Schulle: *Die "Judendeportationen" aus dem Deutschen Reich 1941–1945*, Wiesbaden: Marix, 2005, 63.

[2] The number of people deported via Nuremberg transport 'Da 32' is stated in the literature as being between 1,008 and 1,027. My investigations discovered that four people – Berthold Bernheimer, Elsa Mannheimer, Flora Kronacher (née Heumann), and Ignatz Julius Selling – were not, as previously thought, among those deported from Nuremberg. However, the following seven people, who have not been stated in the literature to date, should be taken into account: Rosa Himmelreich, Jakob Koschland, Frieda Lärmer, Lina Walfisch, Karl Stein, Regine Stein (née Hecht), and Maria Stein. I would like to thank Michaela Fröhlich, Nuremberg, for the reference to Flora Kronacher (née Heumann) and other relevant information. Furthermore, I would like to thank Dr Ekkehard Hübschmann, Gefrees, for the reference to Ignatz Julius Selling and other relevant information. According to the current state of research, the Nuremberg 'Jew transport' comprised 1,012 people.

∂ OpenAccess. © 2023 the author(s), published by De Gruyter. This work is licensed under the Creative Commons Attribution-NonCommercial-NoDerivatives 4.0 International License.
https://doi.org/10.1515/9783110746464-019

the same day, the chief of the Reich Security Main Office (RSHA) Reinhard Heydrich sent out invitations to the planned Wannsee Conference, which was originally intended to take place on December 9, 1941, but was then postponed until January 1942.

The people who were deported came from eight Franconian places of departure: Bamberg, Bayreuth, Coburg, Erlangen, Forchheim, Fürth, Nuremberg, and Würzburg. 52 of them survived the Shoah. According to my current knowledge, six people are still alive today.

This contribution is intended to show, in the form of a case study, what happened to the 1,012 deported people between November 29, 1941, and the German surrender on May 8, 1945, and what the paths of persecution were following deportation. The transports in the first few months after deportations began in October 1941 were not yet oriented towards the systematic murder of the victims of persecution. Many of those deported were initially imprisoned in various ghettos and camps, where they were conscripted for forced labor. Their chances of survival were thus sometimes greater than those of people on subsequent transports from Germany, which ended directly in Auschwitz or other extermination sites.

For the people concerned, deportation represented a transition from the previous deprivation of rights and marginalization within German society into the SS system of terror and the concentration camp system with the constant threat of being murdered. In this article, all aspects of an individual deportation train from Germany are examined by evaluating the social ties of those who were deported, the chances of survival and survival strategies of the people concerned are investigated in detail. The article is intended as a preliminary appraisal; research into the transport is not yet complete. In the following discussion, I will outline the various departure points for those deported with the transport on November 29, 1941, (hereinafter: Nuremberg transport) in the period from December 2, 1941, to the end of the war, and the events associated with this. Alongside reconstructing the individual paths of persecution, the number of survivors from the transport will also be ascertained and statistically evaluated according to their place of origin.

Sources and State of Research

In his comprehensive standard reference on deportations from Germany, *Der verwaltete Mensch,* published in 1974, H.G. Adler primarily refers to the files of the Würzburg Gestapo preserved in the Würzburg State Archive and thus to part of the transport on November 29, 1941.³ Adler's analyses comprise, among other things, the organization of the Gestapo, the transfer of the victims to the assembly camps (*Sammellager*) and the forced cooperation of the Jewish Community. He also outlines the fate of individual deportees. Both the surviving Gestapo files and Adler's early analysis – both prerequisites that do not exist in the same way for other locations within the '*Altreich*' – form an important basis for this research into the transport on November 29, 1941. They are supplemented by the transport lists preserved in the Nuremberg City Archives and the Würzburg State Archive.⁴ The Arolsen Archives also hold documents containing the names of deportees, including a postwar compilation from the residents' registration office of Nuremberg.⁵

A further key source is the photo album containing photographs from the three deportations from Franconia in the years 1941 and 1942, which has been preserved by the Würzburg State Archive.⁶ The 119 photographs contained in this, a further 19 pictures that originally belonged to the album but found their way to the USA after the war, and an additional photo handed over during a trial in Würzburg in 1949 represent the largest known collection of deportation photographs from the Deutsche Reich. The 139 photographs were taken by an official from the Würzburg Gestapo and also show Jews from Würzburg being searched as part of preparations for the transport on November 29, 1941. Photographs also show people being brought to Würzburg train station, climbing onto the connecting train to Nuremberg, and the loading of luggage.⁷

---

3 H.G. Adler: *Der verwaltete Mensch. Studien zur Deportation der Juden aus Deutschland*, Tübingen: J.C.B. Mohr (Paul Siebeck), 1974.
4 An official list entitled 'Deported Jews, 1st wave' lists the Jews from Nuremberg who were deported on November 29, 1941. The list can be found in the Nuremberg City Archives, holding C 31/I, No. 26, 2–15. No original transport lists of deportees from Nuremberg have been retained. A 'List of Jews to be evacuated from Würzburg' can be found in the Würzburg State Archive (holding Gestapo 18874, 9–18). See also Thomas Freier: "Nürnberg – Würzburg nach Riga". Available at: https://www.statistik-des-holocaust.de/list_ger_bay_411129.html. Last accessed: 10.01.2022. Freier assumes that 1,010 people were deported. My research has resulted in 1,012 deportees, see footnote 2.
5 Deportation from Nuremberg to Riga/Jungfernhof, 29.11.1941, 1.2.1.1/11195000–11195006/ITS Digital Archive, Arolsen Archives; deportation from Würzburg via Nuremberg to Riga, 27.11.1941, 1.2.1.1/11195523–11195532/ITS Digital Archive, Arolsen Archives.
6 Photo album, Gestapo 18880a, Würzburg State Archive. The album, which had been considered lost, was rediscovered by historian Edith Raim in 2001 in the ancillary papers for postwar proceedings at the Nuremberg-Fürth public prosecutor's office. See also the article by Christoph Kreutzmüller in this volume.
7 Further photographs document the 2nd and 3rd deportation from Franconia on March 24, 1942, and April 25, 1942. For a critical analysis of the album and a detailed presentation of the orga-

Images that document the departure of the first eight Forchheim Jews represent a further photographic source.[8] Finally, some portraits of the deportees exist,[9] mostly passport photographs from the identity cards of the Jewish residents of communities and towns, photographs from the family albums of surviving relatives,[10] or from other forms of identification in administrative files.[11] Further information about the transport can be found dispersed in relevant research publications about the Shoah and in publications on local and regional history.[12]

---

nization of the transports and the structure of the Gestapo in Würzburg and Nuremberg see Albrecht Liess (ed.): *Wege in die Vernichtung. Die Deportation der Juden aus Mainfranken 1941– 1943*, Munich: Directorate General of the Bavaria State Archive, 2003. All 139 photographs are shown in this exhibition catalogue. The photo album with 119 photographs is held in the Würzburg State Archive under the signature Gestapo 18880a. 19 original photographs found their way to the USA, see RG 238, NG 2421, National Archives, Washington.
8 Rolf Kilian Kiessling: *Juden in Forchheim. 300 Jahre jüdisches Leben in einer kleinen fränkischen Stadt*, Forchheim: Verlag Kulturamt des Landkreises Forchheim, 2004. Eight out of a total of fourteen photographs are published on pages 205–209.
9 The portraits are pictured in various regional memorial books for the Jewish victims of National Socialism. See for Bamberg: Verein zur Förderung der jüdischen Geschichte und Kultur Bambergs e.V. (ed.): *Gedenkbuch der jüdischen Bürger Bambergs*, Bamberg: Erich Weiß, 2008, 449; see for Bayreuth: Historical Museum Bayreuth: "Gedenkbuch der Stadt Bayreuth für die Opfer des Nationalsozialismus". Available at: https://gedenkbuch.bayreuth.de. Last accessed: 12.01. 2022; see for Erlangen: Ilse Sponsel: *Gedenkbuch für die Erlanger Opfer der Schoa*, Erlangen: Bürgermeister- und Presseamt der Stadt Erlangen, 2001; see for Fürth: Gisela Naomi Blume: "Memorbuch für die Fürther Opfer der Shoah". Available at: https://www.juedische-fuerther.de/index.php/memorbuch-opfer-der-shoah. Last accessed: 20.02.2022; see for Forchheim: Kiessling, Juden in Forchheim, 205–209; see for Nuremberg: Gerhard Jochem and Ulrike Kettner: *Gedenkbuch für die Nürnberger Opfer der Schoa*, Nuremberg: City Archive, 1998; idem: *Gedenkbuch für die Nürnberger Opfer der Schoa*, Nuremberg: City Archive, 2002; see for Würzburg: Jüdisches Leben in Unterfranken – Biographische Datenbank e.V: "Jüdisches Leben in Unterfranken". Available at: https:/juedisches-unterfranken.de/. Last accessed: 10.02.2022.
10 Numerous photographs can be found in the holdings of the Fürth and Nuremberg City Archives and in the Nuremberg State Archive.
11 Photographs from passports of Jewish citizens (up to 1938) and registration cards from the residents' registration office have been preserved in the holdings of the community and city archives in the places of departure, such as Würzburg, Nuremberg, and Fürth. Photographs of Jewish club members from the 1929 to 1955 membership records of the soccer club 1. FC Nürnberg, rediscovered at the end of 2020, are held in the club's archive. These included two Jewish members, who were deported to Riga-Jungfernhof and Stutthof.
12 Cf. in particular Ekkehard Hübschmann: "Die Deportation von Juden aus Franken nach Riga", in *Frankenland. Zeitschrift für fränkische Landeskunde und Kulturpflege*, 5, 2004, 344– 369. Available at: http://www.agfjg.de/deportationen/huebschmann2004a.pdf. Last accessed: 15.01.2022.

Despite the relatively good sources, systematic research into the paths of persecution for those deported from Nuremberg on November 29, 1941, and an investigation into the prisoner community have so far been a research desideratum.

Origin of Deportees, Transport to the Assembly Camp, and the Nuremberg Gestapo

The selection of the deportees in the eight Franconian places of departure Bamberg, Bayreuth, Coburg, Erlangen, Forchheim, Fürth, Nuremberg, and Würzburg, and the drafting of deportation lists were handled in different ways. According to Christopher Browning, the Jews in Nuremberg were chosen for transport by the police using a register of the Jewish Community, probably a members' register, while the police in Würzburg only specified the number of people to be deported. The local Jewish Community then had to select the names themselves by order of the Gestapo and produce a corresponding list.[13]

The place of birth and place of departure were identical for a good quarter of the Jews in the Nuremberg transport (27.05 percent). The influx of Jews to larger cities, particularly Würzburg, Fürth, Nuremberg, and Bamberg, mainly took place for economic reasons, for example, setting up companies, or in connection with marriages, before 1933. There were also Jews who had immigrated to Franconian towns from Poland. After 1933, people primarily moved due to persecution; many Jews sought protection from antisemitic hostility in the anonymity of larger towns. For example, Fritz and Lina Kimmelstiel from Forth (Middle Franconia) moved to Nuremberg in October 1938 with their children Albert and Max. They had been forced to sell their property, their house with a shop in Forth, to neighbors just a few months before.[14] The majority of those who moved to the cities came from smaller Franconian towns and villages in the surrounding area following the November pogroms in 1938. Their new accommoda-

---

13 Christopher Browning: *Die Entfesselung der "Endlösung". Nationalsozialistische Judenpolitik 1939–1942*, Munich: Propyläen, 2003, 551. However, according to Beate Meyer, the addresses of the Jews deported from Nuremberg were taken from the residents' register by the Gestapo. Cf. Beate Meyer: "Handlungsspielräume regionaler jüdischer Repräsentanten (1941–1945)", in Birthe Kundrus and Beate Meyer (eds.): *Die Deportation der Juden aus Deutschland. Pläne – Praxis – Reaktionen 1938–1945*, Göttingen: Wallstein, 2005², 63–85, here 76.
14 Martina Switalski: *Shalom Forth. Jüdisches Dorfleben in Franken*, Münster: Waxmann, 2012, 188–192.

tion was usually compulsory apartments in what were known as '*Judenhäuser*' ('Jews houses') or '*Judenwohnungen*' ('Jews apartments').[15]

The deportees with the Nuremberg transport came from various social classes. Alongside tradespeople, doctors, and other independent workers, there were also teachers, domestic workers, and pensioners. The people from Würzburg mainly came from agricultural professions, such as cattle and horse traders, farmers, and wine merchants.

The proportion of family or kinship relationships within the groups from the eight places of departure was as follows: Bamberg 75.4 percent, Bayreuth 93.5 percent, Coburg 76.9 percent, Erlangen 100 percent, Forchheim 75.0 percent, Fürth 68.1 percent, Nuremberg 76.7 percent, and Würzburg 86.1 percent.[16]

Once the Jewish people selected for deportation on November 29, 1941, were handed their 'evacuation orders' on November 23, 1941,[17] the possibility of escaping this threatening situation was extremely low: Emigration had no longer been possible since October 1941 and going underground was essentially futile.[18]

One example shows how fatal a sense of responsibility could be. Master baker Hugo Schuster and his family were Orthodox Jews. As the 'matzot baker of Fürth',[19] he supplied matzot to the Jewish communities of Fürth and the whole of Middle Franconia.[20] Schuster, his wife Recha Rachel, and his daughter Nelly had already held an immigration certificate to Palestine since 1933 thanks to the help of his brother-in-law Hugo Oppenheimer. However, the master baker

---

15 Cf. Hübschmann, Die Deportation von Juden aus Franken nach Riga, 345–346; Verein zur Förderung der jüdischen Geschichte und Kultur Bambergs e. V., Gedenkbuch der jüdischen Bürger Bambergs, 449; Norbert Aas (ed.): *Juden in Bayreuth 1933–2003. Verfolgung, Vertreibung – und das Danach*, Bayreuth: Bumerang, 2008, 59–63; Hubert Fromm: *Die Coburger Juden. Geduldet – Geächtet – Vernichtet*, Coburg: Evangelisches Bildungswerk Coburg e. V. and Initiative Stadtmuseum Coburg, 2012, 126–127; Kiessling, Juden in Forchheim, 204; Gisela Naomi Blume and Raphael Halmôn: *Zum Gedenken an die von den Nazis ermordeten Fürther Juden 1933–1945*, Fürth: City Archive Fürth, 1997, 13–14; Jochem/Kettner, Gedenkbuch für die Nürnberger Opfer der Schoa, volume 1, 463–464.
16 The family and kinship links between all of the transport participants were investigated (families, spouses, siblings, relatives). The sources come from research into the biographies of the deportees.
17 Hübschmann, Die Deportation von Juden aus Franken nach Riga, 355.
18 Only 23 Jews, who lived in 'mixed marriages' or were hidden, survived the Shoah in Fürth. See Barbara Ohm: *Geschichte der Juden in Fürth*, volume 2, Fürth: Geschichtsverein Fürth, 2014, 268.
19 Hugo Schuster only produced kosher baked goods, e. g. normal matzot, Shmurah matzot or the traditional Shabbat bread berches, at his bakery in Fürth. I would like to thank the nephew of Hugo Schuster, Uri B. Oppenheimer, for this information.
20 Blume/Halmôn, Fürther Juden, 389. Matzot is the unleavened bread for Passover.

decided to stay out of a sense of duty because "he was the last baker in Franconia who could supply his community with matzot".[21] The whole family was deported with the transport on November 29, 1941.[22]

Between November 25 and 28, 1941, the persons selected for deportation were collected from their homes by the Gestapo, SS or criminal police; with the exception of those from Würzburg, who had to go to the assembly point at Würzburg city hall on November 26, 1941. A short time later, they were transferred from the assembly points in the eight places of departure to the assembly center in Nuremberg-Langwasser by the SS or criminal police by bus, truck, car, or train.[23]

The Reich Security Main Office (RSHA) based in Berlin was responsible for coordinating the deportations throughout Germany. The main responsibility for organizing the transports from the three Franconian administrative regions (Lower, Middle, and Upper Franconia) lay with the Staatspolizeistelle in Nuremberg-Fürth. This organized the deportation of Franconian Jews in collaboration with its subordinate field office in Würzburg. The formal overall management of the transport was conducted by the Polizeipräsident in Nuremberg-Fürth and the Höherer SS- und Polizeiführer Main, Benno Martin. Within the Staatspolizeistelle, SS-Sturmbannführer and Kriminalrat Theodor Grafenberger was entrusted with organizing the transport as the head of Department II (Executive) and head of the Nuremberg '*Judenreferat*', a department responsible for matters relating to Jews. Grafenberger's colleague in the '*Judenreferat*', Kriminalkommissar Christian Woesch, was responsible for the practical work involved in all 'transport matters'. His main task was to select the people to be deported from Fürth and Nuremberg and create lists. He also conducted all of the negotiations with the Reichsbahn with regard to ordering trains and requesting means of transport, such as trucks and cars to collect the deportees and their luggage.[24]

The Würzburg field office of the Staatspolizeistelle Nuremberg-Fürth, led by Kriminalkommissar Ernst Gramowski, played a major role in carrying out the deportation. The head of Department II/2 (churches, Jews, emigration, and the

---

21 Uri B. Oppenheimer in a telephone conversation with the author, 13.10.2021. He obtained the information from conversations with his father, Hugo Oppenheimer.
22 Cf. Blume/Halmôn, Fürther Juden, 389–390.
23 Cf. Hübschmann, Die Deportation von Juden aus Franken nach Riga, 355–361.
24 Hübschmann, Die Deportation von Juden aus Franken nach Riga, 346.

press) and deputy head of the Würzburg field office, Kriminalinspektor Michael Völkl, was responsible for the specific implementation on site.[25]

Police Commissioner Benno Martin selected five large wooden barracks at *Waldlager 2* (forest camp 2) outside Nuremberg, on the site of the Nuremberg Rally in Langwasser, to serve as short-term accommodation and assembly camp for the people scheduled for deportation. Around one kilometer from the camp was Märzfeld train station, from which the deportation train departed for Riga.[26]

Before the victims reached their barracks accommodation at the actual assembly camp, each person was once again 'channeled' through four rooms.[27] As part of this *Schleusung*, their luggage was thoroughly searched and all valuables, identification papers, and securities were seized. The victims also underwent a degrading body search and were forced to strip naked. In the last room a bailiff issued each victim a *Vermögenseinziehungsverfügung* (seizure of assets order). This meant that their entire assets were seized to the benefit of the German Reich.[28] While preparations were being made for the transport, the 11th Decree to the Reich Citizenship Law[29] was issued on November 25, 1941, which provided pseudo-legal justification for the expropriation of the deported Jews.[30]

At 3.00 pm on Saturday, November 29, 1941, transport train number 'Da 32' carrying 1,012 people left Nuremberg-Märzfeld train station heading for the city of Riga in Latvia, 1,600 kilometers from Nuremberg. The special train (*Sonderzug*) comprised 22 to 27 cars.[31] There is no specific evidence to date regarding the exact route taken by the train from Nuremberg to Riga. It can be assumed

---

25 Herbert Schott: "Die ersten drei Deportationen mainfränkischer Juden 1941/42", in Albrecht Liess (ed.): *Wege in die Vernichtung. Die Deportation der Juden aus Mainfranken 1941–1943*, Munich: Directorate General of the Bavaria State Archive, 2003, 73–166, here 76.
26 Alexander Schmidt: *Das Reichsparteitagsgelände in Nürnberg*, Nuremberg: Sandberg, 2014, 157.
27 The procedure of searching the people selected for deportation and issuing official papers in the places of departure, such as in Würzburg, was repeated in the same way for a second time in Nuremberg.
28 Hübschmann, Die Deportation von Juden aus Franken nach Riga, 362–363.
29 Reichsgesetzblatt (RGBl.), I, 722–724.
30 Martin Friedenberger: *Fiskalische Ausplünderung. Die Berliner Steuer- und Finanzverwaltung und die jüdische Bevölkerung 1933–1945*, Berlin: Metropol, 2008, 274. Cf. also Adler, Der verwaltete Mensch, 500–503.
31 The train consisted of 15 3rd-class cars (each wagon accommodating a maximum of 66 people plus young children, where applicable) for the Jewish victims, two 2nd-class passenger cars for the escorts, and five to ten goods cars for the luggage. The author's own research based on an estimated extrapolation: Official occupancy of a car at 66 people per car x 15 cars = 990 people + young children.

with some certainty that the route, as was the case for most mass transports heading to Riga, led via Berlin in a northeast direction via Landsberg (Warthe) – Kreuz – Schneidemühl – Firchau to Riga.[32]

Arrival in Riga and the Jungfernhof Camp

The Nuremberg transport was one of twenty transports with German, Austrian, and Czech Jews, who were deported to Riga between November 27, 1941, and February 6, 1942.[33] There were plans to temporarily house them in the Riga ghetto.[34] This had been sealed on October 25, 1941, when there were more than 29,600 Latvian Jews living there. More than 27,500 of them were murdered on November 30, 1941, 'Riga Bloody Sunday', and one week later on December 8/9, 1941, to make room for the Jews deported from the German Reich to Riga.[35] Those murdered also included all 1,053 occupants of the 7th deportation transport to the East from Berlin, which had reached Riga on November 30, 1941. This mass murder in the forest of Rumbula took place on the orders of the Höherer SS- und Polizeiführer for Ostland and Rußland-Nord, SS Obergruppenführer Friedrich Jeckeln, who acted on his own authority.[36]

The train from Nuremberg arrived at its destination Riga just a few days after 'Bloody Sunday'. On December 2, 1941, after three days and two nights, it reached the Riga-Skirotava freight yard, which is located in a suburb in the south-east of the city and served as the destination station for transports to Riga.[37]

As the clearing of the Riga ghetto and the murder of the ghetto inhabitants had not yet been completed, those deported from Nuremberg were taken from

---

32 There is evidence of the route of the transport train from Düsseldorf with train number Da 38, which took the same route via Berlin to the destination Riga-Skirotava (Jungfernhof). See transport report by Polizeihauptmann Paul Salitter, 26.12.1941, printed in Raul Hilberg: *Sonderzüge nach Auschwitz*, Mainz: Dumjahn, 1981, 130–138. Yad Vashem assumes the same transport route via Berlin, see Yad Vashem: "Transport, Zug 'Da 32' von Nürnberg nach Jungfernhof". Available at: https://deportation.yadvashem.org/index.html?language=de&itemId=9437978&ind=-1. Last accessed: 15.01.2022.
33 Gottwaldt/Schulle, Judendeportationen, 110.
34 The Riga ghetto only represented an interim solution. Cf. Andrej Angrick and Peter Klein: *Die "Endlösung" in Riga. Ausbeutung und Vernichtung 1941–1944*, Darmstadt: WBG, 2006, 199.
35 Gottwaldt/Schulle, Judendeportationen, 111; Angrick/Klein, Endlösung in Riga, 180.
36 Richard Rhodes: *Die deutschen Mörder. Die SS-Einsatzgruppen und der Holocaust*, Bergisch Gladbach: Lübbe, 2004, 318–320.
37 Gottwaldt/Schulle, Judendeportationen, 122.

Skirotava to the Jungfernhof estate, six kilometers from the center of Riga.[38] The journey there involved the occupants of the transport traveling 1.5 kilometers on foot.

Jungfernhof, a former farming estate for the city of Riga, which had been taken over by the Security Police (SiPo) following the German occupation of Latvia, served as a detention camp, labor camp, and temporary assembly point. It was not originally intended as a prisoner camp and thus, compared to other camps and ghettos, it represents a special case within the Nazi camp system. There were plans to create a large model agricultural business to ensure supplies to SS units stationed in and around Riga. The camp commander and estate manager was farmer and SS-Unterscharführer Rudolf Seck, who came from Süderdithmarschen.[39]

Jungfernhof was in a dilapidated state when the Nuremberg deportees arrived. The 200-hectare estate extended between the Dünaburg (Daugavpils) highway and the bank of the Daugava River. The farm complex consisted of a walled farmhouse, three large wooden barns, five small houses, and various cattle sheds. The barns were in a dire condition, the building completely unsuitable for housing several thousand people. In November 1941, multi-story wooden bunk beds had been set up in a hurry in the unheated barns and sheds by Soviet prisoners of war and civilian workers.[40] Survivor Albert Kimmelstiel wrote in 1945: "The accommodation of the people was a catastrophe. 500 [men] in one open barn, without doors and without window frames, the roof completely rotten, snow, rain, and wind [...] at 32 degrees below zero".[41] Alongside the structural inadequacies came the complete overcrowding of the site. The Nuremberg transport was followed a few days later by a transport from Stuttgart, one from Vienna, and one from Hamburg, each with around 1,000 people. Just under 4,000 Jews thus lived crammed together in a very small space in the worst living and weather conditions. Around 850 people from the four transports died within their first four months at the Jungfernhof camp due to the cold, hunger, illness, and mass shootings.

The 'prisoner community' at Jungfernhof consisted of Germans and Austrians. Life together involved less conflict than the imposed communities in

---

38 Ibid., 134.
39 Wolfgang Scheffler: "Ein historischer Überblick", in idem./Diana Schulle: *Buch der Erinnerung. Das Schicksal der in die baltischen Staaten deportierten deutschen, österreichischen und tschechoslowakischen Juden 1941–1945*, volume 1, Munich: Saur, 2003, 1–43, here 9–13. There has so far been insufficient research into the history of the Jungfernhof labor camp.
40 Gottwaldt/Schulle, Judendeportationen, 114.
41 Albert Kimmelstiel quoted in Switalski, Shalom Forth, 169. Translation by the author.

other transit ghettos, in which 'Western Jews' had to share living space with the local Jewish population.

The arrivals spent the first few weeks after arriving at Jungfernhof organizing their own food. A separate emergency kitchen was gradually set up for each transport, which took care of the meagre food supplies for the prisoners.[42] Working on the farm was currently unthinkable as it was the middle of a cold winter. Labor details (*Arbeitskommandos*) were later formed, who cleared for example the streets of Riga and the surrounding areas from snow or who tried to obtain firewood. A labor detail at the train station, consisting of younger men, had to unload and clean the transport trains arriving at Skirotava train station. There was also a quarry labor detail, which left the camp for work each morning.[43] As the weather became warmer, the establishment of a farm began. The prisoners had to sow vegetables and grow potatoes[44] on the former runway, which originated from the construction of an airport that was begun on the estate site during Soviet occupation.[45] Male prisoners had previously been conscripted to perform heavy physical labor to remove large granite slabs from the runway. The women removed mounds in large, heavy tubs to form level areas of farmland.[46] Prisoners, such as Käthe Frieß, also had to work in the shoe and clothing storage rooms, or as blacksmiths and carpenters.[47]

Despite the hopeless situation and the busy and exhausting everyday life, the prisoner community at Jungfernhof nevertheless found opportunities to establish a cultural and religious life that gave them back a little 'normality' and 'privacy'.

The Jews who were deported into the Riga area in December 1941 were not scheduled for organized systematic murder at that time. On March 15, 1942, SS-Sturmbannführer Rudolf Lange, Commander of the SS Security Police and the SD in Latvia, issued the order to convert the Jungfernhof labor camp into an estate. This order was based, among other things, on the insistence of camp commander Seck to decimate the camp population by removing old and incapacitated people.[48] Following this conversion, the SS organized the '*Aktion Dünamünde*' at

---

42 Christin Sandow (ed.): "*Schießen Sie mich nieder!*" *Käte Frieß' Aufzeichnungen über KZ und Zwangsarbeit von 1941 bis 1945*, Berlin: Lukas, 2017, 32.
43 Angrick/Klein, "Endlösung" in Riga, 225.
44 Hanneliese Reinauer (survivor from the Bayreuth group) in an interview with the author on November 21, 2011.
45 Scheffler, Historischer Überblick, 9.
46 Sandow, Käte Frieß' Aufzeichnungen, 48.
47 Ibid., 34–37.
48 Hans-Hermann Seiffert: *Eine Sehnder Jüdin kehrt zurück*, Konstanz: Hartung-Gorre, 2016, 59.

Jungfernhof on March 26, 1942. All camp inmates over 50 years of age, the sick, and children under 14 years of age with their mothers were to be moved to a new, allegedly better camp.[49] Lange falsely claimed that the prisoners were being taken to Dünamünde, where they would allegedly find much easier working conditions and better accommodation at a fish cannery.[50] A district of Riga named Dünamünde did actually exist approx. 30 kilometers to the north-west of Jungfernhof. However, there were no fish canneries there. Instead, the SS took between 1,700 and 1,800 elderly and sick people to the Bikernieki forest to be shot by the Latvian SS. Those killed included the majority of older men and women, as well as mothers with their children, from the Nuremberg transport.[51] However, it is no longer possible to determine the exact number.

The 'Aktion Dünamünde' represented a crucial turning point in the lives of the prisoners who remained at Jungfernhof.[52] It meant that each of the survivors from the Nuremberg group lost at least one close family member, relative, or friend. Whole families were wiped out overnight, mothers killed with their children, old, sick, and weak individuals murdered. Men were separated from their families and lost their wives and children.

The mass shooting on March 26, 1942, meant that the 450 prisoners who were still alive now had more space and food at Jungfernhof. On the very next day after the massacre, the SS ordered the building of new heated accommodation barracks with toilets, washrooms, and recreation rooms. Seck released potatoes and vegetables from the fields; the rations also included meat. Seck believed that he could best achieve his goal of creating a model farming estate at Jungfernhof with strong, healthy prisoners.[53] The improved conditions were intended to keep sickness away from the camp while retaining and boosting forced labor.

Although the Jungfernhof camp was isolated and did not have an enclosing fence, any camp lighting, or watchtowers, and was only controlled by a mobile patrol of 15 to 20 Latvian auxiliary police officers (Hilfspolizisten), there is no

---

49 Ibid.
50 Scheffler, Historischer Überblick, 11.
51 It is certain that, with the exception of two children from Nuremberg (Peter and Samuel Stern), all of the children under six years of age from the Nuremberg transport were killed during this operation. Cf. Gerhard Jochem: "Zum 80. Jahrestag der Deportation von Nürnberg nach Riga-Jungfernhof am 29. November 1941. Das Beispiel der Familie Stern". Available at: https://stadtarchive-metropolregion-nuernberg.de/zum-80-jahrestag-der-deportation-von-nuernberg-nach-riga-jung fernhof-am-29-november-1941-das-beispiel-der-familie-stern/. Last accessed: 16.02.2022.
52 Sandow, Käte Frieß' Aufzeichnungen, 170.
53 Ibid., 45.

evidence of a single escape or escape attempt by any of the around 4,000 prisoners. This may have been due to the rough terrain, the foreign country, the language barriers, and the unfavorable weather conditions. Without (Latvian) assistance, no one could survive on the run outside the camp for a prolonged period of time. However, a large proportion of the Latvian population held antisemitic views, which meant that there was not much prospect of assistance and there was a risk of being betrayed.[54]

Salaspils, Auschwitz, Riga Ghetto, Riga-Kaiserwald, and Stutthof

The surviving prisoners were taken from Jungfernhof to various camps and ghettos. These included the Salaspils police detention camp (*Polizeihaftlager*), which had been set up around 12 kilometers to the south-east of Jungfernhof at the beginning of December 1941 under the leadership of SS-Obersturmführer Gerhard Maywald. Male prisoners from Jungfernhof and the Riga ghetto were brought there to perform the toughest forced labor in order to build barracks and watchtowers.[55] These also included around 56 members of the Nuremberg group, strong, healthy men between 16 and 50 years of age, who were transferred to Salaspils shortly after the transport arrived on December 4/5, 1941.[56] Due to the catastrophic conditions there – it was cold and the accommodation and food supplies were completely inadequate – many of them died in Salaspils. Mass executions also took place there.[57]

The SS had already used the Riga ghetto at the beginning of 1942 to house parts of the Nuremberg group. Following the mass murder of Latvian Jews in the ghetto on November 30 and December 7/8, 1941, the ghetto was divided into two parts: The largest section was named the '*Reichsjudenghetto*' ('German Jew ghetto'), in which the deportees from the German Reich had to live. The smaller section, the '*Kleine Ghetto*' ('Small ghetto'), was inhabited by Latvian Jews. In early 1942, around 200 women from Jungfernhof, including some from the Nuremberg

---

54 Scheffler, Historischer Überblick, 11. Only two men from the Nuremberg group managed to escape during their persecution after their forced stay in Jungfernhof: Ludwig Gutmann from the Maly Trostinez camp in 1944 and Henry Behrens during the Allied bombing of his transport in Germany in 1945.
55 Cf. ibid., 14.
56 Ibid., 14, footnote 61.
57 Ibid., 9–16; Josef Katz: *Erinnerungen eines Überlebenden*, Kiel: Neuer Malik Verlag, 1988, 39–40.

group, came to the larger section of the ghetto. More followed in the subsequent months. Between April 1942 and August 1943, all of the prisoners who remained at Jungfernhof – apart from around 80 forced laborers, who had to stay until Jungfernhof was closed in 1944 – were gradually transferred to the Riga ghetto. Some of the women who came to the ghetto in January 1942 had voluntarily registered for work there. They were divided into work crews (*Arbeitskolonnen*) to clear snow in the city and to perform tidying and sorting work in the ghetto. Some of them were forced to work on the moor near the city in summer 1943.[58]

In an order dated June 21, 1943, Heinrich Himmler instructed Friedrich Jeckeln that "all Jews still present in ghettos in the Ostland region are to be brought together in concentration camps".[59] The Latvian SS closed the '*Reichsjudenghetto*' in Riga on November 2, 1943. Following a selection process, some of the inhabitants, particularly the elderly, sick, and those unfit for work, were taken to Auschwitz by train.[60] The majority of the former ghetto occupants, Jews who were fit for work, were taken to the Riga-Kaiserwald concentration camp, which had been set up in March 1943.[61] Franziska Jahn ascertained that around 5,550 to 5,900 German, Czech, and Austrian Jews from the Riga ghetto were transferred to Kaiserwald between July and November 1943.[62] From August 1943, the Riga-Kaiserwald concentration camp was the only main camp in occupied Latvia to which all sub-camps were connected.

At Riga-Kaiserwald, the prisoners were re-registered, had their heads shaved, and were given striped uniforms. 15-year-old Hanneliese Reinauer from Bayreuth found the cutting of the hair to be the most degrading aspect.[63] From the reception procedure onwards, the identity of the prisoners now only consisted of a prisoner number. The former inmates of the Riga ghetto, including at least 192 survivors from the Nuremberg group,[64] were distributed between the sub-

---

58 Scheffler, Historischer Überblick, 11–13; Lilly Menczel: *Vom Rhein nach Riga. Deportiert von Köln: Bericht einer Überlebenden des Holocaust*, Hamburg: VSA, 2012, 36.
59 Heiner Lichtenstein: *Im Namen des Volkes? Eine persönliche Bilanz der NS-Prozesse*, Cologne: Bund-Verlag, 1984, 156. Translation by the author.
60 Ibid.
61 Wolfgang Benz and Barbara Distel (eds.): *Der Ort des Terrors. Geschichte der nationalsozialistischen Konzentrationslager*, volume 8, Munich: Beck, 2008, 15–87; Franziska Jahn: *Das KZ Riga-Kaiserwald und seine Außenlager 1943–1944. Strukturen und Entwicklungen*, Berlin: Metropol, 2018.
62 Jahn, Riga-Kaiserwald, 437.
63 Norbert Aas: *… und trotzdem wieder Bayreuth. Hanneliese Reinauer-Wandersmann*, Bayreuth: Bumerang, 2011, 80.
64 The number results from the number of survivors of the massacre on March 26, 1942, from the Nuremberg group (183 people) plus nine surviving men from Salaspils.

camps Spilve, Strasdenhof, Dondangen, and Eleja-Meitene near Mitau (Jelgava), which were subordinate to the Riga-Kaiserwald main camp. They were also brought to other sub-camps within Riga to perform forced labor: Heereskraftfahrpark (army motor vehicle repair), Mühlgraben (army clothing supply), Lenta (repair shop for the SS), SS-Truppenwirtschaftslager, Riga (Reichsbahn) and Allgemeine Elektrizitätsgesellschaft (AEG, general electric corporation).[65] Families with older children and married couples, who were initially able to stay together in the ghetto, were torn apart and separated by gender. However, they were able to contact each other, see each other, and talk to each other through the barbed wire.[66]

Franziska Jahn calculated the actual number of surviving former prisoners of the Kaiserwald complex to be at least 2,170. It is, however, possible, that up to around 3,500 people could have survived the Kaiserwald concentration camp.[67] The others, the old, weak, and children, died in the sub-camps and in the main camp, where the SS organized two murder campaigns: The brutal *'Kinderaktion'* ('children's raid') and the *'Krebsbachaktion'* ('Krebsbach action'), named after site doctor Eduard Krebsbach, from spring 1944.[68]

Due to the advancing Soviet front, all Jewish prisoners from the Baltic region were relocated to camps further towards the German Reich from summer 1944 and the Kaiserwald complex was closed.[69] The destination for the prisoners in the Riga area was the nearest Stutthof concentration camp near Danzig (Gdańsk). This had serious consequences for the camp inmates at Kaiserwald concentration camp and the prisoners housed in the barracks, who once again had to undergo a selection process and withstand the exhausting 'evacuation' by land and sea over the Baltic Sea to Stutthof concentration camp 600 kilometers away. The journey by land initially led to the port city of Libau (Liepāja) 200 kilometers to the west of Riga. The first transports left there on August 6, 1944, on ships that reached Stutthof via Danzig (Gdańsk) on August 9, 1944.[70]

The Stutthof camp, which was set up in 1939 as a 'civilian prison camp' (*Zivilgefangenenlager*) and received the status of 'Grade I concentration camp' on

---

65 Lichtenstein, Im Namen des Volkes, 157; Jahn, Riga-Kaiserwald, 344–347.
66 Menczel, Vom Rhein nach Riga, 11 and 41.
67 Jahn, Riga-Kaiserwald, 438.
68 Ibid., 415–420. According to my current knowledge, not a single prisoner from the Nuremberg group is known to have died during internment at the Kaiserwald concentration camp or the sub-camp.
69 Ibid., 407–431.
70 Benz/Distel, Der Ort des Terrors, volume 8, 52–53.

January 19, 1942,[71] was already overcrowded when the prisoners from Riga arrived. The hygiene conditions there and the supplies of food and medications to the prisoners were catastrophic. The health of the prisoners brought here from Riga deteriorated noticeably. The women were mainly conscripted to perform forced labor in the Stutthof sub-camps. From there, individual prisoners went to Neuengamme and later to the Fuhlsbüttel Gestapo prison in Hamburg. However, most of the men were taken by Reichsbahn to other camps in the German Reich shortly after arriving at Stutthof concentration camp, the majority of them to Buchenwald concentration camp, others to the concentration camps in Bergen-Belsen, Natzweiler, Dachau, Neuengamme, Auschwitz-Monowitz, Sachsenhausen, Dachau-Kaufering, Mauthausen, and Libau (Liepāja)/Latvia.[72] Individual prisoners from Riga, including members of the Nuremberg transport, were part of the inhumane death marches, which left Stutthof concentration camp from January 26, 1945, and the sub-camps heading towards the West.[73] In the subsequent months until surrender, the prisoners who survived the death marches, predominantly women, were, in some cases, liberated by members of the Soviet Army or were left behind by fleeing SS guards.[74]

Prisoner Community and Chances of Survival

The people from the Nuremberg group were increasingly decimated by illness, selection processes, and shooting over time in the various places of detention following deportation to Riga. At least 193 out of the 1,012 deportees were still alive following the '*Aktion Dünamünde*' on March 26, 1942. And at least 135 peo-

---

71 Karin Orth: *Das System der nationalsozialistischen Konzentrationslager. Eine politische Organisationsgeschichtes*, Hamburg: Hamburger Edition, 1999, 155.
72 Scheffler/Schulle, Buch der Erinnerung, volume 1, 42 and volume 2, 533–567.
73 Danuta Drywa: "Stutthof-Stammlager", in Wolfgang Benz and Barbara Distel (eds.): *Der Ort des Terrors. Geschichte der nationalsozialistischen Konzentrationslager*, volume 6, Munich: Beck, 2007, 477–530, here 514. Concerning the 'evacuation routes' see overview map in Jahn, Riga-Kaiserwald, 427.
74 The two prisoners from Bayreuth, Friedel and her daughter Hanneliese Reinauer, had been sent from a sub-camp in Thorn to Bromberg with a group of 40 to 50 people in January 1945. On January 26, 1945, the SS guards left them at night and thus they were liberated. Cf. Aas, Juden in Bayreuth, 85–87.

ple were still living upon registration at Stutthof concentration camp on August 9 and October 1, 1944.[75]

If we consider the mortality rates of the prisoners from the Jungfernhof in the first five months (December 1941 to April 1942), we can see that the majority of the people already died during this short period due to the tough weather conditions, due to freezing, and mass murder (89 percent). A total of around 850 people at Jungfernhof fell victim to the hard winter of 1941/1942 with hunger and temperatures down to minus 32 degrees centigrade. After March 26, 1942, only 450 mostly younger workers remained at Jungfernhof, at least 183 of whom were members of the Nuremberg group.[76]

Of the 3,991 people deported in the transports from Nuremberg, Stuttgart, Vienna, and Hamburg, only 150 of the 'Jungfernhofers' survived, 52 of whom belonged to the Nuremberg group.[77] The survivors from the Nuremberg transport were aged between 6 and 60 years, their average age 30.5 years.[78]

Some people survived because their manual skills as a farmer, gardener, carpenter, chef, metalworker, etc., were needed, others because they were in a good physical condition, others because they had attachment figures, such as mothers, fathers, daughters, or sons, who supported them during their detention in the camp. In the following, I will take a closer look at the extent to which these social ties increased the chances of survival.

---

75 When ascertaining the change in the number of survivors, three key dates were compared: 26.03.1942 ('*Aktion Dünamünde*'), 09.08.1944/01.10.1944 (registration in Stutthof concentration camp), and 08.05.1945 (end of the war).

76 Cf. fig. 1. There were also at least 10 men conscripted to perform forced labor at the Salaspils camp at this time.

77 Gottwaldt/Schulle, Judendeportationen, 115. The 148 survivors mentioned by Gottwaldt and Schulle must be corrected to 150 due to Irene Gerstl and Justin Zeilberger, who have not been recorded as survivors in the literature to date. For Irene Gerstl, see Reiner Strätz: *Biographisches Handbuch*, volume 1, Würzburg: Ferdinand Schöningh, 1989, 191; for Justin Zeilberger, see Hübschmann, Die Deportation von Juden aus Franken nach Riga, 365. – The number of survivors from the Nuremberg transport should be reduced by two people, Ignatz Julius Selling, who was from Stuttgart, and Ludwig Ramsfelder, who was not deported. However, Irene Gerstl and Justin Zeilberger, who had not been recorded as survivors in the literature to date, need to be taken into account. The number of survivors thus remains unchanged.

78 Age on 08.05.1945.

Tab. 1: Chronological presentation of the decimation of the Nuremberg group[79]

Chronology/places of departure	BA	BY	CO	ER	FO	FÜ	NU	WÜ	Transport
Occupants of transport 'Da 32' on November 29, 1941	118	46	25	4	8	94	515	202	1,012
Survivors 'Aktion Dünamünde' on March 26, 1942	21	8	1	4	0	26	86	37	183
Living men on March 26, 1942 at the Salaspils camp	1	3	-	-	-	-	4	2	10
Survivors on March 26, 1942 total	22	11	1	4	0	26	90	39	193
Alive on January 1, 1945	5	4	1	3	0	7	27	24	71
Died between January 1, 1945 and May 8, 1945	2	-	-	-	-	3	7	7	19
Survivors on May 8, 1945	3	4	1	3	0	4	20	17	52

Legend: BA = Bamberg; BY = Bayreuth; CO = Coburg; ER = Erlangen; FO = Forchheim; FÜ = Fürth; NU = Nuremberg; WÜ = Würzburg

Alongside the provision of food and maintaining health, belonging to a social group within the prisoner community was an important factor when it came to the chances of survival. Living under the care of a group could guaranteed support from familiar people. It provided safety and offered a better supply of food and an emotional bond. However, the larger and closer the kinship relationship with other transport participants, the more frequently families and individuals were confronted with the death of their relatives and friends.

Those deported included various family groups, married couples, kinship and friendship groups, and relationships that arose during the detention at Jungfernhof. An investigation into the family and kinship relationships and ties among the transport participants found that at least over three quarters of the deportees (78 percent) were related either directly or by marriage to other people in the transport. The majority were nuclear families (mother, father, children) with 38.8 percent. This was followed by married couples without children with a share of 29 percent. Only around one in five people in the deported group was an individual without any kinship relationship to another transport participant (see fig. 2).[80]

---

[79] Cf. Scheffler/Schulle, Buch der Erinnerung, volume 2, 545–566. The table was created by the author and supplemented with data from his own research. The death data for deportees on 26.03.1942, 01.01.1945, and 08.05.1945 was compared.

[80] My research comprised ascertaining the family and kinship links between all the transport participants. The investigation concerned family groups (father, mother, with children, spouses

These links became fewer and fewer over time and largely existed until at least March 26, 1942 ('*Aktion Dünamünde*'). Following this, very few families still existed among the prisoners. Alongside the family group, partnerships and marriages formed the second most common social tie. Social groups were generally retained, even when changing camps or ghettos.[81] For many people, social ties were helpful and crucial for survival. Of the 135 prisoners from the Nuremberg group who were registered on arrival at Stutthof concentration camp, it can be shown that over half of them (72 people) had a kinship relationship or social tie, i.e. were accompanied by at least one family member. In turn, one in every three of these (25 out of a total of 52 survivors) had survived the Shoah.[82] One reason for the high proportion of survivors with family connections is that this early transport originated directly in the home region of the deportees. In later transports from the home region and between the concentration camps, in contrast, the age structure and the composition of the social groups changed significantly.

At least 265,000 people were deported from the 'Greater Germanic Reich' for extermination, 24,685 of these were transported to Riga. From the 25 transports to Riga in 1941/1942, only 1,082 people survived the Shoah, 609 of these were women and 473 men.

Of the 52 survivors from the Nuremberg group, 38 people emigrated to the USA after liberation, two each to Palestine/Israel and the United Kingdom, and one person to Chile. Justin Zeilberger died a week after his liberation. Only eight people returned to their former home Franconia.

The history of an individual transport and the reconstruction of the paths of persecution for the people who were deported on it represents an often little-noticed chapter in the written history of the Shoah.

The existence of biographical sources for the individual victims is essential in order to allow their many individual fates to be traced and to reconstruct the history of a transport. In the case of the researched transport from Nuremberg, documents have been retained for some of the deportees, while only names

---

with children), siblings, brother-in-law or sister-in-law, and individuals, for whom no kinship relationship with another transport participation could so far be demonstrated.
81 Jahn, Riga-Kaiserwald, 338–339.
82 The development of the number of survivors from the Nuremberg transport at the time of the registrations at Stutthof concentration camp on August 9, 1944, and October 1, 1944, (135 people) was compared with the number of survivors on May 8, 1945. The number of registered prisoners from the Nuremberg group at Stutthof concentration camp was taken from Scheffler/Schulle, Buch der Erinnerung, volume 2, 567.

and places and dates of birth are known for others. An evaluation of the sources makes it possible to identify kinship relationships within the group of deportees.

Tab. 2: Social links of Jews from the transport 'Da 32' on November 29, 1941

Place of departure	Number of deportees	Total kinship relationships with regard to the departure transport		of which family members		of which married couples (number of people)		of which individuals without kinship/family relations	
		Pers.	%	Pers.	%	Pers.	%	Pers.	%
Bamberg	118	89	75.4	36	30.5	42	35.6	28	23.7
Bayreuth	46	43	93.5	19	41.3	18	39.1	3	6.5
Coburg	25	20	80.0	6	24.0	14	56.0	6	24.0
Erlangen	4	4	100	4	100	-	-	-	-
Forchheim	8	5	62.5	3	37.5	2	25.0	3	37.5
Fürth	94	64	68.1	36	38.3	26	27.7	21	22.3
Nuremberg	515	395	76.7	196	38.1	150	29.1	116	22.5
Würzburg	202	174	86.1	96	47.5	42	20.8	38	18.8
Total	1,012	789	78.0	393	38.8	294	29.1	216	21.4

The figures may deviate slightly. The percentages relate to the respective departure transport/total transport.[83]

Most people from this specific Nuremberg transport were not alone on the way to their deaths. They were accompanied by spouses, family members, relatives, acquaintances, and friends. The suffering was made all the more intolerable when whole families were wiped out, grandmother or grandfather, mother or father, mothers with young children, brother or sister, brother-in-law or sister-in-law were killed, such as in the mass graves in Bikernieki forest or other murder sites, and the family members were forced to witness this within close proximity.

It is to be assumed that most camp prisoners would still have died from hunger, freezing, illness, old age, group executions, selection procedures, and due to 'extermination through labor' even if the large-scale 'Aktion Dünamünde' had not

---

83 Cf. ibid., 545–567.

existed. There was no escape to freedom for the prisoners.[84] Their only salvation lay in the collapse of National Socialism and the end of the war.

---

84 Comment in the meeting protocol about the "Final Solution of the Jewish Question" on January 20, 1942 (Wannsee Conference): "Any final remnant that survives will doubtless consist of the most resistant elements. They will have to be dealt with appropriately because otherwise, by natural selection, they would form the germ cell of a new Jewish revival." Quoted in Mark Roseman: *The Wannsee Conference and the Final Solution: A Reconsideration*, New York: Metropolitan Books, 2002, 157–172, here 164–165.

Daan de Leeuw
Mapping Jewish Slave Laborers' Trajectories Through Concentration Camps

Abstract: After victims had been deported from their home countries to concentration and death camps, the Germans transported prisoners selected for forced and slave labor to places where the war industry needed them. The movement of Jewish slave laborers from camp to camp was a central feature of the Holocaust. This paper scrutinizes this phenomenon through the experiences of a group of Dutch Jewish women selected in Sobibor. For most of their time in the Nazi concentration camps, they managed to stay together. Drawing upon wartime and postwar documents in the Arolsen Archives and survivor testimonies, this paper reconstructs and visualizes their pathways through geographic information system (GIS) and cartographic tools. The maps are not mere illustrations; they help us grasp and understand the protagonists' trajectories and experiences. The microhistory case presented in this paper is part of a larger doctoral study which follows over two hundred Dutch Jewish slave laborers through the concentration camp system.

Introduction

A train of 1,105 Dutch Jews in regular passenger coaches left '*Judendurchgangslager*' Westerbork in the Netherlands on March 10, 1943. Travelling for three days via Bremen, Hamburg, Berlin, Breslau, Łódź, and Lublin, it reached its final destination, Sobibor, on Saturday March 13 (see fig. 1).[1] The Germans selected some thirty women and forty men and relocated them to the Lublin camp system for slave labor. All the other deportees were murdered in the gas chambers of that Operation Reinhardt death camp. Most of the approximately seventy slave laborers who had escaped immediate annihilation that day would perish before war's end; only thirteen of them – all women – survived the Holocaust. Arriving in Sobibor marked the end of both the journey and the lives of those killed there; for the selected slave laborers it meant the beginning of continuous suffering, struggle for survival and, for most of them, deferred death.

---

[1] For the train route and details, see Yad Vashem: "Transports to Extinction: Holocaust (Shoah) Deportation Database". Available at: https://deportation.yadvashem.org/index.html?language=en&itemId=6517696&ind=1. Last accessed: 15.03.2021.

ə OpenAccess. © 2023 the author(s), published by De Gruyter. [(cc) BY-NC-ND] This work is licensed under the Creative Commons Attribution-NonCommercial-NoDerivatives 4.0 International License.
https://doi.org/10.1515/9783110746464-020

The March 10 transport was the second to leave the Netherlands for Sobibor. Deportations to the East had started on July 15, 1942, and continued until September 13, 1944, during which 112 trains with some 107,000 Jews left the country.[2] From July 1942 until March 1943, 51 trains with 46,454 people went to Auschwitz-Birkenau.[3] The Germans sent nineteen transports with 34,313 persons to Sobibor between March and July 1943. Only 18 of those deportees survived, including 13 from the March 10 group. Most Jews were killed upon arrival in Auschwitz and Sobibor; some were selected for slave labor. The exact number remains unknown, but the figures suggest that 20,000 to 30,000 of the 107,000 deported Dutch Jews served as slave laborers.[4] Many of them were transferred frequently to various camps. The majority died from the harsh work conditions and unhygienic circumstances in the camps, or were murdered by the guards. Only 5,200 Dutch Jewish deportees survived the war.

The Germans relocated those deportees selected for slave labor from site to site depending on where their labor was needed. Inmates worked as slave laborers for the SS, the Wehrmacht, other Nazi authorities, and private companies. Labor shortages prompted almost every sector of the German war economy to make use of detainees 'supplied' by the SS. Hundreds of sub-camps were erected at extant or newly established production facilities in the final war years. The main camps became hubs of a network of forced and slave labor sites. For the prisoners this meant that they were transferred again and again to places of incarceration where they had to fight anew for a position within the inmate hierarchy.

The movement of Jews from camp to camp was a central feature of the Holocaust. Yet, few studies of Jewish slave labor address this aspect. What happened

---

2 Loe de Jong: *Het Koninkrijk der Nederlanden in de Tweede Wereldoorlog: Deel 8, Gevangenen en gedeporteerden*, The Hague: Martinus Nijhoff, 1978, 708; David Barnouw, Dirk Mulder, and Guus Veenendaal: *De Nederlandse Spoorwegen in oorlogstijd 1939–1945: Rijden voor Vaderland en Vijand*, Zwolle: WBOOKS, 2019, 116–122.

3 German Federal Archives: "Chronology of Deportations from the Netherlands". Available at: https://www.bundesarchiv.de/gedenkbuch/chronology/viewNetherlands.xhtml?lang=en. Last accessed: 15.03.2021. Around 3,400 men aged 15–55 years were taken off the train in Cosel (Koźle), 80 kilometers before Auschwitz-Birkenau, to work for the Schmelt Organization. See Herman van Rens and Annelies Wilms: *Tussenstation Cosel. Joodse mannen uit West-Europa naar dwangarbeiderskampen in Silezië, 1942–1945*, Hilversum: Verloren, 2020.

4 This estimate is based on De Jong, Het Koninkrijk, 708, 888; Jens-Christian Wagner: "Work and Extermination in the Concentration Camps", in Jane Caplan and Nikolaus Wachsmann (eds.): *Concentration Camps in Nazi Germany: The New Histories*, London: Routledge, 2010, 127–148, esp. 154; Debórah Dwork and Robert Jan van Pelt: *Auschwitz: 1270 to the Present*, New York: W.W. Norton & Company, 2008 (revised edition), 347–348.

to inmates after they left a specific site is beyond the scope of most concentration camp studies.[5] The authors cast camps as static sites of labor, which in essence they were. But that is not how the victims experienced their imprisonment. This article will scrutinize the phenomenon of prisoner transferal. It will drill down on the fate of the approximately 30 women of the March 10 transport selected in Sobibor by applying a microhistory lens and following the thirteen survivors' trajectories through the camp system.[6] Survivors' postwar witness statements elucidate the group's experiences. I have been able to identify twenty-eight of the thirty women. To understand these slave laborers' experiences, I will explore who initiated the relocations and what these shifts meant to the deportees. In general, did the Germans select Jews and send them off to another camp, or did Jews exert some form of agency over their site of incarceration? And, very specifically, how did the March 10 group stay together for such a long time?

Documents from the Arolsen Archives, in combination with survivor testimonies, have been crucial to reconstruct the victims' pathways. The convergence of these sources allowed me to trace their movements between camps. In some cases, the exact date of transfer could not be determined but only guesstimated after careful scrutiny of the available records and literature. I collected the spatial data obtained from the archival documents in a database, which I used to create maps with a geographic information system (GIS) and cartographic tools. A similar approach can be found in historian Henning Borggräfe's re-

---

[5] See, for example, Felicja Karay: *Death Comes in Yellow: Skarżysko-Kamienna Slave Labor Camp*, Amsterdam: Harwood Academic Publishers, 1996; Wolf Gruner: *Jewish Forced Labor under the Nazis: Economic Needs and Racial Aims 1938–1944*, Cambridge: Cambridge University Press, 2006; Bella Gutterman: *A Narrow Bridge to Life: Jewish Forced Labor and Survival in the Gross-Rosen Camp System, 1940–1945*, New York: Berghahn Books, 2008; Christopher Browning: *Remembering Survival: Inside a Nazi Slave-Labor Camp*, New York: W.W. Norton & Company, 2010; Marc Buggeln: *Slave Labor in Nazi Concentration Camps*, Oxford: Oxford University Press, 2014.

[6] Survivors' experiences have been discussed briefly in Jules Schelvis: *Sobibor: A History of a Nazi Death Camp*, London: Bloomsbury, 2007, 128–130. Schelvis erred on some points: "Sophie van Praag" should have been Debora van Praag; Jetje Veterman did not end up in Theresienstadt but stayed behind in Bergen-Belsen and was liberated there; Bertha and Debora van Praag were part of the group sent to Trawniki as well; Trawniki was evacuated by mid-May 1944 and not in early June 1944; the evacuees of Lublin-Majdanek were put on trains in Ćmielów instead of Chmielów (the latter being another Polish village on the other side of the Vistula river); one and not all four Dutch women died in Bliżyn due to tuberculosis; Bertha and Celine Ensel and Sientje Veterman did not travel via Buchenwald to Lippstadt but were brought there directly from Auschwitz-Birkenau.

search.⁷ Borggräfe followed a group of 297 inmates on a macro level using GIS. I use similar techniques here, yet I have included survivor testimonies to scrutinize prisoner relocation on a micro level. These witness statements are key to understanding why deportees were transferred and how they experienced these shifts. The maps in this article serve a more robust function than mere illustration. Following historian Richard White's argument, they are part of the research process itself as they allow both the author and the audience to comprehend the spatial extent of this history.⁸ The geovisualizations show the relocations of the group of women from site to site and as dispersed over time. Thus, the interplay between the maps, survivor testimonies, and archival material offers a new and more nuanced lens on the experiences of these Jewish slave laborers.

Deportation from the Netherlands to German-Occupied Poland

The Germans assembled the majority of Dutch Jews in Westerbork transit camp before deporting them to concentration and annihilation camps in the Reich and in occupied Poland. They concealed their true intentions and made the Jews believe they were to be sent to labor camps in the East. Camp commandant SS-Obersturmführer Albert Gemmeker ordered the Jewish Council in Westerbork to assist with the preparations for each deportation. Among other obligations, Jewish Council members had to compile the transport list and announce names the evening prior to departure. On the day itself, it fell to the Jewish Council to help with the logistics of getting the targeted people aboard the train and provide food parcels to the deportees.⁹ Most people on the 10 March transport

---

7 Henning Borggräfe: "Die Rekonstruktion von Verfolgungswegen im NS-Terrorsystem. Eine Fallstudie zu Opfern der Aktion 'Arbeitsscheu Reich'", in Henning Borggräfe (ed.): *Freilegungen: Wege, Orte, und Räume der NS-Verfolgung*, Göttingen: Wallstein, 2016, 56–82.
8 Richard White: "What is Spatial History?", in *Stanford University Spatial History Project, Spatial History Lab*, Working Paper, 2010, 1–6. Available at: https://web.stanford.edu/group/spatialhistory/media/images/publication/what%20is%20spatial%20history%20pub%20020110.pdf. Last accessed: 26.07.2021.
9 Cato Polak, 250d Kampen en Gevangenissen buiten Nederland, inventory 759, NIOD Institute for War, Holocaust, and Genocide Studies, Amsterdam; Mirjam Blits: *Auschwitz 13917: Hoe ik de Duitse concentratiekampen overleefde*, Amsterdam: Elsevier, 1961, 13. Blits's book is an adaption of her testimony written shortly after she returned to the Netherlands. The events described in both sources are the same, yet in the book, all persons have been assigned pseudonyms and the text has been edited for publication. For the original testimony manuscript, see Mirjam Penha-Blits, NIOD 250d, inventory 750.

had been in Westerbork for only a few days or weeks. As they boarded the train, the sisters Debora (born March 6, 1926) and Bertha (born May 9, 1928) van Praag were warned by Jewish aides not to volunteer for anything when incarcerated in the camps. They were told to do only what the Germans told them to do as they would not know what they were actually volunteering for.[10] It is unclear whether the helpers gave this advice to the sisters alone or whether it was a general instruction communicated to all deportees. Other testimonies do not provide any indication of such warning. After the transport left Westerbork, Gemmeker sent a telex message to various German authorities, including the Reichssicherheitshauptamt Department IV B 4 in Berlin and SS- und Polizeiführer in Lublin, Odilo Globocnik, notifying them about the departure and estimated time of arrival. Globocnik passed on this information to the commandant of Sobibor.[11]

The train wagons deployed on 10 March were in bad shape, yet the windows allowed the deportees to look outside which made the journey somewhat bearable. Still, people feared what awaited them.[12] Mirjam Blits (born June 5, 1916) was deported together with her husband Elias Penha (born January 24, 1912). They met the couple Menno (born April 13, 1909) and Annie (born September 29, 1917) Troostwijk in their coach. Menno found Blits a brave woman and asked her to look after Annie; Blits agreed and asked him to look after her husband in return. The train halted in Breslau and the deportees saw Jewish slave laborers for the first time, as the latter were working on the railway tracks. Blits looked out the window hoping to see her father who had been deported in November 1942, and she shouted his name. She grew upset when she did not see him, and Penha calmed her down by saying that her father, an upholsterer, was surely working in an airplane factory. As they moved on, Blits and others in the wagon threw food to the Jews laboring outside. The SS guards responded by firing at the laborers and the train.[13] This was the first time the Dutch Jews experienced the deadly violence that awaited them.

Arriving in Sobibor, the deportees were beaten out of the train. They had no idea where they were. The Germans needed 25 to 30 women as slave laborers. The SS asked nurses, seamstresses, washers, and household maids to identify themselves. Only six stood forward, and an SS man randomly chose another

---

10 Debora Sessler-van Praag, interview 25384, segment 27, Visual History Archive (VHA), USC Shoah Foundation, 1995. Last accessed: 15.01.2020.
11 Schelvis, Sobibor, 50–51.
12 Blits, Auschwitz, 11–12; Polak, NIOD 250d, inventory 759; Debora Sessler-van Praag, interview 52693, segments 101–102, VHA, 1995. Last accessed: 16.01.2020.
13 Blits, Auschwitz, 11–13.

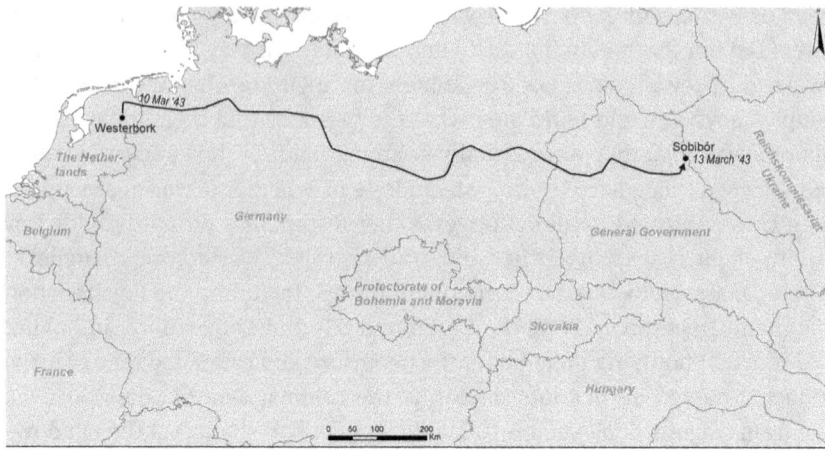

Fig. 1: This map shows the route of the March 10, 1943, deportation train travelling from Westerbork via Bremen, Hamburg, Berlin, Breslau, Łódź, and Lublin to Sobibór. Borders as of February 28, 1943. Basemap: Michael De Groot: *Building the New Order: 1938–1945*, Stanford University: Spatial History Lab, 2010. Copyright Daan de Leeuw.

20 or so, almost all young women aged 15 to 40.[14] When Blits was selected but Troostwijk was not, Blits boldly approached the SS man and asked if Troostwijk could join the group as well. He allowed her to do so. Blits thus intervened directly in the drafting process, managed to keep her new friend close and, even though unaware of it at the time, saved Troostwijk from imminent death. The

---

14 A few women in their forties were selected as well, including Henderiene den Arend-van der Reis (b. 19.06.1896), Auguste Berliner (b. 28.09.1901), and Hilde Beate Blumendal (b. 22.09.1902). See Penha-Blits, NIOD 250d, inventory 750, 3; Blits, Auschwitz, 17; Surry Polak and Suze Polak, NIOD 250d, inventory 761; Transport List 10 March 1943, 804 Onderzoek–Vernietigingskamp Sobibor, inventory 55, NIOD, Amsterdam; List Camp Majdanek-Lublin by the American Jewish Joint Distribution Committee (AJDC), Paris, 1.1.23.1/1205094–1205097/ITS Digital Archive, Arolsen Archives; List 138 Lublin Wlodowa by the AJDC, Paris, 1.1.23.1/1205106–1205109/ITS Digital Archive, Arolsen Archives. See further individuals' entries at Joods Monument website. Available at: https://www.joodsmonument.nl/. Last accessed: 01.12.2021. The AJDC lists are early postwar documents and cannot be verified as completely accurate. Some ITS index cards refer to them as "Doc[uments] of doubtful value" (e.g., 0.1/48464342 and 97962884/ITS Digital Archive, Arolsen Archives). Still, these documents are among the few sources that include names of Dutch Jews selected in Sobibor for slave labor. Names that appear on the lists and referred to in this article have been cross-checked with survivor testimonies, the 10 March 1943 transport list, the Amsterdam Jewish Council index cards, and individuals' entries at the Joods Monument.

SS also selected some 40 men: doctors and nurses. The entire selection process took a few hours and then the group of men and women was sent to camp Lublin-Majdanek on the same train with which they had come. Anxious about what lay ahead, the deportees hardly spoke with one another.[15]

In Lublin, the women were quartered in a barrack, and these strangers had a moment together for the first time. Blits recalled that she spoke to the group:

> The SS disappeared and finally we were alone. I felt called to address the girls and I asked for a moment of silence. I remember having said something along these lines: Girls, I am almost one of the oldest, 26 years old and married, and actually I am just a greenhorn like you all are, but perhaps, as I come from a working-class family and having been raised as a socialist, I know something about comradeship. I do not know you, I do not know anything about you or your social relationships, but let us learn to tolerate each other here, not to be angry or fight over nothing. Girls, we need each other badly, be strong and steadfast in your feelings towards each other. Help each other to endure this life, that is being made unbearable, bearable. Girls, give each other a hand, let good intentions inspire you, because where there is a will, there is a way.[16]

Blits reported that she received much support immediately. The other survivors did not mention this speech in their postwar witness statements. Perhaps Blits remembered her plea so vividly as she was the one who had spoken. Still, the group managed to stay together for a long time, and Blits's extensive testimony records countless examples of group solidarity such as food sharing and mutual protection in fights with other inmates.[17]

Jewish Slave Labor in the Midst of Genocide

The following day, March 14, 1943, the group of 30 women was brought by foot from Lublin-Majdanek to Lublin Alter Flughafen (Old Airfield), a sub-camp where goods from murdered Jews were collected, sorted, and shipped to Germa-

---

15 Polak, NIOD 250d, inventory 759; Sophia Huisman, NIOD 250d, inventory 592; Judith Eliazar and Bertha Ensel, NIOD 250d, inventory 510; Polak and Polak, NIOD 250d, inventory 761; Jetje Veterman, NIOD 250d, inventory 906; Sessler-van Praag, VHA 25384, segment 15; Sessler-van Praag, VHA 52693, segments 113–114; Blits, Auschwitz, 15–16.
16 Penha-Blits, NIOD 250d, inventory 750, 3–4. Cf. Blits, Auschwitz, 20. Translation by the author.
17 For example Blits, Auschwitz, 25–27, 49, 66; Mirjam Mullaart-Blits, interview 21341, segments 27–28, VHA, 1996. Last accessed: 04.01.2021.

ny.¹⁸ Here the Dutch women learned about the mass killing of Jews in gas chambers. Until then they had been unaware of what was about to happen to the people who had remained in Sobibor. They also met female Polish Jewish prisoners for the first time. Cultural, religious, and linguistic barriers led to animosity between them. The Dutch Jews felt that the Polish Jews held them in contempt because they were not Orthodox and did not speak Yiddish. This spurred the March 10 group to bond with and support each other. Throughout their time in the camps, they fought physically with Polish Jewish women frequently.¹⁹ This was not their only problem. Much worse: The conditions in Lublin Alter Flughafen were harsh and at least four Dutch women died of disease, violence from the guards, or were sent to the gas chambers. Henderiene den Arend-van der Reis, Hilde Beate Blumendal, and Marga Cohen (born September 2, 1909) were selected by the SS and murdered in the gas chambers of Lublin-Majdanek. Sophia Cohen (born March 10, 1915) was raped by an SS man and subsequently gassed as well.²⁰

The group split up half a year later, when the Germans selected six seamstresses in Lublin Alter Flughafen, including survivors Celine Ensel (born April 9, 1926) and Sophie Verduin (born April 30, 1926), and forcibly transported them (in late September 1943) to the Lublin-Majdanek sub-camp of Bliżyn, with its armaments factory and stone quarry (see fig. 2). The victims were powerless with regard to the transfer; the SS forcibly relocated them to another site where their labor was needed. The Dutch women were assigned to a textile workshop. The camp population comprised 5,000 to 6,000 Polish Jews; the six women were the only Dutch people there. Grim conditions, poor hygiene, and SS terror led to hundreds of dead prisoners. Hester Fresco (born June 19, 1926) and Lotje Stad (born May 30, 1914) died from exhaustion, Lena Verduin (born Oc-

---

18 Eliazar and Ensel, NIOD 250d, inventory 510; Huisman, NIOD 250d, inventory 592; Polak, NIOD 250d, inventory 759; Penha-Blits, NIOD 250d, inventory 750; Sessler-van Praag, VHA 25384, segments 16–18.
19 Penha-Blits, NIOD 250d, inventory 750, 4–5; Blits, Auschwitz, 22–26; Polak and Polak, NIOD 250d, inventory 761; Sessler-van Praag, VHA 25384, segments 16–20.
20 Penha-Blits, NIOD 250d, inventory 750, 6–7; Blits, Auschwitz, 30–31, 40–42; Polak and Polak, NIOD 250d, inventory 761; Sophia Engelsman-Huisman, interview 11233, segments 32–34, VHA, 1996. Last accessed: 25.06.2021. Suze and Sury Polak also referred to Juurtje van Praag and "Miss Wurms" who had died in Lublin Alter Flughafen. I have been unable to identify them in the other testimonies, nor on the transport list or AJDC lists. Miss Wurms could have been Clara Wurms-Hamburg (b. 21.06.1880) or Hendrika Canes-Wurms (b. 08.04.1882), mentioned on the transport list, however, the Joods Monument website states that both women were murdered in Sobibor on 13 March 1943.

tober 6, 1927) of typhus, and Charlotte Zeehandelaar-Andriesse (born September 23, 1917) perished from tuberculosis.[21]

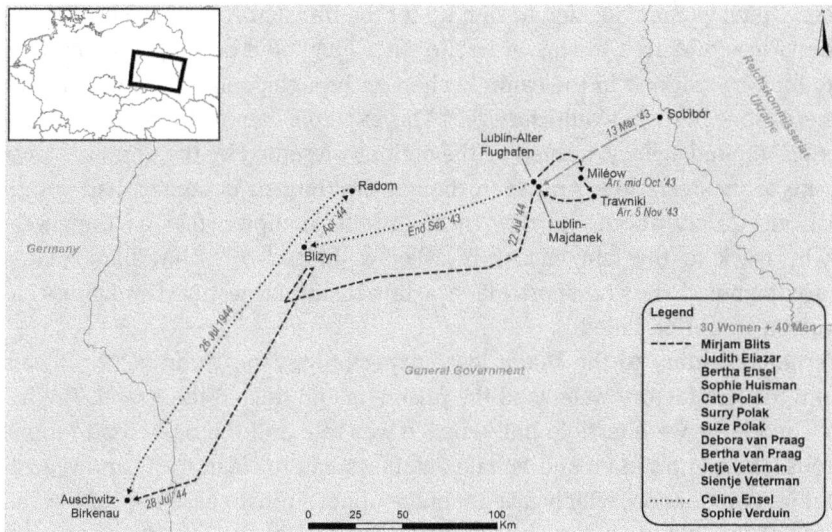

Fig. 2: This map illustrates how the group of Dutch women was transferred through the concentration camp system between March 1943 and July 1944. Note how a large section of the group stayed together until the summer of 1944. The indicated transfer from Lublin-Majdanek to Auschwitz-Birkenau follows the exact route of the death march (see also fig. 3 in this article). Borders as of December 31, 1943. Basemap: Michael De Groot: *Building the New Order: 1938–1945*, Stanford University: Spatial History Lab, 2010. Copyright Daan de Leeuw.

In mid-October, the women of the original group remaining in Lublin Alter Flughafen were given a chance to escape the horrible conditions of that site when the SS sought 40 to 50 volunteers to work in a jam factory at another camp.[22] The women weighed their options. The sisters van Praag remembered the aides' counsel in Westerbork not to volunteer for jobs. Debora van Praag re-

---

21 Sophie Verduin, NIOD 250d, inventory 904; Eliazar and Ensel, NIOD 250d, inventory 510, 4; Polak, NIOD 250d, inventory 759; Martin Dean: "Bliżyn", in Geoffrey P. Megargee (ed.): *Encyclopedia of Camps and Ghettos, 1933–1945*, volume I, part B, Bloomington, Indiana: Indiana University Press, 2009, 880–882.
22 Correspondence file Judith Eliazar, 6.3.3.2/101230678–101230683/ITS Digital Archive, Arolsen Archives; Huisman, NIOD 250d, inventory 592. Correspondence file Judith Eliazar states "mid-Oct" as arrival date in Milejów and 5 November as departure date. Huisman said the group was in Milejów for 18 days. Hence the date should have been on or around 18 October 1943.

called: "My sister said, 'We are not going to volunteer, are we?' And I said, 'Well Bep [Bertha], we are dying here, we might as well volunteer. I am dying here, we are going to be dead in no time, I am going to volunteer.' So, we volunteered".[23] Thirteen Dutch women decided to sign up for the transfer. A few March 10 transport deportees preferred to stay in Lublin Alter Flughafen because they had access to food by working in the camp kitchen or through connections with Polish prisoners. None of them would survive.[24] This example demonstrates an instance of victims' limited agency, framed by the options presented by the Germans, over their site of incarceration. And even though the thirteen detainees had volunteered, uncertainty about the new location still prompted fear as they were taken by truck to the jam factory in Milejów. Indeed, the Ukrainian guards who accompanied the transport made a throat-slitting gesture, implying that the women would be killed.[25]

Perhaps contrary to the Dutch Jews' expectations, the Wehrmacht officials who ran the jam factory welcomed the prisoners and treated them well. The hygienic conditions were terrible but violence was rare and the daily food rations generous. The camp's male and female detainees had to clean fruits and vegetables for jam production, which gave them the opportunity to eat the peels secretly. Blits felt she had made the right decision. The Dutch group stayed for almost three weeks in Milejów. It was just during this time that Heinrich Himmler, spooked by the Jewish uprisings in Warsaw, Białystok, Vilna, Treblinka, and Sobibor, decided upon the so-called Operation Harvest Festival in the Lublin district. Some 42,000 Jews remaining in the region, most of them camp slave laborers, were murdered on November 3 and 4, 1943. The prisoners in Milejów were spared. The Germans kept these inmates alive as their labor was considered

---

23 Sessler-van Praag, VHA 25384, segment 27. Sophia Huisman said in her postwar testimony that her friend Cato Polak was also reluctant to volunteer as Polak was afraid what awaited her in the new camp. In the end, both women decided to volunteer too. See Engelsman-Huisman, VHA 11233, segments 40–41.
24 Flora Blok (b. 07.08.1913) and Fanny Landsman (b. 01.11.1924) decided to remain in Lublin Alter Flughafen. See Penha-Blits, NIOD 250d, inventory 750, 9–10; Blits, Auschwitz, 46. Auguste Berliner, Naatje Roodveldt-Moffie (b. 07.01.1916), and Judith Swaab (b. 28.12.1924) must have stayed there too. They most likely died in Lublin Alter Flughafen before or during Operation Harvest Festival (3–4 November 1943). See AJDC, Paris, List Camp Majdanek-Lublin, Arolsen Archives; AJDC, Paris List 138 Lublin Wlodowa, Arolsen Archives; Transport List 10 March 1943, NIOD 804, 55; Individuals' Entries on Joods Monument.
25 Penha-Blits, NIOD 250d, inventory 750, 9–10; Blits, Auschwitz, 46; Huisman, NIOD 250d, inventory 592; Polak, NIOD 250d, inventory 759; Sessler-van Praag, VHA 25384, segments 27–30; Sessler-van Praag, VHA 52693, segments 140–146.

indispensable to finish the gruesome action, and they were sent to Trawniki to do so the day after the massacre.²⁶

Thousands of Jews had been killed in Trawniki during Operation Harvest Festival. Jewish men brought in from Milejów were forced to burn bodies for two weeks after which they themselves were executed. The Jewish women had to extract gold teeth and sort the plundered goods and possessions, and sometimes assist with burning bodies. After the men were murdered, around 40 women prisoners remained in the camp for six months to sort the looted goods of the Jews killed in Trawniki and the Lublin district. Despite their predecessors' gruesome fate, incarceration in the camp allowed the Dutch women to recuperate, as they could acquire better clothes and food and the guards were relatively nonviolent. Still, Troostwijk contracted tuberculosis and died during this time. By mid-May 1944, with the advance of the Red Army, the Germans forcibly relocated the prisoners to Lublin-Majdanek. The Dutch Jews were afraid they would be killed there.²⁷

The women were not gassed. They were put to work in the camp laundry, sewing shop, and farmland. As the Red Army was advancing toward Lublin, the SS evacuated the site on July 22, 1944, and the victims were involuntarily uprooted once more. Before the 1,000 to 1,200 inmates marched westward in the direction of Auschwitz (see fig. 3), escorted by SS men and Wehrmacht soldiers, they saw the gas chambers and crematoria blown up. Soviet airplanes flew over the marching column and fired at it. The Germans fell on the ground and the prisoners had to protect their guards with their own bodies by laying over them. According to Blits, the Red Army pilots flew off when they were close enough to identify the striped prisoner uniforms. In the confusion of the attack, many lost their blankets, shoes, and food. The prisoners had to walk for days with hardly any rest. Klaartje Gompertz (born April 14, 1905) was shot by the guards because she was no longer able to move. Debora van Praag was exhausted too but her sister Bertha pushed her to continue. One day in the town Kraśnik,

---

26 Correspondence file Judith Eliazar, Arolsen Archives; Blits, Auschwitz, 46–47; Eliazar and Ensel, NIOD 250d, inventory 510; Huisman, NIOD 250d, inventory 592; Polak, NIOD 250d, inventory 759; Polak and Polak, NIOD 250d, inventory 761.
27 Sessler-van Praag, VHA 25384, segments 28–32; Eliazar and Ensel, NIOD 250d, inventory 510; Huisman, NIOD 250d, inventory 592; Penha-Blits, NIOD 250d, inventory 750, 10–34; Polak, NIOD 250d, inventory 759; Polak and Polak, NIOD 250d, inventory 761; Veterman, NIOD 250d, inventory 906; Blits, Auschwitz, 50–152; Peter Black: "Trawniki", in Megargee, Encyclopedia of Camps and Ghettos, volume I, part B, 893–897. The transfer date is based on Blits and Black. The other sources referenced – as well as the correspondence file on Judith Eliazar in the Arolsen Archives – claim dates in June and July 1944, but this is impossible as Trawniki was closed in May 1944.

the Germans chose the attic of a brick factory as a shelter for the night, right above the ovens below, so the prisoners could dry up after marching in the rain. The space became unbearably hot and those without shoes burned their feet. The Germans allowed the German inmates, Christian Poles, and Soviet POWs to leave the attic. The SS men wanted to set the building afire with the Jewish prisoners inside, but (allegedly) the Wehrmacht soldiers and privileged evacuees managed to change their minds. For some reason, the temperature in the attic dropped again, and the following day the death march continued. On the morning of the fifth day, the prisoners crossed the Vistula and shortly thereafter were loaded onto open train wagons in Ćmielów. The transport reached Auschwitz-Birkenau the following day, July 28. Only 452 men and 156 women had survived the march, including 11 Dutch women of the March 10 transport.[28]

It remains unclear whether the Germans intended to kill the Majdanek prisoners in Auschwitz. Three survivors asserted that an Oberfeldwebel had given the order not to murder them, apparently because they had protected the German soldiers and SS men when the Soviet fighter jets had attacked. In the event, the entire Majdanek group was detailed to slave labor in Birkenau.[29] The newly arrived prisoners were quarantined for three weeks, and then the 11 Dutch women were assigned to the '*Scheissekommando*'. They and 20 female Polish Jews had to pull a horse cart with an excrements tank on top to a site beyond the camp enclosure and emptied the container there.[30]

---

28 Penha-Blits, NIOD 250d, inventory 750, 35–46; Blits, Auschwitz, 153–201; Eliazar and Ensel, NIOD 250d, inventory 510; Huisman, NIOD 250d, inventory 592; Polak, NIOD 250d, inventory 759; Polak and Polak, NIOD 250d, inventory 761; Veterman, NIOD 250d, inventory 906; Sessler-van Praag, VHA 25384, segments 36–38; Sessler-van Praag, VHA 52693, segments 193–205; "Map Death March Lublin", in *Death Marches: Routes and Distances*, volume II, UNRRA Central Tracing Bureau, 28.05.1946, 5.3.3/84619474/ITS Digital Archive, Arolsen Archives; Schelvis, Sobibor, 130; Daniel Blatman: *The Death Marches: The Final Phase of Nazi Genocide*, Cambridge, MA: Belknap Press of Harvard University Press, 2011, 58; Elissa Mailänder: *Female SS Guards and Workaday Violence: The Majdanek Concentration Camp, 1942–1944*, East Lansing: Michigan State University Press, 2015, 35. According to Blits, Eliazar and Ensel, Huisman, and Cato Polak, and correspondence file Judith Eliazar (Arolsen Archives), the death march took place in August, but this is impossible because Lublin-Majdanek was evacuated on 22 July 1944.
29 Blits, Auschwitz, 205–206; Polak and Polak, NIOD 250d, inventory 761. See also Sessler-van Praag, VHA 52693, segments 230–231. According to Cato Polak (NIOD 250d, inventory 759) and the sisters Surry and Suze Polak, camp commandant SS-Hauptsturmführer Josef Kramer was present at the evacuees' acceptance into the camp. This implies that he must have approved the decision not to murder the Lublin-Majdanek evacuees.
30 Penha-Blits, NIOD 250d, inventory 750, 49–52; Blits, Auschwitz, 214, 220–227; Eliazar and Ensel, NIOD 250d, inventory 510; Huisman, NIOD 250d, inventory 592; Polak, NIOD 250d, inventory 759; Polak and Polak, NIOD 250d, inventory 761. Cato Polak and the sisters Surry and Suze

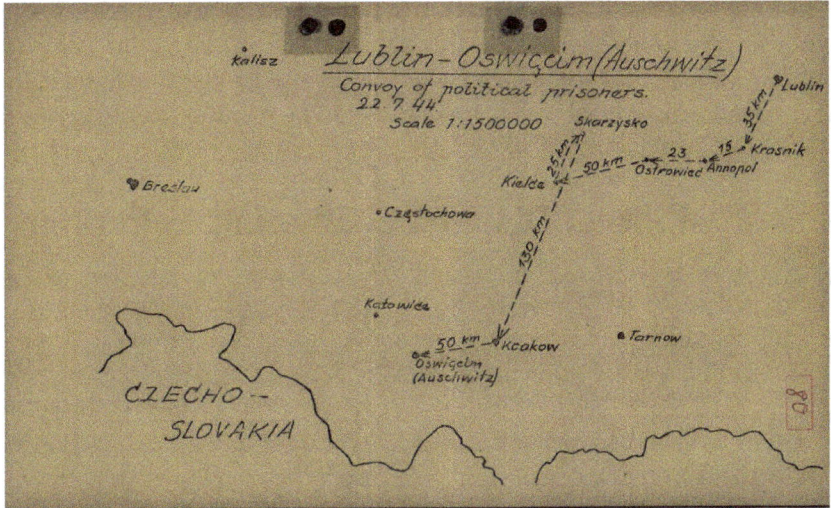

Fig. 3: UNRRA map of the death march from Lublin to Auschwitz July 22, 1944. This early postwar map held by the Arolsen Archives has been made by the United Nations Relief and Rehabilitation Administration's (UNRRA) Central Tracing Bureau (CTB) and was published in *Death Marches: Routes and Distances* in May 1946. In addition to providing relief and support to World War Two refugees and Displaced Persons, UNRRA also investigated the fate of the deceased victims and the location of mass graves. Establishing the exact routes of death marches supported this action. UNRRA map, 5.3.3/84619474/ITS Digital Archive, Arolsen Archives.

The group met other Dutch prisoners in Auschwitz-Birkenau, including Celine Ensel and Sophie Verduin, whom they had last seen in Lublin Alter Flughafen a year earlier.[31] From the six Dutch women sent to Bliżyn only Ensel and Verduin had survived. The Germans had brought them by lorry to Radom in April 1944, where they worked in agriculture until that incarceration site was evacuated on July 26. The prisoners were relocated to Auschwitz-Birkenau by trucks and train (see fig. 2). Verduin's postwar testimony does not indicate who decided on these transfers, but it is almost certain the Germans initiated them in re-

---

Polak mentioned that they worked in the grass sods commando before being assigned to the 'shit commando'. The other testimonies do not mention this.

31 Penha-Blits, NIOD 250d, inventory 750, 49–56; Blits, Auschwitz, 204–224; Eliazar and Ensel, NIOD 250d, inventory 510; Huisman, NIOD 250d, inventory 592; Polak, NIOD 250d, inventory 759; Polak and Polak, NIOD 250d, inventory 761; Veterman, NIOD 250d, inventory 906.

sponse to the Soviet military advances.³² One day Verduin and Ensel saw the other women in another section of Auschwitz-Birkenau. They were not allowed to meet each other, but sisters Bertha (born May 23, 1924) and Celine Ensel managed to speak to each other from afar. They would be reunited later.³³

The Final Months: Dispersal, Ongoing Suffering, and Survival

Continuous selections and relocation transports fractured the group in Auschwitz-Birkenau into smaller segments. And as the German military situation worsened in fall 1944, the SS began to evacuate Auschwitz. The gassings in Birkenau stopped, the gas chambers were dismantled, and tens of thousands of prisoners were transported to concentration camps in central Germany to work in the armaments industry.³⁴ During a selection in early November, SS doctor Josef Mengele found most March 10 deportees sufficiently fit to be relocated to the West. Some were ordered to stay in Auschwitz: Sientje Veterman (born April 17, 1922) and Debora van Praag had scabies, and Bertha van Praag pleurisy and typhus. Bertha and Celine Ensel remained there too. The forced separation caused much despair. The women bound for Germany thought their friends would be gassed.³⁵ However, they were not: the Ensel sisters and Veterman were transported to Lippstadt later that month,³⁶ Bertha van Praag was brought to the *Revier* (the camp hospital), and her sister Debora continued working as a slave laborer, no longer in the '*Scheissekommando*' but in a textile workshop. Four months later she fell ill and was taken to the *Revier*, too. Debora happened to be placed

---

32 Verduin, NIOD 250d, inventory 904; Evelyn Zegenhagen: "Radom [aka Radom (Szkolna Street)]", in Megargee, Encyclopedia of Camps and Ghettos, volume I, part B, 892–893. Verduin stated in her testimony that she stayed "until the spring" in Bliżyn and remained in Radom for three months. Radom was evacuated on 26 July 1944, so Verduin and Ensel must have been transferred to Radom in April 1944.
33 Eliazar and Ensel, NIOD 250d, inventory 510; Huisman, NIOD 250d, inventory 592.
34 Nikolaus Wachsmann: *KL: A History of the Nazi Concentration Camps*, New York: Farrar, Straus and Giroux, 2015, 553.
35 Penha-Blits, NIOD 250d, inventory 750, 55–56; Blits, Auschwitz, 236–240; Huisman, NIOD 250d, inventory 592; Veterman, NIOD 250d, inventory 906. Veterman referred to Josef Mengele as the one who conducted the selection. Mengele is often adduced by survivors, as he became such an infamous figure in later postwar decades. Still, Veterman's reference can be regarded as trustworthy because at the time of her witness statement in August 1947 Mengele was still an (almost) unknown figure in the public discourse about Auschwitz-Birkenau and the Holocaust.
36 See footnote 47.

in the bed right next to Bertha. The van Praag sisters were thus reunited and liberated in the hospital shortly thereafter, on January 27, 1945.[37]

The prisoners deemed fit in the early November selection were loaded onto a train. The guards gave them an exceptionally large food ration consisting of a loaf of bread, a big chunk of butter, and a thick slice of sausage. This prompted the Jewish slave laborers to believe they would not be killed because they were needed for the war effort: a correct assessment. The train left Auschwitz-Birkenau in the evening and took three nights and three days to reach North Germany (see fig. 4).[38]

Arriving in Celle, the prisoners were forced to walk for a few hours through the forest and moorland to Bergen-Belsen. The women were disillusioned when they saw the dreadful conditions of the camp. Bergen-Belsen had been set up as a detention site to hold privileged Jews to exchange with the Allies for German captives or to initiate peace negotiations. Its function changed in spring 1944 when the SS began to dump inmates from other camps no longer able to work into Bergen-Belsen, officially to recuperate. Without medical care, the debilitated laborers died soon after arrival. In addition, a tent camp was built to function as a transit camp for evacuated female Jews from Auschwitz-Birkenau in fall 1944. These prisoners were assigned to work in the German armaments industry. Overpopulated and in a deplorable state, Bergen-Belsen became a "de facto death camp".[39]

The Dutch women were assigned to a tent, which was destroyed by a storm on the third day. The detainees slept in the open air for two cold November nights until they were quartered in a barrack. The survivors recalled the lack

---

37 Sessler-van Praag, VHA 25384, segments 39–40; Sessler-van Praag, VHA 52693, segment 217; List of Dutch Liberated at Auschwitz, 3.1.1.3/78786333–78786334/ITS Digital Archive, Arolsen Archives.
38 Penha-Blits, NIOD 250d, inventory 750, 55–56; Blits, Auschwitz, 241–243; Eliazar and Ensel, NIOD 250d, inventory 510; correspondence file Mirjam Blits, 6.3.3.2/104382807–104382818/ITS Digital Archive, Arolsen Archives; correspondence file Judith Eliazar, Arolsen Archives. The transfer most likely took place on 4–7 November 1944. Correspondence file Mirjam Blits states that she was brought to Bergen-Belsen "Anfang November 1944" (at the beginning of November). Blits's and Eliazar's correspondence files note that they were relocated to Fallersleben on 17 November 1944. In her testimony, Eliazar recalled she was in Bergen-Belsen for ten days. As the transport lasted three days and nights, it is most likely that they arrived in Bergen-Belsen on 7 November, and departed from Auschwitz-Birkenau on 4 November.
39 Thomas Rahe: "Bergen-Belsen Main Camp", in Megargee, Encyclopedia of Camps and Ghettos, volume I, part A, 278–281.

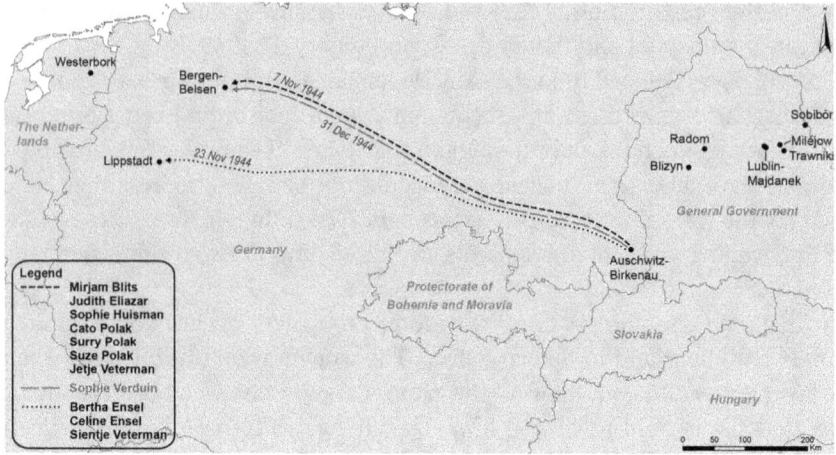

Fig. 4: In the fall of 1944, the March 10 group dispersed due to selections and relocation transports. This map tracks the deportees' movements from August 1944 until the end of that year. Borders as of October 31, 1944. Basemap: Michael De Groot: *Building the New Order: 1938–1945*, Stanford University: Spatial History Lab, 2010. Copyright Daan de Leeuw.

of food, abominable hygienic conditions, and insufficient medical care in the camp which resulted in rampant disease and a staggering number of deaths.[40]

The women met other Dutch Jewish slave laborers in Bergen-Belsen, including one referred to as Julia Wijnrothe.[41] The guards sent her to another incarceration site as a punishment for talking across the barbed fence to her boyfriend who was held in another section of the camp. Although they disciplined her, the guards allowed Wijnrothe to bring three women with her; she asked Blits whom she deemed very brave. Blits agreed and voluntarily chose to join her, as did Judith Eliazar (born December 3, 1914). Blits recalled that she had already decided to get out of Bergen-Belsen when the opportunity would present itself. She felt that the harsh conditions of the camp drained her of all her strength and her wish to survive. Her desperation stripped her of her solidarity with the other

---

40 Penha-Blits, NIOD 250d, inventory 750, 56–60; Blits, Auschwitz, 244–252; Polak, NIOD 250d, inventory 759; Polak and Polak, NIOD 250d, inventory 761.
41 Penha-Blits, NIOD 250d, inventory 750, 60; Blits, Auschwitz, 256–263; Eliazar and Ensel, NIOD 250d, inventory 510. The name Julia Wijnrothe does not appear on the Westerbork transport lists, the Jewish Council index card system, and the Vught prisoner registration forms. I have been unable to determine her identity. See 1.1.46.1 List Material Westerbork, 1.2.4.2 Index Cards from the 'Judenrat' ('Jewish Council') File in Amsterdam, 1.1.12.1 List Material Herzogenbusch/ITS Digital Archive, Arolsen Archives.

Dutch Sobibor women; they were no longer on her mind when she chose to accompany Wijnrothe, Blits admitted. The others wanted to come too but they were not allowed to do so. As this instance demonstrates, prisoner agency and powerlessness could sometimes exist in the same moment.[42]

After ten days in Bergen-Belsen, the remainder of the March 10 transport group was thus fragmented once more (see fig. 5). Blits and Eliazar were taken by cattle car to Fallersleben (*Volkswagenwerke*) on November 17, 1944, together with Wijnrothe, another Dutch woman, Jeanette de Vries-Blits (born March 20, 1910), whom Blits had met in Auschwitz-Birkenau, and 46 Hungarian Jewish women. In this Neuengamme sub-camp, the inmates worked in an armaments factory.[43] The conditions were relatively good, although the food portions grew smaller as the Allies approached. The camp was evacuated on April 8, 1945, and 1,600 women were shipped by train to Salzwedel. Even though the two camps were rather close to each other, the journey in cattle cars took over a day. The locked wagons without windows blocked all light and air; conditions inside Blits's and Eliazar's car were so horrible that five women were asphyxiated from the heat and lack of oxygen. In Salzwedel, another Neuengamme sub-camp, the prisoners were not forced to work. The Americans liberated Blits and Eliazar there on April 14, 1945.[44]

Sophia Huisman (born January 22, 1926), Cato Polak (born December 4, 1920), Surry Polak (born September 18, 1912), and Suze Polak (born February 7, 1926) were relocated from Bergen-Belsen to Raguhn on February 7, 1945. Their testimonies do not provide any information as to whether choice was involved. Together with another 496 female Bergen-Belsen inmates they were

---

[42] Penha-Blits, NIOD 250d, inventory 750, 60; Eliazar and Ensel, NIOD 250d, inventory 510; Huisman, NIOD 250d, inventory 592; Polak, NIOD 250d, inventory 759.

[43] Penha-Blits, NIOD 250d, inventory 750, 60; Eliazar and Ensel, NIOD 250d, inventory 510; correspondence file Judith Eliazar, Arolsen Archives; correspondence file Mirjam Blits, Arolsen Archives; Therkel Straede: "Fallersleben (Volkswagenwerke)", in Megargee, Encyclopedia of Camps and Ghettos, volume I, part B, 2009, 1107–1108. Blits's and Eliazar's correspondence files state that they were transferred to Fallersleben on 17 November 1944; Straede's encyclopedia entry mentions 18 November 1944. The difference can be explained by the possibility that the women were perhaps registered as inmates the day after their arrival.

[44] Blits, Auschwitz, 264–300; Eliazar and Ensel, NIOD 250d, inventory 510; correspondence file Mirjam Blits, Arolsen Archives; correspondence file Judith Eliazar, Arolsen Archives; Straede, Fallersleben; Dietrich Banse: "Salzwedel", in Megargee, Encyclopedia of Camps and Ghettos, volume I, part B, 1170–1172; Marc Buggeln: *Slave Labor in Nazi Concentration Camps*, Oxford: Oxford University Press, 2014, 292, 297. According to Blits's and Eliazar's correspondence files and Buggeln, the evacuation of Fallersleben to Salzwedel took place on 8 April 1945. Straede mentioned 7 April.

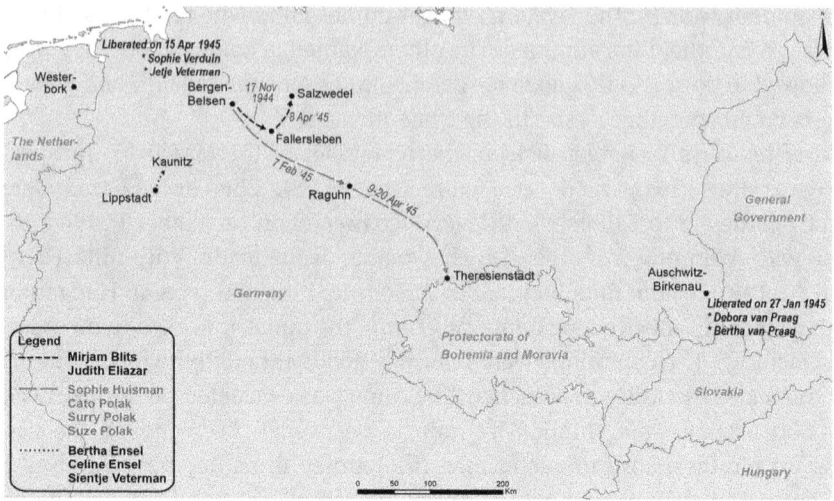

Fig. 5: Prisoner transfers continued during the final months of World War Two. The group of Dutch Jewish slave laborers fell into smaller segments. The women mentioned in the legend were liberated in the final site of their trajectory. Borders as of January 31, 1945. Basemap: Michael De Groot: *Building the New Order: 1938–1945*, Stanford University: Spatial History Lab, 2010. Copyright Daan de Leeuw.

the camp's first prisoners; all Jews except for two. Raguhn, one of the last Buchenwald sub-camps for women to be established, was located close to a factory where the slave laborers produced Junker airplane parts. The plant made use of forced civilian laborers as well, including some Dutch men with whom the four women connected secretly. The conditions in the camp and on the worksite were abhorrent: tiny food rations and hygienic circumstances so bad that many inmates contracted typhus. Civilian laborers fled the site, something the Dutch women considered too, yet before they could prepare sufficiently the SS evacuated the camp. The approximately 500 prisoners were pushed onto a train on April 9. The journey through Germany lasted 12 days and at least 60 women died from typhus, hunger, and cold. The survivors shared the wagon with the dead until the transport reached Theresienstadt on April 20. Perhaps the transfer took so long because the destination had not been determined upon departure or the train had difficulty crossing the country in the midst of chaos and breakdown. The four Dutch Jewish slave laborers were liberated in Theresienstadt on May 8, 1945.[45]

---

45 Huisman, NIOD 250d, inventory 592; Engelsman-Huisman, VHA 11233, segments 79–85;

Jetje Veterman (born June 3, 1923) and Sophie Verduin ended up in Bergen-Belsen. Veterman had been transferred there with the other women in early November 1944, and while the rest of the group was relocated to various camps, she remained in Bergen-Belsen. Veterman contracted typhus for a second time while incarcerated in the camp system. Perhaps her illness was the reason she stayed behind; her postwar testimony is silent on this question. Yet the witness statement does report a remarkable turn of events: she received a note from her sister Sientje Veterman (born April 17, 1922) through a woman prisoner who had been brought to Bergen-Belsen. Sientje wrote that she was in Lippstadt and that she had to work very hard. This short letter was the only news Jetje received from her sister.[46] Verduin stayed in Auschwitz-Birkenau until New Year's Eve 1944/1945 when she was transported to Bergen-Belsen. The archival documents do not provide any insight as to whether she volunteered. It seems Verduin and Veterman did not see each other in that camp, at least their testimonies do not indicate that they did. The British army liberated both women in Bergen-Belsen on April 15, 1945.[47]

The sisters Bertha and Celine Ensel and Sientje Veterman had remained in Auschwitz-Birkenau until the Germans brought them with 300 other female prisoners to the Buchenwald sub-camp Lippstadt on November 23, 1944. The survivors' testimonies do not say whether these Dutch Jewish slave laborers had any agency over their relocation. The SS had established the site as a women's camp for the Lippstadt Eisen- und Metallwerke (LEM) in summer 1944. The barracks stood on the factory premises, guarded by a small contingent of SS men and women overseers. LEM produced armaments such as ammunition and airplane parts. The inmates worked long hours, received little food, and were subjected to beatings and humiliations by the guards. The living and medical conditions in the camp were grim. The SS evacuated the camp at the end of March and

---

Polak, NIOD 250d, inventory 759; Polak and Polak, NIOD 250d, inventory 761; Transport list Bergen-Belsen–Raguhn, 07.02.1945, 1.1.3.1/3393363–3393409 and 1.1.5.1/5289324–5289346/ITS Digital Archive, Arolsen Archives; Evelyn Zegenhagen: "Raguhn", in Megargee, Encyclopedia of Camps and Ghettos, volume I, part A, 409–410. The NIOD testimonies state that the women were liberated on May 9. The correct date is May 8. See Vojtěch Blodig and Joseph Robert White: "Terezín", in Martin Dean and Mel Hecker (eds.): *Encyclopedia of Camps and Ghettos, 1933–1945*, volume II, part A, Bloomington, Indiana: Indiana University Press, 2012, 180–184.
46 Veterman, NIOD 250d, inventory 906.
47 Verduin, NIOD 250d, inventory 904; Veterman, NIOD 250d, inventory 906; correspondence file Jetje Veterman, 6.3.3.2/100387401–100387407/ITS Digital Archive, Arolsen Archives; List of Dutch Jews Released from Various Camps, 1.1.47.1/5157920–5157922/ITS Digital Archive, Arolsen Archives; Dutch Released from Bergen-Belsen and Buchenwald now in Eindhoven, 1.1.47.1/5157923–5157927/ITS Digital Archive, Arolsen Archives.

marched the prisoners by foot in the direction of Bergen-Belsen. When the evacuees reached the village of Kaunitz on Sunday April 1, 30 kilometers northeast of Lippstadt, the guards fled. American soldiers liberated the women a few hours later.[48]

Conclusion

The 13 surviving Dutch women endured over two years in the Nazi concentration camp system. They lost family and friends and, as we have seen, were relocated continuously. With each transfer, the deportees faced entry in a new camp with its own unique geography, terror regime, slave labor circumstances, hygienic conditions, and prisoner hierarchy. At least 15 deportees of the March 10 transport selected in Sobibor did not survive the camps to which they were sent. Nine died in the Lublin-Majdanek camp system: the Germans sent four women to the gas chambers, as witnessed by the survivors; the others must have died before or in Operation Harvest Festival. The women who had been transferred to Bliżyn and Milejów were not killed in this murderous action. Bliżyn was not affected by Operation Harvest Festival as it was located in Radom district and not in Lublin district, where Himmler had ordered all Jews to be murdered. Prisoners in Milejów were spared to burn the dead Jews' bodies in Trawniki; after their task had been completed the Germans murdered the male prisoners but let the female prisoners live to work in the camp. Still, one of the March 10 women in Trawniki fell ill and died there. Four Dutch inmates in Bliżyn perished

---

48 Eliazar and Ensel, NIOD 250d, inventory 510; Veterman, NIOD 250d, inventory 906; Transport List Auschwitz-Birkenau to Lippstadt, 23.11.1944, 1.1.2.1/129637261–129637266 and 1.1.5.1/5289152–5289158/ITS Digital Archive, Arolsen Archives; Individual Documents Bertha Ensel, Buchenwald, 1.1.5.4/7553458–7553462/ITS Digital Archive, Arolsen Archives; Individual Documents Sertina (Celine) Ensel, Buchenwald, 1.1.5.4/7553466–7553472/ITS Digital Archive, Arolsen Archives; Individual Documents Sientje Veterman, Buchenwald, 1.1.5.4/7748244–7748251/ITS Digital Archive, Arolsen Archives; Evelyn Zegenhagen: "Lippstadt (Lippstädter Eisen- und Metallwerke) [aka LEM, SS-Kommando Lippstadt I]", in Megargee, Encyclopedia of Camps and Ghettos, volume I, part A, 384–386. In her NIOD testimony, Bertha Ensel recalled that she was transported via Bergen-Belsen and Buchenwald to Lippstadt. Extensive research in the Arolsen Archives, the Dutch Red Cross Archive, and Memorial Center Camp Westerbork has proven that this was not the case, and that she was transferred directly from Auschwitz-Birkenau to Lippstadt on 23 November 1944, together with her sister Celine Ensel and Sientje Veterman. See Email to author, Arolsen Archives, date 22.03.2021; Email to author, Memorial Center Camp Westerbork, date 30.03.2021.

from exhaustion and sickness. The last to die of the group of 30 deportees succumbed during the death march from Lublin-Majdanek to Auschwitz.

For the survivors, liberation put an end to their incarceration and the constant relocations. Blits expressed how she felt when the US Army liberated Salzwedel:

> Everybody went crazy, completely wild. When we calmed down for a brief moment I suggested we leave the camp, to get out of that mess and lice plague and [return] to Holland. It sounded like music, Holland. I could return to my fatherland, there, where I belong. I was allowed to walk down the street freely once again, to board streetcars, and go to bars and cinemas. I was free again, free, free![49]

Transfer through the concentration camp system was common for most prisoners. Many deportees, who were not murdered on site, did not stay in the camp where they first arrived; sooner or later they found themselves on yet another transport to yet another unknown site. The longer the war lasted the more urgent the labor shortage became. Heinrich Himmler and Albert Speer tried to fill this void through the allocation of concentration camp inmates. Forced and slave laborers had to work for the German war effort in the armaments industry and in infrastructural projects. The main camps became the central points whence prisoners were shipped to sub-camps close to factories and work sites. The Germans sent the detainees where the war industry needed them.

Most of the time, the Nazis determined who was sent where. Very often the selections and transports were met with fear by the inmates as they did not know what awaited them. The possibility of being selected for the gas chambers was omnipresent for every Jewish slave laborer. Most of them were indeed murdered by the SS when their labor was no longer needed or when the terrible work and camp conditions had deprived them of all strength and energy. Each relocation could thus mean life or death.

The survivors' testimonies show that in some cases the inmates could exert some form of control over their site of incarceration. Sometimes the SS asked prisoners to volunteer for another camp; they left the decision to stay in or leave a certain site with the detainees. And on rare occasions, Jews affected the selection process by direct interaction with German guards, and thus managed to keep their relatives and friends close and to remain together. In these instances, the victims exerted some agency in a system of oppression and terror. The space that was occasionally given to prisoners problematizes the typical perspective of the SS concentration camps as a system in which the inmates were

---

49 Blits, Auschwitz, 301. Translation by the author.

helpless and without any agency. By scrutinizing the Jewish slave laborers' trajectories on a microlevel, my study has unearthed instances of both power and powerlessness that shaped their experiences in the concentration camps.

The maps help us understand those experiences. On a macro level, GIS can be used as an analytical tool to plot the trajectories of hundreds of deportees, as Borggräfe's article has shown.[50] Visualizing prisoner transfers with GIS can reveal unknown patterns in their pathways through the camp system. Yet GIS alone cannot explain why inmates followed certain routes; we turn to survivor testimonies and German bureaucratic documents to fully understand this history. Combining both approaches and considering geovisualizations as part of the research process allow for a more fine-grained analysis of Jewish slave labor during the Holocaust, as my contribution has sought to do.

---

50 Borggräfe, Rekonstruktion von Verfolgungswegen.

Alexandra Patrikiou
Escaping the Death Train
The Survival Strategies of Errikos Botton[1]

Abstract: This contribution deals with the escape of Errikos Botton from a death train on the way from Greece to Auschwitz. Errikos Botton was born in 1919 in Salonika, he started his studies in chemistry in Athens before the war and thus managed to avoid deportation in the first wave in 1943. However, in early June 1944 the German occupiers arrested him in Athens and sent him to Chaidari concentration camp. He was stacked in a train along with other Jews arrested from Dodecanese Islands of Rhodes and Kos. In the border region of Slovakia and German-occupied Poland he managed to escape along with three other young men, and to return safely to Salonika in July 1945.

Using Botton's typescript memoir and two Oral History interviews, this article narrates his story, which reveals a series of conscious choices and decisions, i. e., his wider survival strategies to confront racial persecutions during World War II. In addition, a closer look at his experience of the train journey in correlation to Errikos' sociocultural background leads to a better understanding of his conscious choice to escape from the death train. Finally, the aim of this article is to look at the deportations from the perspective of the victims; in other words, not as a horrible means of mass transport of anonymous and submissive individuals to almost certain death, but as one episode in the life of an individual as a historical subject.

Introduction

On February 12, 1946, Errikos Isaac Botton asked the Jewish Community of Athens (JCA) to verify his deportation by the German occupiers a year and a half earlier in order that his cancelled food stamps could be reissued:

> On August 2, 1944 after spending fifty days in Chaidari camp I was deported along with the Jews of Rhodes to Poland. During the journey near the Slovak-Polish borders, I escaped along with three other men, who have already returned to Athens. After a lot of suffering on the mountains of Slovakia, I managed to survive and return to Salonika on July 27,

---
1 An earlier version of this article was written in collaboration with Dr Maria Vassilikou, whom I would like to thank for her insightful comments in all versions of the text.

∂ OpenAccess. © 2023 the author(s), published by De Gruyter. [CC BY-NC-ND] This work is licensed under the Creative Commons Attribution-NonCommercial-NoDerivatives 4.0 International License.
https://doi.org/10.1515/9783110746464-021

> 1945 (approximately). Ten days ago, I came back to Athens, where I live permanently [...]. Two witnesses that escaped with me confirm my testimony.²

Botton's request was quite common for all survivors who were trying to begin their lives from scratch.³ To start anew and to get some kind of aid survivors had to briefly describe their experiences of the Shoah and, indeed, to have them verified. However, Botton's rather extraordinary case falls into the numerically small category of those Jews who were arrested and deported but successfully escaped from the trains heading to the extermination camps.

By presenting and analyzing Botton's story this contribution aims to look at the deportations from the perspective of the victims; in other words, not as a horrible means of mass transport of anonymous and submissive individuals to almost certain death, but as one episode in the life of an individual as a historical subject. A closer look at his experience of the train journey in correlation to his sociocultural background also leads to a better understanding of his conscious choice to escape from the death train. Furthermore, Botton's case will be put into broader context of flight and escape during the Shoah in Europe in order to see whether it confirms the typology proposed in other countries.⁴ Finally, examining this one case will allow a thorough analysis of the factors, which might have increased or decreased the chances of escaping from the deportation transports.

The primary sources used for this article include a 62-page unpublished typescript in Greek, which Botton wrote in 1991 with the benefit of hindsight, as well as his two audiovisual interviews deposited at the Visual History Archive of the Shoah Foundation⁵ and the Fortunoff Archive at Yale University.⁶ A photocopy of the typescript was donated to the Jewish Museum of Greece (JMG) in

---

2 Non-catalogued Archive of the Jewish Community of Athens (JCA). I would like to thank Philip Carabott for providing me with a copy of this document and critically reading and discussing this article. Translation by the author.
3 Indicatively, see numerous such examples in Leon Nar: *Ξανά στη Σαλονίκη*, Athens: Polis, 2018, and Rika Benveniste: *Αυτοί που επέζησαν. Αντίσταση, Εκτόπιση, Επιστροφή. Θεσσαλονικείς Εβραίοι στη δεκαετία του 1940*, Athens: Polis, 2014.
4 Tanja von Fransecky: *Escapees: The History of Jews Who Fled Nazi Deportation Trains in France*, trnsl. Benjamin Liebelt, New York, Oxford: Berghahn Books, 2019.
5 Anry Mpotton, Interview 42858 in Greek by Pauline Matathias, Visual History Archive (VHA), USC Shoah Foundation, 01.04.1998.
6 Henry B., Interview 3017 in French by Jaša Almuli, Fortunoff Video Archive for Holocaust Testimonies (Fortunoff Archive), 12.12.1999.

1991.⁷ The typescript constitutes a type of memoir, a 'life narrative' as he calls it, even though he focuses mostly on the period 1940 to 1945 and offers little information on his prewar or postwar life. His aim is to describe the extent of the brutality during the Shoah; an impossible and frightful task.⁸ It should not go amiss that these are narratives, both the typescript and the interviews, shaped by the cultural, social and political framework of Shoah commemoration, and thus limit our perspective on Botton's contemporaneous views. The story is contextualized by an interview of his brother Markos to the Visual History Archive,⁹ as well as Sam David Nehama's interviews in the Oral History Archive of the JMG¹⁰ and the Visual History Archive.¹¹ Sam, a 13-year-old boy at the time, was deported along with members of his family (originally from Bitola) in the same cattle wagon, as Botton was. Therefore, we have the unimaginable fortune of being able to better contextualize Botton's story as well as to hear of what happened after the escape.

A Jew from Salonika in German-Occupied Athens

Botton's decision to escape the death train to Auschwitz was not out of the blue. It was one decision in a series of decisions during the Shoah. This one decision was part of a wider survival strategy to confront the racial persecution. What was his life up to his arrest and deportation like? How does this particular decision fit in with the rest of his Shoah experiences? These questions help us frame and comprehend his story. Errikos Bottton was born on August 10, 1919, in Salonika.¹² Salonika had rather recently been incorporated into the Greek state in 1912 after the successful outcome of the First Balkan War. The multicultural city was home to the largest Sephardic Jewish community in the Balkans. Its incorporation into the Greek state signified the increase of the country's Jewish population from

---

7 Errikos Botton's Typescript, JMG Archival Collection (from now on Typescript). The typescript was donated to the Museum by Errikos Sasson in the memory of his parents Laura Nachmia and Solomon Sasson. JMG 2015.039, JMG Archival Collection, Jewish Museum of Greece, Athens.
8 Typescript, 1.
9 Markos Mpotton, Interview 43906 in Greek by Pauline Matathias, VHA, 05.05.1998.
10 Oral History Archive of the Jewish Museum of Greece (JMG/OHA/070). Special thanks to the JMG for letting me use its archival collection and its Oral History Archive.
11 Samuel Nehama, Interview 687 in English by Bonnie Gurewitsch, VHA, 25.01.1995.
12 Details on his family were found in both his interviews, while the typescript mentions only a few things.

less than 10,000 to circa 90,000 after 1912.¹³ Salonikan Jewry, while diminishing in numbers during the interwar period due to immigration mostly to France and Palestine and rising antisemitism, constituted a vibrant, flourishing, and multifaceted community before World War Two. Nevertheless, due to a number of factors, such as the Great Fire of 1917 and the influx of refugees from Asia Minor after 1922, the city's Jewish character was progressively fading.

Errikos was born in a "petit-bourgeois"¹⁴ family with four children – Marios, Sarah, himself and Markos. His father Isaac was a peddler, who went out of business during the financial crisis of 1929 to 1932 that led the family to extreme poverty. They lost their house and merchandise to debt. Isaac never managed to recover his business and the two older siblings, Marios and Sarah, supported the family financially. Marios was working at a bike store, while Sarah was tutoring young children in French. Before the financial destruction of the family, all the children were attending or had finished foreign language schools (the French Jean Baptist de la Salle and the Italian Uberto Primo). Learning foreign languages was a vital and inherent characteristic of the complex framework of Jewish education in Thessaloniki.¹⁵ The Botton family was no exception.

Errikos attended the French primary school, graduated from a Greek public high school and went on to study chemistry at the University of Athens, as this was "the science of the future".¹⁶ He arrived in Athens in 1938 during the Metaxas Dictatorship (1936 to 1941), which provided impoverished students with coupons for lunch and dinner. In order to pay his rent, he was tutoring young Jewish students in mathematics and sharing a room with two other Jewish friends: Marios Avraam Benaroyias (born Athens 1920) and David Avraam Allalouf (born Salonika 1922).

The Jewish presence in Athens was fairly new, especially compared with Salonika, with the first Ashkenazi Jews arriving with the Bavarian King Otto in the 1830s. Only in 1890 did the Jews of Athens formulate the first non-Christian brotherhood recognized by the Greek State.¹⁷ By the 1930s, the Jewish Communi-

---

13 Devin E. Naar: *Jewish Salonica. Between the Ottoman Empire and Modern Greece*, Stanford: Stanford University Press, 2016, 25.
14 VHA interview, 42858. Translation by the author.
15 For the importance of schools during and after the transition of the city to Modern Greece, cf. Naar, 166–167.
16 VHA interview, 42858. Translation by the author.
17 Philip Carabott: "Μικρές ιστορίες με άρωμα νεωτερικότητας (1890–93): Η Ισραηλιτική Αδελφότης Αθηνών και 'Η ανθρωποθυσία παρά τοις Ιουδαίοις'", in Kaiti Aroni-Tsichli, Stephanos Papageorgiou and Alexandra Patrikiou (eds.): *Η Ελλάδα της Νεωτερικότητας. Κοινωνικές κρίσεις και ιδεολογικά διλήμματα (19ος – 20ός αιώνας)*, Athens: Papazisis, 2014, 113–142.

ty of Athens was a flourishing community of approximately 3,000 people, the second largest in the country. During World War Two, approximately another 3,000 from the German and the Bulgarian zones of Occupation found temporary refuge in practically Italian-occupied Athens, as the Italians were unwilling to comply with the German intentions of persecuting the Jewish population.

In 1943, Botton had joined the youth organization United Panhellenic Organization of Youth (EPON) of the communist-led resistance organization (National Liberation Front, EAM) but did not manage to join its military wing, the Greek People's Liberation Army (ELAS), although he tried.[18] It is estimated that at least 650 Jewish men and women, from almost all the Jewish communities in the country, joined EAM, ELAS and/or EPON. When he attempted to find the necessary liaison to flee to the mountains and join ELAS, he was told that everyone was in danger, and he was no exception to that.[19] Not being able to join ELAS made him feel that he had not done enough: "This was my weakness. We weren't doing any high-quality resistance, i.e., armed".[20] In addition, he believed that the fact that he was not armed was partly to blame on his arrest in 1944. Despite that feeling of worthlessness regarding his participation in the youth resistance organization, that same participation is evidence of a broader active stance towards the German occupation and racial persecution. Joining EPON as a university student was not an isolated or exceptional event. During the Occupation, a massive youth movement was created with numerous organizations, the largest of which was EPON, which is said to have more than 500,000 members.[21] Jewish experiences in EPON were no different from everyone else's.[22] Botton says: "We were going out at night and we were writing [slogans] on the walls. [...] The entire university was in EPON".[23] Their participation constituted a moment of overcoming oneself, a turning point in their lifetime and a passport to adulthood.[24] Despite Botton's questioning the efficacy of his participation in EPON, it is certain that this experience further intensified his stance of taking matters into his own hands; i.e., not leaving everything to chance.

---

18 On Jewish participation in the communist-led resistance, see Iassonas Chandrinos, *Συναγωνιστές. Το ΕΑΜ και οι Εβραίοι της Ελλάδας*, Athens: Psifides, 2020. See also JMG digital exhibition in English "Synagonistis: Greek Jews in the National Resistance" https://www.jewishmuseum.gr/en/synagonistis-greek-jews-in-the-national-resistance-8/. Last accessed: 04.03.2022.
19 VHA interview, 42858.
20 Ibid. Translation by the author.
21 Odette Varon-Vassard: *Η ενηλικίωση μιας γενιάς. Νέοι και νέες στην Κατοχή και στην Αντίσταση*, Athens: Estia, 2009, 269–314.
22 Chandrinos, Συναγωνιστές, 57.
23 VHA interview, 42858. Translation by the author.
24 Varon-Vassard, Η ενηλικίωση μιας γενιάς, 520–521.

The deportations of the Jews from Greece essentially took place in two phases, one in 1943 and the second in 1944. This was largely due to the partition of the country into three different zones of occupation, German, Italian and Bulgarian, which demonstrated the secondary importance of Greece for the Third Reich and practically hindered the implementation of the Nuremberg laws, as the Germans had to convince their Italian partners.[25]

In early February 1943, Adolf Eichmann's agents, Alois Brunner and Dieter Wisliceny, arrived in Salonika in order to implement the 'Final Solution' on the 50,000 Jews who constituted 25 percent of the prewar city's population.[26] Preparations for the deportations began immediately.[27] From February 6, all Jews had to wear a yellow star and had to gather in the newly formed ghetto quarters. Within the next few days, Jews were forbidden to use the telephone, the tram or to own any professional or corporate organization. On March 1, they were ordered to register all of their belongings, and on March 15, 1943, the first cattle train with approximately 2,400 people from the Baron Hirsch ghetto-district began its gruesome journey to Auschwitz. Another eighteen transports would follow until August 1943, almost completely destroying the centuries-long Jewish presence of the city.[28]

Until the storm of anti-Jewish legislation in early 1943, Jews and Christians of Salonika largely shared the 'abnormal normality' of everyday life under German occupation: terror, fear, hunger, yearning for freedom.[29] Among the Salonikan deportees were Errikos' parents, his sister Sarah and his brother Marios. They were all murdered in Birkenau. Only his brother Markos managed to avoid deportation and joined EAM. Markos, who was a student of the Faculty of Agronomy, decided to disobey the first anti-Jewish mass action that took place in Salonika on Saturday, July 11, 1942, and did not present himself for registration. Instead, he was watching from afar the humiliation and violence his coreligionists were suffering.[30] Thanks to his contacts through the university, he succeeded in finding the necessary liaison to flee to the mountains along with few other young

---

25 Iason Chandrinos and Anna Maria Droumpouki: "The German Occupation and the Holocaust in Greece: A Survey", in Giorgos Antoniou and Dirk Moses (eds.): *The Holocaust in Greece*, Cambridge: Cambridge University Press, 2018, 15–35, here 17.
26 Steven Bowman: *The Agony of Greek Jews 1940–1945*, Stanford: Stanford University Press, 2009, 82.
27 Chandrinos-Droumpouki, German Occupation, 21.
28 For a chronicle of all the deportations from Greece, cf. Bowman, Agony, 80–93.
29 Benveniste, Αυτοί που επέζησαν, 61.
30 Ibid., 68; VHA interview, 43906.

male Jews from Salonika.³¹ Since he was in Athens, Errikos managed to avoid the first wave of deportations in 1943.

In autumn 1943, the Italian capitulation meant the extension of the German authority on the rest of the country, including the Dodecanese Islands, which at the time were not part of the Greek state, and subsequently the beginning of the end for the Jews residing and/or hiding in these areas. Jürgen Stroop, an SS commander who had crushed the Warsaw ghetto uprising in spring 1943, was appointed Higher SS and Police Chief (*Höherer SS und Polizeiführer*) in Athens. Dieter Wisliceny, SS officer and deputy to Adolf Eichmann in the Jewish affairs department of the Reich Security Main Office (*Reichssicherheitshauptamt*), arrived in Athens after having completed his mission in Salonika and demanded from Rabbi Elias Barzilai lists of all Jews in Athens. Barzilai claimed that the lists were destroyed by the collaborationist pro-Nazi ESPO (Greek Socialist Patriotic Organization) and actually fled to the mountains with the assistance of EAM,³² thereby giving a signal of non-compliance to his coreligionists. Faced with this predicament, Stroop issued a decree on October 4, 1943, according to which all Jews in Athens had to register immediately at the synagogue.³³ According to the decree, a Jewish Council ('*Judenrat*') was to be created, a strict curfew was imposed and anyone caught to assist in any way a Jew would be deported. Refusing to comply with the decree carried the penalty of death.

Naturally, Errikos Botton and his two roommates got worried. According to Errikos, they were worried not only because of the decree but also because rumors were starting to circulate from those Jews who had been sent from Salonika to forced labor camps in Central Greece (Karya, Lianokladi and Thebes) in March 1943 and had managed to escape. Indeed, there were quite a few men escaping from the forced labor camp in Thebes.³⁴ Botton actually commented on these escapees saying that there should have been more. He distinguished the two main factors that could lead to the decision to escape: one factor was willpower, i.e., determination, courage and strength to carry out a tough decision, and the se-

---

31 For several individual stories of how young male Jews from Thessaloniki joined ELAS, see. Benveniste, Αυτοί που επέζησαν, 47–81.
32 Bowman, Agony, 68.
33 Mark Mazower: *Inside Hitler's Greece. The Experience of Occupation*, New Haven and London: Yale University Press, 1993, 250–251.
34 Leon Levy describes his own escape in Michael Matsas: *The Illusion of Safety. The Story of the Greek Jews During the Second World War*, New York: Pella Publishing, 1997, 134–137. Moshe Halegoua also mentioned people escaping the same hard labor camp. See Errika Kounio-Amarilio and Albert Nar: *Προφορικές Μαρτυρίες Εβραίων της Θεσσαλονίκης για το Ολοκαύτωμα*, Thessaloniki: Ets-Ahaim, Paratiritis, 1998, 411–413. Benveniste, Αυτοί που επέζησαν, 72, 76, 79.

cond one were familial concerns. Those sent to hard labor were 'comforted' by the Germans that their families back in Salonika will be safe (in the sense that they would not get deported) as long as they were still working in the hard labor camps.[35] Little did they know that the deportations had already begun. It was an obvious attempt by the Germans to create an atmosphere of security, to maintain compliance and hence to hinder any possible attempt of escape, while safeguarding their financial interests. Willpower, courage and strength, all possible signs of youth, and the lack of family ties, also a potential sign of youth, describe the circumstances under which one may reach the point of escaping incarceration, according to Errikos. Moshe Halegoua from Salonika agreed with Errikos. When Moshe, who knew that the deportations had already started, was sent to Thebes for forced labor and was asked why he did not try to escape, his answer was: "How? [...] I had my parents in Salonika".[36]

Expressions of regret about missed opportunities of escaping were not exclusive to Botton. Shlomo Venezia, a '*Sonderkommando*' survivor, was asked whether he thought it was actually possible to escape the ambush in the Athens Synagogue in March 1944. He answered:

> Yes, because I knew what had happened in Salonika. [...] We might have been able to force the doors and get out instead of waiting there until it was way too late. We could have, we should have, tried to escape. Some would have lost their lives but we were all walking towards death anyway. People thought that if they obeyed to what they were told, they would not be killed. Unfortunately, the opposite was true.[37]

At first not many Jews from Athens complied with Stroop's decree and as time went by and hardly any arrests were made a false sense of 'trust' was being established.[38] This statement might be somewhat exaggerated, in the sense that trust is too positive of a concept to encompass the range of different and conflicting emotions among Jews in hiding. It is certain that this attitude of inaction on behalf of the Germans gave a false sense of security. Furthermore, it certainly put a lot of strain on those Jews who could no longer afford to remain into hiding because they had run out of money and, as 'outlaws', could not use their food stamps. These conditions are briefly described by Botton himself:

---

[35] Kounio/Nar, Προφορικές, 413.
[36] Ibid. Translation by the author.
[37] Shlomo Venezia: *Sonderkommando μέσα από την κόλαση των θαλάμων αερίων*, Athens: Pataki, 2008, 49. Translation by the author.
[38] Michael Molho and Joseph Nehama: *In memoriam: hommage aux victimes juives des Nazis en Grèce*, Salonika: Nicolaïdès, 1948, 222.

This was a great lure for the poorer families that didn't have the means to support themselves in hiding, pay large amount of money in rent and probably even supporting the hosts who were starving. Hence, these poor people timidly started registering to the community's offices and spreading the word that there was no danger.[39]

In addition, survivors mention that people did not know how to react to the constantly tightening cord,[40] i.e., did not know which survival strategy would work best. It is important to highlight this notion of oscillation felt by the Jews in Athens before deciding to register to the Synagogue. It is also vital to keep in mind the constantly changing atmosphere of uncertainty in order to better understand the range of choices available to the persecutees as well as the circumstances under which these choices were finally made.

For his part, Errikos had managed to provide himself with a false ID card from the police station, a potential life-saving document. According to his testimony, he went to a police officer at Koumoundourou Square, where he knew they were issuing false papers and got one under the surname Dimitriadis.[41] Along with his roommates, he decided to flee from the neighborhood where they were staying and were recognizable, and search for a "secluded area, where no one knew them".[42] They reached Nea Elvetia, a suburb northeast of Athens at the foot of Mount Hymettus. However, they did not stay for long there. They moved to another refugee suburb in southern Athens, Nea Smyrni.

The fact that Botton had a false ID card, whereas his roommates did not, empowered him to move freely and, in turn, be responsible for getting bread.[43] Thus Botton was among those Jews who had actively sought and succeeded in obtaining false papers and contrary to Stroop's decree decided not to present himself to the Synagogue every week and thus avoid the March 24, 1944, round up. On that day, the Germans arrested approximately 800 Jews. Thereafter, the Germans continued sporadically to arrest Jews who remained hidden. Botton and Sam Nehama[44] mentioned that around 200 people had been arrested this way.

In early June 1944, a known collaborator, David Cohen, who had been baptized and went by the name Christos Michailidis, arrested Botton at a bakery for fraud and dragged him to the Gestapo headquarters in Merlin Street to check his papers. The German officer saw the papers, reacted rather nonchalantly and told

---

39 Typescript, 2. See also Fortunoff Archive, 3017. Translation by the author.
40 Errikos Sevillias: *Athens – Auschwitz*, transl. Nikos Stavroulakis, Athens: Lycabettus Press, 1983.
41 VHA interview, 42858.
42 VHA interview, 42858. Translation by the author.
43 Fortunoff Archive, 3017.
44 JMG/OHA 070.

him to wait. However, the Recanati cousins, Pepo and Ino, the infamous Jewish collaborators[45] that happened to know him from Salonika, recognized him and betrayed him to the Germans. Thereafter, he was arrested and imprisoned in Chaidari concentration camp, located eight kilometers west of central Athens,[46] where he claims to have spent at least one month, if not more.[47] However, it does sound peculiar that Michailidis dragged him to the Gestapo Headquarters without knowing he was a Jew. If indeed he was taken to Merlin at first, most likely Michalidis already knew he had arrested a Jew, as arrested Jews in Athens were taken directly to the Gestapo headquarters. In any case, Botton did not miss a chance to characterize his arrest as an avoidable mistake and a mere foolishness.[48]

Along with the 200 other people in hiding arrested in the wider area of Attica in spring/summer 1944, there were the Jews from Rhodes and Kos (the two of the Dodecanese Islands that were not yet part of the Greek state) who had been arrested and also held at Chaidari. On July 18, 1944, Jews from the island Rhodes had been ordered to gather with all their valuables at the city center. Five days later, all members of the community, more than 1,700 people, were forced to go to the harbor and from there they were brought by the Germans to nearby Leros. Another ship carried 120 Jews from Kos. These ships travelled for eight days under horrible conditions and finally arrived at the port of Piraeus. The human cargo was transferred to Chaidari, where they spent several days there performing forced labor and being tortured.[49] Botton described their chaotic arrival at the camp as "a first step towards Dante's hell",[50] an often-cited reference

---

45 The Recanati cousins were among those coreligionists arrested, tried and convicted for collaborating with the Germans in 1947 for threatening and abusing Greek citizens of Jewish faith. Michailidis was not arrested, he was tried in absentia. Molho, In memoriam, 326–327; Philip Carabott: "Να εξαφανισθούν οι καταδότες από το πρόσωπον της γης: Εβραίοι 'δοσίλογοι' και η σκιά της προδοσίας (1944–63)", in Evangelos Chekimoglou and Anna Maria Droumbouki (eds.): *Την επαύριον του Ολοκαυτώματος*, Salonika: Jewish Community of Thessaloniki, 2017, 102–122.
46 On Chaidari, see Anna-Maria Droumpouki: *Μνημεία της Λήθης. Ίχνη του Β' Παγκοσμίου Πολέμου*, Athens: Polis, 2014, 147–190.
47 VHA interview, 42858.
48 Ibid. There is no description of his arrest in the typescript. This 'omission' might be accounted for in this context of feeling his arrest being an 'avoidable mistake'. And hence he did not want to include it in his memoir, while in the interviews he can not avoid answering the interviewer's question.
49 Anthony McElligott: "The Deportation of the Jews of Rhodes 1944: An Integrated History", in Giorgos Antoniou and Dirk Moses (eds.): *The Holocaust in Greece*, Cambridge: Cambridge University Press, 2018, 58–85.
50 Typescript, 4. Translation by the author.

to provide identification with an epic voyage and a descent to the abyss.[51] What is also very peculiar in Errikos' case is that he was not deported with the twenty-first transport, which left Athens on June 21, even though he had been already arrested and taken to Chaidari.

All these arrestees formed the twenty-second and last deportation transport from Greece that left Athens on August 3, and arrived in Auschwitz on August 16, 1944. It consisted of approximately 2,500 Jews, out of which only 600 were admitted to the camp; the others were murdered in the gas chambers upon arrival.[52] As mentioned above, that is the fate that Botton actually managed to avoid; either death upon arrival or – given his age – most probably a life as a slave laborer where chances of survival were next to nothing.

A Small Window of Opportunity

On August 3, 1944, Botton was crammed in a cattle wagon of the twenty-second transport. One day before arrival at Auschwitz, near the border region of Slovakia and German-occupied Poland he escaped along with three other men: the street vendor Alfred Isaac Abraham (born Sofia 1921), the plumber Samuel Joseph Asseas (born Athens 1917) and the pharmacist Nissim Elias Azouvi (born Larissa 1906). Botton chooses to describe the conditions in the cattle wagon in a composed manner, without failing to spare his readers/listeners of the horrible details:

> We were all crammed in the train at gunpoint. Entire families. Crowded with practically no food. Loaves of moldy bread, a bag of raisins mixed with dirt and several onions. What a chaos? [The despair continued] for two or three days and then the crying subsided. [The temperature reached] 45 degrees. Everyone took his clothes off. [We were] full of lice. That was the worst. The lice had nested in the boards. A constant crying [was heard]. Women undressed themselves to avoid the lice.[53]

Indeed, his words sound sober and controlled, especially when compared to other emotionally overwhelming moments, such as his bursting into tears

---

51 Simone Gigliotti: *The Train Journey. Transit, Captivity, and Witnessing in the Holocaust*, New York: Berghahn Books, 2009, 96.
52 Bowman, 80–93. Danuta Czech: *Auschwitz Chronicle 1939–1945. From the Archives of the Auschwitz Memorial and the German Federal Archives*, New York: Owl Books, 1997, 688.
53 Typescript, 5–7. Fortunoff Archive, 3017. Translation by the author.

when mentioning the executions of partisans at the Chaidari camp or the assistance offered to him by unknown Slovakians after his escape.[54]

There are three descriptions of his escape. Each description highlights a different aspect. The interview in the Fortunoff Archives offers a calm description:

> During the first hours and days of the train journey, when someone would say that they were going to try and escape, people reacted because they were under the impression that the Germans kept records of how many people were in each carriage. They thought they would have to suffer the consequences of the escape and that they would be punished by the Germans. So, they refused to let us escape in the beginning. Around the tenth or eleventh day, they were so tired that they could not react anymore. And that is how three men and I managed to escape. [...] Our escape took place around midnight. One of them was about forty years old, and was a pharmacist. The other, he was well-built. The third was called Freddy Abraham, and now lives in Israel. We had not actually planned the escape together. I escaped last. I noticed that they had torn the wire of the window, and they escaped. I was left last and I decided to follow them. I fell on the rails, on the rocks. Unfortunately, I did not run into the three others in Slovakia, and I was by myself all the time. The train was not too fast. There were two engines: one in the front and one at the back. It was in the mountains [when we escaped]. The window was high up, and they actually stepped on the people who were sitting beneath it. It was not too difficult. I got hurt when I fell on the ground. I was very poorly dressed. I was wearing a pair of trousers, and a shirt. I did not have any shoes, because they had taken my sandals away from me.[55]

The typescript description is more sentimental:

> I cannot recall the exact date of my escape. [...] What I remember the most was the freezing cold; I was barefoot and was wearing only a pair of trousers, underpants and a shirt. [...] For a moment, the thought crossed my mind that I had done the fatal and last mistake of my life. Maybe my fellow passengers would have found bearable conditions upon arrival at the concentration camp. However, instantly the thought, that one may not yearn for survival and freedom waiting passively for the executioner's mercy prevailed. It's better to have fought with whatever force you may have for your survival, while being free, and lose [rather than not to have fought at all]. These are not just hollow words.[56]

As is also the VHA description:

> I had not done any previous arrangements. When I saw the others jump, I also jumped. We either live or die. [I jumped] unprepared, on an impulse. Almost naked. We were all in the same boat. The carriage did not stop. That was very important.[57]

---

54 VHA interview, 42858.
55 Fortunoff Archive, 3017. Translation by the author.
56 Typescript, 23. Translation by the author.
57 VHA interview, 42858. Translation by the author.

All three descriptions reveal agency, a struggle for life, a firm response to racial persecution; in short: they reveal a survival strategy.

Escaping the Death Train: A Survival Strategy

The fact that Botton characterized his arrest as an avoidable mistake obviously does not reveal the actual responsibility he had over his arrest. Far from it. It reveals the agency he still felt after all these years; the fact that in other crucial moments he managed to evade mortal danger. My use of the verb *evade* is deliberate. In a sense, it encapsulates a large part of his Shoah experience. By remaining in Athens after the outbreak of the war and the German occupation of his native city, he *evades* the first phase of deportations. By participating in the organized resistance and having a fake ID he *evades* the Synagogue round-up of March 24 (and the arrest for the second time). By escaping from the death train to Auschwitz, he *evades* death, despite the fact that the Germans had arrested and deported him.

In categorizing Jewish behavior during the Shoah, evasion was one of the survival strategies that describe any attempt to escape persecution by hiding, fleeing, assuming a false identity or even jumping from a moving train.[58] Historian Evgeny Finkel proposed a typology of survival strategies in which the Jews could and did engage during the Holocaust: cooperation and collaboration, coping and compliance, evasion, and finally, resistance. Finkel distinguishes, and rightly so, 'evasion' from 'resistance',[59] but as we realize – more often than not – analytic categories do not match perfectly actual realities and should not be used as rigid monolithic categories, but rather as intertwined paths. Botton's case could also be placed in the category of resistance, if the focus was on his participation in the youth resistance organization.[60] Botton's escape from the death train constitutes just a part of a wider survival strategy, one choice, – as crucial as it was – that led to his survival, which was accomplished in the end thanks to a number of structural and circumstantial factors, a number of people and a number of individual choices.

All these observations, of course, are made with the benefit of hindsight and should not conceal the fact that choosing a survival strategy, i.e., making a life

---

58 Evgeny Finkel: *Ordinary Jews. Choice and Survival during the Holocaust*, Princeton and Oxford: Princeton University Press, 2017, 126–158.
59 Ibid. 159–190.
60 For the youth resistance organization (EPON) with references to the Jewish participation, see Varon-Vassard, Η ενηλικίωση μιας γενιάς, 331–514.

or death decision without knowing the end result is an unthinkable or even unbearable situation; a decision that might be seen within the range of Lawrence Langer's 'choiceless choices'.[61] Despite the fact that Langer was referring to camp life, where morality and human dignity were completely absent or inversed, his term could be loosely applied to the death trains as well. Death trains constitute literally the transition from the illusion or deception that deportation may suggest survival to the realization of the death camp; from relocation to murder.[62] The journey was the transition to a place where human dignity and morality had been altered so much that a new language had to be constructed, as Primo Levi put it:

> If the lagers (camps) had lasted longer a new, harsh language would have been born; and only this language could express what it means to toil the whole day in the wind, with the temperature below freezing, and wearing only a shirt, underpants, cloth jacket and trousers, and in one's body nothing but weakness, hunger and knowledge of the end drawing near.[63]

However, the train journey itself was part of the genocidal process called 'Final Solution'. The terrorizing conditions of compressed space and indeterminate journeying were chosen explicitly to break morale and hinder any thought of resistance or escape.[64] The deportees were literally dealing with severe hunger, deteriorating health and unhygienic conditions, and the overpowering and choking stench of excrement, urine and vomit.[65]

Langer, when talking about 'choiceless choices', was basically talking about impossible moral choices between 'dreadful' and 'impossible'.[66] Although Botton's choice does not have a moral dimension, this does not make it any less impossible. Jumping from a moving train with no shoes and no orientation was indeed a jump into the unknown. It is now in retrospect that we know that this was the 'correct' decision to take; correct in the sense that it led to the path of survival. However, in that moment there, things might not have been that clear. Mo-

---

[61] Lawrence Langer: "The Dilemma of Choice in the Deathcamps", in *Centerpoint: A Journal of Interdisciplinary Studies*, 4/1, 1980, 53–59; reprinted in John K. Roth and Michael Berenbaum, (eds.): *Holocaust: Religious and Philosophical Implications*, New York: Paragon House, 1989, 222–232.
[62] Gigliotti, Train Journey, 4.
[63] Primo Levi: *Survival in Auschwitz. The Nazi Assault on Humanity*, New York: Touchstone, 1996, 123.
[64] Gigliotti, Train Journey, 4.
[65] Ibid., 97.
[66] Langer, Dilemma, 226.

ments after he jumped, Botton questioned his decision: "Up in the mountains the cold was such that my moral was shaken. Maybe it was a mistake, [maybe it was] madness to escape!"[67] In our noble and academically vital willingness to depict survivors as active agents, we should not forget that these viewpoints on agency are given by survivors with the benefit of hindsight and their will to protect their image as self-determining human beings.[68] Escaping the train was just one decision that led to survival and as important and crucial as it was, it was definitely not the only one.

Botton does not mince his words when referring to three basic reasons that made him take the decision to escape: a) The specific circumstances; b) His will to survive; and c) The fact that he was alone, having responsibility for nobody. "If I had a family, I would never have tried to escape",[69] he mentions in both his interviews and the typescript. The circumstance that he saw three other men jumping from the train was the sparkle that motivated him to do the same. The barbed wire covering the narrow slot in the wagon had been removed, so there it was, 'a window of opportunity' leading, possibly, to freedom and survival. Botton seized the chance, jumped and managed to survive. This attitude was definitely not exclusive to Botton. Undoubtedly, Botton had realized the unthinkable moral dilemma involved in this situation on the edge and the subsequent moral burden of his decision to escape, as family ties were seen as an insurmountable obstacle:

> I would never have decided to escape if I was in the wagon with a member of my family. [...] How to leave your old parents and underage siblings to get lost into the unknown while you were saved. What can you do with such a life? The family bond within the Jewish family was not only strong but indestructible. So, being without the presence of my own family in the coffin-carriage, I was able to play with my life.[70]

This 'will to survive' included the will to escape, whenever possible, which brings us to a sociocultural observation made by Botton himself regarding his constant choice to react as part of his survival strategy. When he was in the carriage, he observed his coreligionists and noted that after the chaos of the first few days "a veil of death"[71] had covered everything and had silenced all screaming and fighting over space or food. Some of the elderly carried with them prayer books and

---

67 Typescript, 11. Translation by the author.
68 Langer, Dilemma, 223.
69 VHA interview, 42858. Translation by the author
70 Typescript, 22. Translation by the author.
71 Ibid., 5. Translation by the author.

started praying as the only hope for survival. Botton found this stance of 'believing in a miracle' as destructively fatalistic and condemned it:

> I never believed that divine forces follow peoples' and societies routes. That's why I was aiming to escape. To keep these 80 people alive, we found in the carriage a bag of black raisins which had 25% of dirt in it, some 10 loafs of moldy bread, a bag of onions and a barrel of 200 liters of water. Most had given up their portion. I ate everything and the moldy bread didn't bother me at all.[72]

His observation on religion and its correlation to a more passive response towards persecution and deportation is obviously a personal one and does not necessarily correspond to specific reactions deportees had. In his typescript, he notes that he was "completely ignorant" of the Jewish faith and hence he became "free of ghosts and prejudices".[73] However, his views do raise the question of how religious beliefs could have shaped choices and survival strategies. It is certain that spiritual comfort through praying provided a psychological refuge inside the self and within the community and protected the individual's cultural identity despite incredibly hostile circumstances.[74] In that sense, this praying in the death train could also be interpreted as an act of spiritual or passive resistance. Instead for Botton it was a manifestation of passiveness and inactiveness; a manifestation of the exact opposite response Botton wanted to follow and actually did follow. His stance, seemingly, was typical among partisans who focused of the futility of such gestures.[75]

Furthermore, this was Botton's specific cattle wagon. In other wagons, the situation might have been quite different. Leon Cohen, who was arrested in Athens in March 1944, deported on April 2 and forced to work as a member of the '*Sonderkommando*' in Birkenau, described a journey full of "ridiculous quarrels and insults", instigated by those who "thought that they were entitled to home comforts".[76] This diversity in circumstances within each wagon of different transports brings to the fore the role and importance of incidental conditions that led Errikos Botton to make the specific decision. Were these circumstances so unique and exceptional that no one else was found in the same situation? Or can we trace the trends that could lead incarcerated people to attempt to escape?

---

[72] Ibid. Translation by the author.
[73] Typescript, 22. Translation by the author.
[74] James Glass: *Jewish Resistance during the Holocaust. Moral Uses of Violence and Will*, London: Palgrave Macmillan, 2004, 103–119.
[75] Ibid., 7.
[76] Leon Cohen: *From Greece to Birkenau: the Crematoria Workers' Uprising*, Tel Aviv: Salonika Jewry Research Center, 1996, 14.

In other words, how unique is Botton's story? He was definitely not the only Greek Jew escaping from a death train. First of all, there were at least another three deportees who successfully escaped from Botton's wagon. Second, there is the case of Dino Uziel from Salonika,[77] a well-known professional boxer.[78] He had escaped Salonika dressed as a railway worker and then failed twice to flee to the Middle East. In April 1944, he was arrested and transferred to Chaidari, where he did some plumbing work and stole some tools and a rail worker's cap. I mentioned earlier the cases of arrestees escaping the forced labor camps in Central Greece.[79] Furthermore, there were the people who escaped from Salonika's ghettoes and avoided deportation. Then there are known cases of escaping the death camps. It is also certain that there were other cases of escape that may have gone unregistered. These are different kinds of escaping a place of incarceration – a death train, a forced labor camp, a ghetto and a death camp – in the sense that different kinds of skills were needed, different conditions and other risks were possible. One thing is common, though: the decision to take matters into their own hands; agency.

Conclusion

In her study on escapes from deportation trains from Belgium, France and the Netherlands, historian Tanja von Fransecky poses two basic research questions: one concerns the overriding structural factors that enabled or hindered escapes regardless of the situation; the other concerns the key incidental factors within the cattle wagon with regard to the decision of escaping or not.[80] In the case of

---

[77] Philip Carabott, "Το νέον κέντρο του εβραϊσμού. Αθήνα 1941–1947", lecture (22.03.2018) in a ten-lecture series organized by the Workshop on the Study of the Jews of Greece and the Netherlands Institute at Athens under the title "The Jews of Greece and the Netherlands: Destruction, reconstruction, restitution" in 2018.
[78] The Jewish Museum of Thessaloniki has organized an exhibition on "Greek Jews in Sport: The Contibution of Thessaloniki". The exhibition's catalogue, one may find a lot of information on D. Uziel. Available at: http://www.maccabi.gr/wp-content/uploads/2013/03/history.pdf. Last accessed: 08.07.2021.
[79] Stiftung Denkmal für die ermordeten Juden Europas: "Karya 1943 – Tödliche Zwangsarbeit im besetzten Griechenland". Available at: https://www.youtube.com/watch?v=VIqXAN8aXlQ. Last accessed: 08.07.2021.
[80] Tanja von Fransecky: *Escapees: The History of Jews Who Fled Nazi Deportation Trains in France, Belgium, and the Netherlands*, New York-Oxford: Berghahn, 2019, 4.

Botton, who was one of the persecuted European Jews that attempted to flee from the trains of death,[81] Fransecky's approach seems to fit.

Botton was a young, clever, healthy, strong man with a fighting spirit. These features urged him to take his fate into his own hands and seek contact with the organized resistance. He was a self-made young man with an impressive curriculum vitae in terms both of academic excellence and his proficiency in no less than four languages (Greek, French, Italian and Ladino). And on top of that, Botton had an extra reason to be confident and endeavoring, for he had acquired all these assets without enjoying any economic support from his impoverished family. His decision to escape was consistent with his whole story and experiences during the war.

Last but not least, Botton was a lonely fighter, a man carrying responsibility for absolutely no one else. Most of his immediate relatives from Salonika had already been deported and murdered in Auschwitz during the first wave of deportations in spring and summer of 1943. Even though Errikos did not know exactly what had happened to them, it is certain that he had not heard from them since spring 1943. This tragic fact gave him a kind of grim 'privilege', which the overwhelming majority of persecuted Jews, who were deported along with their entire families, never had. Moreover, the setting of his escape was much more than a stroke of circumstance. It was a conscious decision; part of a series of decisions constituting his survival strategy during the Shoah. The window in the cattle wagon was already open. There were three other men, who made the herculean step to jump off the moving train first thus inspiring Botton to attempt the same. The speed of the train was not high, so his escape did not necessarily equal a suicide attempt.

It goes without saying, that Botton's story is unique, at least in as much his survival strategies met with success, and highlights individuality. It demonstrates a series of distinct and, in his case, successful decisions that led to survival, made by a man who was particularly clever, daring and courageous as well as fully conscious of the surrounding conditions of his existence. Essentially, his very story is an exemplary story of a textbook survival strategy. And probably, the same qualities of his character accompanied him also throughout his life after the Shoah, for, as we listen to his interviews, one is struck by the same comprehensive, critical and thorough spirit of his descriptions. But what does this particular story of a single individual tell us about the deportations to the death camps or the Shoah in general? If we look at the historical events from the perspective of the victims, as Yehuda Bauer and Saul Friedländer call us to do, with-

---

[81] Ibid.

in these horrible transports we do not just witness victimhood. Instead, we see individuals with different experiences and backgrounds, as well as men, women and children with some excruciating difficult moral choices in front of them. This particular story gives us a glimpse into that specific train. This particular story reframes the deportees' experiences as experiences of active agents, of people with conscious thoughts, unfulfilled wishes, hidden fears, moral courage rather than passive victims taken to their deaths by force.

Johannes Meerwald
The DEGOB Protocols and the Deportations of Jewish Prisoners to the Dachau Camp Complex

A Critical Source Analysis

Abstract: In the early postwar period, the organization Deportáltakat Gondozó Országos Bizottság (DEGOB, engl. National Committee for Attending Deportees) ran an extensive project to interview Hungarian survivors of the Holocaust. The resulting protocols contain detailed information about the experiences of Hungarian Jews during the Holocaust. Like many sources dating from the early postwar period, the protocols have so far been little analyzed in terms of specific criteria. Due to the fact that Jewish concentration camp prisoners from Hungary had to endure deportations and subsequent transports between camps in a relatively short time, narratives about these forced movements constitute a central element of the protocols. Therefore, this contribution examines DEGOB's protocols for their relevance to the research of deportations. On the basis of selected texts, the article will critically examine the extent to which the protocols can contribute to a deeper understanding of persecution routes. Furthermore, it will be illustrated what qualitative information they contain about the deportations and what perspectives they can open up on topics that are only inadequately covered by common historical sources. To ensure a coherent analysis, the essay will limit itself to the deportations of Hungarian-Jewish prisoners to the Dachau concentration camp complex, which played a central role in the Nazis' policy of exploitation and extermination in the late phase of the Holocaust.

Introduction

During the second half of 1945, approximately 121,500 Jewish Holocaust survivors returned to Hungary or the formerly Hungarian-occupied territories from the liberated concentration and labor camps as well as the death marches.[1]

---

[1] However, a large part of the Hungarian survivors did not return to their country of origin as a result of their experiences during the Holocaust. They prepared their emigration overseas or to Palestine. Cf. Götz Aly and Christian Gerlach: *Das letzte Kapitel. Realpolitik, Ideologie und der Mord an den ungarischen Juden 1944/1945*, Stuttgart: Deutsche Verlags-Anstalt, 2002, 409; Regi-

 OpenAccess. © 2023 the author(s), published by De Gruyter. This work is licensed under the Creative Commons Attribution-NonCommercial-NoDerivatives 4.0 International License.
https://doi.org/10.1515/9783110746464-022

Most of the returnees had to cross Budapest. In many instances the repatriates arrived both physically and mentally in critical states, often unable to return to their former homes. The Jewish organization Deportáltakat Gondozó Országos Bizottság (DEGOB, engl. National Committee for Attending Deportees), which had already been founded in the last days of the war, reached out to survivors in need, passing or arriving the Hungarian capital. DEGOB provided them with food, clothing, and shelter. Besides social work, one of the main activities of the organization became gathering information about the persecution, extermination and exploitation of the Hungarian Jews during the Second World War.[2]

The majority of DEGOB's interviewees had belonged to a group of roughly 176,000 Hungarian[3] concentration camp prisoners whom the Nazis and their collaborators had deported from Hungary to the territory of the German Reich for forced labor in the last year of the war.[4] Of them, 17,800 had been imprisoned in the Dachau concentration camp complex.[5] The fate of this group reveals that, unlike in the earlier years of the war, the Germans had no longer deported Jews exclusively from 'West to East' for their destruction, but in the late phase of the Holocaust also from 'East to West' for forced labor.[6]

With its documentation work, DEGOB left behind an important pool of historical sources referring to this phenomenon of deportations. Hence, this contribution extract the information from the protocols concerning the deportees' routes into the Dachau concentration camp complex. Thereby, it will be highlighted how the protocols convey survivors' experiences and memories on

---

na Fritz: *Nach Krieg und Judenmord. Ungarns Geschichtspolitik seit 1944*, Göttingen: Wallstein, 2012, 83–84; Dirk Riedel: "Masseneinlieferungen im letzten Kriegsjahr. Das KZ Dachau und die Juden aus Ungarn", in Sybille Steinbacher (ed.): *Transit US-Zone. Überlebende des Holocaust im Bayern der Nachkriegszeit*, Göttingen: Wallstein, 2013, 60–80, here 73–75.

2 In fact, early DEGOB members have loosely been starting to collect interviews clandestinely before being liberated by the Red Army in February 1945. Cf. Rita Horváth: "Jews in Hungary after the Holocaust: The National Relief Committee for Deportees, 1945–1950", in *The Journal of Israeli History*, 19, 1998, 69–91, here 86.

3 For the sake of simplicity, the terms 'Hungarian Jews' or 'Jews from Hungary' will be used in the following to refer to the entire Jewish population living on Hungarian territory in 1944 and who were directly affected by Hungarian or Nazi policies.

4 Cf. Regina Fritz: "Einleitung", in idem. (ed.): *Die Verfolgung und Ermordung der europäischen Juden durch das nationalsozialistische Deutschland 1933–1945. Volume 15: Ungarn 1944–1945*, Boston: De Gruyter, 2021, 13–84, here 64 and 76.

5 Cf. Riedel, Masseneinlieferungen, 61.

6 This direction of the deportations also affected, among others, the Jewish survivors of the ghettos or camps in the Baltic States, e.g. the Kaunas and Riga ghettos, who were 'evacuated' from the Red Army in autumn 1944. Cf. Karin Orth: *Das System der nationalsozialistischen Konzentrationslager. Eine politische Organisationsgeschichte*, Zürich: Pendo, 2002, 270–271.

those deportations and which factors could contribute to differentiating narratives. In addition, it will be examined what conclusions these statements allow us to draw about the practices of the Nazis in their extermination and deportation policy.

Both the protocols' contents and the deportations of Hungarian Jewish prisoners into the German concentration camp system constitute understudied objects of historical analyses so far. In 2013, Dirk Riedel published a paper on the deportations of Hungarian Jewish prisoners to the Dachau camp complex. He outlined the deportation routes and opened a perspective on the DEGOB protocols, which had received very little attention at the time. Riedel also provided a plausible explanation for the gap in research concerning the Hungarian Jewish concentration camp prisoners. According to him, the history of this group remained in the shadow of the fate of the more than 320,000 Hungarian Jews who were murdered by the Nazis in Auschwitz.[7] One reason for this may also have been that until a few years ago, scholars also faced difficulties in accessing relevant sources concerning the history of Jewish prisoners. Particularly in the field of deportations research, historians were therefore often forced to resort to documents of official provenance and to accordingly reproduce what Yehuda Bauer calls the 'history of the perpetrators.'[8]

The DEGOB protocols can help to challenge this approach and to open up a perspective of the victims, which apparently has remained unnoticed for a long time. Only in recent years, the results and sources of so-called early Holocaust research have received more attention.[9] Although Rita Horváth presented a profound study on the work of the organization in 1998 and researchers increasingly use the protocols as sources for their work,[10] the outcome of DEGOB's documentation work and the content of the protocols have so far remained unanalyzed.[11] In 2013, the Hungarian historian Ferenc Laczó distilled the experiences of former Jewish prisoners of the Buchenwald concentration camp from the DEGOB protocols.[12]

---

[7] Cf. Riedel, Masseneinlieferungen, 62; Fritz, Einleitung, 64.
[8] Cf. Yehuda Bauer and Klaus Binder: *Der Tod des Schtetls*, Berlin: Suhrkamp, 2013, 36. Translation by the author.
[9] Cf. Laura Jockusch: *Collect and Record! Jewish Holocaust Documentation in Early Postwar Europe*, Oxford: Oxford University Press, 2012.
[10] For one example of current research using DEGOB protocols, see Dora Pataricza's article in this volume.
[11] Cf. Horváth, Jews in Hungary after the Holocaust.
[12] Ferenc Laczó: "'I could hardly wait to get out of this camp, even though I knew it would only get worse until liberation came'. On Hungarian Jewish Accounts of the Buchenwald Concentration Camp from 1945–1946", in *Hungarian Historical Review*, 2, 2013, 605–638.

Hence, the article's first part critically examines the general representation of the deportations in DEGOB's protocols and confronts them with other sources of Holocaust research. The second section analyzes the qualitative information regarding the deportations to the Dachau concentration camp complex entailed in the protocols' contents, embeds the survivors' memories within their historical contexts, and sets these narratives in relation to other relevant sources. Using selected sample protocols in which the deportations are thematized in a particularly vivid manner, this section chronologically traces the deportation processes from Hungary, via the ghettos and Auschwitz or Hegyeshalom at the German-Hungarian border, to the Dachau camp complex.

The DEGOB Protocols and the Deportations

DEGOB conducted up to 4,600 interviews with survivors of the Holocaust until June 1946.[13] In at least 250 transcripts, Jewish survivors of the Dachau camp complex shared their memories regarding their experiences during the Holocaust. Conducting the interviews with the Jewish returnees, DEGOB staff followed a questionnaire which consisted of 304 specific questions subdivided into twelve core areas. The all in all 29 interviewers aimed at chronologically tracing the interviewees' personal experiences during the Holocaust, ranging from their lives before the Holocaust, during the ghettoization and deportation, inside the concentration camps, throughout the death marches, in the light of the liberation, as well as during their journeys back to Hungary. Eventually, also the witness' plans for the future were covered in the interviews.[14] Today, almost all of the minutes can be viewed online or in the archives of the Hungarian Jewish Museum.[15]

---

13 Cf. DEGOB: "The Protocols". Available at: http://degob.org/index.php?showarticle=201. Last accessed: 15.05.2021; Horváth, Jews in Hungary, 75; Jockusch, Collect and record, 186.
14 Cf. Horváth, Jews in Hungary, 87–88; Laczó, On Hungarian Jewish accounts, 610.
15 Almost all the transcripts can be found in digital form at DEGOB: "Online database in English and Hungarian". Available at: www.degob.hu and www.degob.org respectively. Last accessed: 04.02.2022. Most of the transcripts accessible there have been translated into English recently. Only a small part of the protocols was translated into English or German already shortly after the war. However, in the texts available on degob.hu the names of the interviewed survivors have been rendered unrecognizable through anonymization. The digital collection of Yad Vashem also contains a large part of the DEGOB transcripts. There, the names of the interviewed persons are generally available. However, very few of them are translated from the Hungarian originals. Cf. DEGOB: "The Protocols". Available at: http://degob.org/index.php?showarticle=201. Last accessed: 09.03.2022.

The scope and the level of detail of the protocols obviously depended on the interviewer's individual approach.[16] From a methodological perspective, the crucial influence of the interviewer marks both a strength and a weakness of the protocols. The interviewers' questions largely aimed to inquire facts concerning concrete events the survivors witnessed during the Holocaust. For one of DEGOB's goals was to contribute sources and documentation for war crime trials in the postwar era.[17] Thus, the protocols in many cases consist of information that frequently appears pointedly prepared and hence valuable for historiographical analyses. In addition, the interviewers questioned the statements of their interviewees and aimed to find out whether the interviewees had experienced the stories themselves or only knew about them from hearsay.[18] However, the strict orientation towards an interview guideline also creates difficulties. The transcripts often lack a personal, subjective touch, as is the case with Holocaust memoirs or more recent oral history projects. In addition, the protocols are strongly influenced by the interest of the respective interviewers. As the historian Jens-Christian Wagner puts it correctly, "the risk of statements being guided by leading questions is particularly high with this type of oral report".[19] Without a doubt, this can diminish the informative value of the protocols and create unified historical images. The motivation and cognitive interest of the interviewers ought to be kept in mind when reading the protocols.

However, as one of the Nazis' central instruments of repression and power, the interviewers devoted particular attention to the deportations. Their specific questions about this topic were aimed at the preparation of the deportations, the period of deportation as well as the conditions during the journey.[20] The survivors had mostly witnessed a complex deportation history, which was linked to various places of persecution within the Nazis' sphere of power ranging from the ghettos to the concentration camps.[21] Therefore, the mentioned questions arose repeatedly in many cases. To simplify, a section located above the transcribed interview provides a concise summary of the personal data of the interviewee

---

16 Cf. Horváth, Jews in Hungary, 87–88.
17 Cf. DEGOB: "The Protocols". Available at: http://degob.org/index.php?showarticle=201. Last accessed: 15.05.2021; Horváth, Jews in Hungary, 75.
18 EHRI: "Deportáltakat Gondozó Országos Bizottság (DEGOB)". Available at: https://portal.ehri-project.eu/units/hu-002736-visszaeml%C3%A9kez%C3%A9sek_gy%C5%B1jtem%C3%A9nye_1945_2010-pih_i_m. Last accessed: 21.05.2021; Horváth, Jews in Hungary, 89.
19 Cf. Jens-Christian Wagner: *Produktion des Todes. Das KZ Mittelbau-Dora*, Göttingen: Wallstein, 2015, 36. Translation by the author.
20 Cf. Horváth, Jews in Hungary, 88.
21 Cf. Aly and Gerlach, Das letzte Kapitel, 380–381.

(place of birth, date of birth, occupation) as well as the dates of entry and exit at the various places of persecution and imprisonment. This reaches from the pre-stages of the deportations, the ghettos and the 'yellow star houses' in Budapest, to the various places of detention ranging from the ghettos into the concentration camp system and mostly ending at the place of liberation. Such a data string, provided by the survivor Salamon Fülöp, could appear as follows:

> Getto: Munkács
> Camps: Auschwitz (May 27 to June 4, 1944)
> Warsaw (June 6 to beginning of August 1944)
> Dachau (mid-August to end of August 1944)
> Kaufering (End of August to end of September 1944)
> Landsberg (End of September 1944 to beginning of February 1945)
> Kaufering (Beginning of February to beginning of March 1945)
> Landsberg (Beginning of March to April 26, 1945)[22]

Between the entries and exits at the respective places of the survivor's detention, in numerous protocols it is therefore possible to roughly identify the periods and routes of the deportations even before reading the protocols' texts. Thus, precise indications of time and space can help to uncover individual routes of deportations of Hungarian Jews through the concentration camp system previously unrepresented by common perpetrator sources such as transfer lists, for example. A major problem with the use of the latter is that they are often fragmentary in nature. In the last days of the war, the Nazis and/or their allies destroyed large parts of their holdings that would have provided insight into the deportations and particularly prisoner transports within the concentration camp system. Moreover, using perpetrator-related sources, the prisoners' trajectories through the concentration camp system can often only be reconstructed with difficulty. Information on specific prisoners must be brought together from various sources, sometimes stored in disparate locations.[23] The DEGOB protocols, in contrast, offer easily accessible information about the individual deportation history of survivors in only one document and therefore contribute to an understanding of the ways of Jewish prisoners through the concentration camp system. Combin-

---

22 DEGOB interrogation transcript of Salamon Fülöp, O.15 E, 534, Yad Vashem Archives. Available at: https://documents.yadvashem.org/index.html?language=en&search=global&strSearch=salamon%20f%C3%BCl%C3%B6p&GridItemId=3542696. Last accessed: 08.03.2022.
23 Cf. Henning Borggräfe: "Die Rekonstruktion von Verfolgungswegen im NS-Terrorsystem. Eine Fallstudie zu Opfern der Aktion 'Arbeitsscheu Reich'", in idem. (ed.): *Freilegungen. Wege, Orte und Räume der NS-Verfolgung*, Göttingen: Wallstein, 2016, 56–82.

ing the protocols with sources from the camp administrations yields a profound insight into the deportations and prisoner transports.

Within the field of Holocaust memoirs the DEGOB protocols prove outstanding informative value. One reason for this is the interviews' and protocols' temporal context of emergence. As has already been mentioned, DEGOB conducted its interviews mainly between 1945 and 1946. Thus, the events described in the protocols have a strong immediate character for the proximity made it easier for the interviewed Jews to recall and state detailed information on their individual deportation histories. Accordingly, it is noticeable that the protocols are more likely to contain more specific dates than other comparable Holocaust memoirs that were mostly published during the later twentieth century until today. Another advantage is that DEGOB preserved the memories of survivors who might never have written down their memories. For example, DEGOB deliberately interviewed people from the remote regions of Carpato-Ruthenia, whose Jewish inhabitants mostly came from highly disadvantaged social classes.[24] DEGOBS' documentation work thus enables us today to access a broad spectrum of the deportation experiences of Jewish survivors, which is not limited by social or regional boundaries.

However, it is imperative to maintain a critical perspective on this data regarding the deportations provided by the survivors. In biographical research, for example, the protocols' usage meets its limits. As shown before, DEGOB's online accessible protocols are mostly made unrecognizable through anonymization. Only a small proportion of respondents are identifiable by name. Accordingly, in some cases it can result difficult to contrast the protocols with other sources. Furthermore, the data stated by the survivors should be critically questioned. Due to the enormous pressure the Jews suffered during their persecution, it could prove difficult for them to memorize places or periods of time accurately. The horrors of the ghettos or camps often overlaid the memory of what must have seemed banalities.

Deportations from Hungary

On March 19, 1944, Germany invaded Hungary. Besides military reasons for the occupation, the Nazis aimed to finally gain influence over the Hungarian Jews. Despite Hungarian anti-Jewish decrees and measures, they had not yet come

---

24 Fritz, Nach Krieg und Judenmord, 93–94.

under the sphere of influence of German anti-Jewish policy until 1944.[25] In addition, the German leadership aimed to deport Hungarian-Jewish prisoners to the Reich, who should then be exploited in the tumbling German armaments industry.[26] Thus, immediately after the invasion, Reichssicherheitshauptamt's (RSHA) '*Judenreferat*' under the direction of Adolf Eichmann ordered several measures against the Hungarian Jews to pave the way for the deportations of the Jews from the country.[27] Until April 4, the occupants, together with representatives of the Hungarian administration, hastily elaborated a so-called masterplan to eject, expropriate and deport the Jews from Hungarian territory. The plan foresaw to divide the country in six geographical and administrative operational zones and to consecutively deport the Jewish population according to these subdivisions. Zone one and two represented the main part of the territories, which Hungary had gained due to its expansion policy between 1938 and 1941: Carpato-Ruthenia, Northeastern Hungary (Zone 1) and Northern Transylvania (Zone 2).[28] These should be followed by Northern Hungary (Zone 3), Southeastern Hungary (Zone 4), as well as Western and Southwestern Hungary (Zone 5, including the Hungarian occupied Bačka), and at last by Budapest and its surroundings.[29]

Hungary – Auschwitz – Dachau

On April 23, 1944, Edmund Veesenmayer, envoy of the Reich and co-responsible for the 'Final Solution' in Hungary, telegraphed to the German Ministry of Foreign Affairs that the ghettoization and deportations of the Jews had begun in

---

25 Cf. Fritz, Einleitung, 50; Aly and Gerlach, Das letzte Kapitel, 249.
26 For the construction of large scale bomb-proof manufacturing bunkers, Hitler advocated exploiting Jewish concentration camp prisoners from Hungary, thus revoking Himmler's decision, made only in September 1942, to ban all Jews from concentration camps within the pre-war borders of the Reich. However, Hitler's decision not only affected the Hungarian Jews, but all 'able-bodied' Jews who were still alive and in the Nazis' sphere of power. Cf. Fritz, Einleitung, 60; Marc Buggeln: *Das System der KZ-Außenlager. Krieg, Sklavenarbeit und Massengewalt*, Bonn: Archiv der Sozialen Demokratie, 2012, 137.
27 Telegram of Gerhart Feine to the German Ministry of Foreign Affairs, 28.03.1944, in Heim et al., Verfolgung und Ermordung, volume 15, document no. 117; extract from the Ministerial Council Protocol (paragraph no. 66), 28.03.1944, in ibid., document no. 119.
28 The government hoped that the fate of the often less assimilated, Yiddish-speaking Jewish population living in Carpato-Ruthenia or Northern Transylvania would raise only little sympathy among the Hungarian Christian majority society. Cf. Randolph L. Braham: *The Politics of Genocide. The Holocaust in Hungary*, Detroit: Wayne State University Press, 2000, 112.
29 Cf. ibid., 113–114, 153.

Carpato-Ruthenia. According to Veesenmayer, 3,000 Jews were to be deported daily from May 15 onwards to Auschwitz. Initially, also those 'fit for work' among the Hungarian Jews who were targeted by the Germans were also supposed to be deported to the extermination camp.[30]

One of DEGOB's interviewees was a young man, who in protocol no. 90 is only marked by his initials GE. GE was born in Nagyszőlős (today Виноградів in Ukraine) in Carpato-Ruthenia, which has been annexed by the Hungarian state in March 1939. GE was 20 years old and worked as a chef, when the Germans invaded his hometown.[31] Another interviewee was a Jewish girl named LZ in DEGOB's protocol nr. 3055; she was a 14-year-old student when the Germans occupied Hungary. She was born and raised in Mezőcsát, not far from Miskolc in northern Hungary and came from a well-situated family. Roughly two months after the occupation, LZ and her family had to leave their homes for the Mezőcsát ghetto.[32]

In mid-May 1944, the Hungarian Gendarmerie began to carry out the evacuation of the ghettos and the entrainment of the Jews in the occupied territories. In a smaller amount, Eichmann's men supervized those actions.[33] After eight days in the Nagyszőlős ghetto, GE and his family were forced on a transport to Auschwitz:

> After six days we set off. By this time many Jews had already died or committed suicide. We were not given food at all and we were driven like animals, pushed and thrown into the freight cars. There were 80 people in a cattle car. I was the commander of the car being responsible for everybody. Escaping from the freight car would have been possible, but I did not want to leave my mother. We travelled for ten days and during that time we were given water only three times. The Hungarians escorted us until we reached Kassa where the Germans took us over.[34]

Alongside the ghettos, the Hungarian authorities established assembly centers in places like brickyards or other abandoned localities as a collection point for the

---

30 Telegram from Edmund Veesenmayer to the German Ministry of Foreign Affairs, 23.04.1944, in Heim et al., Verfolgung und Ermordung, volume 15, document no. 147.
31 DEGOB: "Protocol Nr. 90". Available at: http://degob.org/?showjk=90. Last accessed: 25.05.2021.
32 Cf. DEGOB: "Protocol Nr. 3055". Available at: http://degob.org/?showjk=3055. Last accessed: 25.05.2021.
33 Cf. Aly and Gerlach, Das letzte Kapitel, 278–279.
34 DEGOB: "Protocol Nr. 90". Available at: http://degob.org/?showjk=90. Last accessed: 25.05.2021.

Jewish deportees, which were to be sent to Auschwitz.[35] Together with the Jews from Mezőcsát ghetto, in mid-May Hungarian Gendarmes brought LZ to a brickyard in Miskolc:

> We could take whatever we could fit into a rucksack. All the small items that looked precious were taken away. Our barrack in the brick factory was open on the sides; we were lying on the ground. The air was unbearable inside [...]. We were guarded by SS men: they beat us so hard that more than one person was beaten to death [...]. Our destination was not yet revealed: we could only hope that we would be taken into the inner parts of the country to work. [...] There were 75 of us in a cattle car. We got some water before we left. Gendarmes escorted us to Kassa and the Germans took over us there. Here we realized that we were taken towards Poland.[36]

The narrations reflect the radical practice of the Hungarian Gendarmerie or the SS, which used brutal violence to round up the Jews and force them into the cattle waggons or to guard them in primitive transitional accommodations. Both survivors also mention the fatal conditions during the ride to Auschwitz, the lack of provisions, and the oppression. The official deportation plan foresaw 70 people per cattle car, however both survivors remember that this number was exceeded in each of their cars.[37] It is remarkable that GE and LZ broach the issue of their expectations about what was happening to them. Statements like these reveal that both the Hungarian and the German forces resorted to well-established Nazi tactics in order to camouflage their real intentions. Guards made Jews like GE and LZ believe that they were to be exploited as forced laborers within Germany.[38] While for GE and LZ this would later even turn out to be true (which neither the SS nor the deportees could know at the time), for most Jews this represented a lie that only served the purpose to prevent resistance among the deportees. Most of them were unaware of what really awaited them.[39]

---

35 Cf. Fritz, Einleitung, 63.
36 DEGOB: "Protocol Nr. 3055". Available at: http://degob.org/?showjk=3055. Last accessed: 25.05.2021.
37 Cf. Aly and Gerlach, Das letzte Kapitel, 276.
38 The Nazis applied this strategy from the very beginning of their deportation policy. From autumn 1941 onwards, German Jews were led to believe that they were being transported to the East for 'labor deployment'. Cf. Akim Jah: "Die Deportationen der Juden aus Deutschland 1941–1945. Zur Geschichte und Dokumentenüberlieferung im Archiv des ITS", in idem. and Gerd Kühling (eds.): *Fundstücke. Die Deportationen der Juden aus Deutschland und ihre verdrängte Geschichte nach 1945*, Göttingen: Wallstein, 2016, 11–29, here 13–15.
39 Cf. Aly and Gerlach, Das letzte Kapitel, 285.

Between May and July 1944, almost all deportations from Hungary led to Auschwitz-Birkenau.[40] After the arrival of the Hungarian Jews, the SS undertook selections among them to separate Jews who were 'able to work' from those who were supposedly not.[41] Protocol nr. 90 reflects GE's memories concerning the arrival and selections in Auschwitz-Birkenau:

> After we arrived in Auschwitz, the Poles [the Polish prisoner functionaries in Auschwitz] threw the children and elderly people out of the freight cars, and I could hardly say goodbye to my mother and my sister in the midst of crying and moaning. Although we were told that they would allow the families to stay together, we were separated. I have not seen my mother since then. Soon they started the selection, during which they separated the ill from those who were incapable of working.[42]

LZ, on the other hand, put forward the following:

> After arriving in Auschwitz in the afternoon of June 8, we had to get off the train, but the luggage stayed in the cattle cars. On the platform we were lined up in rows of three; I was queuing up with my mother, but a German officer separated us and ever since I have not heard anything from my poor mother.[43]

Alongside 100,000 Jews from Hungary, the SS declared both LZ and GE as 'fit' for forced labor. In the chaotic moments of arrival and selection, the SS separated them from their mothers, who were – like roughly 320,000 Hungarian Jews – murdered promptly after the selection in Birkenau's gas chambers.[44] The practice of selections, however, finds little place in the accounts of the two survivors. They are noticeably overshadowed by the horror of arriving at Auschwitz-Birkenau and, in particular, the trauma of having lost closest family members.

Shortly after the arrival and the selections, the SS transported most of those selected for labor to workplaces outside of the extermination camp. Hence,

---

40 Cf. Fritz, Einleitung, 64.
41 The selection practices of the SS often seem arbitrary and apparently followed only loose guidelines. In general, however, it can be stated that the SS doctors selected children, older people, pregnant women, sick and injured persons as well as parents with children as 'not fit for work'. Cf. Nikolaus Wachsmann: *KL. Die Geschichte der nationalsozialistischen Konzentrationslager*, Bonn: Bundeszentrale für politische Bildung, 2016, 530.
42 DEGOB: "Protocol Nr. 90". Available at: http://degob.org/?showjk=90. Last accessed: 25.05.2021.
43 DEGOB: "Protocol Nr. 3055". Available at: http://degob.org/?showjk=3055. Last accessed: 25.05.2021.
44 Cf. Fritz, Einleitung, 64–65.

Auschwitz-Birkenau only constituted a transition place for those prisoners.[45] LZ stated concrete data concerning one of these transports: "In ten days ca. 800 of us were put on a laborer's transport and taken to Plaszow, near Krakow. We arrived there after ten days of travel in cattle cars with 50 prisoners each".[46] In Plaszow, the SS forced LZ to work in a quarry. After an undefined period, LZ once again had to enter a cattle car, this time leading back to Auschwitz-Birkenau. The prisoner transport would take a very long time for the relatively short distance between Plaszow and Auschwitz: "[W]e were taken back to Auschwitz. We travelled for two days again; only a sliver of bread was distributed and only for a few people".[47] GE on the other hand had to work in Auschwitz's infamous 'Sonderkommando' ('special work unit') until he managed to get on a transport to Warsaw concentration camp. There, the SS obliged male Jewish prisoners to clear the remains of the former Warsaw ghetto.[48]

End of May 1944, however, the SS began the transports from the concentration camps in the east to those in the west within the 'Altreich' whose concentration camps had been declared 'judenfrei' ('free of Jews') just one year before.[49] Simultaneously the SS began to transport roughly 9,000 Hungarian Jews, mostly via Auschwitz but also via Warsaw, to the Dachau camp complex. There they were imprisoned in newly established sub-camp complexes outside of Dachau's main camp like Kaufering, Mühldorf or Allach. For the most part, Jewish prisoners had to work on large-scale construction sites of the Organization Todt (OT) in these camps to build armament bunkers for the aviation industry.[50] A minority, in this period mostly women, were forced to work in the armament industry itself.[51]

As the Red Army was advancing towards the Polish capital in end of July, the SS dissolved the Warsaw concentration camp. Among roughly 4,000 other prisoners, the SS drove GE from Warsaw on a gruelling march in direction to Kutno, a

---

[45] The SS labelled such prisoners, who were to stay only a short time in Auschwitz as *Depothäftlinge* (depot prisoners). Cf. ibid., 65.

[46] DEGOB: "Protocol Nr. 3055". Available at: http://degob.org/?showjk=3055. Last accessed: 25.05.2021.

[47] Ibid.

[48] Cf. Andreas Mix: "Warschau", in Wolfgang Benz and Barbara Distel (eds.): *Der Ort des Terrors. Geschichte der nationalsozialistischen Konzentrationslager*, volume 8, Munich: Beck, 2008, 100–104.

[49] Cf. Wachsmann, Geschichte, 512.

[50] Cf. Sabine Schalm: *Überleben durch Arbeit? Außenkommandos und Außenlager des KZ Dachau 1933–1945*, Berlin: Metropol, 2009, 123–124; Riedel, Masseneinlieferungen, 64.

[51] Cf. Schalm, Außenkommandos und Außenlager, 193.

town in the Warthegau. There the SS forced them in cattle wagons and set them off to Dachau:

> After that there was a terrible retreat. About 5000 people were driven on foot towards a destination 130 kilometres away. We marched 30 kilometres a day in heavy rain. For the whole journey we received only one third of a loaf of bread. Each of us had to carry three blankets. We had to sleep on those wet, completely soaked blankets under the open sky, in pouring rain. We were entrained at a place 130 kilometres from Warsaw. The Germans started to beat and chase us again. Later we suffered from the terribly hot weather and we did not have any water for four days. [...] [O]ne of my townsmen died of thirst in the lap of his son. He was moaning and begging for water, but we could not help him. That man even tore his gold teeth out of his own mouth and gave them to the SS guards [...]. After travelling for six days without food and water we arrived in Dachau. By the time we got off the freight car, 14 out of 60 people had already been dead.[52]

Also LZ was assigned for forced labor within Germany. Prior to her transport, the SS once more examined her working capability:

> Selections were frequent at the end of August. On September 2, 500 of us were put on a transport again and were taken to Augsburg. There were perhaps 60 prisoners in a freight car. We got a whole loaf of bread and some sausage for the four-day travel.[53]

In August and September 1944, both of the exemplary cases arrived in the Dachau concentration camp complex. After the horrifying march and transport from Warsaw GE arrived in the main camp whereas LZ had to work in Augsburg's Michelwerke factory, a supplier for Messerschmitt. Therefore, the SS interned her in Dachau's sub-camp Augsburg-Kriegshaber.[54]

The histories of GE and LZ permit the conclusion that the deportation practices transformed during the summer of 1944. From 1941 onwards, the mass deportations of Jews led from the German Reich or other countries within Nazis' sphere of power to ghettos, concentration or extermination camps within the occupied territories in the east and served as pre-stage for extermination.[55] With the mass transports in the opposite direction, of Jewish slave laborers into the Reich's heartlands, this practice changed. Both GE's and LZ's unvoluntary jour-

---

[52] DEGOB: "Protocol Nr. 90". Available at: http://degob.org/?showjk=90. Last accessed: 25.05.2021.
[53] DEGOB: "Protocol Nr. 3055". Available at: http://degob.org/?showjk=3055. Last accessed: 25.05.2021.
[54] Cf. Wolfgang Kucera: "Augsburg-Kriegshaber", in Wolfgang Benz and Barbara Distel (eds.): *Der Ort des Terrors. Geschichte der nationalsozialistischen Konzentrationslager*, volume 2, Munich: Beck, 2014, 286–288.
[55] Regarding the deportations of Jews from Germany cf. Jah, Dokumentenüberlieferung, 13–15.

neys towards Dachau formed part of this pattern. However, this did not mean that these Jewish prisoners were exempt from the Nazis' extermination policy. The execution of the transports in this phase of the Holocaust strongly proves this. During 1944 and after the arrival of Hungarian Jews in Auschwitz, the SS-Wirtschafts-Verwaltungshauptamt (WVHA) did not cease to demand more Jewish forced laborers for the concentration camps in the Reich.[56] The SS sent Jewish prisoners from camps in the eastern areas, such as the overcrowded Auschwitz camp complex or the camp in Warsaw, on inhumane transports to fulfil the WVHA's target.[57] The transport from Warsaw to Dachau was, and resulted aggravating for the prisoners, not only a forced laborer but also an evacuation transport from the dissolved Warsaw concentration camp.

These transports were accompanied by SS men from the eastern concentration and extermination camps who had previously distinguished themselves by their willingness to participate in the extermination of Jews.[58] Treating Jews as workers whose labor force was to be preserved, was far from their minds. The authority of the WVHA or Himmler, which in theory demanded physically 'able-bodied' prisoners for the needs of the industry, rarely prevailed on such transports.[59] GE's (and many others') narratives of the detached, brutal violence of the SS men underline this moment particularly strongly.[60] Practically, deportations and prisoner transports could perform a double function: transport and extermination went hand in hand. Such as forced labor, deportations constituted an instrument of power that not only moved prisoners from one place to another but also decimated those, who after all, according to Nazi's concept of the 'Final Solution' were supposed to be murdered eventually, be it in Auschwitz, Dachau or during the transports.

---

56 In his memoirs which he wrote in a Polish prison shortly before his execution in 1947, the Auschwitz camp commander Rudolf Höß discusses the labor force demands of the WVHA. His remarks must admittedly be read critically, but they appear plausible since they are backed up by further source material. Cf. Rudolf Höß: *Kommandant in Auschwitz. Autobiographische Aufzeichnungen des Rudolf Höß*, edited by Martin Broszat, Munich: DTV, 1998, 246.
57 Cf. Andrea Rudorff: "Einleitung", in idem. (ed.): *Die Verfolgung und Ermordung der europäischen Juden durch das nationalsozialistische Deutschland 1933–1945. Volume 16: Das KZ Auschwitz 1942–1945 und die Zeit der Todesmärsche 1944/45*, Boston: De Gruyter, 2021, 13–97, here 40.
58 Concerning the fanaticism of SS men from the 'eastern concentration camps', cf. Wachsmann, Geschichte, 656–657.
59 Cf. Orth, Politische Organisationsgeschichte, 272–273.
60 After the war, the transport leader of the Warsaw transport, Alfred Kramer, openly stated that he was an enemy of Jews and confessed the mass murder of Jews during the march and transport from Warsaw to Dachau. Cf. Interrogation transcript Alfred Kramer, 51 Js 46/77, State Archive Augsburg.

In this analysis GE's experiences have in the main proven this apparent inconsistency within the deportation and extermination policy. Still, LZ's experiences underline the ambivalent nature of the deportation practices in the late stage of the Holocaust as well. In the interview, the Hungarian girl highlighted that the SS provided her an unusual and relatively appropriate level of provisions before entering the transport to Bavaria. The transport to Augsburg was long and arduous, but unlike other transports it was significantly less marked by incidents. This somewhat better treatment undoubtfully was no symbol of any act of humanity of the SS. It much rather shows that in individual cases the perpetrators tried to comply with the WVHA's and the industry's request for physically healthy Jewish prisoners. The use of prisoners in industrial factories rarely amounted to extermination measures, since companies like the Michelwerke were interested in employing forced laborers for longer periods of time.[61]

LZ and GE were among roughly 9,000 other Hungarian Jews whom the SS transported from Auschwitz or Warsaw to the Dachau concentration camp complex in summer 1944.[62] The SS forced LZ to perform slave labor in the armament industry but also to work in the fields next to the Mühldorf sub-camp complex in April 1945. In the last days of the war, LZ once more had to embark one of the so-called death trains, before US-American troops liberated her in Seeshaupt.[63] GE, however, stayed in Dachau only for a short time. Two weeks after his arrival in Dachau, the SS sent him to Buchenwald and back to the Majdanek camp in occupied Poland from there. His history of persecution reminds of an odyssey, as from Majdanek, the SS sent him once more back to Bavaria, this time to Mühldorf, to work for the OT.[64]

Budapest – Hegyeshalom – Zurndorf – Dachau

After the deportations from the Hungarian provinces, the Germans' gaze turned to the Jews in Budapest. On July 6, 1944, however, Edmund Veesenmayer tele-

---

[61] Regarding the forced labor employment of Jews and especially Jewish women in the armament industry from 1944 onwards, cf. Buggeln, System, 124–127.
[62] Cf. Riedel, Masseneinlieferungen, 64.
[63] Cf. DEGOB: "Protocol Nr. 3055". Available at: http://degob.org/?showjk=3055. Last accessed: 25.05.2021.
[64] Cf. DEGOB: "Protocol Nr. 90". Available at: http://degob.org/?showjk=90. Last accessed: 25.05.2021.

graphed to Berlin that Miklós Horthy had halted the deportations to Auschwitz.[65] In doing so, Horthy primarily bowed to the international pressure that was being put on him due to the deportations of the Jews from the Hungarian provinces.[66] In July 1944, solely the Jews of the capital and the members of the Jewish labor service remained in Hungary.[67] Their destiny remained uncertain and a tug-of-war between the German occupiers and the Hungarian administration started over the Jewish Community of Budapest and those forced to work in the labor battalions. Yet the German leadership, most notably Heinrich Himmler, seemingly accepted the Hungarian move – at least temporarily. Their biggest concern was the risk of losing yet another ally in the war, particularly after Romania's retreat.[68] Despite these anticipations, Miklós Horthy and the Hungarian Lakatos-government pursued the target to drag the country of the war, whose continuation was unmistakably to no avail, considering the military situation at the eastern front.[69] On October 15, 1944, Hungary's state leader Horthy indeed announced Hungary's withdrawal from the alliance with Germany. The Nazis promptly intervened and ultimately conducted a yet organized *coup d'état* to bring their confidant Ferenc Szálasi, the leader of the Arrow Cross (*Nilyas*) Party, to power.[70] Immediately after Szálasi's antisemitic and quasi-National Socialist Arrow Cross government had taken control over the Hungarian state and its institutions, they once more resumed anti-Jewish measures. On October 17, the Hungarian regime signed Eichmann's demands of the systematic persecution and deportation of the remaining 300,000 Hungarian Jews to Germany.[71] The extermination machinery at Auschwitz-Birkenau was already being shut down by this time and the war situation prevented rail transports urgently needed for the front from being made available for mass deportations.[72] Thus, Eichmann urged the Hungarian Gendarmerie to guard death marches to the German-Hungarian border. Only those not able to work, however, ought to be left in Budapest's specially established ghettos.[73] Around 20,000 of those remaining Jews

---

65 Telegram Edmund Veesenmayer to Joachim von Ribbentropp, 06.07.1944, in Heim et al., Verfolgung und Ermordung, volume 15, document no. 237.
66 Cf. Fritz, Einleitung, 71.
67 Cf. Braham, Politics of Genocide, 158–164.
68 Cf. ibid., 166–170.
69 Cf. ibid., 181.
70 Cf. ibid.,181–184.
71 Cf. ibid., 185.
72 Cf. Verena Walter: "Auschwitz. Endphase und Befreiung", in Wolfgang Benz and Barbara Distel (eds.): *Der Ort des Terrors. Geschichte der nationalsozialistischen Konzentrationslager*, volume 5, Munich: Beck, 2007, 79–173, here 154; Fritz, Einleitung, 75.
73 Cf. Braham, Politics of Genocide, 185–187.

were murdered or died of the poor living conditions during the last weeks of the war in Budapest.[74]

On November 8, the Arrow Cross government re-initiated the deportations. In a first step, the Arrow Cross militias herded Jews in several assembly centers, often brickyards such as the one in Óbuda in the northern outskirts of the capital.[75] One person to be affected by this development was VR, a 30-year-old Jewish tailor from Budapest. Like many other Jews in these days, shocked by the antisemitic violence of the Arrow Crows militias, she hoped to find aid at the Swiss Embassy in Budapest. There, Arrow Cross militias trapped and arrested her among others.[76]

In addition, KD, a Jewish merchant, and his wife were unexpectedly arrested by Arrow Cross men on October 14. As KD was already 64 years old, he had not reckoned to be arrested, much less to serve as a forced laborer.[77] Both examples demonstrate how unprepared the Jews of Budapest were, when the Arrow Cross regime began to execute the deportations. KD mentions his gentile neighbors' attempts to warn him being fruitless. In addition, the quoted protocols reveal the brutal recklessness that characterized the deportations carried out in late 1944. According to VR, the paramilitaries insulted and threatened the deportees. In the overcrowded Óbuda brickyards, the guards largely stole from the internees and at the same time refused to facilitate medical supplies nor food. The behavior of the Arrow Cross men and the Gendarmerie was described in a horrendous manner. In particular, the Arrow Cross militias were deeply indoctrinated with fanatic antisemitism and eager to contribute to the 'Final Solution'. The Red Army however, was already very close to Hungary's capital. Poisoned by anti-Jewish propaganda, they saw the Jews as scapegoats for their looming defeat in the war.[78]

The Hungarian security forces lost no time in initiating the deportations of the last Jews from the country. Typically, the Jews had to leave the brickyard in Óbuda after only a few days. Even though they were supposed to serve as slave laborers in Germany, Arrow Cross men and the Gendarmerie forced nearly everyone onto the death marches to the border – old or young, male or female, sick or 'able-bodied'.[79] In the DEGOB interview VR remembered the following:

---

74 Cf. Aly and Gerlach, Das letzte Kapitel, 374.
75 Cf. Braham, Politics of Genocide, 187–188.
76 Cf. DEGOB: "Protocol Nr. 2054". Available at: http://degob.hu/?showjk=2054. Last accessed: 25.05.2021.
77 Cf. DEGOB: "Protocol Nr. 3043". Available at: http://degob.org/?showjk=3043. Last accessed: 25.05.2021.
78 Cf. Braham, Politics of Genocide, 184–185.
79 Cf. ibid., 188.

> The next day they set off on foot for Piliscsaba, and the whole way they amused themselves by shooting a few people. The next day, on the way to Dorog, we were escorted by National Guardsmen who rivalled the Arrow Cross in brutality. Our next stop was Süttő. They drove in forced marches, there were days when we covered 40–50 kilometres. It rained all day and all night, we got soaked, and many of us had to give up our shoes. We were not even taken under shelter for the night, we spent the night in the dirty, muddy fairgrounds. We looked awful. On top of all this, we were given food every 3–4 days: a soup or two, nothing else.[80]

The guards also drove KD and his wife out of the brickyard on foot:

> We started our march through Piliscsaba, where I learned in the market square, where we slept in the open, that 48 people from the previous transport of 3,000 people had died, out of whom 30 committed suicide and the rest were frozen in the cold. In our group only 16–18 people passed away. On our way to Komárom we saw women and men lying in the ditch, most of them had already departed this life […].[81]

These passages narrate the unambiguously dreadful nature of the marches to the Hungarian border vividly, which is in alignment with historian Randolph L. Braham labelling them as "horribly barbaric" or "highway[s] of death".[82] Arrow Cross guards and Gendarmerie policemen treated the marching Jews in the worst way conceivable. Both survivors underline those horrors with clear figures and data. Especially KD lists the numbers of those who died or had been murdered in detail. The exemplary passages shown here demonstrate how the Hungarian guards refused the Jews any 'humane' treatment. KD and VR mention the extremely strenuous walks they were forced to take. The cited protocols show that the deportees suffered greatly from the harsh weather conditions and were provided with only very inadequate provisions. The marches resembled a large-scale extermination campaign in which the guards willingly and actively participated.

The Hungarian-German border served as a handover point for the Jewish deportees to the SS. From there, the SS brought the Jews to the concentration camps in the Reich. Out of the nearly 76,000 Jews who had been displaced in November 1944, the SS deported nearly 5,000 to the Dachau concentration camp complex.[83] From Zurndorf, VR was brought to the Kaufering sub-camp:

---

[80] DEGOB: "Protocol Nr. 2054". Available at: http://degob.hu/?showjk=2054. Last accessed: 25.05.2021. Translation by the author.
[81] DEGOB: "Protocol Nr. 3043". Available at: http://degob.org/?showjk=3043. Last accessed: 25.05.2021.
[82] Braham, Politics of Genocide, 188.
[83] Cf. Fritz, Einleitung, 76; Riedel, Masseneinlieferungen, 67.

We continued on foot to Zürndorf [sic], where we were wagoned in and transported for three days, without food or water, in a sealed wagon. On the way many people died of starvation, in our wagon there were 66 living and 2 dead on arrival. On November 21 we finally arrived in Landsberg.[84]

KD however was already put to a cattle car in Komárom, a town by the Danube and halfway between the capital and the border. In Komárom Arrow Cross men separated him from his wife:

They sorted out people day after day but we hoped that some political change might save us soon from deportation to Germany. But this did not happen. On December 16 we were put into freight cars. There were around 1,500 of us and each of us received a loaf of bread, some kind of sausage and cheese and later on the way also some jam. We were in horrible condition because we could not move, since there were around 60 of us crammed into a freight car. This unpleasant travel made us terribly exhausted but we still cherished the hopes that people older than 60 might be singled out at Hegyeshalom and sent back. Unfortunately, this was not the case. On the December 21 we got off the train at Dachau.[85]

At the border the Germans crammed them into cattle wagons. It is also clear that the SS did not treat the prisoners any better than the Hungarian guards. Although the interviewees did not mention any active physical abuses committed by their guards, the SS did not seem to be interested in a proper treatment of the deportees either. Also, in this stage of the deportation, the Jews had to suffer lack of food, water and especially space.

At this point, particularly KD's protocol illustrates the farce of the 'ability to work' of the Jewish deportees in this phase. In the first place, the Germans had indeed demanded 'able-bodied' workers for their armament industry and construction sites within the Reich. Hence, Rudolf Höß, who was responsible for the takeover of Jews at the border at this time, complained about the condition of the deportees, whom he did not consider suitable for doing forced labor in many cases.[86] This led so far, that occasionally the Germans refused Jews at the border, who, in their perspective, were not 'fit for work'.[87] Statements like

---

[84] DEGOB: "Protocol Nr. 2054". Available at: http://degob.hu/?showjk=2054. Last accessed: 25.05.2021. Translation by the author.
[85] DEGOB: "Protocol Nr. 3043". Available at: http://degob.org/?showjk=3043. Last accessed: 25.05.2021.
[86] Eichmann's role in this dispute is controversial, as he supervised the deportations and originally most strongly pursued the complete extermination of the Jews. On 9 November 1944, however, he allegedly opposed the deportation of Jews who were not 'fit for work'. Cf. Aly and Gerlach, Das letzte Kapitel, 362.
[87] Cf. Fritz, Einleitung, 75.

in the quoted passages nourish the assumption that the goal to deport merely 'able bodied' workers to the Reich was later on more and more disrespected. On November 21, Foreign Minister von Ribbentropp demanded the extradition of all Jews living in Hungary. The Hungarian Arrow Cross government complied with this and drove Jews, regardless of their age, towards the Reich border.[88]

In Dachau, KD had to endure the horrors of the concentration camp and the maltreatment by SS and Kapos. Nevertheless, and most probably due to his age, the SS did not deploy him as a forced laborer. In the last days of the war, KD had to embark on a freight train once again, before the US-Army finally liberated him in Seefeld, Tyrol.[89] In contrast, VR had to perform heavy slave labor for the OT at the construction of an armament bunker. There she witnessed severe atrocities and the death of thousands of Jews from Hungary, Lithuania, Poland, and other European states. In the *'Endphase'* ('final phase'), the SS forced her onto yet another death march, this time directed towards Allach where US-American forces liberated her on April 30, 1945.[90]

According to Aly and Gerlach, around 65,000 Hungarian Jews who were deported to the Reich by the Nazis in the last year of the war, did not survive the Holocaust.[91] At least 5,000 of them died in the Dachau camp complex.[92]

Towards an Integrated History of the Deportations During the Holocaust

DEGOB left to posterity an essential and easily accessible source collection that particularly provides insights into the fate of the roughly 176,000 Hungarian-Jewish prisoners who were transported to the concentration camps within the prewar borders of the Reich in the last year of the war. They reflect the survivors' narratives of persecution of this yet insufficiently researched group of Holocaust victims. On the basis of selected example protocols, it has been shown that they shed light on the deportations of the aforementioned group to concentration camps in the Reich, show the Odysseys of the deportees through the camp sys-

---

88 Cf. László Varga: "Ungarn", in Wolfgang Benz (ed.): *Dimension des Völkermords. Die Zahl der jüdischen Opfer des Nationalsozialismus*, Munich: Oldenburg, 1991, 331–351, here 349.
89 Cf. DEGOB: "Protocol Nr. 3043". Available at: http://degob.org/?showjk=3043. Last accessed: 25.05.2021.
90 Cf. DEGOB: "Protocol Nr. 2054". Available at: http://degob.hu/?showjk=2054. Last accessed: 25.05.2021.
91 Cf. Aly and Gerlach, Das letzte Kapitel, 409.
92 Cf. Riedel, Masseneinlieferungen, 73.

tem, and reflect the experiences they made on these forced journeys. This yields qualitative information about several stages of the deportations during the Holocaust in its last phase: the ghettoizations, the mass transports from Hungary to Auschwitz in the summer months of 1944, and the transports to the Reich in the second half of the year. For the second deportation phase from Hungary, we learn particularly about the experiences of the deportees during the roundups in Budapest, the death marches to the border, and the transports from there to the Reich. Due to the temporal context in which the protocols were created, it was often possible for the survivors to give access to information which is essential for the reconstruction of deportations and prisoner transports. Nevertheless, the content of the transcripts varies and is highly dependent on the interviewer's way of conducting the interview and the survivor's personal background. Therefore, despite their high source value, the protocols must be read carefully.

Furthermore, the narratives transmitted in the DEGOB protocols open up perspectives not only on the survivors' personal experiences during the Holocaust, but also sharpen our understanding of how the perpetrators conducted the transports. Thus, we learn about the significance of the deportations during the different stages of the Holocaust in Hungary and the forced labor deployment of Hungarian Jews, the practices the Nazis and their collaborators applied before, during and after the transports (such as violence or deception methods), and the various perpetrators who took part in them. These specifics often seem inadequately depicted by conventional sources of deportation research.

The portrayed survivors' voices prove especially essential with regard to the history of deportation. In the past, research on the Holocaust and particularly on deportations has largely been dominated by analyses of perpetrator sources, the use of which is problematic for numerous reasons. Centrally, they are often only available in fragments and intensively biased by the ideology of the Nazis and their supporters. Scholars have been seeking alternatives to such one-sided approaches and referred strongly to the voices of the survivors. However, in the past, historians have repeatedly discussed the potentials and limits of prisoner narratives. Considering the source-related peculiarities of the protocols, the survivors' accounts can help to, as Danuta Czech puts it, close gaps within the available sources.[93] Another example is Saul Friedländer's general suggestion of an integrated history as well as the publication of the monumental source edition series *Die Verfolgung und Ermordung der europäischen Juden*, which both con-

---

93 Cf. Danuta Czech: *Kalendarium der Ereignisse im Konzentrationslager Auschwitz-Birkenau 1939–1945*, Hamburg: Rowohlt, 1989, 13.

front the perspective of the perpetrators and the bystanders with the experiences of the survivors.[94] The DEGOB protocols, which convey the memories of a cross-section of Jewish survivors from Hungary, should be taken into account as a contributing source to an integrated history of the Holocaust.

---

[94] Cf. Saul Friedländer: *Den Holocaust beschreiben. Auf dem Weg zu einer integrierten Geschichte*, Göttingen: Wallstein, 2007, 7–27.

After the Arrival in Ghettos and other Deportation Destinations

Ingo Loose
Deportations of Jews to the Ghetto of Litzmannstadt (Łódź)

Some Thoughts on the State of Research, on Older Discussions and Open Questions

Abstract: Using a memorial book from 2009 for more than 4,200 Berlin Jews deported to the ghetto of Litzmannstadt as a starting point, the article outlines the state of research on the ghetto and especially on the deportations from a number of cities in the Reich in autumn 1941. Second, it discusses the significance and position of Litzmannstadt in Shoah research, the desiderata and – in some cases even significant – gaps in our knowledge, but also the uneven reception and evaluation of the preserved sources, i.e. archival findings as well as survivors' testimonies. This includes also the question to what extent the choice of sources influences the nature of the questions we ask about the history of a given ghetto or the Shoah in general.

Introduction: What We Do Know

The ghetto in Łódź (or Litzmannstadt in German, when the town was renamed between 1940 and 1945) in occupied Poland (i.e., in the annexed western territories, the so-called Reichsgau Wartheland or Warthegau) was in terms of size and population after the Warsaw ghetto the second biggest ghetto the Nazis imposed in Eastern Middle Europe and lasted until summer 1944. At this time, the overwhelming majority of European Jews was already murdered in the Shoah. Although Łódź had a numerous Jewish population before September 1, 1939, tens of thousands of Jews were brought to the ghetto also from other regions and from many smaller ghettos in the 'Warthegau' between autumn 1941 and the end of 1942. In the following, I would like to pursue the question of whether the current state of research indicates significant scholarly gaps and what this could mean for further research into the ghetto of Litzmannstadt and for the history of deportations in general.

In 2009, a memorial book was published for the more than 4,200 Jews deported in four transports from Berlin to Litzmannstadt between mid-October and the beginning of November 1941. These were four out of 25 transports (i.e. including five transports with Roma from the Austrian Burgenland region) to

Litzmannstadt, which, apart from a few previous deportations between October 1938 and early 1941, marked the beginning of countless other transports 'to the East'. This marked also the beginning of the industrial dimension of the Shoah through stationary killing camps in autumn 1941, when the erection of the Kulmhof death camp 70 km in the north of Litzmannstadt was already under way.[1] Following the opening of the Radegast commemoration site in Łódź in 2004, this memorial book emerged from a research project for students in cooperation with the State Archives of Łódź and the Foundation Topography of Terror in Berlin. On the basis of preserved transport lists and numerous other archival findings especially in Łódź not only almost all deportees from Berlin (and from Emden, from where Jews were included in the second Berlin transport) were identified, but their individual fate, too, could be precisely described in the context of the ghetto. The documentation includes information on the death of more than 40,000 people within the ghetto, the murder of tens of thousands in the Kulmhof extermination camp and finally on the mass deportations of almost 70,000 Jews to the Auschwitz-Birkenau death camp in August 1944 which marked the liquidation of the Litzmannstadt ghetto as one of the very last ghettos in German occupied Europe.

Since then, several other memorial books have been published – partly concerning other transports from Berlin (e. g. to Minsk),[2] partly for other deportees being sent from the Reich to Litzmannstadt, for example, from Prague, Vienna, Düsseldorf, Luxemburg/Trier,[3] in the fall of 1941.[4] These memorial books have

---

[1] Ingo Loose (ed.): *Berliner Juden im Getto Litzmannstadt 1941–1944. Ein Gedenkbuch*, Berlin/Łódź: Foundation Topography of Terror, 2009; Polish edition: Ingo Loose (ed.): *Żydzi Berlińscy w Litzmannstadt Getto 1941–1944. Księga pamięci*, Berlin/Łódź: Fundacja Topografia Terroru, 2009; Ingo Loose (ed.): *Die Verfolgung und Ermordung der europäischen Juden durch das nationalsozialistische Deutschland 1933–1945. Volume 10: Polen. Die eingegliederten Gebiete August 1941–1945*, Berlin/Boston: De Gruyter, 2020.

[2] Anja Reuss and Kristin Schneider (eds.): *Berlin – Minsk. Unvergessene Lebensgeschichten. Ein Gedenkbuch für die nach Minsk deportierten Berliner Jüdinnen und Juden*, Berlin: Metropol, 2013; Clara Hecker: "Deutsche Juden im Minsker Ghetto", in *Zeitschrift für Geschichtswissenschaft*, 58, 2006, 823–843; Julia Berlit-Jackstien and Karljosef Kreter (eds.): *Abgeschoben in den Tod: Die Deportation von 1001 jüdischen Hannoveranerinnen und Hannoveranern am 15. Dezember 1941 nach Riga*, Hannover: Hahn, 2011.

[3] Angelika Brechelmacher, Bertrand Perz and Regina Wonisch (eds.): *Post 41. Berichte aus dem Getto Litzmannstadt. Ein Gedenkbuch*, Vienna: Mandelbaum, 2015; Pascale Eberhard (ed.): *Der Überlebenskampf jüdischer Deportierter aus Luxemburg und der Trierer Region im Getto Litzmannstadt. Briefe Mai 1942*, Saarbrücken: Blattlausverlag, 2012; Angela Genger and Hildegard Jakobs (eds.): *Düsseldorf / Getto Litzmannstadt. 1941*, Essen: Klartext, 2010; Rolf Uphoff: *Reise ohne Wiederkehr, Wege in das Grauen. Die Deportation der letzten jüdischen Bürger Emdens, Nordens und*

chosen sometimes comparable, sometimes different approaches to the topic of deportations and the Jewish deportees. However, what these publications have in common with their claim not only to historical reconstruction, but also with the intention of commemoration, is the individualization of the victims, not only the listing of their names, but also the exploration of their private life before the deportation. The intention is to portray them as individual human beings, as personalities and not alone as victims, all the less as nameless victims being deported somewhere 'in the East'. What some of these memorial books also strive for, albeit to a different extent, is the connection with the places to which the deportees were involuntarily brought to, that is: in a completely alien and catastrophic world, in which they remained alive for more or less long, or died from the severe living conditions shortly after their arrival or in the long run were murdered in the death camps.

However, the biggest surprise, when working on the memorial book mentioned above, were the numerous reactions from all over the world, emails and letters from relatives and even from a few survivors from Australia to South America, Europe, the USA and Israel. It turned out that there was a large (albeit hardly coherent) community of descendants who followed every new publication on the topic. And what was perhaps even more surprising and satisfying at the same time was that the research also acquired a religious dimension in that many relatives finally, since the exact date of death of the deportees became known for the first time, could say '*yorzeit*' or *kaddish* on the day of death of their beloved ones.

Deportations were a central pillar of the Nazi mass crimes in Europe before (namely in October 1938) and especially during the Second World War and served different motives. First, the expulsion of the Jews was the one and first political goal and central mobilizing ideology of Hitler and the NSDAP since its first days in the early 1920s. Second, the Nazi regime deported Jewish, as well as non-Jewish laborers to work.[5] Third, prisoners were deported to all kinds of camps, Jews to hundreds of ghettos, in order to allegedly fight diseases,

---

Aurichs, Emden: Stadt Emden, 2011; Richard Seemann: *Ghetto Litzmannstadt. Dokumenty a výpovědi o životě českých židů v lodžském ghettu*, Praha: self-published, 2000.
4 For a concise overview of all deportations of Jews from the Reich during the Shoah, see Alfred Gottwaldt and Diana Schulle (eds.): *Die "Judendeportationen" aus dem Deutschen Reich 1941– 1945. Eine kommentierte Chronologie*, Wiesbaden: Marix, 2005.
5 Wolf Gruner: *Jewish Forced Labor Under the Nazis. Economic Needs and Racial Aims, 1938– 1944*, New York: Cambridge University Press, 2006; Dieter Maier: *Arbeitseinsatz und Deportation. Die Mitwirkung der Arbeitsverwaltung bei der nationalsozialistischen Judenverfolgung in den Jahren 1938–1945*, Berlin: Hentrich, 1994.

for the enrichment of the perpetrators and to make room for Germanization. Finally, above all, deportations were a crucial aspect of the Shoah: Three million Jewish victims out of six million altogether were deported in some way, as well as tens of thousands of Roma and Sinti, whose deportations and their fate in general are still insufficiently scrutinized, if not grossly neglected.[6]

If we look at the state of research, Litzmannstadt can probably be considered one of the best-researched ghettos of all, alongside Warsaw. And it should be added that it is also the one with by far the most preserved original sources – from the perpetrators as well as from the victims. Editions, for example the famous chronicle of the ghetto,[7] books, research papers, memorial texts, huge photo collections from Jewish and non-Jewish perspectives,[8] source editions, some of which appeared immediately after the end of the war, are available to researchers today. The same applies to the most diverse forms of commemoration on site and at the places where the deportation trains to Litzmannstadt departed. Finally, the many stumbling stones (*Stolpersteine*) in the places of last residence for deportees should be mentioned as well.

A considerable number of monographs, for example from the pen of Isaiah Trunk or Henryk Rubin,[9] in recent years from Michal Unger, Andrea Löw, and others,[10] prove the good but in some respect still insufficient state of knowledge of the overall history of the Litzmannstadt ghetto. In addition, there are also se-

---

[6] Cf. Birthe Kundrus and Beate Meyer (eds.): *Die Deportation der Juden aus Deutschland. Pläne – Praxis – Reaktionen 1938–1945*, Göttingen: Wallstein, 2005².
[7] Julian Baranowski et al. (eds.): *Kronika getta łódzkiego/Litzmannstadt Getto 1941–1944*, Łódź: Wydawnictwo Uniwersytetu Łódzkiego, 2009; German edition: Sascha Feuchert, Erwin Leibfried and Jörg Riecke (eds.): *Die Chronik des Gettos Lodz/Litzmannstadt*, Göttingen: Wallstein, 2007.
[8] Ingo Loose (ed.): *Das Gesicht des Gettos. Bilder jüdischer Photographen aus dem Getto Litzmannstadt 1940–1944 / The Face of the Ghetto. Pictures taken by Jewish Photographers in the Litzmannstadt Ghetto 1940–1944*, Berlin: Foundation Topography of Terror, 2010; Tanja Kinzel: *Im Fokus der Kamera. Fotografien aus dem Getto Lodz im Spannungsfeld von Kontexten und Perspektiven*, Berlin: Metropol, 2021.
[9] Isaiah Trunk: *Lodzsher geto. A historishe un sotsiologishe shtudie mit dokumentn, tabeles un mape*, New York: Marstin Press, 1962; English edition: idem.: *Łódź Ghetto. A History*, Bloomington/Indianapolis: Indiana University Press, 2006; Icchak (Henryk) Rubin: *Żydzi w Łodzi pod niemiecką okupacją 1939–1945*, London: Kontra, 1988.
[10] Hanno Loewy and Gerhard Schoenberner: *"Unser einziger Weg ist Arbeit." Das Getto in Łódź 1940–1944*, Vienna: Löcker, 1990; Michal Unger (ed.): *The Last Ghetto. Life in the Lodz Ghetto 1940–1944. Ha-geto ha-akharon. Ha-khaym ba-geto lodzh 1940–1944*, Jerusalem: Yad Vashem, 1997³; Andrea Löw: *Juden im Getto Litzmannstadt. Lebensbedingungen, Selbstwahrnehmung, Verhalten*, Göttingen: Wallstein, 2006; Carlos Alberto Haas: *Das Private im Ghetto. Jüdisches Leben im deutsch besetzten Polen 1939 bis 1944*, Göttingen: Wallstein, 2020.

veral detailed studies, for example on the judiciary of the ghetto[11] or on the German administration authorities[12] or even on stamps and money in the ghetto.[13] The role that the deportations played in the decision-making process in Berlin and on the periphery for the murder of European Jews in the fall of 1941 is also described, although it is not exhaustingly studied, especially not in a comparing way.[14] At the same time, in recent years, research results and the commemoration of the victims in the city of Łódź, especially since the 60th anniversary of the liquidation of the ghetto in 2004, have met with intense interest, as reflected in the genesis of the Radegast memorial at the former railway station where the deportations from the Reich arrived and the transports towards the Kulmhof death camp departed,[15] the Park of the Rescued (Park Ocalałych w Łodzi) and the Marek Edelman Dialogue Center.

All in all, it is not entirely presumptuous to say that we know a lot about the Litzmannstadt ghetto, the German plans and goals for it, the involuntarily inhabitants and victims, the deportations from the Reich, Vienna, Prague and Luxembourg, but also from the Reichsgau Wartheland to Litzmannstadt. Furthermore, quite few is known about the responsible perpetrators on site, in the Warthegau's 'capital' Posen (Poznań) and finally also in Berlin.

With this short and incomplete backdrop in mind, one may ask which questions or topics have not yet met sufficient – if any – historical research and which questions are still to be discussed in order to broaden our overall knowledge and maybe to establish new areas of research especially when it comes to

---

11 Svenja Bethke: "Regeln und Sanktionen im Getto Litzmannstadt. Die Bekanntmachungen des Judenratsvorsitzenden Rumkowski", in *Zeitschrift für Genozidforschung*, 1/2, 2013, 30–52; idem: *Tanz auf Messers Schneide. Kriminalität und Recht in den Ghettos Warschau, Litzmannstadt und Wilna*, Hamburg: Hamburger Edition, 2015.
12 Peter Klein: *Die "Gettoverwaltung Litzmannstadt" 1940–1944. Eine Dienststelle im Spannungsfeld von Kommunalbürokratie und staatlicher Verfolgungspolitik*, Hamburg: Hamburger Edition, 2009; Adam Sitarek: *"Otoczone drutem państwo". Struktura i funkcjonowanie administracji żydowskiej getta łódzkiego*, Łódź: Instytut Pamięci Narodowej, 2015.
13 Manfred Schulze and Stefan Petriuk: *Unsere Arbeit – unsere Hoffnung. Getto Lodz 1940–1945. Eine zeitgeschichtliche Dokumentation des Post- und Geldwesens im Lager Litzmannstadt*, Schwalmtal: Phil-Creativ, 1995. See also the article by Anna Veronica Pobbe in this volume.
14 See above all Michael Alberti: *Die Verfolgung und Vernichtung der Juden im Reichsgau Wartheland 1939–1945*, Wiesbaden: Harrassowitz, 2006; Gottwaldt and Schulle, "Judendeportationen" aus dem Deutschen Reich; Wolf Gruner: "Von der Kollektivausweisung zur Deportation der Juden aus Deutschland (1938–1945). Neue Perspektiven und Dokumente", in Kundrus and Meyer, Pläne – Praxis – Reaktionen, 21–62.
15 Cf. Ingo Loose: "Das Vernichtungslager Kulmhof am Ner (Chełmno nad Nerem) 1941 bis 1945", in Beate Meyer (ed.): *Deutsche Jüdinnen und Juden in Ghettos und Lagern (1941–1945). Łódź. Chełmno. Minsk. Riga. Auschwitz. Theresienstadt*, Berlin: Metropol, 2017, 54–75.

the deportations of Jews to the Litzmannstadt ghetto or from the ghetto to the death camps.

Precisely where things seem familiar and well researched to us, historical research can and should focus on three central tasks in addition to knowledge production as such: reflecting on our explanatory models, criticizing methods, and reassessing the preserved sources. In the following, I would like to reduce this to three questions, namely: What do we not yet know? How does the existing knowledge influence and affect research and the public understanding of historiography of the Shoah,[16] of the ghettos, and the deportations in particular? And finally, already in the form of a conclusion: What can the future hold for our perception of the deportations to Litzmannstadt and of deportations during the Shoah in general?

What We Still Do Not Know

Since the researchers' but also the general public's interest in knowledge is constantly changing, depending on our current historical, social and political circumstances, the idea is misleading from the start, that historical research is more or less like a puzzle, in which all is about finding missing parts and inserting them correctly until the finished picture finally lies in front of us. At first sight it seems to be easy, in a certain way additively, which is just as legitimate as it is important, to expand the level of knowledge about the deportations to Litzmannstadt, for example by pressing ahead with research on the still unexplored cities in the Reich from which transports with Jews were directed to the Litzmannstadt ghetto. Primarily this is being done on the micro level with a considerable number of publications in recent years, mostly in Poland and Germany. However, the many different presentations at the conference *Deportations in the Nazi Era – Sources and Research* in November 2020, on which this volume is based, showed how complex the amount of detail quickly becomes.

It has long been known that the deportations from the Reich to the Reichsgau Wartheland had a central function for the radicalization of the Nazi persecution of Jews and their subsequent systematic extermination.[17] Since October

---

[16] On the term Shoah itself, see Dan Michman: "Why Is the Shoah Called 'the Shoah' or 'the Holocaust'? On the History of the Terminology for the Nazi Anti-Jewish Campaign", in *The Journal of Holocaust Research*, 35/4, 2021, 233–256.
[17] Ian Kershaw: "Improvised Genocide? The Emergence of the 'Final Solution' in the Warthegau", in *Transactions of the Royal Historical Society*, 2/6, 1992, 51–78; Peter Klein: "Die Erlaubnis zum grenzenlosen Massenmord – Das Schicksal der Berliner Juden und die Rolle der Einsatz-

1938 at the latest, when 17,000 Jews of Polish nationality were forcibly deported from the Reich to the Polish border, the Nazi leadership had been thinking about how Jews could be deported 'to the East'. Soon after the occupation of Poland in September 1939, large areas, i.e. annexed Western Poland, were designated as territory to be Germanized. With regard to the Reich, it was Reinhard Heydrich, who stated at the Wannsee Conference of January 20, 1942, that "housing issues and other socio-political necessities"[18] added to the urgency of deportations. Apart from deportations from Vienna and Prague, it was the big cities in the '*Altreich*' or rather the cities with the biggest Jewish population, most of them already hit by Allied air raids, from which the Jews started to be deported in autumn 1941. In October 1941 alone more than 8,000 Jews from the '*Altreich*' were brought to Litzmannstadt, altogether approximately 20,000.[19]

However, the first deportations of Polish Jews (and Polish Gentiles) from the Warthegau region to the 'General Government' took place in late autumn and winter 1939/40 to make space for 60,000 Baltic German 'resettlers' who mostly settled in the 'Warthegau' and demanded housing and jobs preferably in towns like Posen.[20] What followed were countless internal deportations within the 'Warthegau' – especially in the context of several 'near plans' for the fast and total 'Germanization' and the operation 'Home to the Reich' ('*Heim-ins-Reich-Aktion*'). Already these transports were accompanied by excessive brutality, mass shootings on site and in the near forests, as research literature has convincingly shown. The next step were transports to the ghettos, labor camps, later to the Kulmhof extermination camp on which research has made significant

---

gruppen bei dem Versuch, Juden als Partisanen 'auszurotten'", in Rolf-Dieter Müller and Hans-Erich Volkmann (eds.): *Die Wehrmacht. Mythos und Realität*, Munich: Oldenbourg, 1999, 923 – 947; Peter Klein: "Die Rolle der Vernichtungslager Kulmhof (Chełmno), Belzec (Bełżec) und Auschwitz-Birkenau in den frühen Deportationsvorbereitungen", in Dittmar Dahlmann and Gerhard Hirschfeld (eds.): *Lager, Zwangsarbeit, Vertreibung und Deportation. Dimensionen der Massenverbrechen in der Sowjetunion und in Deutschland 1933 – 1945*, Essen: Klartext, 1999, 459 – 481; Ingo Loose: "Wartheland", in Wolf Gruner and Jörg Osterloh (eds.): *The Greater German Reich and the Jews. Nazi Persecution Policies in the Annexed Territories 1935 – 1945*, New York/Oxford: Berghahn, 2015, 189 – 218.
18 Cited from the Protocol of the Wannsee Conference, January 20, 1942, in Politisches Archiv des Auswärtigen Amtes (PAAA), R 100857, fol. 166 – 188, here fol. 173, p. 8 of the protocol. Translation by the author.
19 Götz Aly: *Hitlers Volksstaat. Raub, Rassenkrieg und nationaler Sozialismus*, Frankfurt am Main: S. Fischer, 2005³, 140.
20 Michael Alberti assumes that the majority of the deportees were Jews. See Alberti, Vernichtung der Juden im Reichsgau Wartheland, 136 – 137, especially footnote 415. Cf. in contrast Maria Rutowska: *Wysiedlenia ludności polskiej z Kraju Warty do Generalnego Gubernatorstwa 1939 – 1941*, Poznań: Instytut Zachodni, 2003, 49.

progress in recent years.[21] However, the successive liquidation of the smaller ghettos in the first half of 1942, etc. have scarcely been investigated, not to mention the situation for Jews in the province.[22] A better understanding of the dynamics or systematics and the immense potential for increasing violence of these deportations would be decisive for a better understanding of when deportations in the 'Warthegau' changed from a policy of 'making space' to systematic mass murder. This would also make the whole range of actors and their fields for maneuver, institutions, district self-administration etc. better visible.

Most research deals specifically with individual transports and/or ghettos and treats them more or less separately from the larger historical context of the deportations. An additional and demanding task therefore would be a comparative approach to a broader set of deportations either from various cities to Litzmannstadt or within the 'Warthegau', because research projects on individual transports often fail in combining their findings and interpretations with other transports, deportations etc. While comparing different ghettos or a certain number of deportations, the problem of scaling, for example, scaling ghettos of different sizes and their respective social structures, etc., can be better detected or even avoided, because what historiography knows about the ghettos in Litzmannstadt or Warsaw is not necessarily correct with regard to smaller ghettos. How do we deal with the knowledge of the approximately 20,000 Reich German, Prague and Luxembourg Jews in Litzmannstadt in relation to smaller ghettos, of which our knowledge often tends towards zero?

Looking from a German perspective alone at the antisemitic persecution in the years after the 'seizure of power' in 1933 on the one hand and at the deportations of Jews from the Reich 'to the East' in autumn 1941 on the other hand, we run the risk of ignoring and disregarding the fate of hundreds of thousands of Jews, especially in East Central and Eastern Europe for several years in which the ghettos continued to exist and Jews continuously got murdered. In the Litzmannstadt ghetto alone, well over 40,000 people died of malnutrition and epidemics as late as 1944. The corresponding number of victims in Warsaw was

---

21 Alberti, Vernichtung der Juden im Reichsgau Wartheland; Bartłomiej and Małgorzata Grzanka: *The Shadow of the Holocaust. The Beginning of the Operation of the German Kulmhof Death Camp in Chełmno-on-Ner*, Luboń: Martyr's Museum in Żabikowo, 2016; Ingo Loose: "Chełmno nad Nerem/Kulmhof am Ner heute begegnen", in Martin Langebach and Hanna Liever: *Im Schatten von Auschwitz. Spurensuche in Polen, Belarus und der Ukraine. Begegnen, erinnern, lernen*, Bonn: Federal Agency for Civic Education, 2017, 206–225.

22 Ingo Loose: "Odkrycie prowincji w historiografii Holocaustu po 1945 roku", in Adam Sitarek, Michał Trębacz and Ewa Wiatr (eds.): *Zagłada Żydów na polskiej prowincji*, Łódź: Instytut Pamięci Narodowej, 2012, 467–479.

still far higher, not to mention the countless other compulsory housing areas, camps, and ghettos in occupied Poland and other occupied countries during the Shoah. At least 600,000 people, perhaps more, are estimated to have perished in the ghettos alone; even more victims were deported from the ghettos to their death.[23]

While many people believe that they have a comparatively precise idea of concentration and extermination camps, this is much less the case for the approximately 1,200 ghettos that the Nazis established in East Central and Eastern Europe during the Second World War.[24] In historiography, the history of the ghettos is not in principle unknown, but there are still considerable gaps in knowledge about the ghettos and even more with regard to the countless translocations of their Jewish inmates.

There are many reasons to take a closer look at the active and self-determined behavior of the persecuted Jews, from mutual social aid to armed resistance, even during the Shoah. Probably based on Ernst Simon's succinct book title *Aufbau im Untergang* (Construction in Decline),[25] in the mid-1960s the phrase 'probation in decline' was coined by Ernst Gottfried Löwenthal, who himself had been able to escape into British exile in 1939.[26] The numerous biographical appraisals from Löwenthal's pen still read today like a pantheon of German-Jewish culture of the twentieth century. However, Löwenthal's collection of hundreds of biographies was not all about prominent Jewish personalities (although not one of them was deported to the 'Warthegau' or Litzmannstadt). He understood the concept of 'probation' as an expression of the fact that the Jews were by no means just passive victims, he rather spoke of the 'fighting German Jewry', especially the women and men who tried their best in the service of the Jewish community to alleviate the growing need, all too often themselves being sooner or later victims of the Shoah. This admittedly broad concept of resistance therefore seems to be well suited when we talk about the possibilities and the obligation to self-organization in the ghettos. The Jewish resistance, especially the armed one, above all the uprising in the Warsaw ghetto in January and

---

23 Dieter Pohl: "Ghettos im Holocaust. Zum Stand der historischen Forschung", in Jürgen Zarusky (ed.): *Ghettorenten. Entschädigungspolitik, Rechtsprechung und historische Forschung*, Munich: Oldenbourg, 2010, 39–50.
24 Christopher Browning: "Mehr als Warschau und Lodz. Der Holocaust in Polen", in idem. (ed.): *Der Weg zur "Endlösung". Entscheidungen und Täter*, Bonn: Dietz, 1998, 127–148.
25 Ernst Simon: *Aufbau im Untergang. Jüdische Erwachsenenbildung im nationalsozialistischen Deutschland als geistiger Widerstand*, Tübingen: Mohr, 1959, 68–69, 72.
26 E.G. Lowenthal (ed.): *Bewährung im Untergang. Ein Gedenkbuch. Im Auftrag des Council of Jews from Germany, London*, Stuttgart: Deutsche Verlags-Anstalt, 1965.

April 1943, but also the uprisings in the Treblinka and Sobibor extermination camps in autumn 1943, not least the uprising of the Jewish '*Sonderkommando*' in Auschwitz-Birkenau in October 1944 were undoubtedly outstanding events of lasting historical importance.[27] Despite the defeat and the following complete destruction of the Warsaw ghetto, the uprising has become a powerful counter narrative to the aforementioned alleged passivity of the Jews during the Shoah for which the 'Jewish Elder' in Litzmannstadt, Mordechai Chaim Rumkowski, who was allegedly compliant with the Germans, became the central symbol. Nevertheless, were there any other options, i.e. during the deportations, for the Jews to resist on their own initiative? This, of course, depended on many factors, not to the least on the age of the deportees who in the case of the Berlin transports to Litzmannstadt were very much older than the average in the ghetto. In the immediate postwar period, however, the image of 'Jewish resistance' was even broader and referred to other aspects of Jewish action and suffering during the Shoah, too. There were probably very few Jewish survivors who, especially in East Central and Eastern Europe, had no personal experience with being deported to one of the countless ghettos. This was often only the starting point, for example, for deportations to a labor or death camp or for fleeing and hiding. However, the first postwar years were a time of systematic gathering of information, above all by the Jewish Historical Commissions that had formed in the liberated cities with formerly important Jewish communities in Poland and elsewhere. Here the foundation stone was laid for a collection today comprising several thousand testimonies in the Jewish Historical Institute in Warsaw, which was accompanied by a rich literature of memoirs, however, predominantly written by Jews for Jews, namely in Yiddish. In this way, around the mid-1950s, hundreds of survival reports and contemporary testimonies of the murdered were already published. Suffice to mention the famous Argentine book series *Dos poylishe yidntum* (The Polish Jewry), in which dozens of important reports appeared about individual ghettos (with Warsaw and Litzmannstadt having the most accounts by Jewish survivors). All of them still impressively demonstrate the diverse efforts to maintain human dignity and solidarity within the Jewish community, even under the unspeakable living conditions in the ghettos.

However, one very important aspect rarely received the attention it deserves, for what the uninformed observer could have understood as the passivity of the Jewish masses and what Aba Kovner in the Vilna ghetto had already addressed in his famous appeal that the Jewish masses should not allow themselves to be

---

27 Arno Lustiger: *Zum Kampf auf Leben und Tod! Vom Widerstand der Juden in Europa 1933–1945*, Erftstadt: Area, 2005, 15–26, 44–56.

led to the slaughter like sheep. This is exactly what reveals a dimension of humanity of its own. The Warsaw based sociologist and historian Barbara Engelking pointed this out using the example of so-called Jewish columns moving from a ghetto – and this could have been equally Warsaw, Litzmannstadt, or any other ghetto – to the train station or the next murder site, supposedly without resistance: "It seems much more understandable to me," Engelking writes,

> that people in the face of death, when the last chance of rescue could presumably be found only in connection with other people, wanted to stay together with their neighbors and relatives and beloved ones. In doing so, they showed love, solidarity, loyalty, and courage. In this common death march I see many positive feelings, many signs of greatness, loyalty and sacrifice. Only the very superficial gaze of an indifferent observer interprets this as a migration of the "sheep to the slaughter".[28]

Shmuel Ron, a survivor from the Upper Silesian forced labor camp system for Jews, describes it very similarly:

> I've always asked myself who can be considered a hero – just the ghetto fighters, or maybe others too? A story that my cousin Sam told me gave an answer to this in a certain sense: Before the selection in Birkenau, Sam stood in the same row as his father. His father was a godly man, he stood there muttering passages of the Talmud that he knew by heart. Sam turned to him and said, "Is this the time to think about the Talmud?" His father replied, "I do mine, and He – pointing to heaven – does his." A few minutes later Sam's father picked up a crying child who was standing beside him, all alone without an adult in his company. "I am your horse now and you ride me," he said to the child in Polish. And so they both went to their deaths.[29]

Similar accounts from the Kulmhof death camp – at least for the first phase between December 1941 and 1943 – do not exist because there were no survivors who could later tell about them. However, this perspective in particular and social history of the Jewish victims in general can be portrayed only through the eyes of the victims themselves. In his path breaking study *Admitting the Holocaust*, Lawrence Langer has stressed that Jewish diaries from the ghettos often describe perpetrators (and bystanders) in a way postwar and post-Shoah re-

---

28 Barbara Engelking: *Jest taki piękny słoneczny dzień ... Losy Żydów szukających ratunku na wsi polskiej 1942–1945*, Warszawa: Stowarzyszenie Centrum Badań nad Zagładą Żydów, 2011, 32. Translation by the author.
29 Shmuel Ron: *Die Erinnerungen haben mich nie losgelassen. Vom jüdischen Widerstand im besetzten Polen*, Frankfurt am Main: Neue Kritik, 1998, 154. Translation by the author.

searchers simply could not and cannot.³⁰ Through a re-reading of the victims' diaries, the focus lies on a perspective from the inside, on the gradual acquisition of knowledge by the victims and on the adaption of their behavior towards the ever-growing pressure from the outside. This includes not only everyday life and suffering as well as the perception of other Jews sharing a common fate in the ghetto, but also how they thought about the perpetrators. Among other diarists this can be impressively studied in the diary of Jakub Poznański written in the Litzmannstadt ghetto, who constantly watched the interactions between German oppressors and Jewish victims during the war.³¹ What is also entirely based on Jewish accounts is the study of culture. Authors like, for example, David Roskies have emphasized the importance of Shoah diaries for a better understanding of Jewish or Yiddish culture and Jewish religion among the ghetto inhabitants.³² This picture is not automatically the same as we most often have in mind or think we are familiar with when reading postwar histories of this period. However, diaries written in Litzmannstadt and other ghettos have their limitations as well, for example, many diarists were well educated, meaning that they were perhaps not at all representative of the entire Jewish population in a given ghetto. This strongly influenced the content of diaries and the way that their authors – and subsequently historians – reflected on living conditions in the ghettos. The task at hand, however, is to fill the gaps in our understanding of underrepresented groups such as women, children, the elderly, religious Jews, the young generation, or the lower socioeconomic strata of the ghetto population.

How limited our knowledge can prove becomes clear when new questions are brought to science from 'outside'. This became evident, for example, a few years ago, in connection with the compensation of former Jewish forced laborers in the ghettos – the so-called ghetto pensions. Historians were confronted with questions, namely about the remuneration of work in the broadest sense (money,

---

30 Lawrence L. Langer: "Ghetto Chronicles: Life at the Brink", in idem: *Admitting the Holocaust. Collected Essays*, New York/Oxford: Oxford University Press, 1995, 41–50; Mark Roseman: "Holocaust Perpetrators in Victims' Eyes", in Christian Wiese and Paul Betts (eds.): *Years of Persecution, Years of Extermination: Saul Friedländer and the Future of Holocaust Studies*, London: Continuum, 2010, 81–100.
31 Jakub Poznański: *Tagebuch aus dem Ghetto Litzmannstadt*, Berlin: Metropol, 2011; Polish edition: Jakub Poznański: *Dziennik z łódzkiego getta*, Warszawa: ŻIH, 2002. On the topic of privat life in the ghettos – including Litzmannstadt – see Haas, Das Private im Ghetto.
32 David Roskies: *The Literature of Destruction: Jewish Responses to Catastrophe*, Philadelphia: Jewish Publication Society, 1988; Robert Moses Shapiro (ed.): *Holocaust Chronicles. Individualizing the Holocaust through Diaries and other Contemporaneous Personal Accounts*, New York: Ktav Publishing, 1999.

food, protection etc.), which were important especially with regard to ghettos such as Litzmannstadt with a numerous set of craft and other workshops and which simply could not be answered on the basis of the existing state of research.[33] In other words: What the German Federal and Regional social courts dealing with ghetto pension cases wanted to know at the time, nobody among the scholars working in the field had asked before.

Such gaps are sometimes embarrassing or even scandalous – for example in the case of groups of victims that have been until now scarcely researched, such as the aforementioned more than 5,000 Roma from the Austrian Burgenland who were deported to Litzmannstadt at the beginning of November 1941 and entirely murdered only a couple of weeks later.[34] The same is true for the persecution and deportations of Roma and Sinti to Auschwitz-Birkenau and elsewhere. In addition, we only slowly begin to understand the crucial connection between the murder of patients and disabled persons and the genesis of the murder of Jews especially in the Reichsgau Wartheland.[35] Most of the time our questions about history are formulated and constructed in the present. As the present changes, so does our attitude towards history and the interest in it as well as, last but not least, the needs of a retrospective creation of meaning – especially in relation to the Shoah. And, of course, we have different questions today than, for example, in the 1960s.

---

[33] "Gesetz zur Zahlbarmachung von Renten aus Beschäftigungen in einem Ghetto vom 20. Juni 2002 (mit Wirkung vom 1. Juli 1997)", in BGBl. I, 2074; Jürgen Zarusky, Ghettorenten; Kristin Platt: *Bezweifelte Erinnerung, verweigerte Glaubhaftigkeit. Überlebende des Holocaust in den Ghettorenten-Verfahren*, Munich: Wilhelm Fink, 2012; ra-online (pt): "Bundessozialgericht erleichtert Zugang zu 'Ghetto-Renten'". Available at: http://www.kostenlose-urteile.de/BSG_B-13-R-8108-RB-13-R-8508-RB-13-R-13908-R_Bundessozialgericht-erleichtert-Zugang-zu-Ghetto-Renten.news7940.htm. Last accessed: 30.12.2021.

[34] Karola Fings: "Sinti und Roma – eine Reise am Abgrund", in Langebach and Liever, Im Schatten von Auschwitz, 386–399; Frank Sparing: "Das 'Zigeunerwohngebiet' im Ghetto Lodz 1941/42", in Christoph Dieckmann and Babette Quinkert (eds.): *Im Ghetto 1939–1945. Neue Forschungen zu Alltag und Umfeld*, Göttingen: Wallstein, 2009, 136–170.

[35] This point was made particularly strong already by Henry Friedlander, a survivor from the Litzmannstadt Ghetto, see Henry Friedlander: *Der Weg zum NS-Genozid. Von der Euthanasie zur Endlösung*, Berlin: Berlin Verlag, 1997.

How the Existing Knowledge Influences and Affects Research and the Public Understanding of Historiography

What are the structures of knowledge and memory that influence our way of doing research today, in five years or 15 years? Does a perception of loss of the deported neighbors in Berlin, Hamburg, Frankfurt am Main, Vienna, or Dusseldorf,[36] imagined by different means of commemoration, lead to stable or an 'improved' awareness of Shoah history, or does it distort or perhaps even obscure the view of the transnational, European dimension of the annihilation of European Jews? In addition to detailed studies, biographies and to the growing but often poorly or at least insufficiently informational commemoration of the past we also need new integrating analyses that put the insights of numerous micro-level investigations into a broader narrative context, revealing, so to speak, the entire picture.

In general, the perspective on the Shoah has changed significantly in the last almost twenty to thirty years, not only in Germany, but also internationally. Shoah research had been part of national historiography for a long time, specifically in those countries that had been occupied or dominated by National Socialism in Europe and whose Jewish population mostly fell victim to Shoah. On the one hand, Jewish memories and national historiographies have often shown a fragile balance even in Western Europe, whereas in Eastern and East Central Europe recent narratives again tend to marginalize the specifics of the Shoah within their national framework.[37] 'National historiography' means that in France, for example, the Shoah was understood as an integral part of the history of France between 1940 and 1945 and that, of course, historians of the Shoah were primarily interested in the fate of French Jews. Regardless of whether in Poland, France or the Netherlands: it was increasingly the perspective of the victims that historians took, even if they usually perceived them as a collective of

---

[36] In the sense of what Bernt Engelmann describes as an inconceivable loss that is still felt today in 'Germany without Jews'. See Bernt Engelmann: *Deutschland ohne Juden. Eine Bilanz*, Munich: Schneekluth, 1970.

[37] Cf. Jan Grabowski and Ingo Loose: "Die Holocaustgeschichtsschreibung – ein Fall für die Gerichte? Zur Gefährdung der Wissenschaftsfreiheit in Polen", in *Zeitschrift für Geschichtswissenschaft*, 69, 7/8, 2021, 647–668; Havi Dreifuss: "The Polish Government's Holocaust 'Truth Campaign' Is a Weird Mix of Authoritarianism, Ignorance, and Injured Pride", in Tablet, 26.02. 2021. Available at: https://www.tabletmag.com/sections/news/articles/poland-holocaust-controversy-yad-vashem-response. Last accessed: 30.12.2021.

victims. On the other hand, for a long time this interest was limited to the Jews who remained in a given country. Those who were deported most often were described as 'perished in the East', and until 1989 the Iron Curtain led to very limited research what the precise fate of the Jewish deportees 'in the East' really had been. Even now, more than 30 years after the fall of the Berlin wall, this filter of perception is still alive, although to a somehow weaker extend. An additional problem is that the historians' knowledge of foreign languages has apparently decreased in recent years, which represents a considerable obstacle to researching the multilingual sources.

As is well known, Shoah research in Germany for a long time focused predominantly on the history of the perpetrators, and this mainly because the most essential impulses for historical studies came from the prosecutors and the courts, where the focus on the perpetrators and their crimes naturally stood in the foreground. Especially the last few years, however, when the awareness increased that only a few years will be left before the last witnesses, the last survivors, will no longer be able to provide any information about their personal experiences, have brought about a change from the perception of victims as 'gray masses' to an individualization of the victims. This can also be observed in the aforementioned large number of memorial books and survivors' accounts that are published. The beginning of this development was marked by the bestseller by Auschwitz survivor Ruth Klüger *weiter leben*, followed by a now almost unmanageable number of publications.

Later on, the complex coexistence of hundreds of thousands of Jews in the ghettos also aroused increased interest. The ghettos were no longer only the 'courtyard to hell', but an object of interest in itself. The opening of many archives after 1989 brought a large number of new files to light, which posed new questions and shaped numerous new topics, especially on the internal perspective of the ghettos and on the Jewish inmates, of which the documents of the perpetrators had not given any information in the years before.

If we understand the deportations to Litzmannstadt as an integral part of the history of the ghetto, one can have the impression that German research in recent years has tended to support commemoration in the places of the departing transports. Whereas in Poland, the transports from the Reich to the ghettos were rather used for introspection in the ghettos, especially about the relationship between 'Eastern and Western Jews' in which the perpetrators and also the individuality of the deportees largely disappeared behind a supposed Jewish 'clash of cultures'.[38]

---

[38] With regard to Litzmannstadt see as an example Krystyna Radziszewska: "Żydzi zachod-

If one follows Raul Hilberg's well-known categorization of perpetrators, victims and spectators, whereby the term bystanders probably better describes the ambivalence with reference to the latter, then in the case of Litzmannstadt we know a lot about the victims and the perpetrators. But only comparatively little is known about the third category, the bystanders, with the possible exception of individual complaints about how inconvenient it was to use the fenced-off German tram through the ghetto. Seeking for new evidence concerning the bystanders as well as the perpetrators, it is impossible not to reach for witness accounts. The perspective of Jews and their writings have most often very few in common with postwar historiography written on the basis of German official sources alone. Nor have many historians even attempted to look at the German perpetrators through the eyes of the Jews.[39] Seemingly, Jewish victims had little or no need to understand Nazi motivations, but they interpreted the behavior of the perpetrators trying to foresee the next steps in the ghettoization and – shortly later – extermination policy.

Reflections on the historian's own attitude towards the subject of his or her topic of interest is a standard procedure in professional historiography. However, this should be even more essential when we reflect on why and how Shoah research is carried out by those who do it. Was and still is ghetto historiography perhaps attractive because this topic offers comparatively little target for historical-political struggles of interpretation, as they have visibly increased in the last few years? The focus on Jews alone completes the perspective on perpetrators, but also on – certainly more controversial – the co-perpetrators, the collaborators and the bystanders. With regard to the Warsaw ghetto and the 'General Government' as a whole, a vivid discussion about Jewish–Gentile relations and the role of non-German collaborators started vehemently at the beginning of the 1990s and especially since the Jedwabne debate in 2000.[40] The fact that the ghetto in Litzmannstadt does not appear in these debates is only due to the fact that

---

nioeuropejscy w getcie łódzkim w świetle dzienników i wspomnień z getta", in Paweł Samuś and Wiesław Puś (eds.): *Fenomen getta łódzkiego 1940–1944*, Łódź: Wydawnictwo Uniwersytetu Łódzkiego, 2006, 309–325.

39 In the field of literary studies cf. Chunguang Fang: *Das Täterbild in der Überlebenden-Literatur. Ein Vergleich der Täterbilder in der frühen und späten Lagerliteratur von Buchenwald und Dachau*, Frankfurt am Main et al.: Peter Lang, 2017.

40 The literary scholar Jan Błoński, who had seen the evacuation of the Warsaw ghetto as a child in 1943, played a prominent role. In 1987, he published an article that was immediately controversially discussed and in which he addressed the passivity of non-Jewish Poles in the face of the Holocaust. See Jan Błoński: *Biedni Polacy patrzą na getto*, Kraków: Wydawnictwo Literackie, 1994; German edition in Marek Klecel (ed.): *Polen zwischen Ost und West. Polnische Essays des 20. Jahrhunderts. Eine Anthologie*, Berlin: Suhrkamp, 1995, 76–93.

the annexed Polish territories during German occupation in recent years have found little research (and public) interest in Poland.

Since 2015 this debate has become – especially in high-circulation newspapers and social media – an increasingly uncompromising one, not seldom intermingled with far right-wing or even antisemitic tendencies. However, these are by no means just historical discourses of right-wing conservative regimes or historical discourses in East Central Europe. In Germany, too, it seems, there are invisible borders beyond which the understanding for the Jewish victims rapidly diminishes, for example in the area of restitution or the slowly begun provenance research on stolen or 'Aryanized' property of those who were later deported and murdered. Incidentally, this also affects deportations and the related question of who under what circumstances and with what help could have been rescued. During the work on the above-mentioned memorial book for the first four transports from Berlin to Litzmannstadt, I recall the failed attempts to find somehow reliable and informative witness reports or notes from Berliners that thousands of Jews for hours long crossed the city mainly by foot to the Berlin deportation station Grunewald in October 1941.

Conclusion: How Future Research on the Ghettos and Deportations May Look Like

The Jewish compulsory communities in the ghettos have found great academic interest in the past decades until today, with all the evaluations, judgments, but also with recognition and the sincere attempt to approach the suffering and horrors in the ghettos. But there is still, as outlined above, even in the case of Litzmannstadt an extensive gap, especially with regard to the social and emotional history of the Jews, the context and the circumstances surrounding their deportations (including their persecution and suffering prior to being deported), and living conditions in the ghetto as a compulsory, yet complex social community. Given the advances in social historiography since the 1960s, this may come as a surprise or even as a scandal.

To improve this unsatisfactory state of affairs there should be at least one aspect kept in mind, namely the constant reconsidering and re-evaluation of the sources. Social history writing long before was methodically declared the royal road of historical writing in the Federal Republic of Germany since the 1960s. Since then it has been only applied scarcely to Eastern European social history of the interwar period, to the time of the Second World War or the Shoah. It is worth mentioning that Jewish social scientists and historians, especially in the context of the famous Ringelblum Archive Oneg Shabat in the Warsaw ghetto, long before adapted similar methods while scrutinizing the living conditions in the ghetto. The contributors were professional historians such as Emanuel Ringelblum himself, Stanisław Różycki, Peretz Opoczyński, who partly had already made careers in the YIVO or elsewhere; others wrote texts for the archive for the first time in their life: Many of these texts have something peculiar to what could be described as methodical modernity. After the death of the last Jewish and non-Jewish witnesses, it will therefore be a necessity to look again at the hundreds of publications especially from the first postwar years (mainly in Yiddish), as well as at extensive archival holdings that are still more or less completely unknown to this day and can easily be found across entire Europe with the help of finding aids like EHRI.[41]

In addition, a lot has happened in the field of digitization, i.e. the online availability of many sources, in the last ten years. In particular, it should be emphasized that the State Archives in Łódź have pushed ahead with the digitization and online placing of archival documents relating to the ghetto like hardly any other archive in Poland. The records of the so-called Elder of the Jews in the Litzmannstadt ghetto are now completely available online.[42] Accompanying holdings such as the several thousand files with documents by the German ghetto administration are also being successively digitized.

Nevertheless, the search for sources and their evaluation or re-evaluation are not finished, they have only just begun. New questions can come up anytime. Many sources on Litzmannstadt and publications, especially from the immediate postwar period, have been forgotten or have hardly ever been perceived by scholars.[43] Although it is important to record the last voices in order to document their experiences, it is also crucial that historians re-evaluate the very first voices as well. Already in the 1960s, Yad Vashem in Jerusalem and the YIVO Institute for Jewish Research in New York started to register bibliographical details of all testimonies published in Yiddish. There are several thousands of these narra-

---

[41] European Holocaust Research Infrastructure: "EHRI Portal". Available at: https://portal.ehri-project.eu/. Last accessed: 01.02.2022.
[42] See National Digital Archive: "Przełożony Starszeństwa Żydów w Getcie Łódzkim". Available at: https://www.szukajwarchiwach.gov.pl/zespol/-/zespol/28211. Last accessed: 15.02.2022.
[43] To mention just a few titles on Litzmannstadt, see Fareynikter retungs komitet far der shtot lodzsh (ed.): *Lodzsher Yizker-Bukh*, New York: Fareyniktes retungs-komitet fun der shtot lodzsh, 1943; Israel Tabaksblat: *Khurbn-lodzsh. 6 yor natsi-gehenom*, Buenos Aires: Tsentral-farband fun poylishe yidn in argentine, 1946; Moshe Pulaver: *Geven iz a geto*, Tel Aviv: Farlag I.L. Perets, 1963; Wolf Yasny: *Di geshikhte fun yidn in lodzh in di yorn fun der daytsher yidn-oysrotung*, 2 volumes, Tel Aviv: Farlag I.L. Perets, 1960–1966.

tives, plus several more thousand authentic reports held in the Jewish Historical Institute in Warsaw, including the Oneg Shabbat archive of Emanuel Ringelblum from the Warsaw ghetto but also numerous accounts from ghetto inmates from Litzmannstadt and the Warthegau in general.[44] In the late 1940s and 1950s, there were literally hundreds and thousands of survival reports and also specialist literature in Yiddish, which even in Israel and the USA is hardly used at all for research.

While at the beginning of the 1990s there was still a kind of optimistic mood to learn the languages relevant for research (mainly Polish and Yiddish), for some years there has been more of a 'retreat', focusing more on the fate of the German Jews during the 1930s. The Iron Curtain has undoubtedly made the decades-long repression of German crimes 'in the East' much easier. This – let us call it – filter effect has by no means dissolved into favor after 1989, but rather modified at best: since there were no longer any restrictions in the archives, maybe ignorance or at least convenience took over. A few hours train journey lie between the Berlin Nazi Memorial sites and literally tens of thousands of archival material on the Shoah in Polish archives, which remain mostly (or at least often) unrecognized and unused by German researchers.

Therefore occasionally there are publications that unfortunately show in detail that an important perspective is missing because either German, Polish or Yiddish sources simply could not be studied. Of course, this is a general problem of the entire, especially comparative, Shoah research, but in my impression one that is clearly neglected in theoretical debates as well as in works of individual researchers. Closely related to this is – almost inevitably – the ongoing nationalization of individual topics in Shoah research.

The comparatively good state of research on Litzmannstadt could finally be the starting point for some considerations as to what this actually means from a comparative perspective, whether Litzmannstadt can be compared, for example, with ghettos in the Wartheland region because of its size, the chronology of deportations, and/or because of the specifics in the 'Warthegau', or with similarly extensive ghettos such as those in Warsaw, Białystok or Lemberg.

---

44 Philip Friedman and Joseph Gar (eds.): *Bibliography of Yiddish Books on the Catastrophe and Heroism*, New York: Marstin Press, 1962; Joseph Gar (ed.): *Bibliography of Articles on the Catastrophe and Heroism in Yiddish Periodicals*, 2 volumes, New York: Marstin Press, 1966/1969; Bolesław Woszczyński and Violetta Urbaniak (eds.): *Źródła archiwalne do dziejów Żydów w Polsce*, Warsaw: Wydawnictwo DIG, 2001.

Anna Veronica Pobbe
Looking for the Money

Using a Bank Account of the Litzmannstadt Ghetto as a Source in the History of Deportations

Abstract: At the end of one of the most prolific decades concerning the studies on the Litzmannstadt ghetto, the State Archive of Łódź (APŁ) became part of a massive project related to the digitization of its documents, especially the ones that dealt with the city's past. Łódź was occupied by the Germans right after the beginning of the Second World War and was included directly into the newly founded district Warthegau, managed by Reichsstatthalter Arthur Greiser. Due to various reasons most of the documents, produced not only by the German administration but also by the Jewish 'self-administration', survived the war and are now part of one of the richest collections dealing with the tragedy of the Holocaust. This article examines a peculiar type of source that is deeply connected to the deportation's management in the 'Warthegau': the bank accounts of the ghetto administration. Thanks to this specific focus we will be able to look at the dynamics concerning not only the interests behind the 'Final Solution', but also the people and institutions involved.

The Ghetto

The Litzmannstadt ghetto[1] was established by a decree of the Regierungspräsident Friedrich Uebelhoer as early as December 1939 and it was sealed in May 1940.[2] Between these six months the municipality of the city, which had the jurisdiction over the ghetto matters, had established a specific agency, named

---

[1] Just to mention few works that were fundamental in the light of this essay: Gustavo Corni: *Hitler's Ghettos. Voices from a Beleaguered Society 1939–1944*, Oxford: Oxford University Press, 2002; Peter Klein: *Die "Gettoverwaltung Litzmannstadt" 1940 bis 1944. Eine Dienststelle im Spannungsfeld von Kommunalbürokratie und staatlicher Verfolgungspolitik*, Hamburg: Hamburger Edition, 2009; Andrea Löw: *Juden im Getto Litzmannstadt. Lebensbedingungen, Selbstwahrnehmung, Verhalten*, Göttingen: Wallstein, 2006; Michael Alberti: *Die Verfolgung und Vernichtung der Juden im Reichsgau Wartheland 1939–1945*, Wiesbaden: Harrassowitz, 2006.
[2] Artur Eisenbach (ed.): *Dokumenty i materiały do dziejów okupacji Niemieckiej w Polsce*, volume 3: *Getto Łódzkie*, Warsaw/Lodz/Krakow: Centralny Żydowska Komisja Historyczna, 1946, 27–31; Raul Hilberg: *La distruzione degli Ebrei d'Europa*, Torino: Einaudi, 1989, 226–227.

ghetto administration (*Gettoverwaltung*), in order to run the businesses concerning the ghetto. Using the term 'businesses' is not anacronistical in the case of the Litzmannstadt ghetto as it became the center of economic interests already in the middle of the year 1940, when the debate between different German institutions began about not only the ghetto's value but also its utility in the war economy.[3] The 'theme' of the economic value soon became a tool for the local authorities in order to present the ghetto as a model, which was used to draw resources and support from higher institutions both on a local and a national level. This pattern, later on, became also a matter of debate inside historiography, as Primo Levi brilliantly pointed out: "[Litzmannstadt] was the longest-lived Nazi ghetto, due to two reasons: one was its value for the Germans and the other one was the enchanting personality of its Elder".[4]

When the 'Final Solution' hit the territories around Litzmannstadt, the narrative of a lucrative business was adapted to a new goal: the extermination of Jews and Sinti and Roma.[5] Three waves of deportations hit the ghetto between January 1942 and September 1942. The victims were deported to and murdered inside the extermination camp of Kulmhof (Chełmno), which was established already in December 1941.[6] Only for the period during 1943 it is appropriate to define the Litzmannstadt ghetto as a 'working ghetto' as only then almost 90 percent of the ghetto population was actually working inside the *Ressorts*, which was the German term used for work shops producing clothes and accessories, especially for the German Army but also for private German companies.[7] From mid 1943 the SS tried to take control over the management of the ghetto, but never succeeded.[8] In February 1944, Greiser made the decision to liquidate the

---

[3] Correspondence, 09.11.1940, O.53/78, 11, Yad Vashem Archives (YVA), Jerusalem.
[4] Primo Levi: *Lilith e altri racconti*, Torino: Einaudi, 1981, 78. Translation by the author.
[5] Especially referring to the German ghetto-managers, Christopher R. Browning has pointed out how those men were able to reinvent themselves when the goals – set by the Nazi authorities – changed. See Christopher R. Browning: *The Origins of the Final Solution. The Evolution of Nazi Jewish Policy, September 1939–March 1942*, Lincoln: University of Nebraska Press, 2004.
[6] Patrick Montague: *Chelmno and the Holocaust. The History of Hitler's First Death Camp*, Chapel Hill: University of North Carolina Press, 2012.
[7] Andrea Löw: "Ghettos", in Shelley Baranowki, Armin Nolzen, and Claus-Christian W. Szejnmann, *A Companion to Nazi Germany*, New York: Wiley-Blackwell, 2018, 551–564, here 559; idem.: "Arbeit, Lohn, Essen. Überlebensbedingungen im Ghetto", in Jürgen Zarusky (ed.): *Ghettorenten. Entschädigungspolitik, Rechtssprechung und historische Forschung*, Berlin: De Gruyter, 2010, 65–79, here 76.
[8] Speech by Arthur Greiser, 09.02.1944, NS 3/30, Federal Archives Lichterfelde-Berlin (BArch). See also Jan Erik Schulte: "Zwangsarbeit für die SS. Juden in der Ostindustrie GmbH", in Norbert Frei, Sybille Steinbacher, and Bernd C. Wagner: *Darstellungen und Quellen zur Geschichte von Auschwitz, volume 4: Ausbeutung, Vernichtung, Öffentlichkeit*, Munich: Saur, 2000, 43–74.

ghetto, which was implemented during the summer of the same year, when almost the entire population of the ghetto was deported to Auschwitz-Birkenau.[9] In its four and a half years of existence, the narrative around the ghetto's productiveness and profitability was constantly used by the local authorities.[10] At the same time, this narrative was a way to drag out every resource from the people that were persecuted. The following pages will address how dragging out money, goods and basically everything that was still owned by the deportees became in fact a fundamental step for the dynamics of power consolidation of the German ghetto administration.

Even right after the first deportations from the ghetto to Kulmhof in the first six months of 1942, it was obvious that the killing operations had a tremendous effect on the manpower at the disposal of the industries involved in the war economy. The documents that will be analyzed subsequently, demonstrate how institutions like the ghetto administration never stopped to have a certain hunger for immediate profits, despite the consequences.

The Bank Accounts

As pre-war experiences had taught the Nazi authorities, drawing resources from Jews was not a simple task. It required new laws,[11] new institutions[12] and most of

---

9 Alan Adelson: *Lodz Ghetto. Inside a Community under Siege*, New York: Penguin, 1991.
10 For suggestions regarding the actual value of the production of the ghetto factories, see Julia Schnaus, Roman Smolorz and Mark Spoerer: "Die Rolle des Ghetto Litzmannstadt (Łódź) bei der Versorgung der Wehrmacht und der deutschen Privatwirtschaft mit Kleidung (1940 bis 1944)", in *Zeitschrift für Unternehmensgeschichte (ZUG)*, 62, 2017, 35–56.
11 One of the first measures that was used by the Nazis, in that sense, was the '*Reichsfluchtsteuer*' law. See Jeanne Dingell: *Zur Tätigkeit der Haupttreuhandstelle Ost, Treuhandstelle Posen 1939 bis 1945*, Frankfurt am Main: Lang, 2003, 12–13.
12 It was especially after the '*Anschluss*' that the Nazis established specific departments for that aim. See Constantin Goschler: "The Dispossession of the Jews and the Europeanization of the Holocaust", in Hartmut Berghoff, Jürgen Kocka and Dieter Ziegler (eds.): *Business in the Age of Extremes. Essays in Modern German and Austrian Economic History*, Cambridge: Cambridge University Press, 2013, 189–203, here 195; Hans Safrian: "Beschleunigung der Beraubung und Vertreibung. Zur Bedeutung des 'Wiener Modells' für die antijüdische Politik des 'Dritten Reiches' im Jahr 1938", in Constantin Goschler and Jürgen Lillteicher (eds.): *"Arisierung" und Restitution. Die Rückerstattung jüdischen Eigentums in Deutschland und Österreich nach 1945 und 1989*, Göttingen: Wallstein, 2002, 61–89; Götz Aly and Susanne Heim: *Vordenker der Vernichtung. Auschwitz und die deutschen Pläne für eine neue europäische Ordnung*, Berlin: Fischer, 1998, 262–269; Martin Dean: *Robbing the Jews. The Confiscation of Jewish Property in the Holocaust, 1933–1945*, Cambridge: Cambridge University Press, 2010, 108–111.

all new administrators, who were willing to overcome the boundaries of jurisdiction and morality.[13] Hence, when the Nazis arrived in Łódź, they were 'armed' with a series of tools in order to exploit the resources of the territory in a very short amount of time. One of those tools were bank accounts that were used to collect what was taken from the occupied territories.[14] Based on the records preserved by the State Archive in Łódź (APŁ),[15] it is known that six bank accounts were opened during the war in order to collect and manage the cash flow related to the Litzmannstadt ghetto.[16] The one account that will be taken into consideration here is the *Sonderkonto 12300* (special bank account 12300), opened at the Stadtparkasse Litzmannstadt right after the beginning of the deportations to Kulmhof.[17] The objective of the bank account was very clear from the beginning: the very first document shows how the *Sonderkonto* was meant to collect everything that was related to '*Aktionen*' (raids) organized in order to deport Jews and Sinti and Roma. The first income is dated February 28, 1942 and refers to the activity of the '*Sonderkommando*' that was based in Kulmhof.[18]

---

13 Peter Longerich: *Politik der Vernichtung. Eine Gesamtdarstellung der nationalsozialistischen Judenverfolgung*, Munich: Piper, 1998, 304; Michael Wildt: *Generation of the Unbound. The Leadership Corps of the Reich Security Main Office*, Göttingen: Wallstein, 2008; Ulrich Herbert: *Best. Biographische Studien über Radikalismus, Weltanschauung und Vernunft, 1903–1989*, Munich: C.H. Beck, 2016.

14 On this matter in general, see Ingo Loose: "Die Beteiligung deutscher Kreditinstitute an der Vernichtung der ökonomischen Existenz der Juden in Polen 1933–1945", in Ludolf Herbst and Thomas Weihe (eds.): *Die Commerzbank und die Juden 1933–1945*, Munich: C. H. Beck, 2004, 223–271; idem.: *Kredite für NS-Verbrechen. Die deutschen Kreditinstitute in Polen und die Ausraubung der polnischen und jüdischen Bevölkerung 1939–1945*, Berlin: De Gruyter, 2007.

15 The archival resources were made accessible as open-access in 2009. The database is still growing and is ment to collect different sources from various archives from all over Poland. See National Digital Archive: "Szukaj w Archiwach". Available at: https://www.szukajwarchiwach.gov.pl/en/strona_glowna. Last accessed: 02.02.2022.

16 Records relating to bank account n. 700, 39/221 Zarząd Getta (Gettoverwaltung), 29662, State Archive of Łódź (henforth APŁ); records relating to *Sonderkonto 12300*, 39/221 Zarząd Getta (Gettoverwaltung), 29663–29700, APŁ; records relating to bank account n. 1600, 39/221 Zarząd Getta (Gettoverwaltung), 29645–29661, APŁ; records relating to bank account n. 00, 39/221, Zarząd Getta (Gettoverwaltung), 29634, APŁ; records relating to the bank account n. 2, 39/221 Zarząd Getta (Gettoverwaltung), 29619–29633, APŁ; records relating to the bank account n. 7, 39/221 Zarząd Getta (Gettoverwaltung), 29636–29644, APŁ.

17 The first transports left the Litzmannstadt Ghetto on 16 January 1942. See Sascha Feuchert, Erwin Leibfried and Jörg Riecke (eds.): *Die Chronik des Gettos Lodz/Litzmannstadt 1942*, Göttingen: Wallstein, 2007, 37–38.

18 Bank statement n. 1, 39/221 Zarząd Getta (Gettoverwaltung), 29664, APŁ. References to the aim of the *Sonderkonto* were also made by Peter Klein. See Klein, Gettoverwaltung Litzmannstadt.

Regarding 'the administrators issue', the Nazis sent to Litzmannstadt Hans Biebow, a late-joiner of the NSDAP, who had made a career in the trade business and who became head of the ghetto administration.[19] The *Sonderkonto 12300* was managed directly by him, who was given the authority by Greiser.[20] The *Sonderkonto* remained active until the liquidation of the ghetto in fall 1944. The transactions of the *Sonderkonto* can give us a precise image of the deportations management for the entire Warthegau area, covering the matters concerning not only the Litzmannstadt ghetto and the extermination camp of Kulmhof, but also the smaller ghettos established in the governmental districts (*Regierungsbezirke*) of Litzmannstadt and Hohensalza and the labor camps established in the district of Posen. The documents referring to the *Sonderkonto* which are collected at the APŁ comprise thousands of pages. For this essay, the sample taken into account consists of about 5,000 documents. These cover the development of the *Sonderkonto 12300* from the beginning to the end of the year 1942 and can be divided into two main types of documents: the actual bank statements (*Bankauszüge*) and the attachments (generally referred to by using the broad term *Belege*). Both types of documents will be analyzed in depth in this paper in order to portrait a complex and kaleidoscopic image of which agencies were involved in the 'business of deportations'. As the analysis of the documents will later show, the *Sonderkonto* is not a static source, its development in fact reflects the evolving situation concerning the persecution and mass murder of the Jewish population especially in the Polish occupied-territory.

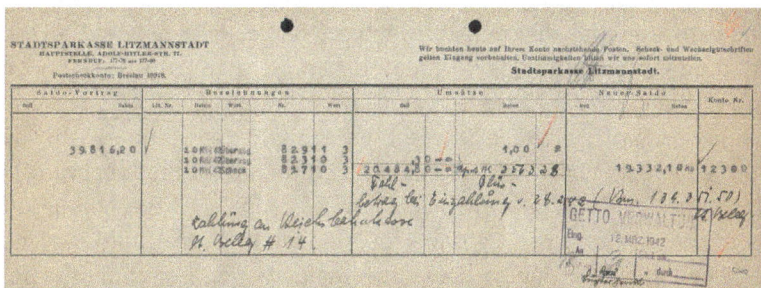

Fig. 1: Bank statement n. March 10, 1942, 39/221, Zarząd Getta (Gettoverwaltung), 29664, State Archive of Łódź (APŁ).

---

19 Anna Veronica Pobbe: *Un manager del Terzo Reich: Hans Biebow e la Soluzione Finale*, Roma: Laterza, 2022 (forthcoming).
20 Klein, Gettoverwaltung Litzmannstadt, 480.

The Bank Statements

The bank statements of the *Sonderkonto 12300* are printed on small pieces of paper, which are divided by columns (see fig. 1). From left to right they read: old saldo, date of transactions, outgoing money and incoming money, new saldo and the number of the bank account from which the money was transferred. Often, near the column related to the outgoing and the incoming money there is a hand-written number as reference to the *Beleg* (receipt). Finally, at the top of the document, there is a stamp of the ghetto administration including the date the transaction was issued. As mentioned before, the first bank statement was issued at the end of February 1942. From this date, the documents enable us to look at the transactions of almost every single day until the end of the year.

In order to evaluate the huge number of documents relating to the *Sonderkonto*, firstly the data was transcribed into an Excel data sheet in a chronological order. After that, the data was translated into a Cartesian graph with the Reichsmarks (RM), divided on a scale of 500,000, on the ordinate and the months of the year 1942 on the axis (see fig. 2). Building a graphic representation of the bank account development was very important because it gives a frame of the general capital growth, before dividing the references into where the money came from and where it went to. In fact, the graphic representation of the bank account shows that it actually took several months until the *Sonderkonto* reached the amount of 1 million RM in September 1942.[21] Especially until the month of June 1942, the bank account was constantly subjected to a series of withdrawals. For example, during the first ten days of May 1942 more than 700,000 RM were taken from the *Sonderkonto*.[22] However, when the withdrawals became less frequent, the bank account started to increase its capital exponentially. Already at the end of September 1942, the *Sonderkonto 12300* reached the amount of 3 million RM.[23] It was not only a growth in terms of capital but the number of transactions increased from the beginning of summer 1942, too: until May no more than five operation per day had been recorded; starting from June the operations were between five and ten per day and from August the operations were constantly more than ten per day. It will be addressed later how this growth was not a coincidence, but that it is strictly connected to the changing reality of the deportations.

---

21 Bank statement n. 110, 39/221 Zarząd Getta (Gettoverwaltung), 29664, APŁ.
22 Bank statements n. 24–27, 39/221 Zarząd Getta (Gettoverwaltung), 29664, APŁ.
23 Bank statement n. 139, 39/221 Zarząd Getta (Gettoverwaltung), 29664, APŁ.

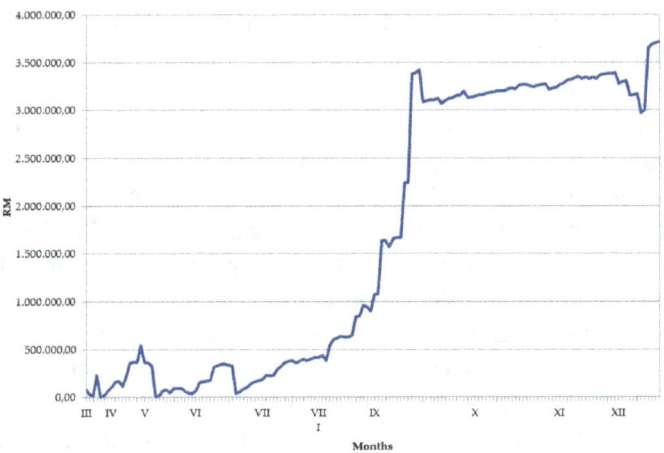

Fig. 2: Cartesian graph representing the account balance of the *Sonderkonto* in 1942 (created by the author).

Quittungen

The transactions recorded in the bank statements were only the pinnacle of an iceberg, built upon many layers of different types of documents that were collected as *Belege* (supporting documents).[24] The term *Beleg*, in this case, is referred to at least two types of documents: *Quittungen* (receipts), which are records of the transactions produced by the bank, and attachments, which are receipts produced by different agencies and businesses. Both types of documents have precise references to the bank statements, which are indicated by the hand-written numbers at the upper margin.

However, the references to the bank statements are not the only important information that is hand-written on the *Quittungen* by bank clerks. In fact, under the printed expression *Quittung* there are often other hand-written notes. The first one, which appears in the supporting documents in the spring of 1942, is the letter S, which is a reference to the Geheime Staatspolizei (Gestapo) Litzmannstadt. In the peculiar organization of the Warthegau, the Gestapo managed all the practical issues regarding the deportations: the power structure,

---

24 *Belege* #0–1000, 39/221 Zarząd Getta (Gettoverwaltung), 29665–29671, APŁ.

set by the Gauleiter Greiser, was based essentialy on a strong collaboration between police forces and civil administration, in which, however, the civil administration had always a leading role in terms of who made the decisions.[25] Interestingly, the references to the Gestapo concern both the incomes[26] and outcomes[27]. On the one hand, due to its role as principal police force in the deportation matters, the Gestapo put money in the bank account; on the other hand, the involvement in the '*Aktionen*' was not free of charge, it was, in fact, paid using transfers made directly from the *Sonderkonto* to the Gestapo. The transactions referring to the activities of the Gestapo were consistently between tens of thousands and hundreds of thousands of RM.

Another important reference that can be found as hand-written notes on the *Quittungen* are the names of places which refer to the smaller ghettos established by the Nazis in the Warthegau.[28] One of the most common references is Pabianice, where the Nazis established a Jewish ghetto that was reconverted into a labor camp in summer 1942. The inmates of this labor camp and former ghetto had to sanitize clothes that were taken from the Jewish deportees in Kulmhof.[29] The labor camp was managed by a specific department inside the ghetto administration of Litzmannstadt: the so-called *Warenverwertung* (recycling of goods). Later on, during the year of 1942, the references to Pabianice were sometimes even accompanied by the expression "Warenverwertung".[30]

---

[25] On the relationship between the Gestapo and the civil administration, see Andreas Mix: "Zwangsarbeit von Juden im Reichsgau Wartheland und im Generalgouvernement", in Elizabeth Harvey and Kim Christian Priemel (eds.): *Working Papers of the Independent Commission of Historians Investigating the History of the Reich Ministry of Labour (Reichsarbeitsministerium) in the National Socialist Period*, 2017. Available at: https://www.historikerkommission-reich sarbeitsministerium.de/sites/default/files/inline-files/Working%20Paper%20UHK%20A1_Mix_1. pdf. Last accessed: 18.02.2022; Catherine Epstein: *Model Nazi: Arthur Greiser and the Occupation of Western Poland*, Oxford: Oxford University Press, 2010.

[26] For example, on 11 March 1942 the Gestapo made a deposit of 214.022,87 RM. See *Beleg* #19, 39/221 Zarząd Getta (Gettoverwaltung), 29665, APŁ.

[27] For example, on 28 May 1942 a transition was made to the Gestapo of 30.000,00 RM. See *Beleg* #83, 39/221 Zarząd Getta (Gettoverwaltung), 29665, APŁ.

[28] From 1939 to mid-1941 in the territories of the Warthegau, the Nazis established almost 60 mostly 'open-ghettos' with a population of a few thousands each. See Geoffrey P. Megargee (ed.): *Encyclopedia of Camps and Ghettos, 1933–1945*, volume 2, Bloomington: Indiana University Press, 2009.

[29] Trial against Erich Czarnulla, 344/88, Żydowski Instytut Historyczny (ŻIH), Warsaw.

[30] For an incoming transfer to "Pabianice Warenverwertung" of 29.571,00 RM, 18.09.1942, 39/221 Zarząd Getta (Gettoverwaltung), 29670, APŁ.

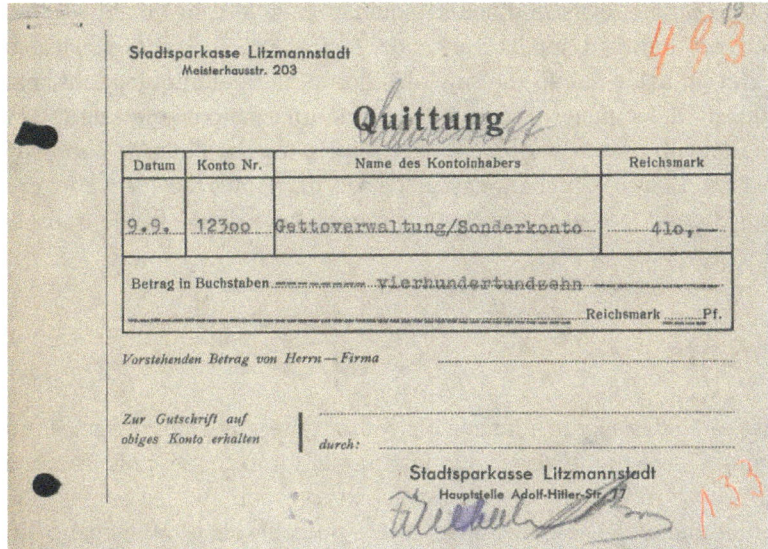

Fig. 3: Income of 410 RM from "Alexandorf" n. 19, 39/221 Zarząd Getta (Gettoverwaltung), 29669, APŁ.

The *Sonderkonto* was also used in order to collect the money from liquidations of smaller ghettos such as the ones in Poddębice,[31] Łęczyca,[32] Służewo,[33] Chodecz,[34] Krośniewice,[35] Widzew,[36] Wieluń,[37] Łask,[38] Zduńska Wola,[39] and Warta.[40] In some

---

31 Income of 25.000,00 RM referring to the deportation of Jews from Poddębice, 05.06.1942, 39/221 Zarząd Getta (Gettoverwaltung), 29666, APŁ.
32 Income of 19.320,00 RM referring to the deportation of Jews from Łęczyca, 05.06.1942, 39/221 Zarząd Getta (Gettoverwaltung), 29666, APŁ.
33 Income of 316,45 RM referring to the deportation of Jews from Służewo, 18.05.1942, 39/221 Zarząd Getta (Gettoverwaltung), 29667, APŁ.
34 Income of 385,25 RM referring to the deportation of Jews from Chodecz, 18.05.1942, 39/221 Zarząd Getta (Gettoverwaltung), 29666, APŁ.
35 Income of 9.433,36 RM from the municipality of *Krośniewice*, 02.07.1942, 39/221 Zarząd Getta (Gettoverwaltung), 29667, APŁ.
36 Income of 9.805,55 RM from the municipality of Widzew, May 1942, 39/221 Zarząd Getta (Gettoverwaltung), 29666, APŁ.
37 Income of 7.000,00 RM from the municipality of Wieluń, 21.09.1942, 39/221 Zarząd Getta (Gettoverwaltung), 29668, APŁ.
38 Income of 71.784,00 RM from Łask, 01.09.1942, 39/221 Zarząd Getta (Gettoverwaltung), 29669, 229, APŁ.
39 Income of 108.707,00 RM from Zduńska Wola, 31.08.1942, 39/221 Zarząd Getta (Gettoverwaltung), 29669, APŁ.

cases, a single *Quitting* refers to different liquidations that were combined into one transaction.[41] Between summer and fall 1942, the *Sonderkonto* reached a peak of capital probably due to the capitalization of different liquidations that happened during the summer. The amount of the transactions referring to the liquidation of small ghettos varied strongly from a few hundred to hundreds of thousands RM. However, in many cases, the specific details like the actual origin of the transferred money or the circumstances of the timing of the transaction are not known.

Attachments

Also catalogued as *Belege*, the attachments comprise receipts that other institutions created and sent to the ghetto administration, for example, bills from the Reichsbahn, whose trains were used in order to transport the Jews from Litzmannstadt to Kulmhof.[42] These documents were probably sent to the ghetto administration in order to receive refund for the respective trains. In case of the Reichsbahn,[43] the costs reflect the travel rates that were applied both to Jewish deportees and to police and SS-personnel: 2.96 RM for every Jew and 5.60 RM for every SS-personnel. The documents show the exact number of Jews in each transport (around 1000) and the accompanying SS-personnel (12). Furthermore, the names of train stations that were used as places of departure, like Radegast, and the destinations, like Koło, are stated.

In addition to *Belege* concerning the transport of people, there are also bills for transferring clothes that were taken from the deportees right before their death in Kulmhof.[44] Small businesses, mostly from Litzmannstadt, were paid regularly by the ghetto administration for this task. The clothes were taken by train to facilities like the one in Pabianice and, once sanitized, they were transferred, this time by truck, to the '*Altreich*'. Private businesses were in charge of organizing the whole transport and billed the ghetto administration for some expenses like fuel. Already during the end of spring 1942, a great part of the clothes was

---

40 Income of 7.290,00 RM from Warta, 18.09.1942, 39/221 Zarząd Getta (Gettoverwaltung), 29669, APŁ.
41 Income of 56.821,20 RM from different '*Aktionen*' in Wielun, Wieruszow, Lututow, Osjakoe, Szadek, Sieradz, Warta, 31.08.1942, 39/221 Zarząd Getta (Gettoverwaltung), 29669, APŁ.
42 *Beleg* #78, payment of 33.731,35 RM for special trains (*Sonderzüge*) to Koło, from 04.05 to 15.05.1942, 39/221 Zarząd Getta (Gettoverwaltung), 29665, APŁ.
43 On the Reichsbahn, see also the contribution by Susanne Kill in this volume.
44 *Beleg* #430, transport from Sieradz, 39/221 Zarząd Getta (Gettoverwaltung), 29669, APŁ.

sent to a specific factory, the Kindler factory in Pabianice managed by the Volksdeutsche Mittelstelle (VoMi).⁴⁵ The VoMi was an agency established to implement the racial population policy of the Nazis in regard of ethnic Germans living outside the boundaries of the German Reich.⁴⁶ If the sanitized clothes were in good condition they were given to charities devoted to the supply of German ethnic families. It is important to point out that there was a differentiation in terms of businesses involved in the transport of clothes. Those involved in the transports from Kulmhof to the facilities were never involved in the transports from the facilities to the '*Altreich*'. However, at this point we do not know why this distinction was made. There are further questions in this context that remain unanswered like who choose the businesses for the transports. Nevertheless, pointing out those peculiarities is important in order to address the wide range of involved institutions, businesses and individuals in the deportations, especially for what concerns the local area surrounding the Litzmannstadt ghetto.

In terms of private businesses, local sellers of cigarettes and alcohol also benefited from some transactions from the *Sonderkonto 12300*. Their mentioning as beneficiaries confirms a common practice during the deportations and the killing operations: the men that were involved in the '*Aktionen*' were rewarded often with cigarettes and alcohol.⁴⁷ All of those companies and agencies made business with the ghetto and profited from the deportations.

Up to now, this article has dealt with deposits that were made directly by the actors involved, like the Gestapo, and payments made for specific services like the ones to the local firms. However, the *Sonderkonto* was often used as the final step of previous transactions to other bank accounts, too. For example, the bank account number 3030–539 had been opened in a small bank near the extermination camp of Kulmhof, probably by the SS. The transactions between this account and the *Sonderkonto* started soon after the opening of the *Sonderkonto* and they refer especially to the '*Sonderkommando*' Kulmhof, which had probably used this account to collect money that was confiscated from Jews murdered in Kulmhof.⁴⁸ But as the time passed, the references to

---

45 *Beleg* #432, payment of 18.284,99 RM to Kindler factory in Pabianice, 39/221 Zarząd Getta (Gettoverwaltung), 29669, APŁ.
46 Peter Longerich: *Heinrich Himmler. A Life*, Oxford: Oxford University Press, 2012, 389.
47 *Beleg* #429, payment of 479,40 RM to the tabacco-seller Fischer, 39/221 Zarząd Getta (Gettoverwaltung), 29669, APŁ. Regarding the alcohol consumption among the perpetrators, see Edward B. Westermann: *Drunk on Genocide. Alcohol and Mass Murder in Nazi Germany*, Ithaca: Cornell University Press, 2021.
48 Payments from the bank account 3030–539, 25.03.1942, 39/221 Zarząd Getta (Gettoverwaltung), 29665, APŁ.

transactions coming from this account changed: in the first six month of 1942 they referred to the '*Sonderkommando*' primarily, then they began to refer to "Judenarbeit"[49] (Jewish Labor).

Furthermore, the *Sonderkonto* also refers to money that was in possession of the murdered Jews at the moment of their death.[50] Most of the *Belege* referring to currency exchange were related to transactions from the end of September 1942 and almost every transaction between September 29 and October 12 of the same year is about currency exchange.[51] The timing of these transactions is an important aspect: for example some *Belege* from the end of November refer to the liquidation of the Wielun ghetto[52] despite the fact that it was liquidated at the end of August.[53]

A changing nature of the deportation process can also be seen during the last months of 1942. At this time, the references to "Judenarbeit"[54] and "Judenlager"[55] appeared in the supporting documents for the first time and then became very frequent. As the deportations in the Warthegau ended, the *Sonderkonto* became in fact the collector of the income of the labor camps' activities. This is proven by the title of the folders referring to the years 1943 and 1944, where there are precise references made to some labor camps.

There were regular withdrawals from the *Sonderkonto* over a longer period of time. In May 1942, for example, a withdrawal of 400,000.00 RM was made in favor of Dr Friedrich Hausler, who was in charge of the Reichsstatthalter's financial office.[56] Another withdrawal of 300,000.00 RM, also to Dr Hausler, was made just a few weeks later.[57] Although 700.000,00 RM were transferred to Dr Hausler in a matter of weeks, it is not clear what his role was, but it most likely had to do with the management of the bank accounts.

---

[49] Payment of 499,80 RM from the bank account 3030–539 for 'Jewish Labor' used from 27.08. until 09.09.1942, *Beleg* #649, 21.09.1942, 39/221 Zarząd Getta (Gettoverwaltung), 29671, APŁ.
[50] Deposits from currency exchange of 76.600,00 RM and 69 grams of gold, 03.04.1942, 39/221 Zarząd Getta (Gettoverwaltung), 29665, APŁ.
[51] *Belege* #500–700, 39/221 Zarząd Getta (Gettoverwaltung), 29670–29671, APŁ.
[52] *Belege* #798–799, 39/221 Zarząd Getta (Gettoverwaltung), 29672, APŁ.
[53] Megargee, Encyclopedia of camps and ghettos, volume II, 114–115.
[54] For the payment of 737,80 RM referring to 'Jewish Labor', see *Beleg* #659, 01.10.1942, 39/221 Zarząd Getta (Gettoverwaltung), 29671, APŁ.
[55] For the payment of 1003,00 RM referring to the '*Judenlager*' of Kosciau, see *Beleg* #578, 28.09.1942, 39/221 Zarząd Getta (Gettoverwaltung), 29670, APŁ.
[56] For the transaction of 400.000,00 RM to Dr Hausler, see *Beleg* #42, 01.05.1942, 39/221 Zarząd Getta (Gettoverwaltung), 29665, APŁ.
[57] For the transaction of 300.000,00 RM to Dr Hausler, see *Beleg* from 04.05.1942, 39/221 Zarząd Getta (Gettoverwaltung), 29665, APŁ.

On September 14, 1942, during the last day of the *'Große Sperre'*,[58] a withdrawal of 350,000.00 RM was recorded as a refund for the *'Judenälteste'*. The practice to refund the *'Judenrat'* for a deportation was established by the Nazis already in 1941, when the Jewish deportees from Germany arrived in the Litzmannstadt ghetto.[59] Back then the German authorities made a transaction of two milion RM. However, this money was tied to the German approval in order to be used by the *'Judenrat'*, which in the end never received the authorization to spend the money for the needs of the community.

The biggest withdrawal happened during February 1943, when four million RM were withdrawn from the *Sonderkonto*.[60] However, we do not have any information about where the money was actually transferred to and what it was used for.

Enrichment – a Misconception

On the one hand, the bank statements and supporting documents enable us to look at the leading role of Biebow, who managed the *Sonderkonto* and became the trust-worthy person in the refunding process. Many *Belege* are in fact signed by Biebow. However, the documents also give hints to the presence of other leading agencies in the ghetto, like the Gestapo. Furthermore, it is revealing to see what is not mentioned in the documents and where the information is incomplete. For example, none of the documents referring to the *Sonderkonto* originate from the period between the end of 1941 and the beginning of 1942, when the killings started in Kulmhof. The main thesis is that this absence is a reflection of the first stages of the destruction process concerning not only the Jewish communities but also Sinti and Roma. At this point in time, the killing operations were not yet 'standardized' in the three-steps process that we often refer to (deportation, killing by gas, burning of bodies),[61] but varied between different killing techniques and evolving practices.

---

58 This is the name of the third deportation wave that hit the Litzmannstadt ghetto. Between 2 and 15 September 1942, mostly children (under the age of 10), elderly (over the age of 65) and sick people were deported and murdered in the death-facilities of Kulmhof. See Montague, *Chelmno and the Holocaust*.
59 Transaction to the *Älteste der Juden* in Litzmannstadt, 15.11.1941, JM/807, YVA, Jerusalem.
60 Transaction from 24.02.1943, 39/221 Zarząd Getta (Gettoverwaltung), 29679, APŁ.
61 Danuta Dąbrowska and Abraham Wein (eds.): *Pinkas ha-kehilot. Encyclopedia of Jewish Communities: Poland, volume 1: Lodz and its Region*, Jerusalem: Yad Vashem, 1976, 103.

Despite the accuracy of some references, until now no traces have been found in the documents connected to the *Sonderkonto* concerning the corruption that was used, especially by Biebow, in order to manage some businesses related to the ghetto.[62] It is more likely that those types of exchanges were not recorded.

There is also a great discrepancy between the amount of sources at our disposal as there are, for example, hardly any attachments from before July 1942 that enable us to look at the data expressed inside the bank statements. On the contrary for the period between August and December 1942, the attachments explain almost every transaction recorded in the bank statements. Additionally, the hiatus between some transactions and the liquidations, as the case of the Wielun ghetto has shown, is still a pending question.

If one looks at bank documents, it is very tempting to think that the local German authorities, from the ghetto administration to the regional institutions, were able to build a lucrative business around the 'Final Solution' and the exploitation of Jewish labor for themselves. This is in some ways true, if we look, for example, at the luxurious life that Biebow lived and as it was reported by some survivors.[63] But despite the profits that the ones directly involved in the deportations were able to gain, talking about enrichment is very much misleading in case of Litzmannstadt. First of all, the profits recorded by the *Sonderkonto* were used by the local Nazi-authorities in order to portray their Gau as a '*Muster-Gau*' (model district).[64] This effort had an undesired effect: at the beginning of 1943, the Ministry of Economy decided to cut the funds destined to the Warthegau, precisely due to the profits that the Reichsstatthalter was able to gain from Jewish forced labor and deportations.[65] Furthermore, the consequences of the deportations had a negative impact on the businesses of other businessmen involved in the Jewish labor exploitation as a case from Zduńska Wola demonstrates: The businessman Neubauer, who was in charge of the Striegel&Wagner factory which exploited Jews to produce garments made out

---

[62] Otto Bradfisch, commander of the Security Police and the SD in Litzmannstadt, mentioned in a report about the ghetto that the system built by Biebow was based upon a strong cronyism. See report by Otto Bradfisch, August 1943, O.51/13, 315–342, YVA, Jerusalem.

[63] See, for example, the video testimonial by Manny Langer from 1998, #41163, Visual History Archive (VHA), USC Shoah Foundation.

[64] Ryszard Kaczmarek: "Zwischen Altreich und Besatzungsgebiet: Der Gau Oberschlesien 1939/1941–45", in Jürgen John, Horst Möller and Thomas Schaarschmidt (eds.): *Die NS-Gaue. Regionale Mittelinstanzen im zentralistischen "Führerstaat"*, Munich: Oldenbourg, 2007, 348–360.

[65] Klein, Gettoverwaltung Litzmannstadt, 501; Epstein, Model Nazi, 257.

of fur, made several complains to Biebow regarding the deportations.⁶⁶ However, his complains had no effect and the liquidation of the ghetto continued.

Secondly, the enrichment was real only if we take into account the personal enrichment of Biebow; however the enrichment was not 'effective' if we take a look at the entire scenario. In fact if we compare the profits registered in the *Sonderkonto* with the costs that the ghetto administration had to deal with in order to manage the Litzmannstadt ghetto, we will have a complete different image than the one that was presented by local authorities. The ghetto administration spent in fact almost one million RM per month in order to run the ghetto; the costs decreased only during January and May 1944 before the actual liquidation of the ghetto.⁶⁷ Those high costs were the result of a vicious circle, created by the Nazis themselves, between profits and food supplies. Based on the 'agreement' made between the ghetto administration and the '*Judenrat*' only 35 percent of the profits were used to buy food supplies for the ghetto. Those supplies were never enough in order to maintain a standard of living for the ghetto inmates, both in terms of quantity and quality of food, which was often only vegetables. The German administration of the ghetto was not only unwilling to increase the food supplies to the ghetto, but they linked the production rates to the food supplies: when the production rates did not meet the expectations, they cut off the supplies.⁶⁸ By setting this vicious circle, Biebow became the main reason for the quick deterioration of the ghetto inmates' living conditions which ultimately resulted in a lower productivity. In order to keep the ghetto capable of production, the ghetto administration, already from 1941 onwards, therefore had to buy some extra food supplies and, later on, some medications in order to try to control the diseases that were endemic inside the ghetto. Nevertheless, these measures cannot be defined as an effort made by the German administration to improve the living conditions of the ghetto inmates. These measures were, in fact, never sufficient and the rations were always kept to a minimum. The German administration rather focused on creating a picture of the ghetto as a productive and profitable business. After all, for the Nazis, the health of the Jews did not matter and production also under inhuman condition brought the desired result, as it was underlined by a commissar in 1943.⁶⁹

---

66 Isaac Neuman: *The Narrow Bridge: Beyond the Holocaust*, Chicago: University of Illinois Press, 2000, 69.
67 "Salden-Bilanz Gettoverwaltung", January to September 1944, 39/221 Zarząd Getta (Gettoverwaltung), 29596, APŁ.
68 See Isaiah Trunk: *Łódź Ghetto. A History*, Bloomington/Indianapolis: Indiana University Press, 2006, 163; Epstein, Model Nazi, 258; Klein, Gettoverwaltung Litzmannstadt, 529.
69 Letters from Dr Lautrich to Hans Biebow, July 1943, 205/141, ŻIH.

Another reason behind the high costs were the raw materials sent to the work shops, which were mostly of bad quality, which ultimately increased the production costs of the clothes – both in terms of aggravated labor and higher quantity of the needed material – disproportionately.

Even the attempt to recycle the clothes that were taken from the murdered Jews in Kulmhof was an economic fail. Already in May 1942, Biebow sent in fact a letter to the VoMi addressing the issue of the conditions of the clothes:

> There is no way that those clothes could be used by Arians because they are so damaged, so dirty and inferior that a new method has to be undertaken: the clothes, that are still wearable, will be given to the Jews, who are working at the station; the rest will be dismembered and the pieces obtained will be spun with the addition of wool, so that the clothes produced can be treated as new.[70]

Conclusion

Despite the actual value of what was portrayed as 'enrichment' by the local authorities, the analysis of the *Sonderkonto 12300* during the year 1942 enables us to look at, first of all, those who were directly involved in the organization of the deportations. Following the pattern proposed by Reichsstatthalter Arthur Greiser,[71] the civil authorities, mostly the ghetto administration, worked hand in hand with the Gestapo and the small businesses around the city of Litzmannstadt. This confirms one of the core patterns of the Holocaust: the division of labor and responsibility which ultimately made deportations and mass murder possible. Inside this scenario, the self-representation of the ghetto administration built a narrative based upon the concept of success.[72]

The capital growth of the *Sonderkonto* was deeply connected to some sort of destructive euphoria[73] felt transversally by the Nazis during the first years of the

---

70 Letter by Hans Biebow to the VoMi, 15.05.1942, 39/221 Zarząd Getta (Gettoverwaltung), 30790, 11), APŁ. Translation by the author.
71 Thomas Schaarschmidt: "Centre and Periphery", in Shelley Baranowski, Armin Nolzen and Claus-Christian Szejnmann (eds.): *A Companion to Nazi Germany*, New York: Wiley-Blackwell, 2018, 147–162, here 155.
72 Schnaus, Smolorz, Spoerer, Rolle des Ghetto Litzmannstadt.
73 Christopher R. Browning: "The decision-making process", in Dan Stone (ed.): *The Historiography of the Holocaust*, New York: Palgrave, 2004, 173–196.

war. That involved also some near territories like the '*Generalgouvernement*'[74] where harsh criticism was expressed by the German Army concerning the killing of Jews who were able to work.[75]

Lastly, but certainly not least important, the very nature of the documents analyzed for this article enable us to look at the deportations in the 'Warthegau' from a new perspective. The financial documents, from the bank statements to the *Belege*, offer precise information on the situation inside the Litzmannstadt ghetto and on the details of the deportations from there. In order to be refunded, the different agencies involved in the economy of the ghetto and the deportations had to present a detailed documentation about the work they had done. The documents relating to the bank account represent the core of the deportation structure not only in Litzmannstadt. All over the place, private firms billed the Gestapo for the services they provided using other *Sonderkontos* like the account W that was used to confiscate and administrate funds from German Jews, or the account R that was used to collect the profits of the '*Operation Reinhard*'.[76]

The uniqueness of the sources presented here is that one can precisely see in one collection how the ghetto and the deportations were administered and which 'stakeholders' and costs were involved, besides the specifics of the Litzmannstadt ghetto. So in the end, following those types of documents is like witnessing a day by day history about the robbery that the German authorities were able to make due to the deportations.

---

74 On the immediate profits and their consequences, see Ingo Loose: "Credit Banks and the Holocaust in the Generalgouvernement", in *Yad Vashem Studies*, 34, 2006, 177–218, here 210–212.
75 Memorandum General Ginant, 18.09.1942, O.4.4/2, YVA, Jerusalem.
76 René Moehrle: *Judenverfolgung in Triest während Faschismus und Nationalsozialismus 1922–1945*, Berlin: Metropol, 2014.

Tomáš Fedorovič
Preparations for and Organization of the Transports from Terezín to Auschwitz-Birkenau in September 1943

Abstract: As many as 5,007 people left the Terezín (Theresienstadt) ghetto in two large transports in September 1943. Their fate in the so-called Terezín family camp in Auschwitz-Birkenau was tragic since virtually all of them, with precious few exceptions, were murdered. This article is aimed at describing the compiling of the transports in Terezín and the factors according to which some groups of inmates had been selected for transport by the SS Command and by the Jewish 'self-administration'. Based on an analysis of more than 2,500 petitions, submitted in a bid to exempt specific inmates from the transports, it is possible to trace their successful or unsuccessful attempts to save themselves from deportation. The article attempts to answer the question what criteria assisted prisoners in their request to be removed from the transport. What weight did parameters such as relationship to ghetto officials, social ties between prisoners, work for the Jewish religious community prior to deportation, work in the ghetto, illness and disability, criminal records, or family circumstances ('mixed marriages') carry in the decision to exclude them from these two transports?

Introduction

Between November 1941 and the end of April 1945, 140,000 Jewish men, women and children passed through the Terezín ghetto.[1] These prisoners came to the ghetto in hundreds of small and larger transports. For a significant number of them, the ghetto became a transit camp. In 60 'eastern transports', 88,000 Terezín prisoners were deported to extermination, concentration and labor camps in Central and Eastern Europe. Of these, only about 3,800 survived until liberation.

---

[1] This research has been supported by GACR grant no. 19–05523S. The analysis presented in this article was part of the research project *Social Structure of a Nazi Ghetto: Analysis of Survival in the Terezín Ghetto*. Independently from the author of this work, the author of the most recent monograph on the Terezín ghetto, Anna Hájková, examined the same convolute of petitions. Hájková summarizes her results in the last chapter of her book, entitled "Transports from Terezín to the East". See Anna Hájková: *The Last Ghetto. An Everyday History of Terezín*, New York: OUP, 2020, 201–238.

Among these transports were 5,007 people on board of two trains on September 6, 1943, to Auschwitz-Birkenau, with designations 'Dl' and 'Dm'.[2] Both these transports ended in the newly established Terezín family camp in Auschwitz-Birkenau[3] and had been declared as 'Protectorate transports', meaning that the transports were to be composed only of prisoners deported to the ghetto from the Protectorate. Benjamin Murmelstein, the last 'Elder of the Jews' ('*Judenältester*') in Terezín, expressed in a postwar testimony that the preparation of these transports might have been related to the desired suppression of "unreliable Terezín elements"[4] as a result of the transfer of archives of the Reichssicherheitshauptamt (RSHA, Reich Security Main Office) from Berlin to Terezín. Loesten's (i.e. Karl Löwenstein's) correspondence with Jehuda Bacon mentioned that an internal struggle within the 'Council of Elders' and attempts at defamation of the Ghetto Guard (*Ghettowache*) by SS-Hauptsturmführer Ernst Moes led to the decision for the two transports.[5]

The transports ushered a spate of tragic events that culminated in March 1944 in Auschwitz-Birkenau. After a six-month quarantine of the Terezín inmates, who altogether had not passed the selection on their arrival and were all placed in one special section of the camp in Birkenau – the so-called Terezín family camp – the decision was taken to completely liquidate them. Only a group of medical and nursing personnel, as well as seriously ill inmates, who were expected to die soon anyway, escaped this extermination. The other inmates, according to an entry by Dr Wolken, a physician in quarantine camp BIIa in Birkenau, a total of 3,752 people were sent to death in the gas chambers.[6] These events

---

[2] The marking of transports to and from the ghetto using a combination of the alphabet or Roman numerals (for transports to the ghetto from Germany, Austria, the Netherlands, Denmark and Slovakia) was carried out by the Jewish authorities. For an overview of deportations from the Terezín ghetto to 'the East', see Alfred Gottwaldt and Diana Schulle: *Die "Judendeportationen" aus dem Deutschen Reich 1941–1945*, Wiesbaden: Marix, 2005.

[3] For basic information about the Terezín family camp in Auschwitz-Birkenau, see Franziska Jahn: "Das 'Theresienstädter Familienlager' (BIIb) in Birkenau", in Wolfgang Benz and Barbara Distel (eds.): *Der Ort des Terrors*, volume 5, Munich: Beck, 2007, 112–115.

[4] Murmelstein's Testimony – Questions for Weinmann and K. H. Frank, n.d., 305–633–1, 112, Archives of the Security Services (ABS), Prague. Translation by the author.

[5] Letter from Karl Loesten to Yehuda Bacon, 18.03.1961, O.64/103, Yad Vashem Archives (YVA). Available at: https://documents.yadvashem.org/index.html?language=en&search=advance&re_value=0.64&re_type=literal&fi_value=103&fi_type=exact. Last accessed: 01.05.2020.

[6] I would like to point out the hitherto erroneous number of 3,792 persons murdered during the liquidation of the family camp given in literature. Somebody probably made this mistake which has since then been uncritically accepted. Cf. "Quarantäne Liste", sign. D-AuII-3/1, inv. No. 29740, kart. 18, Archive of the Auschwitz-Birkenau State Museum (APMA); Miroslav Kárný: "Terezínský rodinný tábor v 'konečném řešení'", in idem., Margita Kárná, and Toman Brod

and the actual purpose of establishing the Terezín family camp have remained a subject of speculations to this day. The most probable purpose of the existence of the family camp, apart from eliminating the insurgent potential of the Terezín ghetto, was primarily its role of concealment. To this end, the Nazis used an innocuous name (Arbeitslager Birkenau bei Neu Berun) to disguise the true name of the extermination camp, keeping the deportees alive for a suitable period of time and forcing them to write antedated letters about their good stay in the camp to Terezín prisoners. Thus the six months stay in Auschwitz functioned as a decoy that the transports were in fact work transports which they were officially passed off as and not liquidation transports, what they had actually been in the end.[7]

These September transports formed part of a continuous line of hundreds of small and large incoming and outgoing transports, making the Terezín ghetto an assembly and transit camp for the Jewish population of occupied Europe. Each transport coming to the Terezín ghetto from Germany, the Protectorate and other German occupied countries was subjected to scrutiny in terms of protection of its newcomers by the Jewish 'self-administration'. In fact, on arrival in Terezín all the inmates, or actually the heads of families, had to fill in questionnaires giving reasons for eventual exemption from the departing transports to 'the East'.[8] For the arriving prisoners, getting protection meant being at least temporarily exempted from the departing transports. The criterion for selection for the so-called commission protection lists with the names of the protected newcomers laid in their previous work for a Jewish religious community and in the protection of the relatives of the ghetto's leading personnel. With the gradual liquidation of the Jewish Community in Prague, these protection lists were getting progressively more extensive. For example, in case of transport 'Di', which left Prague on July 13, 1943, 236 people (i.e., 28 percent) of the total of 838 deportees were entered in the commission protection list.[9]

These lists of (temporarily) protected persons were revised before the departure of the September 1943 transports. The reason for the revision of these lists by

---

(eds.): *Terezínský rodinný tábor v Osvětimi-Birkenau*, Prague: Terezínská iniciativa-Melantrich, 1994, 35–49.
7 For an evaluation of the research carried out so far, for clarification of starting points as well as the potential significance and purpose of the Terezín family camp, see Tomáš Fedorovič: Propagandistická role Terezína a terezínský rodinný tábor v Auschwitz-Birkenau, in *Terezínské listy*, 46, 2018, 32–40.
8 Order of the day No. 67, 05.03.1942, and order of the day No. 91, 03.04.1942, Terezín collection, inv. No. 144, Jewish Museum in Prague (hereafter JMP).
9 Transport list Di, 06.08.1943, O.64/47 – 116–119, Yad Vashem Archives (YVA).

representatives of the Jewish ghetto leadership was to update the really indispensable and important persons for the running of the ghetto. According to the so-called Renunciation list No. 1 (*Verzichtliste Nr. 1*) from August 7, 1943, i.e. just one day after the start of registration for the September 1943 transports, 153 names were crossed out from the commission protection lists.[10] However, an additional list of artists (*Zusatzliste der Künstler*) was drawn up on August 21, 1943, intended to protect 45 employees of the Free Time Organization Department (*Freizeitgestaltung*, FZG).[11]

The decisive role in the preparation of the transports was played by the top representatives of the Jewish authorities on the orders of the SS. For the purposes of the SS, the Jewish 'self-administration' was a transfer institution, which had the main task of mediating all the demands of the SS to the prison community. As Benjamin Murmelstein himself recalled after the war, the Jewish 'self-administration' had to participate in six tasks while organizing transports to 'the East':

1. Compiling the transports
2. Notifying inmates selected for the transports
3. Establishing a checking point (so-called Schleuse or channel)
4. Providing food and medication for the deportees
5. Registering actually deported inmates
6. Boarding deportees and loading luggage into freight (cattle) wagons[12]

The purpose of this study is to map out the first item of the preparatory stage in the context of the transports to Auschwitz in September 1943, and to valid the findings to some extent at least for the December 1943 transports. The analysis is based on more than 2,500 petitions, which were submitted to the officials of the Jewish 'self administration' in a bid to exempt specific inmates from the transports. They all are documenting the efforts of more than 4,200 individual prisoners, family members, prominent inmates as well as members of the 'Council of Elders', and eventually of individual departments of the Jewish 'self-administration', to protect potential deportees from their final call-up.[13] Beyond the in-

---

10 "Verzichtliste Nr. 1" compiled by Beck and Zucker, 07.08.1943, O.64/47 – 122–123, YVA.
11 Additional list of artists, 21.08.1943, O.64/47 – 150, YVA.
12 Benjamin Murmelstein's testimony concerning the organization of transports, 14.03.1946, 305–633–1, ABS.
13 This unique set of documents was collected as part of the so-called Documentation Action, which was driven by the prominent Zionist and later diplomat Yochanan Zeev Shek. Some of these materials were later transferred to Israel and form part of the O.64 (Terezín Collection) of the Yad Vashem Memorial, files 10.1–21.2 and partially file 23. Files 22.1 and 22.2 are con-

dividual cases, the petitions show the logic behind the selection policy of the Jewish 'self-administration'. Since hardly any official entries on the internal rules of the Jewish 'self-administration' have survived, these sources are also instructive for the study of its activities in general.

In the following, I will describe the strategy adopted by the inmates called up for deportation in their struggle for exemption from the transports. I will first give an overview of the compilation of the transports in regard to the different institutions within the Jewish 'self-administration' and the filing of petitions to these different departments. Next, I will show the function of the so-called protection lists, which were held by the various functionaries of the 'self-administration', and will, by means of various categories of prisoners, discuss who was actually deported and who was saved.

Compiling the Transports and Filing Petitions

The organization of transports, including the compilation of the names and exemptions from it, known as preparatory work (*Vorarbeiten*), was left to the Terezín Jewish 'self-administration', or entrusted to what were called the Large Transport Commission and the Small Transport Commission.[14] Its instructions were to be put into effect by the Transport Department headed by Vilém Cantor, falling under the Central Secretariat, managed by Leo Janowitz. The Transport Department received not only all the information on inmates which were to be put on a specific transport, but also of those who should be removed from it.[15] The Large Transport Commission was made up of some dozens representatives of national commissions and individual departments of the Jewish 'self-administration'.[16] In contrast, the Small Transport Commission consisted only of se-

---

cerned with exemptions and information on inmates enrolled in the December 1943 transport to the family camp in Auschwitz-Birkenau. See Yad Vashem: "Yad Vashem Document Archive". Available at: https://documents.yadvashem.org/index.html?language=en&search=advance&re_value=O.64&re_type=literal&fi_value=103&fi_type=exact. Last accessed: 13.09.2022.

14 Vilém Cantor's protocol for the National Security (Police) Directorate in Prague, 13.02.1946, 305–633–1, 192–194, ABS. See on this and the following also Hájková, The Last Ghetto, 201–207.

15 Cf. description of W. Cantor in H.G. Adler: *Terezín 1941–1945. Das Antlitz einer Zwangsgemeinschaft*, Tübingen: Mohr (Paul Siebeck), 1960, 287.

16 Murmelstein's testimony, given in the Prague-Pankrác Police Prison, b.d., 305–633–1, 48, ABS. The name Walter Wiener also figured among the people serving on the Transport Commission. See petition filed by the Youth Welfare Department (*Jugendfürsorge*) to exempt the family of Oskar Fuchs from transport, 16.08.1943, O.64/19.1 – 1809, YVA.

nior representatives of some departments of the Terezín 'self-administration' and decided in case of disagreement by the Large Transport Commission.[17]

We know that the initial selection of the persons intended for deportation was made by the Large Transport Commission. Reasons for exemption were evaluated before each 'Eastern transport'. Persons who were selected for the September 1943 transports had the opportunity to complete a special questionnaire, giving five chief reasons for exemption.[18] Inmates had to take such questionnaires with them, when summoned to the camp's SS Command to be inspected.[19] Even though every inmate called up for a transport could read already in a printed form that petitions for exemption from labor deployment transports were inadmissible,[20] around 4,200 prisoners were going through the petition process in an effort to save themselves or a third person from deportation to 'the East'. The two transports were officially declared as labor deployment transports (*Arbeitseinsatz-Transporte*). However, the prisoners were kept in the dark about the true purpose of the deportations and therefore sought to exercise their exemption.

The petitions were addressed to the Jewish 'self-administration' or to some of its members by name. There are as many as 4,239 names of Terezín inmates in the preserved petitions and material associated with requests for exemptions from these transports, kept in the volume dealing with exemption from the September transports. 3,721 of them filed petitions in their own name, trying to escape their own deportation. 518 persons acted on behalf of their close relatives, asking for their exemption from the transports.

The fate of inmates for whom a petition was filed depended on the reasons and criteria under which they were eventually removed from the transport or were left on the list. We know that 1,674 failed in their exemption petitions, thus accounting for 33 percent of all the deportees. 2,047 inmates originally registered for a transport were eventually taken off the transport lists, while inmates who did not receive any such life-saving protection had to go instead of them.

It remains to be explained why petitions of the remaining two thirds of 5,007 deportees called up for transports have not been preserved. Did they not file

---

17 Friedmann's petition addressed to Placzek, 28.08.1943, O.64/18.1 – 1661, YVA.
18 The reasons were: (I.) bearer of military distinctions (Iron Cross first class, gold medal for bravery, Order of the Crown, and other major distinctions), (II.) war invalid and also whether he or she was permanently unfit for transport as a result of injury, (III.) those who drew in pension or annuity, (IV.) whether inmates had relatives outside Terezín, (V.–VII.) fields of questions concerning 'mixed marriages' and offsprings born from such marriages. See questionnaire of Zdenek Baar, b.d., O.64/10.2 – 107, YVA.
19 Petition of Abraham Fink, 16.08.1943, O.64/14.2 – 925, YVA.
20 Call-up form of Gustav Friedmann, b.d., O.64/10.1 – 7, YVA.

them, or did they just not survive in the archives? Or perhaps they did not petition at all? Is it possible that these people reconciled themselves with their summons to transports, being convinced that their grounds for exemption failed to be adequate? Or was there a role played here by the obfuscation that these were not deportations to 'the East', but transports for labor deployment? So far, research has not been able to provide answers to these questions.

During a reorganization of Terezín's Jewish 'self-administration' in January 1943, the camp's SS Commandant Siegfried Seidl ruled that Paul Eppstein would bear the main responsibility for the operation of the ghetto in the new triumvirate of former high-ranking Jewish officials from Berlin (Eppstein), Prague (Edelstein) and Vienna (Murmelstein).[21] Before, these responsibilities were in the hands of Jakob Edelstein. This transfer of final decision-making power (or rather lack of it) was accompanied by the targeting of petitions for exemption. Paul Eppstein, in these days active as the 'Elder of the Jews', received several times more petitions than the other high-ranking officials of the 'self-administration', including the previous 'Elder of the Jews', Jacob Edelstein.[22] As a matter of fact, it was Eppstein, as the 'Elder of the Jews', that had the last say primarily in those controversial cases on which the Small Transport Commission could not reach consensus.[23] We may suppose that Eppstein, as the 'Elder of the Jews', did see and analyze many of those cases, having attached his initial E with a date, eventually with a request for a further consultation on the petitions.[24]

Accepted and Rejected Petitions

In the following, I will refer to petitions for exemption from the two September transports to elaborate on the reasons why some of the prisoners were taken off the transport list and why some were deported.

Some of the major factors conducive to an inmate's inclusion into a transport or exemption therefrom were undertakings given by individual leading officials of the Jewish 'self-administration'. If such a pledge was undertaken by the 'Elder of the Jews', the resultant decision carried maximum weight. Marta Krai-

---

21 Official entry No. Ed/Ek from Terezín, 27.01.1943, collection Terezín, inv. No. 146, JMP.
22 Edelstein received 28 petitions, Murmelstein 28 as well, Zucker 80, and Eppstein 473. 463 other petitions were addressed to the 'Council of Elders', 464 eventually to the management (*Leitung*) or Transport/Exemption/Polish Commission; 473 have not been included in the overview.
23 Vilém Cantor's protocol for the National Security (Police) Directorate in Prague, 13.02.1946, 305–633–1, 192–194, ABS.
24 Petition for exempting Gustav Steger, 09.08.1943, O.64/18.2 – 1800, YVA.

nerová, a member of the Jewish 'self-administration', pleaded for herself, her mother Ida and her brother Bruno Fuchs, a former member of the Ghetto Guard to be exempted from the transport. While Marta and Ida were successful, Bruno's name had also been removed from the transport list on September 4, 1943, but on the following day, he received a new registration number.[25] Eppstein's secretary Alice Myrants approached the head of the Transport Department, Cantor, with the request to exempt Fuchs definitely. But due to a shortage of time and possibly owing to tensions, mounting among the members of the Jewish 'self-administration', the request had not been granted, and Fuchs departed from Terezín in one of the September transports. It is evident that the later a person submitted his or her petition, the lesser chance for success he or she had. With every day prior to transport departure the chances for success and exemption from the transport increased by one percentage point. If Bruno Fuchs hypothetically petitioned ten days earlier, he would have raised his chance of staying in the camp by ten percentage points, as compared with those whose records of exemption are not available (control group).[26]

Ghetto inmates also realized that a face-to-face meeting with Eppstein and presentation of their reasons for being taken off the transport list enhanced their chances for staying in Terezín. During their efforts to arrange a personal meeting with Eppstein, his closest colleagues played an important mediating role. His secretary Alice Myrants was requested by many petitioners to arrange such face-to-face encounters.[27] One of the aspects that have not yet been accentuated in historical research was the role of the spouses of the ghetto's high-ranking officials.[28] At the time of the September transports, it was primarily the wife of the 'Elder', Hedwig Eppstein, who interceded on behalf of some of the prisoners.[29]

Protection Lists

The most important and widespread mechanism of protection consisted in establishing strong bonds with persons among the Jewish 'self-administration' be-

---

25 Petition of Marta Krainerová, b.d. (04.09.1943?), O.64/10.1 – 83, YVA.
26 The project led by Professor Štěpán Jurajda from CERGE-EI: *Social Structure of a Nazi Ghetto: Analysis of Survival in the Terezín Ghetto* (GAČR 19–05523S).
27 Petition of Dr Bauer, 15.08.1943, O.64/20.1 – 2036, YVA.
28 As an example, see petition for exemption of Růžena Ziemlichová from the transport to Treblinka in the fall of 1942, O.64/94 – 9–12, YVA.
29 Note on the exemption of the Rosenberger family, b.d., O.64/10.1 – 54, YVA.

lieved to have the power to arrange an inmate's exemption from transport. To have ones name on the personal protective list (*persönliche Schutzliste*) of a member of the 'Council of Elders', in case of registration and call up for transport, offered a high degree of protection indeed.

Thanks to their privileged position, members of the 'Council of Elders' had the possibility of protecting some of the inmates from deportation. Egon Popper, head of the Internal Administration Department (*Innere Verwaltung*), kept 57 names on his personal exemption list.[30] In a similar vein, we know the names on the protection lists of other members of the 'Council of Elders', namely Jakob Wolffing[31] or Robert Stricker.[32]

Even though not a member of the 'Council of Elders', Richard Friedmann, a former chief of the division for dealing with authorities at the Jewish religious Community in Prague and a Terezín notable, reminded the 'Council of Elders' that he had been given a mandate to nominate seven people "whose protection had been promised to me". This particular request is accompanied by Eppstein's initial and the words "correct/kindly see to exemption".[33]

Although some inmates knew that the respective departments of the 'self-administration' would intercede on behalf of their next of kin summoned for transport, they made use of every opportunity to address other people who could also significantly help them. For instance, Lydia Altmannová wrote in her exemption letter to the management that Leo Janowitz, member of the staff of the 'self-administration' (*Stab*), Head of the Central Secretariat and her former university colleague and youth friend, promised her, half an hour before his arrest, that he would do everything in his power to prevent her inclusion in the transport, literally "to inhibit my inclusion".[34]

Furthermore, Max Popper, an employee of the Labor Center (*Arbeitszentrale*), put on the list of a transport reserve, tried unsuccessfully to save his family from the transport on the day of its departure. He approached Erich Österreicher, Head of the Economic Department – Production (WAP), with a plea for further assistance since the latter's promises given to him earlier had been to no avail. What is quite bewildering in this case is the helpless obsequiousness Popper dis-

---

30 Egon Popper, personal exemption list containing people up to the age of 60, b.d., O.64/47 – 131, YVA.
31 Petition of Jakob Wolffing, 31.08.1943, O.64/12.1 – 425, YVA.
32 Petition of Robert Stricker, 28.08.1943, O.64/12.1 – 426, YVA.
33 Both quotes from petition of Richard Friedmann, 03.09.1943, O.64/11.1 – 203, YVA. Translation by the author.
34 Petition for exemption from transport on behalf of Lydie Altmannová, 03.09.1943, O.64/15.1 – 1041, YVA. Translation by the author.

played, although he had already seen for himself that in this way he could not achieve his sought-after goal.[35]

The petitions filed by the departments of the Jewish 'self-administration' on behalf of their protégés proved to have a much greater impact on the outcome of eventual exemptions than those submitted by individual inmates on their own behalf or by some of their relatives. In mathematical terms, the actual weight of such petitions was 14 percent greater with the 'Council of Elders', and even 19 percent higher in case of the Jewish 'self-administration'.[36]

Each department of the Jewish 'self-administration' had its own protection list. Until its abolition in mid-August 1943, the protection list of the Ghetto Guard had as many as 348 slots.[37] The Youth Welfare Department (*Jugendfürsorge*) that had at its disposal 15 protected places also sought to exempt Alžběta Hirschová, one of the leaders in a children's home. Exempted from a transport, she was then transferred to take care of the Białystok children with whom she later found death in Auschwitz-Birkenau.[38]

Protection lists were also known to have their own specific order of names, which turned out to be an important factor considered on many occasions, as proved by the preserved petitions. Alice Ehrlichová, a chief disinfecting specialist, was exempted from transport, as she had figured in the 14th place on the list of 186 names of the inner staff of the Insect Control Department (*Entwesung*).[39] The Bank of the Jewish 'self-administration' was another division for which we have a definite idea of the scope of its protected persons. The bank stated in its exemption list that out of the 37 inmates of Protectorate nationality, 20 people were registered, or rather enrolled, in labor transports. The entire protection list of the Bank of the Jewish 'self-administration' contained 87 names.[40] The Technical Department (*Technische Abteilung*) sent to the Transport Commission a list of persons over 60 years of age, defining three major groups for exemption. Group A was reserved for workers deemed indispensable for the department, group B contained workforce necessary for Barracks Construction (*Baracken-*

---

35 Petition of Max Popper, 06.09.1943, O.64/21.2 – 2374, YVA.
36 Professor Jurajda's research concerning the transports 'Dl' and 'Dm', in an e-mail to the author, 29.09.2020.
37 Exemption of Karel Schnürmacher, 04.09.1943, O.64/10.1 – 1, YVA.
38 Petition filed by Bedřich Prager, an official of the Youth Welfare Department, on behalf of Alžběta Hirschová, 16.08.1943, O.64/15.2 – 1142, YVA.
39 Petition of Josef Pacovský, head of the Insect Control Department, 03.09.1943, O.64/13.2 – 797, YVA. Cf. Youth Welfare Department to Zucker, O.64/12.2 – 559; 15.1 – 1045; 17.1 – 1457, YVA.
40 Exemption list of the Bank of the Jewish 'self-administration', 04.09.1943, O.64/14.1 – 803, YVA. Cf. also petition filed by the bank on the exemption from transport of its two colleagues, b.d., O.64/17.1 – 1452, YVA.

bau), while group C featured family members of reliable employees of that particular department.⁴¹ Attached to the Technical Department, the Railroad Construction Division (*Bahnbau*) insisted on the protection of its 30 workers critically needed for railroad maintenance. Interestingly, the list comprising 30 names was compiled at the instigation of the SS headquarters.⁴² Endeavors to keep the employees of the individual departments or divisions in the ghetto are attested to by their insistence on the stipulated protection quotas.⁴³

The extant correspondence maintained between the various departments and its senior Jewish officials with the Transportation Department indicate that the assignments of their personnel were not classified as intentional, but rather as 'errors' that had to be speedily corrected.⁴⁴ Julius Grünberger, head of the Technical Department, wrote in his letter to Eppstein, that he was inclined to believe that, as concerned the exemption petition on behalf of carpenters Oskar Beer and Isidor Zehngut from the Barracks Construction Division, the head of the Transport Department Cantor had not shown what Grünberger termed "correct grasp of the matter", and that was why he called for their "authentic exemption".⁴⁵

Besides the protection lists of the 'Council of Elders' and the individual departments of the Jewish 'self-administration', there were preserved lists drawn up by the Jewish municipality containing the names of persons working for the German SS Camp Command or the 'Berlin "M" headquarters', hence the archive of the RSHA in Terezín. Their protective effect for September transports was surprisingly slight.⁴⁶ The protective effect of the list kept by the 'Berlin "M" headquarters' was quite intriguing in that it did not provide any protection at all. Even though the list, comprising the names of 16 men, was compiled for the protection of persons against transports in September 1943, ten inmates were called up precisely for those transports. None of them survived.⁴⁷

---

41 Petition filed by the Technical Department, 23.08.1943, O.64/19.3 – 1994, YVA.
42 Petition of Bruno Knöpfelmacher, foreman of the first company, and Bedřich Stern, O.64/14.2 – 995, YVA. Their petition had been ignored and both were put on the transport.
43 Petition filed by the K-production concerning the additional list, 23.08.1943, O.64/18.2 – 1799, YVA.
44 WAP to the Central Secretariat/Transport Commission, 04.09.1943, O.64/10.1 – 17, YVA.
45 Both quotes from Julius Grünberger's letter to Paul Eppstein, 04.09.1943, O.64/13.1 – 602, YVA. Translation by the author.
46 Permanent cleaning service for the headquarters, including the clubhouse for SS officers, December 1943, O.64/22.2 – 3125, YVA.
47 Protection list of the parties permanently working in the Bodenbach Barracks who were listed as protected, 05.09.1943, O.64/16.1 – 1248, YVA.

Deported and Saved Prisoners

Despite the fact that the fate of the Terezín prisoners may have been influenced to some extent by the Jewish 'self-administration' of the Terezín ghetto, whether Terezín inmates succeeded in staying in the ghetto or not depended primarily on the directives issued by the SS headquarters. One of the directives why Terezín inmates could end up in transports was an entry in their criminal records in the ghetto or their incarceration.[48] A criterion for inclusion was the fact that inmates had been imprisoned in one of the Terezín jails for over two weeks.[49] Furthermore, the WAP added that the SS Command insisted on inclusion into transport by order (*Weisung*) for those sentenced for more than three months.[50]

In addition to the instructions and guidelines derived from those directives, the Jewish 'self-administration' laid down its own internal criteria, taking into account some groups of prisoners. Also relevant for protection against deportation was the exploitation of the prisoners' labor. The so-called K-production (*K-Produktion*), for example, located on the main square inside the ghetto, i.e. the manufacture of boxes for equipment facilitating starting engines of army vehicles at low temperatures, ranked among the production sectors vital for the war economy and was managed and manned by ghetto inmates. According to order of the day No. 328 dated June 1, 1943, some 1,000 people were slated to be deployed in this branch.[51] However, the total numbers in this case speak of something very different than the fact that the requirements of meeting the Wehrmacht orders were also accompanied by the need to protect this production sector. According to Dr. Kussy, head of the K-production, the name of its worker Eliška Picková was on a list of 30 protected persons of the K-production. However, Picková was summoned for a transport in December 1943 after the relevant production was terminated.[52] Even though other instructions issued by the SS headquarters in Terezín

---

[48] Egon Preiss said that he had been included in a transport with his whole family, namely together with other protectorate inmates who found themselves in jail. Petition of Egon Preiss, 01.09.1943, O.64/17.2 – 1515, YVA.

[49] To punish violations of SS prohibitions and orders, the so-called Jewish ghetto court was in operation in Terezín. It sentenced minor offences to the so-called Jewish prison, while some serious offences were dealt with in the prison at the SS Headquarters or by sending them to the nearby Gestapo police prison in the Little Fortress.

[50] Petition by the WAP, 29.08.1943, O.64/19.1 – 1862, YVA.

[51] Order of the day No. 328, 01.06.1943, A 3389, Terezín Memorial Archive.

[52] Petition of Dr Kussy on behalf of Eliška Picková, 14.08.1943, O.64/14.1 – 818, YVA.

were aimed at protecting vitally important sectors for war production,[53] not all of the workers were automatically saved. A petition filed by the WAP concerning Otilie Saarová, one of the best seamstresses in the Uniform Mending Department (*Uniformkonfektion*), noted that she should be exempted from the transport as "we refer to the instructions issued by the SS headquarters"[54]. This protective arrangement concerned the 13 best workers employed in the vital war production sectors, an understanding promised on September 4, 1943, by the station's civilian employee, inspector Friedrich Komarek, to Gustav Korngold, head responsible for this division. Of those 13 allegedly "indispensable"[55] women mentioned in the official document for Karl Schliesser, head of the Economic Department, another eight women were called up for transports in September 1943.

Members of the Ghetto Guard (GW) constituted a sizable group heavily afflicted by call-ups for the September transports. At the instigation of SS Commandant Burger, the total number of GW members was to be reduced through transports, and as many as 150 of them were to be summoned for the September transports. Three former GW members, Kurt Singer, Viktor Drechsler and Richard Nettl, approached Eppstein with the argument that according to the official record, parents and children under 14 years of age and persons from 'mixed marriages' were eligible for exemption from transports. In their opinion, there were some 20 'Aryan'-related inmates as well as 50 people with children under the age of 14 years among some 300 GW members. If these persons were to be exempted from the transport, another 230 persons, i.e. "enough other material",[56] would have remained for selecting 150 people for the transport.

Social capital also played a seminal role in many cases for exemption from a transport. The great importance of social bonds established among Terezín inmates either prior to their deportation or during incarceration in Terezín is illustrated in the correspondence of Kurt Bauer from the Transport Department who interceded for a brother and a sister-in-law of Max Löbl from the Central Secretariat in Terezín. As a reason for exemption he argued – in addition to knowing the family from Brno – that these were reliable and charitable people; he added that Löbl spent three months in the Sudeten Barracks as his "bed neighbor".[57]

---

53 Information for Otto Zucker on the requirements of the SS headquarters (Moes and Bartels), 03.09.1943, O.64/17.2 – 1589, YVA.
54 Petition filed by the WAP, 04.09.1943, O.64/11.1 – 218, YVA. Translation by the author.
55 Official record for Mr. Schliesser, petition of Gustav Korngold, 04.09.1943, O.64/11.1 – 230, YVA. Translation by the author.
56 Petition of Viktor Drechsler, Kurt Singer, and Richard Nettl, 28.08.1943, O.64/17.2 – 1534, YVA. Translation by the author.
57 Petition of Dr Bauer, b.d., O.64/20.3 – 2153, YVA. Translation by the author.

The importance of the social ties originating in the rooms of Terezín's buildings and halls is also documented by Bauer's other petition pertaining to the exemption from transport of the wife and son of Julius Singer who had died of typhoid:

> Her husband, Ing. Julius Singer, [...] lived for more than a year with us in the room for staff officials No. 124 and later 239 [...]. During his illness we, his roommates, promised him [...] that whatever happens we would stand behind his wife and his sick child [...]. [T]hey are threatened, and I dare to express a polite request on my own behalf and on behalf of all the friends of the deceased [...] to provide them the greatest possible protection.[58]

Quite surprisingly, well-known personalities of Terezín's life were also included in the September transports. Karel Švenk, an actor, producer and composer, who was called up for the second September transport ('Dm'), can be counted in this category. His petition for exemption and that of his parents was supported by Rafael Schächter and seven other artists.[59] A great deal of credit for his exemption from the transport went to Otto Zucker, member of the 'Council of Elders' in the Terezín ghetto responsible for the youth, cultural life and work commitment of the prisoners, to whom Švenk wrote the following words: "Dear Sir! Overjoyed, I hasten to express my profound thanks. Now I will dedicate my life to arts, fulfilling my legacy and so forth. I thank you once again, greeting you, yours Karel Švenk".[60]

The 'elite' of Terezín's contemporary theater and cultural life also interceded on behalf of Rudolf Weiss, expert in theater make-up, wigs and beards, "the only one who had any knowledge of the art of make-up as well as of making aids for make-up designers"[61] and head of the barber shop in the Hannover Barracks. However, not even the signatures of Karel Švenk, Gustav Schorsch, Hans Hofer, Otakar Růžička, Karel Lustig or Eugen Weisz could stop Weiss's deportation.

Foreign nationals were also among those who were removed from transport lists. As mentioned before, the September 1943 transports had been declared by decision of the SS as transports made up of participants from the Protectorate transports. The Jewish 'self-administration' had to accept these guidelines and therefore it comes as a surprise that names of deportees from Germany, Austria and the Netherlands were also among the exemption petitions. The inmates thus

---

58 Petition of Kurt Bauer concerning the exemption of the Singer family, 04.09.1943, O.64/13.1 – 643, YVA. Translation by the author.
59 Petition of Karel Švenk, 30.08.1943, O.64/18.1 – 1607, YVA.
60 Karel Švenk's transport number, 05.09.1943, O.64/21.2 – 2464, YVA. Translation by the author.
61 Petition filed by the members of the Free Time Organization Department, 13.08.1943, O.64/23–10, YVA. Translation by the author.

involved were well aware of this restriction and rightly and successfully took advantage of it. Persons who had arrived in some of the earlier German, Austrian or Dutch transports (a total of 230 people, i.e. 4.6 percent of all the deportees in both transports) were eventually called up for the transports, because the 'self-administration' had registered them as stateless.[62] Another reason for why their names had been put on the transport lists could be their criminal records.[63] However, prisoners with German nationality, who had come to Terezín with transports from the Protectorate, were not taken into account.[64]

There were also foreign nationals coming to Terezín in transports from Germany and Austria. Bertha Frommerová with her daughter were former Slovak nationals and there are reasons to believe that an existing agreement between the Slovak state and Germany on the deportation of Slovakian Jews was the main cause of their summons to the September transports.[65] The fact that German nationals were not supposed to get deported with the September 1943 transports offered a chance for many inmates from the Protectorate and Slovakia to get their names off the transportation lists. Many Protectorate inmates could refer to their marriage with German nationals in Terezín. Slovak national Alice Klopstocková was not deported, being the common-law wife of Otto Pollak, a German national who had come to the camp in a Vienna transport.[66] On the contrary, the German national Lieselotte Schönfeld, who had been deported to Terezín with the 95th Berlin transport, had to get a permission from the 'Elder of the Jews' Eppstein for her voluntary inclusion into transport to accompany her non-German fiancé Ervín Hecht, deported from Prague in transport 'AAw' in August 1942.[67]

Another internal directive for automatic exemption from transports hinged on inmates' previous post of a regional head of Jewish religious communities and their families.[68] However, this did not apply to all former heads of the Jewish communities in the Protectorate. Judging by the notes attached to the petition filed by Arnošt Löwy, who had stood at the helm of the Jewish religious Community in Uherský Brod for 15 years, we may assume that in his case the 'self-admin-

---

62 Petition of Lilly Schatzmann deported to the ghetto from Dortmund, 04.09.1943, O.64/13.2 – 703, YVA.
63 Note on the person of Anna Reisz, b.d., O.64/13.1 – 602, YVA.
64 Petition of Max Körner, 28.09.1943, O.64/19.2 – 1925, YVA.
65 Petition of Bertha Frommerová, 01.09.1943, O.64/19.2 – 1918, YVA.
66 Note on the person of Alice Klopstocková, b.d., O.64/13.1 – 602, YVA.
67 Information of the Transport Commission concerning Lieselotte Schönfeld, 06.09.1943, O.64/19.3 – 1993, YVA.
68 Petition of Rudolf Steiner, b.d., O.64/10.2 – 103, YVA.

istration' itself sought to argue for his removal from the transport. Dr Wiener from Transport Department dismissed a postscript that could have meant survival for Löwy with a laconic reply: "Ernst Löwy [...] does not figure on any of the objective protection lists".[69] This eventually led to the inclusion of the whole family in the transport.

People of mixed descent ('*Mischlinge*') and persons related to 'Aryans' through 'German-Aryan mixed-marriages' ('*Deutsch-arische Mischehen*', DAM) constituted a large group of inmates who proved to be successful in their struggle to be exempted from the September transports. Contrary, prisoners from 'Czech[=Protectorate]-Aryan mixed-marriages' ('Č[=*Tsch*]*echisch-arische Mischehen*', ČAM) were universally included in the transport, unless other successful reasons for exemption were given.

All the efforts of the Jewish 'self-administration' were focused on preserving – to the greatest possible extent – families together. A major factor the 'self-administration' was obliged to take into consideration was the bulk of 285 petitions filed to prevent the separation of families (*Familienzerreissung*). A total of 151 of such appeals were accepted, and the petitioners were, indeed, exempted from transports. Some of the life stories, as described by the preserved petitions, are truly heart-rending. Such was the case of Kamila Seidlerová who petitioned for her three daughters, all of them aged around 50, to be removed from the transport list. Since all three had been included in the transport together, their mother asked for their exemption on the grounds of family separation, and if not possible, pleaded that at least one of them should be left in Terezín. Neither Alice Seidlerová nor her two other sisters had been saved from the September transport. Mother Kamila, who was deported later, was reunited with her daughters in the Terezín family camp in December 1943, and probably witnessed their murders in the Auschwitz-Birkenau gas chambers in March 1944.[70]

Nearly 14 percent of all the submitted petitions for exemption (62 percent of them successful) were related to the petitioners' work for the ghetto. Protection from transports based on inmates' labor deployment proved its worth primarily in case of professional and skilled jobs in great demand. Inmates, who held very specialized jobs and were indispensable, could (at least) temporarily protect their parents as well. A case in point was František Süssland, the only roofer in the ghetto. Thanks to his 'unique' job, he was not even sent to outside com-

---

69 Petition of Arnošt Löwy, 16.08.1943, O.64/20.3 – 2156, YVA. Translation by the author.
70 Petition of Kamila Seidlerová, 28.08.1943, O.64/20.1 – 2045, YVA.

mandos to Oslavany or Kladno. He was in a position to arrange the exemption of his parents from the September transports.[71]

In addition, professional lobbying also helped in keeping a given person in the Terezín ghetto. A prominent figure in the ghetto, Hans Pick, former chief engineer of the Association for Chemical and Metallurgical Production in Ústí nad Labem, a leading personality of former Czechoslovakia's chemical industry, interceded for his colleague and fellow prisoner Max Freund, a chemical engineer and member of the Delousing Division.[72]

Out of the 3,721 persons, who asked for exemption from the September 1943 transports, 493 of them gave as one of the reasons their inability to manage the transport due to illness. For their purposes in the matter of exempting petitioners from transports on medical grounds, the Jewish 'self-administration' made use of the services of the official physician (*Amtsarzt*) Hugo Holzinger.[73] Based on the data from the extant medical files, his official statements on the health of potential deportees decided about their temporary rescue or call-up for deportation. Medical testimonies and records on medical cards played a significant role in the process of putting inmates on or off the transport lists.[74] Hugo Richter and his family members, all prisoners in Terezín, were seriously affected. Richter himself suffered from cardiomalacia and asthma, and his wife and son were mentally ill. Their petition was examined by Holzinger who added a note to their petition, saying, "their exemption from a medical point of view is not justifiable".[75] However, according to Holzinger, the critical factor for exemption from transport was not fitness for work but rather severe physical damage.[76] Although the September transports had been declared as deportations to labor camps, some of the inmates, in spite of their incapacity for work entered in their work cards, were still included in the transports.[77]

A relatively large portion of prisoners, at least 157 persons, included in the September 1943 transports, were volunteers. Their volunteer registrations were also filed through petitions. There were three categories of petitions concerning voluntary reports for transports. The first type comprised an unconditioned participation in the transport by the petitioner. The second one relates to the so-

---

71 Petition of František Süssland, 04.09.1943, O.64/13.1 – 619, YVA.
72 Petitions by Hans Pick and Karl Schliesser, 04.09.1943, O.64/11.1 – 245, 245a, YVA.
73 Petition of the War Invalids Department, 04.09.1943, O.64/12.2 – 540, YVA.
74 "(He) is not reported sick. No reason for exemption. (Signed) Holzinger." Holzinger's note on the petition of Josef Wantoch, 16.08.1943, O.64/19.1 – 1840, YVA.
75 Medical testimony, 20.08.1943, O.64/13.2 – 672, YVA. Translation by the author.
76 Holzinger's medical opinion on Julius Lappert, 01.09.1943, O.64/19.3 – 1964, YVA.
77 Petition of Kamil Upřímný, 05.09.1943, O.64/13.1 – 625, YVA.

called voluntary but conditional inclusion – *bedingt freiwillig*. This means that the petitioner was enrolled in a transport only if another mentioned person in the petition was exempted from the transport.[78] The last, third type featured what was called compensatory exchange. In such cases, individual inmates or a department of the Jewish 'self-administration' briefed the Transport Department that their exemption from transport would be compensated for by voluntary replacement with another inmate.[79] Several similar petitions have been preserved in the files of documents of the Transport Department. A conditional exchange is also known to have transpired, this time successfully, between Tomáš Kosta and František Eisenschimmel. With his offer, the latter, a famous member of the Construction Commando, actually saved Tomáš Kosta's life.[80]

Final Remarks and Conclusion

As many as 5,007 people had left the Terezín ghetto with the two transports in September 1943. After the compilation, the deportees had to board the trains, which each consisted of 50 freight wagons. Via the train station Bohušovice nad Ohří, just approx. two kilometers away, where the control over the train was taken over from the gendarmes by members of the Schutzpolizei (Schupo), the trains departed to Auschwitz. The first 50 wagons left Bohušovice at 2 p.m. on September 6, 1943, and the second set of 50 wagons departed at 8 o'clock in the evening of the same day. After the departure of the transports 'Dl' and 'Dm' life in the ghetto was gradually settling down to its old ways. Already three days after the transport departure the Magdeburg Barracks housed the Terezín premiere of Mozart's "Magic Flute" (*Zauberflöte*) and nobody could then suspect that only less than one percent of the more than five thousand deportees would live to see their liberation.

The petitions are a rare testimony to the assembly of two transports and the attempts of the deportees to escape being transported away. Unaware of their tragic fate, they had tried to use every possibility to avert their inclusion in

---

[78] Petition of Ettie Gottesmann, O.64/13.2 – 756, YVA.
[79] If a member of a department volunteered for a transport, the respective department could suggest the exemption of another of its members called up for that transport. For instance, the Agriculture Department asked for the exemption from transport of Hermína Polláková in exchange of volunteer Anna Felsenbergová. See petition filed by the Agriculture Department on behalf of Hermína Polláková, 04.09.1943, O.64/10.1 – 30, YVA.
[80] Notification concerning František Eisenschimmel's conditional voluntary report, b.d., O.64/10.2 – 135, YVA.

the transport. It is sad reality that almost half of all preserved documents in this convolute documents the failure of the Terezín prisoners. We must note that some of the documents, applications or lists requesting exemption from the transports contained the names of both groups of prisoners – those included in the transports and those removed from the lists.

Based on an analysis of almost 2,500 petitions for exemption, it is possible to trace the petitioner's successful or unsuccessful attempts to save themselves from deportations. The study of this particular file of documents is conducive to understanding the actual range of possible actions by the inmates themselves and of the Jewish 'self-administration', which was obliged to abide by the SS instructions in Terezín. In addition to unique information about the life of the Terezín prisoners, these applications provide micro surveys of important aspects of the coerced community, such as the importance of sponsorship by individual departments and/or the 'Council of the Elders', social ties between prisoners, value of labor or the lobbying and excellent protection for individual craftsmen in short supply. We could also examine a statistical effect of the time of application or the form of application. We observe protection of certain groups of prisoners (artists, agricultural workers, partly K-production), not significant effect of illness, an impact of the family relations (e. g., through marriages with non-Jewish Germans or Czechs).

Escaping a form of certain 'self-selection' through the Jewish administration required having, at the appropriate time, the appropriate 'key' accepted by the SS and applied by the Jewish administration. These 'keys' in the form of labor, transport incapacity (sickness), and relations with the 'Aryan' population constituted defense mechanisms of 'ordinary' prisoners. The above all most important and widespread mechanism of protection was the creation of important ties to the alleged 'power-full'.

Murmelstein, in his postwar testimony, stated that working on the transport committees carried with it a heavy burden of responsibility, since the elimination of one person resulted in the inclusion of another. Although exemption claims were in the end in most cases without factual basis, they had a great psychological effect as evidence of good will on the part of the leadership of the Jewish 'self-administration'.[81] Such evidence of goodwill, however, only amounted to a 'temporary' reprieve. Of the 2,047 persons excluded from deportation to 'the East' in September 1943, only 291 were not deported by further 'Eastern transports', to see their liberation.

---

81 Deposition of Benjamin Murmelstein in his own case, 11. 02.1946, 305 – 633 – 1, ABS.

Viorel Achim
The Petitions of Roma Deportees as a Source for the Study of the Deportation Sites in Transnistria

Abstract: Researching the deportation of approximately 25,000 Roma from Romania to Transnistria in the years 1942 to 1944 benefits from a large amount of documents, preserved in various archives in Romania and Ukraine, which facilitate a detailed study of this historical phenomenon. A special category of documents is represented by the petitions that deported Roma sent to the Romanian occupation administration in this territory, at different levels. Some were individual petitions, others spoke on behalf of a group of deportees. The content of the petitions is very different. In many petitions, especially in the first months after deportation, the petitioners demanded the repatriation of themselves and their families. But in many others the Roma complained about the miserable conditions in the deportation sites, asked the authorities to give them shelter, food and clothes, and to ensure them a better treatment, enabling them to survive. Also, the Roma required to have a place to work or to be allowed to exercise their crafts in the villages they were placed in or in the vicinity.

In the first part, this article discusses this type of sources, with their specificity and potential. The Roma petitions are important not just for the historical information they contain, but also because they provide insights into the contemporary deportees' perspective on the deportation and the state of affairs in deportation sites. In the second part, based on the petitions, living condition of deported Roma in the Eastern part of Transnistria as well as relations with the local Ukrainian population will be discussed.

Introduction

The deportation of Roma to Transnistria is the story of approximately 25,000 Romanian citizens – of which more than 11,000 were considered 'nomads' and about 14,000 'sedentary' –, originary from all regions of the country. The government lead by Marshall Ion Antonescu deported them in the summer and autumn of 1942 to the Soviet territory situated between the rivers Dniestr and Bug, which then was under Romanian military occupation. The 25,000 Roma were selected according to certain criteria from a total Roma population of 208,700, as estimated by the Central Institute for Statistics in Bucharest.¹ This deportation was related to the population policy of the Antonescu government, more precisely to the project of ethnic homogenization of the country. The Roma were settled at the border of or inside villages located in Eastern Transnistria, on the bank of the Bug in the districts of Oceacov, Berezovca, Golta, and Balta.² The living conditions at the deportation sites were extremely harsh, which explains why until the spring of 1944, when the survivors returned to Romania, about 11,000 deported had died, mostly due to inhuman conditions of accommodation and food, cold and epidemics. Most of them passed away during a typhoid epidemic that broke out in the middle of December 1942 in the so-called Gypsy villages in the northern part of Oceacov district.³

The Roma were the second largest population group that the Antonescu government deported to Transnistria, after the approximately 160,000 Jews, almost all from the provinces of Bessarabia and Bukovina, who were deported in several waves between October 1941 and October 1942.⁴ In some places in Transnistria, Jews and Roma deportees lived in the same locality and worked on the same farm or construction site.

The history of deportation of Roma to Transnistria has a rich documentary base. The most important sources in terms of quantity and information are historical documents, which are collected in various archives in Romania and Ukraine. Most of these files on the deportations were created by the authorities and institutions at the central or local level in Romania, but also in Transnistria, and have been preserved to this day.

---

1 A statistical study of the Roma population in Romania in its borders from 1942, based on the data of the general census of 1930, was made by the Central Insititute for Statistics in September 1942. See Lucian Nastasă and Andrea Varga (eds.): *Minorități etnoculturale. Mărturii documentare. Țiganii din România (1919–1944)*, Cluj-Napoca: Centrul de Resurse pentru Diversitate Culturală, 2001, doc. 207, 333–412.

2 In this article the districts and rayons in Transnistria, which were created by the Romanian occupation administration, appear with their Romanian name, which was official between 1941 and 1944. Instead, for villages, communes and towns in Transnistria, the Ukrainian names are used, from that time but also today.

3 On the deportation of Roma to Transnistria, see Viorel Achim: *The Roma in Romanian History*, Budapest, New York: CEU Press, 2004, 163–188; Tuvia Friling, Radu Ioanid, and Mihail E. Ionescu (eds.): *International Commission on the Holocaust in Romania. Final Report*, Iași: Polirom, 2005, 223–241; Viorel Achim: "La déportation des Rroms en Transnistrie, les données principales", in *Études tsiganes*, 56/57, 2015, 68–89.

4 On the deportations of Jews to Transnistria, see Jean Ancel: *Tansnistria, 1941–1942. The Romanian Mass Murder Campaigns*, volume 1, Jerusalem: The Goldstein-Goren Diaspora Research Center, Tel Aviv University, 2003; Radu Ioanid: *The Holocaust in Romania: The Destruction of Jews and Gypsies Under the Antonescu Regime, 1940–1944*, Chicago: Ivan R. Dee, 2008, 176–224.

Among the archival documents, a special category are the petitions that the deported Roma addressed in those years to the Romanian occupation authorities in Transnistria (the governor of Transnistria, the prefects of the districts, the praetors of the rayons, other authorities, the management of some state farms, etc.) or to autorities in the country (the Presidency of the Ministry Council, Marshall Ion Antonescu, the *Conducător* of the State, the Ministry of Internal Affairs, etc.). There are hundreds of petitions preserved in the Ukranian regional archives of Odessa and Mykolaiv or in the National Archives of Romania in Bucharest. Of these, about 30 have been published,[5] and some have been used in various publications on the deportation of Roma. With a multitude of issues which they refer to, these petitions are a valuable source for those who study the deportations to Transnistria.

In the first part of this contribution I will discuss this category of sources, with their specificity and potential. The petitions are important not just for information on historical events, but also because they show how the Roma reacted to the deportation and how they tried to survive. These first-person testimonies, written while suffering persecution, are also important because they allow us to understand the Roma's own perspective on the deportation. In the second part, the article reconstructs, based on the petitions, some internal realities of the groups of deported Roma in the villages, farms, ghettos and camps in the Eastern part of Transnistria, where these people were settled. As I will show, the petitions speak about lack of shelter, starvation, cold, epidemics, the death of a large number of people, the work that the Roma did in the kolkhoz or sovkhoz, for the local mayor's office and some construction sites, but also about the relations between the Roma and the local Ukrainian population.

The Phenomenon of Roma Petitions

Petitions of deported Roma are an important type of source from several points of view. First of all they exist in relatively large numbers. Romanian and Ukrainian archives hold several hundred petitions from Roma deported to Transnistria. In contrast, in Germany and other countries under German occupation or in the orbit of Nazi Germany documents from the years of the Porajmos coming from the Roma are very few. The project *Voices of the Victims*, coordinated by Karola Fings and published in 2018 at the RomArchive website, dealt with this category

---

5 Viorel Achim (ed.): *Documente privind deportarea țiganilor în Transnistria*, volume I and II, Bucharest: Editura Enciclopedică, 2004.

of documents and published 60 pieces from 20 European countries, including three documents from Romania.⁶ These are letters, petitions, protests, appeals for help, witness statements, and some interviews taken immediately after the end of the war.

The special situation in Romania is explained by the fact that the deported Roma, as they did not lose their Romanian citizenship, were allowed to communicate with the authorities in Transnistria and those in the country – notwithstanding of restrictions which were in place. Also, to some extent, they were able to communicate with their relatives in the country, in cases where not the whole family was deported. Naturally, this situation materialized in documents written or dictated by deported Roma, in which they speak in first person.

Most petitions concern a group, not an individual. There are no petitions that speak on behalf of all Roma deported to Transnistria or on behalf of all Roma in a district or a rayon. There are only a few petitions where signers of the same petition come from several neighbouring or even more remote villages. All of these petitions ask for repatriation and were sent together with lists of names of tens of people from several villages in Transnistria.

Petitions come from places where there was a larger number of Roma, from a few dozen to several hundred, and where the Roma had a certain level of organization, i.e. in places where the Transnistrian authorities had concentrated the deportees into some sort of ghetto. This means that the group was headed by a leader appointed by the Transnistrian authorities, who had authority over the group but also some responsibilities for it, and was interested in having 'his people' in acceptable living conditions. Often this man was the traditional leader of the group, as was the case in Romania even before the deportations. The large concentrations of Roma with an organization of this kind were called 'Gypsy villages' (in Romanian '*sate de țigani*') by the authorities and here the head was called, in the official language, 'Gypsy mayor' or 'mayor of Gypsies' (in Romanian '*primar de țigani*' or '*primarul țiganilor*'). In these places as a rule the 'Gypsy mayor' was the person who wrote the petitions on behalf of himself as the head, or on behalf of the entire group. However, there are also petitions from ordinary people. In contrast, there are hardly any petitions coming from Roma who lived in small numbers in an Ukrainian village.

While most petitions were written or dictated by men, in the archives there are also petitions from women. Among the deported 'sedentary' Roma were hun-

---

6 See Dokumentations- und Kulturzentrum Deutscher Sinti und Roma e.V.: "Rumänien". Available at: https://www.romarchive.eu/de/voices-of-the-victims/romania/. Last accessed: 30.07.2021.

dreds of women as heads of family, which can be explained mainly by the fact that their husbands were mobilized into the army. Some of these women communicated with the Transnistrian authorities or with the country's authorities through petitions.

Yet, petitions are not the only documents from those years produced by the deported Roma. There are also statements made by Roma to the Transnistrian and Romanian authorities on various occasions. These sources are quite numerous. For example, Roma who had fled Transnistria and were caught on the road or in their place of origin in Romania, were headed to the gendarmes or police precinct where they were taken a statement about their escape. In these statements Roma described not only how they managed to escape from Transnistria, but also why they did. Besides, we also find letters, postcards, and telegrams sent by the deportees. However, just few of these sources exist, because the families did not keep them. Only those pieces have reached the archives that have either been intercepted by the authorities or were later included in a file related to a repatriation request.[7] Diaries kept by Roma deportees or other personal records kept by them are not known or have not been preserved.

The Content and Dynamics of Roma Petitions

The petitions of the Roma deported to Transnistria cover a multitude of issues. In many petitions, the petitioners demanded the repatriation of themselves and their families. But in many others the Roma complained about the miserable conditions in the deportation sites, asked the authorities to provide shelter, food and clothes, and to ensure them a better treatment in order to enable them to survive. Also, the Roma required to have a place to work or to be allowed to exercise their crafts in the villages they were placed in.

As many petitioners, when they appeared before the authorities with their requests, wrote about the difficult situation in the places where they were thrown, the petitions are thus important sources for the knowledge of the deportation of Roma to Transnistria. The fact that the petitions come from people who have directly experienced deportation makes them an indispensable sources for understanding the destiny of these people. However, there is a dynamic regard-

---

7 For a telegram of this category, dated March 22, 1943, send from Vradiivka, Transnistria, by a deported Roma to a fellow villager from Dobreni, Ilfov County, Romania, see Achim, Documente, volume II, doc. 347, 153–154.

ing the content of the petitions. In the beginning, almost all petitions asked for repatriation, then the petitions addressed more and more diverse issues.

Petitions existed everywhere in Transnistria. The 'nomadic' Roma too made petitions which, because they usually were illiterate, were dictated by them and put on paper by other people: a man from the occupation administration (for example, a gendarme from the gendarmes precinct in the commune), a deported Romanian Jew living in the same place as a deportee, or another person who knew Romanian.

The problems faced by the deported Roma were about the same everywhere in Transnistria. Yet, there were some local differences in terms of treatment, food, epidemics, sanitary situation, as well as the mortality and survival rate. The deportees knew the living conditions in other parts of the region and this explains why some of them asked to be removed, under the pretext of finding the family, but in fact to improve their living situation.[8]

The latest known petitions by Roma in Transnistria were written in March 1944, a few days before the Romanian occupation administration withdrew from Transnistria. They originated from Roma on the Sukha Balka farm in Berezovca district, who asked the prefect of the district to issue them authorizations for the sale of the bone combs they made. They sold their goods in their area, but also at greater distances in Transnistria.[9] In March 1944, the survivors had already begun to leave en masse the deportation sites. On April 10, 1944, the Red Army crossed the Bug, and the Romanian army and administration withdrew from this territory and with them Roma and Jewish deportees. However, deportees continued to petition the authorities even on their way home, in Romania, in the spring and summer of 1944.[10]

---

[8] To give an example: Alexandru Păun, head of eight Roma families deported to the commune Hrushivka, Golta District, requested in October 1943 for these families to be moved to one of the kolkhozes from Birzula (since 2016: Podilsk), where they had relatives and former neighbours. See Achim, Documente, volume II, doc. 520, 357–358.

[9] Two of these petitions were published in Achim, Documente, volume II, doc. 604, 454–455 and doc. 605, 455.

[10] For two petitions from this phase see Achim, Documente, volume II, doc. 628, 481–482 and doc. 637, 491–493.

Realities from the Deportation Places in Transnistria as Reflected in Petitions

In the following, with the help of published and unpublished petitions, I will discuss some internal realities of the groups of deported Roma in the villages, farms, ghettos and camps in the Eastern part of Transnistria, where the deportees were settled, and I will review some petitions to show the range of issues covered by this category of documents.

Repatriation Requests Describing Conditions at Deportation Sites

As mentioned above, numerous petitions deal with requests for repatriation. Usually they are individual petitions, but there are collective petitions as well, some with dozens of signatures. Most of these petitions come from the Roma from Oceacov and Berezovca districts, i.e. from the 'sedentary' Roma. In contrast, 'nomad' Roma wrote only few petitions of this kind, because the Ministry of Internal Affairs forbade from the beginning the repatriation of this category. However, there are still about 20 petitions of 'nomads' asking for repatriation. With the 'sedentary' Roma the situation was different, because they could request repatriation and, if the investigation that normally had to be done following a petition proved that the deportation was conducted in violation of the orders in force, they in fact could be repatriated, as has happened in many cases.

Especially in the first months after the deportation, among the Roma in Transnistria, and especially the 'sedentary', there was a lot of hype around the repatriation. Many people asked to be repatriated and even those who did not petition for this believed they would be able to go back soon. As written in a report on the deportees in the commune Velyka Korenykha, Oceacov district, from April 13, 1943, "[a]lmost all Gypsies are sitting with their luggage"[11] waiting to be repatriated.

Petitions generally focused on demonstrating the illegal nature of the deportation. Petitioners motivated their requests for repatriation in that they were not one of the categories which, according to the orders of the Ministry of the Interior, were to be deported. They showed that they were 'military elements' (Roma

---

[11] Report of the Praetura of Varavarovca rayon to the Prefecture of the Oceacov District, in Achim, Documente, volume II, doc. 362, 170–171, here 171.

who fought in the First or Second World War, Roma mobilized and Roma eligible for mobilization together with their families), that they had property in the country (so they were not poor elements) or that they had no criminal record. In some petitions they claimed that the deportation was made through the abuse of the local gendarmerie or police, that it was a violation of the orders, and that as a result the petitioner and his/her ones shouldt be repatriated.

Some of the petitions requesting repatriation talk about the situation of Roma in the deportation sites. These are a few lines or a paragraph in which the petitioner mention miserable living conditions in the village, camp, etc. in Transnistria where he/she was taken, the shortages of all kinds, and diseases that haunted the deportees. The petitioner sometimes pointed out that people in that place starved to death and, where appropriate, showed that members of his/her family had died because of the inhuman living conditions.

A petition in this category is that of Margareta Dodan, a woman from the city of Iași, who was deported to Transnistria with her children. On December 16, 1942, in Odessa, she submitted to the governor of Transnistria a petition requesting repatriation:

> The undersigned Margareta Dodan with five children, widow for a year and six months [sic], my husband has fallen wounded by a shell splinter on the battlefield and we are now without any help and at some point we've been brought to Transnistria and we've sold everything good we had and we're now starving and dying from cold here in the village Covaliovca [Kovalivka] distr[ict] of Oceacov and I came Mr. Governor with the request and with tears in my eyes because I couldn't stand the cold and the hunger I walked for 140 Kilometers to reach you with the request to give me an authorization to go to the country with my children to my dear home. We kiss your hands and feet Mr. Governor [and] I am waiting for this answer from your Highness.[12]

As one can see, in this petition Margareta Dodan describes in simple language the desperate situation of her and her deported children. The petition, which is written by another hand, is signed only with the names of Margareta Dodan and of the children Maria, Anica and Ileana Dodan, and Iacob Varlan. Margareta Dodan and her children were deported in September 1942, when about 14,000 'sedentary' Roma were taken to Transnistria. The Police Questure Iași had put this woman and her children on the list of "Gypsies who have no means of living

---

12 Petition by Margareta Dodan, in Achim, Documente, volume II, doc. 263, 47–48. Translation by the author.

or precise occupations from which to live honestly",[13] and the Ministry of Internal Affairs had decided to send her to Transnistria.

The Kovalivka village, located in Oceacov district (in the middle of December 1942 it became part of the Berezovca district), was one of the so-called Gypsy villages on the Bug river. In mid-October 1942, in Kovalivka, approximately 1,100 Roma were installed in 54 houses, representing about half of this village's houses. From the beginning, the conditions in which the deported lived were extremely tough. Deportees suffered from hunger, cold and illness. In the winter of 1942/1943, about half of the deportees in Kovalivka died, most of them because of an epidemic of exantematic typhus which broke out at the end of December 1942 and lasted until March the following year. The situation in Kovalivka is documented in many sources, either petitions of the Roma, or acts of the administration, as is the report made by one of the three commissions that the General Inspectorate of the Gendarmerie sent to Transnistria to investigate the situation of the Roma deportees in Oceacov and Berezovca districts. The report made by the Commission III, headed by Colonelul Sandu Moldoveanu, that worked in the Kovalivka-Andriivka-Varyushyne area from December 12 to 19, 1942, gives relevant information about the Roma in Kovalivka.[14]

The petition submitted by Margareta Dodan on December 16 was sent by the Governorate on December 31, 1942 to the Gendarmerie Inspectorate of Transnistria, with an order to investigate this case.[15] But this was not needed anymore, because in the meantime Margareta Dodan's case had been reported by the commission mentioned above. The commission put Margareta on a list with persons proposed for repatriation. She asked to be repatriated on the grounds that she had a house in Iași and that she had two sons who were earning their living as musicians. The investigation conducted by the Police Questure Iași approved the repatriation of this family. However, the repatriation was delayed until May 1, 1943, due to the typhus epidemic. Meanwhile, four of Margareta's children died, probably because of the typhus. Finally, Margareta and Anica returned to Iași after May 1, 1943.

Along with Margareta Dodan, on the same day, Ștefan Feraru, another deportee from Kovalivka, who also made the trip on foot to Odessa, also a native

---

13 Fond Direcția Generală a Poliției, dosar 185/1942, Arhiva Națională Istorică Centrală, 113–119, here 116. Translation by the author.
14 Achim, Documente, volume II, doc. 270, 59–64, here 61. The report dates from December 21, 1942.
15 Letter accompanying the petition of Margareta Dodan, fond 2242, opis 1, delo 1912, Derzhavnyi arkhiv Odes'koi oblasti, Odessa, Ukraine, 50, RG-31.004M, reel 6, United States Holocaust Memorial Museum, Washington.

of Iași, submitted a repatriation request to the governor of Transnistria. He was deported along with his wife, child and mother-in-law. He says that "so far what we have had as thrifty people, money, things, what we could, we sold and now we were dying of hunger and cold".[16]

Petru Drângoi, a Roma deported to Nechayane commune, Oceacov district, in his petition to the governor of Transnistria, in July 1943, wrote that "[h]ere I fell ill with pulmonary tuberculosis, I am absolutely deprived of livelihood and doomed, along with my wife and two minor children".[17]

On October 4, 1943, Ștefan Bejan, 'mayor of Gypsies', asked the governor of Transnistria for the repatration of the Roma from the villages of Varyushyne, Novoandriivka and Yasna Polyana, Berezovca district, most of them originary from Dolhasca commune, Baia County. On this occasion he as well expressed the miserable conditions in these villages in Transnistria:

> We are Romanianized Gypsies, who paid the taxes to the State like every Romanian citizen, and we are now undressed around winter, so that we can't go out to get water, because our children laugh at us, at the way we look. We live tens of souls in one room.[18]

The last repatriation requests mentioned here were rejected. The three commissions sent by the General Inspectorate of the Gendarmerie to investigate the deportees' complaints found that a large number of them were well-founded. Based on the reports prepared by the commissions,[19] a favorable repatriation notice was given for 311 heads of families with 950 members, a total of 1,261 people.[20]

---

16 Petition by Ștefan Feraru, in Achim, Documente, volume II, doc. 262, 46–47, here 46. Translation by the author.
17 Petition by Petru Drângoi, in Achim, Documente, volume II, doc. 428, 256. Translation by the author.
18 Petition by Ștefan Bejan, in Achim, Documente, volume II, doc. 498, 331–332, here 332. Translation by the author.
19 For the three reports see Achim, Documente, volume II, doc. 267, 51–54 (report from December 17, 1942), doc. 269, 56–59 (report from December 19, 1942), doc. 270, 59–64 (report from December 21, 1942).
20 These data appear in a report prepared by the General Inspectorate of the Gendarmerie, 05.02.1943, in Achim, Documente, volume II, doc. 306, 107–108.

Petitions Dealing with the Harsh Conditions in the Deportation Sites

Other petitions address solely the situation of Roma in the deportation places, combined with the request for improvement of the living conditions. The petitioners ask to be provided with shelter, to receive the necessary food, to get clothes and shoes or to have the opportunity to buy them. Furthermore, they asked to have a place to work or be free to exercise their crafts. Some petitions describe the extremely harsh situation the Roma were living in and sometimes they even speak about the death of fellow deportees as well as abuses committed by authorities.

A significant example is a petition from September 16, 1943, sent by Ion Stan named Natale, 'mayor of the Gypsies' from the Farm Sukha Balka (Berezovca district), to the governor of Transnistria. The mayor shows the difficult situation of the 499 Roma, all originary from the commune Țăndărei (Ialomița County) and requests the improvement of their situation:

> Since July this year we have been working at the state farm Suha Balca [Sukha Balka], rayon Mostovoi, district Berezovca, doing agricultural work. By consulting the necessary information, you will see that we have only done agricultural work for the farm where we have been kept in good conditions. Since seasons have changed and winter approaches, we hereby ask you to be so kind as to examine our situation and give the necessary orders. We are naked and without clothes, all clothes we had have torn, especially since we came to Transnistria we have worked honestly and have kept ourselves out of our work, a thing that can be verified at any time by consulting the respective authorities. Please, Mr. Governor, be so kind and give the necessary orders for us to be given clothes and to be accommodated in decent houses during the winter, since it is impossible for us to live in huts.[21]

The 'mayor of the Gypsies' in Sukha Balka was supported in his approach by the director of the farm, engineer Teodor Apolzan, who sent this petition to the Prefecture of Berezovca District on September 17, 1943. By this occasion he emphasized that most of the Roma on the farm were naked and barefoot and that the farm did not have housing for their accommodation during the winter. He asked the prefect to intervene to the Governorate for the procurement of the materials necessary for building the huts for Roma and for solving the problem of clothing and footwear.[22]

---

21 Petition by Ion Stan, in Achim, Documente, volume II, doc. 483, 314–315. Translation by the author.
22 Letter by Teodor Apolzan, in Achim, Documente, volume II, doc. 484, 315–316. A paragraph from this document reads: "The majority are completely naked and barefoot. In this situation,

The Prefecture of Berezovca District took the necessary steps at the Governorate of Transnistria on September 29, 1943, regarding the "tragic situation of the Gypsies from the Sukha Balka farm and the other Gypsies in the district". In this document the prefect wrote: "The winter is not far away, and to help these miserable ones, in order to save them from the winter frost, for them, as they are now, the winter is a sure death".[23] The Prefecture proposed the collection of old clothes from the Roma in the country.

In another petition from July 13, 1943, to the prefect of the Golta district, the 'mayor of the Gypsies' from the commune Yasenove Druhe, Dumitru Cristea, complained about the fact that the deportees had been given neither work, nor food:

> I have come to you, with a deep feeling of respect, to complain about the fact that we, the Gypsies distributed in the commune Iașii Noi II [Yasenove Druhe], don't have any working place and aren't given any food by the town hall of the commune Iașii Noi II [Yasenove Druhe], being in such a difficult situation, that I am forced to come to you, who is entitled to take action, because otherwise we are forced to commit robberies, thefts and other things in order to secure our daily existence.[24]

Thefts referred to by this 'mayor' were in fact a reality at that time in Golta district, as recorded in archival documents, resulting in tensions between the Roma and the locals, but also between the Romanian occupation administration and the Ukrainian communes. The authorities at communal and rayon level found that the thefts were due to the lack of livelihood and, when they proposed measures to improve the situation of the Roma, they justified them also through the need to ensure public order.[25]

---

when the weather will tighten they will not be able to withstand the cold and will die of cold." (Translation by the author.)

23 Letter by the Prefecture of Berezovca District, 29.10.1943, in Achim, Documente, volume II, doc. 522, 358–359, here 359. Translation by the author.

24 Petition by Dumitru Cristea, in Achim, Documente, volume II, doc. 420, 249–250. Translation by the author.

25 Some documents that speak about these aspects, from July to August 1943, with special reference to the Roma deportees from Golta district can be found in Achim, Documente, volume II, doc. 439, 267–268, doc. 452, 281–282, doc. 453, 282–283, doc. 456, 285, doc. 462, 291–292, doc. 464, 293–294, doc. 468, 298–299, doc. 472, 302.

Accommodation, Food and Clothing

The accommodation of the deportees was a big problem almost everywhere. In the villages of Oceacov District, after all, almost all the Roma were housed, but crowded, sometimes two or three families in one room. In the other districts, many Roma were accommodated in barns, warehouses, or stables. There were also Roma who lived for a while in huts or even in the open air. These people complained about the miserable accommodation conditions or even the lack of shelter. A petition of this category was sent to the governor of Transnistria in early October 1942, by seven Roma deported to the villages Nechayane (Oceacov district), Tryduby and Domanivka (Golta district). They request that their families, "which at present have not been given a shelter and have to stay all day long with only the sky as a roof", be given a shelter. They ask for an urgent solving of their request, "since, due to the cold weather, our children will die of cold before the approval of the Ministry of the Interior reaches this Governorate".[26] The signators mentioned that they had already asked for their repatriation at the Ministry of the Interior.

In the villages where the Roma were placed, the Governorate of Transnistria provided food for them through the town hall, which in turn took the food from the quota that the local kolkhoz had to give to the Governorate. In this chain, dysfunctions often intervened, not to mention the fact that in some places the authorities – either the Romanian occupier or the local mayor's office – paid almost no attention to the deportees. The food ration established by the Governorate was not small, if we take into account the conditions of war, but the local authorities reduced it. In addition, in many places the ration was not distributed in time. Sometimes there were delays of weeks. In some places in Transnistria people starved to death, especially in the winter of 1942/1943.[27]

There are several petitions in which Roma complained that they were not given the food ration on time or that the ration was insufficient. We saw above that Margareta Dodan and Ștefan Feraru, deported to Kovalivka commune in Oceacov district, or the 'Gypsy mayor' Dumitru Cristea from Golta district, complained to the authorities, among others, about the lack of food. In another petition from September 1943, Ioan Stancu, 'mayor of the Gypsies' in the com-

---

26 Petition by seven Roma, in Achim, Documente, volume I, doc. 176, 265–266, here 265. Translation by the author.
27 This is documented not only in the deportees' petitions, but also in documents of the Romanian occcupation authorities; see for example Achim, Documente, volume II, doc. 249, 24–29, here 28.

mune Kamiana Balka, addressed to the prefect of the Golta district and denounced the fact that Roma did not receive sufficient food:

> During the day we work at the kolkhoz, but during the night we patrol at the precinct, they give us very little food, 300 grams of flour, 500 grams of potatoes and 10 grams of salt per person, without any other kind of food, we haven't been given oil for 8 months. [...] Please be so kind as to order for us to receive more food, since these quantities are not sufficient and we are not able to work.[28]

Another head, Ion Rădulescu, *vătaf*[29] in the village of Burylove in Golta district, complained to the praetor of Crivoi Ozero rayon, in October 1943, that, after returning from the work they did for a few months in a village in the area, his people were not given food rations and, in addition, they needed clothes:

> The undersigned Ion Mihai D. Rădulescu, *vătaf* of 25 Gypsy families with 141 souls, so far we have worked at the church in Secretarca [Sekretarka] as brickmakers, currently we are without clothes, the cold has come, we are not fed like the other Gypsies, our children die of hunger and cold. Please, Mr. Praetor, decide on us.[30]

The situation with the food ration was difficult in the summer and autumn of 1943 in many places in Golta district. The head of the Gendarmes Section Crivoi Ozero described that, on the occasion of the inspection he made on July 28, 1943, in the 'Gypsy camp' in Krasnen'ke commune, the Roma had complained that the food ration was not enough for them and that they did not receive even the little that was fixed for them in June and July 1943. In his report, he noted that due to hunger the Roma had left the camp and invaded neighbouring communes, where they commited theft and only with great difficulty could be gathered and redirected to the camp.[31] The remaining products for June and July were given to the Roma on July 31.[32] The mayor of Krasnen'ke commune was found guilty of delaying the delivery of food, and was punished with a three-day pay cut.[33]

---

[28] Petition by Ioan Stancu, in Achim, Documente, volume II, doc. 488, 319. Translation by the author.
[29] *Vătaf* was a traditional head of a 'nomadic' or 'seminomadic' group in some parts of Romania.
[30] Petition by Ion Rădulescu, fond 2689, opis 2, delo 18, Derzhavnyi arkhiv Mykolaivs'koi oblasti, Mykolaiv, Ukraine, 37. Translation by the author.
[31] Report by the chief of the Gendarmes Section Crivoi Ozero to the praetor of the rayon Crivoi Ozero, 30.07.1943, fond 2689, opis 2, delo 18, Derzhavnyi arkhiv Mykolaivs'koi oblasti, Mykolaiv, Ukraine, 19.
[32] Report on the distribution of the remaining products, 03.08. 1943, in ibid., 18.

In this case the Romanian occupation authorities took into account the complaint of the Roma. There were further cases in which some measures were taken to improve the situation of the deportees following the complaints made by them. However, most petitions remained without any effect.

Another major problem faced by the deported Roma was the lack of clothing and footwear. The clothes they brought from home were worn or sold to locals in exchange for food. We saw that the 'mayor of Gypsies' from the farm Sukha Balka complained to the governor of Transnistria that his people were naked and barefoot and asked to be given clothes. The local authorities notified the Labour Directorate from the Governorate of Transnistria about this issue. It was not until the autumn of 1943 that the Labour Directorate approved the sale of clothing and footwear to the Roma who were almost naked and threatened to die of cold. But they had nothing to pay with. Only a few comb makers at Sukha Balka farm had money and asked to be given clothes and shoes for cash.[34] In these conditions, it was ordered that the clothes be given 'in account' (i.e. without payment on the spot), following that their price would be recovered from the remuneration that the deportees would receive for their work in the spring.[35] Clothing and footwear were also very expensive: a men's suit (made of sackcloth) cost 180 RKKS,[36] a women's suit 150 RKKS, a cotton flannel 30 RKKS, a pair of boots with a wooden sole 50 RKKS and a pair of pigskin sandals 20 RKKS. To put these prices in context: in the few places where the forced labor of Jews and Roma was paid, their remuneration in the summer of 1943 was between 2 and 4 RKKS per day.[37] The clothes distributed to the Roma in 1943 and 1944 were made in the workshops in Balta, and the footwear in the workshop in Bershad, both belonging to the Governorate, where the labour force was provided by Jewish deportees. Such a request for clothing and footwear came on January 31, 1944, when the aid of

---

33 Report by the chief of the Agricultural Office of the Crivoi Ozero rayon, 04.08.1943, in ibid., 19.
34 For documents concerning the selling of clothing and footwear to the Gypsies, see Achim, Documente, volume II, doc. 494, doc. 495, doc. 499, doc. 502, doc. 512, doc. 516, doc. 519, doc. 522, doc. 523, doc. 528, doc. 548, doc. 556, doc. 558, doc. 559, doc. 570, doc. 574, doc. 575 and doc. 586.
35 Governorate of Transnistria, the Labour Directorate, Accountancy Service to the Prefecture of Balta District, 08.01.1944, in Achim, Documente, volume II, doc. 574, 421.
36 The official currency in Transnistria during the Romanian occupation, between 1941 and 1944, was *Reichskreditkassenschein*, abbreviated *RKKK*, also called *Mark*. This was the currency introduced by Nazi Germany in the occupied Eastern Territories.
37 For the issue of the remuneration of the Jewish and Roma labour in Transnistria, see Viorel Achim: *Munca forțată în Transnistria. "Organizarea muncii" evreilor și romilor, decembrie 1942– martie 1944*, Târgoviște: Editura Cetatea de Scaun, 2015, 74–85.

the 'mayor of the Gypsies' from the farm Sukha Balka, Călin T. Marin, asked the prefect of Berezovca district for 38 sweaters, nine pairs of sandals and seven pairs of boots to be sold to them.[38]

Labour of Roma Deportees in Transnistria: Petitions Asking for Work

The Romanian occupation authorities in Transnistria used the Roma for various works, especially since the spring of 1943. Usually organized in teams, able-bodied Roma did agricultural work on farms and kolkhozes. Many of those who had a trade, especially blacksmiths, were repairing agricultural tools or worked in workshops. Some of the deportees found a niche in the economy of the village where they lived, performing certain crafts and works for the locals. Some worked for local town halls. Others were sent to cut logs in the forests. In addition, in 1943 and 1944, hundreds of Roma worked on the large construction sites of military interest in Southeastern Transnistria managed by the German army.[39]

In Transnistria, the work was important for survival. In some places and some times the food ration was given only to those who worked. In any case, where there was work and where the deportees worked in the places indicated by the authorities or on their own, the survival rate was higher than where there were no work opportunities.

There are several petitions of Roma asking to be given work in order to secure their existence. A petition of this kind is that of Preda Pavăl and Nichifor Pleşa, blacksmiths at the kolkhoz no. 48 Voroshilov from February 1943 to the praetor of the rayon Crivoi Ozero, Golta district. It contains the information that the petitioners had completed the work on this particular kolkhoz and that they asked for approval to work on the kolkhoz in Lukanivka, where they were required by the head of the kolkhoz.[40]

The praetor of the Crivoi Ozero rayon did not approve the request and ordered them to stay in place. At Lukanivka and in the other villages in the rayon that did not have the needed blacksmiths for spring agricultural works the praeture sent blacksmiths from Krasnen'ke camp, located in the same

---

[38] Petition by Călin T. Marin, in Achim, Documente, volume II, doc. 586, 433.
[39] For the labor of the Roma in Transnistria, see Achim, Munca forțată; Viorel Achim: "The Forced Labour of the Gypsies in Transnistria: The Regulation of December 1942 and the Reality on the Ground", in *Historical Yearbook*, XI–XII, 2014–2015, 209–224.
[40] Petition by Preda Pavăl and Nichifor Pleşa, fond 2689, opis 2, delo 18, Derzhavnyi arkhiv Mykolaivs'koi oblasti, Mykolaiv, Ukraine, 1a.

rayon. In autumn 1942 the Krasnen'ke camp consisted of 500 huts, and about 4,200 Roma, among them a big number of blacksmiths. This was the largest Roma colony in Transnistria. Blacksmiths were important for the local economy, they were very required at kolkhozes and farms. Thus, generally, blacksmiths and other craftsmen found opportunities to work in Transnistria and most of them survived with their families.

In December 1942, the Governorate of Transnistria set out to organize workshops for Jewish and Roma deportees in order to use skilled labour from the two communities. Decision no. 2927 of December 7, 1942 'on the organization of the labour of Jews in Transnistria' and Decision no. 3149 of December 18, 1942, regarding the Roma, were issued, which dealt with the workshops.[41] In the following months workshops were set up in some Jewish ghettos in which Jews qualified in the respective profession were employed. However, the same did not happen with the Roma. In some places, work teams were set up with Roma craftsmen who worked as blacksmiths or otherwise at the kolkhoz, on the farm or for the local population, but these were improperly called workshops by the authorities. In fact, they did not have the structure of a Jewish workshop, as they were not professionally organized, for example, they did not work on the basis of tariffs, did not have a management, etc.[42]

In Transnistria there was only one economic organization comprising a large number of Roma who practiced the same craft, the so-called comb making workshop from the Sukha Balka farm in Berezovca district.[43] In Berezovca district at the end of 1943 and the beginning of 1944, a number of 1,800 people (including their families) earned their living from making and selling combs. As Ion Stan named Natale, the 'mayor of the Gypsies' from Sukha Balka farm, wrote in a petition sent to the prefect of Berezovca district on March 11, 1944:

> We received nothing from the farm or the state for four months and we live only from our work and the income we make by selling the combs. With the income we made by selling the combs, we managed to dress and feed ourselves decently this winter.[44]

---

[41] See Achim, Munca forțată, 40–50.
[42] See ibid., 70.
[43] On the comb making workshop from the farm Sukha Balka, see Viorel Achim: "The Deportation of Gypsies to Transnistria", in Achim: Documente, XXXIV–XXXV; Achim, Munca forțată, 90–91.
[44] Petition by Ion Stan, in Achim, Documente, volume II, doc. 605, 455. Translation by the author.

The work was not paid in any way by the Governorate, but the comb makers were helped to procure the raw material (cattle horns from the Odessa slaughterhouse) and had the freedom to sell their products in the localities in the region.

From the Roma in Sukha Balka farm approximatively 20 petitions have been kept, many of them written by the 'Gypsy mayor', the deputy 'mayor' and the foreman of the comb workshop. The petitions concern two aspects: some petitions refer to the procurement of the raw material for the workshop, and others refer to the question of the authorizations for marketing the combs.

In January 1944, the comb makers asked the prefect of Berezovca district for travel permits to Odessa to buy the horns of cattle needed to make combs. A request of this kind is signed by nine people, led by the 'Gypsy mayor'.[45] Others are signed by a single person, who asks for authorization for several people.[46] To Odessa they went in a group of three people accompanied by a gendarme, this being a 'delegation'.[47]

Requests for an authorization for selling combs are relatively numerous because they had to be renewed. At the beginning of March 1944, when the front reached the borders of Transnistria, a military administration was installed in this territory, which canceled all the authorizations for mobile trade – a situation that created problems to the Roma there. That is why we see that on March 11, 1944, both the foreman of the comb workshop, Păun N. Marin,[48] and the 'mayor of the Gypsies' from the farm Sukha Balka, Ion Stan named Natale,[49] came with a petition addressed to the prefect of the Berezova district, requesting a new authorization for selling combs, this time in Anan'iv, a town approximately 50 kilometers from Sukha Balka.

Difficult Relations of Roma Deportees with the Local Population

The relations of the Roma deportees with the local population were not everywhere and always good. It seems that most problems were in the district of Oceacov. Here, the 'sedentary' Roma brought from Romania were placed in the houses

---

[45] Petition by nine Roma, in Achim, Documente, volume II, doc. 572, 419.
[46] See for example the petition by Gheorghe Constantin named Porumbiță, 22.01.1944, in Achim, Documente, volume II, doc. 581, 428–429.
[47] As specified by the Prefecture of Berezovca District, the Labour Bureau, 01.02.1944, when it approved a request of this kind, see Achim, Documente, volume II, doc. 588, 435.
[48] Petition by Păun N. Marin, in Achim, Documente, volume II, doc. 604, 454–455.
[49] Petition by Ion Stan, in Achim, Documente, volume II, doc. 605, 455.

of local Ukrainians. Some villages on the bank of the Bug river were entirely evacuated, the population being relocated into the interior of the district. In other places, half of the village was evacuated, the inhabitants here being moved to the houses of their villagers in the other half of the village. These compact Roma settlements were the so-called 'Gypsy villages' from the Oceacov district. The Ukrainians were dissatisfied that they were evacuated from their households. The fact that in the winter of 1942/1943 the Roma from 'Gypsy villages', being deprived of the necessary fuel for heating and food preparation, burned the woodwork from the roofs, the floors, etc. and thus destroyed the houses, complicated the relations between the local population and the Romanian occupation authorities, which saw themselves forced to compensate the owners.[50] Also, the inhabitants who remained in the village and those from the neighboring villages were dissatisfied with the fact that the Roma, not having food and heating fuel, indulged in theft and destruction.

The archival documents created by the occupation authorities refer to these problems and tensions between the Ukrainian commune and the Roma. They also express that the local administration did not give the Roma the food provided in the ration or did not give them the food on time. A report of one the three commissions of inquiry sent to the 'Gypsy villages' in Oceacov district in December 1942 said that the inhabitants "had to arrange security guards in communes and villages and not infrequently these guards mistreated to the blood the Gypsies caught in thefts".[51]

A petition from August 1943 talks about the problems faced by Roma deportees from the Ukrainian commune. At the beginning of August 1943, Ion Ghica, the 'mayor of the Gypsies' in Katalyne commune, Oceacov district, addressed a petition to the prefect of the district about the harsh situation of the Roma deported to that locality. Ion Ghica showed here that the Roma were forced to work on the kolkhoz hungry, because the mayor of the Katalyne commune did not give them the necessary provisions. He asked for food to be given to the Roma in time. Ghica also wrote that the mayor of the commune had told the Roma that he no longer needed them because the work at the kolkhoz was done. He also required a permit under which

---

[50] Besides official documents, these issues are also mentioned in a 1945 memorandum of the former prefect of Oceacov district, Lt.-Col. Vasile Gorsky. He had held the position until April 1, 1943, and made several efforts to repatriate the Roma and improve their situation. See Achim, Documente, volume II, doc. 641, 495–500, here 499–500.

[51] Report, in Achim, Documente, volume II, doc. 270, 64. Translation by the author.

he could travel to Ochakiv for matters that concerned the Roma, first of all for provisions and clothing.⁵²

How did the prefect of the Oceacov district deal with the petition of Ion Ghica? After receiving the 'Gypsy mayor's' petition, the prefect sent the act to the Praetura of the Oceacov rayon, "for investigation and to take measures to correct things".⁵³ On August 19, 1943, the Praetura ordered the local administration of Katalyne commune to

> [t]ake measures to ensure that the Gypsies receive in time all the food they need to feed their families, so that they do not give way to such complaints. If we receive such complaints from the Gypsies, we will take the most drastic measures to punish the culprit.⁵⁴

At the same time, the Praetura made an investigation in the sense that it called on the mayor of Katalyne commune to give some clarification about what the 'mayor of the Gypsies' complained. The results of the investigation are summarized in a report to the prefect of the Oceacov district, dated September 2, 1943, which partially acknowledges the claims of Ion Ghica, but presents more the views of the Ukrainian mayor. It does not speak of the food ration that the Roma should have received and which they were not given. And as to the lack of salt, it recognizes that the Roma were not given salt, but in the formula "[salt] could not have been distributed to them for some time"⁵⁵; although it was notorious that until that moment the Roma in this rayon had never received salt, which was often claimed by the deported from different sites. Instead, the report accuses the Roma of refusing to work at the kolkhoz ("it was found that most Gypsies refuse to work in the field"⁵⁶) and that they do not even want to dig the potatoes they need in order to cook their food. At the end, however, the rayon report says that "now measures have been taken to distribute in time all the food available in the commune for the feeding of these Gypsies".⁵⁷

---

52 Petition by Ion Ghica, fond 1592, opis 2, delo 38, Derzhavnyi arkhiv Mykolaivs'koi oblasti, Mykolaiv, Ukraine, 22.
53 Letter by the prefect of the Oceacov district to the Praetura of the Oceacov rayon, 10.08.1943, fond 1592, opis 2, delo 38, Derzhavnyi arkhiv Mykolaivs'koi oblasti, Mykolaiv, Ukraine, 21. Translation by the author.
54 Order by the Praetura of the Oceacov rayon, fond 1592, opis 2, delo 38, Derzhavnyi arkhiv Mykolaivs'koi oblasti, Mykolaiv, Ukraine, 20. Translation by the author.
55 Report by the Praeture of the Oceacov rayon to the Prefecture of Oceacov District, fond 1592, opis 2, delo 38, Derzhavnyi arkhiv Mykolaivs'koi oblasti, Mykolaiv, Ukraine, 18. Translation by the author.
56 Ibid.
57 Ibid.

The report is an obvious attempt to cover up this case. Here and in many other cases when the Roma claimed abuses from the Ukrainian communes, the Romanian occupation authorities that had to arbitrate between the commune and the deported Roma favored the commune.

Conclusions

This article primarily dealt with the historical information contained in the petitions of Roma deported to Transnistria, which helps to understand the situation in the villages, camps, farms and kolkhozes where the deportees were placed, including their daily life. Of course, other documents from the Transnistrian authorities, Ukrainian locals (individuals, local administration, kolkhozes) or other individuals and institutions that came into contact with these deportees also talk about these realities. When I presented a few petitions, I put them in connection with archival documents from the authorities, which confirm the information in those petitions, possibly offering a partially different perspective.

Some information that appears in the petitions cannot be found elsewhere. One such detail was the long march of 140 kilometers from Kovalivka, on the banks of the Bug, to Odessa, that the petitioners Margareta Dodan and Ștefan Feraru mentioned above undertook to submit their petitions. Usually, Roma travelling to Odessa with permission or illegally used the train or other means of transport. In addition, the shame that Ștefan Bejan, the 'mayor of the Gypsies' from three villages in Berezovca district, describes that the 'Gypsies' felt when they had to leave the house with torn clothes, that "our children laugh at us, at the way we look", of course, could not be recorded in an official document, which was not interested in what the deportees felt.

There is, of course, other small and sometimes strictly local information that appears only in Roma petitions and that helps to understand the realities at places of deportation, including the hunger, diseases and death of many deportees. However, the information contained in the petitions is not likely to change the overall picture we have of the deportation of Roma to Transnistria, which is based mainly on the large amount of documents created by the authorities involved in one way or another in the deportation. Yet, there are some details that the petitions bring and which are precious, especially when it comes to studying the destiny of an individual, a family or a Roma group.

The petitions must of course be discussed not only in relation to other documents produced at the time, but also to existing oral history interviews.[58] Taken only from the mid-1990s, interviews with special documentary value – i.e. those from people who were adults in the years of deportation – are of course more detailed in describing life in deportation sites and the treatment of deportees. When it comes to sensitive issues, such as the relations that the deportees had with the local population, the two categories of sources differ. In interviews, the survivors speak almost only positive about the Ukrainian peasants with whom they came into contact. On the contrary, Roma petitions also contain descriptions of tensions between the two groups. It seems that 50 to 60 years after the deportation, the asperities mentioned in the petitions have been forgotten.

To the documentary value of the petitions is added the fact that they make known the perspective of the deportees on the deportation and on the events that took place in the Roma settlements in Transnistria, as it was in those years. As time passed, the survivors were able to think differently about the experience they went through. However, petitions must also be subjected to other types of analysis, starting with language. In general, these petitions were written or dictated under the rule of suffering, and they express pain and despair.

Nevertheless, with a multitude of problems which they refer to and by showing how the Roma reacted to the deportation and which were their survival strategies, the petitions are an incredibly important type of historical source for those who want to study the deportations to Transnistria, and the living conditions as well as the suffering of the deportees.

---

58 For collections of interviews with Roma survivors of the deportation to Transnistria, see Lucian Năstasă and Andrea Varga (eds.): *Minorități etnoculturale. Mărturii documentare. Țiganii din România (1919–1944)*, Cluj-Napoca: Centrul de Resurse pentru Diversitate Etnoculturală, 2001, 591–626; Luminița Cioabă (ed.): *Deportarea în Transnistria. Mărturii*, Sibiu: Neodrom, 2005; Luminița Cioabă (ed.): *Lacrimi rome. Romane asva*, Bucharest: Ro Media, 2006; Radu Ioanid, Michelle Kelso, and Luminița Mihai Cioabă (eds.): *Tragedia romilor deportați în Transnistria (1942–1945). Mărturii și Documente*, Iași: Polirom, 2009, 55–264.

Alexandra Pulvermacher
'Aktion Zamosc' and its Entanglements with the Holocaust

Abstract: During *Aktion Reinhardt*, the murder of one and a half million Jews, Himmler and Globocnik planned the next mass crime, *Aktion Zamosc*, which served as a test run for the *Generalplan Ost*. This largest deportation plan in history, which already presupposed the murder of the Jews, envisaged the expulsion of at least 31 million Slavs and the simultaneous settlement of hundreds of thousands of 'ethnic Germans'. Only three days after *Aktion Reinhardt* in the district of Lublin was officially completed on November 9, 1942, Himmler proclaimed the Zamość-region the first German settlement area. Subsequently, 50,000 Poles were deported, the majority for forced labor to the German Reich or to the Auschwitz concentration camp, and several thousands, who were considered unfit for work were brought to so-called retirement villages. Thousands of Poles, fearing deportation, fled into the forests, where they joined the underground. Even though the German occupiers according to their National Socialist racial ideology made a clear distinction between Jews and Poles, an increasing radicalization towards the Polish population can be seen in *Aktion Zamosc* which was also a consequence of the numerous personnel continuities in the organizations of the occupation apparatus.

Introduction

On February 25, 1943, Zygmunt Klukowski, doctor and head of the hospital in Szczebrzeszyn, a small town south of Lublin, wrote the following lines in his diary:

> I also had a patient in the hospital who had been resettled from the Poznań area together with her parents three years ago. A few weeks ago, in the course of the resettlement of the village of Kąty near Zamość, her husband was taken away and sent to Auschwitz, she was held "behind the wire" in Zamość, while the five children were taken by train to the Garwolin area. Finally, she herself was also deported to Germany to work. The brave woman escaped from the train on the way and got to Garwolin, found all five children there, who had been placed with various farmers, and returned to Zamość. All these bad experiences caused her to miscarry in the fourth month of pregnancy with very heavy bleeding.[1]

---

1 Christine Glauning and Ewelina Wanke (eds.): Zygmunt Klukowski: *Tagebuch aus den Jahren*

OpenAccess. © 2023 the author(s), published by De Gruyter. This work is licensed under the Creative Commons Attribution-NonCommercial-NoDerivatives 4.0 International License.
https://doi.org/10.1515/9783110746464-027

In his diary entry, Klukowski describes the brutal actions of the German occupiers against the non-Jewish Polish population in a region that has been addressed in research primarily in the context of the Holocaust.

On November 24, 1942, the German occupiers began deporting non-Jewish Poles[2] from the area around Zamość, which Heinrich Himmler, Reichsführer-SS and Reich Commissioner for the Consolidation of German Nationhood (*Reichskommissar für die Festigung deutschen Volkstums*, henceforth RKF) had declared a German settlement area shortly before. This area was of interest to the German occupiers for several reasons: They had discovered traces of alleged German colonists there from the time of Austrian rule, who now were to be 're-Germanised'.[3] The soils around Zamość were extremely fertile, and several important transport routes ran through the area.[4]

Originally, a 'Germanization' of the 'General Government', the central part of occupied Poland in which Zamość was located, had not been envisaged – it was rather to serve as the "Homestead of the Polish People"[5] ("*Heimstätte des polnischen Volkes*"), as a reservoir of labor and as a deployment area of the *Wehrmacht* for the war against the Soviet Union. Only the so-called incorporated areas in Western Poland, which had become part of the Reich, were to be 'Germanised'.[6] As early as September 1939, the German elites developed concrete plans for the reorganization of the population structure in the annexed territories.[7] In this context, the creation of a 'Jewish reservation' near Lublin was

---

der Okkupation: 1939–1944, Berlin: Metropol, 2017, entry dated 25.02.1943, 413 (all translations by the author).

2 Henceforth, when referring to Poles, this refers to non-Jewish Polish citizens.

3 W. Gradmann's note on the conditions of a 'Germanisation' of Zamość and the Zamość county, Łódź 19.03.1942, in Czesław Madajczyk (ed.): *Zamojszczyzna – Sonderlaboratorium SS. Zbiór dokumentów polskich i niemieckich z okresu okupacji hitlerowskiej*, volume 1, Warsaw: Ludowa Spółdzielnia Wydawnictwo, 1977 (henceforth Zamojszczyzna 1, document titles are translated to English by the author), 53–60.

4 Zamojszczyzna 1, 12.

5 Werner Präg and Wolfgang Jacobmeyer (eds.): *Das Diensttagebuch des deutschen Generalgouverneurs in Polen, 1939–1945*, Stuttgart: dva, 1975 (henceforth Diensttagebuch), entry dated 25.02.1940, 117.

6 Günther Häufele: "Zwangsumsiedlungen in Polen 1939–1941: Zum Vergleich sowjetischer und deutscher Besatzungspolitik", in Dittmar Dahlmann and Gerhard Hirschfeld (eds.): *Lager, Zwangsarbeit, Vertreibung und Deportation: Dimensionen der Massenverbrechen in der Sowjetunion und in Deutschland 1933 bis 1945*, Essen: Klartext, 1999, 515–534.

7 Already on 21.09.1939, Reinhardt Heydrich had presented a plan providing for a swift deportation of all Jews and the remaining Polish intelligentsia living in the incorporated territories; cf. Christopher Browning: *The Origins of the Final Solution: The Evolution of Nazi Jewish Policy, September 1939–March 1942*, London: Arrow Books, 2005, 36.

also discussed. In October 1939, deportation plans had been increasingly linked to the resettlement of 'ethnic Germans' from the Baltics and Soviet-occupied eastern Poland to the annexed territories.[8] By March 1941, the Central Emigration Office (*Umwandererzentralstelle*, henceforth UWZ) succeeded in deporting 410,000 Polish citizens to the 'General Government'.[9]

At the government meeting on March 25, 1941, after a talk with Hitler,[10] 'General Governor' Hans Frank announced an abrupt change of the objective of the 'General Government':

> The General Government, as we know it and as we have worked for, will be much richer, happier, will receive more support and, above all, will be de-Jewified. Yet, it will also lose the characteristic sight of a still predominant Polish life; for with the Jews the Poles will also leave this area. The Führer is determined to make this area a purely German country in the course of 15 to 20 years. The word of the home of the Polish people will no longer be applicable to this area of the former General Government [...].[11]

The SS and police leader of the Lublin district, Odilo Globocnik, who had been commissioned by Himmler on July 17, 1941, to establish the SS and police bases in the new eastern territories, had been pressing ahead with this change of direction ever since. He advocated settling the entire district of Lublin with 'ethnic Germans'. In the long term, this was to create a German-populated 'ethnic bridge' from the Baltics to Transylvania. Those Poles who lived in the areas to the west of it were to be encircled in terms of settlement and, step by step, economically and biologically "crushed".[12] On July 30, 1941, during one of his many visits to Lublin and Zamość, Himmler ordered the expansion of the 'Search for German Blood' campaign to the entire 'General Government'. At the same

---

8 Circular by Wilhelm Koppe, Higher SS and Police Leader (HSSPF) of Reichsgau of Wartheland, 12.11.1939, concerning preparations for the mass deportations, in Werner Röhr (ed.): *Europa unterm Hakenkreuz: Die faschistische Okkupationspolitik in Polen (1939–1945)*, Heidelberg: VEB, 1989, 138–139.
9 Order by Himmler concerning the mass deportation of the Polish and Jewish population, 30.10.1939, Federal Archives Berlin (henceforth BArch) R 49/4, fol. 20.
10 Diensttagebuch, entry dated 17.03.1941, 332–333.
11 Diensttagebuch, entry dated 25.03.1941, 335–336; According to Martin Broszat, the decision to include the 'General Government' in the German settlement area in the East was made as early as 1940. See Martin Broszat: *Nationalsozialistische Polenpolitik 1939–1945*, Frankfurt am Main: Fischer Bücherei, 1965, 165.
12 Helmut Müller's status report on the conditions in Lublin, directed to the head of the Main Race and Settlement Office (RuS), Otto Hoffmann, 15.10.1941, in Symon Datner, Janusz Gumkowski, Kazimierz Leszczyński: "Wysiedlanie w Zamojszczyznie", in *Biuletyn Głównej Komisji Badania Zbrodni Hitlerowskich w Polsce*, volume 13 (henceforth BGKBZHwP 13), 1960, F 3–5.

time, he declared his plans to create a large settlement area near Zamość.¹³ In a test run initiated by Globocnik, 2,089 inhabitants were expelled from seven villages in the Zamość region and moved to the Hrubieszów county in November 1941.¹⁴

In the summer of 1942, when *Aktion Reinhardt* – the murder of mainly Polish Jews – in the Lublin district was at its peak, Globocnik pushed ahead with the elaboration of a plan for the expulsion of the entire Polish population from the Zamość area – the so-called *Aktion Zamosc*,¹⁵ which can be seen as the first phase of the *Generalplan Ost*. This gigantic demographic resettlement project, developed by Nazi German planning elites since the summer of 1941, envisaged the expulsion of at least 31 million people in East Central Europe and already presupposed the extermination of the Jews.¹⁶ Thus, it was no coincidence that on July 19, 1942, Himmler, who again stayed with Globocnik in Lublin, ordered the deportation – i. e. the murder – of almost the entire Jewish population in the 'General Government' to be completed by the end of the year. Accordingly, after this date, Jews were only to remain in labor camps.¹⁷

---

13 Note on the detailed order of the Reichsführer-SS, issued during his inspection tour to Lublin and Zamość, concerning the resettlement plans in the Lublin district, Lublin and Zamość on 30.07.1941, in Zamojszczyzna 1, 26–27.
14 Janina Kiełboń: *Wysiedlency z Zamojszczyzny w obozie Koncentracyjnym na Majdnku 1943*, Lublin: Państwowe Muzeum na Majdanku, 2006, 34.
15 Letter of U. Greifelt to the Reichsführer-SS regarding the designation of the 'General Government' as settlement area, Berlin on 03.07.1942, in Zamojszczyzna 1, 127; minutes of the meeting regarding the resettlement plans in the district of Lublin; participants: the HSSPF East Friedrich-Wilhelm Krüger, state secretary Dr Bühler, governor of the district Lublin, Ernst Zörner, General Governor Hans Frank, 04.08.1942, in Diensttagebuch, 540–541.
16 "Generalplan Ost. Rechtliche, wirtschaftliche und räumliche Grundlagen des Ostaufbaus", presented by Prof Dr Konrad Meyer, Berlin-Dahlem, June 1942, in Czesław Madajczyk (ed.): *Vom Generalplan Ost zum Generalsiedlungsplan: Dokumente*, Munich: Saur, 1994, 124. After reading Meyer's draft, Himmler pointed out in his letter to Greifelt that he [Himmler] had obviously been misunderstood: he wanted the "Germanization" of the entire 'General Government' within 20 years, not just the establishment of bases, 12.06.1942, in Madajczyk, Vom Generalplan Ost, 133–134.
17 Order of the Reichsführer-SS Himmler to complete the murder of the Jewish population in the 'General Government' by the end of the year, the order was dated 19.07.1942, but actually sent from Hegewald to the HSSPF East, Friedrich Wilhelm Krüger on 29.07.1942, in Klaus-Peter Friedrich (ed.): *Die Verfolgung und Ermordung der europäischen Juden durch das nationalsozialistische Deutschland 1933–1945. Volume 9: Polen: Generalgouvernement August 1941–1945*, Munich: De Gruyter-Oldenbourg, 2013, 337; Peter Witte, Michael Wildt, Martina Voigt, Dieter Pohl, Peter Klein, Christian Gerlach, Christoph Dieckmann and Andrej Angrick (eds.): *Der Dienstkalender Heinrich Himmlers 1941/42* (henceforth: Himmlers Dienstkalender 1941/42), Hamburg: Christians, 1999, entries dated 18.07.1942 and 19.07.1942, 493–496.

Until November 9, 1942, most of the remaining ghettos in the district were dissolved. Of 50,000 Jews residing in the Zamość region, 44,000 Jews had been killed in the extermination camps Bełżec and Sobibór, about 3,000 had been murdered on the spot or during the transports. It was hardly by chance that Globocnik chose November 9 as the end of *Aktion Reinhardt* – after all, it was a Nazi Memorial Day.[18] Only three days later – on November 12, 1942 – Himmler declared the Zamość region the "first German settlement area".[19]

This article focuses on the *Aktion Zamosc* as well as on its entanglements with the Holocaust and tries to clarify to what extent there were continuities in the policies of the occupiers. Furthermore, the question arises as to how the local population perceived these two crimes and related them to each other, and how people responded to *Aktion Zamosc*. The Holocaust in Poland cannot be viewed in isolation from other German mass crimes. In particular, the deportations of Jewish and non-Jewish Poles were strongly intertwined. The example of *Aktion Zamosc* and its entanglements with the Holocaust illustrates the complexity of German crimes in Central and Eastern Europe.

Despite solid source material, *Aktion Zamosc* – the deportation and eviction of about 50,000 Poles from the Southern counties of Hrubieszów, Zamość und Biłgoraj, carried out from November 1942 until August 1943 – was studied almost exclusively by Polish historians until the 1980s.[20] Zygmunt Mańkowski extensively dealt with this topic in the 1970s.[21] Particularly noteworthy is the comprehensive source edition *Zamojszczyzna*[22] published by Czesław Madajczyk in 1978. The diary entries of Zygmunt Klukowski[23] are also extremely valuable, as they provide an outstanding illustration of the increasing escalation of violence in this area.

---

18 Dieter Pohl: *Von der "Judenpolitik" zum Judenmord: Der Distrikt Lublin des Generalgouvernements 1939–1944*, Frankfurt am Main: Peter Lang, 1993, 134–136; Christian Ingrao: *The Promise of the East: Nazi Hopes and Genocide*, 1939–43, Cambridge: Polity Press, 2019, 205; cf. Tatiana Berenstein: "Martyrologia, opór i zagłada ludności żydowskiej w dystrykcie lubelskim", in *Biuletyn Żydowskiego Instytutu Historycznego*, 21, 1975, 21–92.
19 General order No. 17 C of the Reichsführer-SS on the designation of the first settlement area in the 'General Government', Berlin-Halensee on 12.11.1942, in Zamojszczyzna 1, 167–168.
20 Exceptions: Gerhard Eisenblätter: *Grundlinien der Politik des Reiches gegenüber dem Generalgouvernement 1939–1944*, unpublished dissertation from the University of Frankfurt am Main, 1969, 207–232; Broszat, Nationalsozialistische Polenpolitik.
21 Zygmunt Mańkowski: *Między Wisłą a Bugiem 1939–1944: Studium o polityce okupanta i postawach społeczeństwa*, Lublin: Wydawnictwo Lubelskie, 1978, 223–242, 264–266.
22 Zamojszczyzna.
23 Klukowski, Tagebuch; cf. Zygmunt Klukowski: *Terror niemiecki w Zamojszczyźnie 1939–1944*, Zamość: Powiatowa Rady Narodowej, 1945.

Expulsions and Selection in the Assembly Centers

The evictions, which started on November 24, 1942, usually followed a similar pattern: Early in the morning, units of SS, Gestapo, Wehrmacht, Gendarmerie, and uniformed police (*Ordnungspolizei*, Orpo) surrounded the respective village. The head of the village (*sołtys*) was ordered to gather all inhabitants, including sick and old people, babies, and pregnant women, in a central place. The people had 15 to 30 minutes to pack some personal belongings and food, but it also happened that they were not allowed to do so.[24] The police behaved brutally towards the expellees, and some who tried to escape or refused to leave their home were shot on the spot or beaten to death.[25] Some people were selected to remain in the village as workers for the settled 'ethnic German' colonists. The majority of the inhabitants, however, were loaded onto carts and taken to the UWZ assembly center in Zamość[26], a former prisoner of war camp that had been adapted only a few days before.[27]

After the registration, 'experts' of the Race and Settlement Office (*Rasse- und Siedlungsamt*, henceforth RuS) screened the deportees and selected them into four main categories according to 'racial value' and ability to work.[28] Similar categories had already been contained in the 'German People's List' (*Deutsche Volksliste*, DVL), which had been applied in the annexed territories and later also in the 'General Government', although not for the purpose of exclusion as

---

24 Himmlers Dienstkalender 1941/42, entry dated 01.12.1942, 625; Helena Kubica: *Zagłada w KL Auschwitz: Polaków wysiedlonych z Zamojszczyzny w latach 1942–1943*, Oświęcim – Warszawa: IPN, 2004, 11–12; cf. Wolfgang Curilla (ed.): *Der Judenmord in Polen und die deutsche Ordnungspolizei 1939–1945*, Paderborn: Schöningh, 2011; Klaus Dönecke and Hermann Spix: "Das Reserve-Polizeibataillon 67 und die 'Aktion Zamość'. Ein Recherchebericht", in *MEDAON* 13, 2013, 1–8. Available at: http://www.medaon.de/pdf/MEDAON_13_Doenecke-Spix.pdf. Last accessed: 02.05.2021.
25 Dönecke and Spix, Reserve-Polizeibataillon 67, 7–8; Genowefa Anna Wójtowicz, "Eviction of the village of Żurawlów", in Zamojszyzna 2, 380–382.
26 Kubica, Zagłada, 11–12; Minutes of the testimonial of Anna Hanas, Zamość on 22.11.1967, in Wacław Szulc (ed.): *Wysiedlanie ludności polskiej w tzw. Kraju Warty, na Zamojszczyźnie oraz popełnione przy tym zbrodni. Biuletyn Głównej Komisji Badania Zbrodni Hitlerowskich w Polsce*, volume 21 (henceforth BGKBZHwP 21), Warszawa: Wydawnictwo prawnicze, 1970, 298–299.
27 Kiełboń, Wysiedlency z Zamojszczyzny, 34.
28 BGKBZHwP 21, 298–299.

in *Aktion Zamosc*, but rather to integrate ethnic Poles considered racially valuable into the German '*Volksgemeinschaft*'.[29]

The RuS categories I and II were to include persons who had 'Nordic' characteristics and were intended for 'Germanization'. They were to be segregated and brought to the UWZ Litzmannstadt (Lodz), where they were to be definitively examined for their 'racial characteristics'.[30] All persons considered 'only of importance in terms of work' (*nur in arbeitsmäßiger Hinsicht von Bedeutung*) were selected into RuS category III. They were to be deported to the Reich as forced laborers, first of all to replace the so-called armament Jews in Berlin. Those selected into RuS category IV were to be deported to the Auschwitz concentration camp. Elderly, sick, and disabled people as well as children between the ages of seven months and 14 years selected into RuS categories III and IV were to be deported to so-called retirement villages (*Rentendörfer*), deserted villages, from which the Jewish inhabitants had previously been deported to the extermination camps.[31]

Living conditions in the assembly center in Zamość were poor: up to 1,500 people were housed in one barrack. The most vulnerable – old, sick, and disabled persons as well as children, were accommodated in the shabbiest barracks – former horse stables where there were neither stoves, nor floor or straw sacks. Thus, the inmates had to sleep on the bare bunks. The roof had holes, so it rained and snowed into the barrack soaking the ground so that the people stood ankle-deep in mud.[32] Insufficient food, the lack of medical care and terrible hygienic conditions led not only to numerous illnesses, but also to increased mortality, especially among children.[33] The already precarious situation of the deportees was made even worse by the sadistic behavior of the camp staff. The camp commander, Artur Schütz, beat, tortured, set his dog on the prisoners, and did not even hesitate to murder inmates.[34]

---

29 Isabel Heinemann: *"Rasse, Siedlung, deutsches Blut": Das Rasse- und Siedlungshauptamt der SS und die rassenpolitische Neuordnung Europas*, Göttingen: Wallstein, 2003, 263–267.
30 Zamojszczyzna 1, 14.
31 H. Krumey's guidelines regarding the classification of the deportees in the Zamość camp, Łódź on 21.11.1942, in Zamojszczyzna 1, 175–176; Kiełboń, Wysiedlency z Zamojszczyzny, 34.
32 Kubica, Zagłada, 14–15; Edward Madyniak, "Eviction of Wisłowiec, camp in Łódź, work in the Reich," in Zamojszczyzna 2, 370–371.
33 Kiełboń, Wysiedlency z Zamojszczyzny, 34.
34 Kubica, Zagłada, 19, 35–168: 1,301 of them were registered, a further 107 persons did not receive prisoner numbers.

Deportations for Forced Labor

All deportees selected into RuS categories III and IV were to be deported for forced labor, either to Germany or to the Auschwitz concentration camp. The first transport from Zamość to Auschwitz took place on December 10, 1942, and mainly concerned farmers from the surrounding villages around Zamość. The transport lasted for three days – the deportees spent this time standing crammed together in sealed wagons, receiving neither water nor food. The numerous stopovers prolonged the hardships. Among the first 632 Poles from the Zamość region, who arrived in Auschwitz on December 13, 1942, was also 14-year-old Czesława Kwoka. According to the death certificate, she died three months later due to intestinal catarrh.[35]

Fig. 1: Picture of Czesława Kwoka, prisoner number 26947, taken by Wilhelm Brasse, by courtesy of Archiwum Państwowego Muzeum Auschwitz-Birkenau w Oświęcimiu.

However, the head of the 'preventive detention-camp' (*Schutzhaftlagerführer*) in Auschwitz, Hans Aumeier, was not satisfied with the incoming deportees regarding their ability to work. As can be read in a memo of his subordinate Heinrich Kinna, dated December 16, 1942, the Poles, in contrast to the Jews, were supposed to 'die a natural death'. The assignment of those who were from the perspective of the Germans unfit for work – such as "handicapped, idiots, cripples and sick people" should be avoided in order to "prevent any useless burden on

---

35 Kubica, Zagłada, 20–21, 86.

the camp and the feeder traffic"[36] that would result from having to liquidate them. Two weeks later, however, Aumeier's demand was undermined by the leader of the UWZ, Hermann Krumey. In his final report for 1942, Krumey advocated that also children under 14 years should be deported to Auschwitz with their parents. Otherwise, they would "reappear biologically" at some later time and thus endanger the "Germanization" project.[37] Subsequently, during the following months, hundreds of children from the Zamość area were killed in Auschwitz by phenol injections.[38] In addition, experiments were carried out on individual children under the supervision of the infamous doctor Mengele, such as infection with typhoid fever or malaria.[39] In total, the mortality rate for Poles from the Zamość region deported to Auschwitz was extremely high at over 80 percent.[40]

The first forced laborers deported to Germany (RuS category III) were to replace the so-called armament Jews in Berlin. Hitler had already been pushing since autumn 1942 to finally remove this yet protected group of Jews. In 1942 alone, 1,310 Poles were brought in four transports.[41] Among them was Czesława Daniłowicz, who was selected for forced labor at the Pertrix Battery Factory in Berlin, where she arrived in January 1943. Later she recalled: "In the whole hall there were nothing but Jewish women. The Jewish women were with us for three weeks. For three weeks, we worked together with them. And then they came and took them away".[42] The Jewish forced laborers had to instruct the Poles, before they were arrested on February 27, 1943, as part of the so-called

---

[36] Both quotes from the report of H. Kinna on the transport of deportees from the Zamość region to the Auschwitz camp, Zamość on 16.12.1942, in Zamojszczyzna 1, 220–222.
[37] Report of H. Krumey on the activities of the Zamość branch of the UWZ from the beginning of the operation in Zamość to 31 December 1942, Lodz on 31.12.1942, in Zamojszczyzna 1, 259.
[38] Danuta Czech: *Kalendarium der Ereignisse im Konzentrationslager Auschwitz-Birkenau 1939–1945*. Reinbek: Rowohlt, 1989, 358–359. Two boys aged eight and nine whose mothers had tried to disguise them as girls. On 17.12.1942, the two – Tadeusz Rycyk and Mieczysław Rycaj – were discovered and later murdered by phenol injections.
[39] Testimonies of Stanisław Głowy and Roland Goryczki, in BGKBZHwP 21, 292–295; Report of Wacława Kedzierska regarding the experiments of Dr Mengele at Auschwitz, quoted from Kubica, Zagłada, 223.
[40] Kinna's report, 16.12.1942, in Zamojszczyzna 1, 220–222.
[41] Krumey's UWZ-report, 31.12.1942, in Zamojszczyzna 1, 256–259.
[42] Interview of Czesława Daniłowicz, NS-Zwangsarbeit Dokumentationszentrum, Zeitzeugenarchiv, dzsw8746, rec. 12.07.2014. Available at: https://www.dz-ns-zwangsarbeit.de/zeitzeugenarchiv/interviews/video/danilowicz-czeslawa/. Last accessed: 20.12.2020.

'factory raid' (*Fabrikaktion*).⁴³ While in total, only about 2,600 Poles were brought to Berlin, several thousand Berlin 'armament Jews' (*Rüstungsjuden*) were deported to Auschwitz, partly on the same trains in which the Poles had been deported to Berlin. Although the SS Main Economic and Administrative Office (*Wirtschaftsverwaltungshauptamt*) had issued instructions to preserve their labor at all costs, most of them were immediately murdered in the gas chambers.⁴⁴

Apart from the non-Jewish Poles who replaced the armament Jews in Berlin, tens of thousands more were deported to the Reich, where they were employed not only in armament but also on large construction sites and in agriculture.⁴⁵

Deportations to the *Rentendörfer*

All those persons selected to RuS categories III and IV, but considered incapable of working, were initially to be taken to the *Rentendörfer*. This included sick, handicapped, and elderly people, children from seven months to 14 years. The latter were brutally separated from their parents, who were deported to the Reich.⁴⁶ The teacher Adam Skora later reported how the formation of such a transport in the UWZ camp in Zamość was carried out:

> After the files were prepared, the people were usually brought to the square in the early evening, where those designated for transport were read out. This lasted until 7 a.m., as the transports were large. During this time, the old, children and cripples lay in the snow. After the transport was completed, several bodies usually had to be removed from the square.⁴⁷

---

43 Interview of Czesława Daniłowicz, NS-Zwangsarbeit Dokumentationszentrum; Akim Jah: *Die Deportation der Juden aus Berlin. Die nationalsozialistische Vernichtungspolitik und das Sammellager Große Hamburger Straße*. Berlin: be.bra, 2013, in particular chapter 7.
44 Krumey's UWZ-report, 31.12.1942, in Zamojszczyzna 1, 257; Gruner, Fabrikaktion, 44, fn. 44, 75; Czech, Kalendarium, 428–429; Jah, Deportation der Juden aus Berlin, chapter 7; Götz Aly and Susanne Heim: *Vordenker der Vernichtung: Auschwitz und die deutschen Pläne für eine neue europäische Ordnung*, Frankfurt am Main: Fischer, 1995, 436–437.
45 Final report on the work of the UWZ in the Reichsgau Wartheland and Generalgouvernement for 1943, Łódź on 31.12.1943, Federal Archives Berlin, BArch R 70-POLEN/263, fol. 162–163.
46 Krumey's guidelines regarding the classification of the deportees in the Zamość camp, Łódź on 21.11.1942, in Zamojszczyzna 1, 175–176; Kiełboń, Wysiedlency z Zamojszczyzny, 34.
47 Zygmunt Klukowski: "Zbrodnie Niemieckie w Zamojszczyźnie", in *Biuletyn Głównej Komisji Badania Zbrodni Niemieckich w Polsce*, 2, 1947 (henceforth BGKBZHwP 2), 62.

There are records of at least six transports with a total of 5,342 persons from the Zamość area to the Warsaw district. The first transport left on December 7, 1942, and reached Garwolin, southeast of Warsaw, three days later with a total of 605 people, including 275 children. Already upon arrival, 13 persons were dead, more died afterwards. On December 11 and 18, the next two transports left the camp with 634 and 974 persons respectively, reaching Sobolew, south of Garwolin, on December 13 and 20, 1942. Upon arrival, the deportees were distributed among the surrounding towns, where they were housed in foster families or temporarily in community facilities, such as schools and community centres.[48] Józef Braciejewski described the arrival of one of these transports at the Sobolew railway station:

> The wagons were gradually opened by the gendarmerie and then a horrifying, terrible sight appeared before our eyes: a crowded mass of people, mangled, frightened, polluted. There was an unbearable stench from these unfortunate people. During the transport, they were not allowed to leave the wagon, so these people had to satisfy their physiological needs one on one, their clothes were soaked with excrement and urine, and one should not forget that it was December. Old people and poor children were not able to leave the wagons on their own, out of exhaustion [...].[49]

On February 2, 1943, in the morning, news spread in Garwolin concerning another expected transport from Zamość, with children only, which finally arrived in the afternoon. Twenty children were already dead upon arrival, 80 children and 40 elderly persons had to be admitted to the hospital. They were mainly sick with pneumonia, stomach and intestinal catarrh or diarrhea – several of them died during the following days. Almost all deported children suffered from frostbite on their hands, feet, and faces. The Central Welfare Council (*Rada Główna Opiekuńcza*, henceforth RGO) and the municipal office provided the arrivals with bread and a warm meal. All those who did not need urgent medical attention were distributed among the locals, who took them to their homes. On February 3, 1943, a funeral procession with 23 white coffins went through the streets to the local cemetery in Cmentarna Street. Up to 4,000 Poles from the surrounding area and Siedlce took part in the ceremony and thus demonstrated their protest against the German occupation regime. The eyewitness Józef Buska, a member of the Polish underground, was later arrested by the Gestapo

---

48 Kozaczyńska, Wysiedlenia mieszkańców Zamojszczyzny, 73–74.
49 Klukowski, Zbrodnie Niemieckie w Zamojszczyźnie, 68–69.

and deported to Auschwitz, as he had taken several photographs during the funeral.[50]

The RGO and other organizations endeavored to rescue as many children as possible, to provide them with medical care and to reunite them with their parents. Private individuals bribed the train staff to buy children out of the transports; others literally 'kidnapped' them. According to an undated report of the Security Service (*Sicherheitsdienst*, henceforth SD) of Warsaw, the transports of children were the talk of the town for weeks and aroused the Polish population to an extent that had not been observed in the previous three years.[51] Partly responsible for this tense atmosphere were several articles in various underground newspapers calling for joint armed resistance against the occupiers. Most of these appeals argued that the Poles were now threatened with a fate similar to that of the Jews.[52]

According to German sources, 7,000 Poles from the Zamość region were deported to the *Rentendörfer*. However, there is a lack of information about the further fate of these victims – many fled from there, the majority of the children were taken into care by Polish organizations or individuals. Often, the children's biological parents could no longer be identified.

Resistance and Retribution

Since the beginning of *Aktion Zamosc*, thousands of Poles, fearing deportation, fled into the woods to join the resistance, who consisted mainly of the divisions of the Polish Peasants' Battalions (*Bataliony Chłopskie*), the People's Army (*Armia Ludowa*) and the Home Army (*Armia Krajowa*). Through countless acts of sabotage, attacks on the German police stations and 'ethnic German' settlers, the so-called people of the forest attempted to prevent the deportations.[53] As a consequence, many 'ethnic German' colonists fled from their new homes or

---

[50] Report of a Siedlce inhabitant, Jozef Buszka, on the assistance of Siedlce inhabitants to the displaced people from the Zamość region, in Kubica, Zagłada, 208–209; Report of the Warsaw office of the Security Service on the effects of the Zamość resettlement action in the Warsaw district, in Zamojszczyzna 1, 380–383.
[51] Report of the SD Warsaw, in Zamojszczyzna 1, 380–383.
[52] See articles in various underground newspapers, published 01.01.1943–07.01.1943, in Zamojszczyzna 1, 271–313.
[53] Bruno Wasser: *Die Neugestaltung des Ostens: Ostkolonisation und Raumplanung der Nationalsozialisten in Polen während der deutschen Besetzung 1939–1944 unter besonderer Berücksichtigung der Zamojszczyzna im Distrikt Lublin*, dissertation from the RWTH Aachen University, Aachen, 1992, 228–229; Mańkowski, Między Wisłą a Bugiem, 272–276.

sold part of the livestock, arguing that one horse and one cow would be enough to make ends meet. The resulting rapid reduction in livestock caused great concern among the German occupiers, as the area around Zamość with its fertile soils deteriorated from an agricultural surplus to a subsidy area.[54]

In response to the exploding resistance, the occupiers carried out so-called pacification operations, which included mass arrests and deportations to the Reich for forced labor, the burning and bombing of villages not yet 'Germanized', and massacres.[55] The first village to be 'pacified' was Kitów in December 1942, where members of the Police Reserve Battalion 67 rounded up 165 villagers – mostly women and children – on the village square and shot them with machine guns. All men aged 15 to 45 had been arrested two days earlier.[56]

Despite or perhaps because of this brutal approach, the occupiers increasingly lost control in the Zamość area and beyond. Since January 1943, there had been several thousands of incidents, including attacks on postal and telecommunication facilities.[57] The leader of the first motorized Gendarmerie Battalion, major Schwieger, reported a veritable uprising at the beginning of March 1943, in which about 800 members of the Polish resistance had taken part. The German police forces were too weak and the Polish police not reliable to successfully fight the resistance. Therefore, according to Schwieger, the deployment of the German Army and Air Force was necessary.[58] In the village of Cieszyn, the former inhabitants, who had evaded the deportations, took revenge on the new 'ethnic German' settlers by burning down 90 farms and killing 160 people. In addition, there were attacks on people working for the Germans, including municipal officials and teachers. The forests were no longer accessible to forestry workers, as they ran the risk of being shot by members of the resistance, and several agricultural businesses had been destroyed.[59] Globocnik, however, overrode all criticism and ruthlessly pursued the goals set with Himmler.[60]

---

54 Report of the SD Warsaw, in Zamojszczyzna 1, 380–383.
55 Wasser, Neugestaltung, 230–231.
56 Anna Pawelczyk, "Pacyfikacja Kitowa", in Zamojszczyzna 2, 390; Klukowski, Tagebuch, entry dated 13.12.1942, 393; Stefan Klemp: *"Nicht ermittelt": Polizeibataillone und die Nachkriegsjustiz. Ein Handbuch*, Essen: Klartext, 2011, 190; Extract from the testimony of SS man Joseph Scharenberg given in Essen on 07.06.1945, in Zamojszyzna 2, 390–391.
57 Ingrao, Promise, 214; Diensttagebuch des deutschen Generalgouverneurs, entry dated 28.05.1943, Archiv des Instituts für Zeitgeschichte (henceforth IfZ Archive), FB 105/29, fol. 7223, 7226.
58 Report of the commander of the first motorized gendarmerie battalion, major Schwieger, to the gendarmerie commander of the Lublin district concerning the Zamość-uprising, Lublin on 04.03.1943, in Zamojszczyzna 1, 472–476.
59 Minutes of the conference on the state of security in the Lublin district on 29.05.1943, Diensttagebuch des deutschen Generalgouverneurs, IfZ Archive, FB 105/29, fol. 7252; Klukowski, Tage-

The negative impact of the forced resettlements intensified opposition from several Nazi officials, including 'General Governor' Hans Frank, Reich Minister of Propaganda Joseph Goebbels and Plenipotentiary of the Four Year Plan, Hermann Göring as well as the Governor of the Distrikt of Lublin, Ernst Zörner.[61] Although there was a consensus that the 'General Government' should be 'Germanized' in the long term, Göring, Frank and Zörner feared unrest in the rear of the front and considerable economic losses.[62] The official physician of Warsaw, Wilhelm Hagen, had already warned of the possible negative consequences of *Aktion Zamosc* in December 1942,[63] but in vain. In March 1943, Himmler even suggested that Hagen should be committed to a concentration camp for his "in his tendency outrageous letter".[64]

To calm his critics, on February 20, 1943, Himmler ordered all planning work for Lublin and Zamość unnecessary for the realization of the settlement of 'ethnic Germans' in the Lublin district to be stopped.[65] Subsequently, the racial examination of the deportees was dropped, the deportations, though, were continued under the pretext of 'bandit fighting' (*'Bandenbekämpfung'*) within the *Aktion Werwolf* – a literal war against the Polish population. Already on June 1, 1943, the village of Sochy was 'pacified': Policemen and soldiers of the Wehrmacht took the village under fire and committed massacres against the

---

buch, entry dated 15.05.1943, 426; Article in the Polish underground newspaper CKRL "Wieś – AI" concerning the partisan action in the village of Cieszyn, Warzaw on 11.02.1943, in Zamojszczyzna 1, 395–396.

60 Minutes of the conference on the state of security in the Lublin district on 29.05.1943, Diensttagebuch des deutschen Generalgouverneurs, IfZ Archive, FB 105/29, fol. 7253; Musiał, Deutsche Zivilverwaltung, 37.

61 Zamojszczyzna 1, 15; Memo from the Governor of the Lublin District E. Zörner to the Governor General of the 'General Government' about the effects of the settlement action in the Zamość district, Lublin on 23.02.1943, in Zamojszczyzna 1, 415–421.

62 Zamojszczyzna 1, 15–16.

63 Letter of protest from Dr W. Hagen, the Warsaw medical officer, to Hitler regarding the alleged planned murder of parts of the population of the Zamość area, Warsaw on 07.12.1942, in Zamojszczyzna 1, 210–212; in this letter, Hagen stood up for the Polish population, but also expressed his consensus with the extermination of the Jews. After the Second World War, Hagen became president of the Federal Health Office. In the 1960s, Hagen successfully sued Joseph Wulf for his book *Das Dritte Reich und seine Vollstrecker* and the arani publishing house; cf. Klaus Kempter: *Joseph Wulf: Ein Historikerschicksal in Deutschland*. Göttingen: Vandenhoeck & Ruprecht, 2013, 249–271.

64 Letter from R. Brandt to the State secretary at the Ministry of the Interior, Leonardo Conti, in the matter of Dr Hagen, field headquarters on 29.03.1943, in Zamojszczyzna 1, 517.

65 Letter of the Reichsführer-SS on the suspension of unnecessary planning work for Lublin and Zamość, field headquarters on 20.02.1943, in Zamojszczyzna 1, 410–411.

population. In addition, planes of the German Air Force bombed the village. A total of 181 inhabitants – mostly women, children and old people – were killed.[66] Able-bodied men aged 15 to 45 years were arrested en masse, interrogated, tortured and partly shot in the infamous Rotunda in Zamość. As the assembly centers in Zamość and Zwierzyniec were completely overcrowded, from June to August 1943 about 9,000 to 16,000 expellees, including many real and alleged resistance fighters, were brought to the concentration camp of Maidanek.[67] The majority of them were subsequently deported to Germany for forced labor. From the beginning of *Aktion Zamosc*, the RGO endeavoured to alleviate the suffering of the resettlers. In the summer of 1943, as part of negotiations with the occupiers, the RGO succeeded in obtaining the release of 2,000 people from Maidanek, whom it also provided with accommodation, food and medical care.[68]

In the summer of 1943, the Zamość region increasingly descended into total chaos – the implementation of the Nazi resettlement plans had obviously failed.[69] However, this did not stop Himmler from adhering to his plans for a 'Germanization' of the Lublin district.[70]

The Persecution and Murder of the Jews, the *Aktion Zamosc* and the Local Population

As early as March 1942, the German occupiers also carried out the murder of more than 33,000 Jews in the Zamość region as part of *Aktion Reinhardt*. Although this officially ended on November 9, 1942, it actually extended well into 1943.[71] Both crimes were strongly entangled; they overlapped in time and were mutually dependent. This affected not only the perpetrators, who used sim-

---

66 Matthias Uhl, Thomas Pruschwitz, Martin Holler, Jean-Luc Leleu, Dieter Pohl, Henrik Eberle, and Wladimir Sacharow (eds.): *Die Organisation des Terrors: Der Dienstkalender Heinrich Himmlers 1943–45*, Munich: Piper, 2020, 207, 211; Kazimiera Świtajowa, "Pazification of the village of Sochy", in Zamojszczyzna 2, 397; Klukowski, Tagebuch, 433–434.
67 Kubica, Zagłada, 13; the transports to Majdanek took place on June 30, as well as July 1 (men's transport), 2, 3, 5, 6, 7 (women and children), 8 and 9, 1943. On 31.07.1943, men and women were brought to Majdanek who were suspected of being active in the resistance, Kiełboń, Wysiedlency z Zamojszczyzny, 38–39, 45–47.
68 Kiełboń, Wysiedlency z Zamojszczyzny, 52–59; Report of the Polish Welfare Committee in Lublin to the RGO in Kraków on the release of Poles deported from the Zamość region from the Majdanek camp, Lublin on 07.09.1943, in Zamojszczyzna 2, 202–205.
69 Cf. Zamojszczyzna 2, 165–211.
70 Madajczyk, Vom Generalplan Ost, 256–288.
71 Curilla, Judenmord in Polen, 699–796.

ilar practices in both actions, but also society, which experienced both crimes as witnesses, perpetrators and/or victims. The Poles experienced the persecution and murder of their Jewish neighbors at first hand,[72] and some even participated in it.[73]

Already during *Aktion Reinhardt*, masses of Jews had fled into the forests to escape certain death in the nearby extermination camps of Bełżec and Sobibór. Partly they joined the underground groups there; partly they tried to go into hiding with the help of non-Jewish Poles. At the same time, the population was obliged by the country chiefs (*Kreishauptmänner*) to denounce and hunt for hidden Jews.[74] Thus, peasants often would hunt Jews in the villages and bring them to town or even kill them themselves. In addition, 'thugs' would kill Jews in the forests; sometimes they would just rob them of their clothes and let them go. The Jewish population could only hope for limited support from their non-Jewish compatriots – partly due to widespread antisemitism, partly because the non-Jewish Polish population also suffered significantly under the German occupation. The *Aktion Zamosc* led to countless initiatives on the part of Polish organizations and individuals.[75] On the other hand, thousands of non-Jews saved Jews, endangering not only their lives but also those of their relatives. Failed attempts are rarely documented, for example, by Zygmunt Klukowski: In his diary, he mentions a non-Jewish Polish peasant who died in his hospital after being seriously injured while fleeing from the German police. The farmer had hidden six Jews in his barn. Not only the six Jews, but also the farmer's wife and their two little children were shot.[76]

Entanglements and Continuities

During the *Aktion Zamosc*, the German occupiers deported about 50,000 Poles, as many fled on their own initiative. According to German documents, about 600 persons were assessed as "re-Germanizable" (RuS category II). Almost 39,000

---

[72] Ingrao, Promise, 205.
[73] See e.g. Klukowski, Tagebuch, entry dated 21.10.1942–26.11.1942, 376–387.
[74] Musiał, Deutsche Zivilverwaltung, 308–312; Shmuel Krakowski: *The War of the Doomed: Jewish Armed Resistance in Poland, 1942–1944*, New York, London: Holmes & Meier, 1984, 80–81.
[75] Klukowski, Tagebuch, entry dated 02.07.1943, 445; Kielboń, Wysiedlency z Zamojszczyzny, 50–55; Jaczyńska, The SS Sonderlaboratorium, 319–339; Ingrao, Promise, 212; cf. Kozaczyńska, Wysiedlenia mieszkańców Zamojszczyzny.
[76] Klukowski, Tagebuch, entry dated 04.11.1942 and 18.11.1942, 383–386; and entry dated 22.03.1943, 417–418.

Poles were deported for forced labor to the Reich (RuS category III, *Arbeitseinsatz Altreich*), more than 1,400 to the labor camp of Auschwitz (RuS category IV). Almost 7,000 persons were sent to *Rentendörfer* and about 814 persons either died in the assembly centers or fled.[77] Thousands were killed during the 'pacifications', which comprised massacres of the inhabitants and the destruction of whole villages or died due to the terrible conditions during the transports. In contrast to the Jews, who were shot on the spot or deported to extermination camps and immediately murdered, the Poles of the Zamość region suffered different fates.

Even though the German occupiers according to their Nazi racial ideology made a clear distinction between Jews and Poles, an increasing radicalization towards the non-Jewish Polish population can be seen in *Aktion Zamosc* which was presumably also related to the numerous personnel continuities, such as in Globocnik's staff. His adjutant Reinhold von Mohrenschildt had already been involved in the resettlement of 'ethnic Germans' from the Soviet sphere of influence in 1940 to the German-annexed territories; in 1942, he became head of the RKF office in Lublin and was thus responsible for the detailed resettlement planning. The Viennese archivist Franz Stanglica had not only participated in the resettlement of Poles and Jews and worked as a guard in the concentration camp of Auschwitz, but also played a leading role in the planning of *Aktion Zamosc*.[78] Ernst Lerch, as Globocnik's adjutant, *Judenreferent* and 'head of the personal office', was his closest and most influential collaborator and thus involved in Globocniks projects. Another close associate of Globocnik was Hermann Höfle, who joined his team in Lublin in autumn 1940. Before he had been active in the 'ethnic German' self-protection militia (*Volksdeutscher Selbstschutz*), which had been involved in the mass shootings of the Polish intelligentsia (*Intelligenzaktion*). Höfle was not only one of the main coordinators of *Aktion Reinhardt*, but as SSPF deputy chief of staff also responsible for the establishment of the SS and police bases and thus involved in *Aktion Zamosc*.[79] Hermann Kintrup was head of Globocnik's SSPF staff in 1941 and promoted to Commander of the Orpo (KdO) in Lublin at the beginning of 1942.[80] In these

---

[77] Krumey's UWZ-report, 31.12.1942, in Zamojszczyzna 1, 256–259; Report of the UWZ Litzmannstadt for 1943, BArch R 70-POLEN/263, fol. 162–163.

[78] Bertrand Perz: "The Austrian Connection: SS and Police Leader Odilo Globocnik and His Staff in the Lublin District", in *Holocaust and Genocide Studies*, 13, 2015, 406–407, 411–412; Pohl, Judenpolitik, 153; Heinemann, Rasse, 406–407; Ingrao, Promise, 175–176.

[79] See e.g. Zamojszczyzna 1, 368–369, 448; Zamojszczyzna 2, 121, 172, 189; Perz, Austrian Connection, 415.

[80] Perz, Austrian Connection, 413.

two functions, Kintrup played a central role in both the extermination of the Jews and the expulsion of the Polish population. In the Zamość region especially the *Polizei-Reiter-Abteilung III*, the Police Regiment 25 with its Bataillon 67 and the *Polizeiabteilung z.b.V. Zamosc* participated in both mass crimes,[81] supported by personnel of the Security Police, the Gestapo as well as the Gendarmerie.[82]

The implementation of the deportations was entrusted to Krumey and his team of the UWZ, who, from September 1939 until March 1941, had already gained considerable experience in the mass expulsion of Poles and Jews from the incorporated territories to the 'General Government'. In the summer of 1941, Krumey had been sent to Croatia to ensure that no 'ethnic Germans' were deported.[83] As Krumey's final report for 1942 shows, the UWZ office Litzmannstadt provided the Zamość branch not only forms, index cards and its fleet of vehicles, but also with staff.[84] Among this staff was race expert Hans Rihl, who had already 'proven himself' within the early deportations from the annexed territories to the 'General Government' as well as in the racial screenings within the deportations in Slovenia.[85]

Thus, methods from the early deportations in the context of the 'Germanization' of the incorporated territories were adopted, raids, selections, rail transport, expulsion, in part also from the 'ghettoization' as well as from *Aktion Reinhardt*, here again rail transport, the establishment of transit zones as well as the

---

[81] The *Polizeiabteilung z.b.V. Zamosc* was headed by Hermann Meurin, who already in the fall of 1941 had been involved in the deportations of German Jews to Minsk: Schutzpolizei Captain Wilhelm Meurin describes his impressions as an escort of a deportation train from Düsseldorf to Minsk, 22.11.1941, in Susanne Heim and Maria Wilke (eds.): *Die Verfolgung und Ermordung der europäischen Juden durch das nationalsozialistische Deutschland 1933–1945. Volume 6: Deutsches Reich und Protektorat Böhmen und Mähren Oktober 1941 – März 1943*, Munich: De Gruyter Oldenbourg, 2019, 199–204; cf. Klemp, Nicht ermittelt, 409–420; Klaus-Michael Mallmann, Volker Rieß, and Wolfram Pyta (eds.): *Deutscher Osten 1939–1945: Der Weltanschauungskrieg in Photos und Texten*, Darmstadt: WBG, 2003, 167–171.

[82] Dönecke and Spix, Das Reserve-Polizeibataillon 67, 1–8; cf. Curilla, Judenmord in Polen, 683–832; Klemp, Nicht ermittelt, 187–191.

[83] LG Frankfurt am Main vom 29.08.1969, 4 Ks 1/63, in Christiaan Rüter and Dick de Mildt (eds.): *Justiz- und NS-Verbrechen: Sammlung deutscher Strafurteile wegen nationalsozialistischer Tötungsverbrechen 1945–1999*, volume XXXIII, Munich: Saur, 2005, Lfd. Nr. 716a, 5–64, here 10–11. In 1944, Krumey played a leading role in the deportations of Hungarian Jews to Auschwitz as a member of Eichmann's staff, BGH dated 22.03.1967, 2 StR 279/66 and Lfd. Nr. 716e, 194–199. He also stayed in Belgrade and Sarajevo – the nature and extent of his activities there are unknown.

[84] Krumey's UWZ-report, 31.12.1942, in Zamojszczyzna 1, 256.

[85] Heinemann, Rasse, 406–407.

'bandit fighting'.⁸⁶ The selection according to 'race' and 'ability to work', as practised in the context of *Aktion Zamosc*, was special in this form. The *Deutsche Volksliste* contained similar categories, but in contrast to the selection in the Zamość region was applied as an instrument for the integration of certain parts of the Polish population. The Jews, on the other hand, were selected only according to their ability to work. Since summer 1942, however, the German occupiers increasingly proceeded to murder all Jews, no matter, if fit or unfit for work.

Although within *Aktion Zamosc*, the Poles were supposed to die a 'natural death', the Germans actively killed thousands of Poles, in particular during the 'pacifications' and in the case of hundreds of children from the Zamość region who were murdered by phenol injections. However there was not such a clear consensus among the responsible Nazi officials regarding the Poles as there was concerning the extermination of the Jews; the majority spoke out in favor of resettlement to certain regions after the "final victory but did not consider mass murder".⁸⁷ While Polish historians since long have regarded *Aktion Zamosc* and the Holocaust as interrelated,⁸⁸ in Western historiography the two mass crimes were discussed rather separately until the 1990s.⁸⁹

The German occupiers pursued further 'Germanization' projects, such as in the Hegewald-colony near Zhytomyr and in the Crimea. However, the Hegewald project did not reach the scope of *Aktion Zamosc* and failed due to increasing partisan attacks, while the idea of a German settlement in Crimea was abruptly rejected.⁹⁰ The comprehensive source material on *Aktion Zamosc* allows also an analysis of the numerous entanglements with the Holocaust and shows how strongly deportation, population policy, the Holocaust and forced labor were intertwined under Nazi rule. The 'armament Jews' were deported from Berlin to Auschwitz on the same trains that had previously brought Poles from the Zamość area to Berlin. In Zamość the settled 'ethnic Germans' were compensated with the property of the Jews previously deported to the extermination camps. Polish deportees from the Zamość area were resettled in villages from which Jews had previously been deported. The organizers and executors of *Aktion Zamosc* had already been involved in

---

86 Diensttagebuch, entry dated 07.12.1942, 583.
87 Eisenblätter, Grundlinien, 216–217, 220–232.
88 Mańkowski, Między Wisłą a Bugiem, 223–242, 264–266.
89 Cf. Aly and Heim, Vordenker der Vernichtung, 432–440; Pohl, Judenpolitik, 153–157.
90 Wendy Lower: *Nazi Empire-Building and the Holocaust in Ukraine*, Chapel Hill: The University of North Carolina Press, 2005, 155–179; Norbert Kunz: *Die Krim unter deutscher Herrschaft 1941– 1944. Germanisierungsutopie und Besatzungsrealität*, Darmstadt: WBG, 2005, 53–73.

the organization and implementation of the deportations from the Warthegau or *Aktion Reinhardt*.

Furthermore, the *Aktion Zamosc* shows what the implementation of the *Generalplan Ost* would have meant for the Slavic population of large parts of East-Central Europe in the event of a German victory and what practices would have been used. However, it also demonstrates that although the German occupiers were able to carry out the comprehensive murder of the Jews without major resistance, they increasingly reached their limits with their practice of rule, which in the East was based primarily on violence and terror. This also raises the question of whether and to what extent they would have been able to implement their gigantic deportation plans even if the course of the war had been different.

Contributors

VIOREL ACHIM is a senior researcher at the Nicolae Iorga Institute of History, Romanian Academy, Bucharest. His research fields include the history of the Roma, ethnic minorities in Romania between 1918 and 1948, population policies in Romania during the Second World War, and the Holocaust. He has published extensively on the deportations to Transnistria during the Second World War including, among others, the two volumes of *Documente privind deportarea țiganilor în Transnistria* (editor, 2004) and *Munca forțată în Transnistria*. "Organizarea muncii" evreilor, decembrie 1942–martie 1944 (2015).

HENNING BORGGRÄFE is a historian and, since 2017, head of Historical Research at the Arolsen Archives – International Center on Nazi Persecution. He earned his PhD in History in 2012 from Ruhr-University Bochum. Before he came to Arolsen in 2014, he worked as a research associate at the Institute for Advanced Studies in the Humanities in Essen. He has published on nationalism, Nazi Germany, the history of sociology, and Germany's dealing with the Nazi past, including the books *Zwangsarbeiterentschädigung. Vom Streit um "vergessene Opfer" zur Selbstaussöhnung der Deutschen* (2014), *A Paper Monument: The History of the Arolsen Archives* (catalogue of the permanent exhibition, co-author, 2019), and *Tracing and Documenting Nazi Victims Past and Present* (co-editor, 2020).

KIM DRESEL studied History and Comparative Religion in Bremen and Berlin and is currently finishing another master's degree in Archival Science at the University of Applied Sciences in Potsdam (FHP). Since 2017, she has been working in the Cataloguing Department of the Arolsen Archives – International Center on Nazi Persecution. Her main responsibilities are processing collections and document acquisition in the context of cooperations with small archives. In 2021, she also started teaching Archival Science at the FHP. In her recently published article "What Counts and Who Does It? Crowdsourcing and Arolsen Archives 2.0" (*Medaon. Journal for Jewish Life in Research and Education*), she discusses the opportunities and challenges of making sensitive metadata from collections on Nazi persecutees available online.

ALFRED ECKERT is a Nuremberg based tax official for the State of Bavaria. As a freelance historian, his research focuses on Nazi persecution of Jews and the deportation of Jews from Franconia. After his Master's in Free Painting and Sculpture/Plastic at the Free Academy of Fine Arts, Essen, he also approaches the topic of the deportation of Jews artistically in paintings and installations. Since 1998, he researches Jewish history in Bavaria, especially the fate of Jewish individuals, and the role of tax offices in the Holocaust. He has published his findings in *Altstadtbläddla*, the bulletin of a local historical society in Fürth. In 2011, he started his research project *Deportation Train 'Da 32' and the Fate of its 1,012 Inmates*.

TOMÁŠ FEDOROVIČ is a historian at the Terezín Memorial. He devoted his PhD to the fate of Jewish mentally ill patients from the Czech lands and Slovakia during the Holocaust. His research of the history of the Terezín Ghetto concentrates not only on the agenda of the Jewish 'self-administration' and its top-ranking officials, but also on the fate of different groups of inmates (e.g. the blind and war invalids). Fedorovič also applies himself to the statistical research of the survival rate of Terezín inmates within the project *Surviving Terezín: The Social Structure of a Nazi Concentration Camp*. At present, he is preparing an edition of Willy Mahler's diary, a member of the middle administrative staff of the Terezín Ghetto administration, whose entries shed a new light on many aspects of everyday life in Terezín.

CHRISTIAN GROH studied History as well as English Language and Literature at Ruprecht-Karls University Heidelberg. He holds a PhD in History and a master's degree in Archival Sciences from the University of Applied Sciences in Potsdam. From 1998 to 2014, he worked in various positions for the municipal archives of Pforzheim, including head of archives. As head of archives at the Arolsen Archives – International Center on Nazi Persecution between 2014 and 2021, he was responsible for the preservation of the original materials and for improving access to the digitized holdings. Since October 2021, he has led the department of exhibitions at MARCHIVUM (municipal archives of Mannheim), which includes the creation of a documentation center on Nazi history and the curation of a memorial site.

AKIM JAH studied Political Science at the Free University of Berlin and received his PhD for his thesis in which he examines the deportations of Jews from Berlin 1941 to 1945 and the assembly camp Große Hamburger Straße. Since 2015, he is a research associate at the Arolsen Archives – International Center on Nazi Persecution. Before he worked freelance as a researcher and political and historical educator. His research activities focus on Nazi persecution, especially in Germany, and its aftermaths as well as on the history of Displaced Persons. He published widely on the aforementioned topics, most recently *Beyond Europe. Findings on the International Refugee Organization (IRO) in Africa and Asia, 1947–1951* (co-editor, 2021).

SUSANNE KILL has been head of the Historical Collection and Department of Business History of Deutsche Bahn AG in Berlin since 1999. She holds a PhD in Modern History and a degree in Political Science and History of Arts from the Johann Wolfgang Goethe University, Frankfurt am Main. She was a researcher in several projects of urban and business history before joining Deutsche Bahn AG. Together with colleagues, she curated exhibitions on the role of the Reichsbahn in democracy and dictatorship.

CHRISTOPH KREUTZMÜLLER is senior historian in the Education and Research Department of the Memorial and Educational Site House of the Wannsee-Conference in Berlin. In the current project #LastSeen he is responsible for developing an interactive educational tool to decipher deportation photos. He has also worked as curator of the segment "Catastrophe" for the new permanent exhibition in the Jewish Museum Berlin. Among his publications are the acclaimed study on the Lili Jacob Album *Die Inszenierung des Verbrechens. Ein Fotoalbum aus Auschwitz* (co-author, 2019) as well as *Fixiert. Fotografische Quellen zur Verfolgung und Ermordung der Juden in Europa. Eine pädagogische Handreichung* (co-author, 2016).

DAAN DE LEEUW is a PhD candidate at the Strassler Center for Holocaust and Genocide Studies, Clark University, USA. He holds a BA and MA in History from the University of Amsterdam. His MA thesis on Nazi doctors who committed human experiments on prisoners in German concentration camps during the Second World War was awarded the Volkskrant-IISG Thesis Award 2014. Prior to his doctoral studies, he worked at NIOD Institute for War, Holocaust and Genocide Studies in Amsterdam as research assistant and as project manager of the European Holocaust Research Infrastructure (EHRI). His doctoral research focuses on Jewish slave labor from a spatial perspective during the Holocaust. He has held fellowships at Yad Vashem and the Center for Holocaust Studies at the Institute for Contemporary History.

THÉOPHILE LEROY is a PhD candidate at the Historical Research Center of the School for Advanced Studies in the Social Sciences (EHESS) in Paris. He studies the persecution of Roma and Sinti in the Rhine area during the Second World War with a focus on Alsace and Moselle, territories annexed to Germany. Using resources from the Arolsen Archives, he works on the reconstruction of the trajectories of individual Sinti and Roma to understand the implementation of German genocidal policies in a western European borderland. His research attempts to loom the dislocation of families targeted by persecution policies.

INGO LOOSE studied History, Philosophy and Slavonic Languages in Hamburg, Warsaw, Moscow and at the Humboldt University in Berlin. He obtained his PhD in 2005 on German banks in occupied Poland 1939 to 1945. From 2000 until 2010, he was a lecturer at Humboldt University and Professor for Holocaust Studies at Touro College Berlin. Since 2010, he has been a researcher at the Berlin branch of the Institute for Contemporary History. His fields of research are the history of Jews in Poland and Russia/Soviet Union in the nineteenth and twentieth centuries, Yiddish literature, Nazi occupation policy in East Central and Eastern Europe, and the economic history of the 'Third Reich'. Recent publications are the article *"Eastern European Shoah Victims and the Problem of Group Identity"* (2021) and volume 10 of *Die Verfolgung und Ermordung der europäischen Juden durch das nationalsozialistische Deutschland 1933–1945 (VEJ), Polen: Die eingegliederten Gebiete August 1941–1945* (2020).

JOHANNES MEERWALD studied History, Political Science and Spanish Studies at the Justus-Liebig University Gießen and the Philipps University Marburg. In 2018, he submitted his Master's thesis entitled *"Spanische Häftlinge im KZ-Komplex Dachau (1940–1945). Deportation, Lagerhaft, Folgen"*. The thesis was awarded the Stanislav Zámečník Studienpreis by the Comité International de Dachau in 2020. Meerwald worked for the Dachau Memorial in a research project on the Dachau-Allach sub-camp complex. Since April 2020, he is working on his PhD at the Fritz Bauer Institut in Frankfurt am Main. His dissertation project focuses on the Jewish prisoners who were deported to the Dachau concentration camp complex for forced labor in the last year of the war.

VERENA MEIER studied History, English Philology, European Art History, and Philosophy at the Ruprecht-Karls University Heidelberg and Hebrew University of Jerusalem. In her previous role at the Documentation and Cultural Centre of German Sinti and Roma she assisted in creating exhibitions. She has also worked at the Working Group on Minority History and Civil Rights in Europe, at the Grafeneck Memorial, the Documentation Centre of North African Jewry during World War Two in Jerusalem, the Memorial for the Murdered Jews of Europe, the Topography of Terror as well as the State Archives Sachsen-Anhalt in Magdeburg. Since August 2018, she has been a PhD candidate at the Research Centre on Antigypsyism (Forschungsstelle Antiziganismus) at the Ruprecht-Karls University of Heidelberg. Her research interests include minority history, the history of ideas, perpetrator history, and research on historical antisemitism and antigypsyism.

DÓRA PATARICZA has MAs in History and Teaching of History, English, and Ancient Greek from Eötvös Loránd University, Budapest. In 2011, she earned a PhD in Classical Philology from the University of Debrecen, Hungary. Pataricza worked at the Szeged Jewish Community in Hungary as a project manager and at the Helsinki Jewish Community in Finland as a project worker. Both projects included the indexing, cataloguing and digitisation of the communities' Jewish archives. She is currently working as a part-time post-doctoral researcher at Åbo Akademi University in Turku, Finland, in a project entitled *Boundaries of Jewish Identities in Contemporary Finland*. Starting in January 2020, she has been project director at the Szeged Jewish Community. The project is funded by the Claims Conference Research Grant and IHRA and aims at the reconstruction of the fates of Holocaust victims deported from Szeged and the creation of a digital memorial wall to commemorate them.

ALEXANDRA PATRIKIOU holds a PhD in Contemporary History from Panteion University on *"Representations of the Old Continent. The 'Dialogue' of Europe in Greece, 1941–1946"*. She has been awarded the State Scholarship for Modern Greek History, a scholarship from the Foundation for Education and European Culture, Nikos and Lidia Tricha, and a library research grant for Princeton University, funded by S. J. Seeger Center for Hellenic Studies. She edited, under the supervision of Alexis Dimaras, the publication of the collected works of Alexandros Delmouzos. Since 2017, she is working as a researcher at the Jewish Museum of Greece and is responsible for Shoah research and education. Her main academic interests focus on political and social history of the twentieth century in Greece.

ANNA VERONICA POBBE holds a PhD in European Cultures from University of Trento and a degree in Modern and Contemporary History from the University La Sapienza Rome. In her thesis she examined the peculiar management of the Litzmannstadt Ghetto under Hans Biebow. She has been Yad Vashem fellow in 2017, EHRI fellow in 2018 and junior fellow at the Institute for Contemporary History in Munich in 2019. Her PhD thesis has been awarded the Ivano Tognarini Prize, the Irma Rosenberg Prize and the Auschwitz Foundation Prize. She is currently the main editor of an issue of the peer review journal *Rivista Storica Italiana* devoted to Holocaust Studies and a postdoc fellow at the Deutsches Historisches Institut in Rome (DHI) and Adjunct Professor at University of Milan.

ELISABETH PÖNISCH is a sociologist and researcher at the chair of Sociology of markets, Organizations and Governance at the Friedrich-Schiller University Jena and a PhD student at the Institute of Sociology at the Albert-Ludwigs University Freiburg im Breisgau. She was a fellow of the Leo Baeck Programme, organized by the Studienstiftung des deutschen Volkes and the Leo Baeck Institute London, and received a Saul Kagan Fellowship in Advanced Shoah Study from the Claims Conference. Additionally, she was a fellow at the Center for Holocaust Studies at the Institute for Contemporary History Munich between January and April 2015. Her research interests include the sociology of culture and organization, research on violence, the sociology of National Socialism and the Holocaust, and social theory.

ALEXANDRA PULVERMACHER studied History and Slavistics at the University of Klagenfurt where she is currently a PhD candidate at the Department of History. In her dissertation project she researches the persecution of organized resistance by NKVD and Gestapo in Poland from September 1939 to June 1941. Her further research interests include the history of the Second World War with a focus on East Central, East and Southeastern Europe and the comparison of dictatorships. From July to August 2020, she was fellow at the Centre for Holocaust Studies at the Institute for Contemporary History in Munich.

MICHAELA RAGGAM-BLESCH is a senior research fellow at the Institute for Contemporary History at the University of Vienna, where she is currently completing her habilitation on 'mixed marriages' and their families during the Nazi period in Vienna, funded by the Elise Richter grant (Austrian Science Fund) and the Fondation pour la Mémoire de la Shoah. From 1999 to 2003, she worked at the Leo Baeck Institute in New York and was among the first fellows of the Center for Jewish History. She is the curator of several exhibitions on the Holocaust. Her research interests include Austrian Jewish history of the nineteenth and twentieth centuries, antisemitism, gender studies, oral history, microhistory of the Holocaust, and genocide studies.

JOACHIM SCHRÖDER studied History and Political Sciences in Düsseldorf, Berlin and Nantes and earned his PhD in 2006. He worked for the Mahn- und Gedenkstätte Düsseldorf, in research-projects about forced labor during the Second World War, as research associate at the Heinrich Heine University of Düsseldorf, and at the NS-Documentation Centre in Munich. Since 2013, he is a research associate at the Forschungsschwerpunkt Rechtsextremismus/Neonazismus and head of the Memorial Alter Schlachthof at the University of Applied Sciences in Düsseldorf. His research and publications focus on the history of Nazism, First and Second World War, socialism and communism.

MAXIMILIAN STRNAD holds a PhD in Contemporary History from the University of Munich. In his thesis he examines the scope of action of 'mixed-marriages' and their non-Jewish relatives in Nazi Germany and in the immediate postwar-period. Strnad is the author of numerous books and articles on topics including National Socialism and the Holocaust, culture of remembrance, and public history. He has been involved in many university- and community-based research undertakings and is curator of several exhibitions and memorials. Strnad is currently a historian at the Institute for Municipal History and Remembrance in Munich.

KRISTINA VAGT studied History, Political Science and Art History in Hamburg and Seville and holds a PhD in Science of History from the University of Hamburg. She is a curator for the planned denk.mal Hannoverscher Bahnhof documentation centre of the Foundation of Hamburg Memorials and Learning Centres Commemorating the Victims of Nazi Crimes. She is currently working, among other things, on the topic of the deportation of Sinti and Roma to Belzec forced labor camp. She has worked on exhibition projects about the Nazi period and on developing the denk.mal Hannoverscher Bahnhof memorial site in Hamburg.

AYA ZARFATI studied Modern European History in Tel-Aviv and Berlin. Since September 2015, she has been a research associate in the Education and Research Department of the Memorial and Educational Site House of the Wannsee Conference. Her work and research focus on German and Israeli remembrance culture, the experience of visitors at memorial sites, the role of the judiciary in the persecution and murder of European Jews, and pedagogical approaches to communicating history and for teaching the topics of flight and escape in a historical perspective.

www.ingramcontent.com/pod-product-compliance
Lightning Source LLC
Chambersburg PA
CBHW070254240426
43661CB00057B/2557